# LEGAL
# ASPECTS OF
# MANAGING
# TECHNOLOGY

**LEE B. BURGUNDER**
Professor of Business Law & Public Policy
Cal Poly-San Luis Obispo

SOUTH-WESTERN College Publishing

*An International Thomson Publishing Company*

| | |
|---|---|
| Acquisitions Editor: | Chris Will |
| Developmental Editor: | Carol Cromer |
| Production Editor: | Robin Schuster |
| Production House: | Trejo Production |
| Cover Design: | Paul Neff Design |
| Internal Design: | Tom Hubbard |
| Marketing Manager: | Denise Carlson |

LE62AA
Copyright ©1995
by SOUTH-WESTERN PUBLISHING CO.
Cincinnati, Ohio

**Library of Congress Cataloging-in-Publication Data**

Burgunder, Lee B.
   Legal aspects of managing technology / Lee B. Burgunder.
       p.   cm.
   Includes index.
   ISBN: 0-538-82664-9
   1. Technology and law.  2. Industrial property—United States.
   3. Copyright—United States.  I. Title.
KF4270.B87   1995
346.7304′8--dc20
[347.30648]                                 94-37946
                                           CIP

1  2  3  4  5  MA  8  7  6  5  4

Printed in the United States of America
I(T)P
International Thomson Publishing
South-Western is an ITP Company. The ITP trademark is under license.

# ACKNOWLEDGMENTS

I am grateful to the following people who reviewed the manuscript: Dr. John Aje, University of Maryland; Dr. Sue Graziano Moto, Bowling Green State University, Ohio; Professor Katharine E. Rockett, Northwestern University; Dr. Linda B. Samuels, George Mason University; and Dr. Alfred Thim, University of Vermont. I also am indebted to Carey Heckman, Co-Director of the Stanford Law and Technology Policy Center, for his helpful comments and insights. In addition, I thank Paul Goldstein, the Stella W. Lillick and Ira S. Lillick Professor of Law at Stanford University, who first introduced me to the world of high-technology law and inspired me through his kind mentorship to pursue a career in that field.

# PREFACE

If you ask any executive to provide an opinion about the most important challenges facing business today, the answer invariably will include the topic of managing technology. The fast-paced world of technology raises special issues for managers, requiring them to adopt new ways of assimilating information and formulating strategic decisions. Universities in the United States and around the world are committed to training future managers who can deal with the rapidly changing environment of technology. To that end, the academic community is devising new courses, and indeed programs, to educate tomorrow's leaders in the ways to best compete in a technological world.

The purpose of this book is to lend critical support to that important educational objective. There is little debate that legal and regulatory policies increasingly impact the strategic decisions that managers must make. But in the world of technology management, the principles of law have taken on added importance. Dominating the newswires today are not stories about securities fraud or deceptive advertising; rather, the notable topics involve multimillion-dollar disputes over rights in technological innovations. Managers of technology appreciate that their most prized possessions are ideas and that ideas may be quickly and easily lost if they are not handled in the appropriate strategic fashion. Clearly, managers want and need to learn about the legal aspects of managing technology. The only question is how those concepts should be presented.

This book is designed specifically for students and businesspersons who need exposure to the legal aspects of managing technology, but who do not have the immediate intention of becoming lawyers. Those interested in managing technologies come from a wide spectrum of disciplines, including management, engineering, architecture, industrial technology, biology, and computer science. The overriding goal of the text is to stimulate and inform such individuals without regard to their background or training. The premise of general accessibility distinguishes this project from most, if not all, of the other texts on the market. Certain books are intended specifically for law schools or for those practicing law, but they are not appropriate for individuals who are not involved with the legal profession. There also are books tailored particularly for management information systems students. Computer law is undeniably a fundamental topic for those who want to learn about the legal aspects of managing technology. Indeed, much of this text is dedicated to that subject. Nonetheless, there are many other important and interesting topics besides computer law, such as biotechnology, digital sampling, and product design protection.

Unlike other texts on the market, this book is unusually current in its treatment of topics. Several major international events unfolded while the work was being produced, such as the completion of both the GATT Uruguay Round and NAFTA, the establishment of the European Union, and the introduction of initiatives to fundamentally change the U.S. patent system. A major objective of this project concerned assimilating these important developments and anticipating potential future directions for change.

One of the fascinating challenges in this project consisted of determining the correct balance between theory and practice. On one level, the book articulates the current state of the law and suggests the practical strategic decisions that logically follow. However, it is my firm belief that strategic decisions also must account for how the law might change in the future. Such an exercise requires a somewhat sophisticated appreciation of the concepts and reasoning that shape legal policies. To that end, this book presents the most important and current judicial cases, as, for instance, *Computer Associates v. Altai* (copyright protection for computer programs), *Sega v. Accolade* (decompilation of computer programs), and *Campbell v. Acuff-Rose Music* (commercial parodies), to name just a very few. All of the cases have been carefully edited so that the reader may focus on the major facts and issues involved in the dispute without being distracted by nuances of the legal system. In addition, the court's original language has been preserved as much as possible. And, unlike most legal texts, the cases are preceded by explanations of what the reader should expect and are followed by summaries of their major principles.

One of the reasons I find this field to be so interesting is that it provides a dynamic and comprehensive example of the public policy process. This book does not simply articulate what the laws are; rather it considers how policies evolved within the checks and balances of government institutions. And as we know, international developments are becoming increasingly important to those who manage technologies. The text therefore embraces the opportunity to explore international policy processes as well.

One final key aspect of this book involved the selection and treatment of topics. The work does not cover every issue that conceivably may be important to someone managing technology. For instance, telecommunications law and computer crimes are not among the subjects. Rather, the objective is to focus on the topics that are important to every person involved with managing technology. In that way, this book serves as a necessary core upon which readers or instructors may select other materials for greater breadth. Thus the book avoids the trap of getting mired in every detail of the law. That aspect is an attribute of so many law-related texts, which makes them unappetizing to readers. The guiding philosophy here is to stimulate the reader by presenting the most pressing and interesting issues without necessarily covering every legal angle that might come into play. The book is not intended to enable its readers to become legal experts. Instead, the goal is to allow managers to understand the fundamental legal issues pertinent to technology management so that they can competently create strategic plans in consultation with their attorneys.

# BRIEF
# CONTENTS

# CONTENTS

# 1

# AN OVERVIEW OF INTELLECTUAL PROPERTY PROTECTION: A POLICY PERSPECTIVE

## INTRODUCTION

You are about to embark on an important journey. This book will guide you through the maze of legal policies that affect the strategic decisions of those managing new technologies. What you will find may surprise you. The pace of inventions is advancing at an ever-increasing rate, constantly challenging the legitimacy of legal frameworks that govern how new technologies should be developed, controlled, and used. You will see how the law struggles to keep up as new realities test traditional legal norms. The chaos in the realm of computer programs, including the notion of "look and feel" protection, is just one of the many examples of the process that you will explore in this book. When the journey is complete, you will have learned a number of principles that will be crucial for your future in high-technology enterprises.

As you might expect, this book provides a current snapshot of the most important legal policies affecting the technological environment. Having knowledge of these key concepts will allow you to make the most informed strategic business decisions possible. However, you will also become painfully aware that the knowledge you acquire from reading this book may no longer be valid when it comes time to implement decisions in the future. Thus, you will come to understand that managers never can rest content with what they have learned. Rather, they must continually find ways to become aware of new developments so that they can appropriately adjust their business strategies. You will find that the best answer is never obvious. Instead, you will see that in the world of high technology, managers are offered a large array of different legal opportunities offering distinct advantages and disadvantages. Thus, this book, by explaining what is possible, provides only the necessary foundation for developing business strategies. It will be up to you, using your business acumen, to determine what choices may be most appropriate for any particular venture.

Finally, you will come to grips with how the complexity of legal issues is compounded when one must deal in the international environment. The multitude of legal systems that have been developed around the globe often are based on far different principles from those in the United States. Managers who focus their attention solely on the laws of the United States often find that their strategic decisions are inappropriate, even devastating, when they decide to broaden operations internationally. Thus, from reading this book, you also will recognize that one needs to consider international options in the early stages of the strategic decision process.

This book will take you into the most rapidly developing and exciting forum that currently exists in the legal environment of business. Those involved in developing new multimedia technologies, for instance, have found that the legal issues are as important and complex as the technologies themselves. Genetic engineering has opened a host of questions about the morality and legality of creating and owning new life forms. Computer programs are written works, in a sense, but they also serve critical functions in machines. This combination has strained the traditional legal doctrines that were designed to treat these subjects differently. Also, the advent of new technologies has magnified certain business and societal problems, such as piracy and intrusions on privacy. It is issues such as these that makes this area of the law so interesting and important.

It is no longer possible to open a newspaper without reading accounts of disputes between the world's most powerful companies over legal rights to technological innovations. For example, Polaroid's patent infringement suit against Kodak garnered a lot of attention in the press in the 1980s, not only because the result effectively drove Kodak out of the instant camera market but also because Polaroid asked the court to award it $12 billion in damages. Making headlines today are controversies between leading computer companies, involving such names as Apple, Hewlett-Packard, Microsoft, Xerox, IBM, and Lotus. Genetic engineering has drawn tremendous publicity, with firms such as Genentech, Amgen, and Genetics Institute battling over rights to erythropoietin, tissue plasminogen activator and other innovative drugs. The international intrigue of industrial espionage has made headlines, as when Hitachi and Mitsubishi stole technological secrets from IBM. Even those companies marketing to children and young adults have been unable to avoid the media spotlight, as the various legal actions against Nintendo demonstrate.

This first chapter sets the foundation for the specific issues, cases, inquiries, and strategic recommendations that follow. Here, we will consider why there are public policies in the United States allowing firms to obtain legal rights to technological innovations. We will also explore how such legal policies are developed in the United States by the various state and federal government institutions. Finally, we will broaden our perspective to the international policy arena, the increasingly important frontier affecting high-technology practices today.

## THE INTELLECTUAL PROPERTY SYSTEM

Many things can make a firm profitable. The innate abilities of the managers and employees, coupled with hard work, are almost always critical to the success of an organization. The business also may have unique situational advantages, such as its proximity to buyers or distributors. In addition, the firm may have access to relatively cheap sources of raw materials and power. All of the above—labor, land, and natural resources—are tangible ingredients for success.

Profitability depends on much more than such tangible aspects, however. Novel production techniques may reduce costs through increasing the efficiency of the physical plants. New managerial methods may lead to better quality control and more industrious employees. Development of unique product features and characteristics may result in greater customer satisfaction and sales. A stylish brand image may create consumer interest. Unlike tangible assets, however, these qualities are more elusive in that their value is derived from the novel implementation of ideas. For this reason, such resources are called intangible or intellectual assets.

In a competitive economy, such as that of the United States, the mere possession of assets, whether they be tangible or intangible, may not be sufficient to generate profits. Implicit in the foregoing was the assumption that the firm's assets were as good as, or better than, those held by competitors. Thus, for example, a piece of land may not be profitable unless that parcel is comparatively well situated for its uses. The land may be relatively close to the firm's customers, for instance, thereby yielding lower transportation costs than those enjoyed by competitors.

The importance of comparative advantages to profitability leads to problems in a free market economy. First, if one possesses a lucrative asset, then competitors will attempt to take it for their own uses. Just consider what might happen if you were the first to discover a gorgeous lake within 50 miles of Los Angeles. As long as you are the only one to know about it, your life will be improved through enhanced recreational freedoms. But when others learn of your advantageous lifestyle, they too will want to share your asset. Soon will come a free-for-all, with numerous individuals using acts of aggression to lay claim to their particular portions of the lake. In order for you to maintain your advantage, you will need to *control* the asset, backed up by the authority of the government. This is one of the reasons that property rights are created and protected by law.

Legal protection of property, even with its private exclusivity, results in social benefits. Reflect again on your newly discovered pristine lake. Certain improvements, such as tastefully conceived lakefront houses, roads, and boating facilities, may be socially desirable. But would you be willing to invest time and money in these construction projects if visitors could freely take them when they were completed? With this prospect in mind, you likely would abandon the concept and refrain from any labor or investments in the region. Only with property rights enforced by law would you be willing to undertake such efforts. This social justification for property conforms to the philosophical teachings of John Locke. Put simply, the premise is that people must be motivated to perform labor, and the best way to encourage and reward it is through property protection.[1]

Property protection is no less vital for intellectual assets than for tangible ones. For example, assume that you believe that you can create a handheld radio capable of clear FM reception from a distance of up to 500 miles. Your theory is based on adjusting such factors as transistor numbers, their placement, circuitry, and materials. After three years of expensive research and development (R&D), your theory is confirmed, and an affordable working prototype is completed. You then embark on production, distribution, and marketing.

After the new radio is publicly distributed, various events may take place in the competitive market. Persons interested in the radio business will take the radio apart to determine how its extended range was achieved. This exercise likely will be much easier than the effort you expended during the initial R&D. Once this knowledge is cheaply in the hands of competitors, they may choose to produce similar radios. However, these firms will be more profitable than yours since they have fewer start-up costs to cover.[2] Also, once firms are in possession of your novel radio ides, they may come up with associated concepts that yield a greater range, or they may make other beneficial improvements. Competitors may now have an even better radio than yours, and again without incurring your initial R&D outlay. Finally, firms that have expertise in mass production may find ways to manufacture your radio more cheaply than you do, again without the initial risks and expenses of development.

These competitive effects are advantageous to the consumer and society, at least on first glance. After all, the result may be a better product produced possibly with fewer resources and sold at a lower price. This is why free competition is cherished in the U.S. economy and why it serves as the fundamental tenet of most social policies.[3] However, under these circumstances, you might be reluctant to risk putting the time and capital into the development of this radio in the first place. Why go through the expense when everyone else can just take a free ride on your efforts when you are done? In this environment, you might logically conclude that you would be better off if you simply waited for some other foolish individual to develop the radio, thereby allowing you to costlessly learn from that person. In the end, rational market participants, such as yourself, likely will forgo useful and creative investments based on ideas. Therefore, if firms are allowed to compete freely without regard to property rights, the net result may be that creativity is stifled to the detriment of social welfare.

Components of the intellectual property system are designed to correct this inherent defect resulting from free competition. Patents in the United States, for instance, provide property rights to creators of innovations that are useful, novel and nonobvious. They also bestow similar benefits on originators of novel and nonobvious ornamental designs. As this book goes to press in 1994, the term of patent protection in the United States begins when a patent is granted, and lasts

17 years for a useful invention and 14 years for a design. However, change in patent durations is forthcoming, possibly as early as 1995, and the result will be that the duration for useful and design patents will be 20 and 17 years respectively. These terms, though, will be measured from the date that the patent application is filed rather than from when the patent is ultimately granted.[4] Whichever system is now in place, inventors have the right to control their new designs and developments while the patent is in force, and have the legal authority to prevent anyone from making or selling in the United States any products that incorporate them. Assuming the improvements are good ones, periods of exclusive control potentially could be very profitable. The duration of the patent is intended to achieve a delicate balance, providing inventors sufficient incentives to undertake the risks of development while returning the inventions as early as possible to the public domain, where free competition can begin. Also, during the lives of patents, the details of the inventions are fully disclosed to the public for scrutiny, thereby increasing the likelihood that competitive improvements will hit the market either immediately on the expiration of protection or sooner if the inventors approve.

Copyright protection serves similar public goals for certain creative expressions. Imagine that you have a writer's gift and an intriguing story to tell. Unfortunately, the novel probably will take two years to develop. Although you look for some assurance that you will be adequately compensated, faith in yourself is all that you gather. Nonetheless, you decide to take the risk and create the piece. When the book is finally completed, you know you have a winner. Based on contemplated sales, you decide to price the book at $29.95, a figure that will both compensate you adequately for your years of effort and reward you for the risks of undertaking a project that could have totally failed.

One week after your novel hits the shelves, however, another author introduces a book exactly like yours, but selling for $7.95. How did this happen? This author simply bought one copy of your novel, scanned the pages into a computer printing system, and created his own copies to sell. His price, albeit much lower than yours, is sufficient to comfortably cover his costs of operation. In addition, this business enterprise has relatively few risks, given that the novel was already completed and so obviously desirable. In the end, you do not make nearly enough money to justify the time and risk you dedicated to the project, but the subsequent author makes a tidy profit. Under these circumstances, it is doubtful that you will ever create another novel. To the world's dismay, your artistic genius never again will be publicly enjoyed.

The U.S. copyright system is designed to prevent others from copying creative expressions that are fixed in tangible media, so that artists will have sufficient incentives to share their talents. Items such as books, sculptures, movies, and paintings clearly may be protected with copyrights. Debate begins, however, when considering artistic creations which also are useful, such as computer programs or handsomely sculpted industrial products. Such issues become important because the period of copyright protection is much longer than with a patent, sometimes lasting well over 100 years. Also, copyright protection is much easier to obtain. As we shall explore in later chapters, the controversy theoretically should be alleviated because the potential rewards from copyrights are expected to be much lower than from patents. However, this may not be the result in practice.

As already demonstrated, providing property protection by way of copyrights follows the Lockean doctrine that labor will not be undertaken without the prospect of potential rewards. However, copyright protection can also be justified in somewhat different philosophical terms. According to Georg Hegel, a person self-actualizes by extending his or her persona to external physical objects. Thus, the labor in creating a painting provides a mirror to one's own being. Property protection of such personal expressions prevents others from interfering with the externalizing process, thereby allowing individuals to continue their growth. An artist may sell paintings to others, thereby allowing the purchasers to express themselves through ownership of the unique piece. However, the painter cannot give up all claim to the work, since to do so would be to totally alienate his or her own personality. Thus, an artist will always have some personal or moral rights to a creation even after disposing of it to others.[5] As we shall see, this view has been adopted by many other countries, and recently it has also been followed to a limited degree in the United States.

Another important component of the intellectual property system is trade secret protection. Trade secret laws protect valuable information that is not publicly known and that is subject to measures to preserve its secrecy. Again, the rationale for protection is to stimulate the development of new inventions, techniques, and other creations, as well as to preserve high moral standards of corporate conduct.

For example, suppose you start a beverage company. You are sure that a combination of prunes, apples, and apricots will make a fabulous new drink, but you do not have the skills to create it. Thus, you hire a product development staff of experts to create a formula based on these fruits. Finally, the staff finds the proper proportions in conjunction with other ingredients needed for coloring, additional flavor, and preservation. If one of these experts could freely take the formula and either start his own company or sell it to a competitor, the potential profitability of your R&D efforts might quickly diminish. Indeed, without some means to prevent such occurrences, one would be reluctant to share ideas or information with others, even employees, in order to commercially improve and develop those ideas. Trade secret laws allow one to control such secret information by preventing those entrusted with the information, or those who otherwise steal it, from using or disclosing it.

The final major arm of the intellectual property scheme is trademark protection.[6] Trademarks serve somewhat different public goals from the goals served by patents, copyrights, and trade secrets. The role of trademarks is not to provide creative incentives; rather, trademarks function to increase distributional efficiency by making products easy for consumers to locate without confusion.

For a simple but illustrative demonstration of the importance of trademarks, imagine that you are in a managerial position at a hypothetical detergent company. Your company invests significant capital in the production of its detergent to ensure that its product is among the best laundry agents on the market. In addition, great pains are taken to guarantee that the quality of the product is consistently maintained so that the purchasing public will be continually satisfied. You package the detergent in a white box, which bears the name "Denton's" on it.

Soon after introduction of the product, you become aware of a menacing competitive response. Another company freely copied the characteristics of your packaging and began selling its detergent in a white box with the name "Denton's" on it. Inside is a cheap and ineffective substance closely akin to sawdust. The effect on your customers was both swift and detrimental.

Many buyers who previously enjoyed your product and who wanted it again purchased that of the competitor by mistake. Of course, when they used the product this time, their clothes were not adequately cleaned. The customers became confused. What is going on here? Maybe this company, which makes "Denton's," doesn't perform enough quality control? Clearly, the negative repercussions on the goodwill of your company may be substantial. Some sophisticated customers may question whether the recently purchased box came from the same manufacturer that made the previous ones. How many Denton's are out there? Committed individuals even may take steps to try to find the right "Denton's." Perhaps your detergent has a different smell. Customers with adequate time may sniff the boxes before purchase. Of course, the competitor may foil these efforts by copying your product's odor also. Other steps might include discussions with the retailer, ripping open boxes, and/or buying substantial quantities when the right cleaner is located.

The ability of the competitor to compete freely by copying your packaging has resulted in a number of socially undesirable consequences. First, your incentive to maintain consistent quality is diminished, since many customers, after being fooled, will attribute their annoyance to spotty production techniques. Also, why should you continue to make a premier product at great expense when competitors can so easily pass off sawdust for the same retail price? Indeed, the competitor's business is the more lucrative, so maybe it is time to move into sawdust sales yourself. In addition, many purchasers are wasting a lot of time and money to search for and obtain your product.[7]

Providing legal exclusivity through property protection of identification symbols and characteristics can solve these problems. If your company had exclusive rights to use the name "Denton's" on the packaging, then the competitor's attempts to fool customers would be foiled, for whenever that name appeared on a box, buyers could be sure that it came from you. No longer would customers have to engage in time-consuming search efforts to find your detergent. All they need do is locate a box marked with "Denton's." Your investments in quality and consistency now would pay off because your customers would be constantly satisfied with their purchases. Also, these benefits could be enjoyed in most situations without any countervailing social harms. Those competitors who try to legitimately compete will not be disadvantaged simply because they cannot use the name "Denton's." Certainly there is nothing special about that word that might give your company an unfair advantage in the marketplace. There are hundreds of other words competitors can use to equally identify their products. In fact, the only persons who will be harmed are those who wish to compete unfairly by misleading your customers.

Although trademarks are not directly related to managing technology, still this book will discuss them briefly in a later chapter. There are several reasons to do this. Most important, the law with regard to trademarks has broadened rapidly in recent years, allowing many new product characteristics to be protected. The "look and feel" of computer software interfaces, for instance, may serve as trademarks. Also, current policy now allows useful and stylish product features to be exclusively enjoyed through trademark protection. Another consideration is that companies dealing with technology, no less than any other kind of business, must be aware of the importance of trademark protection. Further, international issues such as the gray market and counterfeiting are increasingly important to those persons involved with managing technology.

In sum, the intellectual property system confers varying degrees of protection on intangible assets. The most important rationale is to stimulate creativity without unduly displacing the benefits that normally flow from free competition. Patents, copyrights, and trade secrets all are grounded substantially on this principle. Patent and copyright protection also encourage public disclosure of ideas and expressions so that the public can learn and enjoy. The intellectual property system also may foster the development of self-identity through the protection of moral and personal attributes. Copyright protection serves as one vehicle for this overseas, while in the United States, such concerns are just starting to arise. Finally, intellectual property, notably by way of trademarks, promotes distributional efficiency and the maintenance of high-quality standards. Exhibit 1.1 outlines the respective roles played by these fundamental forms of intellectual property protection in the United States.

## THE PUBLIC POLICY PROCESS IN THE UNITED STATES

### The Power Struggle: Federal vs. State

Public policies in the United States emanate from an interrelated structure consisting of federal and state domains. When separate spheres of influence attempt to expand their respective realms of control, tension usually results. The public policy process that establishes the ground rules for managing technology provides a classic example.

The founding of the United States was a difficult feat requiring the union of separate and distinct state governments, which theretofore had controlled the policies within their respective borders. As you can imagine, state participants were extremely wary of relinquishing power and control to a federal government. After all, a state is only one of many voices within a national entity, whereas in

**Exhibit 1.1  Important Forms of Intellectual Property Protection in the United States**

| Form of Protection | What It Protects | Standards for Protection | Length of Protection |
|---|---|---|---|
| Patent | | | |
| —Utility | Inventions | Useful, novel, nonobvious | 17 years after patent issues* |
| —Design | Designs | Ornamental, novel, nonobvious | 14 years after patent issues+ |
| Trade Secret | Information | Secret, valuable | Unlimited |
| Copyright | Expressions in tangible media | Original | Life of author plus 50 years† |
| Trademark | Identifying symbols | Capable of distinguishing source of goods | Unlimited |

*The utility patent term likely will be changed to 20 years after the filing date.
+The design patent term likely will be changed to 17 years after the filing date.
†For certain works, the length of copyright protection is 75 to 100 years.

its own state policy structure, it is the sole determinant. The U.S. Constitution provided the great compromise that brought the states together by defining and limiting the authority that the federal government could exert over the various state governments.

Article I, Section 8, of the U.S. Constitution specifically lists those activities in which the federal government may engage if its policy makers so choose. The list is actually fairly short, including such things as the power to tax, spend, regulate foreign affairs, and provide military forces. Of most importance for this book, also included are the rights (1) to promote the progress of science and useful arts by securing for limited times to authors and inventors exclusive rights to their writings and discoveries and (2) to regulate commerce among the several states. Clearly the federal government has the authority to regulate patents and copyrights, as it has done. However, by virtue of its power over interstate commerce, the federal government also may make policies regarding trademarks and trade secrets, as long as a business is involved in some interstate activity. As we shall see, the federal government is substantially involved in trademark policy but is largely absent from the trade secret arena. In addition, the federal government has the authority to regulate other aspects of interstate commercial activity, such as contractual relationships and liabilities for product defects, but here again, it has remained somewhat on the sidelines.[8]

A few additional points are worth noting here. First, Article I of the U.S. Constitution, with few exceptions, delineates the entire permissible sphere of federal influence. If an activity is not on the list, or is not at least somehow necessary and proper to accomplish a power on that list, it is subject to state control only. Second, state governments generally have simultaneous authority to regulate in those areas that are listed. This is why we see state governments making laws affecting trademarks and trade secrets, as well as contracts and products liabilities. However, this state power is qualified by the Supremacy Clause, which provides that federal policies are the supreme laws of the land. Thus, if the federal government passes a law, then the states cannot do anything that undermines the intent of the federal policy.

Supremacy issues sometimes are simple to resolve, but more often they are complicated and contentious. The easy situations are when the federal law explicitly articulates that the federal policy is to be exclusive and that the states are forbidden from exercising any authority. In such a situation, there is no question that any state law regulating the same activity would undermine the very clear intent of the federal law. The federal copyright law provides a good example. Section 301 of the federal copyright law provides that no person may receive equivalent protections under state law. Thus, the states are restricted from passing laws that protect expressions written on tangible media. However, as we shall see later, the federal copyright laws do not extend to oral expressions or ideas. Thus, the explicit federal supremacy related by the copyright law does not apply to state influence over these matters.

The more difficult situations result when the federal law does not explicitly preempt state regulation. In that case, the intent of federal lawmakers must be indirectly discerned. Usually, supremacy will be established when a state law stands as an obstacle to the accomplishment of the purposes and objectives of federal lawmakers.[9] When a state law serves to strengthen or otherwise further the federal policy, the two may coexist. The mutual existence of federal and state trademark policies serves as an example. However, when a state law detracts from federal policy, then that state law, including its requirements, prohibitions, and penalties, must fall. *Bonito Boats, Inc. v. Thunder Craft Boats, Inc.* provides a comprehensive and illustrative example of these principles.

## BONITO BOATS, INC. V. THUNDER CRAFT BOATS, INC.
*United States Supreme Court, 1989*

### Facts

Bonito Boats, through substantial efforts, completed a hull design for a recreational boat in 1976. A set of engineering drawings was prepared, from which a hardwood model was created. The model was sprayed with fiberglass to create a mold, which was then used to produce the finished boats, marketed as Model 5VBR. No patent application was ever filed.

In 1983, after Model 5VBR had been publicly available for over six years, the Florida legislature enacted a law making it unlawful for any person in the state to use the direct molding process to duplicate any manufactured boat hull or to knowingly sell within the state hulls or components developed through that technique. The direct molding process was the most effective and inexpensive means to copy product designs. Violation of the law carried substantial monetary penalties to be paid to those damaged.

In 1984, Bonito Boats sued Thunder Craft, alleging that Thunder Craft had used the direct molding process to duplicate the 5VBR hull and had knowingly sold such duplicates in Florida. In its defense, Thunder Craft asked the court to review whether the Florida law conflicted with the federal patent laws, thereby making it invalid under the Supremacy Clause. The trial court and the Court of Appeals determined that the statute was invalid because it undermined federal patent policy. Bonito Boats appealed to the U.S. Supreme Court.

## Decision and Reasoning

From their inception, the federal patent laws have embodied a careful balance between the need to promote innovation and the recognition that imitation and refinement through imitation are the very lifeblood of a competitive economy. Patent protection is offered to whoever invents or discovers any new and useful process, machine, manufacture, or composition of matter or any new and useful improvement thereof. Protection is also available for any new, original, and ornamental design for an article of manufacture.

The patent laws exclude from consideration for patent protection any knowledge that is already available to the public. This is because the creation of a monopoly in such information would not only serve no socially useful purpose but would in fact injure the public by removing existing knowledge from public use. Also, the public sale of an unpatented article (for over one year) acts as a complete bar to federal protection of the idea embodied in the article thus placed in public commerce. The federal patent scheme creates a limited opportunity to obtain a property right for an idea. Once inventors have decided to lift the veil of secrecy from their work, they must choose between the protection of a federal patent and the dedication of their product ideas to the public at large.

The inventor may keep an invention secret and reap its fruits indefinitely. However, in consideration of its disclosure and the consequent benefit to the community, a patent is granted. An exclusive enjoyment is guaranteed the inventor for 17 years, but upon expiration of that period, the knowledge of the invention inures to the people, who are thus enabled without restriction to practice it and profit by its use.

The attractiveness of such a bargain, and its effectiveness in inducing creative effort and disclosure of the results of that effort, depend almost entirely on a backdrop of free competition in the exploitation of unpatented deigns and innovations. The requirements of patentability embody a congressional understanding that free exploitation of ideas will be the rule, to which the protection of a federal patent is the exception. Moreover, the ultimate goal of the patent system is to bring new designs and technologies into the public domain through disclosure. State law protection for techniques and designs whose disclosure has already been induced by market rewards may conflict with the very purpose of the patent laws by decreasing the range of ideas available as the building blocks of further innovation. The offer of federal protection from competitive exploitation of intellectual property would be rendered meaningless in a world where substantially similar state law protections were readily available. To a limited extent, the federal patent laws must determine not only what is protected but also what is free for all to use.

State trademark (often called "unfair competition") protection was scrutinized previously for conflicts with federal patent policy by the Supreme Court in *Sears, Roebuck & Co. v. Stiffel Co.* In that case, Stiffel sold lamp designs that were not sufficiently novel and nonobvious to merit federal patents. Sears purchased unauthorized copies of the lamps and was able to sell them at a retail price practically equivalent to the wholesale price of the original manufacturer. Stiffel sued Sears for violating Illinois unfair competition laws, which prohibited within the state competitive actions causing consumer confusion based on product simulation.

The U.S. Supreme Court determined that the unlimited protection against copying, which the Illinois law accorded an unpatentable item whose design had been fully disclosed through public sales, conflicted with the federal policy embodied in the patent laws. The Court stated that a publicly disclosed but unpatentable article or design, such as one on which the patent has expired, is in the public domain and may be made and sold by whoever chooses to do so.

Read at the highest level of generality, this decision could be taken to stand for the proposition that the states are completely disabled from offering any form of protection to articles or processes that fall within the broad scope of patentable subject matter. Since the potentially patentable includes anything under the sun that is made by man, the broadest reading of *Sears* would prohibit the states from regulating the deceptive simulation of trade dress or theft of trade secrets. Yet, the decision in *Sears* clearly indicates that the states may place limited regulations on the circumstances in which designs are used in order to prevent consumer confusion as to source. Thus, while *Sears* speaks in absolutist terms, its conclusion that the states may place some conditions on the use of trade dress indicates an implicit recognition that all state regulation of potentially patentable but unpatented subject matter is not ipso facto preempted by the federal patent laws.

State trade secret protection also was previously considered by the Supreme Court. In *Kewanee Oil Co. v. Bicron Corp.*, the Court ruled that state trade secret laws do not frustrate the achievement of congressional objectives served by the patent laws. Despite the fact that state trade secret protection is available for ideas that clearly fall within the subject matter of patent, the court concluded that the nature and degree of state protection do not conflict with the federal policies of encouragement of patentable invention and the prompt disclosure of such innovations.

Since public awareness of the information is limited in the trade secret context, the Court held that trade secret protection does not conflict with the patent policy that says that matter once in the public domain must remain in the public domain. Also, trade secret protection is far weaker because the public has the right to reverse-engineer, or otherwise attempt to determine, the secrets through dismantling and studying a lawfully obtained article. This point was central to the Court's conclusion that trade secret protection does not conflict with either the encouragement or disclosure policies of the federal patent laws.

Finally, certain aspects of trade secret law operate to protect noneconomic interests outside the sphere of congressional concern in the patent laws. A most fundamental human right, that of privacy, is threatened when industrial espionage is condoned or is made profitable. There is no indication that Congress had considered this interest in the balance struck by the patent laws, or that state protection for it would interfere with the policies behind the patent system.

The Court believes that the Florida statute at issue in *Bonito Boats* so substantially impedes public use of the otherwise unprotected design and utilitarian ideas embodied in the unpatented boat hulls as to run afoul of these principles. It is readily apparent that the Florida statute does not operate to prohibit "unfair competition" in the usual sense that the term is understood. The general concern over unfair competition is about protection of *consumers*, not protection of producers as an incentive to product innovation. In contrast to the operation of unfair competition laws, the Florida boat hull statute was intended to create an inducement for the improvement of boat hull designs. Moreover, it does so without the high standards of innovation and limited monopoly contained in the federal scheme. That the Florida statute does not remove all means of reproduction and sale does not eliminate the conflict with the federal scheme. In essence, the Florida law prohibits the entire public from engaging in a form of reverse engineering of a product in the public domain. This is clearly one of the rights vested in the federal patent holder, but it has never been a part of state protection under the law of unfair competition or trade secret.

For both state unfair competition and trade secret laws, state protection is not aimed exclusively at the promotion of invention itself, and the state restrictions on the use of unpatented ideas are limited to those necessary to promote goals outside the contemplation of the federal patent scheme. Both laws have coexisted harmoniously with federal patent protection for almost 200 years, and Congress has given no indication that their operation is inconsistent with the operation of federal patent laws.

Indeed, there are affirmative indications from Congress that both of the laws of unfair competition and trade secret protection are consistent with the balance struck by the patent laws. The federal trademark laws, for instance, recognize many of the same concerns that underlie state unfair competition laws. State trade secret laws and the federal patent laws have coexisted for many, many years. During that time, Congress has repeatedly demonstrated its full awareness of the existence of the trade secret system and without any indication of disapproval. The case for federal preemption is particularly weak when Congress has indicated its awareness of the operation of state law in a field of federal interest and has nonetheless decided to tolerate whatever tension there is between them. The same cannot be said of the Florida statute at issue here, which offers protection beyond that available under the law of unfair competition or trade secret, without any showing of either consumer confusion or breach of trust or secrecy.

Congress has considered extending various forms of limited protection to industrial designs either through the copyright laws or by relaxing restrictions on the availability of design patents. Congress has explicitly refused to take this step in the copyright laws, and despite sustained criticism for a number of years, it has declined to alter the patent protections currently available for industrial designs. It is for Congress to determine whether the present system of design and utility patents is ineffectual in promoting the useful arts in the context of industrial design. By offering patentlike protection for ideas deemed unprotected under the present federal scheme, the Florida statute conflicts with the strong federal policy favoring free competition in ideas that do not merit patent protection. We therefore agree that the Florida law is preempted by the Supremacy Clause.

---

*Bonito Boats* typifies the struggle between the federal and state domains over control of intellectual property. Members of the Florida legislature resolved to protect the research and development efforts of Florida boat manufacturers from those competitors using the direct molding technique. Why the Florida legislature was motivated to pass such a law is open to debate, an exercise that will not be entertained here. However, you can easily imagine a scenario wherein all 50 states pass a multitude of such laws in a variety of contexts. If allowed, the resulting patchwork of intellectual property laws would severely restrain commercial activity on any but a local scale. Likewise, the effectiveness of federal patent policy, which is designed to provide uniformity in this context, would be extremely hampered. That is why the Supreme Court repeatedly has struck down such forays by state governments to control intellectual property. However, as *Bonito Boats* indicates, protection of trade secrets by state governments does not conflict with federal patent policy, nor with any other federal policy to date. Likewise, state trademark or unfair competition laws do not run afoul of federal policies as long as they are carefully tailored only to protect consumers from confusion. But when such laws serve to protect companies from competition, then they are overreaching into the realm of federal patent policy. This is the defect that doomed the Illinois unfair competition law in *Sears*.

The net result can be summarized as follows. The federal patent laws serve as the national umbrella policy to provide the proper level of incentives for inventive activity in useful products. Although most state laws that insulate useful inventions from competition are not tolerated, state trade secret protection survives. The essential element of secrecy and the limited contexts for protection bring such protection outside the purview of patent policy. Federal copyright laws explicitly direct that all similar state protection schemes are void. Thus, there are no state laws that protect creative works of authorship expressed in tangible media. Federal trademark laws, as we shall see, were developed for the most part to rectify certain procedural deficiencies in existing state trademark policies and were intended to work hand in hand with the various state laws. Therefore, one finds policies to combat customer confusion simultaneously at both the fed-

**Exhibit 1.2**

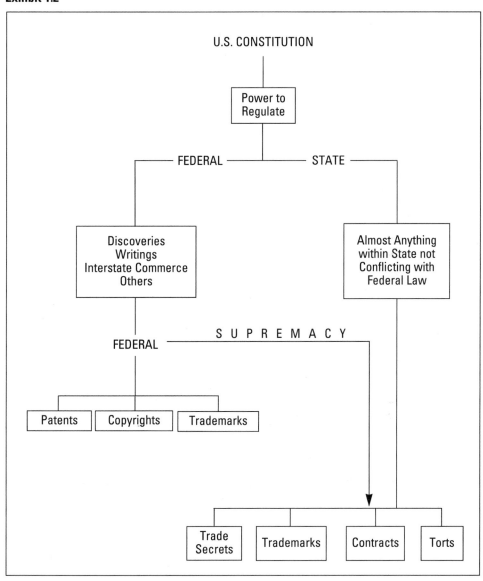

eral and state levels. Exhibit 1.2 illustrates how these principles have been applied to allocate power between the federal and state systems of regulation.

### How Intellectual Property Policies Are Made in the United States

Intellectual property policies are made in similar fashions at both the federal and state levels. We will review the basic concepts here to provide a framework for understanding the more specific elements presented in the chapters that follow. The discussion focuses on the federal policy process, but the principles can be applied readily to the various state methods.

The dynamic nature of the policy process can best be understood by first taking a quick look at patents. When Congress passes a statute, it usually will speak in broad terms. The representational nature of Congress often makes agreement on specifics impossible. Also, details may best be left to experts acting within the general directives from Congress. The Patent Act, for example, provides that one is entitled to a patent upon inventing a novel and nonobvious process, machine, manufacture, or composition of matter. Which governmental body should decide whether these criteria have been met in particular cases? In 1990, there were nearly 175,000 requests in the United States for patents.[10] Clearly, neither Congress nor the president has the time to focus on such minutiae. Therefore, as it has done for most statutes requiring administration, Congress formed an administrative agency to make these determinations. For patents (as well as trademarks) Congress created and funded the Patent and Trademark Office (PTO) to review such applications. The PTO is within the Department of Commerce and is headed by a commissioner, who serves at the pleasure of the president.

Let's assume that the PTO receives a request to patent a genetically engineered living bacterium that is useful for dispersing oil floating on water. If you were the expert at the PTO in charge of examining this file, would you grant the patent? Did Congress intend that living things be patentable? This is certainly a far cry from the more typical situations involving machines or chemicals. Obviously, your job would be easier if Congress had specified in the statute the fact that bio-engineered microorganisms may be patented, but unfortunately nothing so explicit was drafted. Ultimately you interpret the vague terms of the Patent Act so as to prohibit patents on living things, and therefore you reject the application. Such an action by agency personnel thereby establishes the policy that living things are not patentable.

The inventor here likely will feel wronged and become bitter, wondering how a single bureaucrat can make such an improper decision, which may ruin an otherwise bright future. Fortunately for the inventor, Congress subjects all administrative agencies, including the PTO, to procedural safeguards, which allows others to review the examiner's decision. In the PTO, the inventor may appeal to a board, which has the power to correct the examiner's interpretation. If the agency appeal board agrees with the examiner's interpretation, then the inventor may appeal that ruling to the federal court system. As we shall study in the next chapter, such a case actually occurred, and the federal courts ultimately interpreted the statute differently, thereby concluding that living things were patentable. This then became the new policy, and the inventor was granted a patent under it.

To summarize, Congress makes policies, in conjunction with the president, through the passing of statutes. Administrative agencies administer the details of those policies. In carrying out their responsibilities, the agencies may have to interpret vague terms and conditions in the statutes, thereby establishing new policies. Likewise, courts make policies by interpreting statutes when deciding cases. This may happen in appeals from administrative actions, as described, or may arise in other contexts, such as disputes between private parties. *Bonito Boats* actually was an example of the power of courts to make policies by interpreting statutes. There, the U.S. Supreme Court interpreted the terms of the Patent Act and concluded that reverse-molding statutes conflicted with the wishes of Congress.

Two other elements of the dynamic are worth noting here. First, if Congress were opposed to the determination by the courts that living things are patentable, it could amend (subject to presidential action) the statute to explicitly state that living things may not be patented. After such a clarification, the door would be closed on those in the PTO or the courts who felt the policy should be otherwise. Thus, in these matters, Congress has the ultimate say. However, Congress moves very slowly, and such clarification amendments often come very late, especially in a field that moves as quickly as technology. The experience with copyright protection for computer software provides an illustrative example of this result and will be studied in some detail later.

Congress also has given the PTO the power to make regulations about patent procedures. A regulation is simply a law passed by an administrative agency, which conforms to the benchmarks articulated by Congress. A host of such regulations passed by the PTO can be found in the Code of Federal Regulations. The PTO also can make guidelines offering its views up front about certain issues. For instance, the PTO has developed guidelines for use by its patent examiners about the patentability of computer programs.[11]

Federal trademark and copyright policies arise through similar dynamics. Trademark policy is controlled by the Lanham Act, with administration conducted, again, by the PTO. Copyright law is derived from the Copyright Act, which is administered by the Copyright Office, a branch of the Library of Congress. As with patents, the administrative agencies in these instances make registration decisions, which are subject to appeal in the federal courts. They also issue regulations. Exhibit 1.3 provides a summary of the federal government policymaking institutions and indicates how each may affect the development of trademark, copyright, and patent policies in the United States.

Policies made at the state level are controlled by analogous principles. Legislatures make laws that are subject to interpretations by courts and administered, if necessary, by administrative agencies. State policies, however, raise a new issue. You can imagine how potentially burdensome it might be for a national or international company to deal with state laws if those laws varied greatly from state to state. For instance, if you had valuable information that was protected by trade secret laws in some states but not all, your advantage could be lost if you do not exercise special care within certain borders. Fortunately, in a variety of contexts, the states have taken steps to unify their individual policies. For ex-

**Exhibit 1.3 Powers of U.S. Government Policymakers**

| Branch | Formal Methods of Policymaking |
|---|---|
| Congress | 1. Pass legislation articulating policy<br>   a. The Patent Act<br>   b. The Copyright Act<br>   c. The Lanham Act<br><br>2. Pass legislation affecting administrative agencies<br>   a. Authorize powers of agencies<br>   b. Designate budgets for agencies<br>3. Approve president's nominees for administrative agencies and courts |
| President | 1. Nominate administrative agency heads*<br>2. Nominate court justices<br>3. Approve or veto legislation<br>4. Manage administrative agencies |
| Courts | 1. Interpret statutes and constitutions |
| Administrative agencies<br>— Department of Commerce<br>   — Patent and Trademark Office<br>— Library of Congress<br>   — Copyright Office<br>— Others | 1. Administrate legislative directives<br>2. Interpret statutes<br>3. Promulgate regulations<br>4. Establish guidelines |

*Exception: The register of copyrights, who heads the Copyright Office, is selected by the librarian of Congress.

ample, trade secret policy has been brought into substantial conformity in many states through adoption of the Uniform Trade Secrets Act, a document that was developed by experts to serve as a model for legislative action. Also, in the contracts arena, all states except Louisiana have adopted Article II of the Uniform Commercial Code, thereby unifying policies dealing with the sale of goods. However, in other realms, policies still vary. One example explored later in this book is that of strict products liability, a contentious issue wherein manufacturers and distributors must compensate for injuries caused by product defects, even when they are not at fault.

Before moving on to the international arena, one should be aware that there has been a substantial trend toward increasing intellectual property protection within the United States. Since 1982, Congress has passed numerous new laws and amendments that have served to strengthen intellectual property rights. Many of these policy steps will be discussed in detail later in this book. However, here is just a small sample of the recent changes made by Congress on the domestic front: (1) The Copyright Act was amended, simplifying the procedures to receive protection and expanding the range of coverage.[12] (2) The federal trademark statute—the Lanham Act—was revised, allowing one to register a trademark earlier and fortifying the breadth of protection under federal law.[13] (3) Changes were made to the antitrust laws, relaxing restrictions on research and development activities and legitimizing certain business techniques used to control patents and the distribution of patented products.[14] (4) Statutes were passed to protect new forms of intellectual property, such as semiconductor chips.[15] (5) The Court of Appeals for the Federal Circuit was created by Congress to hear appeals in patent, trademark, and other cases.[16] As will be seen, the most important consequence of this new court has been to substantially increase the validity of patent rights granted by the PTO.

The other players in the U.S. policy process reinforced the expansion and solidification of intellectual property rights. Presidents Reagan and Bush were committed to strengthening intellectual property protection both at home and abroad. This was demonstrated not only in their speeches and legislative proposals but in their various governmental appointments as well. Those appointed to head the relevant administrative agencies worked diligently to modernize and improve their departments. For example, the PTO embarked on a program to computerize its operations and otherwise utilize new technologies in order to handle the rapidly increasing number of patent and trademark applications.[17] The PTO made other administrative adjustments as well so as to respond to the burgeoning number of patent filings in the new technology fields such as biotechnology and data processing.[18] Those in the intellectual property agencies also liberalized their interpretations as to protectible assets. One striking example was the decision of the PTO in 1988 to issue a patent on a genetically engineered mouse. Seemingly, patent protection is now available for any form of nonhuman life.[19] In addition, the enforcement agencies contributed to the power of those companies holding intellectual property rights. For instance, the Justice Department's Antitrust Division, which polices the markets for anticompetitive actions, clearly indicated in its enforcement guidelines that businesses could exercise more control over the uses of their intellectual property.[20]

Judges appointed by Presidents Reagan and Bush to the federal bench consistently held conservative judicial philosophies, thereby disposing them also to support a strong system of intellectual property protection. It is interesting to note, for instance, that patent rights are upheld in 80% of cases now, whereas before 1982, the likelihood was closer to 30%.[21] In addition, the courts, through their interpretations, have expanded the range of intellectual property protection to new varieties of technology, such as computers and biotechnology. Indeed, there now is growing criticism that the courts have been overzealous in protecting intellectual property, such as in the computer copyright area.[22] In any event, U.S. companies obviously have noticed the sympathetic ears turned by the courts toward their intellectual assets. In 1990, for instance, U.S. businesses filed more than 5,700 intellectual property lawsuits compared to 3,800 in 1980.[23] Undoubtedly, the heat has been turned up within the domestic technology policy arena. It should come as no surprise that developments are occurring rapidly within the international domain as well.

## AN INTERNATIONAL POLICY PERSPECTIVE

The U.S. policy process clearly has recognized the importance of protecting intellectual property. To that end, numerous laws have been constructed to allow firms operating in the United States to profit from their investments in creativity and to enjoy the fruits of their valued names. Laws on the books, however, would not be enough without enforcement. Predictably, U.S. policy makers have provided for effective enforcement of these laws as well. The various statutes generally articulate that wrongdoers must cease their activities and are responsible to compensate their victims. And the courts have carried out their role in ordering these remedies by using the various tools of authority at their disposal.

If the United States were an insular economy, then one probably could rest comfortably with the aforesaid state of affairs. However, markets now are unquestionably global, within which the United States is only one, albeit important, piece of the puzzle. Most high-technology firms now compete and trade on an international scale. If laws are not developed and enforced within other borders as in the United States, protection may be lost. The United States does not have the authority to dictate policy within other sovereign countries or to enforce its own laws within those other jurisdictions. Thus, U.S. companies managing high technologies are dependent on foreign governments to establish strong intellectual property protection policies, such as those that have been established in the United States. If those policies are not developed, then the ground rules may be completely different when firms engage in commercial activities in international zones. Even if intellectual property protection is established by law overseas, it may be useless if the enforcement mechanisms are insufficient. It is one thing to state that something is wrong; it is quite another to do something about it.

The problems have become especially acute as technology has advanced. It is becoming increasingly easy and inexpensive to transmit, store, copy, and print hugh volumes of data in very short periods of time. The time has passed when effective enforcement could be aimed at a few major business users, distributors, or manufacturers.[24] Now, substantial violations may occur in even the smallest of homes. Under these circumstances, therefore, enforcement may be problematic even in the United States. In countries with less developed intellectual property protection mechanisms, the magnitude of the issue is extreme. And withdrawing operations from those countries does not necessarily avoid the problems. Access to the valued information anywhere in the world allows pirates to make duplicates within the hospitable environments and then channel their copies into the international distribution network. Exports of intellectual property assets from the United States have more than doubled in the past eight years, now accounting for more than 25% of total U.S. exports.[25] By some estimates, inadequate international protection of U.S. patents, trademarks, and copyrights costs the U.S.

economy $80 billion in sales and 250,000 jobs every year.[26] A recent study puts the sales losses for the U.S. software industry alone at over $9 billion, suggesting that software piracy is the norm in a host of countries, including Thailand, Taiwan, Japan, Spain, Italy, Mexico, Colombia, and Venezuela.[27] It is no wonder that international protection of intellectual property ranks high on the U.S. foreign policy agenda.

Raising the level of intellectual property protection across the globe to that level currently enjoyed in the United States and other industrialized countries is a formidable task. After all, there is no world government with the power to establish international intellectual property laws and the authority to enforce their provisions without regard to sovereign boundaries. Therefore, other avenues must be used to reach such uniformity.

Of course, it would be convenient if all governments developed economic policies based on the same philosophical principles as does the United States. Then one might expect at least some continual movement toward continuity among world governments. However, the wide diversity of cultural, economic, political, and social backgrounds that defines the various policies of the independent nations precludes the occurrence of a natural transformation. For example, many developing countries, especially in Latin America and Asia, consider intangible ideas, forms, symbols, and processes as belonging to the common heritage of mankind.[28] Treating such public goods as private property is inconsistent with those countries' cultural orientations, especially when the intangible items are controlled by foreign entities. National pride is an imposing force in such domains. In addition, these countries believe that it is in their economic self-interest to deny protection. Inexpensive access to the developed world's technology is seen as the quickest way to move along the modernization curve.[29] Indeed, piracy-based business ventures do thrive in several countries, such as Argentina, Brazil, China, India, Korea, Mexico, Singapore, Taiwan, and Thailand.[30] Clamping down with intellectual property protection may have serious short-term consequences to the current economic bases of these and other nations. The least developed nations logically fear that stronger intellectual property laws would raise their prices for consumption goods and for key components to their manufactured items while simply transferring additional profits outside their countries.[31] Thus, if one can find intellectual property policies at all within those borders, they are usually weakly drawn and even more casually enforced. Expecting those nations to reform these fundamental notions on an independent basis would be a naive hope.

Deterrence of international pirating activities can be accomplished through unilateral, bilateral, and/or multilateral means. Unilateral options usually are the easiest to implement but tend to be the least effective, especially for companies with widespread international marketing activities. Bilateral agreements are an improvement, but they lead to a patchwork of varying international standards. Multilateral methods should provide the most extensive protection but can be frustrating to achieve. We will review some important considerations and developments on all of these fronts.

## Unilateral Steps

A unilateral action can be defined as an independent step by a country, such as the United States, to protect its citizens from foreign pirating activities. It is a law or measure designed to protect businesses within the national borders. Given that it has only national extent, such a law is most useful for firms that concentrate their marketing activities within those borders. Organizations with more multinational visions will find that other efforts are needed to combat the global effects of piracy on their operations.

The U.S. patent, copyright, and trademark laws all provide remedies for the importation of pirated copies into the United States. Thus, if Lotus 1-2-3 were pervasively copied in Korea, for instance, then Lotus is entitled to legal recourse if these copies are imported into the United States. So, if Lotus discovers a distributor in Seattle, Washington reselling the pirated software, Lotus can bring suit against that distributor in a federal trial court located in that area. If it can persuade the court that the distributor is selling illegal copies, then the court may order the distributor to compensate Lotus for lost profits from forgone sales, and it may also forbid the distributor from selling any more pirated Lotus items in the state.

Although these laws provide some measure of protection for Lotus, their overall effectiveness, even within the United States, can be somewhat limited. First of all, litigation in the United States often takes three to five years, a long period in any context, but especially burdensome in the fast-paced technology climate. Second, and more important, the suit by Lotus is against an individual distributor. If the overseas pirating activity is widespread, then the illegal copies likely will reach U.S. markets through a large number of different importers and distributors throughout the land. To control the situation, Lotus will have to institute a wide array of lawsuits against the multitude of resellers all across the country. Clearly, the magnitude of such a task may be daunting.

There are various laws and regulations in the United States that allow the Customs Service to block the importation of goods violating U.S. intellectual property rights. These, too, may be viewed as examples of unilateral measures established by the United States. Section 337 of the U.S. Tariff Act, which was amended by Congress in 1988 to make it more effective, offers the most general and far-reaching relief to aggrieved intellectual property owners in the United States.[32] Under Section 337, a U.S. industry may file a complaint with the International Trade Commission (ITC) alleging that pirated goods are being imported. If the ITC, after an administrative hearing, determines that the imported goods do violate U.S. patents, copyrights, mask works, trade secrets, or trademarks, it may effectively prevent further imports of those goods at the U.S. door.[33] This route offers a number of advantages to a company such as Lotus. The most obvious difference is that Lotus no longer has to chase sellers around the country. As opposed to trial court litigation, which concerns the wrongdoing of the parties being sued, the ITC hearing is aimed at the offending articles. Once the Section 337 proceeding is successfully completed, the ITC and the Customs Service will act as watchdogs for Lotus, excluding the entry of all offending copies of 1-2-3 before they enter the stream of U.S. commerce. Also, Section 337 requires that the ITC make its determinations within 12 to 18 months, a considerably shorter time period than traditional litigation. On the downside, the ITC does not have the power to compensate Lotus for damages caused by sales made before the exclusion order. Lotus must use the normal trial court channels for that or use the ITC action as leverage to gain monetary settlements with the offending distributors. Nonetheless, for a company that is being injured in the United States by pirated goods, Section 337 may be an effective weapon indeed.[34]

The federal copyright and trademark statutes, in conjunction with Customs Service regulations, have more particularized procedures whereby the Customs Service may restrict the entry of goods violating registered copyrights and trademarks that have been recorded with that office.[35] These Customs Service procedures offer many of the same benefits as Section 337. In fact, they provide an additional advantage in terms of convenience and money, since it is up to the Customs Service to identify infringing products and to take the requisite legal steps to block the imports.[36] However, this bonus obviously evaporates if the Customs Service does not recognize that imports are infringing in the first place.[37] Also, one should consider that the relevant decision makers at the Customs Service may not have sufficient expertise to handle intellectual property matters in certain contexts.[38] In addition, the Customs Service currently does not apply these procedures to many types of intellectual property, such as patents. Finally, as with Section 337, the Customs Service has no power to order the payment of damages for infringements.

## Bilateral Arrangements

For companies selling outside the United States, other measures will be required to protect their intangible investments. The goal of bilateral and multilateral agreements is to alter legal policies in other countries so that those countries elevate the importance of intellectual property protection within their borders.

Bilateral agreements are promises between two sovereigns to conduct their policy affairs in certain ways. For instance, assume that pirates in Thailand are having a significant worldwide negative effect on certain powerful U.S. businesses. These businesses might be able to convince the president to negotiate an agreement with the government of Thailand wherein Thailand pledges to improve its protection of intellectual property. Of course, the United States will have to offer a sufficient concession in return, thus providing Thailand the incentive to go along.

Bilateral arrangements often have successfully resulted in intellectual property reforms overseas. An agreement between the United States and the Soviet Union in 1990, for instance, committed both countries to further the protection of various forms of intellectual property.[39] More recently, the United States entered bilateral agreements with former republics of the Soviet Union such as Estonia and Moldavia.[40] Another example of a bilateral mechanism is provided by the Semiconductor Chip Protection Act. This statute protects within the United States those chip designs owned by U.S. nationals. Chip designs owned by foreign nationals are not initially protected by the act. However, if the foreign national comes from a country that provides similar semiconductor protections to U.S. nationals within its borders, then the foreign national will receive U.S. protection. In effect, this is an offer that may be accepted by another country when it develops similar laws. Through this avenue, 19 other countries have now adopted legislation protecting semiconductor chip designs.[41]

Another bilateral tool used by the U.S. government to induce changes in the intellectual property policies of foreign countries is based on Section 301, a provision of the U.S. Trade and Tariff Act. Section 301 allows the U.S. Trade Representative (USTR), with the approval of the president, to take retaliatory actions against any foreign country that condones unreasonable or discriminatory trading practices that unduly burden U.S. trade or foreign investment. Such practices include providing subsidies to domestic firms, denying market access to U.S. businesses, and, of most relevance for this book, failing to adequately protect the intellectual property of U.S. enterprises. Thus, rather than offering carrots to reward countries for improvements to their intellectual property laws, this section uses the stick approach by giving the president the power to withdraw benefits, such as preferential tariff treatment, or to impose additional punitive tariffs when protection is deemed insufficient. For those countries largely dependent on trade with the United States, this has proven to be a potent weapon.

In 1988, section 301 was enhanced by what are called the Super and Special 301 provisions of the Omnibus Trade and Competitiveness Act.[42] Super 301 is aimed at those countries that impede U.S. export potential, while Special 301 is more particularly concerned with foreign nations that threaten U.S. intellectual property rights. Under Special 301, the USTR establishes three lists of countries by the end of April of each year, based on relative levels of concern about intellectual property protection. The "watch list" consists of those countries to which the USTR wishes to signal that improvement is desired. No immediate tariff action by the United States is contemplated, but this could change in the future if steps are not initiated through bilateral negotiations. In 1993, the USTR announced that 17 countries had been placed on the watch list.[43] Of these, Cyprus, Italy, Pakistan, Spain, and Venezuela were notified that they were the subjects of some heightened concern and that their policies would be reviewed in advance of the regular cycle to determine if reclassification were necessary.

The middle tier is the "priority watch list." It indicates those countries where the need for change is more immediate. Being placed on this list is a strong signal that bilateral negotiations had better proceed. In 1993, the USTR reported that Argentina, Australia, Egypt, the European Union, Hungary, Korea, Poland, Saudi Arabia, Taiwan, and Turkey were within the priority watch list classification. Here again, the USTR reported that some of these countries were especially troublesome and slated them for early reviews. These were Argentina, Egypt, Korea, Poland, and Turkey. In addition, the USTR raised particular objections about the intellectual property efforts of Taiwan and Hungary. The concern with Taiwan was that it often passes laws in a symbolic sense to meet U.S. demands but fails to effectively enforce them.[44] Hungary's problems involved its pharmaceutical patent and copyright laws. These two countries were instructed to present immediate action plans to the USTR and were told that they might be reclassified for retaliatory action if U.S. requirements were not satisfactorily addressed.[45] As a result of this directive, Taiwanese officials approved certain substantial reforms to the country's intellectual property policies in June and July of 1993. These actions satisfied U.S. officials enough to prevent reclassification of Taiwan to the "priority foreign country" list but were not deemed sufficient to move it down to the watch list, as Taiwan had hoped.[46]

The highest level is the Special 301 priority foreign country list. A country is placed on this list when its intellectual property practices have the greatest adverse impact on U.S. trade. Under Special 301, nations designated as priority foreign countries are subject to a six-month fast-track investigative procedure during which the USTR substantiates its concerns and imposes retaliatory trade sanctions if improvements are not made.[47] On April 30, 1993, the USTR indicated that Brazil, India, and Thailand were priority foreign countries. Brazil and India were criticized for ineffective patent policies.[48] Thailand was accused of providing insufficient copyright enforcement.[49] Overall, the clout of trade sanctions offered by Special 301 has been credited with improving intellectual property protection practices in a number of foreign countries.[50] Special 301 also symbolically established the importance of intellectual property matters to the U.S. government.

Despite numerous successes with bilateral arrangements, multilateral bargains, which commit a number of governments to common principles, are greatly preferred. One problem with bilateral methods involves continuity. A concession granted to one country may be demanded by others. Also, bilateral successes may allow other developed countries to enjoy the benefits without paying the concessions.[51] Finally, the limited scope and hodgepodge nature of bilateral agreements does not promote worldwide trade as well as more far-reaching multilateral approaches.

### Multilateral Approaches

Multilateral approaches reach beyond bilateral agreements in that many countries together agree to conform to a policy framework. Currently there are several important multilateral agreements pertaining separately to patents, copyrights, and trademarks. In addition, extensive multilateral negotiations on a comprehensive scale have recently been completed within the General Agreement on Tariffs and Trade (GATT). Exhibit 1.4 provides a list of the most important multilateral agreements affecting the protection of intellectual property. These agreements will be touched on here to establish context for the more detailed considerations this book undertakes in later chapters.

In the patent arena, the most important multilateral accords are the Convention of the Union of Paris for the Protection of Industrial Property (Paris Convention), the Patent Cooperation Treaty, and the European Patent Convention.

**Exhibit 1.4 Major International Multilateral Agreements**

| Field | Agreements |
|---|---|
| Patents | Paris Convention<br>Patent Cooperation Treaty<br>European Patent Convention |
| Copyrights | Berne Convention<br>Universal Copyright Convention |
| Trademarks | Paris Convention<br>Madrid Arrangement<br>Madrid Protocol |
| Comprehensive | General Agreement on Tariffs and Trade<br>Treaty of Rome and Maastricht Treaty<br>　　(European Union)<br>North American Free Trade Agreement |

The members of the Paris Convention, totaling around 80 nations, have agreed that inventors from foreign signatory countries should be accorded the same rights under a member's patent laws as enjoyed by citizens of that member. Thus, since the United States and Canada both are members of the Paris Convention, an inventor from Canada is entitled to the same protections under U.S. patent laws as received by a U.S. citizen. Likewise, a U.S. citizen enjoys the same rights in Canada as does a Canadian native. Such reciprocity, called national treatment, is common to many of the major multilateral intellectual property treaties. Note that national treatment provided by the Paris Convention does not specify any common standards for patentability. Therefore, the patent laws of each member can and do vary widely. For example, when there are two or more creators of the same invention, laws differ on who is entitled to the patent, some granting it to the first to make the invention and others issuing it to the first to file for protection. Also, there are substantial differences in the extent to which certain kinds of inventions, such as biotechnology and computers, can receive patents.

The Patent Cooperation Treaty, signed by more than 55 countries, provides for certain procedural advantages in filing patent applications within member nations.[52] Similarly, the more regional European Patent Convention simplifies the task of filing for patents within 17 European nations. However, the European Patent Convention is more ambitious than the Patent Cooperation Treaty because it also requires the participating nations to accept certain substantive principles of patent protection. Indeed, the European Patent Convention has established something very close to a European-wide patent. It therefore serves as a model for future multilateral patent accords.

Currently, the World International Property Organization (WIPO), an agency affiliated with the United Nations, is attempting to develop a treaty to harmonize substantive patent policies on a more global scale (Patent Harmonization Treaty).

Negotiators within WIPO have made substantial progress in ironing out some key differences currently existing between the patent laws of various countries. Indeed, the latest proposals would require the United States to change a fundamental principle of its patent system, which awards patents to the first person to conceive an invention. This will be discussed further in Chapter 2. However, the momentum for completing the negotiations stalled in 1993, when the United States requested the postponement of a Diplomatic Conference that was scheduled for the end of July to finalize the treaty. The United States made this request after the American Bar Association surprisingly voted to oppose the major change to U.S. law.[53] There are still reasons to be optimistic that the Patent Harmonization Treaty will soon be completed and signed by a large portion of the international community, including the United States. This is especially true given the recent strides made by the international community via other multilateral accords to unify other aspects of patent protection policies.[54]

International copyright policy is dominated by two multilateral arrangements: the Universal Copyright Convention and the Berne Convention. Until 1988, these two separate multilateral accords might have been considered of equal importance in terms of world international trade. The Universal Copyright Convention could boast the United States as a signatory country; the Berne Convention was older and had the broader membership. However, on October 31, 1988, the Berne Convention established itself as the dominant multilateral agreement when the United States became its 79th participant.

The fundamental principle of both copyright conventions is the same: Foreigners from signatory countries must be granted national treatment under the copyright laws of any other member country. This is the same philosophy guiding the Paris Convention. The two conventions part ways, however, in that each also requires adherence to a small but differing set of substantive standards. Under the Universal Copyright Convention, participants must comply with certain formalities for protection such as a copyright notice and possibly registration. An important tenet of the Berne Convention, on the other hand, is that "the enjoyment and the exercise of (copyright) shall not be subject to any formality."[55] Historically, notice and registration requirements were such a fundamental component of the U.S. copyright system that the United States shunned the Berne Convention. Indeed, its reluctance to alter its system of copyright protection caused the United States to lead the effort within the United Nations to create the alternative Universal Copyright Convention.[56] In addition, the Berne Convention establishes that authors must have protection for "moral rights" under the laws of the member countries.[57] Such a Hegelian concept of intellectual property protection does not conform well to the more Lockean philosophy underlying U.S. law. This too made Berne somewhat hard for the United States to swallow.

That the United States was so stubbornly unwilling to join the dominant international copyright code raised the hackles of a number of important trading partners. Many nations criticized the United States for not being fully committed to the international protection of copyrights.[58] At the same time, the United States was calling for greater standards for the international protection of intellectual property. The position by the United States on copyrights, however, was seen as a double standard, greatly weakening its international bargaining position.[59] By joining the Berne Convention in 1988, the United States climbed to philosophically higher ground. Its willingness to compromise on copyrights should strengthen its leadership in establishing better international protections across a broad range of intellectual property issues.

International trademark policy is governed primarily by three multilateral agreements. The Paris Convention has provisions that extend the principle of national treatment to trademarks. It also specifies a few substantive minimum requirements for trademark protection, and requires signatory countries to provide effective protection against unfair competition. Another important trademark agreement is the Arrangement of Madrid Concerning the International Registration of Trademarks (Madrid Arrangement), joined currently by 29 nations but not the United States. The Madrid Arrangement is similar to the Patent Cooperation Treaty in that it provides certain procedural and administrative advantages for protection within member countries. The third major multilateral trademark accord is the Madrid Protocol. The Madrid Protocol is a direct descendent of the Madrid Agreement, but is expected to have wider appeal because it deals with certain objections that some nations, such as the United States, have had with the Madrid Agreement. As with the major patent and copyright conventions, these three international trademark arrangements have little if anything to say about the substantive content and enforcement of each member's trademark laws. One important effort to harmonize trademark policies and procedures in a more regional, multilateral context has been developing within the European Union.[60] In December 1993, for instance, the European Union established the European Union Trademark Office to administer a unionwide trademark registration system.

For nations such as the United States that are committed to stronger intellectual property protections around the globe, the aforementioned set of multilateral approaches suffers from two glaring defects. First, the promise of national treatment does not require anything in terms of the level of protection within a country. All that is required is that foreigners be treated the same as nationals. If a developing country chooses not to protect the intellectual assets of its citizens, then it can allow substantial copying of foreign products as well. Second, even when there is a pledge to have some protection, as with the Berne Convention, this is no guarantee that the laws will be effectively enforced. For this reason, the United States and other developed countries aggressively pursued the adoption of minimum substantive standards for intellectual property protection through the GATT.

GATT was first drafted in 1947 to establish a new international trading order and to eliminate protectionism. The contracting parties, which now number over 115 and represent more than 80% of the total volume of world trade, have agreed to a set of guiding principles and a detailed system of maximum tariffs. Unlike the other multilateral conventions, the GATT system provides substantive standards of international law and includes a dispute resolution settlement process. The major principle of the GATT system is nondiscriminatory treatment. Such nondiscrimination is furthered primarily by the application of what is called unconditional most-favored-nation trade (MFN). Unconditional MFN means that when a GATT party extends some privilege to another GATT member (such as a lower tariff rate), then that privilege is automatically extended to all other GATT participants. The principle of nondiscrimination also is accomplished through national treatment policies, just as we have seen in other, more specific contexts. There are other fundamental notions underlying GATT as well. These include both a basic philosophy that restraints on the movement of goods and services should be kept to a minimum and an understanding that the conditions of international trade should be developed within multilateral frameworks.

When trading disputes develop, complaints are brought by national governments before a council within a newly formed GATT administrative body, called the World Trade Organization. If the council finds that a nation has violated a promise made through the GATT, then it will authorize the complaining party to take defensive actions, such as by withdrawing the offending nation's MFN status or by imposing other retaliatory measures. In addition, and possibly more important, the ruling legitimizes the retaliatory actions of the complaining nation in the eyes of the international community. This puts added pressure on the offending party to come into compliance with GATT principles.

Since the inception of GATT, the contracting parties have completed eight major rounds of multilateral trade negotiations, each aimed at reducing tariffs and trade barriers in various sectors of the international economy. The final effort, called the Uruguay Round, was completed in December 1993 after seven years of intense and often frustrating trade discussions. One component of these negotiations was devoted to trade-related aspects of intellectual property, or TRIPs. Many of the developed countries strongly advocated in the TRIPs discussions that GATT adopt at least some minimum level of substantive protection standards backed by effective internal enforcement mechanisms.[61] Indeed an official of the Office of United States Trade Representative declared that a TRIPs agreement was one of only three must-have items for the United States, the other two being agriculture and services.[62] However, certain less developed members of GATT, such as India, Brazil, and Argentina, vigorously opposed the adoption of minimum standards.[63] As previously discussed, these countries have philosophical and economic objections to intellectual property reforms within their boundaries. The various members also disagreed on the specifics of minimum standards that might eventually be adopted. New technologies based on computers and genetic engineering raised a host of vexing issues that divided the members. In addition, several important procedural aspects of protection, especially in the patent realm, proved to be very contentious.[64]

The completion of the Uruguay Round in December 1993 can be viewed as somewhat of a miracle. Each succeeding round of GATT negotiations has involved a larger and more diverse set of participants. By 1993, 117 nations representing all levels of economic development were included in GATT. In addition, the parties have attempted to tackle more complex and divisive issues at each stage. The goals of the Uruguay Round initially were extremely far-reaching, calling not only for lower maximum tariffs on a host of products but also for consistent international trade policies on such difficult nationalistic arenas as agriculture, textiles, airline manufacturing, financial services, movies, and intellectual property. During the seven years that the Uruguay Round was debated, the parties naturally found that extensive compromises were essential for any deal to be struck. This was no less true for TRIPs than for the other components of the multilateral trade accord. Nonetheless, the completion of the Uruguay Round, and the basic understandings that ultimately prevailed regarding intellectual property, should prove to be crucial to those managing technologies in the international environment.

The Uruguay Round GATT agreement is scheduled to become effective in July 1995. The governments of the member nations must independently approve the agreement before they become bound by its terms. As this book is being finalized, expectations are very high that the U.S. Congress will approve the deal. Most, if not all, of the other countries also will likely adopt it. Therefore, those managing technology should now plan to operate in an international environment governed by the new GATT regime. The most important elements of the Uruguay Round that relate to intellectual property are summarized below.

1. ADMINISTRATION
   a. A Council on Trade-Related Aspects of Intellectual Property Rights will be created for a variety of administrative tasks such as publicizing the laws adopted in member states and monitoring the operation of the TRIPs agreement.

2. TRANSITIONAL COMPLIANCE DATES
   a. Developed nations have 1 year following the effective date of the Treaty to implement its terms. Developing nations (such as India and Thailand) have 5 years and the least developed nations (such as Bangladesh) have 11 years.

3. PATENT ISSUES
   a. Members are required to comply with the Paris Convention.
   b. Patents must be available for products and processes.
   c. Patentable subject matter must be broad, but may exclude plants and animals (other than microorganisms). These exclusions constitute a blow to the goals of the genetic engineering industry.
   d. Patent protection must last for 20 years after the date of filing a patent application. This seemingly will require an adjustment to United States laws, and may be the springboard for a wholesale change to a first-to-file priority system.
   e. Developing nations may delay granting product patent protection to areas of technology that were not protected within their borders when the treaty comes into force. The delay can be for up to 5 additional years (beyond that allowed under transition). Thus, these nations may

delay protection for certain products, such as pharmaceuticals, for up to 10 years after the effective date of the treaty. Although the delay was opposed by the U.S. pharmaceutical industry, there at least is a defined date when protection is supposed to begin.

f. Nations may still require owners of patented technologies to license them to local businesses (compulsory licensing). However, opportunities for compulsory licensing are circumscribed to make them more acceptable to U.S. interests. For instance, compulsory licenses must be non-exclusive, the licensee must first attempt to secure a negotiated license with the patent holder, reasonable remuneration must be paid under a compulsory license, and the duration of a compulsory license must be limited. In the case of semiconductor technology, compulsory licensing shall only be for public non-commercial uses, or to remedy an anti-competitive practice.

g. Patents must be available without discrimination as to the place of invention, the field of technology and whether products are imported or locally produced. Part of this is aimed at the United States, which heretofore has discriminated against inventions made in foreign countries in terms of its first-to-invent priority system. If the Untied States moves to a first-to-file priority system, as expected, this issue becomes moot.

4. TRADE SECRETS

a. Protection for information is required if the information is secret, has commercial value because it is secret, and has been subject to reasonable steps to keep it secret. The conforms to state trade secret policies in the United States.

b. Testing data submitted with applications to obtain government marketing approval of pharmaceutical and of agricultural products which utilize new chemical entities shall be protected against unfair commercial use.

5. INDUSTRIAL PRODUCT DESIGNS

a. Protection is required, but may be limited to those designs which are significantly different from known designs. The United States design patent laws meet this criterion.

6. COPYRIGHT

a. Members are required to comply with the Berne Convention, except for provisions relating to moral rights. This exclusion benefits the United States, which was concerned that moral rights under GATT might exceed the privileges granted under U.S. law.

b. Computer software and compilations of data must be protected by copyright.

c. Copyright owners in computer programs and sound recordings have the right to authorize or prohibit rentals of their products.

7.  TRADEMARKS

    a.  Members are required to comply with the Paris Convention.

    b.  Use of a trademark may not be a condition for filing an application for registration. However, use may be a requirement for registration. The United States came into compliance in 1988 when it started to allow intent-to-use applications.

8.  ANTI-COMPETITIVE PRACTICES

    a.  National laws may specify which, if any, licensing practices have an adverse effect on competition, as long as they are otherwise consistent with the TRIPs principles.

9.  ENFORCEMENT

    a.  Nations are required to provide in their national laws for "effective" action against infringement of intellectual property rights. The procedures should not be unnecessarily costly or complicated, and should not entail unreasonable time limits.

    b.  Expeditious remedies are required. These include, with some qualifications, injunctions and preliminary injunctions.

    c.  Criminal procedures are required for willful trademark counterfeiting and copyright violations on a commercial scale.

    d.  Judicial review of administrative decisions must be provided.

The Uruguay Round GATT will diminish the importance of Section 301 as a tool to convince other nations to improve their intellectual property laws and enforcement. Although the United States did not agree to give up its Section 301 retaliatory powers altogether under the GATT, it will curtail its use. Trade disputes, such as those involving alleged dumping or intellectual property protection deficiencies, will be brought before a panel or council within the newly organized World Trade Organization. Since the new GATT now requires member nations to protect intellectual property rights at levels considered acceptable to U.S. interests, there is some likelihood that decisions rendered by the World Trade Organization will be favorable to the United States, thereby allowing the United States to threaten retaliation if necessary. Thus, the GATT procedures should accomplish the same results as were achieved through Section 301.

Even though the Uruguay Round has now been successfully completed, one should not forget the tremendous hurdles that had to be overcome to finalize the agreement. Due to the inherent difficulties in formulating worldwide multilateral accords, smaller sets of countries, often in geographical proximity and/or with similar economic development patterns, strive to reach more regional multilateral agreements.[65] A substantial number of nations in Europe, for instance, have made great strides in unifying their policies regarding trade and development through multilateral agreements. The most important European effort began in 1957 when six nations signed the Treaty of Rome, which established the European Community. The original goals of this multilateral agreement were to establish a common market and to promote harmonious development of economic activities. In 1986, the members of the European Community, which by that time numbered twelve, signed the Single European Act. The intent of this Act was to strengthen the ability of the members to achieve harmonization, and to further economic integration. In November 1993, the members of the European Community formed the European Union when they signed the Maastricht Treaty on European Union. Through the European Union, the members hope to achieve greater monetary and political union, as well as attain certain social principles. As of mid-1994, there were 12 members of the European Union, but it is expected that this number may soon increase to 16.[66]

The European Union has several governing bodies, including the Council, the Commission, the Assembly, and the Court of Justice. The Council and the Commission have the power to issue regulations and directives for the purpose of harmonizing policies among the member states. A regulation can be likened to a transnational law because it directly controls transactions and behavior within all the member countries of the European Union. A directive provides a policy objective, but requires the individual members to pass their own laws to attain that goal. The Council and Commission have focused their attentions on numerous topics that are substantially important to those involved with managing technology. For example, they have proposed or passed legislation in the forms of regulations and directives for such topics as copyrights and computer software, semiconductors, protection of databases, privacy, trademarks, semiconductors, and biotechnology. Many of these will be discussed in later chapters of this book. For consistency, the text ascribes all directives and regulations to the European Union (rather than the European Community), even though most of them were originally proposed or became effective prior to the formalization of the European Union.

The United States recently negotiated with Canada and Mexico another regional trade pact called the North American Free Trade Agreement (NAFTA). This agreement, which became effective on January 1, 1994, created the world's largest free trade zone, affecting more than 350 million consumers.[67] Of particular interest for managers of technology, it also provides for greater harmony of patent, copyright, trademark, and trade secret standards in the region, and it obliges member countries to enforce their laws effectively. Technology areas that substantially benefit from the accord include computers, pharmaceuticals, sound recordings, and motion pictures.[68] In 1991, as a prelude to NAFTA, Mexico passed an enhanced intellectual property protection law, which achieved in Mexico much of what NAFTA now requires.[69] However, enforcement of that law, which had been subject to criticism, was a key issue in the NAFTA negotiations.[70]

Acceptance of NAFTA by the United States was initially frustrated by various concerns, especially over environmental issues and possible loss of employment opportunities.[71] One potential stumbling block was averted when an appellate court reversed a lower court decision that had required the Clinton Administration to file an environmental-impact statement, evaluating the environmental effects of the trade accord.[72] Organized labor opposed the agreement vigorously, claiming that lower U.S. tariffs on imported goods from within the region would induce U.S. manufacturers to relocate, especially to Mexico. After an extremely narrow and contentious vote in the House of Representatives, NAFTA finally was approved by Congress in November 1993. This paved the way for its eventual adoption in all three countries soon thereafter.

## PRINCIPLES OF STRATEGY FOR MANAGING TECHNOLOGY

The making of business strategy is an enormously complex task, relying on a wide range of variables.[73] It is highly dependent on the nature of an organization and the environment that surrounds it. For instance, corporations often are built on different core philosophies about how business should be conducted. Looking simply at the computer software industry, one can find companies that advocate and practice the free interchange of ideas as well as others that expect information to be protected at great lengths. The core philosophy of firms can affect what strategic steps executives should take in managing technology. For instance, as will be discussed in Chapter 4, trade secrets must be protected with reasonable security measures. If the core philosophy of a firm is not compatible with such actions, then choosing this form of protection may not be a good strategy for managers to take. Other aspects within the organization that affect strategy formulation are the leadership styles employed by its executives and the flexibility of the internal systems established to implement policies. Looking externally, managers who formulate strategies must account for the social, political, economic, and competitive environments in which the business operates. In addition, they must recognize the constraints of laws, including those that are imposed by nature and created by man. It is here, of course, where this book fits in, by providing insights into the legal aspects affecting management decisions.

With this as a basis, managers devising strategies should be mindful of a number of principles. First, it is important to anticipate what the competition will do, so that appropriate measures can be taken to keep the firm profitable. Second, managers should strive to incorporate the strengths of the competition. This means that they should learn about the core competencies of competitors and assimilate them when appropriate. It also suggests that firms should seek to take advantage of the resources held by competitors. This principle does not instruct managers to steal those resources, but it informs them that working with rivals, through perhaps strategic alliances, can be mutually beneficial. Some attributes of strategic alliances will be explored in Chapter 9. One also can learn from this doctrine that there may be times when it is better to share information rather than hoard it. This book spends a lot of time discussing various methods that might be used to protect intellectual property. This does not mean, however, that the best strategy is to use every available means to protect one's ideas. Indeed, it might be a better strategy, depending on the circumstances, to simply give ideas away in the hopes of building a market. To substantiate this, one only has to reflect on a strategy once pervasively used by several computer hardware companies wherein they effectively gave software to the public for free. This made sense at the time because software tied the customers to a particular type of hardware, which then was by far the more profitable aspect of the industry.[74]

There are other key aspects of strategy that should guide how decisions are made. For instance, managers must fully understand the particular business that they are in, including the products, the market, and the competition. A strategy that is appropriate for a tobacco concern may have little relevance for a computer company. Also, strategies must be flexible, having the capability to adapt to changes. Strategies are best when they involve constant planning rather than relying on static long-term plans. Periodic intellectual property audits, for instance, are based on the notion of change and on having the ability to respond to change in ways that best meet the strategic needs of the enterprise.

While reading this book, you should always keep these principles in mind. The book provides the legal framework under which strategies are formulated. As a student of business or technology, it is up to you to use this knowledge to determine the strategy that is best for a company to adopt. This, of course, is highly dependent on the particular situation, as defined by the variables previously discussed. The book provides a lot of information about techniques that are available to carry out business strategies for managing technology. But it is ultimately up to you to determine which techniques are most prudent for a company to adopt and how it should plan to carry them out.

In order to help illustrate and pull together the range of legal opportunities that are available to managers of any technology enterprise, the book presents a hypothetical example at the beginning of the next chapter and then refers to it throughout the text. By focusing on this example, the book makes it clear that technology can be protected in many different ways, often by more than one system at any given time. Also, it demonstrates that managers of all technologies face many of the same problems, but that the solutions may differ depending on the managers' particular strategic situations.

## CONCLUSION

This chapter has provided a bird's-eye view of the legal environment affecting those companies managing technology. You now have a preliminary feel for what intellectual property is and why it is often protected by law. You also should be somewhat comfortable with the dynamics of policymaking within the United States. Further, you have had a glimpse of the complicated web of international policies shaped by the dynamics of world affairs.

This book proceeds to focus more in depth on the important legal issues and considerations bearing on the management of technology. The orientation chosen is that of a company based in the United States. Therefore, there is a pronounced emphasis on U.S. laws and policies. However, the book does respect the critical importance of international policy aspects to those managing technologies from the United States.

The next six chapters are dedicated to the major fields of the intellectual property system: patents, trade secrets, copyrights, and trademarks. Chapters 8 and 9 then introduce other topics critical to managers of technological products. Chapter 8 deals with the legal responsibilities imposed on companies when their products or sales staffs harm their customers. Specifically, the chapter discusses negligence, strict liability, fraud, and privacy. Chapter 9 is dedicated to contract issues. Much of the presentation regards sales and warranty concerns. But the chapter also serves to bring together many of the concepts developed earlier in the book by examining the rise of strategic alliances. In addition, Chapter 9 examines other ways to resolve disputes rather than by litigation, and it provides an understanding of how antitrust might affect the strategic plans of a technology concern. By the end of this book, you will have a sophisticated and comprehensive understanding of the legal framework that will guide your strategic decisions regarding technology.

## NOTES

1. J. Hughes, "The Philosophy of Intellectual Property," 77 Georgetown L.J. 287, 302-303 (1988).
2. In a perfectly competitive market, the innovative firm would not be profitable at all. Once the technology has been introduced, the market would price it at the marginal cost of replication. The price, therefore, would not be sufficient to cover the R&D outlays, yielding a negative net profit for the innovator. See K. Maskus, "Intellectual Property Rights and the Uruguay Round," Federal Reserve Bank of Kansas City Economic Review (First Quarter 1993) at 13.
3. Eastern Wine Corp., v. Winslow Warren, Ltd., 137 F.2d 955, 988 (2d Cir.), cert. denied, 320 U.S. 758 (1943).
4. Because patents generally take about two years to issue, the net effect on the length of patent protection for most inventions will not be significant. However, biotechnology firms fear that this change may cause them substantial hardships because they sometimes face substantially longer periods of examination before their patents issue. See V. Slind-Flor, "Pending Patent Problems," The National L.J. (May 23, 1994) at A1.
5. J. Hughes, "The Philosophy of Intellectual Property," 77 Georgetown L.J. 287, 330-339 (1988).
6. There are other, more specific components of the intellectual property system. For example, federal law protects semiconductor chips, or mask works, under a separate (sui generis) system. 17 U.S.C. §§901-914 (1984).
7. For a thorough discussion of the role of trademarks in reducing search costs, see Folsom & Teply, "Trademarked Generic Words," 89 Yale L.J. 1323 (1980).
8. The federal government often regulates contracts and torts within the context of other specific regulatory areas such as drugs, motor vehicle safety, securities, and cigarettes. Also, Congress currently is debating a more general products liability law under the title the Product Liability Fairness Act.
9. Silkwood v. Kerr-McGee Corp., 464 U.S. 238, 248 (1984); Hines v. Davidowitz, 312 U.S. 52, 67 (1941).
10. T. McCarroll, "Whose Bright Idea?" Time (June 10, 1991) at 45.

11. Patentable Subject Matter—Mathematical Algorithms and Computer Programs, 1106 O.G.4 (September 5, 1989).
12. Berne Convention Implementation Act of 1988.
13. Trademark Law Revision Act of 1988.
14. National Cooperative Research Act of 1984; Intellectual Property Antitrust Protection Act of 1989.
15. The Semiconductor Chip Protection Act of 1984.
16. Federal Courts Improvements Act of 1982.
17. J. Pegram, "Technology Aids Trademark Practice," National L.J. (April 29, 1991) at S10; P. Barrett, "Lost in Paper," Wall Street J. (February 24, 1989) at B5.
18. J. Woo, "Biotech Patents Become Snarled in Bureaucracy," Wall Street J. (July 6, 1989) at B1.
19. J. Barton, "Patenting Life," Scientific American (March 1991) at 40.
20. Department of Justice Enforcement Guidelines for International Operations, reprinted in 1988 Trade Regulation Reports, CCH, No. 24 (November 10, 1988), section 3.6.
21. T. McCarroll, "Whose Bright Idea?" Time (June 10, 1991) at 45; P. Dwyer, "The Battle Raging over Intellectual Property," Business Week (May 22, 1989) at 79.
22. J. Burgess, "The Battle over Software Protection," Washington Post (April 2, 1989) at H1; "Scientists Protest Rash of Computer Software Suits," L.A. Times (May 25, 1989) at 3; W. Bulkeley, "Lotus Trial May Clarify Copyrights," Wall Street J. (February 6, 1990) at B1.
23. T. McCarroll, "Whose Bright Idea?" Time (June 10, 1991) at 44.
24. A. Branscomb, "Who Owns Creativity?" Technology Review (May/June, 1988) at 41.
25. T. McCarroll, "Whose Bright Idea?" Time (June 10, 1991) at 44.
26. T. McCarroll, "Whose Bright Idea?" Time (June 10, 1991) at 44. Other studies indicate that the losses, albeit significant, may not be as high as these estimates suggest. See K. Maskus, "Intellectual Property Rights and the Uruguay Round," Economic Review (First Quarter 1993) at 19-20.
27. "Software Pirates Wreak Worldwide Plundering," San Luis Obispo County Telegram-Tribune (June 10, 1993).
28. J. Pitts, "Pressing Mexico to Protect Intellectual Property," Wall Street J. (January 25, 1991).
29. R. Benko, Protecting Intellectual Property Rights, American Enterprise Institute for Public Policy Research (1987) at 28.
30. G. Hoffman and G. Marcou, "Commercial Piracy of Intellectual Property," 5 The Computer Lawyer (November 1988) at 10.
31. K. Maskus, "Intellectual Property Rights and the Uruguay Round," Federal Reserve Bank of Kansas City Economic Review (First Quarter 1993) at 17-18.
32. For thorough discussions of Section 337, see P. Victor and E. Naftalin, "Section 337 of the Tariff Act of 1930: A Proven Tool for The Protection of Intellectual Property," 2 J. of Proprietary Rights (June 1990) at 10; J. Lever, et al., "The Impact of the 1988 Omnibus Trade Act on Litigation before the International Trade

Commission under Section 337," 5 The Computer Lawyer (November 1988) at 13.

33. The president may overrule the determination of the ITC for any reason. Normally, the president invokes this power for international trade and policy reasons, such as when President Reagan rejected an ITC exclusion order of certain semiconductor "DRAMs" in 1987. P. Victor and E. Naftalin, 2 J. of Proprietary Rights (June 1990) at 115.

34. Section 337 has been found to violate a guiding principle of the General Agreement on Tariffs and Trade (GATT) that foreigners be treated in the same way as nationals. This is because imports are subject to Section 337 proceedings but products of U.S. origin are not. Changes to Section 337 can be expected soon to bring U.S. policies into conformity with GATT. See P. Victor & E. Naftalin, "Section 337 of the Tariff Act of 1930: A Proven Tool for the Protection of Intellectual Property," 2 J. of Proprietary Rights (June 1990) at 16-17.

35. 17 U.S.C. §§602-603; 15 U.S.C. §1124. Customs Service regulations can be found in Volume 19, Code of Federal Regulations. Trade names that have been used for at least six months also may be recorded with the Customs Service. 19 C.F.R. §§133.11-133.15.

36. Dratler, Intellectual Property Law: Commercial, Creative and Industrial Property, Law J. Seminars-Press (1993) at paragraph 13.02[1].

37. Ibid.

38. Ibid.

39. J. Brown, "The Protection of High Technology Intellectual Property: An International Perspective," 7 The Computer Lawyer (December 1990) at 17.

40. "U.S. and Moldavia Enter Trade Agreement and OPIC Agreements," J. of Proprietary Rights. (August 1992) at 38; "U.S. and Estonia Announce Pact," J. of Proprietary Rights (November 1992) at 29.

41. See 56 Fed. Reg. 32180 (July 15, 1991).

42. Omnibus Trade and Competitiveness Act of 1988, Pub. L. No. 100-418, title I, section 1303, 102 Stat 1179 (August 23, 1988), codified in 19 U.S.C. §2242 and 2411 et seq.

43. The 1993 "watch list" consists of Chile, China, Colombia, Cyprus, Ecuador, El Salvador, Greece, Guatemala, Indonesia, Italy, Japan, Pakistan, Peru, the Philippines, Spain, the United Arab Emirates, and Venezuela.

44. F. Wang, "Taming the Infringers," The National L.J. (May 17, 1993) at S.28.

45. On June 25, 1993, Taiwan's cabinet approved a comprehensive action plan for the protection of intellectual property rights.

46. See "Taiwan to Remain on Priority Watch List," 5 J. of Proprietary Rights (September 1993) at 34.

47. The six-month period may be extended if there are especially complex issues to resolve or if the country is making substantial progress toward correcting them.

48. See M. Margolis, "Tougher Patent Law Expected from Brazil," L.A. Times (April 26, 1993) at D2, D7.

49. See K. Stier, "Thai Piracy Likely to Top U.S. Hit List," L.A. Times (April 26, 1993) at D2, D7.

50. B. Turnbull, "Intellectual Property and GATT: TRIPS at the Midterm," 1 J. of Proprietary Rights (March 1989) at 11-12.

51. G. Hoffman and G. Marcou, "Commercial Piracy of Intellectual Property," 5 The Computer Lawyer (November 1988) at 10.

52. On February 16, 1993, Kazakhstan became the 57th member of the Patent Cooperation Treaty.

53. PTC Newsletter, American Bar Association, Vol. 11 (Spring 1993) at 1-2. The American Bar Association's Section of Intellectual Property Law approved the change by a wide margin (102–8), but the House of Delegates narrowly defeated it (99–90).

54. Some of those who opposed a move by the United States to a first-to-file priority system felt that the change should be made only after the international community raised various patent standards. Successful completion of NAFTA and GATT may persuade these opponents that the time is now right for the United States to yield on its adherence to the first-to-invent system.

55. Berne Convention 1886, Article 5(3).

56. S. Strauss, "Don't Be Burned by the Berne Convention," Publication of the State Bar of California Intellectual Property Section (Spring 1989) at 7.

57. Berne Convention 1886, Article 6(b).

58. S. Strauss, "Don't Be Burned by the Berne Convention," Publication of the State Bar of California Intellectual Property Section (Spring 1989) at 7.

59. R. Benko, Protecting Intellectual Property Rights, American Enterprise Institute for Public Policy Research (1987) at 6-7, 33.

60. K. Kotenberg, "Providing Overseas Protection," National L.J. (April 29, 1991) at S2; "The Procedural Aspects of Community-Wide Patent, Trademark, and Copyright Law," 2 J. of Proprietary Rights (April 1990) at 9.

61. B. Turnbull, "Intellectual Property and GATT: TRIPS at the Midterm," 1 J of Proprietary Rights (March 1989) at 10.

62. Ibid.

63. G. Hoffman and G. Marcou, "Commercial Piracy of Intellectual Property," 5 The Computer Lawyer (November 1988) at 10.

64. B. Turnbull, "Intellectual Property and GATT: TRIPS at the Midterm," 1 J. of Proprietary Rights (March 1989) at 15-16.

65. Examples of existing or proposed regional accords include the European Free Trade Zone, Benelux, the Andean Common Market, Mercado Común del Ser Mercosur, the African Economic Community, Asia Pacific Economic Cooperation, the Association of South East Asian nations, and the North American Free Trade Agreement. For a full discussion of these regional pacts, see R. Schaffer, B. Earle, and F. Agusti, International Business Law and Its Environment, 2d ed., West Publishing Co (Minneapolis/St. Paul, 1993) at 83-87.

66. The members of the European Union are Belgium, Denmark, France, Germany, Greece, Ireland, Italy, Luxembourg, Netherlands, Portugal, Spain, and the United Kingdom. Four other nations are undergoing negotiations for European Union membership. These are Norway, Sweden, Finland, and Austria.

67. See, T. Robberson, "A Cloud Drifting over Trade and Texas," Washington Post National Weekly Edition (June 28–July 4, 1993) at 16.

68. For a detailed discussion of these requirements, see C. Del Valle, "Intellectual Property Provisions of the NAFTA," 4 J. of Proprietary Rights (November 1992) at 8-11.

69. Ley de Fomento y Protección de la Propiedad Industrial, Diario Oficial (June 27, 1991).

70. C. Del Valle, "Intellectual Property Provisions of the NAFTA," 4 J. of Proprietary Rights (November 1992) at 8-11.

71. See T. Robberson, "A Cloud Drifting over Trade and Texas," Washington Post Weekly Edition (June 28–July 4, 1993) at 16-17; M. Lavelle, "Free Trade vs. Law," National L.J. (March 29, 1993) at 1.

72. "Court Rejects Need For EIR on NAFTA," San Luis Obispo County Telegram Tribune (September 25, 1993) at C-7; B. Davis & A. Nomani, "Federal Judge's Ruling Could Be Death Blow to Free-Trade Accord," Wall Street J. (July 1, 1993) at 1.

73. I wish to thank Carey Heckman, lecturer, Stanford Law School and codirector, Stanford Law and Technology Policy Center, for these insights, which he based on R. L. Wing, The Art of Strategy (Dolphin, 1988).

74. See P. Heckel, "The Software-Patent Controversy, 9 Computer Lawyer (December 1992) at 17.

# 2

# THE U.S. PATENT SYSTEM: FUNDAMENTAL CONDITIONS FOR PROTECTION

## INTRODUCTION

Scenario: You are an electronics engineer who loves music, especially rock and roll. You have made the transition to compact disc technology in your living room, so much so that you no longer can listen to your large assortment of favorite rock and roll LPs. Somehow, the crackles, skips, and hisses of that old Jethro Tull album now seem to ruin an experience that once was totally enjoyable. It occurs to you that it would be nice if you could use digital technology to filter out the unwanted annoyances and boost the clarity of the desirable material. Then you could appreciate your old classics and not be burdened with investigating whether they have been rereleased on expensive new compact discs.

You and some friends set out to develop a machine that can achieve this goal. You are certain that such a device would be a hot item among the 30 to 50 age bracket and would be extremely profitable if the price were manageable. After two years of effort and experimentation, your team is on the verge of a solution: a machine that uses modified standard digital technologies along with a computer program uniquely suited to identify and eliminate unwanted audio characteristics. As the time for marketing what you have coined the Audio Enhancement System (AES) comes near, you begin to wonder whether your efforts should have legal protection.

Like most persons dealing with new and potentially lucrative technological inventions, you are inclined to focus first, if not exclusively, on whether it is possible to obtain patent protection. There are several reasons why most inventors have a heightened level of awareness of patents within the spectrum of intellectual property rights. Of most importance is the somewhat common knowledge that patents provide substantial benefits. Only with a patent, for instance, may an inventor keep others from independently creating and marketing the same invention. Reinforcing this basic awareness of the power of patents are periodic newspaper accounts of huge, multimillion-dollar returns obtained by patent holders in patent infringement lawsuits or from contractual agreements. Polaroid's highly publicized $909-million judgment against Eastman Kodak certainly garnered media attention.[1] Honeywell's $96-million judgment against Minolta for infringing its patents covering autofocus and automatic flash technologies broadly affected manufacturers of cameras and motivated seven other companies to quickly seek settlements totaling $124 million.[2] More recently, a jury concluded that Honeywell infringed Litton Industries' patent on an airplane guidance device, and it determined that damages totaled $1.2 billion.[3] Also, the patent granted to Gilbert Hyatt in 1990 for the single-chip microprocessor shocked the computer industry, which now faces the prospect of paying hundreds of millions of dollars annually to Mr. Hyatt for the right to continue using his patented invention. Similarly, a patent issued to Compton's New Media in 1993 for a multimedia search-and-retrieval system brought cries of disbelief from industry participants who feared that the breadth of the patent might cover many of their interactive products. In fact, the reaction was so vociferous that the Patent and Trademark Office (PTO) decided to reexamine its decision to issue the patent just months after the patent was granted and ultimately overturned the patent in 1994.[4]

Undoubtedly, you may derive rich rewards from a patent. However, there are numerous drawbacks to the patent system that also must be considered before you determine if it is the best or only means to protect AES. First, in order to be issued a patent by the PTO, you have to demonstrate that your machine is the type of invention deemed suitable for patent protection and that it meets a variety of criteria, such as novelty and nonobviousness. Second, a patent costs money, possibly lots of money. There are fees to obtain a patent and to maintain it. Specialized attorneys are almost always needed, which can magnify the expenses of getting the patent. Also, if you plan to broaden your horizon to international markets, you can expect those expenses to increase severalfold, with such possible additional categories of expenses as for translators, communication, and travel. And then, even after you have the patent, you will bear the burden and expense of tracking down and enforcing your patent rights against alleged infringers. Third, a consequence of receiving the patent is that your invention is suitably disclosed to the public so that one skilled in the art may replicate it. If a court later judges that your patent was inappropriately granted by the PTO—an occurrence that is more likely than you might suspect—then your fully informed competitors are free to develop and market their own versions of your creation.

Clearly, an inventor must seriously consider the long-term advantages and disadvantages of patent protection. Chapters 2 and 3 strive to provide a feel for the basic concepts that underlie patent protection, as well as the benefits and pitfalls that attend protection. This can be only the beginning of the inquiry, however. Before reaching a final decision, the inventor must also factor in the pros and cons of alternative methods of protection, such as trade secrets and copyrights. Only then can the inventor arrive at the most suitable comprehensive strategic plan for protecting the valuable elements of the invention.

The two chapters on patents are divided as follows: Chapter 2 focuses on the essential characteristics that make an invention suitable for patent protection in the United States. Here we consider what it takes for an invention to be novel and nonobvious. Also, we will investigate how the envelope of patent protection has expanded recently to cover new forms of technological frontiers, such as computers and biotechnology, and how the extension has led to questions, confusion, and controversy. The chapter also provides a basic understanding of how design patents might apply to technological products.

Chapter 3 provides a feel for the hurdles that an inventor must overcome to obtain and defend a patent in the United States and abroad. The chapter focuses first on the United States by illustrating the essential components of a U.S. patent application, the typical process that one follows to obtain a U.S. patent, and the difficulties one may encounter to prove infringement of that patent. The goal of these discussions is not to enable you to handle the U.S. PTO without an attorney. In fact, just the contrary is intended—you should clearly recognize that the realm of patent protection constitutes highly specialized, technical, and complicated waters that can be navigated only with the aid of an experienced attorney. Following this exposition, Chapter 3 considers the rapidly changing international environment. As the lines of domestic and international economic affairs have become increasingly blurred, so has the ability of the American inventor to concentrate on U.S. laws. This is especially true in the patent arena, where foreign policies not only may be very different from those in the United States but also may form the basis of substantive international patent agreements likely to be achieved through WIPO. Chapter 3 thereby alerts you to the overall strategic implications that foreign laws and international treaties bear on your ultimate decision to pursue patent protection.

## OVERVIEW OF PATENT POLICIES AND PROCESSES

The fundamental rationales for patent protection in the United States, as well as in most foreign jurisdictions, are to stimulate research and development of new inventions and to encourage thorough and rapid disclosures. Patent protection can be likened to an agreement with the government wherein the inventor promises to divulge sufficient information about a new invention so that others may readily understand and replicate it and have the opportunity to consider improvements to it. In return for those disclosures, the government provides the inventor a narrowly circumscribed and temporally limited right to exclusively control who makes, uses, and sells the invention within the nation's borders. In effect, the government is bestowing a limited monopoly over particular claims to the invention so that the inventor may be amply rewarded for creative energies. As you might have guessed, patent policy has had a contentious history in the United States, owing to the fundamental antipathy its citizens share toward publicly sanctioned monopoly control in the marketplace. One must always be mindful of that tension when embarking on a patent protection strategy. The tension not only explains many of the difficulties one may encounter in obtaining patent protection but should also raise red flags of caution when deciding to enforce monopoly privileges against alleged infringers.

The U.S. patent system is governed by the Patent Act, which was first established in 1790 and has been amended on numerous occasions thereafter. The Patent Act provides that a person is entitled to a patent for an invention if that invention is novel, nonobvious, and a proper subject for protection. As we shall see, the details about meeting the standard of novelty, delineated in Section 102 of the act, are somewhat technical but are based on three principles: The first is that a person may not stake claim to an invention that was publicly available before the person invented it. The second is that if two or more persons allege that they are entitled to patent rights in the United States for the same development, then priority will be given to the person deemed to have invented first. This is the so-called first-to-invent standard of the United States, which differs from the first-to-file system of almost all other countries, wherein priority is granted to the first inventor to file for the patent. The third guiding principle, based on the rapid-disclosure rationale for patents, is that there are reasons not to delay too long after completion of an invention before filing for a patent. Here again, one with an international vision will find differences abroad, where the policies of some countries provide even more incentives to file as early as possible.

The standards for nonobviousness are provided in Section 103 and essentially require that an invention must be something more than that which would be obvious, in light of publicly available knowledge, to one who is skilled in the relevant field. The proper subjects for patent protection are given in various sections of the Patent Act. Section 101 controls utilitarian inventions; here the guiding principle is that all things made by human ingenuity are patentable but naturally occurring elements are not. This concept is at the center of the debate over the patentability of computer programs and biotechnology. Section 171, which covers design patents, provides that product designs may be patented if they are primarily ornamental. In this regard, important questions are arising in the computer field, as for instance about the patentability of screen displays. These basic standards, which will be discussed at length in this chapter, are outlined in Exhibit 2.1.

In contrast to copyrights and trade secrets, an inventor must undertake an arduous examination and approval process to receive patent protection. The inventor initiates the process by filing a patent application with the PTO. As will be discussed in some detail in Chapter 3, the Patent Act and PTO regulations set out the requirements for the application. The most important components are (1) a description of the invention, which is sufficient to enable one skilled in the art

**Exhibit 2.1  Conditions for Patentability in the United States: Utility and Design Patents**

### Novelty (Section 102)

- Knowledge of invention was not publicly available at the time of invention.
- The patent application was filed in time.
  — One-year grace period
  — Experimental use
- First-to-invent priority
- Case: *Dunlop Holdings v. Ram*

### Nonobviousness (Section 103)

- Not obvious at the time the invention was made to one skilled in the art
- Case: *Panduit v. Dennison*

### Appropriate Subject Matter

- Utility patents (Section 101)
  — Useful
  — Anything under the sun made by man
    = Biotechnology
  — Not abstract ideas, laws of nature, or manifestations of nature
    = Mathematical algorithms and computer programs
  — Cases: *Diamond v. Chakrabarty, Diamond v. Diehr, Arrhythmia v. Corazonix*
- Design patents (Section 171)
  — Primarily ornamental
  — Case: *Avia v. L.A. Gear*

to practice it; (2) an illustration of the best mode of carrying out the invention known to the inventor at the time of filing the application; (3) all information known to the inventor that may bear on the patentability of the invention, such as pertaining to its novelty or its obviousness; and (4) the precise aspects of the invention claimed for patent protection. All information presented to the PTO is treated in confidence until a patent is granted, at which time it becomes publicly available. However, one must note that a policy change is looming here. Soon, the information provided in the patent application will be held by the PTO in secrecy for only a designated period of time, most likely 18 months, after the application is filed. As we shall see, the term of secrecy under either procedure is important to an inventor who may want to rely on trade secret protection if it turns out that the patent avenue is not promising or available.

If the PTO is satisfied from the application and subsequent discussions that the invention is novel, nonobvious, and a proper subject for protection, then it will issue a patent. Currently, it usually takes from 1½ to over 3 years for a patent to issue, depending often on the type of invention and its complexity. For instance, biotechnology and computer applications take more time for their patents to issue than do those claiming conventional inventions. Once granted, the patent entitles the patent holder to take action against infringers of the patent. Infringers include those who make, use, or sell the invention in the United States without permission. In addition, when the patented invention is a process, one becomes an infringer by selling articles in the United States that were produced in other countries according to the patented process. A patent holder can challenge alleged infringers in the federal district courts and if successful, is entitled to a variety of remedies, including injunctions and damages. The duration of U.S. patent protection begins when the patent issues, and lasts 17 years for useful inventions (and plants) and 14 years for designs. Be aware, though, as noted in Chapter 1, that some change is imminent in this regard. Under the new system, the length of patent protection begins to toll when the patent application is filed, and lasts 20 years for useful inventions and 17 years for designs. After the patent expires, the inventor no longer enjoys the exclusive privileges of patent protection. Anyone else, then, is free to practice the invention, unless some other form of federal protection, such as perhaps copyright or trademark, is found to apply.

This simplified exposition of U.S. patent protection makes the road appear smooth and clear. However, you will learn over the course of the two chapters on patents that there are pitfalls at every step. The concepts of novelty, nonobviousness, and subject matter raise numerous difficult hurdles. Meeting the requirements of the patent application also may prove challenging. In addition, even after receiving the patent, an inventor may find the task of enforcing the patent against infringers to be troublesome, even overwhelming and economically dangerous.

That final statement may have surprised you. What could be so financially devastating once a patent is granted? Assume that you and your somewhat expensive patent attorney spent nearly two years persuading the PTO that you deserved a patent and you finally obtained one. You then locate a manufacturer in Idaho who you believe is infringing the patent. When your attempts at negotiating with that manufacturer are rebuffed, you decide to defend your patent rights in an Idaho federal district court. This action demands a great deal of your time and will involve your attorney substantially, again at great expense. The manufacturer likely will defend itself on a number of grounds. First, it probably will argue that its products do not infringe the narrow parameters of the patent claims. However, it may also allege that the patent was invalidly granted by the PTO. For instance, it may claim that the PTO erred in its determination that the invention was novel or nonobvious. According to the Patent Act, a patent granted by the PTO is presumed to be valid. Thus, one challenging the patent has the burden of overcoming that presumption. However, one never knows how heavily a court will weigh the presumption. Thus, the Idaho court may look at the invention in light of the history considered by the Patent Office and may determine that the PTO was simply wrong in issuing the patent. Possibly the invention just seems so obvious to the judge reviewing the case that that judge cannot back the PTO's decision. Or the manufacturer may dig up and introduce evidence not even found or reviewed by the PTO. In such an instance, the Idaho court likely will reduce even further its deference to the PTO, given that the PTO's decision was based on an incomplete record of previous information about the invention. Whatever the reason, if the court determines that the patent is invalid, then you have wasted a huge amount of time and money obtaining and trying to defend your patent. But worse, critical information about how to make the invention became publicly available when your patent was issued.[5] A court determination that the patent was invalid, coupled with the disclosure, enables any manufacturer to cheaply learn how to duplicate your efforts.

With the advice of your attorney, you might try to consider which court forum is most likely to respect the validity and breadth of an issued patent, and to bring the case there if possible. However, even this attempt at forum-shopping may be foiled by a potential competitor who is allowed to initiate a court proceeding for the purpose of obtaining a judgment declaring that the patent claims are narrow or invalid (called a declaratory judgment). The competitor, of course, will in turn try to select the forum most likely to doubt the determination of the PTO. And, of course, when this action is brought, you and your attorney have to defend it. Needless to say, one cannot breathe easy once a patent is issued. An inventor must be willing to invest time, energy, and resources in defending a patent for it to be meaningful. In addition, one must factor in the very real prospect that the patent could be lost along with all the attendant problems of disclosure.[6]

In 1982, Congress made a change to the judicial landscape that relieved some of the anxieties faced by patent holders. In that year, it created the Court of Appeals for the Federal Circuit, a new, specialized court with jurisdiction over a limited set of legal matters. One of its duties is to hear appeals by inventors who are dissatisfied with negative judgments from the PTO about patent issues. More important, appeals from district court decisions regarding patents also must be made to the Federal Circuit. Prior to the creation of this court, appeals from the district courts followed the usual routes to their respective regional courts of appeals and, finally, to the Supreme Court. This led to varying standards across the nation about patent matters, which were dependent on the disparate views of the justices sitting on the appellate courts. Some jurisdictions were positively hostile to patent protection and were more likely to strike down a patent than uphold it. Indeed, by some estimates, patent claims were upheld only 30% of the time prior to 1982. Now, however, all patent appeals go to the same place—the Federal Circuit. Thus, a patent holder who is given an unsatisfactory decision at the district court level, whether from an infringement or a declaratory judgment action, no longer must wonder what principles might be applied by the relevant appellate court. Instead, no matter where the first action took place, the appeal goes to the Federal Circuit. And during its first decade, the Federal Circuit has proven to be a relatively hospitable place for patent holders, upholding patent claims close to 80% of the time.[7] Also, the Federal Circuit's regard for patent validity filters down to the district court justices, whose judgments are subject to the unified standards from the sole appellate court. Thus, the creation of the Federal Circuit has greatly reduced the dangers of forum-shopping, even at the initial stages of legal proceedings. None of this means that a patent holder is home free; one still must be financially willing to defend a patent and consider the possibility of losing its protections. However, the forum-shopping risks that used to put a cloud over all patents have now been substantially reduced.

## NOVELTY

The concept of novelty in the United States, as well as in most other countries, is based on the principle that patent protection is a reward for disclosing new innovations to the public. This notion can be broken down into two fundamental requirements. The first is that one should not be allowed to receive patent protection for knowledge that is already available to the public. The conferring of patent rights to existing knowledge is contrary to underlying patent philosophy, for it removes from the public something it previously possessed rather than ultimately presenting something new to it. The second principle recognizes that the public stands to gain from the disclosures that attend patent protection, especially when the disclosures are provided as early as possible. To account for this, there are embedded within the concept of novelty disincentives for an inventor to unreasonably delay in filing a patent application.

Another key determinant of novelty, this one somewhat peculiar to the United States, is that when two or more persons have applied for patents covering the same invention, the patent will be granted to that person who invented first. In almost all other countries, patent decisions regarding competing applications for the same invention favor the first person to file a patent application. In the early 1990s, negotiators for the United States within WIPO and GATT made it clear that the United States may be willing to abandon its first-to-invent priority system in favor of the first-to-file system if certain other concessions, such as that concerning the scope of patentable subject matter, are adopted by other countries. Since some of these issues have been addressed with passage of the 1993 GATT accord, one can anticipate that the United States is on the threshold of making this important change.

The requirements to satisfy novelty in the United States are provided in Section 102 of the Patent Act. Three subsections—102(a), 102(b) and 102(g)—are particularly important, and we will restrict our discussion to those:

### Section 102. Conditions for Patentability; Novelty
A person shall be entitled to a patent unless—

(a) the invention was known or used by others in this country, or patented or described in a printed publication in this or a foreign country, before the invention thereof by the applicant for patent, or

(b) the invention was patented or described in a printed publication in this or a foreign country or in public use or on sale in this country, more than one year prior to the date of application for patent in the United States, or

(g) before the applicant's invention thereof the invention was made in this country by another who had not abandoned, suppressed or concealed it. In determining priority of invention there shall be considered not only the respective dates of conception and reduction to practice of the invention, but also the reasonable diligence of one who was first to conceive and last to reduce to practice, from a time prior to conception by the other.

Section 102(a) serves mainly to ensure that patentees do not claim publicly available knowledge as their own, although as we shall see, it also provides some incentive to disclose new inventions rather than maintain them in secrecy. The role of Section 102(b) is to encourage inventors to file patent applications soon after they begin to commercialize or otherwise disseminate information about their inventions. Section 102(g), with some reinforcement from Section 102(a), establishes the first-to-invent priority system within the United States. Section 102(g) also works in tandem with Section 102(a) to dissuade inventors from relying too heavily on trade secret protection in certain situations. As noted, this subsection, as well as Section 102(a), may undergo substantial change in the near future as part of an international patent accord.

Sections 102(a), (b), and (g) are extremely technical, and it is easy to get lost in the statutory verbiage. You should notice first that these sections cover instances when an inventor would not be permitted to get a U.S. patent. For that reason, these criteria are often called statutory bars to protection. Sections 102(a) and (g) are drafted so that the pivotal events are in terms of what other people besides the patent applicant knew or had done before the applicant's date of invention. Section 102(b) addresses activities that anyone, *including the applicant*, had done more than one year prior to the date the applicant filed the U.S. patent application. Exhibit 2.2 strives to bring some clarity to the nine statutory bars listed in Sections 102(a), (b), and (g) by logically separating them into relevant components.

**Exhibit 2.2  Statutory Bars in the United States: Sections 102 (a), (b), and (g)**

| Section 102(a) | | | |
|---|---|---|---|
| **Activity** | **Where** | **By Whom** | **When** |
| Publicly known | U.S. | Others | |
| Publicly used | U.S. | Others | Before the date |
| Patented | Anywhere | Others | of invention |
| Printed publication | Anywhere | Others | |

| Section 102(b) | | | |
|---|---|---|---|
| **Activity** | **Where** | **By Whom** | **When** |
| Patented | Anywhere | Anyone | More than one |
| Printed publication | Anywhere | Anyone | year before the |
| Use | U.S. | Anyone | filing date of the |
| On sale | U.S. | Anyone | U.S. patent application |

| Section 102(g) | | | |
|---|---|---|---|
| **Activity** | **Where** | **By Whom** | **When** |
| Made | U.S. | Others | Before the date of invention |

### Is the Invention New?

The thrust of Section 102(a) is to keep a patentee from controlling knowledge that was previously available to the public. Therefore, it prevents an applicant from obtaining a patent if the claimed invention was in the hands of the U.S. public prior to the date of invention. Publicly available information that is printed is considered accessible in the United States, no matter where in the world it is published or in what form it is preserved. However, other demonstrations of public knowledge or use must be within the United States to bar the patent.

Looking solely at Section 102(a), our attempts to acquire a patent for certain aspects of the Audio Enhancement System should be unsuccessful if those aspects were previously described by another inventor in a technical journal or even in an obscure paper published in a small foreign nation. The only requirements are that the paper make the information accessible to interested members of the public and that it describe the invention in sufficient detail to enable one ordinarily skilled with the technology to duplicate it without further research or experimentation. Similarly, if the claim were subject to someone else's existing patent in another country, then our U.S. patent should be barred.

The more difficult issues often are whether use or knowledge is publicly available in the United States. Suppose we claim a specific technique to convert analog signals to digital ones via a computer. Clearly, if another person had made a public demonstration at a convention illustrating how the invention works, then our claim should be barred. However, what if another company had used this process to accomplish tasks within its confines but had taken great lengths to maintain the secrecy of the process? If we later arrive at the same invention, should we be barred because of that previous secret use? What if that company used the process to improve recordings and then distributed the recordings to the public? Does that weaken our position? Or going to the other extreme, what if the company actually sells machines that employ the technology but does not otherwise disclose to the public how the machine operates?

To answer these questions, one must interpret Sections 102(a) and (g) in light of patent policy. Patents are designed to bring forth new knowledge so that it can be shared by the public at the end of the patent term. The issue of protection, therefore, devolves to how much the public knows and how much it is likely to find out if a patent is not granted. If someone already has made the invention, then it can be assumed that, in most instances, information about the invention will naturally spread to those in the public who have an interest in it. Thus, a patent normally is not required to inform the public of those inventions already in existence. However, if the invention were made by someone who does absolutely nothing with it or who actively takes steps to ensure that the public will not learn about it, then the presumption about eventual public disclosure is less compelling. This explains the language of Section 102(g) that forbids the patenting of an invention that was previously made by another who had not abandoned, suppressed, or concealed it. It also helps interpret what public knowledge or use under Section 102(a) entails. Use or knowledge is public, even without specific disclosure about the invention, if the public is likely to learn of the invention based on what is said or done. For example, if the public could study distributed products and thereby understand the invention in less than 17 years, then a patent would not be socially beneficial because the public would be able to share the invention earlier if left alone. Therefore, a patent should be denied in such circumstances. *Dunlop Holdings Limited v. Ram Golf Corporation* discusses these considerations about new inventions.

## DUNLOP HOLDINGS LIMITED V. RAM GOLF CORPORATION
*Seventh Circuit Court of Appeals, 1975*

### Facts

Dunlop received a patent for golf balls with covers made of certain synthetic materials, such as Surlyn. Ram produced and sold golf balls made of Surlyn, and Dunlop sued for patent infringement. Ram alleged that the invention was made and publicly used by a third party named Butch Wagner before Dunlop's date of invention, although Wagner had not disclosed his formula to the public. The trial court agreed and determined that the patent was invalid. Dunlop appealed.

### Opinion

The patent covers the discovery that certain synthetic materials, when fabricated by themselves (or with minor amounts of compatible materials), produce a golf ball cover with exceptional cutting resistance. An example of the material described in the patent is Surlyn. The date of invention claimed by Dunlop is February 10, 1965.

In April 1964, Du Pont was trying to find a commercial use for its Surlyn, a recently developed product. Shortly thereafter, Butch Wagner, who was in the business of selling re-covered golf balls, began to experiment with Surlyn as a golf ball cover. He first made some sample balls by hand and then, using a one-iron, determined that the material was almost impossible to cut. He then made several dozen experimental balls, trying different combinations of additives to achieve the proper weight, the proper color, and a texture that could easily be released from an injection molding machine. By November 5, 1964, he had developed a formula he considered suitable for commercial production and had decided to sell Surlyn-covered balls in large quantities.

During the fall of 1964, Wagner provided friends and potential customers with Surlyn-covered golf balls. At least three golfers used these balls that fall for rounds of golf played at a country club in Los Angeles. By February 1965, Wagner had received orders for over 1,000 dozen Surlyn-covered balls, and by the end of 1965, he had ordered enough Surlyn to produce more than 900,000 such balls. Wagner died in October 1965.

Dunlop's patent claims are broad enough to encompass any golf ball cover made principally of Surlyn, and there is no doubt that Wagner had made a large number of such golf balls and successfully placed them in public use. The only novel feature of this case arises from the fact that Wagner was careful not to disclose to the public the ingredient that made his golf ball so tough. Dunlop presented evidence that an acknowledged expert on golf ball construction failed to discover the Surlyn content of the cover in an analysis of Wagner's ball. Dunlop also relies on the secretive manner in which Wagner gave the formula to his daughter "to keep in case something ever happens to me."

Dunlop relies on a case involving a patent on a machine that had previously been developed by a man named Haas. Haas had used the machine in his own factory under tight security. The output from the machine had been sold, but the public had not been given access to the machine itself. In holding that Haas had concealed the invention, Judge Hand drew a distinction between the secret use of an invention and a noninforming public use. Haas had made only a secret use of his machine.

Wagner's situation involves neither abandonment nor a mere secret use. The evidence clearly demonstrates that Wagner endeavored to market his golf balls as promptly and effectively as possible. The balls themselves were in wide public use. Therefore, at best, the evidence establishes a noninforming public use of the subject matter of the invention.

If Wagner had applied for a patent more than a year after commencing the public distribution of Surlyn-covered golf balls, his application would have been barred notwithstanding the noninforming character of the public use or sale [this is provided by Section 102(b), which will be discussed later], for inventors must exercise reasonable diligence if they are to be rewarded with patent protection. Although Wagner may have failed to act diligently to establish his own right to a patent, there was no lack of diligence in his attempt to make the benefits of his discovery available to the public.

In view of his public use of the invention, we do not believe he concealed or suppressed the discovery, even though the use did not disclose the discovery. There are three reasons for this. First, a noninforming use, such as this, gives the public the benefit of the invention. If the new idea is permitted to have its impact in the marketplace, it surely has not been suppressed in an economic sense. Second, even though there may be no explicit disclosure of the inventive concept, when the article itself is freely accessible to the public at large, it is fair to presume that its secret will be uncovered by potential competitors long before the time when a patent would have expired if the inventor had made a timely application and disclosure to the PTO. Third, inventors are under no duty to apply for a patent; they are free to contribute ideas to the public, either voluntarily—by an express disclosure—or involuntarily—by a noninforming public use. In either case, although they may forfeit their entitlement to monopoly protection, it would be unjust to hold that such an election should impair their right to continue diligent efforts to market the product of their own invention.

We hold that the public use of Wagner's golf balls forecloses a finding of suppression or concealment. We therefore affirm the decision of the district court that Dunlop's patent is invalid.

*Dunlop Holdings* alludes to some potential strategic dangers from relying too heavily on trade secret protection. After a reading of Chapter 4, it will be clear that there may be instances in which companies will decide to protect their technological investments by preserving their secrecy rather than by pursuing patent protection. Usually when this is done, the company believes that the greatest downside is that the secret may get out, at which time protection is lost. However, by keeping an invention secret, the company risks the possibility that another inventor will develop the invention on its own. If this inventor then files for a patent, the PTO may issue one given the lack of disclosure about the previous use. Although it may seem unfair, this patent then may effectively block the originating company from using what it discovered first, because its continued use would constitute patent infringement. The original company might be able to argue that its invention, although secret, was in public use. Clearly, from *Dunlop Holdings*, it will be better off if its secret is an aspect of distributed products rather than a process used only to manufacture them. In any event, Section 102 potentially raises the stakes for those who choose the trade secret route for protection.

In an examination of an invention for novelty under Section 102, the question is whether the previous public source of information completely embodies what the inventor claims for protection. Thus, a slight modification in what is claimed over the previous "art" releases one, strictly speaking, from the statutory bars of novelty. However, one must always be careful to read the novelty provisions of Section 102 with the demands of nonobviousness in Section 103. A good example is provided by the litigation over the patentability of PCR (polymerase chain reaction), a biotechnology process used to locate and regenerate strands of DNA (deoxyribonucleic acid). Cetus Corporation obtained several patents covering the process of PCR in the mid-1980s. When Cetus refused to license the technology to Du Pont, Du Pont challenged the validity of the patents. Du Pont's primary basis for asking the court to strip patent protection was that the invention was predated by both an article published in the *Journal of Molecular Biology* in 1971 and a subsequent report publicly released by the same authors in 1974. Although the PCR process was not exactly that described in these papers, Du Pont argued that it was obvious in light of them.[8]

The possibility of such challenges, especially with lucrative inventions such as PCR, highlights the potential risks of patent protection. Competitors who wish to use the process will have a tremendous incentive to search aggressively around the globe for information that "anticipates" the prized patented claims. If something is found, as was the case with PCR, then the company owning the patent will face expensive litigation, and possibly loss of its patent privilege. This is one reason why an inventor should diligently perform a patent search prior to obtaining a patent. Otherwise, the PTO, with its somewhat limited resources, may miss a pertinent piece of prior art, thereby exposing an issued patent to risk of loss. The importance of patent searches will be explored further in Chapter 3.

The issue of whether an invention is new raises one final question. You probably have been wondering what date constitutes the date of invention. After all, one does not invent at a particular instance of time. Rather, invention normally is a continuous process beginning with conception of the idea, which leads to drawings, then possibly to models, and through other steps until finally it is reduced to a working prototype. According to Section 102(g), which we will soon look at more closely, the date of invention for patent purposes is the date of conception, as long as the subsequent steps are carried out diligently. Otherwise, the date of invention will be later—either when the invention is reduced to practice or when the patent application is filed.

When dealing with the patent office, or when faced with litigation questioning a patent's validity, determination of the exact date of invention may be crucial. For instance, what if you conceived of AES in March 1988 but did not reduce it to practice until April 1992? In the interim, an article describing the technique was published—let's say, on June 14, 1991. The public release of this article will serve to bar your ability to patent AES unless you can prove that your conception of the idea for AES predated the release and that you diligently put the idea into practice with reasonable and continuous efforts. The importance of such proof means that inventors must clearly document through lab notebooks—or otherwise—all progress made on development of an idea. It also raises a host of uncertainties about patent validity and priority between simultaneous inventors. These issues, which are most troublesome in the context of Section 102(g), explain why other countries reject the first-to-invent standard and rather employ a system based on the filing date, something that is easy to define and prove. These frustrations with the system also reinforce the willingness of the United States to abandon it in the context of a comprehensive international patent treaty.

### Was the Patent Application Filed in Time?

Section 102(b) encourages rapid filings by inventors interested in patent protection. On the one hand, it serves as a wake-up call for an inventor when others enter the field. This is especially true for those inventors who ploddingly develop their ideas and/or who regard patent filing with a lax attitude. The section accomplishes its intended result by giving inventors one year to file their patent applications once other inventors make knowledge of the invention public through performing one of the listed activities in the requisite location (see Exhibit 2.2). So, consider again the example wherein you conceived of AES first and worked on it diligently to reduce it to practice by April 1992. The June 14, 1991, publication of the article describing the invention means that you have to turn on the burners somewhat to complete and file a patent application. If you have not done so before June 14, 1992, you will be barred from receiving a patent. This is true regardless of your ability to prove that you were the first inventor to conceive of AES and that you diligently reduced it to practice.

Frequently, the most unrecognized aspect of Section 102(b) is that it also establishes a one-year filing deadline when the inventor discloses the information. This comes especially as a surprise to unsuspecting entrepreneurs who unwittingly learn when discussing the prospects for patent protection with an attorney that they have already blown their chances through their own activities. For instance, engineers who publish articles in academic journals describing recent experiments may be surprised to find that the article will prevent them from getting a patent if they do not file the patent application within one year after publication. Most alarming to uninformed businesspersons, however, is the requirement that they file patent applications within one year of the first public use or sale of their inventions in the United States. These considerations are most insidious because of the wide latitude courts have taken in defining what constitutes a "public" use and a "sale."

When a business is in the process of finalizing a new invention, there ordinarily is a lot of excitement and energy devoted to determining whether the invention works as anticipated, whether customers will want it, how much they will pay, and what aspects they prefer. There also is some degree of urgency to beat competitors to the punch by announcing and demonstrating the invention as early as possible. Thus, when a prototype of AES is completed, you probably will send it to an independent lab so that it can conduct a variety of experiments to test its operational characteristics. As part of the testing procedures, the lab may invite a number of typical potential customers to use the machine, possibly in their home, so that certain functional characteristics can be judged in a standard environment. After the bugs in the functional elements have been ironed out, you then may engage a marketing consultant to help determine pricing policies, customer acceptance levels, media techniques, and other strategies to help move the product. As part of this effort, demonstrations may be made at important audio products trade shows to arouse interest and to test potential demand.

Obviously, much of this activity involves a use of the product in a public environment. But a lot of it is not so much to use the invention as to determine what final form it should take when it ultimately is released for use by the public. Nonetheless, public use is interpreted to have such wide scope that much of this behavior is covered. Essentially, any demonstration of the product to a person who has not promised to maintain its secrecy constitutes a public use, unless it was for experimental purposes. Saying this another way, a use is not public if:

1. it involves persons sworn to secrecy, or
2. it is undertaken for experimental purposes.

So, when employees use the product, they usually are not engaging in a public use because they have an implied duty by their position to maintain the secrecy of new product developments. In addition, they probably signed an express contractual agreement promising to maintain the confidentiality of new inventions. Similarly, certain outsiders retained to test the product may have signed agreements to maintain confidentiality. Under these circumstances, therefore, they also use the product in a nonpublic sense. Agreements such as these to maintain secrecy will be discussed further in Chapter 4.

The experimental-use component theoretically could cover all the testing recommended for AES. However, it does not. Rather, activities are considered experimental only if performed to test the operational aspects of the invention. This would cover experiments to perfect the invention, such as beta testing. However, commercial and marketing investigations, such as customer acceptance tests and pricing experiments, are deemed public and initiate the one-year filing period. And clearly, the trade show demonstration would be a public use.

Public use also has a broader reach when applied to activities by the applicant rather than the knowledge of third parties. What this means is that a use of an invention by the applicant can be public even if third parties could not figure out how the invention operates. For instance, a secret use of a process or machine to make goods that are then publicly distributed would trigger the one-year filing requirement for the applicant under Section 102(b). However, as we know, this would not be the sort of public use to bar the ability of others to obtain a patent.

The term "sale" also has been given widespread effect. It does not take a completed sales transaction of an invention to toll the one-year filing period. The time when the first offer to sell is sufficient—even if the invention is not yet finalized and even if that offer ultimately is rejected. Thus, a sales solicitation presentation that displays samples of the invention triggers the one-year period, even if production facilities are not prepared to deliver on orders.

If you dealt with AES in an unsophisticated fashion and only considered the possibility of patent protection more than one year after making a public use or sale, you probably would engender deep feelings of resentment. Here is another technical rule to trip up the small businessperson! However, from an international perspective, the one-year grace period can seem extremely generous. This is because many countries are more stringent, demanding absolute novelty before a filing. To be eligible for patent protection in these countries, there can be no public use or sale of the invention at any time prior to filing. The one-year period in the United States, assuming one is aware of it, allows inventors to engage in various forms of commercial tests for up to a year before determining if it is worth investing their time and money in patent protection. In several other countries, the decision has to be made before one objectively tests commercial viability. And for some, testing or sales anywhere in the world, not simply within national boundaries, negate the possibility for patent protection. So, given that your vision for AES reaches international dimensions, you must thoughtfully consider the countries in which you ultimately might need protection and the requirements of those countries' laws before you engage in any commercial activity putting AES in public use or on sale. Ways to simplify the task of preserving overseas rights so that marketing activities can begin as expeditiously as possible will be discussed in Chapter 3. Also, it should be noted that one of the objectives of U.S. negotiators within WIPO is to establish a unified novelty standard permitting the one-year grace period before filing.

### Who Gets the Patent When There Are Multiple Inventors?

Section 102(g) provides that the first inventor to make an invention has priority for obtaining a patent, unless that inventor has suppressed, concealed, or abandoned his efforts. This establishes the first-to-invent principle in the United States, a standard it shares internationally only with the Philippines and Jordan. The majority of other countries rely on a much simpler formula: The first inventor to file a patent application gets priority. As noted previously, the United States may soon give up its isolating adherence to the first-to-invent scheme as part of an international agreement providing for elevated substantive patent principles worldwide. In fact, legislation has been introduced in Congress to implement that change.[9]

According to Section 102(g), the determination of the first inventor is based on the dates of conception and reduction to practice. An inventor who conceives the invention at the earliest time is the first inventor if that inventor also reduces it to practice first. The more difficult scenario arises when one inventor conceives the invention first but reduces it to practice subsequent to another. Again, the inventor who conceives the invention at the earliest time is the first inventor, but in this case only as long as the inventor was reasonably diligent in reducing it to practice beginning from a time just prior to the other inventor's conception. Exhibit 2.3 illustrates the pertinent aspects of this analysis. Of course, all of this opens the door to a lot of questions: (1) What is conception? (2) What is reduction to practice? (3) What is reasonable diligence? and (4) How does one prove the timing and existence of each?

One of the difficult aspects of the first-to-invent standard is the ill-defined nature of the important determinants for priority. The time of conception, for instance, is a nebulous but obviously critical juncture. Clearly, conception is a mental criterion. However, it is not simply the first time the idea for the invention arises. Rather, conception does not occur until the details of the invention are sufficiently advanced so that a person of ordinary skill could make it operational without further creative actions.

Conception, by itself, is not enough to "make" an invention. Rather, conception is only the beginning of the inventive process. What normally follows are continuous and deliberate steps to reduce an idea into practice by completing a working finished product, such as a functional prototype or a useful composition. An invention does not have to be in its commercially optimal form for it to be judged reduced to practice. All that is necessary is that it work as expected. Thus, after an invention's reduction to practice, one may still make changes to improve production techniques or to increase customer acceptability.

The Patent Act establishes another way to reduce an invention to practice. One may constructively reduce an invention to practice by filing a patent application that discloses the invention sufficiently to meet the enabling requirements of the statute. These will be discussed in Chapter 3, but essentially the application must describe the invention in enough detail so that a person of ordinary skill could reduce it to practice without undue experimentation. Once again, we see the disclosure rationale at work here, encouraging inventors to file as quickly as possible after conception. This also raises a procedural point about rapid disclosure. Because filing equates with reduction to practice, inventors who file first have a leg up on proving who was first to make an invention. This is because without more evidence, first filers have proven that they completed the invention, albeit constructively, prior to those who later file applications. Subsequent filers therefore will have the burden of demonstrating earlier conception dates and reasonable diligence in reducing to practice, either actually or by filing.

Reasonable diligence is a very subjective standard, depending considerably on the personal situation of the inventor. The determination often comes down to

**Exhibit 2.3  First-to-Invent Priority**

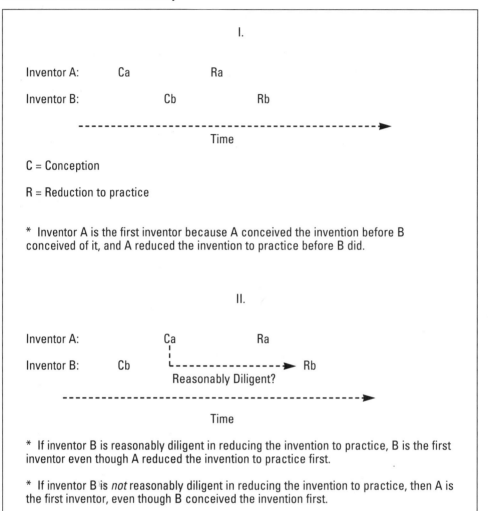

I.

| Inventor A: | Ca | Ra |
| Inventor B: | Cb | Rb |

Time

C = Conception

R = Reduction to practice

\* Inventor A is the first inventor because A conceived the invention before B conceived of it, and A reduced the invention to practice before B did.

II.

Inventor A:        Ca          Ra

Inventor B:    Cb  ┗- - - - - - - - - - - -▶ Rb
                    Reasonably Diligent?

Time

\* If inventor B is reasonably diligent in reducing the invention to practice, B is the first inventor even though A reduced the invention to practice first.

\* If inventor B is *not* reasonably diligent in reducing the invention to practice, then A is the first inventor, even though B conceived the invention first.

whether the inventor had the time and financial means to proceed more quickly but chose not to do so. In addition, activity to reduce to practice is more likely to be viewed as reasonably diligent if it is deliberate and continuous.

Because patent priority in the United States is held by the first inventor, it is extremely important for a person who desires a patent to have sufficient evidence to prove the date of conception, the date of reduction to practice, and the reasonable diligence used in the effort. Oral testimony by the applicant is not very persuasive in this context. Rather, corroboration through physical evidence and the testimony of disinterested third parties are usually needed. Thus, inventors are well advised to consider techniques that document on a routine basis their efforts to conceive an invention and reduce it to practice. The use of bound and consecutively numbered lab manuals wherein the inventor routinely records and dates inventive activity is very persuasive in the demonstration of key times and reasonable diligence. In addition, having witnesses attest to the documentation and dates presented within the lab book can help eliminate such allegations as that the book was contrived after the fact and backdated.

That the U.S. patent system rests on the first-to-invent standard has two important drawbacks. First, the system has the tendency to increase litigation expenses, because it raises a host of uncertainties.[10] Under the first-to-file standard, it is easy to determine priority. Also, an inventor who relies on the first-to-invent system to gain priority over those who file more quickly may succeed in the United States but may lose patent rights in almost all other countries in the process. Thus, once again, reliance on U.S. patent law may be commercially hazardous to those with an international vision. On the other hand, the first-to-invent policy does have an underlying sense of fairness to it. The inventor should be rewarded for creative actions and not for technical steps such as filing patent applications. Such a principle applies especially to the small inventor, who often is not fully cognizant of patent requirements until it is time to commercialize the invention. In addition, small inventors are the ones that are most likely to want extra time before deciding if an invention is worth the expense of hiring an attorney and filing a patent application.[11] And as we know, motivating the entrepreneurial spirit of the small businessperson continues to be an important philosophical norm guiding U.S. policy. Advocates of the first-to-invent standard also point out that the system has worked remarkably well in the United States for over 200 years and that it would be a mistake to tinker with success. Finally, supporters argue that establishing a race to the patent office may lead inventors, in their haste, to resort more often to crash development programs and to file less thoughtful patent applications.

During the final months of 1993, the international community adopted two major trade accords. NAFTA was signed by the United States, Mexico, and Canada and was approved by the legislature of each. Implementation of NAFTA began January 1, 1994. More globally, a new GATT framework was approved by negotiators representing GATT's 117 participants. The United States, as well as most other countries, will individually approve this historic agreement before it becomes effective in 1995. In both accords, the United States successfully convinced other nations to accept provisions raising standards for intellectual property protection within their borders. As a consequence, the United States now may finally be ready to abandon its almost singular adherence to the first-to-invent standard. Indeed, as legislation is drafted to bring U.S. policies into conformity with NAFTA and GATT, one should not be surprised if the long-debated Patent System Harmonization Act emerges from Congress for presidential signature.[12] As this book goes to press in 1994, one can only surmise what specific changes would be included in a move to the first-to-file priority system. However, based on legislative proposals previously considered by Congress,[13] one should expect the following major principles to be included:

- The first to file a patent application will be entitled to priority.
- Novelty principles will be altered so that they are based on the filing date, rather than the date of invention. Thus an invention will be novel unless:
  a. The subject matter was publicly known or publicly used in the United States, or patented or published anywhere in the world, before the filing date of the patent application.
     — However, if the applicant is responsible for the public disclosure of the subject matter, then the applicant may file within one year of the disclosure.
  b. The subject matter was on sale in the United States more than one year before the filing date of the application.
- A person will not infringe a patent if that person, in good faith, commercially used or sold the invention (or earnestly prepared to do so) before the filing date of the patent application.
- Patent applications will be confidential until the PTO makes them public. The PTO will open the application for public inspection 18 months after the filing date, or earlier if the applicant so requests.
- If the patent ultimately issues, those who use the invention after publication by the PTO will have to pay a reasonable royalty (for the period of time up to issuance of the patent).
- The term of a utility patent will begin when the patent issues and will expire 20 years after the patent application was filed.
- The term of a design patent will begin when the patent issues and will expire 17 years after the patent application was filed.

## NONOBVIOUSNESS

For an invention to be patentable, not only must it meet the standards of novelty under Section 102, but also it must be nonobvious, as defined in Section 103. Section 103 provides:

> A patent may not be obtained though the invention is not identically disclosed or described as set forth in Section 102 of this title, if the differences between the subject matter sought to be patented and the prior art are such that the subject matter as a whole would have been obvious at the time the invention was made to a person having ordinary skill in the art to which said subject matter pertains.

That an invention must be something more than new in order to merit a patent demonstrates the basic antipathy toward the monopoly attributes of a patent. The thoughts of Thomas Jefferson, who served on the first patent commission in the United States, are instructive on deciphering the rationales for the nonobvious requirement. According to Jefferson, a key issue in determining patentability is "drawing a line between the things which are worth the public embarrassment of an exclusive patent, and those which are not."[14] Jefferson did not believe that patents should be granted for small details, obvious improvements, or frivolous devices. Thus, there had to be some decisional means for weeding out those inventions that would not be disclosed or devised but for the inducement of a patent.[15] The condition that an invention be nonobvious is supposed to satisfy those additional concerns.

In contrast to the novelty concept, with its somewhat precise definitions of predisclosure and timing, the nonobviousness requirement is extremely nebulous. The Supreme Court has articulated the thinking process one should follow in reaching a determination about obviousness. However, in reality, its procedure adds little in the way of comfort to those who want greater predictability about the implementation of this standard. In *Graham v. John Deere*, the Supreme Court interpreted Section 103 as requiring that the obviousness or nonobviousness of a particular subject be determined in light of a three-part analysis:

1.  The scope and content of the prior art are to be determined;
2.  Differences between the prior art and the claim at issue are to be ascertained; and
3.  The level of ordinary skill in the pertinent art is to be resolved.

The Supreme Court added that there might also be "secondary considerations," which may serve as relevant indicia to substantiate a determination of nonobviousness, such as commercial success, long felt but unresolved needs, and failure of others.[16]

In terms of predictability, none of this is too helpful for the makers of an invention, such as AES. AES is certainly novel, in that no one has written about or made the invention before. And it nicely solves certain problems that audiophiles have with listening to their old records. However, it is hardly an earth-shattering work of extraordinary genius. Rather, the inventors logically integrated a variety of technologies used in different contexts with some personal adaptive measures to produce a machine capable of providing compact-disc-quality sound. Is this enough to be nonobvious? How big do the differences with the prior art have to be? What if all the elements of the invention already existed in the prior art but they were scattered in different contexts? How much skill is ordinary skill? As the Supreme Court indicated, "What is obvious is not a question upon which there is likely to be uniformity of thought in every factual context." So, how does one even begin to approach this standard?

In reality, one can only pull together the factors that shed light on the question of obviousness. For instance, that the invention merely combines concepts, inventions, and principles that were known before does not make for a great start. However, the statute is clear that the invention must be considered *as a whole* and not element by element in isolation. If there was in the prior art documentation that suggested that the elements might be combined to make an audio enhancement product, this would suggest obviousness. On the other hand, maybe the prior art indicates that audio improvement cannot be achieved with the various technologies. Or possibly the prior art alludes to audio improvement but does not contemplate the degree of clarity achieved. Demonstrations of unexpected, unusual, or synergistic results are strong evidence of nonobviousness, although they are not necessarily required.

The statute provides that the point of reference is one ordinarily skilled in the art at the time of making the invention. One trap to which the PTO and judges easily fall victim is the so-called problem of hindsight. In this phenomenon, what appears to be difficult may seem easy and obvious once one knows how to do it. In other words, whoever is deciding the question of obviousness has to be careful not to use the invention against the inventor. Rather, one must forget the solution taught by the inventor and step back to a time before that solution was devised. However, advanced knowledge invariably taints one's perception, and the apparent simplicity of a solution, once learned, may be difficult to ignore.

Often, the best evidence that an inventor will have in order to demonstrate nonobviousness is more objective. Normally, the argument follows the logic of "If this invention is so obvious, then why has X occurred?" For instance, why is this invention selling like gangbusters if it had been so obvious? Of course, it could be because the price is so low, or because of a marketing campaign, but clearly commercial success may be relevant to the value society places on the invention. Or, one might ask how an invention can be perceived as obvious when others in the field had tried to solve the problem but had not reached the inventor's solution. Or, one might inquire why competitors immediately abandoned old technology in favor of the inventor's solution if the new approach were so obvious. These are the factors the Supreme Court called secondary considerations, but often they are the best definitive indicator one has on the issue of nonobviousness. Indeed, the Federal Circuit has embraced the evidentiary importance of these factors. It has done so, first, symbolically by designating them objective factors rather than secondary considerations, thereby placing them on the same plane of importance as the three basic criteria. It has also done so explicitly, both by claiming that such objective factors may constitute the most pertinent, probative, and revealing evidence available to aid the obviousness decision and by requiring them to be considered whenever such evidence is available.[17] Exhibit 2.4 depicts the basic concepts underlying the nonobviousness inquiry.

The review for nonobviousness is a fact-dependent exercise that cannot adequately be appreciated with a simple set of rules or guideposts. *Panduit Corporation v. Dennison Manufacturing* is an important Federal Circuit court opinion that demonstrates the many variables that may bear on the obviousness question and how this key court handled those variables in one particular fact context.

## PANDUIT CORPORATION V. DENNISON MANUFACTURING
*Federal Circuit Court of Appeals, 1985, 1987*[18]

### Facts

Jack Caveney, the founder of Panduit, began a research program in 1961 to develop a one-piece plastic cable tie to be used to bind a bundle of cables or insulated wires. That program lasted nine years and cost several million dollars.

## Exhibit 2.4  Nonobviousness

### Nonobviousness determined in light of:

- Scope and content of prior art
- Differences between prior art and claims at issue
- Level of ordinary skill in pertinent art

### Reference point for nonobviousness is the time the invention is made.

- Problem of hindsight

### Aspects that may be persuasive in finding nonobviousness:

- The invention causes disproportionate, unexpected, surprising, or unusual results.
- The prior art relates to an entirely different field.
- There is no suggestion in the prior art to combine the references to achieve the invention.
- Secondary considerations—objective factors
  - Long-standing problem or need in the field solved or satisfied by the invention
  - Failure of others to solve the problem
  - Invention copied by others
  - Infringer's abandonment of prior art machines in favor of patented machine
  - Commercial success

Caveney received three patents: the '146 patent (filed in 1968, issued in 1970), the '869 patent (filed in 1969, issued in 1972), and the '538 patent (filed in 1969, issued in 1976), which represents the culmination of his work.

One-piece cable ties have a strap that wraps around a bundle, with one end of the strap passing through an opening in a frame in the other end. Teeth on the strap engage with a locking device on the frame. Optimally, the tie would be easy to engage but difficult to withdraw. However, before Caveney's tie, those ties that took little force to engage also had undesired low withdrawal forces and those that provided high withdrawal forces required a high insertion force. Caveney was first to make a cable that was easy to insert and difficult to withdraw, requiring only a ½-pound insertion force but yielding a withdrawal force of 80 pounds. First sold in 1970, the cable tie achieved annual sales of $50 million by 1984.

Dennison Manufacturing began working on a one-piece cable tie development program in 1968. This project lasted for ten years at great expense but with no success. Dennison copied the '869 patent in 1976, and soon thereafter the '538 patent when it issued. It failed to succeed with its own research, but it became the second-largest supplier of one-piece cable ties with its copy of the '538 tie.

Panduit sued, alleging infringement of all three patents. The district court held that the three patents were invalid on the grounds of obviousness. Panduit relied heavily on the fact that the prior art did not show any inventions even close to those claimed in its patents. However, the district court stated that Panduit had given insufficient attention to what is taught by general principles of engineering and physics and by the common experience of mankind.

The district court found the '146 patent to be obvious in light of both a previously patented tie system that used one tooth, and two other references, which disclosed the use of multiple teeth. The court concluded that multiple teeth represented an obvious solution to the disengagement problem of the one-tooth system and that any intelligent reader of that patent would have placed the teeth as did Caveney.

The '869 patent improved compression by changing the orientation of the locking mechanism within the frame and using a ledge to absorb compressive force. The district court cited three references showing a ledge to absorb compressive forces and thus found the invention obvious, indicating that the result achieved was altogether expected.

The '538 patent addressed a problem with the '869 tie—that the teeth tended to break off because of insufficient flexibility. The district court found that the only difference over the '869 patent was the use of a "discrete hinge"—something that was shown in the '146 patent, albeit in a different way, and in four other patents.

Panduit appealed the district court's determinations of invalidity.

## Opinion

En route to its decision on obviousness, the district court made several errors:

1. It employed the benefit of hindsight.
2. It misinterpreted the claimed inventions.
3. It misevaluated the prior art.
4. It misconstrued its role.
5. It applied an improper and impossible standard of obviousness.
6. It gave too little weight to the objective evidence of nonobviousness and the real world story reflected in that evidence.

**1. Hindsight.** The present record reflects the insidious and powerful phenomenon known in patent law as the use of hindsight. The test is whether the subject matter of the claimed inventions would have been obvious to one skilled in the art at the time the inventions were made—not what would be obvious to a judge after reading the patents in suit and hearing the testimony. In this regard, the decision maker confronts a ghost, that is, "a person having ordinary skill in the art," not unlike the "reasonable man" and other ghosts in the law. To reach a proper conclusion under Section 103, the decision maker must step backward in time and into shoes worn by that "person" when the invention was unknown and just before it was made. However, the record compels the conclusion that the district court, having heard many days of testimony from the inventor Caveney, was unable to cast its mind back to the time the invention was made. Instead, the court consulted the knowledge taught by the inventor in his patents and in his testimony, and then it used that knowledge against its teacher.

**2. Misinterpretation of the Claimed Inventions.** The statute requires that the subject matter of the claimed invention be considered "as a whole." Dissecting claims into individual elements to determine the obviousness of each element in isolation is improper. In the present case, the district court interpreted the claims of the '146 patent as though they were drawn to "multiple teeth," those of the '896 patent as though they were drawn to a "ledge," and those of the '538 patent as though they were drawn to a "hinge." But validity is to be determined on the basis of the claimed subject matter as a whole, not in respect of a single element.

Dennison argued that if the court upheld Panduit's patents, it would be telling the entire industry that you can't have more than one tooth, you can't have a ledge in the frame, and you can't use a hinge inside the frame. This is not true. Upholding the patents in suit will not preclude any worker in the art from employing multiple teeth, ledges, and hinges in whatever combinations the worker may desire, so long as those combinations are distinct from those claimed in the present patents. The sole effect of the grant to Caveney of the property right to exclude others for a limited time from unauthorized use of his inventions is to require that others avoid the claimed structure newly disclosed to the public in the patent documents.

**3. Misevaluation of the Prior Art.** The well-established rules of law are that each prior art reference must be evaluated as an entirety and that all of the prior art must be evaluated as a whole. Inventions have often been held to have been obvious when no single reference disclosed the claimed invention. That result was compelled because the art as a whole in those cases suggested the combination claimed. At the same time, inventions have been held to have been nonobvious when neither any reference, considered in its entirety, nor the prior art as a whole suggested the combination claimed. Nowhere did the district court indicate where in the prior art there might be a suggestion for combining the teachings of individual references. Rather, it speculated on a "problem" of how prior art devices might be reconstructed to match the claimed structure, with the benefit of hindsight aided by the inventor's engineering testimony about the inventions in suit.

Virtually all inventions are necessarily combinations of old elements. The notion that combination claims can be declared invalid merely upon finding similar elements in separate prior patents would necessarily destroy virtually all patents and cannot be the law under Section 103. Indeed, that the elements noted by the court lay about in the prior art, available for years to all skilled workers without suggesting anything like the claimed inventions, is itself evidence of nonobviousness.

The district court made a fundamental error by refusing to credit the real-world environment surrounding the inventions disclosed in the references and in the patents in suit. The court paid no attention to insertion and withdrawal forces in the reference structures or to the striking differences in the references, treating them as equivalents of each other. The court specifically stated, "I don't need to know all the details about how all these other things work or don't work." But "how things work" is critical to encouragement of every research and development activity and to every advancement of the useful arts.

It was precisely "how things work" that made the prior-art cable ties failures and the cable tie of the patent in suit the most successful in the history of the industry. It was "how things work" that caused Dennison's ten-year development to fail and led Dennison to copy the tie of the patents in suit. It was "how things work" that enabled Caveney alone to achieve a ½- to 80-pound ratio between insertion and withdrawal forces. And it was a refusal to consider "how things work" that caused the court to cite isolated minutiae from various references while ignoring critically important structural distinctions that significantly affect the different achievements of which the reference and claimed structures are capable.

The record is compelling that the inventing of cable ties is not a simple matter. Panduit invested nine years and several million dollars before achieving success. Dennison tried for ten years and failed. Indeed, it was only the district court who believed that cable tie inventing was a simple, obvious, routine matter of finding elements in the prior art and modifying them in accord with "principles of physics" and "common experience." To reach that belief, the court had to ignore what workers of ordinary skill actually did in the real world with that same experience over the years.

**4. Misconstruence of the Role of the Court.** Courts are not bound by the decisions of the PTO. However, the statute mandates a presumption of validity, and it places the burden of proving facts compelling a conclusion of patent invalidity on the party asserting invalidity. This court has said the burden of proving facts compelling a conclusion of invalidity must be carried by clear and convincing evidence. Though the district court referred to the presumption of validity, mere lip service is insufficient.

The district court said it had been "going back and forth" on the questions of obviousness. It said that there was room for difference of opinion based on the overwhelming record of objective evidence. The court said it was not easy to reach its obviousness conclusion because the patent was an excellent and preeminent commercial product. Such uncertainty should have ended the obviousness inquiry in favor of the patentee.

**5. Improper and Impossible Standards:** a. General Principles and Common Experience. The district court in reaching its obviousness conclusion relied heavily on what it thought was taught by general engineering principles, general principles of physics, and the common experience of mankind. It cannot be the law that the only inventions patentable are those that cannot be explained by any known principles of engineering and physics. Whatever the unidentified principles of engineering and physics the court intended, and whatever the nondescribed common experience of mankind the court had in mind, those principles and that experience were fully available to all who tried and failed before Caveney succeeded. They cannot serve as a basis for holding that the claimed inventions in suit would have been obvious under Section 103.

b. Unexpected Results. The district court, in finding the cable tie obvious, stated that Caveney's invention produced no "unexpected result." The Federal Circuit has specifically pointed out that, whereas an "unexpected result," like "synergism," may be *evidence* of nonobviousness, it is not a *requirement*. Moreover, it there were a requirement for an "unexpected result," then that requirement would have been fully met here. That the achievement of a ½- to 80-pound ratio between insertion and withdrawal force was unexpected is fully reflected in the totality of the evidence.

**6. Objective Evidence.**  That respect is required for the effect to be given objective evidence of nonobviousness, when the evidence is present, has been stated by the Federal Circuit.

The cable tie of the patents in suit was an outstanding commercial success, selling at $50 million a year by 1984 and becoming, early on, the unquestioned leading tie on the market. The district court did not explain why, if Caveney's superior cable tie had been so obvious, the many inventors who preceded Caveney had not found it so. It is extremely difficult to believe that Panduit and Dennison would have invested years and millions of dollars in an effort to achieve what had been obvious all along to all those with ordinary skill in the art. Dennison's conjectural argument that Panduit's success with the ties is due to other factors besides the invention is refuted by its own handsome success with its copied product.

That many others, including Dennison, had tried for years and failed to create a superior cable tie is virtually irrefutable evidence that the superior tie of the patents in suit would not have been obvious to those skilled in the art when it was invented.

That earlier workers were, as the district court said, "going in different ways" is strong evidence that inventor Caveney's way would not have been obvious.

That Dennison, a large corporation with many engineers on its staff, did not copy any prior art device but found it necessary to copy the cable tie of the claims in suit is equally strong evidence of nonobviousness.

Dennison's suggestion that Panduit's success is due to unclaimed features, its advertising, or sales staff is either unsupported or contradicted in the evidence.

For all of these reasons, the district court was clearly erroneous in its conclusion on obviousness, and its judgment is reversed.

---

There are many lessons from *Panduit*, all of them encouraging to the prospective inventor. Obviousness should not be an impossible hurdle. The PTO and the courts are instructed to be careful with the use of hindsight; what may seem obvious today may have been hard to fathom when the inventive activity occurred. Also, an invention is not obvious simply because it builds on old technologies and employs natural laws of physics. Rather, the inventive enterprise must be reviewed as a whole to judge whether there is a nonobvious result. In addition, the Federal Circuit clearly was impressed by the real-world story. Objective factors that demonstrate that an invention was not obvious now may be a decisive factor in one's favor. Finally, once a patent is received, the patentee can take solace in the due respect that the Federal Circuit now requires the courts to give to the PTO's decision to award that patent. Obviously, a patent based on such a fuzzy notion as nonobviousness may be extremely risky if a judge has a free rein to substitute personal interpretations for those of the PTO. And that was pretty much the state of patent affairs prior to the 1980s. However, as indicated in *Panduit*, the Federal Circuit now has affirmatively articulated that the one who is challenging patent validity is the one who must bear the burden of proof by way of clear and convincing evidence. This turns the tables, for it is difficult to be clear and convincing about something that is not very clear from the beginning.

## PATENTABLE SUBJECT MATTER

### Introduction

The patent system has been devised to provide incentives for the creation and disclosure of new inventions and commercial designs. Section 101 is the fundamental patent provision governing the types of useful inventions that are proper subjects for patent protection. Section 101 provides:

> Whoever invents or discovers any new and useful process, machine, manufacture, or composition of matter, or any new and useful improvement thereof, may obtain a patent therefor, subject to the conditions and requirements of this title.

The statutory language of Section 101 is extremely broad. Indeed, one might argue that its only restriction is that the invention be useful. However, the courts have not interpreted this provision as having infinite scope. Rather, they have recognized on public policy grounds that there are certain inventions and discoveries over which no person or entity should be entitled to exclusive control. For instance, Albert Einstein is widely credited for discovering that there is a scientific relationship between energy and mass. Should the patent system allow an inventor, such as Einstein, to receive a patent for the discovery of a basic law of nature? If so, then the inventor will control a large spectrum of intellectual and commercial practices, for the application of a law of nature transcends any particular device or field of use. Similarly, a mathematician or scientist may determine that a particular mathematical formula can solve certain problems because it accurately addresses fundamental natural relationships. Can the application of the formula to solve problems be considered the discovery of a useful process under Section 101? Again, exclusive control may have far-reaching implications. What about patent protection for the discovery of a new, exotic tree bark that helps cure cancer? Or—to go to the logical extreme—consider the potential social and economic repercussions of allowing patent protection for abstract ideas. Wouldn't it be nice to have patent protection for, say, the process of selling sugared cereals by placing them on the lowest shelf in the grocery store?

The courts have determined that patent protection cannot be boundless. Protection would be too broad if it covered the laws of nature, mathematical algorithms, materials common to nature, or unapplied ideas. In a sense, patent protection for these fundamental building blocks of nature would overreward the patent holder to the detriment of the public welfare. Thus, the courts are careful not to allow inventors to use the patent system to lay claim to the basic physical and theoretical resources of nature. Rather, those resources are bestowed to the public by nature for all to use freely.

The debates over patent protection for biotechnology and computer systems essentially come down to these issues. What are the limits to patent protection? How do we distinguish between what is given by nature and what is made from nature? Do computer systems do anything more than solve mathematical algorithms? If so, will patent protection for AES be excluded because it utilizes computer processes? This book now addresses the evolving patent policies in these realms.

## Biotechnology Protection

As technology moves to new frontiers, it inevitably raises questions about the suitability of patent protection for unforeseen discoveries. Nowhere is this debate more heated than in the realm of biological and genetic engineering. The fundamental question is whether it is morally and economically appropriate to grant an inventor exclusive rights to new life forms. Or, in short, should one be able to obtain a patent on living things? The issue is not altogether new. Congress has addressed it previously in the context of plants. But now the issues have risen to higher plateaus—to microorganisms, to proteins that fight human disease, to strands of human DNA, even to new types of animals. The Supreme Court set the stage for the new revolution in biotechnology with its landmark decision in *Diamond v. Chakrabarty*.

## DIAMOND V. CHAKRABARTY
*United States Supreme Court, 1980*

### Facts

In 1972, Chakrabarty filed a patent application that claimed a human-made, genetically engineered bacterium, capable of breaking down multiple components of crude oil. Chakrabarty's patent claims were of three types: first, process claims for the method of producing the bacteria; second, claims for an inoculum composed of a carrier material floating on water—such as straw—and the new bacteria; and third, claims to the bacteria themselves.

The patent examiner allowed the claims that fell into the first two categories but rejected the claim to the bacteria. His decision rested on two grounds: (1) that microorganisms are "products of nature" and (2) that as living things microorganisms are not patentable subject matter under Section 101. Chakrabarty appealed to the Patent Office Board of Appeals, which affirmed the patent examiner's rejection. Chakrabarty appealed to the Court of Customs and Patent Appeals (today, such an appeal would go to the Federal Circuit), which reversed. The Commissioner of Patents and Trademarks appealed to the Supreme Court.

## Opinion

The question before this Court is a narrow one of statutory interpretation, requiring us to construe Section 101 of the Patent Act. Specifically, we must determine whether Chakrabarty's microorganism constitutes a "manufacture" or a "composition of matter" within the meaning of the statute.

In cases of statutory construction, we begin with the language of the statute. Unless otherwise defined, words will be interpreted according to their ordinary meaning. And courts should not read into the patent laws limitations and conditions the legislature has not expressed. In choosing such expansive terms as "manufacture" and "composition of matter," modified by the comprehensive "any," Congress was contemplating that the patent laws would be given wide scope.

The relevant legislative history, too, supports a broad construction. The Patent Act of 1793 embodied Jefferson's philosophy that ingenuity should receive a liberal encouragement. The committee reports that accompanied the 1952 amendments to the act inform us that Congress intended statutory subject matter to "include anything under the sun that is made by man."

This is not to suggest that Section 101 has no limits or that it embraces every discovery. The laws of nature, physical phenomena, and abstract ideas have been held not patentable. Thus, a new mineral discovered in the earth or a new plant discovered in the wild is not patentable subject matter. Likewise, Einstein could not patent his celebrated law that $E = mc^2$; nor could Newton have patented the law of gravity. Such discoveries are manifestations of nature—free to all persons and reserved exclusively to none.

Judged in this light, Chakrabarty's microorganism plainly qualifies as patentable subject matter. His claim is not to a hitherto unknown natural phenomenon, but to a non–naturally occurring manufacture or composition of matter: a product of human ingenuity having a distinctive name, character, and use. A previous case underscores the point. A scientist discovered six naturally occurring root-nodule bacteria that could be mixed into a culture and used to inoculate the seeds of leguminous plants. This court denied patentability, ruling that what was discovered was only the handiwork of nature. The combination of species produced no new bacteria, no change in the six species of bacteria, and no enlargement of the range of their utility. Their use in combination did not improve in any way their natural functioning. They served the ends nature originally provided, and they acted independently by any effort by the scientist.

Here, by contrast, Chakrabarty has produced a new bacterium with markedly different characteristics from any found in nature and one having the potential for significant utility. Chakrabarty's discovery is not nature's handiwork but his own. Accordingly, it is patentable subject matter under Section 101.

Two contrary arguments are advanced, neither of which we find persuasive. The commissioner's first argument rests on the enactments of the 1930 Plant Patent Act, which authorized patent protection to certain asexually reproduced plants, and the 1970 Plant Variety Protection Act, which authorized protection for certain sexually reproduced plants but excluded bacteria from its protection. In the commissioner's view, the passage of these acts evidences congressional understanding that the terms "manufacture" and "composition of matter" do not include living things; if they did, the commissioner argues, neither act would have been necessary.

We reject that argument. Prior to 1930, two factors were thought to remove plants from patent protection. The first was a belief that plants, even those artificially bred, were products of nature and therefore not subject to patent protection. The second was that plants were believed not amenable to the written description requirements of the patent laws. Because new plants may differ from old only in color or perfume, differentiation by written description was often impossible. In enacting the 1930 Plant Patent Act, Congress addressed both of these concerns by articulating that the works of plant breeders may be patentable inventions and then by relaxing the written description requirement. In the legislative history of the act, there is a suggestion that the terms "manufacture" and "composition of matter" cover only inventions and discoveries in the field of inanimate nature. However, there is more persuasive evidence in the legislative history that the relevant distinction for patentability is not between living and inanimate things but between products of nature—whether living or not—and human-made inventions. Here, Chakrabarty's microorganism is the result of human ingenuity and research. Hence, the passage of the Plant Patent Act affords the government no support.

Nor does the passage of the 1970 Plant Variety Protection Act support the government's position. Sexually reproduced plants were not included in the 1930 act because new varieties could not be reproduced true to type through seedlings at that time. By 1970, however, such breeding was possible, and the 1970 act therefore extended protection to it. There is nothing in the legislative history to suggest that the 1970 act was enacted because Section 101 did not include living things.

The specific exclusion of bacteria from this act does not support the commissioner's view. It may merely reflect the view that bacteria are not plants. Or the exclusion may have been included because prior to 1970, the Patent Office had issued patents for bacteria under Section 101.

The commissioner's second argument is that microorganisms cannot qualify as patentable subject matter until Congress expressly authorizes such protection. Its position rests on the fact that genetic technology was unforeseen when Congress enacted Section 101. The commissioner argues that the legislative process is best equipped to weigh the competing economic, social, and scientific considerations involved and to determine whether living organisms produced by genetic engineering should receive patent protection. In support of this position, the commissioner relies on this court's recent statement that the judiciary must proceed cautiously when asked to extend patent rights into areas wholly unforeseen by Congress.

It is, of course, correct that Congress, not the courts, must define the limits of patentability, but it is equally true that once Congress has spoken, it is the province and duty of the judicial department to say what the law is. Congress has performed its role in defining patentable subject matter in Section 101; we perform ours in construing the language Congress has employed.

Broad, general language is not necessarily ambiguous when congressional objectives require broad terms. This court frequently has observed that a statute is not to be confined to the particular applications contemplated by the legislators. This is especially true in the field of patent law. A rule that unanticipated inventions are without protection would conflict with the core concept of the patent law that requires novelty for patentability. Congress employed broad, general language in drafting Section 101 precisely because such inventions are often unforeseeable.

To buttress their argument, the commissioner and others point to grave risks that may be generated by research endeavors such as Chakrabarty's. Their briefs present a gruesome parade of horribles, suggesting that such research may pose a serious threat to the human race. It is argued that this Court should weigh these potential hazards in considering whether Chakrabarty's invention is patentable. We disagree. The grant or denial of patents on microorganisms is not likely to put an end to genetic research or its attendant risks. Legislative or judicial fiat as to patentability will not deter scientific minds from probing into the unknown any more than King Canute could command the tides. Whether Chakrabarty's claims are patentable may determine whether research efforts are accelerated by the hope of reward or slowed by want of incentives, but that is all.

The choice we are urged to make is a matter of high policy for resolution within the legislative process after the kind of investigation, examination, and study that legislative bodies can provide and courts cannot. Whatever their validity, the contentions now pressed on us should be addressed by the Congress and the executive, but not the courts. Congress is free to amend Section 101 so as to exclude from patent protection organisms produced by genetic engineering or to craft a statute specifically designed for such living things. But until Congress does, the Court must construe section 101 as it stands. And that language embraces Chakrabarty's invention.

Accordingly, the judgment of the lower court is Affirmed.

Chakrabarty received a patent on the genetically engineered bacterium in 1981. However, by 1992, the organism had yet to be used in a commercial application. This is not for want of a practical use, however. Recent studies have shown that living microbes, such as Chakrabarty's, may effectively break up oil by releasing soaplike sulfcants that emulsify oil into droplets small enough for bacteria to convert into carbon dioxide and water. This, of course, could be extremely useful for major oil-spill cleanup efforts, such as that needed after the Exxon *Valdez* spilled its cargo in Alaska. Indeed, the microbes may be less toxic and more biodegradable than traditional methods using chemicals. But the stumbling block for this technology, as with most biotechnology concerns, is fear.[19]

Whenever living organisms are introduced into new environments, public anxiety buttons are pushed.[20] This is true even when living things that have been developed by nature are taken from their natural habitat and moved into new regions. One only has to consider what happened when a few African killer bees were shipped to South America, or when the Mediterranean fruit fly made its way to California. Clearly, the balance of nature is a delicate and complex matter well beyond the total grasp of human understanding. Any human action that would serve to upset the natural chain of life in a region, therefore, is rightly met with concern, hostility, and scrutiny. And obviously, the reaction will be many times as strong when the issue is not simply the displacement of natural life, but rather the introduction of new life forms not yet contemplated in the natural scheme of Earth.

For these reasons, the difficult issues pertinent to patent protection for living things, of which there are many, may be only the beginning of the frustrations for biotechnology enterprises. Beyond typical patent concerns regarding the propriety and extent of legal control, biotechnology inventions must bear additional social, ethical, and political burdens. Thus, a biotechnology business that successfully navigates the extremely uncertain waters of patent protection typically has only begun its journey through the legal and public policy process.[21] This is particularly true when the newly engineered life forms will be released into the open environment as opposed to being controlled in a laboratory setting. For instance, field tests for evaluating genetically altered crops have met stiff resistance from environmental groups and burdensome oversight from government regulators.[22] Companies involved with biotechnology therefore must be prepared to contend with regulations from a myriad of administrative agencies, even after a patent is granted. For example, the Environmental Protection Agency, the Department of Agriculture, the Occupational Safety and Health Administration, and the Food and Drug Administration may all have some role in regulating bioengineered food products.[23]

As the science of biotechnology advances, the patent issues become increasingly contentious and complex. A primary concern is just how far up the ladder of life proprietary rights through patents should be allowed. It is one thing to grant a patent on genetically altered microorganisms. It may seem quite another to permit ownership of a strain of celery or a breed of mice or cows. But patent protection now clearly extends to such higher forms of life. In 1985, the PTO Board of Patent Appeals and Interferences (the board) held that seeds, plants, and plant tissue cultures are patentable subject matter under Section 101.[24] In early 1987, the board went further, holding that Section 101 covers non–naturally occurring oysters in which polyploidy was induced by hydrostatic pressure.[25] Soon thereafter, on April 21, 1987, the PTO issued a policy statement indicating that it considers all non–naturally occurring nonhuman multicellular living organisms, including higher animals, to be patentable subject matter under Section 101. In 1988, the PTO granted the first patent for a transgenic nonhuman mammal: a mouse into which a gene is inserted to make it more susceptible to developing cancerous tumors. By mid-1993, the PTO had granted patents for three other mice and a rabbit, and it was reviewing 140 other patent applications filed with that office.[26]

So far, the majority of the transengenic animals have been developed to aid in drug research. Human genes responsible for specific diseases or maladies are introduced into the animal, causing it to carry the genetic disorder. For example, researchers have created transengenic animals that are especially susceptible to afflictions such as AIDS, enlarged prostate, sickle-cell anemia, and cystic fibrosis.[27] These animals have great medical potential because they may serve as laboratories for experiments aimed at curing or preventing afflictions. But they also raise hostile objections, particularly from animal rights activists and opponents of genetic engineering. For example, the Foundation on Economic Trends aggressively challenged attempts by scientists at the National Institutes of Health to perform AIDs research on mice that were genetically altered to improve the study, arguing that the experiment posed an undue danger if the animals were to escape.[28]

Genetic engineering may prove to revolutionize agribusiness. Whereas classical crossbreeding of, say, a tangerine and a pomelo to yield a tangelo, is an imprecise science, manipulation of specific genes could allow the creation of an unlimited number of tangelos having a precise selection of desired characteristics.[29] By proper selection and introduction of genes, plants can be made to be more resistant to normally harmful microorganisms, pests, and weather conditions, and animals can be tailored to be more efficient for human uses, such as by growing more lean on less food or by producing more milk.[30] In addition, it is now possible to inject into the embryos of animals certain genes that trigger the production of useful human proteins in controlled locations such as in mammary glands. When the animal matures, it then can be used for "pharming," the derivation of drug proteins from animal milk supplies.[31]

The introduction of the Flavr Savr tomato, which was developed by Calgene, Inc., raised an important and highly publicized issue involving genetically altered food products. The Flavr Savr tomato takes advantage of a genetic engineering technique called antisense technology.[32] In highly simplified terms, antisense technology works by neutralizing the messenger responsible for the production of unwanted proteins. A natural tomato, for instance, produces proteins as it ripens, which cause the cell walls to soften. This process occurs because a strand of DNA creates proteins that break down compounds essential for stiffness. To be more specific, the DNA links with what is called messenger RNA and creates a template. The messenger RNA then travels outside the cell nucleus and meets up with a ribosome that reads the template and produces the softening proteins according to its instructions. The Flavr Savr tomato is designed to stay firm longer by blocking this messenger RNA from reaching the ribosome. This is done by introducing a synthetic strand of DNA that is the mirror image to the messenger RNA produced by the natural DNA. Since the synthetic DNA and the messenger RNA are direct complements, they have a tendency to bind together, thereby preventing the messenger RNA template from ever traveling to the ribosome. The result is that fewer of the softening proteins are manufactured by the cells of the tomato.[33]

Calgene, which patented the antisense process for its tomato, received permission from the Department of Agriculture in 1992 to begin commercial marketing of its genetically altered food.[34] This resulted in a storm of protest, led by the Foundation on Economic Trends. Some consumers called for regulations requiring supermarkets to identify genetically altered products, such as the Flavr Savr. Then 1,000 prominent chefs throughout the United States refused to use the tomato in their recipes.[35] In response to this public outcry, the Campbell Soup Company announced in 1993 that it was backing away from using the tomato in its products until the item was better accepted by the public.[36] All of this clearly demonstrates that those involved with genetic engineering in agribusiness have to be very sophisticated in handling public perception of their products.

Those opposing the use of bioengineering in agribusiness point to a variety of potential concerns. For one, they are not convinced that bioengineering techniques are as safe as the industry claims. In support of their doubts, they point to some surprising issues resulting from the injection of recombinant bovine growth hormone (rBGH) into cows to increase milk production. rBGH is made through a genetic engineering technique based on a cow gene responsible for growth. Some studies indicate that cows treated with rBGH have a higher incidence of mastitis, requiring treatment with antibiotics. If the additional levels of antibiotics pass into the milk supply, they possibly could result in harmful consequences.[37]

A large set of other concerns centers on the long-term affects of tinkering with nature. Since life can mutate, reproduce, and migrate, there are a host of containment issues. For instance, a herbicide-resistant plant might pollinate in other areas where that plant is not wanted. Ridding it then could necessitate the increased use of more lethal weed killers. Ecological fears also are compelling. As already mentioned, there are constant worries about the delicate balance of nature. A fish that is engineered to achieve greater size may be beneficial for food production, but its introduction into the environment might substantially alter the ecosystem. Less obvious are questions about biodiversity. If agriculture comes to depend on a smaller set of bioengineered food products bred for specific superior traits, then the diversity of living plants may diminish. This could render the world food supply extremely vulnerable to disease, pests, or changing weather conditions.[38] In addition, world debate has begun to focus on the extent of access and control that countries should be given to genetic technologies that depend on raw materials originally grown in their lands. The United States failed to sign the Biodiversity Convention at the Earth Summit in Rio de Janeiro in 1992 based, in part, on objections from the biotechnology industry to certain principles of access and compensation. Since that time, the industry has softened its opposition, and the Clinton Administration ultimately signed the international agreement in 1993.[39]

On an associated front, an extremely contentious issue is whether plant and animal patents should cover progeny. In the context of traditional machine patents, one who purchases a machine is entitled to use it without restriction. Thus, the buyer is allowed to tear the machine apart or transform it into something else. What the buyer may not do is duplicate the machine. Plant and animal patents strain the traditional constructs because the subject matter of the invention—the plant or animal—can reproduce naturally. May purchasers of a patented plant or animal breed it without permission, or must they contract to pay royalties for the harvested seeds or offspring?[40] Clearly, this is a critical issue for those engaged in agribusiness ventures.

Unless the patent laws are amended to specifically address this issue, it is likely that animal patents will extend to progeny. Otherwise, many inventors of transengenic animals and plants will conclude that their most profitable course of action is to maintain the invention in secrecy and to distribute only the final products. That outcome is contrary to the disclosure principles of patent policy. It also might tend to consolidate the production of agricultural products.[41] Therefore, it is logical to assume that breeding that duplicates the protected features will be covered by a patent. But what if a purchaser of a patented animal breeds the animal with one from another species, resulting in some different variation of life? What if the animal runs loose and mates wildly in nature? Is the purchaser liable to pay royalties for all the resultant offspring? These issues are of such concern to farmers that they have aggressively lobbied Congress to either place a moratorium on animal patents or amend the patent laws so as to allow farmers to breed, use, and sell patented farm animals and their offspring.[42]

The problems escalate when viewed from an international perspective. For instance, suppose that an inventor has a U.S. patent on a strain of corn. If protection for that variety is not obtained or is not available in another country, then purchasers can grow several generations of corn with seedlings. Can imports of the corn be prohibited? What if the corn is legally made into meal or into tortillas? Can these types of indirect products be barred from importation into the United States? Although a strict reading of Section 337 would appear to cover such indirect products, there clearly will be practical problems of enforcement as well as sensitive issues of international relations.

That the processes and products of genetic engineering are alive leads to numerous other complicated legal and social issues, especially in the pharmaceutical area. One excellent example is provided by the litigation between Amgen and Genetic Institute over patent rights to erythropoietin (EPO), a hormone secreted by the human kidney, which when purified may be used to treat anemia.[43] Genetics Institute received a patent on the purified hormone in 1987. This alone might surprise you because EPO is a natural product of the kidney. However, there is precedence in the chemical field, indicating that if a chemical can be found in nature only in an unpurified form, then a patent can be received on the purified form. Likewise, if EPO exists in nature only in an unpurified form, then the purified version is eligible for patent protection as an invention made through human ingenuity.

EPO is secreted by human kidneys in such minute quantities that its production from that source is not commercially viable. Therefore, Genetics Institute entered into a race with Amgen to develop the drug through genetic engineering. For genetic engineering to occur, one must locate within the DNA the gene sequence that contains the instructions for a cell to manufacture the desired protein. The gene sequence then is placed into a DNA molecule of an appropriate living cell, which, as it multiplies through natural division, serves as a production factory of the protein. Amgen was the first to discover the appropriate gene sequence, and in 1987 it received a patent on it. Amgen also discovered that a Chinese hamster's ovary cell served well as an EPO factory, and the company received another patent on the transformed version of that cell.

Genetics Institute found a similar way to genetically engineer EPO and used the method to manufacture and sell EPO in the United States. It also licensed a Japanese pharmaceutical company to market EPO worldwide. In the ensuing litigation, Amgen argued that its patents were infringed by Genetics Institute's technique of producing EPO through genetic engineering. Genetics Institute alleged that it had sole rights over purified EPO to treat anemia and that the sale of purified EPO by any unauthorized company infringed its patent, no matter how it was made. In effect, what could have resulted was a standoff, wherein one company owned the useful final product but another owned the only viable way to make it.

If patents on purified proteins take precedence over the biotechnological means to make them, this could have a chilling effect on the biotechnology industry. The Genetics Institute/Amgen litigation did not settle the question, because the appeals court found Genetics Institute's patent to be invalid.[44] Genetic Institute's version of EPO was no more pure than that found in nature. Therefore, Amgen could continue to sell EPO using its biotechnology technique and could block the use of that technique by Genetics Institute in the United States. The larger question regarding the precedence of valid purified protein claims thus survived this dispute. The few other cases that have considered this issue have been extremely complex, as was the case with EPO, and the debate still remains somewhat unresolved.[45] However, evidence is mounting that the courts support the priority of the purified protein claims.[46] Hopefully, the courts will reach a definitive consensus on this important issue soon.

A key aspect of genetic engineering is determining the gene sequence that produces an identified useful protein. Human cells each have 23 pairs of chromosomes, which consist of two twisted strands of DNA. The problem is that not all of the DNA is composed of genes that make proteins. In fact, the 100,000 genes that are thought to exist make up only about 3% of DNA. The rest of the DNA logically is called junk DNA. The problem of fully identifying gene sequences is magnified because each gene consists of between 2,000 and 2 million pairs of nucleotides. Therefore, the endeavor to locate and identify the full makeup of all the genes in human cells is a major undertaking indeed. To achieve this understanding, a major multinational effort, called the Human Genome Initiative, was initiated in 1988 to map and sequence all the human genes.[47]

As noted previously, U.S. law allows a gene sequence to be patented if it does not exist in nature in its isolated form. Other countries may not go so far as to allow the patenting of gene sequences. Rather, a patent may be available only for a new organism created by the introduction of the gene sequence.[48] In 1991 and 1992, the National Institutes of Health (NIH) raised the controversy one more notch by filing patent applications for 2,700 genes and gene fragments it located through use of a new identification technique.[49] The most contentious point of these applications was that although the genes had been located, their function and utility were not yet known. Many experts questioned whether a utility patent is appropriate for an invention before one knows the utility that the invention might accomplish. NIH, on the other hand, worried that if it published its findings without filing for a patent, then scientists who later discovered the function of the genes would be precluded from enjoying patent rights, based on a lack of novelty.[50] The applications caused an international stir, igniting a frantic response by the British government to withhold information on its gene research discoveries and to begin efforts to patent genes located by its scientists.[51] Also, the applications raised substantial speculation that other governments and private companies would join in a global race to file patents for as many genes and gene fragments of the human body as they could locate. In September 1992, the PTO rejected the applications, citing the utility concerns as well as other problems.[52] Tremendous uncertainty remains, however, on how this saga ultimately will unfold. NIH, for instance, might appeal the decision or amend its applications. Clearly, any international accord dealing substantively with the patentability of bioengineered inventions will have to deal carefully with this issue.

Biotechnology raises a host of other patent concerns, some of which will be touched on in the next chapter. As you might suspect, patent applications for biotechnology inventions take a long time for the PTO to process, ranging from about 2½ to 4 years.[53] Although the patent office has upgraded its efficiency and has poured more resources into biotechnology review, it has had a hard time keeping up with the recent huge increases in biotechnology applications.[54] Just to put it into perspective, of the 19,750 biotechnology applications filed through 1990, 9,385 were filed in 1990 alone.[55] The resultant time lags serve to increase the already high level of risk for those who do business in the biotechnology field.

There are many issues involving the requirements of the patent application. One of the most troubling is that new organisms often cannot be described in words, thereby requiring the deposit of viable living specimens into public facilities. This has led to serious questions about the timing and extent of permissible public access. In this regard, the United States is a signatory of the Budapest Treaty, an international accord administered by WIPO, which prescribes standards for approved locations, maintenance, and replacement of deposited organisms.[56]

Heated and controversial discussions are now taking place in the international arena over the propriety and means of protection for biotechnology inventions. In Europe, there is substantial disparity in the amount of protection provided for biotechnology inventions by different countries.[57] The European Union has been working on a Directive intended to harmonize intellectual property rights for biotechnology inventions among its members. The main elements of that Directive provide for patents on living organisms, including plants and higher life forms, and extend protection to progeny.[58] However, the Directive became bogged down in the European Parliament in 1993 due to proposed amendments allowing farmers to harvest and plant seed from patented plants and requiring compulsory licensing in certain situations.[59] Several other countries such as Japan, Canada, and Switzerland provide biotechnology patent protection, but many others do not.[60] The successful conclusion of the Uruguay Round of GATT should improve the situation but will not end the disparities. The participants of

GATT agreed that patents must be available without discrimination as to the field of technology. However, member countries are allowed to exclude plants and animals, other than microorganisms, from patentability. Also, developing countries have ten years to implement new policies regarding biotechnology patent protection.

Complex issues arise in other patent contexts as well. For instance, there are difficult questions regarding the breadth of patent claims allowed by the PTO and the extent of protection the claims provide against potential infringers.[61] Overall, the advent of biotechnology has seriously strained traditional patent concepts and principles. The vast array of social and legal questions, coupled with huge investment risks and enormous potential payoffs, has made biotechnology legal policy a very important topic for national and international debate.

## Patent Protection for Computer Programs

Another significantly important concern on the part of certain high-technology companies is whether computer programs, and those machines and processes that utilize them, may be patented. The proposed AES, for instance, depends on a computer program to properly filter out unwanted noises and to enhance desired frequencies. Within the program, streams of data relayed from various digital sources are run through a logical series of mathematical relationships and decision steps to yield the optimal solutions to the filtering and enhancement problems. Because the laws of nature and the mathematical formulas that explain them are not patentable subject matter, one may reasonably wonder whether a patent may issue on AES. In other words, may a system such as AES be patented when part of that system consists of nonpatentable subject matter?

In the 1970s, the Supreme Court reviewed two computer-related patent cases, and in both, it determined that the inventions did not involve patentable subject matter.[62] This led to the general view that patents were not the appropriate vehicle to protect this form of technological innovation. For this reason, computer programmers typically relied on other forms of intellectual property protection, notably trade secrets and copyrights, to protect their innovations. In 1981, the Supreme Court clarified in *Diamond v. Diehr* that the sweeping generalization about the nonpatentability of computer processes was inappropriate and that computer-related inventions could be subject to patent protection. *Diamond v. Diehr* thus is a landmark patent decision representing a pivotal point for the protection, within the United States, of inventions utilizing computer programs.

## DIAMOND V. DIEHR

*United States Supreme Court, 1981*

### Facts

The claimed invention is a process for molding raw, uncured synthetic rubber into cured precision products. Achieving the perfect cure depends upon several factors, including the thickness of the article to be molded, the temperature of the molding process, and the amount of time that the article is allowed to remain in the press. It is possible using well-known time, temperature, and cure relationships to use the Arrhenius equation to determine when to open the press and remove the cured product. Nonetheless, the industry had heretofore not been able to obtain uniformly accurate cures because the temperature of the molding press (a key variable in the equation) varied as the press heated up and it could not be precisely measured at any moment of time. The result was that rubber often was overcured and sometimes was undercured.

The invention by Diehr and Lutton (D&L) is a process that constantly measures the actual temperature inside the mold and feeds the data to a computer that repeatedly recalculates the cure time by use of the Arrhenius equation. When the appropriate time from the equation equals the elapsed cure time, the computer signals a device to open the press. According to D&L, the continuous measuring of the temperature, the feeding of the information to a computer that constantly recalculates the cure time, and the signaling by the computer to open the press are all new in the art.

The patent examiner rejected the patent claims on the sole ground that those steps carried out by a computer under control of a stored program are not statutory subject matter under Section 101. The Patent and Trademark Office Board of Appeals agreed with the examiner, but the Court of Customs and Patent Appeals (which has currently been replaced by the Federal Circuit) reversed. The Commissioner of Patents and Trademarks appealed to the Supreme Court.

## Opinion

To decide this case, the Court must interpret the meaning of the word "process" in Section 101. In so doing, we must be mindful that Congress intended statutory subject matter to include anything under the sun that is made by man. A process is a mode of treatment of certain material to produce a given result. It is a series of acts performed upon the subject to be transformed and reduced to a different state or thing. Transformation and reduction of an article to a different state or thing thus constitutes the clue to patentability of a process claim.

That D&L's claims involve the transformation of an article—in this case uncured synthetic rubber—into a different state or thing cannot be disputed. That conclusion is not altered by the fact that in several steps of the process, a mathematical equation and a programmed digital computer are used.

The Supreme Court has undoubtedly recognized limits to Section 101, and every discovery is not embraced within the statutory terms. Excluded from such patent protection are laws of nature, natural phenomena, and abstract ideas.

Our recent holdings in two computer-related cases are consistent with this policy. In *Gottschalk v. Benson*, we determined that an algorithm that is used to convert binary code decimal numbers to equivalent pure binary numbers is unpatentable. We defined "algorithm" as a procedure for solving a given type of mathematical problem, and we concluded that such an algorithm or mathematical formula is like a law of nature, which cannot be the subject of a patent. In

*Parker v. Flook*, we held unpatentable claims drawn to a method for computing an "alarm limit." An alarm limit is simply a number, and the application sought to protect a formula for computing the number. The application did not purport to explain how the variables were to be determined, nor did it disclose the chemical processes at work, the monitoring of process variables, or the means of setting off an alarm or adjusting an alarm system.

In contrast, D&L seek to patent not a mathematical formula but a process of curing synthetic rubber. The process admittedly employs a well-known mathematical equation, but D&L do not seek to preempt the use of that equation. Rather, they seek only to foreclose from others the use of that equation in conjunction with all of the other steps of the claimed process. These include installing rubber into the press, closing the mold, constantly determining the temperature of the mold, constantly recalculating the appropriate cure time through the use of the formula and a computer, and automatically opening the press at the proper time. Obviously, one does not need a computer to cure natural or synthetic rubber, but if the computer use incorporated in the process patent significantly lessens the possibility of overcuring or undercuring, the process as a whole does not thereby become unpatentable subject matter.

A claim drawn to subject matter that is otherwise statutory does not become nonstatutory simply because it uses a mathematical formula, computer program, or digital computer. It is commonplace that an *application* of a law of nature or mathematical formula to a known structure or process may well be deserving of patent protection. That is, although a scientific truth, or the mathematical expression of it, is not a patentable invention, a novel and useful structure created with the aid of knowledge of scientific truth may be.

The Arrhenius equation is not patentable in isolation, but when a process for curing rubber is devised that incorporates in it a more efficient solution of the equation, that process is not barred at the threshold by Section 101. In a determination of the eligibility of a process for patent protection, the claims must be considered as a whole. It is inappropriate to dissect the claims into old and new elements and then to ignore the presence of the old elements in the analysis. The novelty of any element or steps in a process is of no relevance in determining whether the subject matter of a claim falls with the Section 101 categories of patentable subject matter. Rather, novelty is of importance only with reference to the requirements of Section 102.

In this case, it may later be determined that D&L's process is not deserving of patent protection because it fails to satisfy conditions of novelty under Section 102 or nonobviousness under Section 103. A rejection on either of these grounds does not affect the determination that the subject matter of D&L's claims was eligible for patent protection under Section 101.

We view D&L's claims as nothing more than a process for molding rubber products and not as an attempt to patent a mathematical formula. We recognize, of course, that when a claim recites a mathematical formula (or scientific principle or phenomenon of nature), an inquiry must be made into whether the claim is seeking patent protection for the formula in the abstract. A mathematical formula as such is not accorded the protection of the patent laws, and this principle cannot be circumvented by attempting to limit the use of the formula to a particular technological environment. Similarly, insignificant postsolution activity will not transform an unpatentable principle into a patentable process. To hold otherwise would allow a competent draftsperson to evade the recognized limitations on the type of subject matter eligible for patent protection. On the other hand, when a claim containing a mathematical formula implements or applies that formula in a structure or process that, when considered as a whole, is performing a function that the patent laws were designed to protect (e.g., transforming or reducing an article to a different state or thing), then the claim satisfies the requirements of Section 101.

Because we do not view D&L's claims as an attempt to patent a mathematical formula, but rather to be drawn to an industrial process for the molding of rubber products, we affirm the judgment of the Court of Customs and Patent Appeals.

---

*Diamond v. Diehr* makes it clear that a process does not become unpatentable subject matter simply because a computer program is incorporated within it. The Supreme Court recognized that computer programs achieve their tasks by solving problems based on laws of nature. However, so do all inventions. For instance, a traditional clock depending on gears keeps the correct time only because the gear ratios have been accurately determined based on mathematical and geometric relationships. All inventions work because the laws of nature allow them to work. Thus, it is not enough that an invention simply uses a law of nature for it to be designated unpatentable. Rather, as the Supreme Court indicated, the invention must be little else *but* a law of nature for it to be designated unpatentable.

Since *Diamond v. Diehr*, the lower courts have clarified the analytical methods for approaching the patentability of inventions using computers, and the PTO has issued guidelines based on these refinements.[63] Essentially, the PTO and the courts utilize a two-step analysis to determine the patentability of computer-based inventions. First, one determines whether the steps involved in the computer process recite a mathematical algorithm at all. If not, then there is no concern that protection of the process will allow the patentee to exercise unwarranted control over such an algorithm. Therefore, if the answer to this inquiry is that no mathematical algorithm is involved, then the invention constitutes patentable subject matter.

Assuming the computer process recites a mathematical algorithm, the second step investigates whether patent protection of the claims would serve to preempt others from lawfully using the algorithm. Here is where one looks to see if the claims involve something other than a natural law. In other words, one strives to understand whether protection might extend to physical relationships other than mathematical laws. Thus, if the mathematical algorithm is implemented in a specific manner to define structural relationships between physical elements in an apparatus or to refine steps in a process, then the invention contains patentable subject matter. Or, viewing the issue another way, one might analyze the invention without the algorithm to determine whether anything that remains, albeit inoperable without the algorithm, is patentable subject matter. If so, then the invention is more than a law of nature, consisting of some technological application of the natural law. In this case, patent protection is entirely appropriate.

Possibly the easiest way to understand these principles is to consider a few examples in which protection is not warranted. The clearest case is when the claims simply extend to the calculation of a number by a mathematical algorithm. For example, a computer process that merely converts binary code decimal numbers to equivalent pure binary numbers is not patentable subject matter.

Often, calculation of a number will be followed by some insignificant post-solution activity. Such minor additional factors, by themselves, will not make an invention patentable. Thus, it is not enough that the invention displays the answer to the calculation or transmits the answer to another location. Similarly, one may not receive a patent for an invention that simply includes the data-gathering steps required to determine the values for the variables in a mathematical algorithm. From these examples, one could surmise that the physical manipulation of data, by itself, is insufficient to render an invention patentable. Rather, the inquiry asks whether there is a transformation of something physical into a different form. In *Diehr*, for instance, the process was patentable because a signal representing heat was transformed into a signal activating the press.

*Arrhythmia Research Technology v. Corazonix* is an important opinion, rendered by the influential Federal Circuit Court of Appeals in 1992, which illustrates how liberally these principles are now being applied. The case also clearly demonstrates that the inclusion of computer processes in inventions no longer raises substantial obstacles to patentability.

## ARRHYTHMIA RESEARCH TECHNOLOGY, INC. V. CORAZONIX CORP.
*Federal Circuit Court of Appeals, 1992*

### Facts

Dr. Michael Simson, a cardiologist, received a patent (the '459 patent) for an invention directed to the analysis of electrocardiogram signals. In the hours immediately after a heart attack, the victim is vulnerable to an acute type of heart arrhythmia known as ventricular tachycardia. Ventricular tachycardia leads quickly to ventricular fibrillation, a condition in which the heart ceases to pump blood effectively through the body. The condition may be treated or prevented with drugs, but the drugs have undesirable and sometimes dangerous side effects. Dr. Simson sought a solution to the problem of determining which heart attack victims are at high risk for ventricular tachycardia, so that such persons can be carefully monitored and appropriately treated.

Heart activity is monitored by means of an electrocardiographic device, whereby electrodes attached to the patient's body detect the heart's electrical signals in accordance with the various phases of heart activity. It was known that in patients subject to ventricular tachycardia, certain anomalous waves having very low amplitude and high frequency—known as late potentials—appear toward the end of what is called the QRS segment of the electrocardiographic signal. Dr. Simson's method of detecting and measuring these late potentials in the QRS segment, and the associated apparatus, are the subjects of the '459 patent.

Dr. Simson's patent application describes the procedures carried out by the invention. Certain of the patient's electrocardiographic signals—those obtained from electrodes designated X, Y, and Z leads—are converted from analog to digital values, and a composite digital representation of the QRS segment is obtained by selecting and averaging a large number of the patient's QRS waveforms. The anterior portion of the composite QRS waveform is first isolated, then processed by a digital high-pass filter in reverse time order (that is, backwards). This type of reverse time order filtering is described as the critical feature of the Simson invention, in that it enables detection of the late potentials by eliminating certain perturbations that obscure these signals. The root mean square of the reverse time filtered output is then calculated to determine the average magnitude of the anterior portion of the QRS segments. Comparison of the output, which is measured in microvolts, with a predetermined level of high frequency energy, indicates whether the patient is subject to ventricular tachycardia. If the root mean square magnitude is less than the predetermined level, then low-amplitude, high-frequency late potentials have been shown to be present, indicating a higher risk of ventricular tachycardia. If the root mean square value is greater than the predetermined level, then high risk for ventricular tachycardia is not indicated.

Certain steps of the invention are described as conducted with the aid of a digital computer, and the patent specification sets forth the mathematical formulas that are used to program the computer. The specification states that dedicated equipment or hardwired logic circuitry can also be used. (Specifications will be discussed in Chapter 3.)

The invention is claimed in the patent both as a method for achieving a result and as an apparatus. (Claims also will be discussed in Chapter 3.) The broadest method claim is as follows:

> A method for analyzing electrocardiograph signals to determine the presence or absence of a predetermined level of high-frequency energy in the late QRS signal, comprising the steps of:
> - Converting a series of QRS signals to time segments, each segment having a digital value equivalent to the analog value of said signals at said times;
> - Applying a portion of said time segments in reverse time order to high-pass filter means;
> - Determining an arithmetic value of the amplitude of the output of said filter; and
> - Comparing said value with said predetermined value.

A representative apparatus claim is as follows:

> Apparatus for analyzing electrocardiographic signals to determine the level of high-frequency energy in the late QRS signal comprising:
> - Means for converting X, Y, and Z lead electrocardiographic input signals to digital valued time segments; and

- Means for examining said X, Y, and Z digital valued time segments and selecting therefrom the QRS waveform portions thereof; . . .

Corazonix challenged the validity of the '459 patent in a Texas district court. The district court declared the patent invalid for failure to claim statutory subject matter. Arrhythmia appealed that determination to the Federal Circuit.

## Opinion

The Supreme Court has observed that Congress intended Section 101 to include anything under the sun that is made by man. There are, however, qualifications to the apparent sweep of this statement. Excluded from patentability is subject matter in the categories of laws of nature, physical phenomena, and abstract ideas. A mathematical formula may describe a law of nature, a scientific truth, or an abstract idea. As courts have recognized, mathematics may also be used to describe the steps of a statutory method or the elements of a statutory apparatus. The exceptions to patentable subject matter derive from a lengthy jurisprudence, but their meaning was probed anew with the advent of computer-related inventions.

Since *Diamond v. Diehr*, the law has crystallized about the principle that claims directed solely to an abstract mathematical formula or equation, including the mathematical expression of a scientific truth or a law of nature, whether directly or indirectly stated, are nonstatutory under Section 101, whereas claims to a specific process or apparatus that is implemented in accordance with a mathematical algorithm will generally satisfy Section 101. In the application of that principle to an invention whose process steps or apparatus elements are described at least in part in terms of mathematical procedures, the mathematical procedures are considered in the context of the claimed invention as a whole.

Determination of statutory subject matter has been conveniently conducted in two stages. This analysis has been designated the Freeman-Walter-Abele test for statutory subject matter. The test first determines whether a mathematical algorithm is recited directly or indirectly in the claim. If so, it is next determined whether the claimed invention as a whole is no more than the algorithm itself, that is, whether the claim is directed to a mathematical algorithm that is not applied to or limited by physical elements or process steps. Such claims are nonstatutory. However, when the mathematical algorithm is applied to one or more steps of an otherwise statutory process claim or to one or more elements of an otherwise statutory apparatus claim, the requirements of Section 101 are met. Although the Freeman-Walter-Abele analysis is not the only test for statutory subject matter, this analytic procedure is conveniently applied to the Simson invention.

Arrhythmia Research states that the district court erred in its determination that the '459 patent is invalid based on nonstatutory subject matter. Although mathematical calculations are involved, Arrhythmia argues that the claims are directed to a method of detection of a certain heart condition by a novel method of analyzing a portion of the electrocardiographically measured heart cycle. This is accomplished by procedures conducted by means of electronic equipment programmed to perform mathematical computation. However, Arrhythmia stresses that the claims do not preempt the mathematical algorithms used in any of the procedures. Corazonix states that the claims define no more than a mathematical algorithm that calculates a number. Corazonix states that in Simson's process and apparatus claims, mathematical algorithms are merely presented and solved and that Simson's designation of a field of use and postsolution activity are not essential to the claims and thus do not cure the defect. Thus, Corazonix states that the claims are not directed to statutory subject matter and that the district court's judgment was correct.

Applying the Freeman-Walter-Abele protocol to the process claims, we first assume for this analysis that a mathematical algorithm is included in the subject matter in that some claimed steps are described in the specification by mathematical formulas. We thus proceed to the second stage of the analysis, to determine whether the claimed process is otherwise statutory; that is, we determine what the claimed steps do, independent of how they are implemented.

Simson's process is claimed as a method for analyzing electrocardiographic signals so as to determine the presence or absence of a predetermined level of high-frequency energy in the late QRS signal. This claim limitation is not ignored in the determination of whether the subject matter as a whole is statutory, for all of the claim steps are in implementation of this method. The electrocardiographic signals are first transformed from analog form, in which they are obtained, to the corresponding digital signal. These input signals are not abstractions; they are related to the patient's heart function. The anterior portion of the QRS signal is then processed by the procedure known as reverse time order filtration. The digital filter selected by Dr. Simson is one of several known procedures for frequency filtering of digital waveforms. The filtered signal is further analyzed to determine its average magnitude by the root mean square technique. Comparison of the resulting output to a predetermined level indicates whether there are late potentials in the anterior portion of the QRS segment, thereby showing if the patient is at high risk. The resultant output is not an abstract number but is a signal related to the patient's heart activity.

These claimed steps of "converting," "applying," "determining," and "comparing" are physical process steps that transform one physical electrical signal into another. The view that there is nothing necessarily physical about signals is incorrect. The Simson process claims are analogous to those upheld in *Diehr*, wherein the court remarked that the applicants do not seek to patent a mathematical formula but seek only to foreclose from others the use of an equation in conjunction with all of the other steps in the claimed process. The Freeman-Walter-Abele standard is met.

The Simson apparatus claims are statutory subject matter under the same principles. The computer-performed operations transform a particular input signal to a different output signal, in accordance with the internal structure of the computer as configured by electronic instructions. The claimed invention converts one physical thing into another physical thing just as any other electrical circuitry would do. Corazonix argues that the final output of the claimed apparatus is simply a number and that the claims therefore are not statutory. However, the number obtained is not a mathematical abstraction; it is a measure in microvolts of a specified heart activity. That the product is numerical is not a criterion for whether the claim is directed to statutory subject matter. The Simson apparatus claims are statutory subject matter. They are directed to a specific apparatus of practical utility and specified application, and they meet the requirements of Section 101.

The judgment of invalidity on the ground that the claimed method and apparatus do not define statutory subject matter is reversed. The case is sent back (remanded) to the district court for resolution of other issues.

---

The analytical discussions in *Diehr* and *Arrhythmia* are directed primarily at physical inventions and processes that utilize computer programs to achieve their ends. However, what if the sole invention is the computer process or the computer program that instructs the computer how to undertake the process? May the computer process or program, in isolation, be patented? According to the courts and the PTO, the same analytical principles as those aforementioned apply to computer processes. Therefore, the computer process or program will constitute patentable subject matter if it does something more than solve a mathematical algorithm.

Although it receives less attention, a related inquiry regarding the patentability of certain computer processes and programs asks whether protection, if allowed, would extend simply to a method of doing business. As noted before, business ideas and methods are not properly the subjects of patent protection; only novel and nonobvious systems implementing those methods are patentable. At one time, many computer programs were thought to be outside the purview of patent protection because they implemented business operations. However, decisions by the courts and the PTO indicate that patents may be received for computer software that implements business methods within an operational system.

In a frequently cited case, a Delaware federal court held that a software computer process implementing the Merrill Lynch Cash Management Accounting (CMA) system was patentable subject matter.[64] Among other things, the system managed up to four types of financial accounts so that idle cash balances were invested promptly in money market funds and so that credit card liabilities were paid most efficiently for customers according to a schedule indicating the cheapest sources of available funds. The court noted that the CMA method would not be patentable if it were done by hand. However, it determined that the patent on the computer system was valid because it demonstrated a method of operation on a computer to effectuate a business activity. In other words, although the method is not patentable, the computerized system to implement it is.

Since that case, many financial services firms have received patents on business software systems. For instance, Lazard Freres & Co. received a patent on a system for restructuring debt obligations by figuring the face value of zero-coupon bonds. And College Savings Bank has a patent on an investment system that pays a variable interest rate linked to the costs of U.S. private colleges.[65] In sum, business applications programs are now clearly viewed as proper subjects for patents. As long as the patent claims are properly tailored to cover only a system for implementing a business activity rather than the business method, itself, then the computer process will be patentable subject matter.[66]

With *Diamond v. Diehr* as a springboard, patent policy has now progressed so that almost all forms of computer processes and computer software are patentable subject matter. The PTO has issued patents for software systems associated with artificial intelligence, language translation, video games, word processing, graphic user interfaces, robotics, computer-aided design, and a host of other applications.[67] The patent office has shown that it will approve patents even for fundamental aspects of multimedia storage and searching systems, as long as the conditions of novelty and nonobviousness are met. This has led some experts to wonder whether the information superhighway will turn into a toll road.[68] Thus, the relevant question no longer is whether computer-related inventions are patentable subject matter in the United States. Rather, the modern inquiry asks whether it makes sense to seek patent protection for such computer processes and programs.

Many issues, such as the cost of obtaining a patent, are no different in the computer field from other fields. However, patent protection in the computer area does raise some interesting special considerations.

**Receiving a Patent from the PTO.** While *Diamond v. Diehr* was under review by the Supreme Court, some 3,000 computer-related applications were held by the PTO pending the decision in that case. Ever since the court announced its decision, the PTO has been playing catch-up with an ever-increasing number of computer-related filings. Whereas patents in other areas may be received in an average of 18 months after filing, the average length of pendency for computer systems, albeit improving, remains at over two years. Coupled with that fact is the rapidity of technological change in this arena. One relevant question therefore concerns the expected life cycle of an invention, because those who wish to clone computer software may do so without restraint from patent policies until the patent issues.[69] While evaluating this, one must bear in mind that patents on computer systems often extend beyond the confines of a particular program. Thus, the relevant life cycle may not simply be that of a defined software product. Rather, the potential family of products to which the invention might apply must be considered.

Because patent protection for computer processes is a relatively new area, the PTO's data bank of prior art may not be fully developed.[70] In addition, there have been allegations that PTO examiners do not have the proper qualifications to sufficiently understand computer software inventions.[71] Some believe that insufficient information at the hands of PTO examiners coupled with inappropriate backgrounds causes those examiners to mistakenly grant patents for computer systems that are not novel.[72] Several recent controversies may illustrate the point, including (1) the patent issued to Compton's New Media for a multimedia retrieval system, (2) a patent received by Software Advertising Corporation covering the use of computer screen savers for advertising, and (3) a patent granted to Roger Billings for a functionally structured distributed data processing system, which some believe may extend to widely used computer networking designs.[73] For those computer programmers who are contemplating patents, these alleged deficiencies within the PTO lead to two concerns, which unfortunately are at odds in making the decision about patent protection. On the one hand, an issued patent may be at risk because a challenge could uncover the overlooked prior art. On the other hand, a patent does carry a lot of power while in force, and the PTO decision to issue one commands substantial deference from the Federal Circuit. Along with this, one must consider that the decision to maintain an invention in secrecy rather than to obtain a patent might open the way for a competitor to claim the invention. Thus, the decision not to pursue a patent carries substantial risks as well.

**Disclosure.** A concern with all patents is how public disclosure of the invention might ultimately be used by competitors to their benefit. Possibly competitors can use disclosure to develop products that do not infringe the claims of a patent. Or, if a patent is found to be invalid, they will then be free to use as they wish the knowledge they obtain. An inventor who fully evaluates these risks might determine that another form of protection, such as trade secrets, may be more appropriate.

The discussion of trade secrets in Chapter 4 shows that computer programs and processes can be successfully protected as trade secrets, particularly if the processes are distributed only in limited contexts amenable to controls ensuring that their secrets will be maintained. However, trade secret protection may not be adequate for mass-marketed products, because customers are free to reverse-engineer products (by decompilation and disassembly), thereby allowing them to learn the sets of instructions that make the processes operate. In addition, the critical features of some inventions, such as with graphical user interfaces, are valuable only in a public environment, limiting the applicability of trade secret protection.

There are other negative aspects about trade secret protection. For instance, if a computer program or process is developed in conjunction with university professors, the professors likely will want to publish the details of the work, thereby making the "secrets" publicly available for competitors to use. Similarly, if a process is developed for or with the federal or a state government, public access often results. Also, trade secret protection does not guard against independent creation of the same process, as does patent protection: strong market demand for an invention means that there likely will be a host of competitors working on achieving the same solution. Depending on the circumstances, these deficiencies to trade secrets suggest that patent protection will be superior if the costs are manageable and the required disclosures are not too extreme.

The disclosure requirements for patent applications will be discussed in the next chapter. Essentially, sufficient information must be disclosed to enable one skilled in the art to make the invention. For a computer process, the application may not have to reveal source or object code to achieve this purpose. Rather, a flow chart presenting the logic of the process may suffice, as long as a skilled programmer could in a reasonable amount of time draft a working program based on the flow chart. In addition, if the computer process is not the entire invention, but rather is one aspect of a broader invention, then the inventor may be able to disclose even less about how to implement the process.[74] The risks from disclosure, therefore, depend greatly on the particular circumstances. *White Consolidated Industries v. Vega Servo-Control, Inc.*, presented in the next chapter, provides a good example of how to evaluate the requisite amount of disclosure for computer processes.

**The Possibility of Copyright Protection.**  The decision to seek patent protection for computer programs carries another wrinkle because, unlike with most other utilitarian inventions, the copyright system represents another viable means of protection. All else being equal, an inventor has reasons to prefer copyright protection because it is much cheaper and easier to obtain, and it enjoys a longer life. However, in theory, everything is not equal, for copyright is designed to protect expressions, whereas patents may protect systems. In addition, copyright protects only against copying, whereas a patent reaches even independent creation of the same invention.

As we will investigate fully in Chapter 6, there is substantial controversy over the amount of protection a computer program may be entitled to enjoy from copyright. The debate comes down to determining just what aspects of the program constitute protectible expression and what parts compose the system to which copyright may not extend. A number of courts have been willing to grant substantial protection to computer programs through copyright. According to them, a copyright on a computer program may prevent competitors from developing programs having the same "look and feel" as the protected program. Although such protection will not prevent competitors from making programs having the same purpose as the copyrighted work, it may severely restrain the ways competitors may go about achieving those ends. Under some circumstances this may be almost as beneficial as protecting the system under the patent laws. However, one must be cautious here, because a new trend is emerging in the courts, which are backing away from such sweeping copyright protection for computer programs. Nonetheless, copyright protection still is clearly applicable. The end result is that managers undertaking a program to protect computer processes must evaluate how copyright protection might fit into their strategic plans. Depending on the circumstances, copyrights may be used either in lieu of patents, in addition to patents, or possibly not at all.

**International Patent Protection of Computer Programs.**  Although there is now little debate in the United States that computer processes and programs may receive patents, such uniformity of opinion certainly does not extend overseas. As of August 1991, only a few major industrialized nations permitted patents to be granted for computer software.[75] Japan represents one example where the trend is to allow patents for computer-related inventions.[76] On the other hand, patent protection for computer programs under the European Patent Convention is not so clear. Although the convention declares that "programs for computers" are not patentable subject matter, the Guidelines of the European Patent Office direct that "patentability should not be denied merely on the ground that a computer program is involved."[77] Thus, in much of Europe a trend may be developing that is analogous to that which has taken place in the United States.[78]

One of the international changes sought by the United States in the Patent Harmonization Treaty being negotiated through WIPO is for enhanced patent protection for computer-related inventions. At this point, it is unclear how successful that effort will be. The TRIPs agreement of the GATT Uruguay Round indicates that all classes of inventions except certain forms of life must be accorded patent protection. However, it does not specifically address whether software-related inventions must be protected. Thus, a company having an international vision must consider the possibility that a novel and nonobvious computer process may enjoy patent protection in the United States and a few countries such as Japan but may not receive patent rights in various other important marketing and manufacturing regions. In those countries, protection, if available at all, will have to be achieved through copyright laws. Clearly, international issues must be considered early in the strategic planning process because the issuance of a patent in the United States will make knowledge of the invention publicly accessible. This, of course, may have devastating consequences if the knowledge is then used to manufacture and distribute products in potentially lucrative trading environments wherein patent protection is unavailable. International considerations for patent protection will be discussed more fully in Chapter 3.

In conclusion, there is no longer any doubt that computer programs may be patented in the United States. Inventions utilizing computers, as well as computer processes and computer software, all are patentable subject matter. Thus, the door is open for patent protection in the United States for an invention such as AES. In addition, it is possible to claim isolated features of AES, such as the computer process or software. However, the ultimate decision to seek patent protection should be made only after one comprehensively considers the full spectrum of ways to preserve rights in the invention, in terms of both their respective positive attributes and their possible negative consequences.

The availability of patent protection for computer software in the United States does not mean that there has been an end to the controversy over the propriety of such protection.[79] As mentioned earlier, many experts in the field believe that the PTO has sometimes issued "bad" patents because of outdated search facilities and insufficient expertise. It is true that those bad patents could theoretically be challenged at any time based on their lack of novelty. However, according to the experts, small companies may not be willing to invest resources in such a challenge, especially with the presumption of validity that attends a PTO decision. Rather, it may make more sense for these companies to accept a license fee from the patentee, thereby leaving the inappropriate patent unchallenged.

Opponents to software patents also note that because software clearly was not patentable before 1981, programmers took steps to protect the secrecy of their computer processes. With the change of position by the courts, the door has opened for companies to claim computer processes that, strictly speaking, may have been secret, but yet still were within the common knowledge of many programmers.[80] Another concern of this group is that computer programs may include a host of patentable processes. If just one of these is already patented, then programmers could be sued for infringement, severely jeopardizing their business operations. Therefore, a programmer must conduct patent searches for all these processes—even without the intention to obtain patents—simply to evaluate the risks of infringement. However, patent searches of computer processes are expensive, possibly totalling up to $2,000 per search.[81] In addition, those against patent protection believe that the large stimulus of a patent is unnecessary for computer programs because programmers do not risk large amounts of capital in their creative endeavors. To confirm this argument, they point to the remarkable growth of the industry in an era when patent protection was not even available. Finally, this opposing group is concerned because the confidentiality of the patent process leads to surprise when the patent issues, thereby requiring computer programming firms, some of which are relatively small, to pay unanticipated license fees. In this regard, one only has to recall how Gilbert Hyatt's patent for microprocessor technology surprised the computer industry when the patent issued in 1990.

Those who approve of patents for computer processes counter these positions with equally compelling arguments.[82] They claim that the PTO must contend with a learning curve for all new technologies. There is nothing particularly special about computer software that makes it more troublesome for the PTO than biotechnology is. Once the PTO identifies its deficiencies in handling new technologies, it takes steps to rectify them. This is currently happening in the computer area. For instance, the PTO is developing a new software classification system, is improving its search facilities, and is increasing its number of software examiners. Proponents also doubt that the industry would continue to advance so rapidly without patents. According to them, the early innovations occurred without patents because the developers were using software to sell hardware. Software now is often extremely complex, making it expensive and risky to develop. In addition, recent court decisions suggest that the copyright system may not be as effective in protecting software as it used to be. Without patents, software developers may be left with little alternative but to rely heavily on trade secrets. Those supporting patents for software also point out that when the United States invariably makes its move to a first-to-file patent system, patent applications likely will be published 18 months after they are filed. This will substantially account for the objections raised by confidentiality and surprise. Finally, they argue that any move to treat software as a special case in the United States may make attempts to achieve uniform protection standards within the international community impossible. From all this, one can easily see that the controversy continues. Indeed, as this book is being finalized in 1994, the PTO is holding hearings so that it can evaluate the use of the patent system to protect software-related inventions.[83] Nonetheless, the policy direction is now firmly established. Patents may be used to protect computer software, and there seems little prospect for turning the clock back, no matter how much one fears the consequences.

## DESIGN PATENTS

Section 171 of the Patent Act provides, "Whoever invents any new, original and ornamental design for an article of manufacture may obtain a patent thereof, subject to the conditions and requirements of this title." There is little doubt among marketing professionals that a product's design may be one of the most important attributes impacting a consumer's purchase decision.[84] As we shall review in Chapter 6, copyright does not offer much opportunity to protect product designs in the United States, although there is a legislative effort for change. The discussion in Chapter 7 will demonstrate that trademark protection is a possibility, but with a lot of qualifications. Thus, the primary means to protect innovative product designs in the United States is through design patents. The following Federal Circuit opinion clearly presents the requirements to receive design patent protection and gives the special considerations that are used to determine if there is infringement of such a patent.

### AVIA GROUP INTERNATIONAL, INC. V. L.A. GEAR CALIFORNIA
*Federal Circuit, 1988*

#### Facts

The subject of this controversy consists of two design patents owned by Avia. The first, termed the '420 patent, claims an ornamental design for an athletic shoe outer sole. The other, designated the '301 patent, claims an ornamental design for an athletic shoe upper. L.A. Gear sold two athletic shoe models—Boy's Thrasher and Boy's Thrasher Hi-Top. Avia sued L.A. Gear, claiming that Boy's Thrasher infringed its '420 design patent and that the Hi-Top model infringed both patents. L.A. Gear alleged that there was no infringement and requested the court to declare that the two patents were invalid because the designs were both obvious and functional. The district court found for Avia, and L.A. Gear appealed to the Federal Circuit.

#### Opinion

**Validity of '420 and '301 Design Patents.**   A patent is presumed valid. The burden is on a challenger to introduce evidence that raises the issue of invalidity. Further, the challenger must establish facts, by clear and convincing evidence, that persuasively lead to the conclusion of invalidity.

The patents in suit are design patents. Under Section 171, a patent may be obtained on the design of an article of manufacture that is "new, original and ornamental" and "nonobvious" within the meaning of Section 103, which is incorporated by reference into Section 171.

*Ornamental versus Functional Designs.*   L.A. Gear correctly asserts that if a patented design is "primarily functional" rather than primarily ornamental, the patent is invalid. When function dictates a design, protection would not promote the decorative arts—a purpose of the design patent statute. There is no dispute that shoes are functional and that certain features of the shoe designs at issue perform functions. However, a distinction exists between the functionality of an article or features thereof and the functionality of the particular design of such article or features thereof that perform a function. Were that not true, it would not be possible to obtain a design patent on a utilitarian article of manufacture or to obtain both design and utility patents on the same article.

With respect to functionality of the design of the '301 patent, the district court made the following observations:

> L.A. Gear took each little aspect of the upper and pointed out that many of the aspects or features in the upper have a function. Even if this is assumed to be true, that would not make the design primarily functional. If the functional aspect or purpose could be accomplished in many other ways than is involved in this very design, that fact is enough to destroy the claim that this design is primarily functional. There are many things in the '301 patent on the upper which are clearly ornamental and nonfunctional such as the location of perforations and how they are arranged, and the stitching and how it's arranged, and the coloration of elements between black and white colors. The overall aesthetics of the various components and the way they are combined are quite important and are not functional.

On the design of the '420 patent, the district court made a similar analysis of various features and drew these conclusions:

> Every function which L.A. Gear says is achieved by one of the component aspects of the sole in this case could be and has been achieved by different components. And that is a very persuasive rationale for the holding that the design overall is not primarily functional. Moreover, there is no function which even L.A. Gear assigns to the swirl effect around the pivot point, which is a very important aspect of the design. This is a unique and pleasing design and its patentability is not offset or destroyed by the fact that the utility patent is utilized and incorporated in this aesthetically pleasing design.

We agree with the district court that the designs in suit have not persuasively been shown to be functional.

*Obviousness.* Design patents must meet a nonobviousness requirement identical to that applicable to utility patents. Accordingly, Section 103 applies in order to determine whether the designs of the '420 and '301 patents would have been obvious to one of ordinary skill in the art.

Four factors must be considered in determining obviousness: the scope and content of the prior art, the differences between the prior art and the claims at issue, the level of ordinary skill in the art when the invention was made, and secondary indicia, such as commercial success and copying.

With respect to a design, obviousness is determined from the vantage of the designer of ordinary capability who designs articles of the type presented in the application. L.A. Gear argues that the designs would have been obvious because they are traditional ones consisting of features old in the art. That some components of Avia's designs exist in prior art references is not determinative. If the combined teachings suggest only components of the claimed design but not its overall appearance, a rejection under Section 103 is inappropriate. There is no evidence that the overall appearances of the '420 and '301 designs would have been suggested to ordinary shoe designers by the references.

L.A. Gear does not contest the commercial success of Avia's shoes manufactured according to the patented designs, but it argues the success is attributable to factors other than the designs themselves, such as advertising. Although commercial success is relevant only if a nexus is proven between the success of the patented product and the merits, Avia provided evidence tending to prove such nexus, and L.A. Gear has only conclusory statements in rebuttal. In addition, the district court referred to L.A. Gear's products as "copies" of the patented designs. Copying is additional evidence of nonobviousness.

On the basis of its evaluation of the four factors outlined above, the district court held that the ordinary designer would not have found the '420 and '301 designs, considered as whole designs, obvious in light of the differences between the prior art and the claimed designs. We agree.

**Design Patent Infringement.**  In a previous case, the Supreme Court established the test for determining infringement of a design patent.

> If, in the eye of an ordinary observer, giving such attention as a purchaser usually gives, two designs are substantially the same, if the resemblance is such as to deceive such an observer, inducing him to purchase one supposing it to be the other, the first one patented is infringed by the other.

In addition to overall similarity of designs, the accused design must appropriate the novelty in the patented device that distinguishes it from the prior art.

The district court correctly applied this test for infringement. It made the following statements:

> L.A. Gear's soles are virtually identical to the '420 patent. In each instance, L.A. Gear has appropriated the novelty of the patented article. One needs only to look at the two soles to see that the infringement exists. But if it is necessary to particularize it, we have in the accused sole copying of the swirl effect, copying of the separate coloration and configuration of the pivot point, though without the red dot. And we have in the accused sole the whole general appearance, which is almost a direct copy of the patented sole. Similar analysis applies to the '301 upper. It is almost a direct copy—much more than the substantially-the-same standard.

Thus, the district court found that L.A. Gear's shoes had overall similarity to the patented designs and incorporated the novel features thereof. For the '420 patent, those features included the swirl effect and the pivot point; for the '301 patent, the novelty consisted of the combination of saddle, eyestay, and perforations.

L.A. Gear points to undisputed evidence that Avia's shoe, made in accordance with the patent, and L.A. Gear's accused models are intended for different customers. Avia's are for tennis players; L.A. Gear's are for children. That fact, according to L.A. Gear, renders the products not "substantially the same" as necessary under the infringement test. But L.A. Gear is grossly in error. To find infringement, the accused shoes need only appropriate a patentee's protected design, not a patentee's market as well. The products of the parties need not be directly competitive; indeed, an infringer is liable even when the patent owner puts out no product. Thus, infringement is not avoided by selling to a different class of purchasers.

For the foregoing reasons, we affirm the decision of the district court that L.A. Gear infringed Avia's valid patents.

---

This case illustrates the basic requirements for a design patent. The design must be "primarily ornamental." This does not mean that the design cannot have attributes that perform functions. Rather, the design cannot be dictated by the utilitarian purposes of the product. In other words, the design must be only one of several equally suitable ways for the product to achieve its useful functions. In addition, as with all patents, the design will have to be novel and nonobvious. This inquiry, as *Avia* demonstrates, is the same as for utility patents. Therefore, it might be possible to receive a design patent for the "look" of the AES stereo component if the design is novel and nonobvious and is not required to make the system operate. Also, as the case indicates, we may receive utility patents for claims to the AES system along with a design patent for its appearance.

In the next chapter, it will be shown that the determination of infringement for utilitarian patents is a complicated affair. *Avia* clearly shows that with design patents, one is on much less technical ground. Essentially, a design infringes a design patent if it looks to an ordinary observer substantially the same as the protected design. This is true even if the design appears on a product sold to an entirely different universe of buyers. Therefore a design patent on AES would be infringed by a machine having a similar design, even if that other machine were sold to auto mechanics to test engine performance.

There is substantial speculation that design patents soon will have an increasingly important role to play in the computer industry.[85] As competition in the field intensifies, industry participants likely will take new steps to differentiate their products in the marketplace.[86] One way for these firms to do this is by securing unique product designs. Obtaining design patents for computer hardware items is an obvious possibility, although computer firms have yet to make widespread use of this practice.[87] Nonetheless, the variety of patents that have issued for computer hardware—such as for monitors, printers, keyboards, laptop personal computers, disk drive units, and modems—demonstrates the potential of this avenue of protection. More controversial is the possibility of receiving design patent protection for graphical user interface screen displays. In 1988, the PTO issued 22 design patents to Xerox Corporation for attributes of screen displays such as icons. However, in 1989, the PTO rejected similar applications made by Xerox. The PTO indicated that screen displays are not the proper subjects for design patents because they are transitory and not affixed to a utilitarian article (the computer). On appeal, the Board of Patent Appeals and Interferences upheld the denial of Xerox's design patent applications, but it did so for procedural reasons dealing with how the applications were drafted.[88] More important, however, the board indicated that graphical displays on computer screens are the proper subjects for design patents, as long as the applications provide the required information in the appropriate fashion. Therefore, unless this decision is reversed on appeal, the way now seems clear for computer firms to receive design patents on screen displays as well as on the ornamental attributes of their hardware.[89]

## CONCLUSION

This chapter focused on the fundamental conditions that must be fulfilled for one to receive a patent. In the give-and-take of international harmonization, one can expect that the United States will adapt aspects of its novelty standard, in particular, the first-to-invent standard, while other countries broaden the scope of patentable subject matter to include biotechnology and computer-related inventions.

The next chapter presents both an overview of the steps one must take to receive a patent in the United States, and the rights a patent provides against alleged infringers. In addition, the horizon is expanded to the international community, giving some insights into the ways that countries have agreed to make it easier for inventors to receive patent protection within their borders. From this exposition, it becomes clear that inventors with more than a domestic vision should understand as early as possible the fundamental principles of international patent protection and should plan their intellectual property strategies accordingly.

## NOTES

1. See, e.g., S. Addanki, "Polaroid v. Kodak: A Meeting of Economics and the Patent Law," J. of Proprietary Rights (November 1990) at 25.
2. C. Scott, "Honeywell Reaches $124.1 Million Pact with Camera Firms," Wall Street J. (August 24, 1992); P. Tirschwell, "Honeywell Chases 15 Camera Makers after Minolta Win," National L.J. (July 27, 1992) at 23.
3. A Pasztor, "Litton-Honeywell Patent War Still Flares," Wall Street J. (September 27, 1993); T. King and J. Miller, "Honeywell Loses $1.2 Billion Suit Filed by Litton," Wall Street J. (September 1, 1993) at A3.
4. See P. Lewis, "The New Patent That Is Infuriating the Multimedia Industry," New York Times (November 28, 1993) at F10; C. MacLachlan, "Multimedia Patent Battle Looms," National L.J. (November 29, 1993) at 3; D. Clark, "Patents May Raise Price of Information Highway," Wall Street J. (November 15, 1993) at B1. In December 1993, the Patent and Trademark Office decided to reexamine the validity and scope of the Compton patent. See also J. Shiver Jr., "Low-Tech Problems with High-Tech Patents," L.A. Times (January 9, 1994) at D1. In March 1994, the PTO overturned its original determination regarding patentability.

5. Once the United States adopts the new policy that provides for disclosure after a prescribed period of time, this information may become public prior to issuance of the patent.

6. J. Caspar, "The Relentless Task of Patent Protection," Wall Street J.; E. Carlson, "For Inventors, Patent Fights May Spoil the Whole Idea," Wall Street J. (December 1990).

7. P. Dwyer, "The Battle Raging over Intellectual Property, Business Week (May 22, 1989) at 79.

8. M. Chase, "Du Pont and Cetus Fight over Patents on New Genetic Tool," Wall Street J. (December 12, 1989) at A1, 5.

9. Patent System Harmonization Act of 1992, S.2605 (102 Cong., 2d Sess.).

10. The legal battle over patent rights to the cancer drug AZT provides an interesting example. See E. Felsenthal, "Who Invented AZT? Big Bucks Are Riding on What Sleuths Find," Wall Street J. (October 21, 1993) at A1.

11. J. Emshwiller, "Patent-Law Proposals Irk Small Inventors," Wall Street J. (April 30, 1992).

12. The Clinton Administration stated in 1994 that it does not intend to include the first-to-file system in the initial package of GATT legislation.

13. See, e.g., Patent System Harmonization Act of 1992, S. 2605 (102d Cong., 2d Sess.).

14. Bonito Boats, Inc. v. Thunder Craft Boats, Inc., 489 U.S. 141 (1989) *quoting* 13 Writings of Thomas Jefferson 335 (Memorial ed. 1904).

15. Graham v. John Deere Co. of Kansas City, 383 U.S. 1, 9-11 (1966).

16. Ibid., at 17.

17. W. L. Gore & Assoc., Inc., v. Garlock, Inc., 721 F. 2d 1540, 1555 (Fed. Cir. 1983), cert. denied, 469 US 851 (1984), on remand, 670 F. Supp 760 (N.D. Ohio 1987).

18. This case was first decided by the Federal Circuit in 1985. The Supreme Court vacated the decision and remanded the case because the Federal Circuit did not adequately address the clearly erroneous standard that must be used to reverse factual determinations on appeal. On remand in 1987, the Federal Circuit restated its previous opinion in terms of the clearly erroneous standard. In the 1987 opinion, it emphasized that its earlier opinion remains on the books and that for a full understanding, both opinions must be read together. This case synopsis is based on language from both opinions.

19. A. Naj, "Scientists Say Alaska Oil Spill Cleanup Would Have Benefited from Microbe Use," Wall Street J. (April 13, 1990)

20. See P. Cox, "Jurassic Park, A Luddite Monster," Wall Street J. (July 9, 1993) at A8.

21. M. Lavelle, "Biotech: The Unknown Frontier for Lawyers," The National L.J. (February 6, 1989) at 1; A. Naj, "Clouds Gather over the Biotech Industry," Wall Street J. (January 30, 1989) at B1.

22. A. Naj, "Clouds Gather over the Biotech Industry," Wall Street J. (Jan. 30, 1989) at B1.

23. M. Lavelle, "Biotech: The Unknown Frontier for Lawyers," National L.J. (February 6, 1989) at 1.

24. Ex Parte Hibbard, 227 USPQ 443 (Bd. Pat. App. 1985).

25. Ex Parte Allen, 2 USPQ 2d 1425 (Bd. Pat. App. 1987).

26. M. Cone, "The Mouse Wars Turn Furious," L.A. Times (May 9, 1993) at A16.

27. Ibid., at A16.

28. M. Lavelle, "Biotech: The Unknown Frontier for Lawyers."

29. J. Adler and L. Denworth, "Splashing in the Gene Pool," Newsweek (March 9, 1992) at 71.

30. A. Manning, "Clones May Wilt Use of Pesticides," USA Today (November 26, 1993) at A1; K. Yamada, "Toward Leaner Meat and Celery Sticks without Strings," Wall Street J. (February 24, 1992) at B1; A. Hagedorn, "Suits Sprout over Rights to Seeds," Wall Street J. (March 5, 1990) at B1; J Adler and L. Denworth, "Splashing in the Gene Pool," Newsweek (March 9, 1992) at 71.

31. D. Stipp, "Animals Altered to Make Drugs in Their Milk," Wall Street J. (August 27, 1991) at B1.

32. Antisense technology might be used in many other contexts besides agribusiness, most notably in the development of drugs. For instance, synthetic DNA might be introduced to block the production of enzymes responsible for causing diseases such as tuberculosis or the growth of certain cancers. See B. Rensberger, "How Genetic Engineers Make Sense of Antisense," Washington Post Weekly (February 22–28, 1993).

33. B. Rensberger, "How Genetic Engineers Make Sense of Antisense," Washington Post Weekly (February 22–28, 1993).

34. G. Hill, "U.S. Approves Use of Calgene's Biotech Tomato," Wall Street J. (October 19, 1992) at C17.

35. S. McMurray, "New Calgene Tomato Might Have Tasted Just as Good without Genetic Alteration," Wall Street J. (January 12, 1993) at B1.

36. Ibid.

37. D. Russell, "Miracle or Myth?" Amicus J. (Spring 1993) at 23–24. The Food and Drug Administration, while noting the possibility of a slight increase in mastitis, approved the marketing of a bovine growth hormone called recombinant somatotropin on November 5, 1993. In the wake of this FDA action, a 90-day moratorium was imposed (through a budgetary provision) on the sale of the product so that information regarding budgetary, social, and economic effects could be reported to Congress. M. Levy, "FDA Gives Formal Approval to Drug That Boosts Milk Production in Cows," Wall Street J. (November 8, 1993) at B7.

38. J. King, "Breeding Uniformity," Amicus J. (Spring 1993) at 27.

39. "U.N. Biodiversity Treaty Signed By U.S.," 5 J. of Proprietary Rights (August 1993) at 29–30; T. Noah, "Clinton to Back International Accord on Environment That Bush Spurned," Wall Street J. (April 22, 1993) at B5.

40. Harvested seeds are not protected under the Plant Variety Protection Act, but they may receive protection when the plants are protected under the regular patent act. J. Barton, "Patenting Life," Scientific American (March 1991) at 43.

41. Ibid., at 43.

42. Transengenic Animal Patent Reform Act, S. 387 (February 16, 1993).

43. Amgen, Inc. v. Chugai Pharmaceutical Co., Ltd., 706 F. Supp. 94 (D. Mass. 1989), aff'd. in part and rev'd. in part, 927 F. 2d 1200 (Fed. Cir.), cert. denied, 112 S. Ct. 169 (1991).

44. Amgen, Inc. v. Chugai Pharmaceutical Co., Ltd., 706 F. Supp. 94 (D. Mass. 1989); aff'd. in part and rev'd. in part, 927 F. 2d 1200 (Fed. Cir. 1991).

45. See Scripps Clinic & Research Foundation v. Genentech Inc., 724 F. Supp. 690 (N.D. CA 1989), aff'd. in part and rev'd. in part, 927 F. 2d 1565 (Fed. Cir. 1991), clarified on reconsideration, 18 U.S.P.Q. 2d 1896 (Fed. Cir. 1991) (litigation over Factor VIII:C); Genentech Inc., v. Wellcome Foundation Ltd., 14 U.S.P.Q. 2d 1363 (D. Del 1990), 798 F. Supp. 213 (D. Del. 1992) (litigation over t-PA).

46. See E. Moroz and W. Feiler, "Biotechnology," National L.J. (November 1, 1993) at S24, which discusses litigations over EPO, Factor VIII:C, and t-PA and, based on them, concludes that purified natural protein claims cover recombinant processes.

47. For a full discussion of the Human Genome Initiative, see D. Karjala, "A Legal Research Agenda for the Human Genome Initiative," Jurimetrics (Winter 1992).

48. J. Barton, "Patenting Life," Scientific American (March 1991) at 42–43.

49. "R. Herman, "The Great Gene Gold Rush," Washington Post (June 16, 1992) at H11; E. Andrews, "Dr. Healy's Big Push on Patents," New York Times (February 16, 1992) at C12; H. Stout, "U.S. Pursuit of Gene Patents Riles Industry," Wall Street J. (February 13, 1992) at B1; M. Waldholzf and H. Stout, "A New Debate Rages Over the Patenting of Gene Discoveries," Wall Street J. (April 17, 1992) at A1.

50. H. Stout, "Gene-Fragment Patent Request Is Turned Down," Wall Street J. (September 23, 1992) at B1.

51. M. Waldholz and H. Stout, "A New Debate over the Patenting of Gene Discoveries," Wall Street J. (April 17, 1992) at A1.

52. H. Stout, "Gene-Fragment Patent Request Is Turned Down," Wall Street J. (September 23, 1992) at B1.

53. J. Yoo, "Biotech Patents Become Snarled in Bureaucracy," Wall Street J. (July 6, 1989).

54. Ibid.

55. S. Sugarawa, "Robbing the Scientist to Pay the Lawyer," Washington Post Weekly (September 23–29, 1991).

56. R. Seide and K. Daniels, "Patent Protection for Animal Inventions," J. of Proprietary Rights (November 1989) at 8.

57. L. Maher, "The Patent Environment: Domestic and European Community Frameworks for Biotechnology," 33 Jurimetrics (Fall 1992) at 105–113.

58. Ibid.

59. "EC Industry Members Slow IP Harmonization Process," J. of Proprietary Rights (May 1993) at 28.

60. R. Seide and K. Daniels, "Patent Protection for Animal Inventions," J. of Proprietary Rights (November 1989) at 9.

61. E. O'Toole, "Amgen and Scripps: Decided and Undecided Issues in Biotechnology," J. of Proprietary Rights (July 1991) at 14; J. Barton, "Patenting Life," Scientific American (March 1991) at 44–45.

62. Parker v. Flook, 437 U.S. 584 (1978); Gottschalk v. Benson, 409 U.S. 63 (1972).

63. L. Barrett, Patentable Subject Matter: Mathematical Algorithms and Computer Programs, 1106 Trademark Office Gazette 1 (September 5, 1989).

64. Paine, Webber, Jackson & Curtis, Inc., v. Merrill Lynch, Pierce, Fenner & Smith, Inc., 564 F. Supp. 1358 (D. Del. 1983).

65. D. Moskowitz, "Using Patents to Protect Innovative Financial Products," Washington Post (August 1990) at F28.

66. See ex parte Murray, 9 USPQ2d 1819 (Bd. Pat. App. and Int. 1988) wherein a patent was denied because it claimed a method of accounting rather than a system implementing the method.

67. J. Lastova and G. Hoffman, "Patent Protection for Software Gives Businesses Extra Leverage," National L.J. (June 26, 1989) at 38; J. Blatt, "A Primer on User Interface Software Patents," Computer Lawyer (April 1992) at 1.

68. D. Clark, "Patents May Raise Price of Information Highway," Wall Street J. (November 15, 1993) at B1; C. MacLachlan, "Multimedia Patent Battle Looms," National L.J. (November 29, 1993) at 3.

69. This could change as the United States moves to a first-to-file priority system since the patent may include rights to reasonable royalties after the date of publication by the PTO.

70. See J. Shiver Jr., "Low-Tech Problems with High-Tech Patents," L.A. Times (January 9, 1994) at D1.

71. B. Kahin, "The Software Patent Crisis," Technology Review (April 1990).

72. W. Bulkeley, "Will Software Patents Cramp Creativity?" Wall Street J. (March 14, 1989) at B1.

73. See M. Groves, "A Patent Dispute: Lawsuit Raises a Hot Issue in Exploding Technology," L.A. Times (February 14, 1994) at D1. The PTO ordered reexaminations of the Compton and Software Advertising Corporation patents. The PTO reversed its decision on the Compton patent in 1994. The reexamination of Software Advertising's patent is pending as this book goes to press.

74. D. Bender and A. Barkume, "Disclosure Requirements for Software-Related Patents," Computer Lawyer (October 1991) at 4.

75. M. Radcliffe, "The Future of Computer Law: Ten Challenges for the Next Decade," Computer Lawyer (August 1991) at 5.

76. Y. Tani, "Preparation and Prosecution of Electronic and Computer Related Patent Application in Japan," Electronic and Computer Patent Law, Practising Law Institute, at 371, 377.

77. J. Brown, "The Protection of High Technology Intellectual Property," 3 J. of Proprietary Rights (January 1991) at 19.

78. Ibid.

79. The following arguments appear in "Against Software Patents," The League of Programming Freedom (February 28, 1991); B. Kahin, "The Software Patent Crisis," Technology Review (April, 1990).

80. Similarly, opponents argue that computer program developers have not been conditioned to publish their achievements in the traditional sense, since the successful operation of a program demonstrates its validity. See J. Shiver Jr., "Low-Tech Problems with High-Tech Patents," L.A. Times (January 9, 1994) at D1.

81. B. Kahin, "The Software Patent Crisis," Technology Review (April 1990).

82. See, e.g., P. Heckel, "The Software-Patent Controversy," 9 The Computer Lawyer (December 1992) at 13–23; J. Sumner and S. Lundberg, "Software Patents: Are They Here to Stay?" 8 The Computer Lawyer (October 1991) at 8–13.

83. In April 1994, Bruch Lehman, the Commissioner of the U.S. Patent and Trademark Office responded to concerns raised in these hearings by announcing several initiatives that the PTO will recommend or implement. First, the Commissioner advocated a system wherein patent applications are publicized rather than held in secrecy. Second, the PTO will hire examiners who are software specialists. Third, the system under which patent examiners gain bonuses based on the number of administrative actions will be modified in the hopes that applications will not be reviewed hastily. Finally, the PTO will use the database created by the Software Patent Institute to help determine the extent of the prior art. G. Zachary, "Patent Commission Outlines Steps to Help Avoid Disputes over Software," Wall Street J. (April 11, 1994) at B6.

84. S. MacDonald, "Designers Assert Role as Artists," Wall. St. J. (November 8, 1988) at B1.

85. See, e.g., K. Liebman, G. Frischling, and A. Brunel, "The Shape of Things to Come: Design-Patent Protection for Computers," 9 Computer Lawyer (November 1992) at 1; R. Barr and S. Hollander, "Design Patents Revisited: Icons as Statutory Subject Matter," 9 Computer Lawyer (June 1992) at 13.

86. K. Liebman, G. Frischling, and A. Brunel, "The Shape of Things to Come: Design-Patent Protection for Computers," 9 Computer Lawyer (November 1992) at 10.

87. Ibid. at 2.

88. Ex parte Donaldson, Appeal No. 92-0546, 1992 Pat. App. LEXIS 6 (Bd. Pat. App. and Interferences, April 2, 1992); Ex parte Strijland, Appeal No. 92-0623, 1992 Pat. App. LEXIS 8 (Bd. Pat. App. and Interferences, April 2, 1992).

89. As this book goes to press, the PTO has scheduled hearings to consider ways of improving the patent examination process for protecting visual elements of software through design patents.

# 3

# PATENT POLICY: OBTAINING AND DEFENDING PATENT RIGHTS

## INTRODUCTION

The patent system provides an inventor a period of exclusive rights to an invention in exchange for thorough information about the invention. The first part of this chapter is designed to give a basic feel both for the steps one must take to get a patent and, more important, for the types of information that must be presented to the PTO for public disclosure. In this regard, there is substantial focus on Section 112. This section of patent law requires a written description of the invention that is sufficiently comprehensive so that one skilled in the art can make and use the invention. Section 112 also demands that the inventor describe the best mode of carrying out the invention.

The chapter then evaluates the potential reach of patent claims to allegedly infringing activities. Here, we will consider some of the rather mechanical doctrines used to evaluate whether an article or process literally infringes the claims of a patent. In addition, there is an investigation into the more nebulous and controversial doctrine of equivalents, which serves to frustrate those who try to gain unfair advantages from strict application of infringement rules. This portion of the chapter concludes with an examination of how damages are ascertained in patent cases.

The final component of the chapter takes a snapshot of the rapidly changing landscape of international patent protection. Most firms no longer may be con-

**Exhibit 3.1  The Patent Application: Key Considerations**

### Who May File the Patent Application

- Inventor
- Employer–employee Relationship
  - Employee is inventor who must file.
  - Contract clauses assign patent rights to employer.
  - Shop-rights—nonexclusive license for employer.

### When to Apply the Patent Application

- Record events proving conception of invention and diligent reduction to practice.
  - Lab notebook: signed, witnessed, and dated
  - Important for determining priority if others are simultaneously working on same invention
- Perform a patent search:
  - Of existing patents, publications.
  - To determine if patentable.
  - To improve the invention.
  - To save attorney's fees.
  - To facilitate prepatent licensing opportunities.
  - To facilitate discussions with the PTO patent examiners.
  - To strengthen the patent.
- File as soon as possible (when disclosure requirements of patent application can be met).
  - May be important to prove priority over other inventors:
    = Confers procedural advantages in the United States.
    = For patents in most other countries, the first to file the patent application establishes priority.
  - Must file within one year of public use or sale.
  - For patents in some countries, must file before public use or sale.

tent with U.S. patent protection alone. The international commercial environment necessitates patent protection on an international scale. This chapter will review some of the important considerations one must evaluate to preserve patent rights on a global basis.

## THE PATENT APPLICATION PROCESS: A BRIEF OVERVIEW

Although the process of obtaining a patent is designed so that the inventor can theoretically accomplish the steps alone, it is normally advisable to retain expert assistance given the somewhat complex and technical requirements involved. It is not the goal of this section to do more than scratch the surface of these demands. There are numerous books and guides available that are devoted solely to providing such assistance.[1] Rather, the purpose here is to raise your understanding

**Exhibit 3.1  The Patent Application: Key Considerations** *(continued)*

### Important Components of the Patent Application

- Summary of the invention
- Enablement
  - Sufficient disclosure so that one skilled in the art can make and use the invention.
  - Case: *White v. Vega Servo-Control*
- Best mode
  - Of the invention contemplated by the inventor at the time of filing the patent application.
  - Case: *Wahl v. Acvious*
- Claims
  - Definite statement of patent monopoly
  - Draftsmanship art
  - Breadth and form of claims
  - Multiple claims
  - Case: *Pennwalt v. Durand-Wayland*
- Information disclosure statement
  - Duty of disclosure—materiality

### Confidentiality

- Until patent issues
- Proposed change to preserve confidentiality only for 18 months after the patent application filing date

---

of the types of issues involved in the process, so that you can meaningfully evaluate the costs and benefits of patent protection, especially in view of other possible techniques to protect inventions. Exhibit 3.1 summarizes important aspects of the patent application process, which should be recognized by those contemplating patent protection.

### Who May File the Patent Application

If you were asked who must file the patent application, your probable initial reaction would be that the inventor is entitled to patent rights to the invention and thus should be the one to file for the privilege of obtaining them. This is precisely the approach taken by the Patent Act. With certain limited exceptions, the inventor (or inventors) must file the patent application with the PTO.

Inventive activity less frequently is within the exclusive domain of individual hobbyists tinkering in their spare time out of a garage. Rather, it usually takes place in the confines of an employment relationship, often while working within an employing company's research and development department. Who has patent rights, for instance, if an employee of IBM develops a novel and nonobvious computer process while at work for IBM in the company labs? You may be surprised that there are situations where the employee will be the owner of the patent rights in the computer process. In fact, the employee will be the owner unless: (1) the employee was hired to create the specific computer process or to achieve its specific objective or (2) the employee signed an agreement assigning the rights in the invention to the employer. Thus, the IBM employee who works without an invention assignment agreement may own the patent rights in the computer process, depending on the specific scope of the employment relationship. This may seem unfair because IBM's facilities were used to develop and perfect the invention. However, the law accounts for this by providing IBM with what are called "shop rights" to the invention. Although the employee is the owner of the patent rights to the invention, through its shop rights, IBM is allowed to make, use, and sell the invention without paying a royalty fee to the employee-inventor. In all other respects, however, ownership and control, in these situations, resides with the inventing employee.

Normally, an employer such as IBM will not be content with only shop-rights to inventions. Rather, the company will want to control who else might be allowed to make, use, and/or sell the invention and will want to be paid for granting those privileges. It can accomplish this result most effectively by entering an agreement with employees stating that employees will assign to the company all rights to their inventions. Normally, this is done in the initial employment contract signed by the employees. Of course, the critical question remains concerning exactly what inventions an employee will be expected to assign to the company. Taking the company's point of view, it likely will want to lay claim to all inventions conceived while the employee works for the company, on the assumption that the company's work environment, facilities, and programs were the motivating force behind the invention. Logically, such reasoning extends to inventions allegedly made in the employee's spare time at home and indeed to inventions made shortly after the employee leaves the company. As you can imagine, the employee will often take issue with the latter demand. Inventors often work at home or in their spare time or in new jobs on creations that are totally separate from what they are doing or what they learned on the job. Unfortunately for the employee, the employer often has a greater bargaining position and will have the ability to demand that the employee sign a far-reaching assignment provision in the employment contract. For this reason, certain states, such as California, undertake to equitably balance these valid and competing interests by restricting to some degree the extent of an employer's reach in assignment clauses. California's Labor Code provides:

> Any provision in an employment agreement which provides that an employee shall assign or offer to assign any of his or her rights to an invention to his or her employer shall not apply to an invention for which no equipment, supplies, facility, or trade secret information of the employer was used and which was developed entirely on the employee's own time, and (a) which does not relate (1) to the business of the employer or (2) to the employer's actual or demonstrably anticipated research or development, or (b) which does not result from any work performed by the employee for the employer. Any provi-

sion which purports to apply to such an invention is to that extent against public policy and is to that extent void and unenforceable.

Although the complex linguistic form of this provision makes it hard to precisely pin down what is or is not permissible, the intent is clear that an employer may not lay claim to an employee's invention that is totally separate and distinct from the employer's business affairs.

A typical employment contract, mindful of the foregoing language, may contain the following simplified provision:

> I hereby agree to notify the Company about all inventions, discoveries, developments, improvements, and innovations (herein called "inventions"), whether or not made or conceived during working hours, which
>
> a. relate to the existing or contemplated business or research activities of the Company, or
> b. are suggested by or result from my work at the Company, or
> c. result from the use of the Company's time, materials, or facilities
>
> and to assign to the Company my entire right, title, and interest to all such inventions.
>
> I will, at the Company's request and expense, execute specific assignments to any such invention and take such further action as may be considered necessary by the Company, during or subsequent to my employment with the Company, to obtain and defend patents in any country.
>
> I agree that an invention described in a patent application filed by me within six months following my employment with the Company shall be presumed to have been conceived or made during my employment with the Company unless I can prove otherwise.

Note that this provision obligates inventors to take such actions as necessary to obtain the patent, even after assigning away their rights. This is because the patent laws require the patent application to be filed by inventors even if they do not own the invention. The normal course of action in this situation, therefore, is for the inventor to file a patent application that indicates for the public record that ownership in the invention and the resulting patent rights have been assigned to the company. As just one example, Chakrabarty's bacterium was developed while he was employed at General Electric Co. As the inventor, Chakrabarty filed the patent application, but the application provided that ownership had been assigned to General Electric.

### When to Apply

Even though the United States bases priority on a first-to-invent standard, an inventor should apply as soon as possible for patent rights to an invention in this country. The reasons for this already have been given in Chapter 2. For example, if several inventors are working on the invention at the same time, then the first person to file the patent application has procedural advantages. Also, the statutory bars of Section 102(b) require filing to occur within one year of certain events, such as publication or a sale. In addition, international considerations, which will be further discussed at the end of this chapter, provide reasons to file early. And of course, once the United States converts to a first-to-file system, the need to apply quickly becomes self-evident.

Prior to filing a patent application, an inventor should keep two steps in mind while working on an invention. As was discussed in Chapter 2, an inventor should keep accurate records throughout the inventive process so as to document the date of conception and that the idea was reduced to practice in a diligent fashion. This normally is accomplished by means of bound lab notebooks, which are signed, witnessed, and dated on a regular, even daily, basis.

The other task worth doing before filing a patent application is conducting a patentability search, which essentially is an investigation by the inventor prior to filing in order to determine whether the invention can meet the standards of novelty and nonobviousness. This is accomplished by reviewing prior art references, such as patents, publications, and advertisements, to ensure that the invention complies with Section 102 of the Patent Act. Such a search is not mandatory. The PTO will make its own independent search to determine whether these patentability standards are met. Indeed, conducting a search may potentially be counterproductive, for inventors are required to disclose to the PTO any information they know may be material to the examiner to determine patentability. Without the search, therefore, information damaging to the prospects of obtaining certain patent claims may never be uncovered. However, it still clearly is advisable to perform a patentability search before engaging in the patent application process.

There are several good reasons to conduct a patentability search. First, the inventor may determine from the search that the invention is not patentable. Abandoning the patent project for the modest fee of a search may save the substantial amount of time and resources that otherwise would have gone into preparing and filing the patent application. Second, information gained from the search may actually help the inventor improve the invention. Third, gathering the information can facilitate the dialogue with the PTO. Approaching the PTO with arguments based up front on all the available knowledge will normally be more fruitful than responding to the discovery of prior art by the PTO examiner. Fourth, if the inventor wishes to license the technology prior to receiving the patent, then potential licensees will feel more secure that a patent is likely to be issued if the inventor can demonstrate the results of a thorough patent search. Fifth, a search may help demonstrate that the invention is nonobvious by perhaps indicating that the bulk of previous efforts to solve a problem used a different approach for the task. Finally, the search may uncover prior art that the patent office otherwise would have missed. Although one might think this is a negative, it normally is not. Remember what happens if the patent issues and then is later challenged based on a prior art surprise, such as an obscure publication. It is far better to find the proper limits of the patent early—before substantial investments are made. In addition, the presumption of validity that attaches to patents is far stronger if the examiner actually reviewed the prior art references raised by the challenging party.[2]

## Dealing with the PTO

Before getting started with the PTO, the inventor should consider how much time and money it will take to receive a patent. The total number of patent applications filed with the PTO rises annually. For example, 164,000 applications were filed in 1990, 168,000 in 1991, and over 170,000 in 1992.[3] Obviously, the enormity of the task facing the PTO is impressive. The PTO, through computerization and other improvements, has managed to reduce the average pendency of a patent application to around 18 months. However, applications in certain technological areas such as computers and biotechnology take somewhat longer. An inventor in these fields should expect to wait between two and three years for a patent to issue.

Filing fees and maintenance fees for patents are rapidly on the rise. The main reason for this was a major funding change instituted by Congress in 1990 that required several federal agencies, including the PTO, to be totally dependent on user-fee income to fund their individual operations.[4] As a result of this act, patent fees increased 69%. Although the patent filing fee remained at $370 ($180 for a small business), the patent issuance fee increased to $1050 ($525 for a small business), and fees to maintain the patent for 17 years rose to $5000. Due to the self-funding requirement, and the increased PTO expenditures on new, automated equipment, additional fee hikes are a virtual certainty.[5] One also should be aware that the PTO has fees for other technical aspects of the application process. In addition, one obviously should not overlook the costs of attorneys and other experts, which ultimately may make the PTO fees pale in comparison.

The types of information that must be in the patent application, and the methods that should be used to present the information are given in the Patent Act and in the Code of Federal Regulations.[6] The regulations provide the proper form, order, and characteristics of the application. According to the regulations, the inventor is to format the application and present information in the following way: (1) the title of the invention; (2) a brief summary of the invention, which often discusses the background of the invention, indicating problems encountered by the prior art and explaining the object and advantages of the invention; (3) descriptions of the drawings if any are included; (4) an enabling description of the invention and the contemplated best mode; (5) a claim or claims; (6) an abstract, which is used by the PTO to quickly identify the nature and gist of the invention; (7) an oath signed by the inventor or inventors; and (8) the drawings if any. In addition, an Information Disclosure Statement must be filed either with the application or generally within three months thereafter.

Clearly, proper disclosure and the scope of the claims represent the core ingredients of the application process. The focus of proper disclosure rests on three key aspects of the application. How much information must be provided to enable one skilled in the field to practice the invention? How does one determine what is the best mode that must be disclosed? These two questions are so controversial and important that they are individually treated with representative cases in the following sections of this chapter.

The third key element of disclosure involves what is required by the Information Disclosure Statement (IDS). In essence, applicants must present to the PTO all material information within their knowledge that bears on patentability. The function of the IDS is to promote candor by the applicant and to ensure that patent examiners have all the relevant information needed to make a proper determination about patentability. What constitutes "materiality" has been the subject of great debate and has tremendous ramifications, because the withholding of information later determined to be material may invalidate an entire patent. Prior to 1992, the applicant had to disclose any information that would be important to a reasonable examiner in ruling on patentability. This was troublesome because honest applicants sometimes mistakenly forget to reveal information that is relevant to the subject of patentability. Under the old standard, applicants might lose patent rights once the mistake were uncovered, even if the information ultimately would not have changed the examiner's decision to grant the patent claims. In an attempt to alleviate the harshness of this outcome, the PTO amended its rules in 1992 to add greater specificity to what must be divulged. Now, the rules articulate that information is material if the information, by itself or in conjunction with other references, compels the conclusion that a claim is unpatentable or is otherwise inconsistent with a position taken by the applicant.[7]

The claims specify the boundaries of the legal monopoly created by the patent. Drafting claims is an art for which expert assistance is highly recommended. Decisions have to be made on the breadth of the claims, their form, and their language. Great care must be given here, for the claims ultimately define the rights of the patent holder against alleged infringers.

The usual goal of the applicant is to maximize the breadth of patent rights. As a simple example, consider how one might claim a new form of cup. A broad claim would recite rights to a device with a bottom, sides attached to that bottom, and no top. When we investigate infringement later in this chapter, it will be clear that if this claim were granted, the patent would be extremely lucrative, extending to almost every variety of cup that might be contemplated to be used in any context and to hold any kind of item. The problem for the applicant is that this claim is so broad that it is not novel or nonobvious. Many previous devices have the claimed general elements. To overcome novelty and nonobviousness, therefore, the applicant must be more specific about the limits of the invention. Perhaps a device with a bottom comprising certain characteristics, with sides of certain characteristics, with a handle of certain characteristics, to hold items of certain characteristics, would have more of a chance. And, of course, how broadly those certain characteristics are defined may be critically important. The downside with specificity, naturally, is that the patent rights to exclude are more narrowly circumscribed, thereby making it easier for competitive inventors to develop similar noninfringing items. Fortunately, the PTO allows the applicant to claim the invention in various ways in the application. Thus, it is common practice to formulate a set of claims ranging from the very broad to the extremely specific. In this way, an applicant might fight hard to receive a broad claim, but if unsuccessful, can still be protected by an allowable narrower position.

The form of expressing the claims is important too. A lawn mower, for example, may be claimed as a machine consisting of various components. Alternatively, it may be claimed as a method for cutting grass consisting of a set of steps. Patent experts in certain fields believe that the form of the claim may affect patentability. For instance, some believe that a computer program is more likely to be viewed as patentable subject matter if expressed as a machine or apparatus rather than as a process or system.[8] The Patent Act also allows drafters the freedom to express a claim as a means for performing a specified function, often called a means-for or a means-plus-function claim. According to the Act, if such a means-for claim is used, then the claim is construed to cover the structure, material, or acts described in the disclosure sections and their equivalents. Claims often are drafted in this form in the computer field, among others, and their breadth has been the subject of considerable controversy. Many questions regarding means-for claims were answered by the Federal Circuit in *Pennwalt Corp. v. Durand-Wayland, Inc.*, a case which is presented later in this chapter to illustrate infringement.

Once the application is filed with the PTO, it will first be scrutinized to determine if it is a candidate for a secrecy order. Secrecy orders may be issued on inventions bearing on national security or utilizing certain circumscribed technologies, such as nuclear materials. A secrecy order restricts the ability to file patent applications in foreign countries, and it limits publication of information about the invention. Assuming a secrecy order is not merited, the PTO will issue a foreign filing license, which grants permission to file for foreign patent protection.[9]

The application then will be referred to an examiner within a group specializing in the invention's filed. For instance, biotechnology inventions go to Group 180. After several months, the examiner will make the first Office Action. Although this action may indicate a notice of allowance, normally it will indicate objections, concerning such aspects as the breadth of claims, defects in the drawings, or the novelty or nonobviousness of the invention. The applicant typically has three months to make amendments or otherwise respond to the first Office Action.[10] Applicants who do not completely agree with the examiner may formulate arguments to persuade the examiner to withdraw certain objections while conforming with other requests. The examiner will issue either a notice of allowance or another rejection. The applicant then has another period to make amendments or reiterate former positions. This process may go on for several cycles, closing the gaps of disagreement. Eventually, the examiner will issue either a notice of allowance or a Final Rejection.

When the applicant receives a notice of allowance, then the patent will be issued after the appropriate fee is paid. At this time, articles using the invention should be properly marked with the patent number. The reason for doing this is to provide notice for potential infringers, thereby making it easier to recover damages for infringement.[11] Prior to one's receiving the patent, but after the application is filed, it is a common practice to mark articles embodying the invention with the term "patent pending." This notice has no legal effect; because the patent has not issued, the applicant has no rights under patent law to exclude others from using the invention. However, it warns others that a patent may issue soon. Knowing this, competitors may pause before investing resources to produce the invention and rather may choose to reduce the risk by entering into negotiations with the patent applicant.

The applicant who receives a final rejection may file an appeal within six months to the Board of Appeals and Patent Interferences—a tribunal of examiners-in-chief within the PTO. The board may either uphold the examiner's decision to refuse the patent or agree with the applicant and instruct the examiner how to proceed. The board upholds the examiner about 65% of the time.[12] When the board upholds the examiner, the applicant may appeal to the federal court system, usually to the Federal Circuit Court of Appeals.[13] The final possible appeal is to the U.S. Supreme Court. Although appeals rarely go that far, we have seen examples in *Diamond v. Diehr* and *Diamond v. Chakrabarty*. Exhibit 3.2 provides a flowchart to illustrate the steps one can expect to encounter after a patent application is filed with the PTO.

Keep in mind that patent issues do not necessarily come to an end just because a patent has issued. Those who wish to use an invention without permission may challenge the validity of the patent either in the PTO or in the federal courts. Alternatively, they may simply use the invention and wait to be sued for infringement. In these situations, they may argue that the PTO erred in allowing the claims, for reasons such as lack of novelty, obviousness, or inappropriate subject matter. As another tack, they may raise deficiencies in the application. The most common points of contention involve whether the disclosure is sufficient to enable one skilled in the art to practice the invention and whether the best mode was revealed. This chapter now looks more closely at these requirements.

## DISCLOSURE: ENABLEMENT AND BEST MODE

Section 112 of the Patent Act requires the patent application to contain a written description of the invention, and of the manner and process of making and using it, in such full, clear, concise and exact terms as to:

1. *enable* any person skilled in the art to which it pertains, or with which it is most nearly connected, to make and use the same, and
2. set forth the *best mode* contemplated by the inventor of carrying out the invention.

These disclosures often are called the *specification* in the patent application, although strictly speaking, the Patent Act also includes the claims within the definition of "specification." The amount of disclosure required by Section 112 clearly is the most contested area of the patent application process.

## Exhibit 3.2  Patent Application Procedures

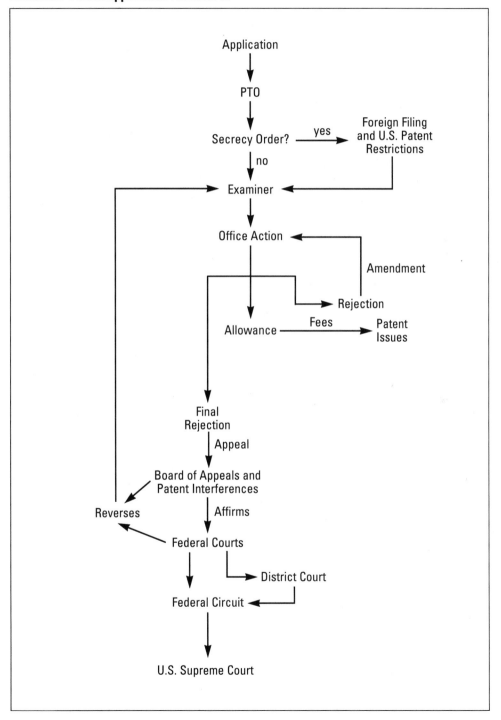

### Enablement

The patent application must provide enough information about the invention to enable one skilled in the art to practice it. There are two frequently encountered problems with that standard. First, it is an objective requirement. What the inventor subjectively believes is enough information to allow others to make or use the invention is not determinative. Rather, the information is judged with reference to a reasonably skilled practitioner. Second, inventors often want to withhold as much information as possible regarding their inventions. For instance, an invention might require use of a component, but the inventor might not want to provide production details of it, possibly because they are considered valuable trade secrets. Similarly, inventions could use computer programs. The inventors may be willing to illustrate what the programs must do, but might not want to provide source code listings that will carry out the specifications. Rather, inventors may believe that their versions of the source code, used to implement the patented claims, are separate "inventions" that do not have to be revealed. In their minds, disclosure of requisite tasks, parameters and logic sequences should be enough for a skilled programmer to practice the invention.

Mindful of these considerations, the courts have determined that a disclosure is not insufficient just because some experimentation may have to be performed by a skilled artisan. However, the amount of experimentation needed to practice the invention must not be undue. The Federal Circuit has offered a set of criteria that illustrate the factors one should consider in determining if disclosure is sufficient:

1. The quantity of experimentation necessary;
2. The amount of direction or guidance presented;
3. The presence or absence of working examples;
4. The nature of the invention;
5. The state of the prior art;
6. The relative skill of those in the art;
7. The predictability or unpredictability of the art;
8. The breadth of the claims.[14]

The following case provides a classic example of how the courts handle high technology cases involving trade secret information.

## WHITE CONSOLIDATED INDUSTRIES V. VEGA SERVO-CONTROL, INC.

*Federal Circuit Court of Appeals, 1983*

### Facts

On June 6, 1972, White Consolidated Industries received a U.S. patent (the '653 patent) for a machine tool numerical control ("NC") system. In an NC system, a machine tool, such as a mill head or a drill bit, is placed under the control of a computer program (the "part program") that defines the operations to be performed by the tool in machining a particular part. The computer part program is created either manually, by writing the instructions directly in machine-readable form (called machine code), or with the assistance of a computer. In the latter situation, the part program is written using an English-like programming computer language that is then translated into machine code by another computer program, called a processor or translator. Processors can be developed so that the translation is completed with a two-step process or in a single pass.

White markets a single-pass NC system called Omnicontrol, which is the subject of the '653 patent. The system provides for two-way conversational communication between the operator and the computer so that the operator may modify the controlling part program while the program is running. The system also includes a universal input feature so that a single part program can be used to control several tools, thereby eliminating the need to create a new part program for each tool. This feature allows one to write the part program in a universal language without considering the specific tool to be used. A language translator in the system converts the part program to the machine code needed to operate the requisite tool. The '653 patent describes the language translator as follows:

> The language TRANSLATOR used in the RUN mode may be a known translator capable of converting, in a single pass, a part program in programming language form into a part program in machine language form, as for example SPLIT (Sundstrand Program Language Internally Translated).

At the time the application for the '653 patent was filed, SPLIT was a trade secret of Sundstrand (Sundstrand subsequently assigned its patent rights to White) and was available only by purchase from Sundstrand.

White sued Vega, charging that Vega manufactured and sold NC systems which infringed the '653 patent. Vega denied infringement and alleged that the patent was invalid. The trial court ruled for Vega, finding the patent invalid for failure to meet the enablement requirement of Section 112 of the Patent Act. White appealed to the Federal Circuit.

## Opinion

Section 112 requires that an invention be described "in such full, clear, concise, and exact terms as to enable any person skilled in the art . . . to make and use the same." White does not claim that SPLIT was disclosed, but rather that the specification contains an enabling disclosure notwithstanding its omission. White says (1) that the '653 patent calls for a known or standard single-pass translator "as for example SPLIT" and specifies the characteristics of such a translator, (2) that SPLIT was only an example, and (3) that there were other known single-pass translators interchangeable with SPLIT. White states that because those other translators, such as ACTION and COMPACT, were known to those skilled in the art and available to them, the enablement requirement is satisfied.

We disagree. It is true that one may refer to an element of a claimed invention held as a trade secret by name only and yet satisfy the requirements of Section

112 if equivalent elements are known, are known to be equivalents, and are available to those skilled in the art. However, there is insufficient evidence here from which to conclude that suitable substitutes for SPLIT were known and widely available.

Testimony that ACTION and COMPACT were takeoffs of, or patterned upon, SPLIT does not establish that those translators were known to be suitable substitutes for SPLIT. That other translators were available when the application was filed is unavailing when there is no basis in the record for finding that a person skilled in the art on reading the specification would know that another single-pass processor would be suitable. Indeed, statements made by Sundstrand employees suggest that the inventors, themselves, originally considered SPLIT the *only* language suitable for operation in the conversational mode of the invention. For instance, Sundstrand announced at a press conference one week after filing, "The system is compatible with programs created by APT or other programming systems; however, we doubt at this time that these systems are compatible with instantaneous reprogramming by use of the 'conversational' part of the system."

White's assertion that SPLIT was itself widely available, albeit only upon purchase from Sundstrand, misses the mark. The sine qua non of a valid patent is a full, clear, *enabling* description of the invention. Though the language translator by itself is not the claimed invention, it is an integral part of the disclosure necessary to enable those skilled in the art to "make and use the same." Were Sundstrand (now White) to maintain SPLIT as a trade secret, it could theoretically extend its exclusionary rights beyond the 17-year life of the patent by controlling access to SPLIT, a result inconsistent with the objectives of the patent system. Sundstrand was therefore obliged to disclose the details of SPLIT or some other language translator, unless suitable substitutes were known and available to those skilled in the art or unless a suitable substitute could be obtained without undue experimentation.

Respecting the latter alternative, White correctly says a disclosure is sufficient even if it required that one skilled in the art must conduct some experimentation. The amount of required experimentation, however, must be reasonable. Richard Stitt, a skilled programmer in the NC field, testified in this case that development of a single-pass translator would require from 1½ to 2 person-years of effort. This is clearly an unreasonable requirement.

White argues that the estimate is irrelevant because it concerns the development of a commercially profitable single-pass translator and that suitable commercial translators were readily available. However, the language of the '653 patent, "a known translator . . . as for example SPLIT," is insufficient to identify which translators could be satisfactorily used, and there is no evidence that one skilled in the art would be able to select or develop a suitable translator without undue experimentation or delay.

It is immaterial that commercial use made, and publications issued, after the filing date of the '653 patent may have established the suitability of other language translators (e.g., ACTION, ADAPT, APT, AUTOSPOT, COMPACT, and UNIAPT). A sufficient disclosure must exist as of the application filing date. That the listed language translators were not specifically identified at that time as suitable substitutes for SPLIT renders futile their citation by White in this case.

White says that APT's suitability was made known three months before the filing date by the following announcement in *Metal Working News*:

> In a status report on its Omnicontrol system for on-line computer control of n/c machine tools, Sundstrand Corp., here, discloses that the "conversational" reprogramming feature has been made compatible with APT-created part programs. Omnicontrol conversational reprogramming originally was restricted to Sunstrand's own SPLIT language.

That announcement supplies an insufficient basis, however, from which to infer that one skilled in the art would know that APT could be used as a direct substitute for SPLIT, particularly when the specification contains no mention of APT's compatibility. An announcement in a news magazine is inadequate proof of such recognized knowledge in the art as will excuse a failure to supply a fully enabling disclosure in a patent application.

For these reasons, White has not demonstrated that the district court erred in concluding that the '653 patent failed to meet the enablement requirement of Section 112. The judgment that the '653 patent is invalid is affirmed.

---

This case not only illustrates what information is needed to make a disclosure enabling, but it also indicates how important it is to be forthcoming with that information in the application process. Although the disclosure in the application was not enough to enable those skilled in the art to use the invention, information released to the public soon after the filing date filled the necessary gaps. Nonetheless, the disclosures were judged lacking in the application, and the patent claims were deemed invalid. This, then, serves as a powerful warning about the importance of disclosure in the application.

### Best Mode

The disclosures in the specification also must reveal the best mode contemplated by the inventor of carrying out the invention. The purpose of this requirement is to prevent inventors from gaining valid patents while concealing from the public what they believe to be the best or preferred embodiment of the invention.

The best mode requirement is drafted in terms of what is contemplated by the inventor at the time of filing. Clearly the inquiry must begin with a subjective analysis: did the inventor subjectively know of a mode of practicing the invention that was considered to be better than any other? If the answer is yes, then one must probe further to determine if the disclosure is adequate to allow those skilled in the art to identify and practice that preferred mode. This part of the evaluation is objective, akin to that used for enablement. Indeed, although best mode and enablement are treated as separate requirements, they clearly are interrelated. The following Federal Circuit case illustrates how the courts handle the dual subjective-objective nature of the best mode requirement.

## WAHL INSTRUMENTS, INC. V. ACVIOUS, INC.
*Federal Circuit Court of Appeals, 1991*

### Facts

In 1975, Wahl became the U.S. distributor of a line of thermochromic temperature indicating materials developed by a Japanese company called Teika. Wahl engaged Parker, an independent engineer, who conceived of using the materials as a cooking aid. The theory was that if the materials were placed in an analog of the food being cooked, then the temperature of the food could be monitored. In 1977, Parker made several prototypes of devices of different compositions and tested them for their suitability as analogs. The devices essentially consisted of two halves of a shape (such as a cylinder or egg), which were sealed in one of various ways (such as with adhesives or bolts) with a layer of thermochromic material sandwiched in between.

Wahl and Parker arranged for Wahl to develop and market the invention for use as an egg timer. They worked with Burton, a plastics fabricator, who suggested modifications in the angles and shapes of Parker's models so that the device could be mass-produced by the embedment-molding technique. Embedment molding consists of layering plastic into a mold, followed by an adhesive pouring, onto which the thermochromic layer is placed, followed by a third pouring to complete the device. Originally, the group used thermochromic paint silkscreened on Mylar, a Teika product. However, to reduce cost, Parker began to make the inserts himself, using paint made by Teika or a U.S. company, Tempil. After much experimentation, Burton's plastics company began producing an embedment-molded commercial version of the egg timer for Wahl and Parker.

Shortly thereafter, on February 6, 1978, Parker filed a patent application, disclosing and claiming the invention in various shapes (domed, cylindrical, and square) and with temperature-indicating materials that were reversible (changes color when a temperature is reached and changes back when the object cools below that temperature) and nonreversible (changes color when a temperature is reached and stays that color even when the object cools below that temperature). Subsequently, the claims were limited to reversible materials only. The patent issued on February 6, 1979.

In 1981, McMillan was hired by Wahl and placed in charge of the project. In 1987, McMillan left Wahl to start a business making a competitive egg timer. McMillan used Burton's plastics company as his fabricator, and he provided the thermochromic materials, which he easily obtained from a supplier. McMillan was sued for patent infringement. In his defense, McMillan claimed that the patent specification failed to disclose the best mode contemplated by Parker of carrying out the invention.

The district court held the patent invalid for failing to disclose numerous specifics about the best manner and mode—known to Parker at the time of filing—for manufacturing the invention, such as (1) the advantages of embedment molding, (2) the fact that the best clear plastic material was polyester resin, (3) the advantages of silk-screening the thermochromic material onto Mylar and die-cutting oval-shaped pieces for use as inserts, and (4) the fact that the best thermochromic paints for silk-screening were those made by Teika and Tempil. Wahl appealed the judgment of the district court to the Federal Circuit.

## Opinion

Under Section 112, a patent specification must "set forth the best mode contemplated by the inventor for carrying out an invention." The purpose of the best-mode requirement is to restrain inventors from applying for a patent while at the same time *concealing* from the public the preferred embodiments of their inventions that they have in fact conceived. The words in the statute are not without ambiguity. This case illustrates that the term "mode" and the phrase "carrying out the invention" are not definable with precision.

The objection here is narrowly focused. The best-mode defense is directed at the undisclosed manufacturing technique by which commercial versions of the egg timer were made and at the materials and sources of supply for materials used. Whereas McMillan's company easily duplicated the Wahl egg timer because McMillan was fully familiar with all aspects of its manufacture while employed by Wahl, McMillan asserts that Parker concealed from others information concerning fabrication of the egg timer, whereby others would not be able to reap the full benefit of the invention upon expiration of the patent. We disagree.

A description of particular materials or their sources or of a particular method or technique selected for manufacture may or may not be required as part of a best-mode disclosure with respect to a device. Indeed, the inventor's manufacturing materials or sources or techniques used to make a device may vary from wholly irrelevant to critical. For example, if the inventor develops or knows of a particular method of making that substantially improves the operation or effectiveness of the invention, failure to disclose such peripheral development may well lead to invalidation. One must look to the scope of the invention, the skill in the art, the evidence as to the inventor's belief, and all of the circumstances in order to evaluate whether the inventor's failure to disclose particulars of manufacture gives rise to the inference that the inventor concealed information that one of ordinary skill in the art would not know.

For example, in *Dana Corp v. IPC Ltd.*, this court held a patent invalid for failure to disclose a production technique using fluoride to treat rubber seals to prevent leakage, even though the technique was generally known in the art. This ruling was made because the inventors at the time of filing contemplated that the fluoride technique was specifically necessary to the invention and affected how it worked—something that those skilled in the art might not know. We face a different situation in Wahl's case, however.

**Embedment Molding.** The patent specification describes a sectional device of two parts between which a layer of temperature-indicating material is used. It states that the two parts may be ultrasonically welded, or joined by adhesive, releasable clamping, or any other suitable or desirable means for incorporating a layer of material within the plastic body. Unlike in *Dana*, there is no evidence that the working of the invention was affected in any way by how the two halves were joined. The embedment-molding method was suggested by Burton for making an egg timer, which was but one embodiment of the invention, because of the suitability, to embedment molding, of an egg shape with one flattened side. Parker also explained that this method was selected because at the expected volume of production, it would be best from a cost standpoint.

There is abundant testimony that embedment molding would be utilized if one in the business of fabricating solid plastic articles were asked to make an egg-timer device depicted in the drawings in the patent. Further, this technique was well-known at the time the application was filed.

Any process of manufacture requires the selection of specific steps and materials over others. The best mode does not necessarily cover each of these selections. To so hold would turn a patent specification into a detailed production schedule, which is not the function of patent specification. The best-mode inquiry is not mechanical. A step or material or source or technique considered best in a manufacturing circumstance may have been selected for a non-best mode reason, such as the handiness of manufacturing equipment, the availability of certain materials, prior relationships with suppliers, or other reasons having nothing to do with development of the invention.

In this case, embedment molding did not affect and was not thought to affect how the invention worked. The method of manufacture was no more than a routine manufacturing choice selected because of expected volume and cost. There is no evidence that Parker thought embedment molding was best for any reason related to the invention other than commercializing a particular embodiment. How to mass-produce the device is not, however, a best mode of the invention or part of what was invented.

**Use of Polyester Resin.** Burton told Parker that polyester resin was more suitable than acrylic for embedment molding and was cheaper. Thus, the choice of polyester resin was made over acrylic. If injection molding had been selected for fabrication, acrylic would have been used. These are matters within the routine knowledge of a plastics fabricator. The specification calls for "a solid body of plastic material" and adequately discloses the best mode of a clear plastic over other materials. The type of plastic is dictated by the need for visibility and heat resistance, information disclosed in the specification. Failure to specify polyester resin does not violate the best-mode requirement.

**Silk-Screened Thermochromic Paint on Mylar and Commercial Sources Therefor.** The specification calls for any suitable material that effects a visual indication at a preselected transition temperature. There is no evidence that Parker selected the procedure of silk-screening thermochromic paint on Mylar over other methods, such as by using cholesteric-type liquid crystals, for functional reasons. The Mylar option may merely be a manufacturing choice of convenience.

Even assuming that the thermochromic Mylar insert was the best mode for carrying out the invention instead of being only a preferred method of mass-producing one embodiment of the invention, the district court should have considered whether this form of insert was so known to those skilled in the art that they would (1) understand to use it, (2) know how to make it, (3) know it was a standard product, and (4) know the supply sources for the paints or entire inserts.

The experts agreed that silk-screened paint on a substrate, such as Mylar, had long been a standard product to use when a flat thermochromic insert was needed, although that was not the only way to make a flat layer of such materials. The district court apparently interpreted as a best-mode decision Parker's decision to make the inserts. However, Parker's decision to make rather than purchase the inserts was merely because of cost. Moreover, his technique of silk-screening was not only an ancient art but long used in connection with placing temperature-indicating paints on a substrate. Parker clearly made no contribution to the art of making such inserts and did not have to disclose how to make a standard product. Also, the sources for thermochromic materials known to Parker were generally known to those skilled in the art or were readily obtainable in the well-known *Thomas Register*. Further, there is no evidence either that special thermochromic paints were created for or selected by Parker or that he believed his invention would not work properly without the silk-screening of paints on Mylar. Finally, it hardly needs to be said that cutting to size is within routine skills. Thus, the only open question is whether those skilled in the art would need more information in order to know that thermochromic inserts on a substrate should be used. While the experts' testimony suggests more information was not needed, it is not entirely one-sided. Therefore, we believe this disputed factual issue must be reconsidered by the district court.

In sum, the burden is on the infringers to show (1) that the thermochromic inserts were part of the best mode of the invention and not simply a manufacturing choice and (2) that if part of the best mode, those skilled in the art were not likely to know from the disclosures in the specification, drawings, and claims that such inserts should be used to carry out the invention. The case is remanded to the district court for determination of these issues. In other respects, the district court decision is reversed.

---

An interesting aspect about the best-mode requirement is that it rarely is raised by the PTO during the application process. An examiner is not going to investigate whether the applicant subjectively knows of a better mode than that disclosed in the application. Thus, an inventor may well receive a patent while concealing the best mode of an invention. However, this is not a toothless tiger to be routinely ignored. Those who challenge the validity of the patent will be keenly interested in what the inventor both believed and disclosed at the time of filing. Even those who are aware of the best mode may challenge any knowledge-disclosure disparity in the application on the basis that others may not have been

**Exhibit 3.3  Patent Infringement**

| Flow Chart of Infringement Issues |
| --- |

- Is there literal infringement?
  — Yes: infringes.
  — No: Go on.
- Does doctrine of equivalents apply?
  — No: Does not infringe.
  — Yes: Go on.
- Does file wrapper estoppel apply?
  — Yes: Does not infringe.
  — No: Infringes.

| Infringement Analysis |
| --- |

- Literal Infringement
  — Section 271(a)
  — Rule of exactness: Defendant literally infringes if (s)he makes, uses, or sells (in U.S.) the invention exactly as recited in the claim.
  — Rule of addition: Defendant literally infringes if (s)he makes, uses, or sells (in U.S.) an apparatus, composition, or process having all the elements, compounds, or steps specified in the claims and adds other elements, compounds, or steps.
  — Rule of omission: Defendant does *not* literally infringe if (s)he omits one or more of the elements, compounds, or steps recited in the claims.
- Doctrine of equivalents
  — Device performs substantially the same function in substantially the same way to obtain the same result.
- File Wrapper Estoppel
  — Equivalent arrangement used by defendant was abandoned by the patentee in obtaining the patent.
- Case: *Pennwalt v. Durand-Wayland*

so well-informed. Therefore, the ultimate strength of a patent greatly depends on fulfilling the best-mode requirement of the Patent Act.

## INFRINGEMENT

Section 271(a) of the Patent Act provides that "whoever without authority makes, uses or sells any patented invention, within the United States during the term of the patent therefor, infringes the patent." Infringement analysis has three components as illustrated in Exhibit 3.3. First, one must determine if there is literal infringement. If so, then infringement is established and that is the end of the inquiry.[15] If there is not literal infringement, then one must evaluate whether the doctrine of equivalents applies. If it does not, then there is no infringement. If it is determined that the doctrine of equivalents is applicable, then before concluding that there is infringement, one must investigate further and consider whether file wrapper estoppel bars the allegations. These principles first will be reviewed; their application then will be illustrated by the landmark case, *Pennwalt Corp. v. Durand-Wayland, Inc.*

### Literal Infringement

A person literally infringes a claim in a patent by making, using, or selling an item in the United States that contains all the elements of the claim. Literal infringement often is evaluated according to one of three rules: the rule of exactness, the rule of addition, or the rule of omission. According to the rule of exactness, one infringes a claim by making, using, or selling an item that exactly conforms to that claim. By the rule of addition, infringement also is present when one makes, uses, or sells an item that not only has all the elements of the claim but also includes other elements. Under the rule of omission, one does not infringe a claim if the item under review omits any of the elements that compose the claim.

A claim for a chair provides a simple example. A broad claim might read:

**A mechanism comprising a level surface, a back, and four legs.**

A person who manufactures a chair with a back and four legs will infringe the patent by the rule of exactness. What happens if a person manufactures a four-legged chair on casters? Does this infringe the patent? According to the rule of addition, the answer is yes. Therefore, even an improvement such as the mobile chair is subject to the patent because it cannot be made without the basic elements claimed in the patent. Therefore, the inventor of the rolling chair will need permission from the patent holder before making and selling the new means to relax.

Now, take this concept a step further. Suppose including wheels on the chair is a novel and nonobvious improvement over the current art—the stationary chair. This means that the mobile chair meets the standards for patentability, and thus its inventor could receive a patent for it. The interesting thing is that even with a patent, the inventor of the chair on rollers would not be able to make it, use it, or sell it in the United States. This inventor is effectively blocked by the patent on the regular chair according to the rule of addition. Likewise, the patentee of the regular chair will be blocked from making a rolling chair; by the rule of exactness, such a chair that has exactly the elements of the mobile chair patent will infringe that patent. This scenario of two patents' blocking the production of an improvement is somewhat common, and it requires the respective patentees to come to some agreement to break the deadlock. A typical solution is a cross-license, wherein the inventor of the mobile chair allows the regular chair patentee to make the rolling variety, and the regular chair patentee gives permissions as to the regular model. As indicated in Chapter 2, blocking patents have raised serious questions in biotechnology such as whether a patent on a purified protein might block production of that protein through genetic engineering. Blocking patents also are frequently encountered in the computer field.

The rule of omission indicates that a person only has to omit one of the elements of the claim to escape literal infringement. Thus, a chair with a back and only three legs would escape liability for literal infringement because it omits an element of the claim. Obviously, this can have a pernicious effect if the inventor is not very careful with drafting the claims, since those who want to make the invention must only find some element that might be replaced with a suitable substitute.

### Doctrine of Equivalents

Strict application of the rule of omission allows individuals to avoid the spirit of a patent because they can simply omit an element and include an obviously similar feature in its stead. Due to the potential harshness of this result, the Supreme Court approved of an equitable inquiry, called the doctrine of equivalents, in *Graver Tank & Mfg. Co. v. Linde Air Products Co.* In that case, the patentee claimed an electrical welding compound consisting of silicates of calcium and magnesium. The alleged infringer omitted magnesium and substituted manganese for it. The Supreme Court stated:

> Outright and forthright duplication is a dull and very rare type of infringement. To prohibit no other would place the inventor at the mercy of verbalism and would be subordinating substance over form. It would deprive [the inventor] of the benefit of his invention and would foster concealment rather than disclosure of inventions, which is one of the primary purposes of the patent system.[16]

The doctrine of equivalents evolved to ensure that one could not practice a fraud on the patent by making obvious changes. Even if a device does not literally infringe, a patentee may proceed under the doctrine of equivalents if the device "performs substantially the same function in substantially the same way to obtain the same result."[17] The Supreme Court offered that an important factor in this judgment is whether a person reasonably skilled in the art would have known of the interchangeability of the element omitted with the one substituted. With reference to the issue before it, the Court found equivalency between the uses of magnesium and manganese in welding compositions and thus found infringement. Infringement here was based not on literal infringement, which was avoided by the rule of omission, but rather on the doctrine of equivalents.

The doctrine of equivalents is somewhat controversial because it takes something that is supposed to be definite—the claims—and makes their reach more nebulous. Patent systems in some other countries, such as Japan, do not recognize the doctrine of equivalents. One of the issues being considered by those involved in efforts to harmonize international patent policies is the future and applicability of the doctrine of equivalents.

### File Wrapper Estoppel

When an individual makes a substitution that falls under the doctrine of equivalents, an additional issue must be considered before finding infringement. Suppose the patent for the chair covered legs made of oak. The alleged infringer makes chairs out of cherry wood, which everyone in the business knows is equivalent for holding a seat above the ground. Thus, this is a good candidate for infringement under the doctrine of equivalents. However, when one looks at the history of the patent application, called the file wrapper, one might find that the patentee took actions that should prohibit extension of rights to cherry wood. For instance, assume that when the patentee filed for the patent, the claims covered legs of oak or cherry wood. However, since the prior art used a lot of cherry wood, the PTO denied these claims as obvious. Ultimately, though, the PTO was persuaded to allow the patent when the claims were narrowed to oak only. Under these circumstances it would be unfair to allow the patentee to take back through the doctrine of equivalents that which the patentee willingly gave up to get the patent in the first place. The doctrine of file wrapper estoppel prevents this unfair result. In effect, the patentee is estopped from claiming rights to cherry wood via the doctrine of equivalents due to conduct in obtaining the patent.

The following case demonstrates the difficulty of applying these seemingly simple doctrines to complex, high-technology patent claims. The evaluation is further complicated because the claims at issue use the means-plus-function technique. Although it can be confusing, recall that literal infringement of such claims covers the means indicated in the specification and those means' equivalents. This analysis is distinct from application of the doctrine of equivalents, which evaluates whether the devices achieve substantially the same functions in substantially the same way. The discussion by the Federal Circuit is enlightening and paints a real-world picture on the entire subject of infringement.

## PENNWALT CORPORATION V. DURAND-WAYLAND, INC.

*Federal Circuit Court of Appeals, 1987*

### Facts

Pennwalt sued Durand-Wayland for infringing certain claims in its patent (the '628 patent) for a sorting invention. The principal object of the invention is to provide a rapid means for sorting items, such as fruit, by color, weight, or a combination of these characteristics.

Pennwalt's invention is claimed using means-plus-function language. The weight sorter recited in claims 1 and 2 conveys items along a track having an electronic weighing device that produces an electrical signal proportional to the weight of the item, along with signal comparison means, clock means, position-indicating means, and discharge means, each of which performs specified functions. The specification describes the details of a hardwired network consisting of discrete electrical components that perform each step of the claims. Essentially, signals from the weighing device are compared to reference signals, and an appropriate signal is sent at the proper time to discharge the item into a container corresponding to its weight. In effect, the invention continuously tracks the positions of the items to be sorted, and it discharges them at the proper times.

The combined sorter of claims 10 and 18 is a multifunctional apparatus whereby the item is conveyed across the weighing device and also carried past an optical scanner that produces an electrical signal proportional to the color of the item. The signals from the weighing device and color sensor are combined, and an appropriate signal is sent at the proper time to discharge the item into the container corresponding to its color and weight.

Durand-Wayland manufactures and sells two different sorting machines: the Microsizer, which sorts by weight, and the Microsorter, in conjunction with the Microsizer, which sorts by weight and color. These machines differ from Pennwalt's in that they use microprocessors and computer programs to store data about weight and color. These machines do not continuously track the position of the items as does Pennwalt's invention; rather, data about the items and the distances to relevant drop points are stored in memory so that, under the direction of software routines, they can be released when the appropriate time intervals have elapsed.

The district court ruled for Durand-Wayland, determining that there was neither literal infringement nor infringement under the doctrine of equivalents. Pennwalt appealed to the Federal Circuit.

## Opinion

**Literal Infringement.** Pennwalt asserts that all limitations set forth in its patent claims can be read literally on Durand's devices. Pennwalt contends that the district court erred in interpreting the claims by both going beyond the means-plus-function language of a claim limitation and comparing the structure in the accused device with the structure disclosed in the specification. Such comparison allegedly resulted in the court's reading nonexistent structural limitations in the claims. Pennwalt relies on the statement in *Graver Tank*: "If accused matter falls clearly within the claim, infringement is made out and that is the end of it."

In view of the breadth of means-plus-function language in the claims, that test for literal infringement would encompass *any* means that performed the function of a claim element. This is not the proper test, however, for means-plus-function limitations. The *Graver Tank* statement predated the inclusion—in the 1952 Act—of the provision specifically permitting means limitations: Section 112, paragraph 6. This paragraph requires that means language be construed to cover the corresponding structure, material, or acts in the specification and their equivalents.

Section 112 rules out the possibility that any and every means that performs the function specified in the claim *literally* satisfies the limitation. Rather, literal infringement occurs only if the accused device uses means to achieve every claimed function that are the same as or equivalent to the structures disclosed in the specification. Of course, if every function cited in the claim is not performed by the accused device, then there cannot be literal infringement.

Thus it was appropriate that the district court made a comparison between Durand-Wayland's structure and the structure disclosed in the specification for performing a particular function. The statute means exactly what it says: To determine whether a claim limitation is met literally—when expressed as a means for performing a stated function—the court must compare the accused structure with the disclosed structure and must find equivalent *structure* as well as *identity* of claimed *function* for that structure. Thus, Pennwalt is in error when it argues that if an accused structure performs the function required by the claim, then there are structural equivalency and literal infringement.

We need not determine whether the district court correctly found no equivalency in structure because the district court also found that the accused devices, in any event, did not perform all the same functions specified in the claims. For example, the accused devices had no position-indicating means for tracking the locations of the item being sorted. The absence of that function negates the possibility of literal infringement.

**Infringement under the Doctrine of Equivalents.**  Under the doctrine of equivalents, infringement may be found if an accused device performs substantially the same overall function in substantially the same way to obtain substantially the same overall result as the claimed invention. That formulation, however, does not mean one can ignore claim limitations. Each element of a claim is material, and the plaintiff must show the presence of every element or its substantial equivalent in the accused device.

Pennwalt argues that the accused machines simply do in a computer what the patent illustrates doing with hardwired circuitry. If Pennwalt were correct that the accused devices differ only in substituting a computer for hardwired circuitry, it might have a stronger position for arguing that the accused devices infringe its claims. The claim limitations, however, require the performance of certain specified functions, for which the microprocessor in the accused devices was not so programmed.

The district court found that certain functions of the claimed inventions were missing from the accused devices and that those that were performed were substantially different. For example, all of Pennwalt's claims require the function of continuously indicating positions of items. Some language from claim 10 is representative:

> first position-indicating means responsive to a signal from said clock means and said signal from said second comparison means for continuously indicating the position of an item to be sorted while the item is in transit between said optical detection means and said electronic weighing means.

> second position-indicating means responsive to the signal from said clock means, the signal from said first comparison means and said first position-indicating means for generating a signal continuously indicative of the position of an item to be sorted after said item has been weighed.

The district court found that the accused devices do not have any position-indicating means to determine the positions of the items being sorted. Rather, it correctly found that the microprocessor stores weight and color data, not the positions of the items to be sorted.

Pennwalt argues that there is a way to find out where an item is physically located on the track of the accused machine. Thus, Pennwalt asserts that the accused devices have position-indicating means. However, the accused machine simply does not do what could be done. The physical tracking of fruit is not part of the way in which the Durand-Wayland sorter works. Although a microprocessor theoretically could be programmed to perform that function, the district court determined that the function performed by the Durand-Wayland machines was substantially different.

Pennwalt also claims that the memory component of the Durand-Wayland sorter, which stores information as to weight and color of an item, performed substantially the same function as claimed for the position-indicating means. The district court found that a memory function is neither the same nor substantially the same as the function of continuously indicating where an item is physically located in a sorter. On this point the record is indisputable that before the words "continuously indicating" were added as an additional limitation, the claim was unpatentable in view of prior art that, like the accused machines, stores the information with respect to sorting criteria in memories but did not continuously track the location.

Thus, the facts here do not involve later-developed technology, which should be deemed within the scope of the claims to avoid the pirating of an invention. On the contrary, the inventors could not obtain a patent with claims in which the functions were described more broadly. Having secured claims only by including very specific *functional* limitations, Pennwalt now seeks to avoid those very limitations under the doctrine of equivalents. This it cannot do.

### Conclusion

In sum, all of Pennwalt's claims require the function of continuously indicating the positions of the items to be sorted. No means in the accused device performs that function and thus there can be no literal infringement. No means with an equivalent function was substituted in the accused devices and thus there can be no infringement under the doctrine of equivalents. The district court's finding of no infringement is affirmed.

A U.S. patent generally protects only against acts of infringement that occur in the United States. Thus if the patent claims an article of manufacture or a machine, then one who makes, uses, or sells that machine in the United States infringes the patent under the terms of Section 271. Alternatively, a person who makes, uses, or sells the article outside the United States does not infringe the U.S. patent. However, note that one who makes the article in a foreign country will not be able to sell it in the United States without infringing the U.S. patent. In this way, a patent on a machine or an article secures the inventor from direct competition within the United States.

## Infringement of Process Patents

One who has a patent on a process used to manufacture products faces a more complicated international scenario. Prior to 1989, infringement under Section 271 occurred only if someone used that process within the United States. Therefore, strictly speaking, one did not infringe a U.S. process patent by using that process beyond U.S. borders to manufacture products and then selling those products in the United States. Without more, the only possible remedy was through the International Trade Commission (ITC) under Section 337. However, actions through the ITC may be a weak deterrent because the ITC can only grant an order excluding further imports; it has no power to order monetary damages.[18]

Congress adopted the Process Patent Amendments in 1988 to defeat competition within the United States by foreign manufacturers using processes protected by U.S. patents.[19] Section 271(g), which was added by the amendments, reads in part: "Whoever without authority imports into the United States or sells or uses within the United States a product which is made by a process patented in the United States shall be liable as an infringer." The aim of the change clearly is against foreign manufacturers who use a patented process and import the resultant products into the United States. However, the reach of the amendments is not so limited. Anyone who uses or sells products impermissibly developed from the patented process infringes the patent. Thus, even retailers and noncommercial users of the product are theoretically subject to infringement actions. However, the act makes them susceptible only if there is no adequate remedy against the primary manufacturers, importers, distributors, or wholesalers.[20] In addition, when a business has inventories of products that infringe process patents, it nonetheless will not be liable for damages if those products were acquired before the business knew or had reason to know about the infringement.[21] Under circumstances such as these, when the business can establish its innocence, it is free to sell the products, notwithstanding the fact that they infringe process patents.

The details of the Process Patent Amendments are extremely complicated, well beyond the scope of this book. The complexity results from the fact that it is difficult to determine the processes by which a product or its components were made. For instance, what steps should a retailer, such as Sears, be expected to take to reasonably assure itself that its bicycle frames, or any of the frames' integral component parts, were not constructed by means of patented processes? The act establishes due diligence procedures by which retailers and others may immunize themselves from liability.[22] In very simple terms, a business can limit its exposure by writing to other manufacturers of similar products, requesting that they disclose any process patents they hold related to the product. Once that information is received, the business transmits it to the manufacturer or supplier of the product in question. If the manufacturer then provides adequate written assurance that the product is not made though the patented processes, then the inquiring business is relatively safe from liability for infringement. The full impact of these amendments has not yet become clear, but certainly the amendments in-crease the risks and the paperwork for wholesalers and retailers in the United States.[23]

## DAMAGES FOR PATENT INFRINGEMENT

One must consider a lot of issues throughout the process of obtaining a patent. Is the subject matter patentable? Is the invention novel and nonobvious? What must be disclosed? How much protection is possible? How much will it cost? The payoff for all this is that a court will enforce the right to exclude others from en-joying the fruits of one's invention. It does this in two ways: by issuing injunc-tions prohibiting further infringement and by ordering that compensation be paid for the infringing acts that have occurred. Compensation awards potentially can reach staggering amounts, and they often are reported in the popular press. A very notable figure was the $909 million that Kodak was ordered to pay Polaroid for its infringement of instant photography patents.[24] Indeed, monetary awards can be so high as to bankrupt companies, such as occurred after Smith Interna-tional was ordered to pay Hughes Tool Co. $134 million for infringement of patents related to rock bit technology.[25]

Section 284 of the Patent Act provides that a patent holder may recover dam-ages for infringement. In particular, the section states:

> Upon finding for the claimant, the court shall award the claimant damages ad-equate to compensate for the infringement but in no event less than a reason-able royalty for the use made of the invention by the infringer, together with interest and costs as fixed by the court. . . . [T]he court may increase the dam-ages up to three times the amount found or assessed.

According to this provision, a patentee is entitled to be compensated for profits lost by virtue of an infringement. Establishing this figure can be a demanding ex-ercise, however. The ultimate inquiry for determining lost profits is, "Had the infringer not infringed, what would the patent holder have made?"[26] Logically, one begins with the sales made by the infringer. But then one must ask whether the patentee would have made all those sales had the infringer not used the patented technology. It could be that the infringer's customers were motivated more by certain unique features on the infringer's products than by the patented technology. Perhaps the infringer's customers would have purchased products employing other technologies outside the purview of the patent. Maybe the patentee's sales staff would not have solicited the customers reached by the in-fringer. Possibly the patentee could not have manufactured the products sold by the infringer because of deficiencies in capacity.

Once the lost sales are determined, then one must figure what would have been the cost to produce the goods. Should one base that on variable costs or factor in fixed costs? And then one can argue that the lost sales resulted in other losses, such as fewer accessory sales. And on top of that, one might make further points, such as that the unlawful competition by the infringer caused the patentee to lower its sales prices below the amount it would have charged without the infringement. All of these are acceptable arguments if the patentee has sufficient proof.

The Patent Act states that the patentee is, at a minimum, entitled to a reasonable royalty for use made by the infringer. This usually means that the patentee will receive a reasonable royalty for those sales made by the infringer that it cannot prove it would have otherwise made. In other words, the patentee normally will receive lost profits for the infringer's sales it would have made and a reasonable royalty for the rest. The reasonable royalty will be based on established rates or on a hypothetical rate determined by the court. In addition to lost profits and a reasonable royalty, the patentee can receive prejudgment interest equal to the amount of interest lost due to the delay between the time the profit or royalty should have been earned and the time it is finally paid by the infringer under court order. Finally, for cases of willful infringement, the Patent Act provides that the court may treble the damage award and have the infringer pay the patentee's attorney's fees as well.[27] The following case provides a comprehensive example of the difficult questions involved in calculating patent damage awards.

## MICRO MOTION, INC. V. EXAC CORPORATION

*District Court (Northern District), California, 1991*

### Facts

The district court found that Exac infringed patents held by Micro Motion for Coriolis mass flowmeters. The opinion that follows regards the determination of damages owed by Exac for its infringing activities.

### Opinion

**Profits due to Lost Sales.**  To receive an award of lost profits, the patent owner must prove that but for the infringement, it either would have made the sales made by the infringer, would have charged higher prices for its patented products, or both. The determination of a damage award is not an exact science, and the amount need not be proven with unerring precision. When damage in fact is clear but the amount of the damages cannot be ascertained with precision, any doubts regarding the amount must be resolved against the infringer.

The most widely accepted method of proving lost profits was set forth in *Panduit Corp. v. Stahlin Bros. Fibre Works, Inc.*:

> To obtain as damages the profits on sales he would have made absent the infringement, i.e., the sales made by the infringer, a patent owner must prove: (1) demand for the patented product, (2) absence of acceptable non-infringing substitutes, (3) his manufacturing and marketing capability to exploit the demand, and (4) the amount of the profit he would have made.

Micro Motion need not present absolute proof of each of these elements; the burden is one of reasonable probability. Micro Motion has met this burden for each element of the *Panduit* test.

*Demand for Coriolis Flowmeters.* Micro Motion's flowmeters were popular because they provided a unique combination of capabilities: they were accurate, measured mass flow directly, were nonintrusive, and saved users a great deal of money. Micro Motion charged a high price for its flowmeters and achieved a high level of profitability. Micro Motion's customers were relatively insensitive to the price of Micro Motion's flowmeters because the flowmeters offered substantial benefits that non-Coriolis flowmeters did not offer. Exac's own documents stress the superiority of and demand for Coriolis flowmeters. For instance, they note that the nearly 300% per year compounded annual growth rate of Micro Motion clearly indicates the market demand for the Coriolis technology. Accordingly, the court finds that Coriolis meters offered significant and distinct benefits to their primary users that distinguished Coriolis from non-Coriolis meters and that created demand for Coriolis meters sufficient to satisfy the first element of the *Panduit* test.

*Absence of Acceptable Noninfringing Substitutes.* Acceptable substitutes are noninfringing products that offer the key advantages of the patented device. An acceptable substitute must offer the advantages that the purchaser of the patented device values. Evidence that a patented device filled a long-felt need of its users and enjoyed commercial success indicates the lack of an acceptable noninfringing substitute.

Micro Motion's invention represented a significant advance over other devices and filled a long-felt need of some users. Exac's own documents state that Coriolis technology transcends the mediocrity of volumetric flowmeters. Although Coriolis flowmeters would sometimes compete with non-Coriolis flowmeters, Coriolis meters offered enough benefits that for many applications—such as oil and gas, food, chemicals, petrochemicals, and paper and pulp manufacturing— non-Coriolis meters were, at best, imperfect substitutes for Coriolis flowmeters. Also, Micro Motion's product enjoyed great commercial success. In the years following its introduction, Micro Motion enjoyed very rapid sales growth while maintaining high prices. Accordingly, the court finds an absence of acceptable noninfringing substitutes for the users who purchased the bulk of Coriolis flowmeters.

*Manufacturing and Marketing Capability.* The court finds that Micro Motion had the ability to manufacture and market most of the flowmeters sold by Exac. Micro Motion need not prove with absolute certainty that it could have made each of the sales it claims it lost to Exac; it need show only that it had the potential capability to manufacture and market those meters. It can meet its burden by showing that it would have expanded its manufacturing and marketing functions to meet the needs of Exac's customers. To make 80% of Exac's sales—the amount Micro Motion asserts it would have made had Exac not entered the market—Micro Motion would have had to increase its output by only 1% in 1985, 5% in 1986, 8% in 1987, 9% in 1988, and 2% in 1989.

*Manufacturing.* Exac points to Micro Motion's 1986–1987 production backlogs as evidence that Micro Motion could not have expanded its production to meet this demand. The court finds this unconvincing. Even a substantial backlog does not necessarily create the inability to expand production; a manufacturing concern may simply find it more economical to work off a backlog. Also, every Micro Motion witness testified that Micro Motion had sufficient capacity to make the number of meters sold by Exac. Accordingly, the court finds that Micro Motion had the capacity necessary to produce the meters sold by Exac.

*Marketing and Selling Capability.* Micro Motion was capable of marketing and selling most of the meters that Exac sold. Because Micro Motion and Exac sold to the same basic industries and had many common customers, one can assume that Micro Motion could have reached most of Exac's customers without expending an inordinately large amount of resources.

Micro Motion, however, would not have made every one of Exac's sales. It might not have found every customer that Exac did; some customers may have needed a feature that only Exac could provide; some customers may have been dissatisfied with Micro Motion and would not have bought from it; and some of Exac's customers may have purchased from a third-party Coriolis flowmeter vendor. Micro Motion estimates that it would have made 80% of Exac's sales of infringing devices. Exac argues that its entry caused no decrease in Micro Motion's sales.

• Sales of Infringing Meters. Exac argues that its aggressive marketing campaign and superior features allowed it to make sales that Micro Motion would not have made. Micro Motion introduced evidence that all but 13% of Exac's sales were made to customers who were earlier-established Micro Motion customers, and all but 4% of Exac's sales were to customers operating in industries in which Micro Motion sold. Although the court notes some deficiencies in these data, it nevertheless indicates the large extent to which Exac depended on past, current, or potential Micro Motion customers for sales.

Exac's meters offered some features not available on Micro Motion's meters. However, Exac offered little evidence that its customers bought its meters because of the meters' distinctive features and would not have bought a Micro Motion meter that lacked one or more of them. Although it is very difficult to determine what features were critical to Exac's customers, it seems likely that the advantages inherent in a Coriolis flowmeter, and not any feature unique to Exac, led the overwhelming majority of Exac's customers to purchase their meters.

To the extent that Exac sold to customers who knew of, but would not buy from, Micro Motion, Exac's sales do not represent a loss to Micro Motion. There is little evidence on this issue except that Micro Motion customers returned as defective 10% of the meters purchased in 1985. There is no evidence about how many of these customers turned to Exac for replacement nor whether they would have done so had Exac not had the infringing meter. The court can infer only that some dissatisfied customers would not purchase from Micro Motion.

Finally, some of Exac's sales would have gone to third-party manufacturers of Coriolis technology. Although they began marketing activities as early as 1985, third-party providers enjoyed little success before late 1987. Based on their market shares and accounting for the fact that Exac's customers might be more likely than others to purchase from third-party vendors rather than Micro Motion, the court estimates that the percentage of Exac's sales that would have gone to third-party vendors was only 3% for 1987, 7% for 1988, and 12% for 1989.

Overall, the court finds that Micro Motion would have made 70% of Exac's domestic sales of infringing models (Models 7100 and 8100) had Exac not entered the market.

- Sales of Noninfringing Meters. The court rejects Micro Motion's claim to lost sales damages by Exac's noninfringing Model 8300 meter sales. Micro Motion argues that the name recognition, customer contacts, and marketing and production knowledge Exac gained by manufacturing and selling its infringing meters allowed it to sell far more Model 8300 meters than it otherwise would have sold. However, the court finds the relationship between Exac's earlier infringement and its later sales of its Model 8300 too speculative to merit compensation.

***Amount of Profit Micro Motion Would Have Made on Its Lost Sales.*** Having determined that Micro Motion would have made 70% of Exac's domestic sales but for the infringement, the court must determine the profit Micro Motion lost on those sales. The first step is to quantify Micro Motion's lost sales. To do this, the court (1) determines Exac's total domestic sales for the infringing period by model, (2) converts Exac's sales for each model into each model's Micro Motion equivalents, (3) determines lost sales units by subtracting the Exac sales Micro Motion would not have made (30%), (4) multiplies the lost sales of each Micro Motion meter by that meter's estimated sales price, (5) adjusts the resulting figure to account for anticipated returns, and (6) adds reasonably expected accessory sales. Using this approach, the court finds that the total meter revenue lost during the infringement period was $6,851,334. Total returns and allowances on the lost sales would have been $203,387. Because Micro Motion historically sold $15 worth of accessories for each $100 of meters it sold, lost accessory sales totals $992,584. Total lost sales revenue thus equals $7,640,531.

Both Exac and Micro Motion presented evidence as to the costs Micro Motion would have incurred had it produced and sold the units that it lost to Exac. The court uses an incremental income approach, which recognizes that it does not cost as much to produce unit N+1 if the first N (or fewer) units produced already have paid the fixed costs. Incremental costs include any costs that increase as production expands over a relevant range—here, 9%. By this approach, the incremental cost associated with the lost meter and accessory sales is $2,762,713. Subtracting this amount from total lost sales revenue gives a profit on lost sales of $4,877,818.

**Price Erosion Claim.** In most price erosion cases, a patent owner has reduced the actual price of its patented product in response to an infringer's competition. But a patent holder who proves that it would have increased prices had the infringer not been in competition can also sustain a price erosion claim.

The experts determined that demand for Coriolis flowmeters was highly inelastic. From the evidence, the court concludes that Micro Motion could have raised prices and indeed would have raised prices more frequently than it did had Exac not entered the market.

Exac's entry into the market for Coriolis flowmeters significantly changed the structure of the market. Exac's entrance subjected Micro Motion to a substantial risk that a price increase in its meters would lead customers to switch to Exac. Between 1984 and 1987, Micro Motion rapidly lost market share to Exac, suffered flat sales, and increased selling expenses. Exac's entry changed what had been exclusively Micro Motion's market into a two-supplier market and thus limited Micro Motion's ability to realize monopolistic profits on its Coriolis meters. The court finds that but for Exac's infringement, Micro Motion would have raised its prices 4% more than it did in both 1985 and 1986.

In the late 1980s, several other flowmeter companies began to get involved in making and selling their own Coriolis mass flowmeters. These third-party competitors enjoyed little success before 1987. However, beginning in 1987, the threat by the new entrants would have kept Micro Motion from raising prices further even if Exac had not infringed. Therefore, for this period, Micro Motion would have imposed the 8% price increase generated in 1985 and 1986 only. Based on these figures, price erosion damages on Micro Motion's actual sales equals $14,073,527, and price erosion damages on Micro Motion's lost sales comes to $575,562. Total price erosion damages, therefore, are $14,649,089.

**Reasonable Royalty Analysis.** Micro Motion would not have made 30% of Exac's infringing domestic sales, nor any of its foreign sales. Micro Motion is entitled to a reasonable royalty for the sales of these infringing items. A reasonable royalty is determined by conducting a hypothetical negotiation between the patent owner and infringer at the time infringement began. There was no established royalty for the patents at the time of the hypothetical negotiation. However, a court can consider a number of factors in determining what a reasonable royalty rate should be. Among these are:

> the parties' relative bargaining strength; the anticipated amount of profits that the prospective licensor reasonably thinks he would lose as a result of licensing the patent as compared to the royalty income; the anticipated amount of net profits that the prospective licensee reasonably thinks he will make; the commercial past performance of the invention; the market to be tapped; and other economic factors that prudent businesspersons would take into consideration under similar circumstances.

Based on these factors, the court finds that the parties would have settled on a royalty rate of 15% on a hypothetical negotiation held in December 1983. Applying this rate to Exac's sales that Micro Motion would not have made itself, the reasonable royalty is $1,294,617.

**Prejudgment Interest.** Prejudgment interest ensures that patent owners are placed in as good a position in terms of earned interest as they would have been had the infringer not infringed. The interest depends on two factors: the appropriate interest rate and the appropriate base of damages. The court has discretion in deciding the rate of interest and whether it should be compounded. Based on the evidence, the court determines that total prejudgment interest equals $5,409,481.

**Willfulness.** Under the patent statute, the court may increase the damages up to three times the amount assessed if it finds willful infringement. It also may award reasonable attorney's fees in exceptional cases. The court does not find this to be an exceptional case of willful infringement. Thus, Micro Motion's request for attorney's fees is denied.

**Conclusion.** Exac shall pay Micro Motion $20,821,525 in damages and $5,409,481 in prejudgment interest, making a total award of $26,231,006.

---

Exhibit 3.4 summarizes the elements one must consider in calculating patent infringement damages, as discussed in *Micro Motion*. The trend in the courts toward patent protection in the United States is very clear: patentees are increasingly winning patent infringement actions and are being awarded higher sums as compensation. This has led to two interesting results. One is that small business entities now are more willing to bring patent infringement actions against large corporations, knowing that the odds of success and the potential payoffs have increased. The second is that royalty fees negotiated for patent licenses have risen markedly in the past decade. A notable example that is being carefully watched regards the patent issued to Gilbert Hyatt in 1990 for a single-chip microprocessor—an integral component for a multitude of products such as personal computers, calculators, and videocassette recorders. By some estimates, if Hyatt were to demand a conservative royalty of 3% for all products using the technology, the patent could be worth $200 million per year.[28] With the high stakes involved, there is likely to be substantial litigation questioning not only the breadth of the claims allowed, but whether Hyatt was even the first inventor.

## INTERNATIONAL PATENT PROTECTION ISSUES

The increasing interdependence between the global economies has intensified the need for companies to pursue international business plans. Although patent protection within the United States is an important aspect of a business venture, its protective reach likely will be too limited for the modern corporation. Therefore, most business concerns now must contemplate patent protection on an international scale. Clearly, it would be easiest if an inventor could file for a global patent, which would give worldwide rights once granted. Although this is the ultimate goal of multinational businesses, it does not currently represent reality. Rather, for the most part, each country has its own patent policies, which it enforces in its own way within its own borders. This leads to substantial hardship and expense for inventors seeking global protection. Fortunately, significant strides are being made toward facilitating international patent protection. This is

## Exhibit 3.4  Damages for Patent Infringement

- Section 284
- Profits from lost sales
  — Based on sales made by the infringer that otherwise would have been made by patent holder
  — Includes lost accessory sales
- Reasonable royalty for sales made by infringer that patent holder nevertheless would not have made
- Price erosion on patented product sales due to unlawful competition by infringer
- Prejudgment interest
- Treble damages and attorneys' fees if willful

occurring on two fronts: on a substantive level wherein countries are attempting to harmonize their standards for patentability, and in a procedural sense, making it easier for inventors to file applications and receive protection within selected international boundaries.

### Substantive Patent Policy Issues

The various patent policies throughout the world, especially among the major developed participants, share significant common ground, although the overlap tends to be overshadowed by important distinctions. Almost all, for example, require that an invention be new and nonobvious to be patentable. Differences, however, abound. Countries have different policies regarding patentable subject matter, length of protection, interpretation of claims, requirements for novelty, confidentiality of applications, and priority between multiple inventors, to name just a few. Currently, efforts are being made within the World Intellectual Property Organization (WIPO) to formulate a Patent Harmonization Treaty with the objective of ironing out those differences. In addition, harmonization of certain important patent issues was recently achieved through the resolution of the Uruguay Round of the General Agreement on Tariffs and Trade (GATT).

As discussed in Chapter 2, there are two substantial differences between the patent policies of the United States and those of other nations, which may serve as a trap for the unwary U.S. inventor. Only three countries in the world—the United States, Jordan, and the Philippines—rely on the first-to-invent priority standard. All other nations use a first-to-file system. This may lead to obvious problems when unsuspecting U.S. inventors decide to internationalize their operations. It also may result in substantial incongruities as to ownership of patent rights for the same invention, depending on the jurisdiction. That the United States ultimately will adopt the first-to-file system is nearly a certainty. The first-to-invent system requires detailed records and can lead to expensive litigation over priority. In addition, sophisticated international corporations already mobilize and file early to protect their patent rights overseas. The first-to-invent standard thus yields little advantage for them, and indeed even raises their risks in the United States. Therefore, there is substantial political support for the United States to adopt this fundamental change.

The other surprise lurking for the U.S. inventor is the way many other countries handle the issue of novelty. Recall that in the United States there is a one-year grace period for filing after certain triggering events such as a sale or publication. Many other countries are not so lenient, however. Some nations deny patent protection if the triggering events occur within their borders at any time prior to filing. Japan is somewhat like this, although it has a six-month grace period for certain limited acts of the inventor, such as making a demonstration at a trade show.[29] Other countries may be even more stringent, barring patent rights if the triggering events have occurred anywhere in the world prior to filing. In this way, inventors who publish an article believing that they have one year to file may unknowingly jeopardize or relinquish patent rights in many important commercial trading areas around the world.

Related areas of controversy surround the ways that triggering events, such as "sale" and "public use," are defined. The United States tends to be relatively strict here, broadly interpreting what constitutes a sale to cover such activities as test marketing and offers. It also considers certain secret uses by the inventor to be public, such as when a process is used to manufacture goods for public sale. It is not totally clear where the debate within WIPO will lead on these issues. WIPO's U.S. representatives have expressed the importance of a grace period, especially as to acts of the inventor, so that technical and market experimentation can be performed. However, they have shown more flexibility on the issues of what constitutes a public use or sale.[30]

The major international patent harmonization goals of the United States are to enlarge the scope of patentable subject matter and to strengthen enforcement of patent rights. There is substantial divergence of opinion worldwide on the patentability of two technologies critical to U.S. trade: computer software and biotechnology. Various countries do not explicitly extend patent protection to computer software. Clearly, the United States has an important interest in revising their positions. The international debate over rights to biotechnology inventions is even more heated, as demonstrated by the failure of the United States to initially sign the Earth Summit Biodiversity Convention. Some nations want ownership rights in biotechnologies that are dependent on their raw materials. Also, various countries are reluctant to allow patent rights for medicinal articles, claiming that protection would be unethical and financially devastating. On the other hand, steps have been taken within the European Union to unify and strengthen biotechnology protection in that region.[31] In addition, resolution of the Uruguay Round of GATT eventually should heighten some aspects of biotechnology and pharmaceutical patent protection virtually worldwide. Of course, gaining protection for new types of subject matter is not very meaningful if enforcement is lax. Currently, there are policy disparities over remedies for infringements, especially as to the availability of injunctions and the amount of damages. Again, the TRIPs agreement of the Uruguay Round should improve the situation, by requiring member countries to raise enforcement standards somewhat. Overall, substantial progress has been made in recent years to unify international patent standards. However, there still is significant ground to cover. Therefore one can expect the United States to continue to press for wider, stronger, and more uniform international protection for emerging technologies, and it may make progress on the WIPO harmonization treaty contingent on such developments.

There are additional differences in foreign patent policies that must be considered by inventors having international visions. One important issue regards the secrecy of patent applications. Currently in the United States, patent application materials are preserved in secrecy by the PTO until the patent issues. If the patent does not issue, then there is no public disclosure of the invention or of information pertaining to it. This can be extremely important to inventors who rely on trade secret law for protection both while their patent application is being reviewed and in the event the claims eventually are not allowed. In many other nations, notably in Europe and Japan, patent application files are opened to public inspection at some period of time, generally 18 months after the filing date. This is done primarily to accelerate public disclosure and so that objections may be raised in opposition proceedings. Although there may be some patent rights in these countries before the patent actually issues, one must consider the implications to trade secret protection plans there and around the world if patentability ultimately is not established. Also, inventors should be prepared for the United States to adopt similar disclosure principles either in conjunction with its move to a first-to-file priority system, or possibly before.

An inventor must note further variations as well. One of them involves the length of protection. Developing countries often have shorter terms, although this soon will be rectified in most cases by the Uruguay Round. Also, most countries measure that term starting from the filing date rather than the issue date. Consider the implications of that difference to an inventor such as Gilbert Hyatt, whose patent for microprocessors issued in the United States in 1990, 20 years after the application was filed. Fortunately, this disparity, too, should soon be eliminated through the Uruguay Round, which requires all signatory countries to provide patent protection for 20 years from the filing date of the application. Some nations, such as Japan, strictly adhere to the terms of the claims, denying broader coverage as in the United States based on a doctrine of equivalents. There also are important differences regarding what it takes to prove infringement of process patents. Although the United States recently made it easier for process patent holders to win infringement actions, the burden is still somewhat more difficult in various other countries. Many foreign countries, unlike the United States, require that the invention be worked, or put into commercial use, in the country within a prescribed number of years. In addition, there are differences in the amount of control bestowed by patent rights. Some countries, for instance, may require patented inventions to be licensed to other businesses at reasonable royalty rates, a practice called compulsory licensing. Also, some nations, such as Japan, allow members of the public to argue before the relevant administrative agencies why a patent should not be granted. Such procedures, called pre-grant oppositions, currently are not used in the United States.

Clearly, an inventor who ventures into the international marketplace faces a complex and often divergent web of patent policies. The resultant complexity and frustrations can be averted only through greater international harmonization. The success of the Uruguay Round has given the international community a taste of how progress can be made in this area. Hopefully, the spirit of cooperation engendered though GATT will carry over to negotiations within other multilateral channels, most notably within WIPO.

### Procedural Patent Policy Issues

An important variable in any business decision is the degree of transaction costs the decision will entail. For a business contemplating an international patent program, such costs could be overwhelming. This is due to the largely uncoordinated set of diverse national patent procedures, which, with few exceptions, must be followed piecemeal on a country-by-country basis. Imagine the difficulty of receiving patent protection in just a few countries, such as Japan, Germany, Australia, Israel, and Mexico. An inventor first has to become advised on the substantive patent laws of each nation. This likely will require advice from specialist attorneys in each country. Applications then have to be filed and defended in each jurisdiction, according to each one's respective laws and policies. Translations obviously will be necessary, not only raising financial costs but also jeopardizing the inventor's understanding of the patent applications and resultant patent rights. Then there are costs to business strategy as well. For instance, if test marketing must be curtailed until applications are filed in all desired countries to preserve patent rights, the delay may carry substantial business risk. Fortunately, several international treaties have been negotiated to alleviate some of these procedural problems. The most important are the Paris Convention, the European Patent Convention, and the Patent Cooperation Treaty.

**The Paris Convention.** The Paris Convention is the oldest and most comprehensive multilateral accord dealing with intellectual property. Almost all the industrialized countries and many developing nations are signatories. One of the provisions of the Paris Convention is crucially important to inventors attempting to overcome the procedural impediments to international patent coverage. Under that provision, the filing date of an application filed in a signatory country will be considered the effective filing date of an application filed in another signatory country if the latter application is filed within one year of the first. Thus, if a patent application is filed for AES in the United States on February 8, 1994, then an application filed in Korea before February 8, 1995 will be treated as if it were filed in Korea on February 8, 1994. This can be extremely important, for instance, when one considers that Korea has no grace period for certain sales or publications.[32] Due to the Paris Convention, we can file a U.S. patent application for the Audio Enhancement System and then perform test marketing, release information, and engage in sales. As long as we file in Korea within one year, these actions will be treated as having happened after the effective filing date in Korea. This is a tremendous benefit. Now, we can file in the United States, and over the next year decide if we want to seek patent protection in other signatory countries. This allows time to test the product, consider business strategies, and consult with legal experts before investing the energy and resources in making patent applications abroad.

When relying on the Paris Convention, one must keep foreign patent laws in mind. For instance, if we release a publication about our invention before the U.S. application is filed, relying on the grace period of Section 102(b), then our application in Korea will not be timely, even if it is filed within one year under the Paris Convention. This is because the patent laws of Korea do not permit any publication, even by the inventor, prior to the relevant filing date—in this case, the date the U.S. application is filed. One must be wary of U.S. laws as well. For example, the one-year grace period of Section 102(b) is not affected by the Paris Convention. Therefore, once a publication has been released, a patent application must be filed in the United States within one year (the grace period) of that publication to preserve U.S. patent rights. Filing in a signatory country within the one-year grace period would not give the inventor an additional year under the Paris Convention to file in the United States.

**European Patent Convention.**   Seventeen nations in Europe have made great strides in establishing the equivalent of a European patent.[33] Under the European Patent Convention (EPC), the participating nations have agreed to a number of substantive patent principles, such as concerns subject matter, novelty, utility, priority, patent length, and interpretation of claims. An inventor seeking patent protection in Europe may file one application with the European Patent Office (EPO), which will search and examine the application under the terms of the convention. One advantage for the U.S. inventor is that the application and correspondences with the EPO can be made in English. Also, if the patent is granted, patent rights are effective in all member countries the inventor designates in the application. The only significant way the EPC differs from a truly European patent is that the patentee must bring enforcement actions separately in each country where infringement occurs. The European Union may erase this hurdle shortly by means of a new initiative, under which enforcement litigation can be handled centrally as well.

As a matter of patent strategy, firms involved in certain technologies, notably biotechnology and computer software, sometimes approach Europe with a conservative, two-tiered approach. Since the EPC ties together the diverse nations of Europe, there are many unsettled questions about the patentability of radical technologies, which inevitably leads to delays and/or denials of a Europe-wide patent. Therefore, businesses may opt to double-bank patent protection by seeking patent rights directly in the most commercially important individual nations in addition to filing with the EPO.[34] Thus, we might choose to file patents for AES in Britain, France and Germany as well as through the EPO. In this way, if the process is held up on the European scale, we may have better success and obtain protection in some or all of the individual countries.

**The Patent Cooperation Treaty.** The Patent Cooperation Treaty (PCT), which by 1993 had grown to 57 member countries, further facilitates the process of obtaining international patent rights. Under the PCT, an inventor can file an international application (IA) with an appropriate receiving office, designating the member countries in which patent protection is sought. Both the U.S. PTO and the EPO serve as receiving offices. The IA uses a standardized format, which can be filed in English. An inventor can follow one of two approaches under the PCT. One option is to request that an international search be conducted by an approved searching authority, such as the PTO. Twenty months after the "priority filing date," the search report will be sent to the selected countries for independent national examinations and actions. Alternatively, the inventor can request that a preliminary search and examination be conducted at the international level. This provides a formal indication of allowability of claims, which is very persuasive with the member nations. If this route is selected, the search and examination reports are sent to the selected nations for their separate actions 30 months after the priority filing date.

The PCT provides us with tremendous flexibility in our attempt to gain international patent protection for AES. The following is one of several possible options: We can initiate the international process by filing a U.S. patent application with the PTO. The date of that application will serve as our "priority filing date" under the Paris Convention. Since we have an international vision, we will file the application before making public sales or publications of the invention. Within 12 months, we will file an IA with the PTO, requesting a search and examination and designating that the reports be sent to, say, 20 countries and the EPO. The PCT works within the Paris Convention in such a way that the filing dates for each of the designated countries and regions will refer back to the date of the initial U.S. application, as long as the IA is filed, as it was here, within 12 months. As discussed before, this will help preserve our patent rights in countries with strict novelty requirements. The IA, the search, and the examination all will be conducted in English. Thirty months after the U.S. application date, the search and examination reports will be sent to the designated countries and the EPO. At this time, we will have to pay national fees and hire translators and local attorneys so that any remaining steps under the laws of the individual countries or regional conventions can be completed.

There are three tremendous advantages of filing through the PCT: improved information, language, and deferral of fees and costs. Using the PCT, we gained an additional 18 months to test the invention in the market before having to file the myriad of foreign national applications and pay all of those applications' concomitant fees and costs. During this period, we may determine that public interest in the invention will not merit an expensive international patent program. Or we may learn that the invention will fly in certain cultures but not others. In addition, the international examination may indicate that the claims are not allowable, thereby giving us good reason to abandon the program before sinking too much into the effort.

The advantage of undertaking the patent process in English is the same here as under the EPC, but on a broader scale. It is hard to overestimate the importance of being allowed to communicate in one's native tongue, especially in an area that demands as much precision as a patent.

Finally, the deferral of the separate national stages of the patent program can substantially alleviate financial burdens. These normally outweigh the additional fees required to undergo the PCT examination process, especially if more than three or four countries are targeted for patent protection. If the IA is filed with the U.S. PTO, fees for the search and examination will run around $1,800, plus

**Exhibit 3.5  International Patent Filing Programs: Some Options**

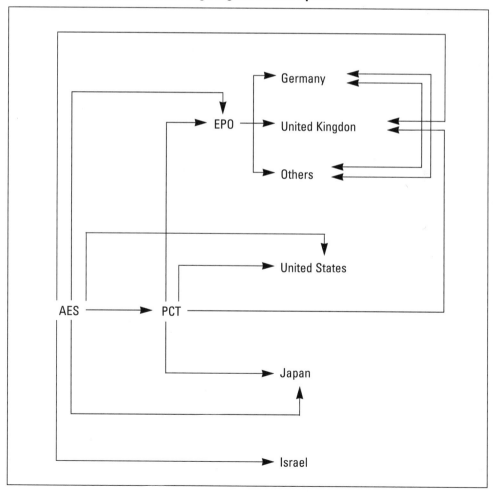

$120 per designated country (up to a maximum of $1,200). Although $3,000 may seem like a lot of money, especially to the small inventor, the importance of deferring the substantially higher national fees and costs must be considered. This is particularly true when one considers the cost of hiring translators and local patent attorneys.

As depicted in Exhibit 3.5, there are innumerable possible options of filing through the PCT. Rather than filing a U.S. patent application first, we could have filed the IA first and designated the United States along with the other countries for protection. If this were done, then the date of filing the IA would constitute the "priority filing date." Thus, the reports would be transmitted to designated countries 20 or 30 months after that filing date, depending on whether search only or examination is selected. Notice also that we selected the EPO to receive the reports. Under this option, we are requesting review under the EPC to cover countries in the European Community. Of course, we also could have designated individual European nations as well as the EPO in order to provide greater security in that region. Clearly, the most appropriate strategy to use via the PCT deserves careful attention. Also, one must always remember that not every country is a party to the PCT. For nonmember countries, national filings should be made within 12 months of the priority filing date (of the U.S. application or the IA), assuming, as is likely, that they are members of the Paris Convention.

## CONCLUSION

Decisions about how best to protect new technologies are extremely complex. Balancing the considerations involved with the patent decision alone are difficult enough. Can the PTO be convinced that the technology is novel, nonobvious, and a proper subject for protection? Will the allowable claims be broad enough? Will too much information have to be disclosed? Is the amount of protection worth the patent fees and the costs of experts and attorneys? Is the inventor/company willing to fight in court, if necessary, to preserve patent rights? Is it possible to come to grips with the vagaries of international patent protection? You now have some feel for the major concerns and benefits that must be weighed in an analysis of patent protection.

Evaluation of patent rights, however, represents only the beginning of a comprehensive business strategy for intellectual assets. Maybe patents do make sense for a particular technology. However, trade secret protection or copyright may be even better. Possibly it would be best to rely somewhat on patents, but reinforce that protection using other available means. This book proceeds to review these other major considerations, which must be strategically assessed by high-technology enterprises.

## NOTES

1. See, e.g., D. Pressman, Patent It Yourself, Nolo Press, 1989.
2. See, e.g., Schwinn Bicycle Co. v. Goodyear Tire & Rubber Co., 444 F. 2d. 295, 300 (9th Cir. 1970).

3. "A new Act . . . A New Challenge," speech by Harry F. Manbeck Jr. in PTC Newsletter (Fall 1991) at 16.

4. Omnibus Budget Reconciliation Act of 1990.

5. By January 1994, the patent application filing fee had risen to $710 ($355 for smaller companies); maintenance fees had increased to around $7,000.

6. 35 U.S.C. 111–115; 37 C.F.R. §§1.51–1.99.

7. Rule 56, effective March 16, 1992.

8. R. Gable, J. Leaheey, and A. Barlow, "The Intelligent Patent Drafter and Compliance with the Requirement of Statutory Subject Matter," Electronic and Computer Patent Law, Practising Law Institute, 1990, at 169.

9. An inventor of an invention made in the United States may not file for foreign patent protection until six months after the U.S. application is filed, unless a foreign filing license has been issued prior to this time. 35 U.S.C. §184.

10. The PTO may give the applicant from 1 to 6 months to respond. 35 U.S.C. §133.

11. 35 U.S.C. §287.

12. D. Pressman, Patent It Yourself, Nolo Press, at 13/43.

13. Certain appeals may go to the D.C. Circuit Court of Appeals. Appeals from this court will then go to the Federal Circuit.

14. In re Wands, 858 F. 2d 731, 737 (Fed. Cir. 1988).

15. There is a minor exception to this conclusion, based on what is called the reverse doctrine of equivalents. For an example of this doctrine, see Mead Digital Systems, Inc., v. A. B. Dick Co., 221 U.S.P.Q. 1035 (6th Cir. 1983).

16. Graver Tank & Mfg. Co., v. Linde Air Products Co., 339 U.S. 605, 607 (1950).

17. Ibid., at 608.

18. See, e.g., S. Rep. No. 100-83, 100th Cong., 1st Sess., 36-38 (June 23, 1987).

19. Title IX, Subtitle A, §§9001-9007 of the Omnibus Trade and Competitiveness Act of 1988, Pub. L. No. 100-418, 102 Stat. 1107, 1563–1567 (August 23, 1988), amending 35 U.S.C. §§154, 271, and 287 and adding 35 U.S.C. §295.

20. 35 U.S.C. §271(g).

21. 35 U.S.C. §287(b)(2).

22. 35 U.S.C. §287.

23. D. Moskowitz, "New Process Patent Law Could Create Headaches for Importers," Washington Post (March 6, 1989) at F16.

24. Polaroid Corp., v. Eastman Kodak Co., 16 U.S.P.Q. 2d (BNA) 1481 (D. Mass. 1990).

25. Oil & Gas J. 64 (March 17, 1986).

26. Aro Mfg. Co., v. Convertible Replacement Top Co., 377 U.S. 476, 507 (1964).

27. Section 285 provides that the court in exceptional cases may award reasonable attorney's fees to the prevailing party.

28. R. Behar, "Who Invented Microprocessors?" Time (September 10, 1990) at 62.

29. E. Radlo, "The Time to Harmonize Is Now," IEEE Grid (April 1992) at 6.

30. See M. Powers and I. Fu, "International Intellectual Property Developments in 1991: A Year of Transformation and Evolution," J. of Proprietary Rights (February 1992) at 7.

31. European Community Commission policy paper on biotechnology patents, April 18, 1991.

32. Korean Patent Law No. 3891, Art. 6(1)(i) (invention anticipated if publicly known or worked in Korea) and Art. 6(1)(ii) (invention anticipated if described in a printed publication distributed in Korea or in a foreign country), reported in Dratler, *Intellectual Property Law: Commercial, Creative, and Industrial Property*, Law Journal Seminars Press (1991 & Supp. 1994) at §2.07[2].

33. The members of the European Patent Convention are: Austria, Belgium, Denmark, France, Germany, Greece, Ireland, Italy, Lichtenstein, Luxembourg, Monaco, the Netherlands, Portugal Spain, Sweden, Switzerland, and the United Kingdom.

34. C. Berman, "Patent Cooperation Treaty: Creating New Horizons," New Matter, State Bar of California (Spring 1989) at 17.

# 4

# PROTECTION OF SECRET INFORMATION: TRADE SECRETS AND UNSOLICITED IDEAS

## INTRODUCTION

As a developer of the Audio Enhancement System (AES), you may now be a little disenchanted with the patent system as a means to protect your valuable creative ideas embedded in the invention. Clearly, the rewards from a patent are significant if its coverage is sufficiently broad. But there are substantial drawbacks as well. The costs of retaining a patent attorney to prepare the patent application and negotiate with the PTO may be hard for a new company to bear. These expenditures are particularly hard to absorb if the PTO eventually decides not to issue the patent. Even if it does, there are the rapidly increasing patent issue and maintenance fees to consider, as well as the enormous costs of seeking protection outside the United States. Further, one must factor in the potentially expensive and exhausting tasks of enforcing the patent.

Then there is the question of whether AES, which embodies computer technologies, is patentable subject matter. Also, one must evaluate whether the invention meets the high standards for patent protection. If it is not patentable, how can the invention be protected? What if the PTO determines that AES is patentable, but a federal court later disagrees? Then the important attributes of the invention will be thoroughly explained for all to use freely. Do the potential benefits from patent protection for AES justify that risk?

Even if we decide to pursue patent protection, what do we do before the invention is sufficiently finalized to file for a patent? Renegade employees entrusted with the project may decide to use the information on their own, possibly hoping to file first in various international patent offices, or simply to market their own versions of the invention. How can we be sure that those entrusted with our valuable information use it properly and maintain its confidentiality?

There are other issues as well. What if we have to approach another company to manufacture and market the system? If we are not careful, that company may attentively learn the essential concepts behind AES, and thereafter not deal with us. How do we ensure that the company pays us for our valuable ideas? Also, we must consider how rapidly the technologies embedded in AES are changing and what the reasonable marketing life of the product may be. For inventions utilizing computer technologies, it may take three years to obtain patent rights in the United States. In foreign jurisdictions, such as Japan, the wait may be even longer. If AES will be obsolete before patent rights can be obtained, then there is little point in pursuing that avenue of protection. So, what strategy should we use during the effective life of the product? In the alternative, albeit unlikely for AES, we may desire protection for a longer period of time than provided by a patent on the assumption that the invention could be lucrative for decades. Is there a reasonable way to accomplish that goal?

As noted in Chapter 1, the federal intellectual property system provides two other principal modes of protection: trademarks and copyrights. The purpose of trademarks is to help consumers identify the sources of products. Although the federal trademark system thereby may protect various external design characteristics of AES, it will not be useful for controlling the fundamental concepts behind the invention. Federal copyright protection extends to expressions, but not ideas and processes. Here, again, protection for AES likely will be insufficient. The only possible exception is for the system's computer programs. As we shall see in Chapter 6, there currently is substantial controversy over the extent of copyright protection for computer programs. Some courts take a very expansive approach, allowing copyright to protect almost all aspects of computer programs. Other courts, however, believe that copyright should play a more limited role in protecting programs. Depending on the importance of the program to the overall utility of AES, copyright protection could be a viable means of protection. At a minimum, it could provide some partial degree of support. However, in all likelihood, we will need something more than copyright to preserve the bulk of our valuable insights from use by competitors.

With all of the foregoing considerations in mind, it is no wonder that businesses turn to state trade secret laws to protect some or all of their valuable creative ideas at various stages of development. The popular press certainly has publicized the importance of trade secrets, especially to high-technology enterprises, and the efforts taken by competitors to acquire them. The dispute between Apple Computer and its founder, Steve Jobs, made headlines when Jobs formed a new company called NeXT after leaving Apple. In that situation, which was finally settled, Apple alleged that Steve Jobs had been improperly using Apple's resources and proprietary secrets to form the new company and its products.[1] More recently, attention focused on IBM's attempts to prevent a former employee from working for Seagate Technology on the grounds that the employee would divulge IBM's trade secrets.[2] Silicon Valley also was shocked by two criminal trade secret cases. The most notable involved allegations that an employee of Borland International Inc. stole valuable secrets when he left the company to join Symantec Corp.[3] In the other criminal proceeding, a former employee of Intel Corp., who later joined ULSI Technology Inc., was accused of stealing technical information and materials from Intel regarding Intel's 80387 math coprocessor.[4] Johnson & Johnson received negative attention in 1991 because of reports that it was being investigated for inappropriately using information stolen from 3M to develop a new casting tape.[5] Other controversies, such as those between Reebok and Spalding over pump technology baseball gloves and between Invitron and Monsanto over cell culture technology secrets similarly have been newsworthy.[6]

Indeed, attention to trade secrets has risen to the level of international intrigue. In 1982, the FBI arrested employees of both Hitachi and Mitsubishi for allegedly paying hundreds of thousands of dollars for stolen data regarding the IBM 3081 computer.[7] According to U.S. intelligence sources, foreign governments are taking extreme measures to acquire the secret information that gives U.S. firms their strategic and technological edge. The measures have included intercepting overseas electronic and satellite communications, using electronic bugs, interviewing foreign nationals working for U.S. firms, and having spies serve as maids in foreign hotels to snoop hotel rooms occupied by executives of U.S. companies.[8]

High-technology companies, almost without exception, have found trade secret protection to be an important component of their strategic intellectual property protection plans. The purpose of this chapter is to familiarize you with the basic concepts of trade secret protection and to propose methods that will help preserve trade secret rights. In addition, this chapter alerts you to common mistakes inexperienced inventors make when attempting to get established companies to "buy" their ideas. You may be surprised just how careful one must be before disclosing potentially lucrative commercial concepts to a major company.

## RATIONALES FOR TRADE SECRET LAWS

State trade secret policies are concerned primarily with enforcing minimum standards of commercial ethics in the competitive marketplace. These policies developed first through the common law; that is, they were created by judges to address business situations that seemed egregiously unfair and unethical. For example, in developing AES, you may have had to entrust certain employees with the novel ideas that will set the invention apart from other types of audio equipment. During the time that these employees worked for you, they may have learned which techniques help make AES succeed and which ones are failures. How would you feel if, after making all the necessary investments to perfect AES, those employees set up their own company and in order to compete with you, immediately used all they learned at your expense? Clearly, you would feel outraged and violated, as if someone had broken into your house and stolen your valuables. Likely, you would go to court, hope to convince the judge of the inequities, and request a remedy. However, unlike with common theft of objects, misappropriated information cannot simply be returned to the rightful owner. Thus, your only hope is that the judge orders the employees both not to use the information and not to tell others who might use it.

The employees may see the situation in an altogether different light. First, they may argue that they did not take anything that really belonged exclusively to you. They may show that the information used was known by others in the field. Sure, they may have learned the information from your business, but that does not mean you have the right to control it. Many employees learn common technical skills on the job. Just because the employer invested in training the employees does not mean the employees cannot use the acquired skills in other jobs. Also, if others know of the information, who is to say that the employees did not learn it from those other sources? On top of this, employees may question how the information could be competitively valuable if competitors already know it. The bottom line of this defense is that if the information was not secret within your business organization and relationships, then the employees have done nothing wrong by using it.

Another argument the employees might raise is that they did not know they were using information you considered to be your secret and expected to be kept in confidence. Employees are exposed to all kinds of information on the job. It would be unreasonable for you to expect them to know just which information you considered to be proprietary and which you did not. Rather, you had some obligation to inform them. Indeed, how could you expect them to treat information as secret if you did not take particular steps to keep the secrets yourself? If you allow documents containing the information to lie on a receptionist's desk in a public waiting room, for instance, it would be hard for you to claim that you expected the information to be maintained in secrecy.

Trade secret policies attempt to balance the claims of the employers with those who wish to use information. The employers' position is that they will not be adequately compensated for their creative investments if those persons who must be entrusted with it cannot be prevented from using it for their personal benefit. Likewise, if competitors can freely use information acquired though inappropriate forms of espionage, then employers will have to concentrate inordinately on fortifying the premises rather than on making valuable contributions to society. The counterposition is that the information was not secret, was not treated sufficiently as a secret, or could not provide a competitive advantage. To balance these concerns, trade secret policies generally protect an employer's information from misappropriation by employees or others if the information is competitively valuable, is secret, and has been the subject of reasonable security measures. Protection is achieved, when appropriate, through court-ordered injunctions against use or disclosure and through monetary damage awards.

Those who oppose trade secret protection also might claim such state laws interfere with federal patent policies. After all, patent laws provide a carefully circumscribed right of protection against the backdrop of free competition in ideas and information. If the information is not the subject of a patent, should it not be free for all to use? The answer to this is a qualified yes. The fundamental notion of free competition does not necessarily condone unethical competition. It is one thing to acquire a product legitimately and tear it apart to figure out how it works. Such a practice, called reverse engineering, fits within the moral constructs of free competition and must be allowed under state law to conform with patent policies. However, stealing the information or using it in violation of a fiduciary responsibility is a whole different ball game, appropriately subject to state law. This is why state trade secret laws prohibit misappropriation but explicitly permit acquisition of the information through reverse engineering. One also may question whether state trade secret laws, which protect the secrecy of information, conflict with the disclosure principles of patent policies. The following landmark Supreme Court case thoughtfully considers the purposes of trade secret policies and addresses why such policies do not conflict with federal patent laws.

## KEWANEE OIL COMPANY V. BICRON CORPORATION

*United States Supreme Court, 1974*

### Facts

In 1949, Harshaw Chemical, a division of Kewanee, commenced research into the growth of synthetic crystals, which are useful in the detection of ionizing radiation. At that time, the company was not able to produce a crystal exceeding 2 inches in diameter. By 1966, as a result of expenditures in excess of $1 million, Harshaw was able to grow a 17-inch crystal, something no one else had done. Harshaw developed many processes, procedures, and manufacturing techniques to accomplish this feat. Many of those techniques it considered to be trade secrets.

The individual defendants were employees of Harshaw. Each of them had signed nondisclosure agreements requiring them not to disclose or use confidential information or trade secrets obtained as employees. These individuals became associated with Bicron, which was formed in 1969 to compete with Harshaw in the production of the crystals. By April 1970, Bicron had grown a 17-inch crystal.

Kewanee sued Bicron and the individuals for trade secret misappropriation under Ohio's state trade secret laws. The district court granted an injunction until such time as the trade secrets had been released to the public or had been obtained by the defendants from sources having the legal rights to convey the information.

The Court of Appeals reversed. Although it found that trade secrets had been misappropriated, it concluded that Ohio's state trade secret laws conflicted with the federal patent laws. The Court of Appeals reasoned that the state of Ohio could not grant monopoly protection to processes that were appropriate subjects for patent protection but that had been in public use for over one year, thereby making them ineligible for patent protection under Section 102(b). Kewanee appealed to the Supreme Court.

## Opinion

The protection accorded a trade secret holder is against the disclosure or unauthorized use of a trade secret by those to whom the secret has been confided under the express or implied restriction of nondisclosure or nonuse. The law also protects the holder of a trade secret against disclosure or use when the knowledge is gained, not by the owner's volition, but by some improper means, which may include theft, wiretapping, or aerial reconnaissance. A trade secret, however, does not offer protection against discovery by fair and honest means, such as by independent invention, accidental disclosure, or by reverse engineering, that is, by starting with the known product and working backward to divine the process that aided in its development or manufacture.

Novelty, in the patent law sense, is not required for a trade secret. However, some novelty will be required if merely because that which does not possess novelty is usually known; secrecy in the context of trade secrets thus implies at least minimal novelty.

The question of whether the trade secret law of Ohio is void under the Supremacy Clause involves consideration of whether that law stands as an obstacle to the accomplishment and execution of the full purposes and objectives of Congress. To determine whether the Ohio law clashes with the federal law, it is helpful to examine the objectives of both the patent and trade secret laws.

The patent laws promote progress in science and useful arts by offering a right of exclusion for a limited period as an incentive to inventors to risk often enormous costs in terms of time, research, and development. In return for the right of exclusion—the reward for invention—the patent laws impose a requirement of full disclosure.

The maintenance of standards of commercial ethics and the encouragement of invention are the broadly stated policies behind trade secret law. Trade secret protection is important to the subsidization of research and development and to increased economic efficiency within large companies through the dispersion of responsibilities for creative developments.

Trade secret laws can protect items, such as customer lists and advertising campaigns, which are not proper subjects for patent protection under Section 101. For these items not amenable to patents, there is no reason to apply for patent protection. Abolition of trade secret protection, therefore, would not result in increased disclosure of these nonpatentable discoveries. On the other hand, keeping such items secret encourages businesses to initiate new and individualized plans of operation, and constructive competition results. This, in turn, leads to a greater variety of business methods than would otherwise be the case if privately developed marketing and other data were passed illicitly among firms involved in the same enterprise.

The question remains whether those items that are proper subjects for consideration for a patent may also have available the alternative protection accorded by trade secret law. Certainly the patent policy of encouraging invention is not disturbed by the existence of another form of incentive to invention. Similarly, the policy that matter once in the public domain must remain in the public domain is not incompatible with the existence of trade secret protection. By definition, a trade secret has not been placed in the public domain.

The more difficult objective of patent law to reconcile with trade secret law is that of disclosure. For this analysis, it is instructive to distinguish between three categories of trade secrets: (1) the trade secret for which the owner knows a valid patent cannot be obtained, (2) the trade secret for which patentability is dubious, and (3) the trade secret for which the owner believes a valid patent could be obtained.

As to the trade secret known not to meet the standards of patentability, very little in the way of disclosure would be accomplished by abolishing trade secret protection. The reasoning is analogous to that for trade secrets of nonpatentable subject matter. In this scenario, trade secret protection does not conflict with disclosure policies and has a decidedly beneficial effect on society. Without trade secret protection, innovative individuals would engage in increased self-help to maintain secrecy. Knowledge would be widely dispersed among the employees of those companies still active in research. Security precautions necessarily would be increased, and officer salaries would have to be made sufficient to ensure their loyalty. Smaller companies would be placed at a distinct economic disadvantage, for the costs of self-help could be great, and the cost to the public to use the invention would increase. Without the ultimate assurance of legal protection against breaches of confidence, innovative entrepreneurs with only limited resources would tend to confine their research efforts to themselves and those few whom they felt they could trust. As a result, organized scientific and technological research could become fragmented and society would suffer.

Another problem that would arise if trade secret protection were precluded is in the area of licensing others to exploit secret processes. The holder of a trade secret would not likely share the secret with a manufacturer who could not be placed under a binding legal obligation to protect the secret. The result would be to hoard rather than disseminate knowledge. Instead of licensing others to use the invention and making the most efficient use of existing manufacturing and marketing structures within the industry, the trade secret holder would either limit the utilization of the invention or engage in the time-consuming and wasteful enterprise of constructing duplicative manufacturing and marketing mechanisms to exploit the invention. The detrimental misallocation of resources and economic waste that would thus take place if trade secret protection were abolished with respect to employees or licensees cannot be justified by reference to any policy that the federal patent law seeks to advance.

The next category consists of trade secrets for which there is a legitimate doubt regarding patentability. In most cases of genuine doubt, the potential rewards of patent protection are so far superior to those of trade secrets that the holders of such inventions will seek patent protection rather than rely on trade secret laws. Some may not wish to undergo the costs and risks of patent protection, even if trade secret protection were not available. Considering them, abolishing trade secret protection would only harm society, as discussed previously. It is true that if trade secret protection were not available, some inventors who are unsure about the patentability of their inventions would more likely give patent protection a try. Some of these would not receive a patent, and the discoveries would remain a secret anyway. Others, however, would receive a patent, and disclosure would take place. Overall, though, we cannot say that this speculative gain outweighs the potential deleterious effect on society that would result from the elimination of trade secret protection.

The final category of patentable subject matter to deal with is the clearly patentable invention. It is here that the federal interest in disclosure is at its peak. If a state law were to dissuade these inventors from relying on the patent system, then the law would have to fall. However, in the case of trade secret law, there is no reasonable risk of deterrence from patent application by those who can expect to be granted patents.

Trade secret law provides far weaker protection in many respects than does patent law. Whereas trade secret law does not forbid the discovery of the trade secret by fair and honest means, for instance by independent creation or reverse engineering, patent law does. The trade secret holder also takes a substantial risk that the secret will be passed on to competitors by theft or breach of confidence in a manner not easily susceptible to proof. Where patent law acts as a barrier, trade secret law functions relatively as a sieve. The possibility that inventors who believe their invention meets the standards of patentability will sit back, rely on trade secret law, and after one year of use forfeit any right to patent protection is remote indeed.

Nor does society face much risk that scientific or technological progress will be impeded from the rare inventor with a patentable invention who chooses trade secret protection over patent protection. The history of the inventive process indicates that even if inventors keep an invention entirely to themselves, there is a high probability that the invention will be independently developed by others. And if the invention, though protected as a trade secret, is put into public use, then the competition is alerted of the inventor's solution to the problem and may be encouraged to make extra efforts to independently find that solution thus known to be possible. We therefore conclude that the extension of trade secret protection to clearly patentable inventions does not conflict with the patent policy of disclosure.

Trade secret law and patent law have coexisted in this country for over 100 years. Each has its particular role to play, and the operation of one does not take away from the need for the other. Trade secret law encourages the development and exploitation of those items of lesser or different invention than might be accorded patent protection, but which still have an important part to play in the technological and scientific advancement of the nation. Trade secret law promotes the sharing of knowledge and the efficient operation of industry; it permits individual inventors to reap the rewards of their labor by contracting with a company large enough to develop and exploit it. Congress, by its silence over these many years, has seen the wisdom of allowing the states to enforce trade secret protection. Until Congress takes affirmative action to the contrary, states are free to grant protection to trade secrets.

The judgment of the Court of Appeals is reversed, and the order of the district court is reinstated.

---

*Kewanee Oil* clearly addresses the recognized purposes of trade secret laws. The Supreme Court put substantial weight on the importance of such protection in a limited distribution environment: to research and development, manufacturing, and marketing efforts within organizations or among different companies working on projects. The court also rested its judgment heavily on the relative weakness of trade secret protection compared to patent protection. In this regard, the ability of consumers or others who legally acquire products to reverse-engineer is seen as critical. You should keep this notion in mind when we evaluate "shrink-wrap licenses" in Chapter 6. Shrink-wrap licenses are used particularly by developers of computer software to keep purchasers of their widely distributed programs from discovering trade secrets through reverse engineering. As we shall see in Chapter 6, one court has found such licenses to violate federal copyright policies. However, in light of *Kewanee Oil*, they also may have dubious legality in the face of federal patent laws.

## IMPORTANT ASPECTS OF TRADE SECRET LAWS

Trade secret policies developed first in the states through the common law. In 1939, the American Law Institute summarized the prevailing common law doctrines of the various states in a treatise called the Restatement of Torts. Although this document has no binding legal effect, it greatly influences judges in various state jurisdictions and over time, has served to unify trade secret principles. In 1979, the Commissioners of Uniform State Laws devised the Uniform Trade Secrets Act (UTSA). The UTSA represents a model for state legislatures to follow in passing legislative statutes that explicitly codify trade secret policies. As of 1994, over 35 states, including California, Connecticut, and Virginia have passed statutes based on the UTSA. Although there are subtle differences between the Restatement and the UTSA, the overall guiding principles are the same. The general discussion that follows concentrates on the language of the UTSA, but it applies equally well to states relying on the common law principles of the Restatement. We shall see this later in this chapter when reviewing *Integrated Cash Management Services*, a New York case that discusses trade secrets in terms of the Restatement and bases its decision on it. Exhibit 4.1 provides a brief overview of the trade secret protection policies that will be considered in this chapter.

## The Uniform Trade Secrets Act

**Definition of Trade Secret.** Under the UTSA, a trade secret holder is entitled to remedies when the trade secret has been misappropriated. Thus, an analysis of one's rights under the UTSA requires an understanding of what information constitutes a trade secret and what type of conduct amounts to misappropriation.

The UTSA defines a trade secret as:

> information, including a formula, pattern, compilation, program, device, method, technique or process, that:
>
> (i) derives independent economic value, actual or potential, from not being generally known to, and not being readily ascertainable by proper means by, other persons who can obtain economic value from its disclosure or use, and
>
> (ii) is the subject of efforts that are reasonable under the circumstances to maintain its secrecy.

This definition indicates that there are three essential components to a trade secret. The first concerns the type of information that may constitute a trade secret. This condition is easy to satisfy since the breadth of the definition seemingly permits trade secret protection to extend to any kind of information, whether it be related to financial, technical, marketing, or organizational topics. Thus, trade secret protection may apply to engineering information, formulas, customer information and lists, sources for raw materials, manufacturing processes, design manuals, operating and pricing policies, market research studies, equipment and machinery, computer software and flow charts, and drawings and blueprints. Indeed, knowledge about negative results—that certain techniques or processes are not effective, for instance—also comes within the ambit of acceptable trade secret information. Clearly, trade secret protection covers a much wider array of business interests than does patent protection, which is limited to useful processes, machines, and compositions.

The second fundamental aspect of a trade secret is that it be economically valuable because it is not known or easily ascertained by those who might benefit from it. Thus, it is not enough that the information have value; it must be valuable because it provides an advantage not yet widely available to others in the industry. For instance, a production technique that improves efficiency may be economically valuable even when those in the industry have thorough knowledge about it and widely use it. However, this form of economic value would not be the type required for a trade secret. Rather, the value has to be derived from the relative secrecy. Also, it is not enough to show that the general public does not know the information. The question is whether those who might profitably use the information know about it. A programming technique, for example, may not be known to the average member of the public, but if it is generally known by computer programmers, or even known by the principal competitor in the field, that will be enough to destroy its trade secret status. Economic value also is a function of how fast others can learn the information by proper means. Here, proper means involves learning about the information through reverse engineering, independent invention, observation in a public forum, or the reading of

## Exhibit 4.1  Important Aspects of Trade Secret Protection Policies in the United States

### State Laws

- Uniform Trade Secrets Act
- Restatement of Torts

### Elements of a Trade Secret

- Valuable information
- Secrecy
- Reasonable security measures

### Offense of Misappropriation

- Acquisition by improper means
- Disclosure or use when reasonably should know that such actions breach fiduciary duties to maintain secrecy
  — Implied through employment relationship
  — Confidentiality agreements
- Disclosure or use when reasonably should know that trade secret comes from a person who used improper means to acquire it
- Disclosure or use when reasonably should know that trade secret comes from a person who breached a fiduciary duty to maintain secrecy

### Proving Misappropriation

- High investment in trade secret
- Access by alleged misappropriator
- Fast development by alleged misappropriator

### Remedies for Trade Secret Misappropriation

- Injunctions
  — For actual or threatened misappropriation
  — Preliminary and permanent
  — Impact on employee mobility
- Criminal remedies

### Case: *Integrated Cash Management v. Digital Transactions*

published literature. For example, if competitors can quickly discern or learn about the unique features of a product once it hits the market, then the secrecy of the information before product release ultimately may yield no commercial benefits. Putting all this in a nutshell, one could say that economic value is simply a function of whether any real advantage can be obtained from secrecy.

The third requirement for trade secret status is that the information be subject to reasonable measures to preserve its secrecy. Since the first two criteria are normally somewhat easy to meet, this factor often is the most important focus of attention. Such a requirement is completely logical. If one does not recognize the importance of secrecy to the value of the information and thus take reasonable steps to maintain that value, then there is no reason to expect the law to come to the rescue. In addition, one cannot expect others to respect the value of secrecy unless one demonstrates a personal commitment to preserving it. Finally, information will not be economically valuable for long if reasonable efforts are not undertaken to maintain its secrecy. The measures one might contemplate to maintain the secrecy of information will be discussed further in the next section.

**Misappropriation.** The UTSA prohibits misappropriation of trade secrets. The definition of "misappropriation" specifically covers a broad range of unethical acts. However, they are all grounded on similar philosophical principles. Misappropriation occurs (1) when one acquires a trade secret by improper means or acquires it from another person reasonably knowing that the person used improper means to get it, (2) when one discloses or uses a trade secret reasonably knowing that such conduct violates a duty to maintain silence, (3) when one who reasonably knows of the impropriety discloses or uses a trade secret that was received from another person who used improper means to get it, or (4) when one who reasonably knows about the fiduciary breach uses or discloses a trade secret that was disclosed by another under a fiduciary duty to maintain silence.[9] Thus, the key elements to misappropriation are whether one acquired the trade secret by improper means, whether one handled the information in a way that breaches a duty to maintain secrecy, and whether there was sufficient awareness about the violation of trade secret rights.

By the terms of the UTSA, improper means includes "theft, misrepresentation, breach or inducement of a breach of a duty to maintain secrecy, or espionage through electronic or other means." This definition is probably just what you expected. In general, activities that illegitimately interfere with a person's expectations of privacy are improper. However, one always must keep in mind the interplay of improper conduct and the security measures the trade secret holder reasonably should take to thwart it. So, consider a competitor who takes a public tour of your facilities. While the group is asking questions, the competitor sneaks into a room and takes pictures. Clearly, this is improper. However, you probably should have taken steps to ensure that the competitor could not wander into private areas of particular importance. Thus, although the conduct may have been improper, it may not be unlawful because the information taken may not have been sufficiently protected to be a trade secret. One final point to remember, as explained in *Kewanee Oil*, is that reverse engineering and independent creation are never improper. Some states that have adopted the UTSA, such as California, make this abundantly clear by explicitly excluding such conduct from the definition of improper means.[10]

Another relevant consideration for certain acts of misappropriation is whether there is sufficient awareness about fiduciary duties to maintain silence. Such a duty to preserve secrecy may arise in two ways: either by implication from one's relationship with the trade secret holder or through express agreement. When a person becomes an employee, the law will imply a confidential relationship even though there was no explicit discussion about maintaining secrets. Therefore, an employee has a duty not to use or disclose information the employee reasonably should know is a trade secret of the employer. When employees appear to have misappropriated trade secrets, employers face the problem of proving that the employees were reasonably aware that they were dealing with secret and valuable information. There are a number of ways that the employer can reasonably inform the employee. How the employer treats the information is a start. If the information is strictly controlled in a guarded environment and released only on a need-to-know basis, for instance, then the employee should be intuitively cognizant that the employer values the secrecy of the information. If the employer puts a written legend on the cover of the information, explicitly stating that it is confidential proprietary information, then the message is even more direct.

The employer can take a further step, however, which strengthens an employee's awareness of fiduciary responsibility and focuses attention on the particular information covered by such confidential obligations. This action, which is highly advisable for all business dealing with trade secrets, is to have employees enter explicit confidentiality agreements. Confidentiality agreements make it very clear to new employees that they will be dealing with trade secrets in the business and that they have a duty to maintain the secrecy of that information by not using or disclosing it during and after the employment relationship. In addition, the agreements should indicate with as much specificity as possible the types of information the employer considers sensitive, and to which the confidentiality obligations clearly apply. Express confidentiality agreements, especially in conjunction with other security measures, are very effective in defeating employees' claims that they knew neither their general obligations to maintain the confidentiality of trade secrets nor the specific information they were supposed to keep secret. In addition, they make it clear at the outset of employment that the employer is very serious about maintaining the security of important trade secret information.

Problems with employees frequently arise when employees use their own knowledge and skills to develop valuable trade secret information. The most pressing question results when an employee leaves the firm and begins work on a similar project elsewhere. The employer has rights to the trade secrets for which it bargained and paid. Valuable secret information developed on the job or under contract rightly belongs to the hiring party. In addition, the employer has trade secret rights to specific information that employees or third parties agree in employment contracts belongs to the employer. The employer does not have rights, however, to the general knowledge and skills that employees originally bring to the job. The problem is that it may be very difficult to determine where the preexisting knowledge ends and the trade secrets begin. In postdeparture disputes, the former employer will claim trade secret misappropriation while the employee will argue that only native skills and abilities are being used in the new project— just as they were for the former employer. This debate is one of the important issues that faced the court in *Integrated Cash Management*, presented later in this chapter.

Fiduciary obligation to maintain secrecy may extend beyond the employment relationship. As indicated in *Kewanee Oil*, firms often must divulge trade secrets to third parties so that they can efficiently assist in achieving certain mutual goals, such as research and development, manufacturing, or marketing. Express agreements to maintain confidentiality are even more important in this setting because proof of implied obligations is harder to sustain. Thus, in dealings outside the firm, it would be a mistake to assume that the other parties know that you expect certain information to be kept secret. Rather, it is critical to have confidentiality agreements signed before any trade secret information is presented. In addition, as will be explained in the next section, the firm will have to implement additional safeguards as well to preserve the secrecy of its valuable information.

Clearly, it is important that those who work for or directly with the trade secret holder understand the sensitive nature of proprietary information. When done appropriately, an employer may seek trade secret remedies against those individuals if they are caught divulging or using the information improperly. However, what if a former employee discloses the information to another party or simply uses it in developing a new product for a subsequent employer? Are there any rights against these recipients? Such an occurrence requires a careful balancing of equitable rights. To understand the complex issues often involved, it is helpful to consider the extremes first. On one end of the spectrum, a competitor who pays a recalcitrant employee specifically to divulge trade secrets is no different from a co-conspirator to the misappropriation. In this situation, it is philosophically easy to treat the competitor as if it had committed the wrongful act and accordingly, hold it responsible to the extent of the law. On the other hand, that same employee may simply take another job and unbeknownst to the new employer, use the information in developing, manufacturing, and/or marketing the new employer's new products. What makes this situation different is the total absence of knowledge. Here, the new employer is just as innocent as the deprived trade secret holder, and it is therefore conceptually difficult to find the new employer legally responsible for what happened. Of course, the equities in most situations are not so clear-cut. For instance, the new employer may hire a technical expert to work on a project knowing the expert had once worked on a similar secret project for a competitor. Although the new employer may not specifically know that secret information is being used, the employer should be on notice of the potential for misappropriation.

The UTSA strives to find the right balance based on the degree of knowledge the recipient should have had under the circumstances. One engages in misappropriation when one acquires, uses, or discloses information knowing that it contains misappropriated trade secrets. An individual also misappropriates if a reasonable person, based on the situation, would have been aware that misappropriated trade secrets were involved. One can apply these standards to the case brought by Minnesota Mining and Manufacturing (3M) alleging that Johnson & Johnson (J&J) had misappropriated secrets from 3M about a new casting tape and had infringed 3M patents.[11] An employee of 3M sent a stolen sample of the new tape to J&J, offering to explain the technology for a fee.[12] J&J did not accept the offer. However, an executive at J&J sent the sample to the J&J laboratory for analysis. J&J chemists were never instructed not to use the results of the analysis in developing J&J products, and so they employed the technology in a competing product.[13] Given these facts, one can conclude that responsible executives at J&J knew or reasonably should have known that J&J's new casting product benefited from trade secret information wrongfully taken from 3M. For this reason, the court ruled that J&J had unlawfully misappropriated trade secrets from 3M. Moreover, the behavior helped persuade the court that J&J willfully infringed 3M's casting tape patents, allowing the court to double the overall damages.[14]

Sometimes, a recipient has no way of knowing about the trade secret status of certain information until the trade secret holder finds out what's going on and then hurriedly brings it to the recipient's attention. If the innocent recipient has done little with the information, it is easy to settle the situation by simply preventing its further use. However, before being informed, the recipient may have invested in new production equipment and begun sales of a new line of products. Now, it might be too harsh to require the recipient to stop manufacturing or sales. To equitably handle this situation, the UTSA allows a judge tremendous flexibility to devise remedies.[15] For instance, rather than issue an injunction, the court may allow the recipient to continue its use of the trade secrets but require it to make reasonable royalty payments for the privilege.[16]

Third parties must be reasonably aware that they are dealing with misappropriated trade secret information before a trade secret holder may have a remedy against them. One technique used by employers is to have employees agree to the following kind of provision in their confidentiality agreements:

> The employer may notify anyone employing me or evidencing an intention to employ me as to the existence and provisions of this Agreement.

Now when the employee changes jobs, the employer may notify the new company about the employee's former duties and the employee's obligations to maintain secrecy about certain kinds of information and projects. Alerting the new company in this manner makes it easier, if necessary, to prove that its executives should have known that the employee would use trade secrets. To protect itself, the new company may take its own steps in its employment agreements. For instance, it likely will make employees promise that they will not use or disclose trade secrets of former employers or others. In this way, the new company tries to demonstrate its good faith in attempting to prevent misappropriation on its premises.

**Proving Misappropriation.** Proving that trade secrets were improperly used or disclosed often is very difficult. For instance, suppose one of your employees quits the job and begins work with a competitor in a similar capacity. Soon thereafter, the competitor comes out with a product that is suspiciously similar to your most important commercial development—one that relies on some carefully guarded secrets. It would be nice if you had direct evidence that the former employee had disclosed or used secret information. Perhaps you could discover a photocopy of a key document in the competitor's files. Or maybe someone will testify how your secrets were used. It is more than likely, however, that such direct proof will be unavailable. Thus, proof will have to be made by circumstantial evidence. Normally, a trade secret holder will try to prove misappropriation circumstantially by showing (1) that it spent large sums of money and spent considerable time developing the secret information, (2) that the alleged misappropriator had access to that information, and (3) that the alleged misappropriator developed its functionally similar product in substantially less time and with fewer resources. The importance of this kind of proof is evident in *Kewanee Oil*, wherein defendants took less than 1 year to produce a crystal that had been developed by the plaintiffs over a 17-year period of expensive trials. Likewise, when you read *Integrated Cash Management*, you will see the same kind of reasoning being used to prove the misappropriation of trade secrets.

Keep in mind the importance of the common employee in these examples to prove access. What if your competitor came out with its similar product but you did not have an explanation such as employee mobility? You are intuitively certain that misappropriation somehow occurred, but you are unable to find the link. Maybe a judge will be persuaded by the similarities alone, if they are sufficiently extraordinary, but that is not likely. Always remember that even if valuable information is misappropriated, trade secret law is not helpful without proof. This is another reason why trade secrets should be closely guarded: not only does such guarding establish the existence of a protectible secret, but it helps ensure that misappropriation, and the associated problems of proof, do not arise at all.

**Remedies for Trade Secret Misappropriation.** The UTSA provides a trade secret holder with a number of remedies for unlawful misappropriation. Of these, the most potent are court-ordered injunctions preventing use or disclosure of the secrets. According to the UTSA, actual or threatened misappropriation of trade secrets may be enjoined. It should not seem surprising that, when a trade secret holder can prove in court that an individual stole trade secrets through espionage, the judge may use judicial powers to prevent use or disclosure of the unlawfully obtained secrets. Similarly, when an employee forms a competitive company and uses the secrets in its operations, a court may issue an injunction preventing further use of the secrets. Likewise, when the employee joins another company and uses the secrets to aid that competitor, then an injunction is appropriate.

All of these are examples of actual misappropriation, and injunctive relief raises little controversy. In such situations, the debate often involves the length of the injunction, that is, the period of time the misappropriator will be prevented from using the secrets. For instance, suppose a company is subject to an injunction for having misappropriated a trade secret. What happens if that information somehow becomes publicly available? Should the misappropriator still be subject to the injunction even after it could otherwise legally obtain and use the information? According to the UTSA, the misappropriator may apply to the court to remove the injunction once the trade secret has ceased to exist. However, the court may continue the injunction for an additional period if needed to eliminate any head-start or other commercial advantage that the misappropriator might enjoy by virtue of the earlier misappropriation.

Judges also have tremendous flexibility to fashion the length of the injunction from the outset depending on the equities of the situation. In one case, for instance, employees who misappropriated confidential customer lists were enjoined for 15 months from soliciting those customers. The length of the injunction was based on the court's determination of the time it would take diligent salespersons to independently discover the valued customer names.[17] *Integrated Cash Management Services* provides another illustration of the flexibility judges have in fashioning injunctions.

## INTEGRATED CASH MANAGEMENT SERVICES, INC. V. DIGITAL TRANSACTIONS, INC.

*United States District Court. New York. 1989*
*Affirmed, Second Circuit Court of Appeals, 1990*

### Facts

Integrated Cash Management Services (ICM) designs and develops computer utility programs. ICM's programs are marketed to banks, which in turn market them to the financial and treasury departments of various corporations. ICM develops generic programs, which may be readily customized to suit a particular client's specifications, thereby reducing the need for computer consultants. The ICM programs at issue are: (1) SEUNIMNT, a generic universal database management system; (2) Telefon, a generic communications program; (3) Menu System/Driver, a treasury workstation program; and (4) Report Writer, a financial report customizing program. The generic programs are able to work together to form a unified generic utility system.

Newlin and Vafa each worked for ICM. Newlin was employed as a computer programmer between 1984 and March 1987. While an ICM employee, Newlin wrote the Communications and Menu modules of the ICM system. He also assisted in writing the SEUNIMNT program in the computer language called C and in writing an initial version of the Report Writer module for ICM. Vafa was employed by ICM as a computer programmer between 1986 and March 1987. Vafa collaborated with Newlin in creating Report Writer and the C-language version of SEUNIMNT. Vafa and Newlin had particular trouble designing Report Writer so that it would work with the rest of the system. ICM expended substantial time and money with different formulations of the Report Writer before developing a suitable version. Both Newlin and Vafa signed nondisclosure agreements with ICM in which they agreed not to disclose or use any confidential or proprietary information of ICM upon leaving the company's employ.

Newlin and Vafa left ICM on March 13, 1987, and formed Digital Transactions, Inc. (DTI), three days later. Within two weeks, DTI had created a prototype database program. That program, and other generic programs subsequently produced for DTI by Newlin and Vafa, were similar to comparable ICM programs. In addition, the overall architecture of the DTI system, which allows the individual programs to work together, was substantially similar to that developed by ICM. ICM sued DTI, alleging that Newlin, Vafa, and another individual formerly linked to ICM had misappropriated trade secrets.

## Opinion

A plaintiff claiming misappropriation of a trade secret must prove (1) it possessed a trade secret, and (2) defendant is using that trade secret either in breach of an agreement, confidence, or duty or as a result of discovery by improper means. DTI contends that the architecture of ICM's system is not a trade secret. This court disagrees.

The most comprehensive and influential definition of a trade secret is that set out in the Restatement of Torts. The definition provides that a "trade secret may consist of any formulation, pattern, device or compilation of information which is used in one's business, and which gives him an opportunity to obtain an advantage over competitors who do not know or use it." In determining whether a trade secret exists, the New York courts have considered the following factors to be relevant:

(1) the extent to which the information is known outside the business; (2) the extent to which it is known by employees and others involved in the business; (3) the extent of measures taken to guard the secrecy of the information; (4) the value to the information to the business and competitors; (5) the amount of effort or money expended in developing the information; and (6) the ease or difficulty with which the information could be properly acquired or duplicated by others.

Applying these factors to the software programs at issue in this case, it is evident that ICM retains a protectible trade secret in its product.

The manner in which ICM's generic utility programs interact, which is the key to the product's success, is not generally known outside ICM. DTI presented evidence that the various components of the ICM system are not secret but are available to the public through books, commercially sold products, and scholarly publications. However, a trade secret can exist in a combination of characteristics and components each of which, by itself, is in the public domain but whose unified process, design, and operation, in unique combination, affords a competitive advantage.

Here, the way in which ICM's various components fit together as building blocks in order to form the unique whole is secret. ICM's combination of programs was not disclosed in ICM's promotional literature, which contains merely a user-oriented description of the advantages of ICM's product. Such limited information does not contain sufficient technical detail to constitute disclosure of the product's architecture. The package as a whole, and the specifications used by ICM to make the parts of that package work together, are not in the public domain.

Clearly, ICM has made reasonable efforts to maintain the secrecy of the source code of its programs. The doors to the premises were kept locked. Also, employees, including Newlin and Vafa, were required to sign nondisclosure agreements, which provided that "when employment is terminated, the former employee agrees not to use, copy or disclose any of ICM's secrets, software products, software tools or any type of information and software which belongs to ICM."

The remaining factors to be considered in ascertaining the existence of a trade secret are also satisfied. The court is satisfied about the value of the programs to ICM and its competitors. Also, it is not disputed that ICM made large investments in research and development. In this regard, the court notes that a significant amount of time and money was spent in investigating alternatives that, in the end, were not fruitful. Such a trial-and-error process is also protectible as a trade secret. Finally, expert testimony reveals that the ICM product's architecture could not be readily duplicated without the secret information acquired by ICM through years of research. Therefore, we find that ICM's winning combination of generic utility programs is a trade secret.

Having found the existence of a trade secret, the court must next decide whether the defendants misused that secret information in creating their own system. The difficulty here results from the need to preserve the proprietary information of ICM while at the same time not unduly restricting Newlin and Vafa from utilizing their admittedly extensive skills, experience, and general knowledge. This is especially the case when, as here, there exists a situation in which no direct copying occurred. Certainly, an employee who achieves technical expertise or general knowledge while in the employ of another may thereafter use that knowledge in competition with that former employer, so long as the employee (or ex-employee) does not use or disclose protected trade secrets in the process.

Certain factors help fashion a just result. One important factor is the existence of a nondisclosure agreement, since it puts the employee on notice about the nature and existence of trade secrets. In this case, Vafa and Newlin were well aware of their duties not to disclose secrets of ICM. Defendants assert that the DTI programs were created from scratch and that Vafa and Newlin approached their tasks with fresh minds. It is a well-recognized principle that when a defendant in a trade secret case claims independent development, the burden shifts to the defendant to show that this was in fact the case. Defendants have not sustained the burden here.

The court does not doubt defendants' good intentions and professional integrity. However, it seems impossible for them to develop a competing system for DTI without dwelling upon their experience from ICM and in the process incorporating into any system for DTI many of the valuable, confidential, and proven-workable features in ICM's systems. Newlin and Vafa made use of information learned while at ICM concerning which functions and relationships among the modules would and would not work in the generic program. That information was maintained as a secret by ICM and was valuable to its business. Newlin and Vafa were simply too bright to make the same mistakes twice in writing the programs. Not general experience, but specific experience with, and knowledge of, those particular types of generic programs for banking and financial applications were utilized, perhaps unavoidably, by Vafa and Newlin when they chose to take up the same task at a new company.

ICM does not attempt to prevent defendants from competing with it on a fair basis. It seeks only to prevent them from creating a substantially similar system of utility programs. The four programs at issue are among approximately 1,000 programs or modules created by defendants. ICM has no complaint concerning the balance of these programs. In light of the equities, and the inadequacy of damages to compensate ICM for the misappropriation of its valuable trade secrets, injunctive relief is appropriate.

Defendants are enjoined for a period of six months from the date of this decision from utilizing, as part of DTI's systems, any versions of the database manager, menu, communications, and report writer programs created in whole or in part by either Vafa or Newlin. In addition, and for the same period, Newlin and Vafa are enjoined from contributing to the creation of any new programs embodying these utilities. DTI is otherwise free to develop new programs, provided that it does not rely on the restricted programs during the development. The period of six months has been chosen with a view to the length of time ICM spent in creating its systems, the increased speed of the current hardware available to programmers, and the need to neutralize the head start gained by DTI from the improper use of ICM's trade secrets.

Defendants also are permanently enjoined from distributing any unmodified versions of ICM's four generic utility programs in existence on the date of this decision. This prevents them from simply shelving the misappropriated information for six months, and then distributing the ICM product as their own.

---

The UTSA also gives courts the power to enjoin threatened misappropriation. The interesting question here arises when a competitor hires away an employee to perform a similar job with the new company. Employees who know valuable trade secrets have an obligation not to use those secrets in a new position. Indeed, an injunction strengthening that duty might be available. However, even an injunction preventing use or disclosure may not be very comforting to the previous employer. That employer intuitively knows that it will be impossible for the employee to work on a similar project without leaking or using some of the valuable information. And the burden of monitoring and proving such misuse may be very difficult to sustain. Thus, the previous employer may feel that the court should enjoin the employee from working in the new job at all. At the greatest extreme, the previous employer might ask the court to prevent employment of any kind for a reasonable period of time with the competitor. More typically, however, the request is to prevent the employee from working on similar projects for the competitor, as we just saw in *Integrated Cash Management*. This also was IBM's position when it sought an injunction barring Peter Bonyhard from working on Seagate Technology's project to develop magnetoresistive (MR) disk drive heads. Mr. Bonyhard had formerly headed IBM's MR development team. The district court initially granted the injunction, as IBM requested, forcing Seagate to reassign Bonyhard to a division not working on the MR heads. However, this injunction was lifted on appeal.[18] As the IBM scenario demonstrates, courts have difficulty with injunctions affecting employment because of the serious economic consequences they may create for persons who have yet to do anything wrong. Nonetheless, injunctions restricting employment have been carried out when the courts were convinced that disclosure was inevitable.[19]

Given the typical backlog in state courts for civil cases, a trade secret holder may have to wait years before fully presenting its case. In the rapidly changing environment of high technology, such a long deferral may make the lawsuit moot. By the time the case is set for trial, the secret may have become public or the technology may be obsolete. For this reason, the courts have set up a preliminary mechanism to stop illicit behavior before a case comes to trial. A trade secret holder may request that a judge issue a temporary restraining order (TRO) preventing an alleged misappropriator from using or disclosing the information until a preliminary hearing can be scheduled. The TRO usually lasts less than 10 days. At the preliminary hearing, the judge will examine the evidence and may issue a preliminary injunction preventing use or disclosure until the completion of a full trial on the merits. To obtain a preliminary injunction, the trade secret holder must prove (1) that it will suffer irreparable harm if the defendant is allowed to use the information before trial and (2) that there is a strong likelihood that it will win when the case comes to trial. A preliminary injunction puts the alleged misappropriator in a difficult position. First, the defendant now must endure the wait to compete in the contemplated way. Second, the judge has sent a strong signal that the trial will not yield positive results. Thus, those subject to a preliminary injunction often try to negotiate a settlement rather than wait for trial.

From the perspective of a company trying to protect its valuable trade secrets, pursuing preliminary and permanent injunctions is simply an honest means to further its legitimate commercial interests. However, competitors may take a different view. Many high-technology enterprises, especially small companies in the start-up phase, consider trade secret suits to be standard operating procedure for established firms to keep the new rivals "down on the farm."[20] From their vantage, established companies use trade secret litigation simply to tie up small companies that are gearing up to manufacture and market competitive products. Such suits can absorb enormous energy and dollars from the new enterprise as it attempts to fend off court-ordered injunctions. In addition, the lawsuits can have a chilling effect on venture capitalists and other financial backers. Ultimately, the small firm may have to cease operations even though its legal position was relatively strong.[21]

Without commenting on the merits of this argument, one must be aware that litigation can have powerful strategic implications. The expenses of legal disputes can be enormous, and they can have disproportionate impacts on smaller firms. On the other hand, it is likely that most trade secret suits brought by large companies do have substantial factual bases, such as employee defections and rapid development of similar products by the competitor. Indeed, the UTSA gives some protection from spurious suits by requiring one who litigates in bad faith to pay the attorney's fees of the innocent party.[22]

The UTSA also provides that a trade secret holder is entitled to damages, or monetary remuneration, for misappropriation. Damages have two components: (1) the amount needed to compensate the trade secret holder for the losses caused by the misappropriation and (2) the unjust enrichment earned by the misappropriator by virtue of the unlawful use or disclosure.[23] The techniques for determining losses for trade secret misappropriation are very similar to those used for patent infringement. For instance, the trade secret holder may demonstrate that there is an established royalty rate for using the information or that the misappropriation had a demonstrable negative affect on profits. The trade secret holder also is entitled to the profits earned by the misappropriator to the degree that they are not already accounted for in the determination of losses. In addition, as with patents, the court has the power to award a reasonable royalty rate if damages to the trade secret holder cannot otherwise be satisfactorily established. Finally, the UTSA provides for double damages and attorney's fees for willful and malicious misappropriation.[24]

Although they are not provided for in the UTSA, criminal remedies also may be applied against those who misappropriate trade secrets. Many states have criminal laws that cover the theft of trade secret information. In addition, federal criminal prosecution for trade secret misappropriation is possible based on such offenses as transporting stolen property across state lines or mail fraud. Criminal proceedings rarely are brought for trade secret misappropriation. However, as alluded to earlier, criminal actions may be on the rise. For instance, a criminal indictment was handed down in March 1993 against the CEO of Symantec Corporation, who allegedly conspired with a departing employee of Borland International to steal trade secrets from Borland. The employee also was indicted. These individuals were charged with violating a provision of the California Penal Code that prohibits theft of scientific or technical information.[25] If convicted, the defendants could be sentenced to up to six years in jail and be fined more than $100,000.[26]

## Trade Secret Protection Measures

High-technology companies with trade secrets to protect must implement an appropriate set of security measures to ensure that the information does not fall into public hands. As previously discussed, information does not rise to the protectible status of being a trade secret under the UTSA unless reasonable security measures are undertaken. In addition, one can go only so far in relying on the law to maintain the value of secret information. Suppose, for example, a competitor learns trade secret information through espionage. The competitor then uses the information in its operations and sells it to various organizations. As the use becomes more widespread, some of the informed sources handle the information in a somewhat relaxed manner. Ultimately, the secret gets out, thereby destroying any relative advantage it had previously bestowed. The UTSA provides for injunctions and damages as remedies for misappropriation. But in the case at hand it is too late for an injunction to be effective. Thus, the victim must rely on monetary damages for relief. However, the victim may find that the assets held by the misappropriators are far less than the losses sustained. And, of course, there is the very real possibility that the victim will never even determine who the misappropriators are. Without adequate proof, the law offers little protection. Therefore, for both legal and practical reasons, security is an important consideration for high-technology companies handling trade secrets.

Most sophisticated businesses give trade secret protection high priority. They recognize that a suitable plan requires a formal process of periodic review, called the trade secret audit. Since the auditors will be evaluating all of the company's trade secrets, they must be extremely trusted personnel. Often the audit team will consist of an engineer who understands the technical nature of the secrets, a security expert, an attorney, and a manager who is knowledgeable about the daily operations of the company. The goal of the team is to act in a proactive manner to continually identify trade secrets and match appropriate measures to secure them.[27]

Some companies erroneously assume that once trade secret protection measures are put in place they operate sufficiently on a form of autopilot. Although these companies think they are being diligent by having a plan at all, they really are opening themselves to trouble. Company personnel have to be constantly reminded what the trade secrets are and how they should be handled. It is surprisingly easy for an employee to be careless with, say, a sales brochure, a speech, or a tour of plant facilities. Companies with high turnover have to be especially concerned that new employees learn the required protection steps and that departing personnel understand their continuing obligations and handle them appropriately. Also, trade secrets change over time. There may be new items that should be subject to security measures. Likewise, there may be information that has lost its value but remains subject to security according to an old plan. This is simply wasteful. Generally, companies that treat trade secrets on a static basis act on the defensive, taking new steps only when some crisis arises. Such defensive management rarely substitutes adequately for conscientious planning and monitoring.

A proactive trade secret protection strategy including periodic audits is the best way to consistently dedicate the appropriate resources to the maintenance of trade secrets. Periodic review by the audit team of trade secrets and security measures enhances the prospects that valuable information will be suitably protected. Such continual evaluation substantially reduces the likelihood that secrets will get into the wrong hands. Indeed, the firm's commitment to security may deter competitors and others from even attempting to misappropriate information. In addition, if secrets are misappropriated and litigation ensues, the company will have an easier time proving to the court that the measures used to protect the secrets were sufficient to be deemed reasonable under the terms of the UTSA. Finally, the attention to security may have a positive influence on employee morale, although this is not universal. At some companies, such as Apple Computer, the degree of security is so high that the atmosphere to some may be akin to that of armed camp.[28] Certain employees may react negatively to such scrutiny, feeling that the company engages in Orwellian tactics because employees are fundamentally distrusted. Others, however, may appreciate the importance attributed by the company to the work they perform. Obviously, the audit team must give some attention to the psychological impact that the security, scrutiny, and paperwork have on employee attitudes and performance.

The duty of the audit team is to identify valuable trade secrets and formulate appropriate security measures. One mistake that companies often make is to instruct employees that everything they learn or hear on the job is valuable proprietary information that must be kept in confidence. Identifying everything as a trade secret has no instructive content; indeed, it is counterproductive. Rather than informing the employees about the items that must be handled delicately, a blanket warning sends the message that nothing deserves special treatment. A wide range of financial, organizational, marketing, and technical information may be suitable for trade secret protection. The job of the audit team is to cull through that information and specifically identify the pieces that are sufficiently valuable to be guarded.

The audit team also must determine the appropriate degree of protection merited by the various pieces of information. This decision must consider the UTSA mandate that security be reasonable. As indicated in *Integrated Cash Management*, the courts usually review whether a firm utilized a suitable combination of security measures. Although this does not provide much specific guidance, it suggests a couple of important considerations. First, it probably would be an error to rely on only one form of security measure to protect a secret. That is, locking a formula in a safe is not enough without considering who has the keys and what those keyholders are allowed to do with the information when they retrieve it. On the other hand, the firm does not have to engage in every conceivable form of security to preserve the secrecy of information.[29] Rather, it should engage in a cost/benefit analysis to arrive at that combination of measures that is appropriate under the circumstances.[30] Such an appraisal will indicate the amount and types of security that should be adopted based on the value of the secret, the ways it could be misappropriated, and the costs of the various measures that could be used for deterrence.

The number of possible security measures the audit team should consider is virtually infinite. The following list provides an overview of the variety of general measures that ought to be reviewed. Keep in mind that an appropriate plan does not have to implement all of these techniques, but rather should strike the proper balance based on a cost/benefit analysis.

*Employee Confidentiality Agreements*
Courts often consider employee confidentiality agreements to be a crucial component of trade secret security plans. As discussed before, these agreements explicitly inform the employee about the importance of trade secrets to the company and the employee's duty to maintain them in confidence. The agreements will define the types of information considered trade secrets in as much specificity as possible to avert possible future disputes about the scope of expectations. Also, the agreements may attempt to clarify ownership issues. For instance, with situations such as that in *Integrated Cash Management* in mind, the employer will

want the employee explicitly to agree that secret information developed by the employee is owned by the employer. In addition, the agreements may address issues such as the removal of important documents from the premises.

Employee confidentiality agreements generally contain other provisions as well. The employees normally agree that the employer can notify subsequent employers about their duties of confidentiality to thwart any claim that the new employer was not aware of the obligations. Employees also will promise not to use or disclose trade secrets of former employers to substantiate, if necessary, that the employer was unaware of any employee impropriety.

### Specifically Inform Employees of Trade Secrets

Employee confidentiality agreements usually can identify only general areas of trade secret concerns. Also, specific trade secrets arise over time. Thus, the employer needs other techniques to continually inform employees about information that must be held in confidence. One prevalent method is to mark sensitive documents with legends that address the trade secret obligations. For example, computer software containing trade secrets may be marked as follows:

> This computer program is proprietary to X Company and contains valuable trade secrets. It is to be kept confidential and not used unless with written consent of the owner.

As mentioned before, the employer should refrain from marking too many documents as confidential since overuse may lead employees to not take the warnings seriously.

Obviously, employees may be informed in other ways. That information is contained in a high-security area should indicate to a reasonable employee that the employer considers secrecy to be important. Also, the employer should periodically discuss continuing trade secret obligations with employees both to ensure that they do not forget their duties and to update their responsibilities.

### Physically Restrict Access to Trade Secrets

If possible, the trade secrets should be physically separated, and access should be granted to those who can demonstrate that they have a need to know the information. The following measures should be considered.

- Keep track of who enters sensitive security areas through written logs, employee badges, and/or electronic-entry security systems.
- Lock gates, cabinets, and doors; establish a routine procedure for checking the locked status, especially at the end of the working day.
- Use security systems such as guards, alarms, and closed-circuit television.
- Have one person be responsible for distributing copies of trade secrets.

### Maintain Computer System Security

Computer systems and programs often contain valuable trade secrets that may be easily accessed and copied unless safeguards are taken. Some measures are as follows.

- Use access restrictions such as passwords, which are changed regularly.
- Restrict software use to hardware within secure areas.

- Fingerprint data with phony code so that copying can be more easily proven.
- Limit distribution of source code.
- Carefully label disks with trade secret legends and use physical security measures to restrict unlawful access.
- Scramble data transmissions.

### Completely Destroy Written Information

Do not throw old documents into the trash. Competitors have a right to and sometimes do rummage though refuse outside the premises and may be able to learn essential information from seemingly innocuous documents. All written materials should be shredded before disposal.

### Do Not Provide Access to Entire Trade Secret

If possible, divide trade secret processes into steps, and have different employees or companies perform the individual procedures. KFC Corporation, for instance, protected its secret chicken recipe by having the seasonings produced in two parts by two separate companies.[31]

### Screen Repair and Service Personnel

Service providers should be referenced, and proper security enforced to limit their access to key data. This may be especially pertinent to computer service technicians.

### Restrict Plant Tours

As part of their civic and community responsibilities, companies will be called upon to demonstrate what they do and how they accomplish it. Plant tours often help serve this important function. Companies must be wary, however, that industrial spies may join these tours to try to learn delicate information. Thus, the public should be restricted from high-security areas. In addition, the tours should be carefully controlled and escorted so that participants do not wander into sensitive areas. Cameras should be forbidden. Also, the escort should be trained in fielding questions so that trade secret information is not unwittingly revealed.

### Screen Speeches, Publications, and Trade Show Materials

Executives often need to highlight the latest achievements of the firm while addressing stockholders, finance professionals, or the public. These speeches should be screened to ensure that they do not unnecessarily reveal important trade secret information about the projects. Marketing personnel trying to land deals at trade shows should be given special attention. They need to be adequately trained to deal with "prospective clients" who may pump for information about upcoming secret design specifications or the names of major clients. In addition, marketing literature and publications should be reviewed.

### Conduct Employee Exit Interviews

Before employees leave the firm, they should be reminded of their contractual and implied obligations to maintain the confidentiality of trade secrets. In addition, the firm should be careful to collect all secret documents, security passes, keys, and badges in the employee's possession.

*Deal with Third Parties Appropriately*
It often will be necessary for the firm to share trade secret information with third parties for such purposes as joint research and development or distribution. Third parties should be treated with precautions similar to those applied to employees. Thus, third-party employees who come into contact with the secrets should be required to sign confidentiality agreements defining the ownership of trade secrets and obligations to preserve secrecy. The trade secret holder also will want assurances that the third party's physical security measures are adequate, that its computer systems are secure, and that its employees are monitored.

If the trade secret holder needs assistance from or furnishes services to a third party but does not want that company to learn trade secrets in the process, then additional steps will have to be taken to prevent disclosure. For example, with computer software, the trade secret holder may provide only object code and require the recipient to pledge not to reverse-engineer that code through decompilation and disassembly. Some computer software companies have gone so far as to extend these steps to ordinary consumers through shrink-wrap licenses. As suggested earlier, such wide-scale attempts to prevent reverse engineering probably run afoul of federal patent and/or copyright policies.

*Make Covenants Not to Compete*
When employees leave a high-technology company, they often have learned several important trade secrets. Although these employees have implied and contractual obligations not to use or disclose the secrets, many companies find such promises to be insufficient protection. For instance, the employee may never have understood the extent of the promises not to use information, or may legitimately dispute whether the alleged trade secret information is owned by the company, or may try to take advantage of the company for personal gain believing that the betrayal will never be proven. Rather than dealing with this uncertainty when employees change jobs, these companies will have their employees promise in their employment agreements that after leaving the company, they will not take competing jobs for a specified period of time within a defined area. Such agreements are often called noncompete clauses or covenants not to compete.

Covenants not to compete are very controversial because of the sweeping ways that they can prevent employees from engaging in their professions and because of their potential effects on legitimate competition.[32] For public policy reasons, courts view the clauses with skepticism and will enforce them only to the extent deemed reasonable under the circumstances. When courts do enforce the covenants, it is only after they have been persuaded that the restrictions are clearly needed to protect the release of trade secrets and are reasonable in terms of their duration and geographic scope.[33]

Courts are more likely to uphold the agreements signed by employees having clear access to trade secrets, such as key executives and scientists, than agreements signed by those less removed from the secrets, such as typists and receptionists. Also, the length of time that the company can keep an employee from competing depends on the circumstances, but it rarely exceeds two years. In addition, courts will enforce the covenant only within the area that the employer conducts business. This may be as small as a city or county, or it may extend around the world. Finally, courts carefully scrutinize the types of job activities subject to the restriction. A narrowly tailored restriction preventing an employee from working for a competitor only in the same capacity as for the employer is more likely to be upheld than a more blanket covenant prohibiting work with the competitor at all.

Some states, notably California, prohibit covenants not to compete. The California code, for example, states that with a few exceptions "every contract by which anyone is restrained from engaging in a lawful profession, trade, or business of any kind is to that extent void."[34] Therefore, in these states, companies have no choice but to rely on confidentiality agreements in conjunction with their other security measures.

## CONCLUDING REMARKS ABOUT TRADE SECRET PROTECTION

The decision about whether trade secret protection should be used for AES is complicated. The answer, in fact, can be given only with reference to particular types of information, their various stages of development, the possible alternatives for protection, and their relative costs. Some of the technical components of AES and some processes that are used to make the system may clearly seem to be patentable. While bearing in mind the pitfalls of patent protection, it would probably be appropriate to file patent applications and embark on a patent strategy for these inventions. There may be other aspects of AES for which patentability is more questionable. Here, it might make sense to file patent applications, but use a trade secret program while the application is pending just in case the patent does not issue. Current U.S. law protects the confidentiality of information in the files until the patent issues, allowing us to use trade secret protection as a fallback position if the patent avenue is closed. Of course, if an international patent program is contemplated, we have to consider that patent files in some countries are opened to public scrutiny after a period of time, usually 18 months. Similarly, it is likely that upcoming changes in U.S. patent laws will create similar publication principles. Thus, we may have to make an election between going for the patent or relying on trade secrets before we know the ultimate disposition about the patentability of AES's features. As will be covered in the next two chapters, we might determine that copyright protection is the best vehicle to protect other attributes of AES, particularly the computer programs. And, of course, there likely will be other types of information and improvements for which neither patents nor copyrights hold much promise. For these, trade secret protection is the only reasonable possibility of retaining a proprietary advantage. Finally, we have to consider that some information simply is not susceptible to trade secret protection. For example, it is hard to use trade secret laws to protect information that can be readily determined through reverse engineering once products are distributed to the public. If we hope to protect these aspects, we have to look to patents, copyrights, or some other specific alternative.

One misconception that should now be clear is that trade secret protection is not necessarily the inexpensive option. The costs of maintaining appropriate security can be staggering, far exceeding the total costs of obtaining patents. Thus, one should resist the initial hesitation to consider a patent strategy due to high filing costs and attorney's fees. It may seem simpler at first blush just to keep the valuable information a secret, but in the end this can be extremely expensive. In addition, trade secret measures may disrupt normal workplace habits and disgruntle certain employees who will resent the apparent Orwellian style of management practices. Thus, trade secrets must be viewed as one of several options providing a set of strengths and weaknesses. The strategic challenge is selecting the most appropriate protective tool for particular information at the right time.

## PRESENTING UNSOLICITED IDEAS TO THIRD PARTIES

When was the last time you thought of a great idea for a product? A wristwatch, say, which wakes up the wearer gently and silently through pulsing vibrations. Did you just laugh it off? Maybe you thought seriously about it for a moment but did not have the desire to make it, experiment with it, or market it. Or maybe you went so far as to develop it but did not know what business steps to take next. How should a person or company proceed in these situations? A natural instinct is to contact a corporation already established in the field, such as Seiko, present it with the idea, and expect appropriate remuneration if the corporation successfully launches the product. However, as we shall see, one who desires compensation must be more cautious when submitting ideas to third parties.

Generally, when it comes to commercial matters, the law will not require a person to do something the person did not somehow promise or agree to do. Contract law is based on the principle of voluntary agreement. Those who enter an agreement are expected to keep their promise. However, one should expect nothing from someone who has not agreed to do anything. A promise does not have to be made explicitly with words. It may be made through conduct or actions. Either way, though, an agreement must be struck before the law will require action.

Suppose we decide to present the watch idea to Seiko executives. If the executives like the idea and choose to use it, we expect to be paid. If they reject it, however, we at least want them to keep the idea confidential so that we might find an alternative way to make money with it. After submitting the concept at a meeting, the executives indicate they are not interested. However, to our surprise, we learn that within a year, Seiko is selling vibrating watches. We naturally feel that our idea has been stolen; we demand compensation; and when that is denied, we march into court knowing that the law will be on our side. However, as the next case demonstrates, the result will only fuel our righteous indignation.

## ALIOTTI V. R. DAKIN & CO.

*Ninth Circuit Court of Appeals, 1987*

### Facts

Shelley Aliotti, a designer of craftwork and toys, worked for Favorite Things, Inc., from 1976 to 1979. She designed soft pillows, stuffed animals, and other items directed toward the children's market.

In November 1978, Bernard Friedman, the president of Favorite Things, telephoned Harold Nizamian, the president of Dakin, to ask whether Dakin would be interested in acquiring Favorite Things. After the conversation, Friedman sent Nizamian a letter and pictures of various products manufactured by Favorite Things. Upon a request for more information from Dakin's board of directors, Friedman sent a presentation booklet, which included data concerning the production and sale of its merchandise. Friedman also sent a current sales brochure, which included photographs of three stuffed toy dinosaurs—Brontosaurus, Stegosaurus and Triceratops—which had been designed by Aliotti and were marketed as the Ding-A-Saur line.

During a March 1979 meeting at Favorite Things' office, Friedman and Aliotti showed two Dakin executives many of Favorite Things' designs, including many products designed by Aliotti. In addition to the three stuffed dinosaurs already marketed by Favorite Things, Aliotti displayed prototypes of three additional Ding-A-Saurs: Tyrannosaurus Rex, Pterodactyl, and Woolly Mammoth. They did not discuss the possibility that Dakin might purchase any particular design. After the meeting, the Dakin executives told Aliotti to contact them if she were interested in being considered for employment at Dakin.

In April 1979, Dakin's board of directors decided not to acquire Favorite Things. In July or August 1979, Dakin began developing its own line of stuffed dinosaurs, called Prehistoric Pets, and started marketing them in June 1980. The six stuffed animals offered by Dakin were of the same six species as those presented to Dakin by Aliotti. The dinosaurs within the two lines had similar postures and body designs and were soft and nonthreatening. In each line, the Tyrannosaurus had its mouth open, and the winged Pterodactyl served as a mobile. The main difference was that Aliotti's dinosaurs appeared dingy, whereas Dakin's depictions were more accurate. Favorite Things became bankrupt in 1982 and assigned all its rights to Aliotti's designs to Aliotti.

Aliotti sued Dakin alleging that Dakin (1) infringed her copyrights by copying the total concept and feel of her toys and (2) unlawfully appropriated her design ideas. Dakin claimed that its employees independently developed Dakin's dinosaur line. The district court judge granted summary judgment, indicating that Aliotti could not win on her claims at trial even if all her allegations were true. Aliotti appealed, arguing that the case should have gone to trial. For the appeal, the Court of Appeals assumes that Dakin appropriated Aliotti's idea of producing stuffed dinosaur toys.

## Opinion

**Copyright Claim.** The court determines that summary judgment was appropriate because there is no substantial similarity of protectible expression between the dinosaurs in the two lines.

**State Law Claims.** Aliotti claims that Dakin breached an implied-in-fact contract by using Aliotti's designs without compensating her and that it committed a breach of confidence by disclosing her designs without permission.

Under California law, for an implied-in-fact contract, one must show (1) that one prepared the work, (2) that one disclosed the work to the offeree for sale, (3) that under all circumstances attending disclosure it can be concluded that the offeree voluntarily accepted the disclosure knowing the conditions on which it was tendered (i.e., the offeree must have the opportunity to reject the attempted disclosure if the conditions were unacceptable), and (4) the reasonable value of the work. If disclosure occurs before it is known that compensation is a condition of its use, no contract will be implied.

Aliotti made her presentation to Dakin not to sell her designs but to help persuade Dakin to buy Favorite Things. She argues that she disclosed her ideas because she hoped to obtain employment with Dakin, but no contract may be implied when an idea has been disclosed not to gain compensation for that idea but for the sole purpose of inducing the defendant to enter a future business relationship. Aliotti argues that by hiring her, Dakin would have obtained her design ideas and put them to work for the company. However, the evidence indicates that Aliotti displayed the dolls before Dakin executives suggested that their company might consider hiring her. No contract will be implied when an "idea man" blurts out the idea without first having struck a bargain, even if the idea has been conveyed with some hope of entering into a contract. Summary judgment on the implied-in-fact contract claim was appropriate.

To prevail on her claim for breach of confidence, Aliotti must show that (1) she conveyed confidential and novel information, (2) Dakin had knowledge that the information was being disclosed in confidence, (3) there was an understanding between Dakin and Aliotti that the confidence be maintained, and (4) there was disclosure or use in violation of the understanding. Constructive notice of confidentiality is not sufficient.

Because three of the Ding-A-Saurs were already on the market, Aliotti could not have conveyed confidential information concerning those dolls. She presented no testimony that Dakin knew that the information was being disclosed in confidence or that the parties agreed that confidence would be maintained. Only constructive knowledge of confidentiality may be inferred from Aliotti's testimony that she was sure there had been some discussion at the meeting about keeping the ideas confidential because "it was presented to them under . . . that these were our ideas, and we were introducing them because they were considering buying the company." Thus, Aliotti's claim for breach of confidence must fall.

The district court properly granted summary judgment to Dakin on Aliotti's claims for copyright infringement, breach of an implied-in-fact contract, and breach of confidence. Affirmed.

---

The lessons from Aliotti are clear. An inventor cannot simply blurt out the idea to a prospective manufacturer and then expect compensation if that idea is subsequently used or revealed. Rather, the inventor must procure an agreement from the company that it will either pay for its use of the idea or keep it in confidence if it ultimately is rejected.

The result from Aliotti may seem harsh at first. However, from the company's perspective, it is entirely logical. It may be that the company had already been working on the concept before the meeting with the inventor. Imagine if Seiko's engineers were finalizing their version of the vibrating watch before our visit to company headquarters. If we had indicated to the Seiko executives the nature of our invention and indicated that compensation was expected for providing further details, they certainly would have refused to listen. For us to claim that they are indebted to us simply because, at our request, they reviewed our idea, would be overreaching. Also, although the invention seemed unique to us, it may be that the concept had already been around for a while. Maybe it had previously been written up in some trade journals. We could hardly expect Seiko to be bound not to use or disclose an idea that others, including its competitors, could freely use.

The end result is that when an inventor approaches a company with an idea, the parties have to deal with different concerns. The inventor needs to ensure that the company somehow agrees, either through words or conduct, to pay for the idea or keep it in confidence. If necessary, the inventor wants the judge or jury that reviews the temporal order of events leading to the disclosure to recognize that the company implicitly understood its obligations prior to the final revelation of the idea. The company, on the other hand, has to make sure that the judge or jury does not misinterpret the chain of events and then erroneously find it responsible to pay for something it did not want.

Companies often are besieged with letters and phone calls containing ideas from inventors. Some of these ideas actually will be good ones, ones that the company eventually adopts, albeit not necessarily because of the unsolicited communications from the inventors. If the company does not deal with these situations carefully, then it may face a litany of lawsuits from outraged inventors who assume that the company took advantage of them. Therefore, most companies have established routine procedures for handling submissions of ideas.

When a company receives a letter containing unsolicited ideas, the letter is immediately forwarded to a clerk in charge of handling such matters. Without reviewing the ideas contained therein, the clerk will return the letter to the sender. Along with the returned letter, there normally will be included an explanation of why the company cannot consider the contents. Here, the company will explain that it does not want any misunderstanding between it and the submitter and that it therefore will deal only after entering an explicit agreement regarding the subject matter. The company will append a written waiver with this explanation. If the inventor agrees to the waiver by signing it, then the company will review the ideas. A sample of such an agreement follows.

### Waiver for Unsolicited Idea

Up to this point, your ideas and materials have not been reviewed by any person in the Company qualified to evaluate them. If you wish that the Company evaluate them, it will do so only under the following conditions:

1.  In consideration for the Company's evaluating your materials, you agree that the Company is released from any liability in connection with your materials except as may result under valid unexpired patents which may have been granted or hereafter may be issued.
2.  No obligations or confidential relationships, either express or implied, are assumed by the Company with respect to any materials submitted.
3.  In order to fully evaluate the materials submitted to the Company, it may have to disclose them to persons outside the Company. Therefore, the Company is under no obligation to maintain the materials in secrecy.
4.  Copies of all materials submitted to the Company may be kept by the Company to prevent misunderstandings regarding the contents of the submissions.
5.  The Company is under no obligation to reveal any information concerning its present or future activities in any field.

If these conditions are acceptable, please sign this form without making changes and return it. Upon receipt of the signed form, the Company will evaluate the materials, and you will be advised of its interest.

By signing this form, the inventor explicitly states that the company is free to do whatever it wants with the ideas without any obligations to pay for them unless the inventor obtains a patent. Unless the inventor has a patent or strongly anticipates that one is forthcoming, the inventor should *not* sign the form.

The language of the waiver and the attached explanatory material strongly urge the inventor to pursue patent rights before working with the company regarding future business arrangements. From a practical standpoint, this makes sense for the company. It may not want to invest time and resources exploring a new idea without knowing that the concept cannot be readily copied by competitors once the product comes to market. However, the advice makes sense for the inventor as well. Since the company is not readily willing to act on a confidential basis, the inventor's only proprietary option for remuneration is through patent rights. For now, patent priority in the United States goes to whoever can establish the earliest date of invention; in most other countries, the first to file gets the patent. In either case, the inventor should at least file for a patent prior to dealing with the other company. This will preserve substantial procedural advantages in case the relationship turns sour in the future and there is a dispute over who did what first and who told what to whom. If the inventor chooses to file after disclosing the invention to the other company, the inventor should be aware of how patent rights are secured in various countries. For the United

States, complete documentation of invention should be kept; for other countries, filing speed may be the critical element. Keep in mind that no matter when filing takes place, by the terms of the waiver, the inventor will have no rights against the company if the patent does not issue. Therefore, if the inventor is not confident about the ultimate outcome in the PTO, the inventor should consider pursuing a different relationship with this company or with another, more receptive entity.

Of course, the whole reason the inventor may have contacted the company in the first place was not wanting to go through all the trouble of pursuing a patent. Or maybe the inventor knows that the idea is not patentable but still can be lucrative for the company that comes to market with it first. If this is the case, then signing the waiver form clearly is not the correct approach. Rather, the inventor should embark on a strategy of sufficiently enticing the company so that it wants to hear more.

The goal for the inventor is to so intrigue the company with general descriptions of the invention that the company becomes willing to enter nondisclosure or remunerations agreements in order to learn the crucial details of the idea. In essence, the inventor will use a dangle-the-carrot approach to arouse the company and motivate it to negotiate on terms more favorable than the waiver form offers. Without hearing all the details of the invention, however, the company still will be reluctant to enter unqualified agreements promising nondisclosure and/or payment. Rather, the most likely outcome is some middle-ground arrangement. For example, the company may become willing to enter the following style of agreement.

> The Company agrees to review the invention and to keep the invention and all materials received in confidence. The Company also agrees to pay a reasonable sum and/or royalty if it uses the invention. However, the Company will not be so obligated with respect to any information that it can document (a) was known to it prior to receipt or (b) is or becomes part of the public domain from a source other than the Company.

This provision can be mutually satisfactory. It protects the inventor as long as the idea is unique. This is normally what the inventor is after. Few inventors expect to receive special treatment when they do not actually contribute something valuable to the company. The company also is protected, for it has no obligations concerning information it already has or can freely obtain. Its only burden is to be able to document its awareness of or access to that information. This is something it would rather not do, especially if such involves a secret proprietary program already under development. However, it may be willing to take on that risk in order to hear the specifics of what may be an exciting new project.

## CONCLUSION

A trade secret protection program must be contemplated by every high-technology business concern. A thoroughly developed strategy using trade secrets in conjunction with patents provides the best way to protect product ideas and information. The other major forms of intellectual property protection—copyrights and trademarks—theoretically are less suitable for ideas and inventions. Copyrights focus on the protection of expressions, and trademarks assist consumers in locating and identifying goods. However, we will find that copyright policy has reached a level of schizophrenia in the high-technology environment, sometimes blurring the distinctions between expressions, ideas, and information. Trademark policy, as well, has reached into new arenas, allowing protection for a host of product characteristics and forms. The next three chapters explore the importance of copyrights and trademarks to those involved with high-technology projects.

## NOTES

1. "Apple Settles Suit against Jobs," Washington Post (January 18, 1986) at C1.
2. M. Miller, "IBM Sues to Silence Former Employee," Wall Street J. (July 15, 1992) at B1.
3. S. Yoder, "High-Tech Firm Cries Trade-Secret Theft, Gets Scant Sympathy," Wall Street J. (October 8, 1992) at A1.
4. V. Slind-Flor, "Charges Fly in Chip War," National L.J. (April 12, 1993) at 1.
5. K. Kelly, "When a Rival's Trade Secret Crosses Your Desk . . . ," Business Week (May 20, 1991) at 48.
6. "Reebok Sues Spalding over Glove," San Luis Obispo County Telegram-Tribune (July 20, 1991) at B-3; J. Miller, "Genentech Charges Invitron, Monsanto with Misappropriation of Trade Secrets," Wall Street J. (February 11. 1988) at A10.
7. R. Eels and P. Nehemkis, Corporate Intelligence and Espionage (1984), at 115-16.
8. W. Carley, "As Cold War Fades, Some Nations' Spies Seek Industrial Secrets," Wall Street J. (June 17, 1991) at A1.
9. Misappropriation may come about in another way. When a person acquires information by mistake and learns that it is trade secret information before relying on it in a material way, then that person misappropriates the information by using or disclosing it. Uniform Trade Secrets Act, §1(2)(ii)(C).
10. Section 3426.1 of the California Uniform Trade Secrets Act states, "Reverse engineering or independent derivation alone shall not be considered improper means."
11. Minnesota Mining & Manufacturing Co. v. Johnson & Johnson Orthopaedics Inc., 976 F. 2d 1559 (Fed. Cir. 1992).
12. When the samples were sent to J&J, 3M had applied for a patent, but one had not yet issued.
13. K. Kelly, "When a Rival's Trade Secret Crosses Your Desk . . . ," Business Week (May 20, 1991) at 48.
14. Minnesota Mining & Manufacturing Co. v. Johnson & Johnson, 976 F. 2d at 1581. The trial court found for 3M and doubled the damages for patent infringement, awarding a total of almost $117 million. The Federal Circuit affirmed this award on appeal.

15. Uniform Trade Secrets Act, §1(2)(ii)(C).

16. Uniform Trade Secrets Act, §2(b).

17. Q-Co Industries, Inc. v. Hoffman, 625 F. Supp. 608 (S.D.N.Y. 1985).

18. M. Miller, "IBM Sues to Silence Former Employee," Wall Street J. (July 15, 1992) at B1.

19. Allis-Chalmers Mfg. Co. v. Continental Aviation & Eng. Corp., 255 F. Supp. 645 (E.D. Mich. 1966); Emery Industries, Inc. v. Cottier, 202 U.S.P.Q. 829 (S.D. Ohio 1978).

20. Statement of Robert Swanson, CEO of Linear Technology Corp., quoted in J. Miller, "Big Firms Pursue Start-Ups with Suits," Wall Street J. (March 24, 1989) at B1.

21. Ibid.

22. UTSA, §4.

23. UTSA. §3(a).

24. UTSA, §§3(b) and 4.

25. California Penal Code, §499c.

26. M. Ratcliffe, "Symantec Execs Face Felony Rap in Borland Case," MacWEEK (March 8, 1993) at 1; V. Slind-Flor, "Silicon Valley Is a Big Battleground," National L.J. (March 22, 1993) at 34.

27. M. Epstein and S. Levi, "Protecting Trade Secret Information," Business Lawyer (May 1988) at 887.

28. G. Zachary, "At Apple Computer Proper Office Attire Includes a Muzzle," Wall Street J. (October 6, 1989) at A1.

29. Surgidev Corp. v. Eye Technology, Inc., 828 F. 2d 452 (8th Cir. 1987); Schalk v. State, 823 S.W. 2d 633 (Tex. Crim. App. Oct. 2, 1991).

30. McKeown and G. Wrenn, "The Stakes on Secrecy Are Rising," National L.J. (February 24, 1992) at 27. See Rockwell Graphic Systems Inc., v. DEV Industries Inc., 925 F. 2d 174 (7th Cir. 1993).

31. M. Epstein and S. Levi, "Protecting Trade Secret Information: A Plan for Proactive Strategy," Business Lawyer (May 1988) at 907.

32. Wadman, "More Firms Restrict Departing Workers," Wall Street J. (June 26, 1992) at B1; W. Green, "Courts Skeptical of Non-Compete Pacts," Wall Street J. (January 11, 1989) at B1.

33. See M. Jacoby, "Protection of Employers in an Era of Shifting Employee Loyalties," J. of Proprietary Rights (October 1990) at 9.

34. California Business & Professional Code, §16600.

# 5

# COPYRIGHT PROTECTION:
# THE BASICS

## INTRODUCTION

Copyright policy may be the most controversial subject in the high-technology legal arena. Federal copyright laws originated in the early 1900s to protect the creative investments of authors and artists from those who otherwise might profit from simply copying their works. This fundamental objective remains the same today, but advances in technology have changed many of the basic parameters for protection. For instance, there are new forms of authorship that were never contemplated in the formative stages of copyright. Clearly, computer programs were not on the minds of legislators in these early periods. New methods have been developed to store and display creative works, such as those used with digital technologies. There also has been substantial change in the ways that works may be copied, reducing the cost and time of reproduction and increasing the quality. Just think how photocopying was a revolution to traditional typesetting systems. And consider how computer and digital techniques are creating change now. Finally, there have been substantial improvements in distribution methods, such as with satellites and optic cables.

As in most areas of the law, change creates new questions, which necessitate new legal solutions. The federal copyright statute has been amended repeatedly to accommodate the forces of change. However, Congress tends to react slowly, thereby leaving temporal gaps where the copyright statute does not satisfactorily

**Exhibit 5.1 Fundamental Aspects of Copyright Protection in the United States**

## What May Be Protected by Copyright

- Original works of authorship (Section 102)
  - Expressions—not ideas
  - Nominal independent creativity
- Relevance to databases
- Case: *Feist Publications v. Rural Telephone*

## Rights Provided by Copyright

- The fundamental rights (Section 106)
  - Reproduce
  - Derive
  - Distribute
  - Perform
  - Display
- Moral rights (Section 106A)
- Fair use (Section 107)
  - Equitable defense for violating rights
  - Application to videocassette recorders
  - Relevance to digital audio recording formats
- Case: *Sony v. Universal*

## Copyright Ownership (Section 201)

- Author
- Works made for hire
- Employees vs. independent contractors
- Joint works
- Cases: *CCNV v. Reid, Aymes vs. Bonelli*

answer the arising concerns. This is especially true, as now, when the pace of change is so rapid. During these periods, it is up to the courts to fashion equitable solutions by transposing the current issues onto the outmoded legislative frameworks. The judiciary's determination that computer programs may be broadly protected by copyright is one of the many examples we will be studying in these chapters. Obviously, such an interpretation has wide-ranging economic effects: benefiting certain businesses and hampering others. The result consists of public outcry, media attention, and congressional appeals to redirect the judicial policy choices.

This chapter and the next review the major copyright concepts bearing on the management of high technologies. Chapter 5 provides an introduction to the basic principles of copyright protection. Here, we shall explore the rights provided by copyright, who may own those rights, and what one must do to obtain them. Such topics as the amount of protection afforded to computer databases and the rights of independent contractors are raised in these sections. The chapter

**Exhibit 5.1  Fundamental Aspects of Copyright Protection in the United States *(continued)***

### Obtaining Copyright Protection

- No action required (Section 408)
- Reasons for registration (Sections 410–412)
  — Prima facie evidence
  — Statutory damages
  — Attorney's fees and costs
  — Litigation
- Reasons for including copyright notice (Section 401)
  — No innocent infringement
- Trade secret protection issues
- Duration of copyright protection (Section 302)

### Infringement (Section 501)

- Substantial similarity analysis
- Clean-room techniques
- Case: *Sega v. Accolade*

### Remedies (Sections 502–506)

- Injunctions
- Damages and profits
  — Statutory damages
- Attorney's fees and costs
- Criminal proceedings

also outlines certain key exceptions to the general rights, most notably the fair-use exception and its applicability to such high-technology issues as home video recording and digital audio recording. Chapter 5 ends with a discussion of how one proves copyright infringement and its relevance to certain corporate practices, such as "clean-room" development techniques. Exhibit 5.1 provides an overview of the topics covered in Chapter 5.

Chapter 6 focuses on selected key copyright issues bearing specifically on the management of technology. Obviously, the protection of computer software by copyright is a major component. This includes the so-called "look and feel" controversy and the protection of user interfaces. The discussion then moves into an associated area—the protection of industrial designs and architecture. Following these sections, the chapter reviews the applicability of trade secret protection within the copyright environment. The controversy over shrink-wrap licenses provides one interesting example. Chapter 6 then concludes by investigating some of the most recent areas of copyright concern, such as digital sampling, digital imaging, and multimedia works.

Within these chapters, we must also consider how copyright might be used to protect certain aspects of the Audio Enhancement System. Will copyright protection extend to the computer program within the AES, even though that program is an integral component of the product? If so, is the entire program protectible, or just portions of it? Can purchasers of the AES tear the system apart and make copies of the program to learn how it works? Who owns the copyright to the program? Is it our company, or possibly another company that made the program for us? Also, can we use copyright protection to keep other companies from duplicating the external appearance of the units? These and other questions regarding copyright protection for the AES will be addressed in these two chapters.

## WHAT MAY BE PROTECTED BY COPYRIGHT

By the terms of the copyright statute, one can obtain copyright protection for *original works of authorship* fixed in any tangible medium of *expression*.[1] The word "original" is not defined by the Copyright Act, and obviously it could be a substantial hurdle to protection depending on the way it is interpreted. After all, your first inclination probably was that "original" raises some objective standard of novelty, possibly akin to that in patent law. However, the courts have interpreted this word to mean that the work must be original to the author.[2] By that interpretation, a work is original to the extent that it manifests some personal creative effort. This is true, even if the resultant work turns out to be exactly like one that is already existing and publicly distributed. As Judge Learned Hand once described it, if by magic a person were to compose anew Keats's "Ode on a Grecian Urn" without having previously known of its existence, then the work would be original and capable of copyright protection.[3] The word "original," therefore, normally does not present a problem for one contemplating copyright protection as long as the work encompasses at least some very minimal amount of personal creativity. Still, there are contexts in which the originality requirement may have substantial financial ramifications. *Feist Publications v. Rural Telephone Service*, presented in this chapter, provides an important illustration with possibly wide-ranging implications.

The phrase "works of authorship," according to the statute, comprises a wide array of categories. One may receive copyright protection for works that are literary, musical, dramatic, or choreographic. Audiovisual works, such as movies, and sound recordings also are subject to copyright protections. In addition, pictures, graphics, and sculptures may be protected through copyright to the extent that they are not inseparable components of useful products.[4] These categories have been interpreted broadly to cover many new forms of technological products. Video games, for instance, are considered audiovisual works, and computer programs usually are seen as literary works. In addition, to bring the U.S. law in conformity with the Berne Convention, the Copyright Act was recently amended to include architectural works within the protectible realm.

Probably the most critical feature of copyright is that it protects only expressions. This is substantiated by that part of the statute that provides that in no case does copyright protection extend to any idea, procedure, process, system, concept, principle or discovery.[5] Here, then, is an important dividing line between

**Exhibit 5.2  Copyrightable Subject Matter**

### Original

- Not copied
- Creative; *di minimis* standard

### Work of Authorship

- Literary
- Musical
- Dramatic
- Pantomimes and choreographic
- Pictorial, graphic and sculptural
- Motion pictures and audiovisual
- Sound recordings
- Architectural

### Tangible, Fixed

- Not oral
- Not transitory

### Expression

- Not an idea, procedure, process, system, method of operation, concept, principle, or discovery

copyrights and utility patents. If one wants federal protection for a product idea, process, or system, then one must look to the patent system rather than copyrights to receive protection. This does not mean that patent protection will necessarily be available. As you know, not every idea is a proper subject for patent protection, and those that are must meet demanding requirements. Still, barring a special federal system of protection such as that for semiconductors, federal protection for ideas can be derived, if at all, only from a patent. Copyright, on the other hand, never protects ideas. Rather, it covers the ways of expressing them. For example, suppose an author writes a book that describes a new system of accounting, and as part of the book provides various forms necessary to implement that system. A copyright in the book would protect only this author's particular version of expressing how the system works. Any person reading the book can use the accounting ideas so expressed. Also, since the forms are an essential component of that system, they may be freely reproduced and used as well.[6]

As we shall see, distinguishing between the ideas and expressions of any work, even the simplest story, is never an easy task. This book, for example, has a great deal of protectible expression, but it also relates numerous ideas and facts about intellectual property protection. Clearly the copyright in this book cannot give the author the exclusive right to relay these essential matters. However, the analysis can become more complicated. For instance, you might consider whether even the particular organization of this book, including the arrangement and selection of topics, constitutes an unprotectible idea about how best to teach this subject. New types of technologies stress the dichotomy between ideas and expressions even further because they integrate creative expression within useful products. For instance, with a computer program, how does one determine where the protectible expression ends and the unprotectible idea or system begins? Similarly, with an industrial design, how does one determine whether a feature is part of the operational system or simply to enhance beauty? The idea-expression dichotomy raises many difficult and substantial questions, which will be pursued later in Chapter 6.

In sum, copyright rewards creativity in expression. Ideas, concepts, facts of nature, and the like are not the subject of copyright; only the ways that they are expressed or communicated are. The expression does not have to be novel; it simply must result from some independent creative process. The following case illustrates the application and interplay of these copyright principles.

## FEIST PUBLICATIONS, INC. V. RURAL TELEPHONE SERVICE

*United States Supreme Court, 1991*

### Facts

Rural Telephone Service (Rural) is a publicly regulated telephone company that solely provides phone service in northwestern Kansas. By law, it is required to issue annually a telephone directory, consisting of white pages and yellow pages. The white pages list in alphabetical order the names, towns, and telephone numbers of Rural's phone service subscribers. Rural obtains this information easily when subscribers sign up for telephone service. Rural distributes its directory free of charge to its subscribers but earns revenue by selling yellow page advertisements.

Feist Publications, Inc. (Feist) specializes in area-wide telephone directories that cover much larger geographical areas than do those of the local phone service companies. Feist also distributes its phone books for free but competes vigorously with local phone companies, such as Rural, for yellow page advertising.

Since Feist lacked easy independent access to subscriber information, it offered to pay the local phone companies for the right to use the information in their white page listings. Rural refused to grant this right. Although Feist attempted to gather the information itself, it had to copy certain listings from Rural's directory to complete its directory.

Rural sued Feist for copyright infringement. The district court determined that the listings were protectible by copyright and that Feist unlawfully copied them. The Court of Appeals affirmed. The Supreme Court granted certiorari to determine whether the copyright in Rural's directory protects the names, towns, and telephone numbers copied by Feist.

### Decision and Reasoning

This case concerns the interaction of two well-established propositions. The first is that facts are not copyrightable; the other that compilations of facts generally are. The most fundamental axiom of copyright law is that no authors may copyright their ideas or the facts they narrate. At the same time, however, it is beyond dispute that certain compilations of facts may be protected by copyright. There is an undeniable tension between these two propositions.

The key to resolving the tension lies in understanding why facts are not copyrightable. The sine qua non of copyright is originality. "Original," as the term is used in copyright, means only that the work was independently created by the author (as opposed to copied from other works) and that it possesses at least some minimal degree of creativity. To be sure, the requisite level of creativity is extremely low. Originality does not signify novelty; a work may be original even though it closely resembles other works so long as the similarity is fortuitous and not the result of copying.

Facts may not be copyrighted because they are not created. Rather, they are discovered. All facts, whether scientific, historical, biographical, or news of the day, are part of the public domain and may not be appropriated by any individual through copyright.

Factual compilations, on the other hand, may possess the requisite originality. The compilation author typically chooses the facts to include, in what order to place them, and how to arrange the collected data so that they may be used effectively by readers. These choices as to selection and arrangement, so long as they are made independently by the compiler and entail a minimal degree of creativity, are sufficiently original to be protected through copyright.

This protection is subject to an important limitation. Merely because a work is copyrighted does not mean that every element of the work is protected. Copyright protection extends only to those components of a work that are original to the author. Copyright protection in factual compilations therefore does not extend to the facts themselves. Only the selection and arrangement of those facts, if original, may be protected. Thus, subsequent compilers are free to use the facts listed; they are restricted by copyright only from copying those aspects of selection and arrangement that are original. To this end, copyright ensures authors the right to their original expression but encourages others to build freely upon the ideas and information conveyed by a work. This principle, known as the idea/expression dichotomy, applies to all works of authorship.

Unfortunately, some lower courts have interpreted the copyright statute inappropriately in the past. These courts extended copyright protection to facts based on a faulty "sweat of the brow" theory that copyright should serve as a reward for the hard work that goes into discovering facts. However, this misplaces the role of copyright. Under the copyright statute, facts are never original. Any protectible originality that may exist in a factual compilation is limited to the way the facts are presented.

However, not every selection or arrangement will pass muster. Originality requires that the author make the selection independently and with some minimal level of creativity. There remains a narrow category of works in which the creative spark is utterly lacking or so trivial to be virtually nonexistent.

There is no doubt that Feist took from Rural's white pages a substantial amount of factual information. Certainly, the raw data are uncopyrightable facts. The question that remains is whether Rural selected and arranged these uncopyrightable facts in an original way. The selection and arrangement in Rural's directory is entirely typical and could not be more obvious. It publishes the most basic information and arranges it alphabetically by surname. The end product is a garden-variety white pages directory lacking the modicum of creativity necessary for copyright protection.

Because Rural's white pages lack the requisite originality, Feist's use of the listings cannot constitute infringement. This decision should not be construed as demeaning Rural's efforts in compiling its directory, but rather as making clear that copyright rewards originality, not effort.

The judgment of the Court of Appeals is reversed.

---

*Feist* is important not only because of its clear exposition of what constitutes copyrightable subject matter but also because of its potential impact on various new, technology-based products. Developers and marketers of computer databases will be particularly affected by this decision. The range of databases has exploded in recent years.[7] Just to provide a small sample, one now finds databases for or regarding creditworthiness, target marketing, legal and financial research, airline flights, television audiences, hospital patients, and business clients and customers.[8] Clearly, tremendous effort is put into developing these bases. However, *Feist* limits the degree of protection provided through copyright. Now it is clear that the individual pieces of data are not protected by copyright; only the selection and arrangement of that data may be covered, and then only if done in a sufficiently creative way. This ruling will affect the ways that many of the companies providing these services do business and may diminish potential profitability. For example, these companies may have to rely more on state trade secret laws than on copyright to protect the valuable aspects of their bases. But as you know, trade secret protection can be cumbersome and difficult to maintain. In addition, trade secret protection may not be appropriate for widely disseminated products and thus may be preempted by federal patent or copyright policy. We will consider that issue further in the discussion about shrink-wrap licenses.

The European Union (EU) proposed a Directive in 1992 that, if passed, will chart a somewhat different course for the protection of databases in Europe.[9] Under the proposal, the role of copyright in protecting databases is very similar to that in the United States. Copyright protection is available for databases, but it extends only to the selection and arrangement of the data and not to the contents themselves. This policy, therefore, conforms to U.S. copyright principles, as articulated in *Feist*. The Directive parts ways with U.S. database doctrines, however, by establishing a sui generis right in the contents of databases. The Directive creates a "right for the maker of the database to prevent the unauthorized extraction or re-utilization, from the database, of its contents, in whole or substantial part, for commercial purposes."[10] The term of the protection is 15 years from the date the database is made available to the public. According to its preamble, the Directive seeks to safeguard the financial and professional investments incurred in collecting data.[11] Therefore, the proposal allows the maker of a database to have exclusive rights to facts, based on the sweat-of-the-brow theory, which was rejected by the U.S. Supreme Court in *Feist*.

The EU-proposed Directive identifies a number of exceptions to the sui generis right for data protection. For instance, the user can extract insubstantial portions of the database for commercial purposes as long as the source is acknowledged.[12] Also, the Directive provides that a fair and nondiscriminatory license to extract materials must be provided if they cannot be independently collected from any other source.[13] One other aspect of the Directive may be important to U.S. database makers if it ultimately is adopted in its current form. The sui generis right against extraction is available to non-EU nationals only if their home country provides comparable protection to databases produced by EU nationals.[14] Since the United States does not provide comparable protection for makers of databases, be they from the EU or from the United States, the proposed EU sui generis right would not apply to U.S. nationals in the EU.

## RIGHTS PROVIDED BY COPYRIGHT

Section 106 of the Copyright Act lists five exclusive rights that one enjoys with a copyright. The first, and probably the most important, is the exclusive *right to reproduce* the work. No one may copy the elements of a work that are protected by copyright without permission. This does not mean that one's entire work is off-limits to copying; only the protected expression is. Thus, copyright protection for a database does not give one the right to prevent others from copying the data. Rather the exclusive right to reproduce extends only to the original selection and arrangement of those data. Similarly, the forms provided in the accounting system book may be reproduced by others because they are a component of the unprotectible idea. In addition, as we shall see, the act allows others to copy even a work's protected expression in certain specific situations.

Copyright protection provides one the exclusive *right to prepare derivative works*. A derivative work is a transformation or adaptation of the protected work, such as a translation, dramatization, motion picture, sound recording, or abridgment. Thus, if one writes a novel, then one has the exclusive right to develop a screenplay based on the novel for television. The act also grants a copyright owner the exclusive *right to distribute* copies of the work, and the *rights to perform* and *to display* the work publicly.[15]

Suppose Harry Hacker develops a BASIC-language computer program, which is protected by copyright. The copyright gives Harry the exclusive rights to make copies and improvements of the program, to distribute them, and to display them publicly. Harry believes that this program could be very popular and might sell for a lot of money. However, Harry's love is programming, not business. Thus, he would like others to market the program for him. Under the Copyright Act,

Harry may give others permission through a license to enjoy any or all of his exclusive rights.[16] Thus, he might make a contract with an established software company, granting to it, for a fee, permission to make copies of the work and to distribute those copies to the public. Harry also thinks that there are potential customers who might prefer the program written in another language such as Pascal. He knows that his friend Tammy is more skilled in that language than he. Thus, if he wants, he may enter into a contractual arrangement with Tammy wherein he gives her permission to make the derivative work in Pascal and for which he promises to pay remuneration. He also may grant Tammy the permission to make and distribute copies of that Pascal program if he also would like her to be involved in marketing. The key is that Harry has complete control over the set of protected rights. He can retain all the rights, or he may divide them and give others permission to enjoy them. Such permission may be exclusive or nonexclusive, depending on the wishes of the parties. Harry may even completely transfer ownership in any individual right or in the whole program if he so chooses. Clearly, Harry has substantial flexibility to profit from his bundle of protected rights.

The Copyright Act, in Sections 107–120, lists a number of exceptions to the set of protected rights. Most of them are quite specific, applying in only very special contexts. However, one should always refer to these sections to ascertain whether they do or do not apply to a contemplated practice. For example, Section 109 states that one who owns a copy of a protected work may distribute that copy without getting permission from the copyright owner. Thus, when you are finished with this book, you may sell or give it to another without asking for permission from the publisher. This exception, called the first-sale doctrine, therefore qualifies the exclusive right of the copyright owner to distribute copies of that owner's work. Other sections provide exceptions for libraries, for certain performances and displays, for sound recordings, for computer programs, and for a variety of other specialized uses. There are even exceptions to exceptions embedded in these sections. For instance, one who owns a copy of a sound recording or a computer program may not rent that copy to another without obtaining permission from the copyright owner, notwithstanding the provisions of the first-sale doctrine.[17]

## The Fair-Use Exception

The most notable and highly publicized exception to a copyright owner's exclusive rights is the *fair-use* exception provided in Section 107 of the Copyright Act. Section 107 states that one may, without permission, make a fair use of a copyrighted work for purposes such as criticism, comment, news reporting, teaching, scholarship, or research. What constitutes a fair use is to be determined by the equities of the particular situation, based on an evaluation of four factors:

1.   The purpose of the use, including whether the use is of a commercial nature or is for nonprofit educational reasons;

2.  The nature of the copyrighted work;
3.  The amount and substantiality of the portion used in relation to the whole copyrighted work; and
4.  The effect of the use upon the potential market for or value of the copyrighted work.

The Copyright Act provides little explicit direction on how to evaluate these factors or on how much proportional weight to give each of them. Thus, if there is litigation, it is up to the court to fashion the appropriate balance for the situation under review. *Sony v. Universal City Studios*, *Sega v. Accolade*, and *Campbell v. Acuff-Rose Music*, three illustrative cases which appear in the copyright component of this book, make it clear that the application of the fair-use doctrine is highly dependent on the equities of a particular situation. Certain general observations about each of the factors can be made, however:

1.  **The purpose of the use**
    - Copying is more likely to be fair if it is undertaken to further teaching or scholarship or to engage in specially protected forms of speech, such as comment or criticism. But as *Sony* illustrates, it is possible to engage in a fair use when these attributes are totally absent.
    - Use of copyrighted material primarily for private commercial benefit weighs strongly against a finding of fair use. As *Sega* and *Acuff-Rose* demonstrate, however, a commercial use may nonetheless be fair when the commercial aspect is of minimal significance or is simply outweighed in importance by other relevant considerations.
2.  **The nature of the work**
    - It is very difficult, although not impossible, to make a fair use of copyrighted works that have not yet been distributed to the public.[18] A recent amendment to Section 107 clarifies that the unpublished nature of a work does not bar a finding of fair use if the equitable balance of the other relevant factors otherwise supports the determination.[19]
    - It is easier to make a fair use of utilitarian or factual works than it is of more expressive materials, such as fiction.
3.  **The amount and substantiality used**
    - The amount of copying should be relatively small, especially if use is made of qualitatively important material. However, this factor is no more controlling than any of the others. *Acuff-Rose* makes it clear, for instance, that a parodist may take enough qualitatively important material as is necessary to conjure up the source of a parody. In addition, *Sony* and *Sega* demonstrate that there may be unique situations in which the copying of entire works may be fair uses.
4.  **Market effect**
    - The effect on the potential market for the copyrighted work often is the decisive determinant of whether the balance tips toward a fair use. A use that reduces the profitability of the copyrighted work is much more unlikely to be a fair use than one that is monetarily benign.

**Fair Use and Video Cassette Recording.** *Sony Corporation v. Universal City Studios* was the significant Supreme Court opinion that legitimized the videocassette recorder (VCR) industry. The ultimate determination in this case depended on a judgment that VCR time-shifting (the act of taping a television show for the purpose of viewing it once at a more convenient time) at home is a fair use. Note that this case was against a VCR manufacturer rather than the users of the machine. The plaintiffs argued that Sony was responsible for the unauthorized copies made by its customers because it provided the means to make those copies. Also, be aware that the Court of Appeals determined that most of the ways VCR owners use their machines are illegal and did hold Sony responsible. Such a decision, if it had not been reversed on appeal by the Supreme Court, would have given copyright owners substantial leverage to negotiate fees from the sale of VCRs and possibly videotapes. In addition, consider carefully how narrow this opinion really is. Although a popular notion, it is a misconception to believe that any home use of a VCR is legitimate. Finally, this case obviously is relevant to home audiorecording, especially with regard to digital audio formats.

## SONY CORPORATION OF AMERICA V. UNIVERSAL CITY STUDIOS, INC.

*United States Supreme Court, 1984*

### Facts

Universal City Studios and Walt Disney Productions own the copyrights on a substantial number of motion pictures and other audiovisual works. Sony is the manufacturer of Betamax, a brand of VCR. The primary use of the machine is time-shifting: the practice of recording a program to view once at a later time, and thereafter erasing it. However, there are other uses of the machine, such as recording tapes to accumulate in a library.

Universal and Disney sued Sony, alleging that individuals used Betamaxes to copy some of their copyrighted works, which had been exhibited on commercially sponsored television. They further contended that these individuals violated their exclusive rights to copy the programs. However, no relief was sought against the individuals. Rather, the studios maintained that Sony was responsible for the wrongful acts of these individuals and as relief sought money damages from Sony and an injunction preventing the further manufacture and sale of Betamaxes. The studios did not raise issues regarding the transfer of tapes or the copying of programs transmitted on pay or cable television systems.

The district court decided that Sony was not liable. It determined that noncommercial home-use recording of material broadcast over the public airwaves was a fair use. It also held that in any event Sony could not be liable for the illegal acts of certain customers since it was not directly involved with them.

The Court of Appeals reversed. It concluded that the home use of a VCR was not a fair use because it did not serve a productive purpose, such as for criticism, comment, teaching, scholarship, or research. The Court of Appeals also determined that Sony was liable for the acts of its purchasers because it knowingly sold Betamaxes for the primary purpose of reproducing television programs, almost all of which were copyrighted.

## Decision and Reasoning

Copyright protection subsists in original works of authorship fixed in any tangible medium of expression. The Copyright Act grants the copyright holder the exclusive right to use and to authorize the use of work in five qualified ways, including reproduction in copies. However, any individual may reproduce a copyrighted work for a "fair use."

Universal and Disney in this case do not seek relief against the VCR users who have allegedly infringed their copyrights. To prevail, they have to prove (1) that users of the Betamax have infringed their copyrights and (2) that Sony should be held responsible for that infringement.

The Copyright Act does not expressly render anyone liable for infringement committed by another. In contrast, the Patent Act expressly imposes vicarious liability on contributory infringers. Although the copyright statute does not mention vicarious liability, it nonetheless exists in this context since vicarious liability is imposed in virtually all areas of law where it is just to hold one individual accountable for the actions of another. And it is appropriate to refer to the patent law cases because of the historic kinship between patent law and copyright law.

The Patent Act provides that the sale of a commodity that is suitable for substantial noninfringing uses does not constitute contributory infringement. Accordingly, the sale of copying equipment does not constitute contributory infringement if it is capable of substantial noninfringing uses. The question is thus whether the Betamax is capable of substantial noninfringing uses. In order to resolve this case we need not give precise content to the question of how much use is substantial, for it is clear that private noncommercial time-shifting in the home meets the standard, however it is understood.

Certain uses of the Betamax clearly are legitimate and noninfringing. Many copyright holders accept private time-shifting. For example, Fred Rogers, president of the company that owns "Mister Rogers' Neighborhood," testified that he had no objection to home taping and expressed that it is a real service to families to be able to record children's programs and to show them at appropriate times. If there are millions of owners of VCRs who make copies of such programs as "Mister Rogers' Neighborhood" and if the proprietors of these programs welcome the practice, then the business of supplying the equipment that makes such copying feasible should not be stifled because the equipment is used by some individuals to make unauthorized reproductions.

Even unauthorized uses of a copyrighted work are not infringing if they constitute a fair use under Section 107. That section identifies various factors that enable a court to apply an equitable-rule-of-reason analysis to particular claims of infringement. The first factor requires that the commercial or nonprofit character be weighed. If the Betamax were used to make copies for a commercial or profit-making purpose, such use would be presumptively unfair. Time-shifting for private home use must be characterized as a noncommercial, nonprofit activity.

Moreover, when one considers the nature of a televised copyrighted audiovisual work and that time-shifting merely enables a viewer to see such a work that the viewer had been invited to witness in its entirety free of charge, the fact that the entire work is reproduced does not have its ordinary effect of militating against a finding of fair use.

This is not, however, the end of the inquiry, because one also must consider the effect of the use upon the potential market for or value of the copyrighted work. A challenge to the noncommercial use of a copyrighted work requires proof that the particular use is harmful or that if it should become widespread, it would adversely affect the potential market for the copyrighted work. Universal and Disney raise numerous fears about the potential effects on television ratings, on theater audiences, on television rerun audiences, and on film rentals. However, the District Court found that harm from time-shifting is speculative, and at worst minimal.

When all these factors are weighed in the equitable-rule-of-reason balance, we must conclude, as did the District Court, that home time-shifting is a fair use. The Court of Appeals erred in its determination that a fair use must be a productive use. The distinction between productive and unproductive uses may be helpful in calibrating the balance, but it cannot be wholly determinative. Copying to promote a scholarly endeavor certainly has a stronger claim to fair use than copying to avoid interrupting a poker game. But that does not end the inquiry.

In summary, the Betamax is capable of substantial noninfringing uses because some copyright owners do not object to private time-shifting and because unauthorized home time-shifting is a fair use. Sony's sale of such equipment, therefore, does not constitute contributory infringement. It may well be that Congress will take a fresh look at this new technology. But it is not our job to apply laws that have not yet been written. Accordingly, the judgment of the Court of Appeals must be reversed.

---

Since there are substantial uses of VCRs that do not violate the exclusive rights of copyright holders, Sony and other manufacturers are free to market these machines. However, it should be clear that not all the ways that individuals use the machines are within the law. For instance, one widespread practice involves making copies to save in a personal library. Do you believe that this is a fair use? Although the first three factors may be no different from the practice of time-shifting, it is probably much easier to prove detrimental economic effects from librarying. After all, one who watches a movie from a personal library might otherwise buy it. Thus, although time-shifting is legal, the act of saving the tape to watch more than once, even at home, probably violates copyrights. You should consider other scenarios too. What about renting a tape and using two machines to make a copy? It is hard to imagine how this could be a fair use. Now think about those video decks with two taping mechanisms built right in. Could a copyright owner prevail in a suit against their manufacturers on the claim of contributory infringement? The answer, of course, comes down to whether there are substantial noninfringing uses of such double decks.

*Sony* also may have some important ramifications on our ability to sell the AES as well. Since the AES is used to upgrade the sound quality of records, one might allege that the system creates derivative works of the records played through it. If this is correct, then customers would need to get permission from the LP (long-playing-record) copyright owners before using the AES. Otherwise, they would be in violation of the exclusive copyright privilege of those copyright owners to control the making of derivative works. Assuming our customers do not take this step, then we could be held liable as a contributory infringer given that there would be few noninfringing uses of the AES.

Fortunately, upgrading sound quality likely would not be considered the making of a derivative work. For if it were, then it would follow that all things that consumers do to alter audio or visual aspects of purchased works would infringe copyrights. For instance, reshuffling the order of songs in a compact disc (CD), under the derivative work theory, would be an infringement. So would playing a 33 RPM record at another speed, such as 45 RPM. Likewise, viewing an art object through rose-colored lenses would infringe. Even boosting the treble on an audio recording, or adding special effects, such as surround sound, might then be an infringement.

A similar scenario to the AES situation was raised in a lawsuit brought by Nintendo against Lewis Galoob Toys for the sale of Game Genie. Game Genie is a microprocessor-equipped box that plugs into Nintendo game cartridges and allows players to electronically alter Nintendo video games to create a variety of new rules or special effects for the original games. Nintendo argued that the game allows users to violate its exclusive rights to create derivative works of its games and that Galoob, by supplying the means for the infringing activity, is a contributory infringer. In 1991, a California district court sided with Galoob, and the court's decision was affirmed on appeal.[20] Thus, it appears that the AES, by improving sound quality, does not create a derivative work. Therefore we do not have to fear being charged with contributory infringement for selling the machine.

**Fair Use and the Controversy over Digital Audio Recording Formats.**  The issues raised in the video context are no less real in the audio world. One should now wonder whether it is legal to create a personal library of analog audiotapes copied from records or CDs for use in one's car audio system. Until recently, there was no definitive answer to this query. But then, no one seemed to care too much either, at least enough to raise a legal case about it. Some scholars believed that the legislative history of the 1976 Copyright Act provided an implicit exception for home analog audiotaping.[21] Even without special treatment, a fair-use equitable-balancing approach very well may have sanctioned the practice. Music recorded on analog tapes has perceptively inferior quality to that on records and CDs. Thus, there generally has been little fear that analog tapes would substitute for the "original." The prospect of playing a recorded tape in the automobile may actually be the decisive factor in convincing one to purchase the CD at all. In addition, recording artists do not worry much about analog "chain-taping" whereby a record is purchased by one individual, who lets a friend tape it, who then lets another friend tape that copy, and so on. This is because analog tape quality deteriorates even more substantially through this process. For these reasons and others, it might have been hard to argue persuasively that home analog audiotape recording could have a negative economic impact on the copyright holders.

Digital audio recording formats (DARs), however, presented a much different picture, and recording artists were not sanguine about the presence of these new technologies. DARs include digital audiotape formats, such as digital compact cassettes, and recordable optical discs, such as MiniDiscs.[22] DARs have the capacity to make identical copies from the original source and can continue to do so from generation to generation in a chain-recording sequence. When DARs hit foreign markets in 1984, the recording industry threatened to bring lawsuits against DAR manufacturers.[23] The theory, of course, was to be contributory infringement: that consumer DAR machines would be used almost entirely to make illegal reproductions of copyrighted programs, which would be saved in private libraries and lent to friends for further reproduction. At the same time, the industry lobbied heavily for legislation requiring all DAR decks sold in the United States to have a "CopyCode" system, which would prevent them from making copies of copyrighted material. In 1987, the National Bureau of Standards determined that the CopyCode system was unreliable, and the legislative proposals were scrapped. However, the DAR manufacturers still feared lawsuits if DARs were marketed in the United States, and so only a limited number trickled into the country. In 1989, representatives from the recording industry and the DAR industry met in Athens, Greece, and agreed to seek legislation worldwide requiring DARs to have a new technical system, called a serial copy management system, or SCMS, which allows recording of commercially purchased CDs or prerecorded digital audiotapes, but which prevents chain-recording. Nonetheless, in 1990, a contributory infringement lawsuit was filed by certain songwriters in the United States.[24] Finally, in 1992, this chapter in copyright history came to a close in the United States when Congress passed the Audio Home Recording Act.[25] The act essentially requires sellers and importers of digital audio recording devices intended for consumer use to pay a 2% royalty on the sales price to the Copyright Office and to integrate the SCMS copy protection system into their products. Similarly, sellers of blank digital audio recording media have to pay a 3% royalty. The royalties are to be distributed by the Copyright Office to musicians, vocalists, recording companies, songwriters, and music publishers. In addition, by expressly prohibiting infringement suits against individuals who make private, noncommercial uses of digital or analog audio recording devices or media, the legislation ends the debate about the potential liability of those who copy audio recordings for home use.[26] Clearly, copyright policy has had a significant impact on the advent of this new industry.

## COPYRIGHT OWNERSHIP

Only the owner of a copyright enjoys the privileges of a copyright. The Copyright Act provides that the initial owner of a copyright is the "author" of a work.[27] As you might expect, the author of a work normally is the person who created it.

Thus, the general rule is that the one who develops original expression initially owns the copyright to that work and has control over the five exclusive rights provided by the copyright. The initial owner may exercise that control in a wide variety of ways. Not only may an owner license to others the right to enjoy any or all of the rights, but an owner also can assign ownership to any or all of the rights.[28] Such assignments serve to transfer complete control over the right or rights to the new owner.

It should be clear that what we are talking about here is ownership in the copyright as opposed to ownership of the material object that "holds" the expression. For instance, when you purchase a book, you own that book. But your ownership extends only to the physical components of the book.[29] The copyright owner of the original expression retains the copyright and all of the benefits from protection. Thus, although you own the book, you may not make copies or prepare derivative works unless you have permission from the copyright owner or such use falls within an exception to the copyright owner's rights, such as fair use.

## Works Made for Hire

The general rule is that the person who creates a work initially owns the copyright privileges to it. There is one notable exception to this rule, however, which is critically important for those developing and managing technology. Section 201(b) of the Copyright Act provides:

> In the case of a work made for hire, the employer or other person for whom the work was prepared is considered the [initial owner] for purposes of this title, and, unless the parties have expressly agreed otherwise in a written agreement signed by them, owns all of the rights comprised in the copyright.

So, if one develops original expression under circumstances that fall within the definition of a work made for hire, then the person for whom the work was prepared is the initial owner. Obviously, depending on how "work made for hire" is interpreted, this could have wide-ranging ramifications. For instance, assume that Jack is a computer programmer who works for IBM. If Jack creates a program while on the job for IBM, is this a "work made for hire"? If so, then IBM initially owns the copyright in the program; if not, Jack does. What if Price Waterhouse, an accounting firm, contracts with Jack to develop in his spare time a program that can carry out a specified set of functions and criteria? Is this a work made for hire? Think about the ramifications if this program turns out to be so good that it is desired by a host of other accountants. Who has the right to make copies and distribute them? Price Waterhouse probably thinks it does because it directed and paid for the development of the program. Jack likely believes that he owns the copyright because the program was built on his creative genius. In his mind, Price Waterhouse only purchased a copy of the program and does not own the copyright to it. What if the contract Jack signed stated that the work is a work made for hire? Will this affect the ownership interest? Clearly, the answer to what makes a work a work made for hire will have tremendous financial implications for Jack and Price Waterhouse.

The Copyright Act defines a work made for hire in Section 101 as:

(1) a work prepared by an employee within the scope of his or her employment; or

(2) a work specially ordered or commissioned for use as a contribution to a collective work, as part of a motion picture or other audiovisual work, as a translation, as a supplementary work, as a compilation, as an instructional text, as a test, as answer material for a test, or as an atlas if the parties expressly agree in a written instrument signed by them that the work shall be considered a work made for hire.

Courts struggled with the meaning of this definition for years, without much agreement. Different courts could review the same facts and come to opposite conclusions about the copyright owner based on their varying approaches to what constitutes a work made for hire. Finally, the Supreme Court settled the matter in 1989 in *Community for Creative Non-Violence (CCNV) v. Reid*. Although this case dealt with an artist who created for a nonprofit organization a sculpture representing the homeless—a somewhat low-tech scenario—numerous persons and companies involved in high technology and informational pursuits eagerly awaited the Court's decision. Indeed, many tried to influence the Court's rendering by filing with the Court certain briefs that supported their differing perspectives. For instance, IBM, Time, AT&T, Dow Chemical, the *Washington Post*, and the *New York Times* supported CCNV; the Graphic Arts Guild and Advertising Photographers of America backed Reid.[30] The ultimate decision that the artist, Reid, was a copyright owner, was a tremendous victory for independent contractors who are commissioned to develop works of authorship.

## COMMUNITY FOR CREATIVE NON-VIOLENCE V. REID

*United States Supreme Court, 1989*

### Facts

Community for Creative Non-Violence (CCNV) is a nonprofit association dedicated to eliminating homelessness in America, and Mitch Snyder is a trustee. In 1985, CCNV decided to participate in the annual Pageant of Peace in Washington, D.C., by sponsoring a sculpture to dramatize the plight of the homeless. CCNV members conceived the idea for the nature of the display: a modern nativity scene in which the traditional Holy Family members appear as contemporary homeless people huddled on a steam grate. CCNV also titled the work "Third World America" and settled on a legend for the pedestal: "and still there is no room at the inn."

James Reid agreed to sculpt the three human figures. CCNV agreed to make the steam grate and pedestal. The parties agreed that the project would cost CCNV no more than $15,000, not including Reid's services, which he offered to donate. The parties did not sign a written agreement. Neither party mentioned copyright.

Reid sent CCNV a sketch of the proposed sculpture. Snyder pointed out that homeless people tend to recline on grates, rather than sit or stand. From that time on, Reid's sketches contained only reclining figures. For two months, Reid worked exclusively on the statue, assisted at various times by people who were paid with funds provided by CCNV. CCNV members often visited Reid to check on his progress and to coordinate CCNV's construction of the base.

The statue was displayed for a month. CCNV then returned it to Reid's studio for minor repairs. Snyder made plans for an extensive tour for the work. Reid objected, contending that the materials were not strong enough. He urged CCNV to cast the statue in bronze or to create a master mold. CCNV declined. Reid then refused to return the statue. CCNV sued Reid, seeking both return of the sculpture and a determination of copyright ownership. The District Court ordered Reid to return the sculpture. Since CCNV had paid for the sculpture, it owned that particular copy and had the right to possess it. The district court also determined that the sculpture was a work made for hire and that CCNV therefore owned the copyright. The court reasoned that Reid was an employee within the meaning of Section 101(1) because CCNV was the motivating force in the statue's production. Reid appealed the judgment as to copyright ownership.

The Court of Appeals reversed, holding that Reid was not an employee under strict agency principles and that the work therefore was not a work made for hire. The court remanded to the District Court to determine whether the sculpture was a joint work, authored and owned by both CCNV and Reid. CCNV appealed to the Supreme Court.

### Opinion and Reasoning

The Copyright Act provides that copyright ownership vests initially in the author or authors of a work. As a general rule, the author is the party who actually creates the work, that is, the person who translates an idea into a fixed, tangible expression. The act carves out an important exception, however, for works made for hire. The contours of the work-made-for-hire doctrine carry profound significance for freelance creators—including artists, writers, photographers, designers, composers, and computer programmers—and for the publishing, advertising, music, and other industries that commission their works.

CCNV does not claim that the statue satisfies the terms of Section 101(2). Quite clearly, it does not. Sculpture does not fit within any of the nine categories of works enumerated in that subsection, and no written agreement between the parties establishes that the sculpture is a work made for hire.

The dispositive inquiry in this case is whether "Third World America" is a work prepared by an employee within the scope of employment. The act does not define these terms. In the absence of such guidance, four interpretations have emerged. The first holds that a work is prepared by an employee whenever the hiring party retains the right to control the product. A second, and closely related, view is that a work is prepared by an employee when the hiring party has actually wielded control over the creation of a work. A third view is that the term "employee" within Section 101(1) carries its common law agency meaning. Finally, some contend "employee" refers only to formal, salaried employees.

In the past, when Congress has used the term "employee" without defining it, we have concluded that Congress intended to describe the conventional common law agency relationship. We agree with the Court of Appeals that this is the correct interpretation of "employee" in Section 101(1).

Neither of the first two tests, supported by CCNV, is consistent with the text of the act. Section 101 plainly creates two distinct ways in which a work can be deemed for hire: one for works prepared by employees, the other for those specially commissioned works that fall within one of the nine enumerated categories and are the subject of a written agreement. The right-to-control-the-product test would mean that many works that could satisfy Section 101(2) would already have been deemed works made for hire under 101(1). Also, the unifying feature of the nine enumerated categories is that they are usually prepared at the direction of a publisher or producer. By their very nature, these types of works would be works by an employee under the right-to-control-test. The actual control test presents similar inconsistencies and there is simply no way to milk it from the language of the statute. We also reject Reid's suggestion that Section 101(1) refers only to formal, salaried employees.

We conclude that a work made for hire can arise through one of two mutually exclusive means: one for employees in the traditional common law agency sense, and one for independent contractors. In determining whether a hired party is an employee under the common law of agency, one considers several factors. Amongst factors relevant to this inquiry are the hiring party's right to control the manner by which the product is accomplished, the skill required, the source of the instrumentalities and tools, the location of the work, the duration of the relationship between the parties, whether the hiring party has the right to assign additional projects to the hired party, the extent of the hired party's discretion over when and how long to work, the method of payment, the hired party's role in hiring and paying assistants, whether the work is part of the regular business of the hiring party, the provision of employee benefits, and the tax treatment of the hired party. No single one of these factors is alone determinative.

In light of these factors, Reid was not an employee of CCNV but was an independent contractor. True, CCNV directed enough of Reid's work to ensure that he produced a sculpture that met their specifications. But the extent of control that the hiring party exercises over the details of the product is not dispositive. Indeed, all the other factors weigh heavily against finding an employment relationship. Reid is a sculptor, a skilled occupation. Reid supplied his own tools. He worked in his own studio in Baltimore, making daily supervision practicably impossibly. Reid was retained for less than two months, a relatively short period of time. CCNV had no right to assign additional projects. Apart from the deadline, Reid had freedom to decide when and how long to work. CCNV paid Reid a sum dependent on completion of a specific job, a method by which independent contractors are often compensated. Reid had total discretion in hiring assistants. Creating sculptures was hardly regular business for CCNV. Finally, CCNV did not pay taxes, provide any employee benefits, or contribute to unemployment insurance or workers' compensation funds.

Because Reid was an independent contractor, whether "Third World America" is a work made for hire depends on whether it satisfies the terms of Section 101(2). This, CCNV concedes, it cannot do. Thus, CCNV is not the author or owner of the sculpture by virtue of the work-made-for-hire provisions of the act.

CCNV nevertheless may be a joint author of the sculpture if, on remand, the district court determines that CCNV and Reid prepared the work with the intention that their contributions be merged into inseparable or interdependent parts of a unitary whole. In that case, CCNV and Reid would be co-owners of the copyright in the work. We affirm the judgment of the Court of Appeals.

---

*CCNV* answers a lot of questions and raises many others. When traditional employees, as determined by standard agency principles, develop works while on the job, these are works made for hire, and ownership resides in the employer. Thus, when Jack created the program for IBM while on the job, the work belonged to IBM, leaving Jack no copyright ownership claims to it. Of course, as the case indicates, the term "employee" is broader than formal salaried personnel, and controversy may result about how to balance the large set of potentially relevant factors. This is amply demonstrated in *Aymes v Bonelli*, the case presented next in this chapter. But it is clear that merely the right to control is no longer sufficient to make one an employee. When independent contractors are engaged, their efforts will not result in works made for hire unless their contributions fall within one of the nine categories enumerated in Section 101(2) and their agreement specifically relates the work for hire relationship. Therefore, when Jack worked at the direction of Price Waterhouse, the final product was not a work made for hire. Be aware that this would have been true even if their contract had stated that the program was a work made for hire; since the program does not fit within any of the nine categories, there can be no work made for hire, even if the parties so agree.

Note also how these principles might be used to determine who owns the rights to copyrightable features of AES, such as elements of the computer program. If a salaried employee of our company develops the program, then the program is a work made for hire, thereby yielding ownership with the company. However, if we commission an independent programmer to design the program based on certain parameters and specifications, then initial ownership of the copyright will reside with the programmer. If this is the case, then we will have to account for those rights before making or distributing the AES. This can be done by acquiring the programmer's copyright interests, as discussed next, or by gaining permission, through contractual license provisions, to enjoy the necessary copyright privileges.

The *CCNV* decision may have widespread effects on existing works. Many industries depend on the services of outside experts and businesses. In the past, the firms needing assistance often retained these parties under the assumption that they were employees by the terms of the act. Due to *CCNV*, they now face the real possibility that they do not own the copyrights to the works they commissioned. This may hold true even in spite of intentions to the contrary. All of a sudden, this may give independent contractors leverage to demand royalties for the continued uses of their creations. It is no wonder that so many companies that frequently hire independent contractors were so interested in the outcome of this case.

There is a technique that can be used by the hiring party to provide it with ownership when a new work is to be developed by an independent contractor. Recall that copyright ownership can be assigned from the owner to another. Therefore, when dealing with an independent contractor, an agreement for services may provide that the contractor will take all necessary steps to assign the copyright upon completion of the work. Since *CCNV*, clauses to this effect in contracts have become much more common. On first glance, one might think that *CCNV* thereby will have little net effect on future business relationships. The hirers will own the copyrights just as they thought they did before *CCNV*. However, there are some differences. The most important effect is on negotiation psychology. Now it will be crystal clear to independent contractors that they are relinquishing all ownership in the work. Before, contracts may not have mentioned ownership, or they may have talked in terms of "works made for hire," a term of art that unsophisticated persons could easily misunderstand. Independent contractors with full knowledge about ownership interests may refuse to sign assignment deals or may demand greater fees. Assignments have other repercussions. For instance, the duration of the copyright is based on the life of the author, rather than the statutory term for works made for hire. Also, the act provides that assignments may be terminated after 35 years.[31] In addition, there is some responsibility to record assignments with the Copyright Office to ensure ownership in case someone else makes a claim.[32]

### Joint Works

At the same time as *CCNV* clarified the works made for hire doctrine, it opened up another can of worms with the "joint-works" scenario. As *CCNV* relates, the act provides for co-ownership when two or more persons jointly develop a work in which they make inseparable contributions. What and how much each must contribute for there to be a joint work is still not clear. Two principles seem to apply, however. First, each person must contribute original expression and not simply ideas.[33] Thus, it is unlikely that Price Waterhouse could claim joint ownership with Jack when it provided him only with the ideas to be embedded in the program. However, as will be explored in the next chapter, it is not always easy to clearly discern what contributions are merely ideas, especially with computer programs. The second principle is that each must contribute more than a *di minimis* amount of expression. One has to contribute something of substance to be a joint owner, although it can be substantially less than one-half or some other defined percentage. In the event that there is joint ownership, each owner can independently make its own decisions about how to profit from the work but must account to the other owners for the profits made from those endeavors. Therefore, if CCNV and Reid are joint owners, and from the facts it seems likely that

**Exhibit 5.3 Works Made for Hire**

Relevant Factors to Distinguish Employees from Independent Contractors

- Right to control how product accomplished
- Skill of hired party
- Source of tools and instrumentalities
- Location of work
- Duration of relationship
- Right to assign other projects
- Discretion of hire party over working hours
- Payment method
- Regular business or hirer
- Employee benefits paid
- Tax treatment

they are, then each must pay the other one-half of the profits made through use of the copyrights. So, for example, if CCNV makes and sells prints of the sculpture, it would have to pay 50% of the profits to Reid.

*Aymes v. Bonelli* was one of the first important court opinions that applied the principles of *CCNV* to the computer industry. Two aspects of the case are particularly instructive. Most critically, the opinion demonstrates the types of analyses courts will use to balance the several factors that *CCNV* relates are relevant to differentiating independent contractors from employees. In this regard, notice how certain factors, such as how the hiring party treats benefits and tax issues, may be given greater weight than others. *Aymes v. Bonelli* also is important because it raises, as did *CCNV*, the thorny possibility that a joint work may have been created. It thus highlights once again that the topic of ownership raises several difficult issues. The case, therefore, should be read as a warning about the importance of dealing with ownership issues clearly and properly in written contracts.

## AYMES V. BONELLI

*Second Circuit Court of Appeals, 1992*

### Facts

In May 1980, Aymes was hired by Bonelli, the president of Island, to work as a computer programmer. Island operated a chain of retail stores selling swimming pools and related supplies. Aymes worked with Island's computer systems from 1980 to 1982. During this period, Aymes created a series of programs called CSALIB under the general direction of Bonelli, who was not a professional computer programmer. CSALIB was used by Island to maintain records of cash receipts, physical inventory, sales figures, purchase orders, merchandise transfers, and price changes. There was no written agreement between Aymes and Bonelli assigning ownership or the copyright of CSALIB. Bonelli did not promise that CSALIB would be used only at one computer and only in one Island office.

Aymes did most of his programming at the Island office, where he had access to Island's computer hardware. He generally worked alone and had enjoyed considerable autonomy in creating CSALIB. That autonomy was restricted only by Bonelli, who directed and instructed Aymes on what he wanted from the program. Bonelli was not, however, sufficiently skilled to write the program himself.

Although Aymes worked semiregular hours, he was not always paid by the hour and on occasion presented his bills to Bonelli as invoices. At times, Aymes would be paid by the project and given bonuses for finishing the project on time. Aymes never received any health or other insurance benefits from Island. Island never paid an employer's percentage of Aymes's payroll taxes and never withheld any of his salary for federal or state taxes. In fact, Aymes was given an Internal Revenue Service 1099 nonemployee compensation form instead of the standard employee W-2 form.

Aymes left Island in September 1982, when Bonelli unilaterally decided to cut Aymes's hours. At the time Aymes left, Island owed him $14,560 in wages. Aymes also requested payment for Island's having made copies of CSALIB so that the program could be used in multiple sites. Bonelli insisted that Aymes sign a release for his rights to CSALIB in order to receive the back earnings. Aymes refused to sign and was not paid.

Aymes sued for copyright infringement and for back wages, among other things. The district court applied the *CCNV v. Reid* multifactored test for determining whether a party is an employee under the work-made-for-hire doctrine. The District Court held that Aymes was Island's employee and had no copyright interest in CSALIB. However, the court ordered Island to pay Aymes for back wages plus interest. Aymes appealed.

### Opinion

It is not disputed that Aymes and Bonelli never signed a written agreement assigning ownership rights in CSALIB. We must therefore consider whether the program was a work prepared by Aymes as an employee within the scope of his employment. If so, CSALIB qualifies as a work made for hire whose copyright belongs to Island as Aymes's employer.

In *CCNV v. Reid*, the Supreme Court addressed the issue of when an individual is an employee under the work-for-hire doctrine. The court concluded that the determination is based on several factors, which, under general agency principles, distinguish an employee from an independent contractor. The court noted that no single factor is determinative.

**Application of the CCNV Test.** We begin our analysis by noting that the *CCNV* test can be easily misapplied, since it consists merely of a list of possible considerations that may or may not be relevant in a given case. *CCNV* established that no one factor is dispositive, but the case gave no direction concerning how the factors were to be weighed. It does not necessarily follow that because no one factor is dispositive, all factors are equally important, or indeed that all factors will have relevance in every case. The factors should not merely be tallied but should be weighed according to their significance in a case.

For example, factors relating to the authority to hire assistants will not normally be relevant if the very nature of the work requires the hired party to work alone. In such a case, that factor should be accorded no weight. Having the authority to hire assistants, however, might have great probative value when the individual claiming to be an independent contractor does exercise authority to enlist assistants without prior approval of the party that hired the individual. This would be highly indicative that the hired party was acting as an independent contractor.

Some factors, therefore, will often have little or no significance in determining whether a party is an independent contractor or an employee. In contrast, there are some factors that will be significant in virtually every situation. These include (1) the hiring party's right to control the manner and means of creation, (2) the skill required, (3) the provision of employee benefits, (4) the tax treatment of the hired party, and (5) whether the hiring party has the right to assign additional projects to the hired party. These factors will almost always be relevant and should be given more weight in the analysis, because they will usually be highly probative of the true nature of the employment relationship.

The district court gave each factor equal weight and simply counted the number of factors for each side in determining that Aymes was an employee. In so doing, the district court over-emphasized indeterminate and thus irrelevant factors having little or no bearing on Aymes's situation. Because we find that the CCNV test was not intended to be applied in a mechanistic fashion, we now review each of the factors and consider their relative importance in this case. We begin by addressing those factors bearing most significantly in our analysis.

*The Right to Control.* It is clear that Bonelli and Island had the right to control the manner in which CSALIB was created. Aymes disputed Bonelli's purported skill at programming, but even without such knowledge, Bonelli was capable of directing Aymes on CSALIB's necessary function. Aymes received significant input from Bonelli in programming CSALIB and worked under the programming limitations placed by Bonelli. Consequently, this factor weighs heavily in favor of finding that Aymes was an employee.

*The Level of Skill.* The district court found that although Aymes's ability as a programmer required skills beyond the capacity of a layman, it required no peculiar expertise or creative genius. We disagree. Aymes's work required far more than merely transcribing Bonelli's instructions. Rather, his programming demanded that he use skills developed while a graduate student and through his experience working at a family-run company. We conclude that the district court erred in relying on Aymes's relative youth and inexperience as a professional computer programmer. Rather, the court should have examined the skill necessary to perform the work. In this case, Aymes was clearly a skilled craftsperson. Consequently, this factor weighs heavily in his favor.

*Employee Benefits and Tax Treatment.* The district court found that Aymes had received no employee benefits from Island, but it disregarded this factor as merely being an indication that Aymes was an employee who worked off the books. Island also did not pay a share of Aymes's Social Security taxes and did not withhold income taxes.

The failure of Island to extend Aymes any employee benefits or to pay any of his payroll taxes is highly indicative that Aymes was considered an outside independent contractor by Island. Indeed, these two factors constitute virtual admissions of Aymes's status by Bonelli himself. Island benefited from treating Aymes like an independent contractor when it came to providing benefits and paying a percentage of his payroll taxes. Island should not be allowed in one context to claim that Aymes was an independent contractor and then ten years later deny him that status in order to avoid a copyright infringement suit. Island deliberately chose to deny Aymes two basic attributes of employment it presumably extended to its workforce. This undisputed choice is completely inconsistent with its defense.

The importance of these two factors is underscored by the fact that every case since *CCNV* that has applied the test has found the hired party to be an independent contractor when the hiring party failed to extend benefits or pay Social Security taxes.

*The Right to Assign Other Projects.* Bonelli had the right to and did assign Aymes other projects in addition to the creation of CSALIB. This is fairly strong evidence that Aymes was an employee, since independent contractors are typically hired only for particular projects. However, this factor carries less weight than those evaluated earlier because the delegation of additional projects to Aymes is not inconsistent with the idea that he was Island's independent troubleshooter who might be asked to intervene as computer problems arose. Accordingly, this factor weighs fairly strongly but not conclusively for Island.

*Remaining Factors.* The remaining factors are relatively insignificant or negligible in weight because they are either indeterminate or inapplicable to these facts. Although none carries much weight, they are addressed in order of their relative importance in this determination.

"The method of payment" is a fairly important factor, but it is indeterminate in this case because there is evidence to support both sides. Aymes was sometimes paid hourly wages and at other times was paid a flat fee for completing a specific task.

"Whether the work is Island's regular business" is a factor that weighs in favor of Aymes's contention that he was an independent contractor. The purpose of this factor is to determine whether the hired party is performing tasks that directly relate to the objective of the hiring party's business. For example, work done by a computer programmer employed by a computer software firm would be done in the firm's regular business. Because Island is in the business of selling swimming pools, however, Aymes's programming was not done in the company's regular business. We find, however, that this factor will generally be of little use in evaluating a claim that a work was made for hire. This factor carries very little weight because pool companies do not survive by merely hiring pool designers and salespeople. For example, most companies hire numerous support personnel such as managers, accountants, secretaries, custodians, and computer programmers. That Aymes did not work in Island's regular business is not strongly indicative of whether he was an independent contractor, even if it does weigh in his favor.

"Whether Island is in business" is a factor that will always have very little weight in this analysis. Here, it weighs negligibly in favor of Island.

"The discretion over when and how long to work" is indeterminate, since Aymes had some degree of flexibility in his hours, but with Island's clearly having control over the project.

"The duration of the relationship" is a similarly inconclusive factor. The relationship between the parties extended over a long period of time, which indicates that Aymes was an employee. Although Aymes worked two years for Island, he did occasional work for others at the same time. Moreover, there were undisputed gaps in his employment, which suggests that he was not a full-time employee. Given the particular facts of this case, this factor has only slight weight in Island's favor.

"The location of the work" was not specifically addressed by the district court. Aymes did most of his programming at Island's offices. However, since Aymes was required to work in Island's offices in order to have access to its computer hardware, this factor would be accorded negligible weight.

Similarly, "the source of the equipment" carries little weight in the analysis. All the equipment Aymes used was located at Island's office. Again, however, the programming by necessity had to be performed on Island's machines.

"The authority to hire assistants" is also virtually meaningless in a situation in which the hired party does not need assistants.

Examining the factors for each side in terms of their importance, we conclude that the only major factor strongly supporting Island is that it directed the creation of the program. Island did reserve the right to assign Aymes other projects, which is a major factor, but under these facts this was not necessarily inconsistent with an independent contractor relationship. Supporting Aymes's argument that he was an independent contractor, however, are several important factor— his skill, and the tax and benefits factors—that outweigh the elements supporting Island. The other factors outlined in *CCNV* are either indeterminate or of negligible importance and cannot outweigh the significance we attach to Island's choice to treat Aymes as an independent contractor when it was to Island's financial benefit. Now that this treatment is no longer to Island's benefit, the company must still adhere to the choice it made.

On balance, application of the *CCNV* test requires that we find Aymes to be an independent contractor when he was creating CSALIB for Island. Consequently, we hold that CSALIB is not a work for hire.

**Issues on Remand.** Aymes cannot realistically dispute the fact that he sold defendants the computer program and that defendants are therefore the rightful owners of the program. Therefore, Island had a clear right to use the program that it had purchased from Aymes. The issue that is unresolved is whether Island made unlicensed copies of the program for other external corporations. We remand this issue to the district court for its determination.

An additional issue on remand arises from Island's argument that Bonelli is a "joint owner" of the copyright to CSALIB under Section 201(a) because of his contribution to its creation. Although CSALIB was not a work for hire, it might still possibly be considered a joint work due to Bonelli's involvement in its development. Because there were no specific findings of fact on this issue, we remand the issue for the district court's determination.

The judgment of the district court is reversed, and the case is remanded for further proceedings.

## Moral Rights

One other issue was discussed in the CCNV litigation, which should be noted before leaving the topic of ownership. The Court of Appeals in CCNV raised the possibility that Reid, as an author, might enjoy certain moral rights independent of his ownership stake. This might give him rights, stated the court, both to prevent CCNV or others from distorting or mutilating versions of the work (rights to integrity) and to ensure that he receives proper credit as an author of the sculpture (rights to paternity or attribution).[34]

Moral rights are likely to receive greater attention in the United States now that this country has signed the Berne Convention. Article 6b of the convention states that independent of an author's economic rights, and even after transfer of them, an author has the rights to claim authorship and to object to any distortion or other derogatory action that would be prejudicial to the author's honor or reputation. When the United States passed the Berne Convention Implementation Act in 1988, no explicit changes in the Copyright Act were then made so as to assimilate the concept of moral rights. The drafters believed such moral rights to attribution and integrity were already protected by other state and federal laws.[35] For instance, federal trademark laws prohibit false designations of origin.[36] Also, many states, such as California and New York, have a variety of laws that extend the rights of authors beyond copyright ownership. For example, California protects a person's "right of publicity" by preventing the unauthorized commercial use of another person's name, voice, signature, or photograph. Due to this state law, it is possible that one who owns the copyright in, let's say, a Bette Midler recording, may not be able to imitate her voice in an advertisement without gaining her permission.[37] In addition, Congress recently amended the Copyright Act so that it protects the moral rights of visual artists.[38] Section 106A of the act now provides that, independent of the Section 106 ownership rights, authors of certain limited-edition works of visual art have rights of attribution and integrity. The protection of moral rights definitely is on the rise in the United States and around the world, and there likely will be repercussions on those managing copyrighted materials. There will be some discussion of possible implications in the next chapter with respect to digital sampling and multimedia works.

# HOW TO OBTAIN COPYRIGHT PROTECTION

## Registration and Deposit

Unlike with patents, copyright protection is inexpensive and easy to obtain. Indeed, the two situations are polar opposites in this regard. Ever since the United States joined the Berne Convention in 1988, the actual procedural requirements for copyright protection come down to one word: none. This is because the fundamental tenet of this international agreement is that the enjoyment of copyright protection shall be subject to no formalities. Thus, the mere act of fixing one's creative expression in a tangible form is sufficient to obtain the rights attendant with copyright. However, although no longer necessary, it still is advisable to register one's work with the Copyright Office and to place a copyright notice on the work. These considerations will be reviewed here.

Even before the adoption of the Berne Convention, registration was not required for copyright protection in the United States. Instead, registration essentially was a means to gain certain technical advantages in case a copyright dispute ever materialized. This situation remains the same today, unaffected by the Berne Convention. The fundamental tenet of the convention is satisfied in that registration is optional, yet there are important reasons why one should consider undertaking it. These reasons are outlined in Exhibit 5.4.

Possibly the most significant consideration in deciding whether to register is that the procedure is so simple and cheap. Essentially, only three things are required: (1) completion of a short form, which requests basic information about the author (name, dates of birth and death, nationality) and the work (its nature, completion date, and publication date); (2) deposit of one or two copies of the work; and (3) payment of a $20 fee. The Copyright Office makes only a perfunctory review of the materials to ensure that the information is correctly provided on the form, that the work is suitable for copyright protection, and that the work comprises some expression entailing at least a minimal amount of creativity. The office does not undertake an exhaustive substantive review to confirm the work's originality or to delineate the protectible expression from the unprotectible ideas. In fact, registration is so routine that an attorney is not really required to satisfy it. Therefore, it normally makes sense to register if one can receive any possible benefit from undertaking the process.

The Copyright Act provides a number of reasons to seriously consider registration. First, if one registers before or within five years of publication (selling or offering to sell copies to the public), then should there be a dispute, the registration and the information contained therein carry substantial evidentiary weight in court. In legal terms, the registration serves as prima facie evidence of copyright validity and of the facts stated in the registration form.[39] For example, Todd develops an original computer program and immediately registers it. After marketing it for several years, he notices that Martha has begun selling a substantially similar program at a lower price. Todd is certain that Martha copied his program, and he brings a lawsuit alleging copyright infringement. Martha challenges the originality of Todd's program, stating that Todd copied other preexisting programs, including her own. Todd's copyright registration will be very important to him in this dispute, since the court will strongly accept its validity and factual statements, including the designated completion date. Since Todd has registered the work, Todd will not have the burden of proving originality; rather, Martha will have the task of convincing the court that the work is not original. In addition, the registration seriously jeopardizes Martha's claim that her work came first, for the court will assume that the date provided in Todd's registration is accurate. Although Martha can rebut this assumption with hard evidence, she is still the one who faces the tough burdens of proof rather than Todd. What could have been an unpredictable battle of credibility thereby will likely evaporate in Todd's favor.

Registration also may improve one's ability to be compensated for copyright infringement. The Copyright Act provides that when copyright privileges are infringed, copyright owners may sue not only for their damages but also, to some extent, for the profits derived by the infringer through its violative activities. Even with these substantial remedial rights, however, copyright owners may find it difficult to be adequately compensated. For example, suppose you own the copyright in a new song that has been distributed in the CD format. A radio station, in theory, has to gain your permission before playing that song. However, the damages imposed on you and the extra profits earned by the radio station from playing that song may be relatively little—so little, in fact, that the radio station might risk playing the song without gaining permission, comfortably knowing that you would not go through the effort to sue it for infringement for such a trivial return. However, if radio stations all over the country did this frequently, your losses could become significant. To alleviate this problem, the Copyright Act provides the copyright owner with an alternative to proving damages and profits. The act allows a judge to grant "statutory damages" for an amount between $500 and $20,000 that, in that judge's discretion, is just and fair under the circumstances.[40] In addition, if the copyright owner can prove that the infringement was willful, then the judge may award up to $100,000.

Statutory damages are important not only because they reduce the burden on the copyright owner to prove damages but also because they impose a nontrivial minimum floor that must be paid for infringement, no matter what real damage a violation has caused. In this way, statutory damages are an additional deterrent for those contemplating infringement. Registration figures into all of this because copyright owners are not eligible to sue for statutory damages unless they have registered the work according to certain time limits specified in the Copyright Act.[41] With some exception, the act provides that a work must have been registered before the infringement occurred. This presents a tremendous incentive to register as soon as possible after a work is created.

Another benefit afforded by registration is that it allows a court to require the infringer to compensate the copyright owner for attorney's fees and costs.[42] As you are probably aware, the prevailing party in a lawsuit is normally responsible to pay for his or her own attorney. This means that even a person who wins a

## Exhibit 5.4  Reasons to Register

### Prima Facie Evidence

- Of copyright validity
- Of facts in registration statement
- Registration within 5 years of publication

### Statutory Damages

- $500–$20,000 ($100,000 if willful)
- Generally, registration must precede infringement.

### Attorney's Fees and Costs

- Generally, registation must precede infringement.

### To Bring Infringement Suit

- Domestic works only

---

lawsuit may end up with little compensation after the attorney and all the other costs of bringing the suit are paid. Attorney's fees and costs, thus, are an important special benefit enjoyed by copyright owners. However, as with statutory damages, one must appropriately register, usually before the infringement, to be entitled to them. This, then, represents another good reason to register promptly.[43]

The importance of registration presents a dilemma for one who wishes to enjoy the full benefits of copyright protection for works containing valuable trade secrets. Section 408 of the Copyright Act specifies that those who register an unpublished work that has not yet been offered or sold to the general public must deposit with the Copyright Office one complete copy of that work. This could be devastating if the work contains trade secrets, because material deposited with the Copyright Office is available for public inspection.[44] The act also requires the deposit of two complete copies of the best edition if the work has indeed been published. Although one usually abandons trade secret protection once public sales have been made, sometimes computer software firms attempt to maintain it by distributing their products only in machine-readable form. Given that the "best edition" of a program is source code, deposits of the program definitely would expose whatever trade secrets it contained. Recognizing that deposits might cause problems in certain contexts, Congress empowered the Copyright Office to permit the deposit of identifying portions of a work instead of a complete copy. Based on this, the Copyright Office generally allows one to apply for special relief when the deposit might cause undue hardship.[45] In addition, because of the widespread concern with computer programs, it has established a set of regulations specifically dealing with them.[46]

The computer program deposit regulations promulgated by the Copyright Office automatically allow owners of program copyrights to deposit less than entire copies. For instance, one can deposit only the first and last 25 pages of source

code. If those portions contain trade secrets, however, then one can choose between a number of alternatives that allow the deposit of smaller portions, or of
portions with the trade secrets blocked out, or of combinations of source code
and machine-readable object code. Deposits in one of these manners usually
allow the copyright owner of a program to retain all the benefits from registration while protecting trade secrets. If trade secrets still would be jeopardized
under any of these alternatives, one even is allowed to simply deposit object code.
However, when that option is selected, the registration will not serve as prima
facie evidence of copyright validity because the Copyright Office examiners are
not able to scrutinize the materials.[47]

One other aspect of registration is worth noting. Before adoption of the
Berne Convention, all persons had to register their works before instituting infringement actions in court. Because this constituted a procedural step that was
needed in order to enjoy one's copyright privileges, it violated the spirit of the
Berne Convention. Therefore, this requirement was modified in 1988, when the
United States became a participant. However, it was altered only with respect to
certain foreign works. Thus, as required by the Berne Convention, foreign
works from Berne participant countries now may protect their copyrights in the
United States without undertaking any procedural steps, including registration. However, domestic works still must be registered before a suit is filed, although this distinction soon may be changed through legislation.[48] Keep in mind
that early registration remains advisable for foreign works so as to retain the
other technical benefits such as prima facie evidence, statutory damages, attorney's fees, and costs. Likewise, if domestic works ultimately are brought into
parity, as one should expect, the same advice would apply equally as well for
them.

### Copyright Notice

Although copyright notice once was a critical aspect of copyright protection in
the United States, it no longer is required. Again, acceptance of the Berne Convention, and its thesis that protection shall be subject to no formalities, was the
reason for the change. Now, one's expression is protected by copyright as soon
as it is fixed in tangible form. A copyright notice does not have to be placed on
a work at any time, either before or after it is publicly distributed.[49]

The Copyright Act nonetheless provides an incentive to place a proper notice
on copies. Those who wrongfully use or copy a work that has no notice might
argue that they did not know they were infringing someone's rights. They might
genuinely claim that had they known that someone claimed ownership in the expression, they would have refrained from impermissible actions. Under the circumstances, they might ask the court to recognize their innocence in the matter
and thus reduce their liability for what they did. The Copyright Act provides
that if a notice of copyright properly appears on the copies seen by the defendant, then no weight shall be given to the defendant's claim that actual or statutory damages should be reduced based on the defendant's claimed innocent in-

fringement.[50] Thus, although such notice is not required, it is still good practice to place one on copies of a work to ensure full compensation for acts of infringement.

The Copyright Act specifies what constitutes proper notice: either the letter "c" in a circle or the word "copyright" or the abbreviation "copr.," followed by the year of first publication and the name of the copyright owner. Thus, if William Styron owns the copyright in a book that is publicly distributed for the first time in 1992, then "© 1992 William Styron" is a correct form of notice. The notice should be placed in a location that reasonably may be seen.[51] The Copyright Office has passed regulations that provide guidance as to what are reasonable locations under certain circumstances. For instance, notice on machine-readable copies of computer programs may appear at the beginning or end of printouts, on a user's terminal either at sign-on or continually, or on labels affixed to containers of the copies, such as reels or cartridges.[52]

Suppose you run a company that has just completed a novel software program. Because the program contains many trade secrets, you plan to distribute it on a very limited basis while taking the necessary trade secret protection steps. However, you also want to fully enjoy copyright protection as well. Therefore you will register the work and deposit a copy so as to conceal the important secrets. Should you also place a notice on the copies? On one hand, if the program somehow is wrongfully released to the public, you do not want infringers to claim that they were innocently misled by the lack of notice. On the other hand, the copyright notice for published works indicates the year of first publication. By using the notice, you may thereby admit that your alleged secrets have already been disclosed to the public, making them ineligible for trade secret protection. A common practice to solve this dilemma is to indicate in the notice that the software is unpublished. Thus, a program written in 1992 by Brittany Bee might have as a notice "© 1992, an unpublished work by Brittany Bee." This will be sufficient to inform potential infringers of the copyright interest, without raising the inference that the program's secrets are already publicly available.[53]

## Duration of Copyright Protection

One of the reasons that copyright protection is so desirable is that it lasts for a relatively long period of time. The general rule is that the protection endures for as long as the author lives and then for 50 more years thereafter.[54] Thus, as soon as one's expression is fixed, one enjoys a substantial period of copyright protection without having to do anything. Certain works have different protection periods, although they all still are somewhat lengthy. The most important exception is for works made for hire. The copyrights in those works last for 100 years from the date of creation or 75 years from the year of first publication, whichever expires first.[55] For most technological products capable of copyright protection, this period more than suffices given that short life cycles are the overwhelming norm.

## INFRINGEMENT AND REMEDIES

A copyright allows its owner to enjoy the fruits of creative energies by providing exclusive control over a bundle of rights to a work's original expression. One who intrudes on any of those rights without permission *infringes* the copyright unless the use falls within an exception such as fair use. Probably a copyright owner's most important benefit is the right to reproduce a work in copies. But proving infringement of that right is most vexing.

There are several extremely difficult issues in proving infringement of the right to make reproductions. What does it mean to reproduce? The Copyright Act does not define the word. Will only an exact reproduction infringe? What if only ideas are copied, but not any expression? How much copying is too much? Also, how does one prove that another person copied a work? Copyright does not prevent another from independently creating the same expression. So how does one convince a court that one work was used in the preparation of another?

Clearly, copying must entail something more than an exact reproduction. Otherwise, one could easily and cheaply take the creative essence of a protected work by making a few minor alterations. Because copyright policy has been designed to preserve the incentives to create original expressions, it should not be so simple to subvert it. Thus, the right to reproduce must be somewhat broader. However, it cannot be so broad to effectively prohibit other persons who see a work from creating works of the same genre.

The balance struck by the courts is that a reproduction is made when one uses a work to make something that is substantially similar. Thus, a work does not have to be an exact replica to be a copy; it only must be substantially similar to the original. The analysis of similarities is not confined to comparisons of notes or words but also extends to plots, structures, and organizations. So, to prove infringement, one step is to provide sufficient evidence that convinces the court the alleged copy is substantially similar to the protected work. At this point, the issue is whether the entire works, in terms of both their ideas and their expressions, are substantially similar.

A complicating factor in the preceding analysis is that copyright infringement requires copying. One must demonstrate, therefore, that the similarities in the works were not the result of two artists' independently arriving at the same creations. It would be nice if alleged infringers admitted that their pieces were derived from that of the copyright owner. But one is not often so fortunate.

When one cannot directly prove that the similarities in the works resulted from copying, then proof must come circumstantially. What would it take to convince you that the similarities in two works did not occur from independent efforts? Of course, if the works are almost exact, then that alone might be sufficient. In such a case, you likely would think it to be unfathomable for such literal duplication to happen by chance. However, when the similarities are more nebulous, you might require something more to be persuaded. One aspect that should strongly affect your determination is whether the alleged infringers had *access* to the copyrighted work before creating their piece. Previous exposure to the work along with the resultant similarities should be sufficient to convince you that the creation of one work was tied to the other. Thus, in infringement actions, one often demonstrates copying by showing that there was access to the copyrighted work as well as substantial similarity. For this investigation, the courts allow experts in the field to present their opinions as to whether copying occurred.

The infringement inquiry does not end, however, with proof that a copyrighted work was reproduced. As you know, copyrights do not protect ideas, facts, and the like. Only expression is protected. Thus, one is allowed to reproduce portions of a copyrighted work and may do so exactly, as long as only the unprotected features are so copied. Proof that one work is substantially similar to another, therefore, may indicate copying but does not necessarily mean there was illicit copying. To satisfy this task, the copyright owner must show that the *expression* in the allegedly infringing work is substantially similar to the *expression* in the protected work. Given that the rationale for copyrights is to reward creative expressions through market incentives, one focuses this inquiry on consumers to determine whether the similarities are sufficient to affect their purchase decisions. Therefore, to judge whether unlawful appropriation of protected expression has occurred, only testimony by laypersons in the purchasing public is relevant. One may satisfactorily prove substantial similarity by showing that the allegedly infringing expression captures the "total concept and feel" of the expression in the copyrighted material. In addition, recognize that it is not necessary to draw upon large segments of expression to capture the "total concept and feel." Usurpation of qualitatively vital creative elements, even if quantitatively only a small portion of the work, can be sufficient.

Of course, before asking the lay audience to determine the existence of substantial similarity in expression, one must adequately factor out the unprotected ideas. This often is the most controversial task in copyright infringement disputes, and it clearly dominates the computer copyright field. Because this specific issue will be considered in depth with the computer materials in the next chapter, we will defer its treatment until then. However, clearly understand that infringement results when one makes a reproduction that is unlawful. The finding of substantial similarity of the entire works is only the beginning. One then must distinguish the ideas from the expressions and ask ordinary consumers to compare the total concepts and feel of those expressions. Exhibit 5.5 summarizes these points.

*Sid & Marty Krofft Television v. McDonald's Corp.* has served as a fundamental precedent for this substantial similarity analysis.[56] The Kroffts created "H. R. Pufnstuf," a children's television show, which included several fanciful, costumed characters, who lived in a fantasyland inhabited by moving trees and talking books. The show was very popular, and the characters were licensed to various manufacturers of children's products as well as to the Ice Capades. The Kroffts discussed the concept of a McDonald's advertising campaign based on the Pufnstuf series with the advertising agency serving McDonald's, but a deal

**Exhibit 5.5  Infringing Reproductions: Elements of Proof**

### Proof that Copyrighted Work was *Copied*

- Direct evidence
- Circumstantial evidence
  - Access
  - Substantial similarity
    = Substantial similarity determined by comparing the entire works, including both the ideas and the expressions in the works
    = Experts in the field may offer opinions.

### Proof that Copyrighted Work was *Illicitly Copied*

- One can legally copy the ideas of a copyrighted work.
- Substantial similarity of expression
  - Distinguish ideas of work from the expression.
  - Would an ordinary observer in the market audience consider the expressions of the two works to be substantially similar?
    = Total concept and feel

was not completed. McDonald's then independently launched its McDonaldland campaign. Licensing revenue from the Pufnstuf series fell dramatically, and the Kroffts sued McDonald's for copyright infringement.

McDonald's admitted in this case that it copied from the Pufnstuf show, so this controversy, as is so often true, centered on whether McDonald's had unlawfully appropriated the expression from the Pufnstuf series. The court determined that the idea of H. R. Pufnstuf was a fantasyland filled with diverse and fanciful characters in action. If this had been the only similarity shared by McDonaldland, then there would not have been infringement. However, both worlds were inhabited by anthropomorphic plants and animals, and they shared similar topographical features such as trees, caves, a pond, a road, and a castle. Both works presented talking trees with human faces and characters with large round heads and long wide mouths. They also both had crazy scientists and a multiarmed evil creature. McDonald's argued that there were still significant differences in the expressions. For instance, Pufnstuf wore a yellow and green dragon suit and a medal, which said "mayor." McCheese wore a pink formal coat with a sash, which also said "mayor" but began with the golden arches.

The court found the expression in McDonaldland to be substantially similar to that in H. R. Pufnstuf. It noted that since the shows were directed to children, the comparison would have to be made through the minds and imaginations of young people. The court recognized that children are not inclined to detect disparities in details. In the end, the Kroffts won the infringement action because McDonaldland, although certainly not an exact or literal replica, had captured the total concept and feel of the Pufnstuf show. The landmark computer cases of *Whelan v. Jaslow*, *Lotus v. Paperback Software*, and *Computer Associates v.*

**Exhibit 5.6  The Clean-Room Process**

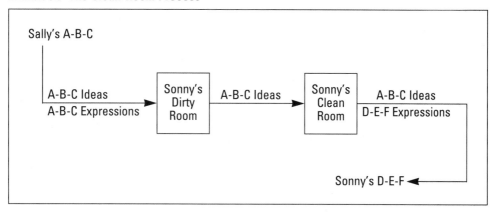

*Altai,* which are presented in the next chapter, provide more detailed examples of how these principles are applied in infringement actions and show how the principles might be misapplied in technology contexts.

## Clean-Room Techniques

The importance of proving access to copyrighted expression has led many computer software firms to develop so-called clean-room techniques to isolate programmers from any copyrighted expression they wish to emulate. Suppose that Sonny's Software, Inc. (Sonny's), wishes to develop a product to compete with Sally Software's popular A-B-C program. Sonny's splits its development personnel into two groups, who occupy two separate rooms. The first group occupies what is called the dirty room. The group thoroughly studies A-B-C and determines what ideas make up the program. Those ideas, and only the ideas, are then transmitted to the other group, who work in the clean room. The group in the clean room then develops an alternative program based on these ideas.

This technique may protect Sonny's if the resultant programs have substantially similar expressions. Sonny's will argue that the similarities in expression did not result from copying, but rather were a consequence of standard programming restraints or by chance. Sonny's will take the position that its programmers copied only the ideas from Sally's program, something it lawfully may do under the Copyright Act. Sally thereby may be frustrated by the clean-room technique because she will not be able to prove that the programmers had access to the A-B-C expression.

Clean-room procedures are routinely used and can be very effective. However, one must be mindful of certain inherent pitfalls. As we shall see in the next chapter, it is not always easy to distinguish the ideas of a computer program, or of any type of work for that matter, from its expression. Therefore, what the dirty room personnel believe to be ideas may turn out to be elements of expression. Since these parts will be given to the clean room, one now can prove that the personnel in the clean room had access to the expression. Also, the personnel in the dirty room must be careful not to violate the copyrights themselves by making illegal copies in that room while attempting to dissect the ideas from the expression. The notes and program listings carried out in this room may be unlawful copies, and this illicit activity may taint the entire procedure.

In 1992, the Ninth Circuit Court of Appeals issued an extremely important decision bearing on the legality of certain clean-room activities. Many computer programs are distributed in object code, a language that only the computer can read. In order for a human being to read the program, the program must be translated into source code, usually by means of a machine called a decompiler. The resultant source code is a copy or derivative of the object code. Under many circumstances, dirty-room personnel who wish to learn the ideas in an object code program may have no choice but to decompile the program into source code. Once the ideas are deciphered from decompiled source code, they are given to the clean room, and the source code is destroyed. The question arises whether the source code listing, made in the dirty room simply to learn the ideas in the program, infringes the copyright in the program. *Sega Enterprises v. Accolade*, which follows, deals with this very important topic.

## SEGA ENTERPRISES, LTD. V. ACCOLADE, INC.
*Ninth Circuit Court of Appeals, 1992*

### Facts

Sega develops and markets video entertainment systems, including the Genesis console. Accolade is a developer, manufacturer, and marketer of computer entertainment software, including game cartridges that are compatible with the Genesis console. Sega licenses its copyrighted computer code to a number of independent developers of computer game software so that they can develop games that can operate in the Genesis console. Accolade has never been one of those licensees.

Accolade used a two-step process to render its video games compatible with the Genesis console. First, it transformed the machine-readable object code contained in commercially available copies of Sega's game cartridges into human-readable source code using a process called disassembly or decompilation. Accolade purchased a Genesis console and three Sega cartridges, wired a decompiler into the console circuitry, and generated printouts of the resulting source code. Accolade engineers studied and annotated the printouts in order to identify areas of commonality among the three game programs. They next loaded the disassembled code back into a computer and experimented to discover the interface specifications for the Genesis console. Accolade then created a development manual that incorporated the information it had discovered about the requirements for a Genesis-compatible game. The manual contained only functional descriptions of the interface requirements and did not include any of Sega's code.

In the second stage, Accolade created its own games for Genesis. In this stage, it did not copy Sega's programs; it relied only on the information concerning interface specifications for the Genesis that was contained in the development manual. Accolade maintains that with the exception of the interface specifications, none of the code in its own games is derived in any way from its examination of Sega's code. Indeed, many of the programs had been developed and marketed for other console systems prior to being adapted for the Genesis console.

Sega sued Accolade for copyright infringement and requested a preliminary injunction. (It also sued for trademark infringement based on facts not provided in this synopsis.) The district court determined that Sega was likely to succeed on the merits and granted preliminary relief. Accolade appealed.

## Opinion

Accolade raises four arguments in support of its position that disassembly of the object code in a copyrighted computer program does not constitute infringement. Three will be considered here. First, it maintains that intermediate copying does not infringe the exclusive rights granted to copyright owners unless the end product of the copying is substantially similar to the copyrighted work. Second, it argues that disassembly of object code in order to gain an understanding of the ideas and functional concepts embodied in the code is always lawful. Finally, Accolade contends that its disassembly of object code was a fair use. Copyright law does not support the first two arguments. However, the third argument has merit. We conclude, based on the policies underlying the Copyright Act, that disassembly of copyrighted object code is a fair use of the work if such disassembly provides the only means of access to those elements of the code that are not protected by copyright, and the copier has a legitimate reason for seeking such access.

**Intermediate Copying.**  The Copyright Act does not distinguish between unauthorized copies of a copyrighted work on the basis of what stage of the alleged infringer's work the unauthorized copies represent. Section 501 provides that "[a]nyone who violates any of the exclusive rights of the copyright owner . . . is an infringer." On its face, that language unambiguously encompasses and proscribes intermediate copying. We hold that intermediate copying of computer object code may infringe the exclusive rights granted in Section 106 regardless of whether the end product of the copying also infringes those rights. If intermediate copying is permissible under the act, authority for such copying must be found in one of the statutory provisions to which the rights granted in Section 106 are subject (such as fair use).

**The Idea/Expression Dichotomy.**  Accolade next contends that disassembly of object code does not violate the Copyright Act because disassembly is always necessary to gain access to the ideas and functional concepts embodied in the code. Because humans cannot comprehend object code, it reasons, disassembly of a commercially available computer program into human-readable form should not be considered an infringement of the owner's copyright. Insofar as Accolade suggests that disassembly of object code is lawful per se, it seeks to overturn settled law.

Accolade's argument, in essence, is that object code is not eligible for the full range of copyright protection. However, the act makes no distinction between the copyrightability of those programs that directly interact with the computer user and those that simply manage the computer system. Nor does the act require that a work be directly accessible to humans to be eligible for copyright protection. Thus, the copyright in a computer program extends to the object code version of the program.

Our refusal to recognize a per se right to disassemble object code does not lead to an absurd result. The ideas and functional concepts underlying many types of computer programs, including word processing programs, spreadsheets, and video game displays, are readily discernible without the need for disassembly because the operation of such programs is visible on the computer screen. The need to disassemble object code arises, if at all, only in connection with operations systems, system interface procedures, and other programs that are not visible to the user when operating—and then only when no alternative means of gaining an understanding of those ideas and functional concepts exists. In our view, consideration of the unique nature of computer object code thus is more appropriate as part of the case-by-case equitable-fair-use analysis authorized by Section 107 of the act.

**Fair Use.** Accolade contends that its disassembly of copyrighted object code is a fair use privileged by Section 107. Because, in the case before us, disassembly is the only means of gaining access to unprotected ideas and functional concepts and because Accolade has a legitimate interest in gaining such access (to determine how to make its cartridges compatible with the Genesis console), we agree with Accolade.

Fair-use analysis requires an equitable balance of the factors noted in Section 107: the purpose of the use, its market effect, the nature of the work, and the amount copied. We proceed to evaluate these factors.

*Purpose.* We observe initially that the fact that copying is for a commercial purpose weighs against a finding of fair use. However, the presumption of unfairness can be rebutted by the characteristics of a particular commercial use.

As we have noted, the use at issue was an intermediate one only, and thus any commercial exploitation was indirect and derivative. Accolade's direct purpose in copying Sega's code was simply to study the functional requirements for Genesis compatibility. There is no evidence that Accolade sought to avoid performing its own creative work. Indeed, most of the games that Accolade released for the Genesis console had been originally developed for other hardware. Nor did Accolade simply copy Sega's code; rather, it wrote its own procedures based on what it had learned through disassembly. On these facts, we conclude that Accolade copied Sega's code for a legitimate, essentially nonexploitive purpose and that the commercial aspect of its use can best be described as of minimal significance.

We further note that we are free to consider the public benefit resulting from a particular use notwithstanding the fact that the alleged infringer may gain commercially. In this case, Accolade's identification of the functional requirements for Genesis compatibility has led to an increase in the number of independently designed video game programs offered for use with the Genesis console. It is precisely such growth in creative expression, based on the dissemination of other creative works and the unprotected ideas contained in them, that the Copyright Act is intended to promote. We conclude that given the purpose and character of Accolade's use of Sega's video game programs, the presumption of unfairness has been overcome and this first statutory factor weighs in favor of Accolade.

*Market Effect.* We must inquire whether there will be an adverse effect on the potential market for the copyrighted work (by way of diminishing potential sales, interfering with marketability, or usurping the market) if the challenged use should become widespread. Accolade sought only to become a legitimate competitor in the field of Genesis-compatible video games. Within that market, it is the characteristics of the game program as experienced by the user that determine the program's commercial success. There is nothing in the record that suggests that Accolade copied any of these elements of Sega's game programs.

By facilitating the entry of a new competitor, Accolade's disassembly of Sega's software undoubtedly affected the market for Genesis-compatible games in an indirect fashion. However, there is no basis for assuming that Accolade's Ishido has significantly affected the market for Sega's Altered Beast, because a consumer might easily purchase both; nor does it seem unlikely that a consumer interested in sports might purchase both Accolade's Mike Ditka Power Football and Sega's Joe Montana Football, particularly if the games are, as Accolade contends, not substantially similar. In any event, an attempt to monopolize the market by making it impossible for others to compete runs counter to the statutory purpose of promoting creative expression and cannot constitute a strong equitable basis for resisting the invocation of the fair-use doctrine. Thus, we conclude that this factor weighs in Accolade's, not Sega's favor, notwithstanding the minor economic loss Sega may suffer.

*Nature of the Work.* Not all copyrighted works are entitled to the same level of protection. Works of fiction receive greater protection than works that have strong factual elements, such as historical or biographical works or works that have strong functional elements such as accounting textbooks. Works that are merely compilations of facts are copyrightable, but their copyright protection is thin. Similarly, since computer programs essentially are utilitarian articles, many aspects of such programs are not protected by copyright.

Sega argues that even if many elements of its video game programs are not protected by copyright, Accolade still copied protected expression. Sega is correct, since disassembly involves wholesale copying. But computer programs are unique: The unprotected aspects of most functional works are readily accessible to the human eye. The systems described in accounting textbooks, for example, can easily be copied without also copying any of the protected expressive aspects of the original works. Computer programs, however, typically are distributed for public use in object code form, embedded in a silicon chip or on a floppy disk. For this reason, humans often cannot gain access to the unprotected ideas and functional concepts contained in object code without disassembling that code, meaning, making copies. Because Sega's video game programs contain unprotected aspects that cannot be examined without copying, we afford those programs a lower degree of protection than more traditional literary works. In light of all these considerations, we conclude that this statutory factor weighs in favor of Accolade.

*Amount Copied.* Accolade disassembled entire programs written by Sega. Accordingly, this factor weighs against Accolade. However, as the Supreme Court explained in *Sony*, the fact that an entire work was copied does not preclude a finding of a fair use.

**Summary.** We are not unaware of the fact that to those used to considering copyright issues in more traditional contexts, our result may seem incongruous at first blush. To oversimplify, Accolade, a commercial competitor of Sega, engaged in wholesale copying of Sega's copyrighted code as a preliminary step in the development of a competing product. However, the key to this case is that we are dealing with computer software, a relatively unexplored area in the world of copyright law. We must avoid the temptation of trying to force the proverbial square peg into a round hole.

Sega argues that the considerable time, effort, and money that went into development of the Genesis and Genesis-compatible video games militate against a finding of fair use. In *Feist*, however, the Supreme Court unequivocally rejected the sweat-of-the-brow rationale for copyright protection.

We conclude that when disassembly is the only way to gain access to the ideas and functional elements embodied in a copyrighted computer program and when there is a legitimate reason for seeking such access, disassembly is a fair use of the copyrighted work. Our conclusion does not, of course, insulate Accolade from a claim of copyright infringement with respect to its finished products. Sega has reserved the right to raise such a claim, and it may do so.

Accordingly, we hold that Sega has failed to demonstrate a likelihood of success on the merits of its copyright claim. Thus, the preliminary injunction issued in its favor must be dissolved.

---

*Sega v. Accolade* is one of a series of cases decided in 1992 that mark a possible reversal of policy respecting the degree of protection afforded computer programs by copyright. Another such case is *Computer Associates v. Altai*, which is presented in the next chapter. Prior to *Sega*, a developer of mass-marketed computer software could effectively protect trade secrets embodied in its programs by distributing them only in object code. Since copying is required to decipher trade secrets written in object code, copyright effectively could prevent reverse engineering of the code to learn the valuable secrets. *Sega*, however, clouds the issue. According to *Sega*, reverse engineering of object code through copying is a fair use if (1) there are no other means to access the program ideas and functional aspects and (2) there is a legitimate reason for seeking access. Although *Sega* provides that one legitimate rationale for decompilation is to achieve interoperability of game programs with consoles, the case does not clearly identify other reasons that may be acceptable. One can expect that more defined guidance will be available only after numerous and diverse cases are decided by the courts. For now, therefore, purveyors of computer programs containing trade secrets must at least consider whether additional measures should be utilized to protect their secrets. One possibility is to form agreements with customers limiting the ways customers may use programs. As we shall see in the next chapter, however, distributors of programs for the mass market may have difficulty enforcing such agreements.

All of this, of course, impacts our ability to protect the computer program used within the AES. We may have decided that since the program is distributed in a form that cannot be read by humans, it could somewhat easily be preserved as a trade secret. Any attempt by other companies to reverse-engineer the program by decompiling or chip-peeling would require a translation into source code. If these actions were to violate the copyright in the program, then we could use copyright policy to help us preserve the secrecy of our program ideas. However, after *Sega*, reverse engineering of the program by methods such as decompilation might be considered a fair use unless there are other ways to access the ideas used within the programs. Thus, although *Sega* was formally a case about copyright protection, its most important impact will be on the viability of trade secret protection strategies used by firms distributing computer programs and the products utilizing them.

### Remedies

Once infringement has been proven, the copyright owner may choose from a wide arsenal of remedies. First, the successful copyright claimant may benefit from court-imposed injunctions—orders requiring the infringer to stop engaging in the infringing activity.[57] Not only can one receive a permanent injunction after proving infringement at trial, but one can also obtain a preliminary injunction before trial if the judge is persuaded that the likelihood of success at trial is high and that irreparable harm will result if the allegedly offending activity is not stopped immediately. Second, the copyright owner may sue for actual damages and the infringer's profits.[58] As previously discussed, these may be hard to prove, so the claimant may opt for statutory damages instead, assuming the work was appropriately registered. In addition, the copyright owner may be able to receive attorney's fees and court costs, again assuming that registration was timely. Finally, one should be aware that it is a criminal offense to infringe a copyright willfully and for private financial gain. Criminal penalties include fines of up to $500,000 and imprisonment for up to ten years.[59]

## CONCLUSION

Copyright protection seems almost too good to be true. Absolutely nothing needs to be done to acquire it. Even those steps that provide extra benefits are extraordinarily inexpensive and easy to perform. And protection may last for over 100 years. Compared to the patent system, therefore, with its expensive and tedious procedures and relatively short period of protection, copyrights are a bargain. Given these enormous disparities, how can patents and copyrights co-exist?

The answer is rooted in the different roles played by the two systems. A patent protects an idea embedded in a product. In a limited sense of the word, a patent provides an owner with monopoly control over a product concept. The market dominance legally bestowed by a patent thereby may be extremely lucrative. A copyright, on the other hand, does not protect an idea, but only a means of expressing it. Normally, there will be a large number of equally suitable ways to convey a concept, and one would expect a host of competitors to adopt them. Therefore, a copyright theoretically gives something less than monopoly power and consequently should provide a lower return than a patent. Also, a copyright, unlike a patent, does not prevent independent creation. This further weakens the market posture of a copyright. In sum, then, copyrights are easier to obtain and last longer than patents but should provide lower economic returns for their owners. Overall, this is a reasonable and balanced trade-off.

The next chapter features some of the most current and controversial copyright issues affecting the management of technology. As copyrights extend to components of useful articles, such as computer programs, one needs to be careful that they do not overstep their rightful bounds. One clear benchmark is that copyrights never should be the basis for market dominance. That would be the best of both worlds—easy protection and monopoly returns—a result that would seriously upset the proper relationship between patents and copyrights. Unfortunately, this basic concept often is overlooked or forgotten.

## NOTES

1. 17 U.S.C. §102(a).
2. Sheldon v. Metro-Goldwyn Pictures Corp., 81 F. 2d 49 (2nd Cir.), cert. den. 298 U.S. 669 (1936).
3. Ibid.
4. 17 U.S.C. §102(a). See the definition of pictorial, graphic and sculptural works in Section 101 of the Copyright Act.
5. 17 U.S.C. §102(b).
6. Baker v. Seldin, 101 U.S. (11 Otto) 99 (1879).
7. Walter, "Databases: Protecting an Asset; Avoiding a Liability," Computer Lawyer (March 1991) at 10.
8. Ibid.
9. For thorough discussions of this proposed Directive, see M. Epstein, "Protection of Databases under U.S. Copyright Law: Feist and Its Progeny," 4 J. of Proprietary Rights (July 1992) at 8-9; American Bar Association, Section of Patent, Trademark and Copyright Law, Annual Report 1991–1992 at 382-387.
10. European Community Proposal for a Council Directive on the Legal Protection of Data Bases, Article 2, paragraph 5.

11. Ibid., preamble, paragraph 28.

12. Ibid., Article 8, paragraph 4.

13. Ibid., Article 8, paragraph 1.

14. Ibid., Article 11, paragraph 1; Preamble, paragraph 38.

15. As of 1994, the Copyright Act does not grant to owners of copyrights in sound recordings the exclusive right to perform their works publicly. Such a right resides only in the owner of the underlying composition. However, there is a strong legislative effort to extend copyright protection to digital performances of sound-recordings. This is due to new digital technologies, which are spawning services that enable customers to request songs to be transmitted (performed) to them digitally. Owners of copyrights in sound-recordings fear that consumers will bypass the purchase of CDs (from which they get their royalties) and obtain the songs via transmissions (public performances). In such a case, the sound recording copyright owners would not be compensated because permissions, and thus royalties, are not required for the transmissions. See the Digital Performance Right in Sound Recordings Act (H.R. 2576, 1993). On an associated front, the Working Group on Intellectual Property Rights of the White House Information Infrastructure Task Force proposed in July 1994 that the right to transmit be added to Section 106.

16. 17 U.S.C. §201(d).

17. 17 U.S.C. §109.

18. Harper & Row Publishers, Inc. v. Nation Enterprises, 471 U.S. 539 (1985).

19. Public Law 102-492 (October 24, 1992) amending Section 107 of the Copyright Act.

20. Lewis Galoob Toys, Inc. v. Nintendo of America, Inc., 964 F. 2d 965 (9th Cir. 1992).

21. For thorough discussions, see Seth Greenstein, "Contributory Infringement the Second Time Around: The Copyright Case against Digital Audio Tape Recorders," 3 J. of Proprietary Rights (July 1991) at 2; Leete, "Betamax and Sound Recordings: Is Copyright in Trouble?" 23 Am. Bus. L.J. 551 (1986).

22. See P. Reilly, "Sony's Digital Audio Format Pulls ahead of Philips's, But Both Still Have Far to Go," Wall Street J. (August 6, 1993) at B1.

23. The initial disputes centered on digital audiotape formats.

24. Cahn v. Sony Corporation, 90 Civ. 4537 (SDNY, 1990). This lawsuit was settled and the case was dismissed by the court in July 1991.

25. 17 U.S.C. §1001 et seq. (1992).

26. 17 U.S.C. §1008.

27. 17 U.S.C. §201(a).

28. 17 U.S.C. §201(d).

29. 17 U.S.C. §202.

30. Kastor, "Whose Art Is It Anyway?" Washington Post (March 27, 1989) at C1.

31. 17 U.S.C. §203(a).

32. 17 U.S.C. §205.

33. Ashton-Tate Corp. v. Ross, 728 F. Supp. 597 (N.D. Cal. 1989).

34. 846 F. 2d 1485, 1498 (D.C. Cir. 1988).

35. Strauss, "Don't Be Burned by the Berne Convention," New Matter (State of California Bar Association), Spring 1989 at 10.
36. Lanham Act, 15 U.S.C. §1125(a).
37. Midler v. Ford Motor Co. 849 F. 2d 460 (9th Cir. 1988).
38. The Visual Artists Rights Act of 1990, Pub. L. No. 101-650,
39. 17 U.S.C. §410(c).
40. 17 U.S.C. §504(c).
41. 17 U.S.C. §412.
42. 17 U.S.C. §§412, 505.
43. As this book goes to press in 1994, Congress is considering a proposal that would allow copyright owners to recover statutory damages, attorney's fees and costs without registering their works. There is a substantial possibility that this legislative initiative will be included within the GATT implementation package. If so, these changes may be implemented as early as 1995.
44. 17 U.S.C. §705(b).
45. 37 CFR Ch. II Section 202.20(d).
46. 37 CFR Part II Section 202.20(c)(2)(vii).
47. 37 CFR Part II Section 202.20(c)(2)(vii)(B).
48. 17 U.S.C. §411. H.R. 897, S. 373, the Copyright Reform Act of 1993.
49. 17 U.S.C. §401.
50. 17 U.S.C. §401(d).
51. 17 U.S.C. §401(c).
52. 37 CFR Section 201.20(g).
53. See Cooper, Law and the Software Marketer, Prentice-Hall, 1988, at 46-47.
54. 17 U.S.C. §302(a).
55. 17 U.S.C. §302(c).
56. 562 F. 2d 1157 (9th Cir. 1977).
57. 17 U.S.C. §502.
58. 17 U.S.C. §504(a).
59. 17 U.S.C. §506; 18 U.S.C. §2319(b).

# 6

# COPYRIGHT POLICY: SPECIFIC TECHNOLOGY APPLICATIONS

## INTRODUCTION

It is difficult to open the newspaper nowadays without noticing some controversy involving copyright protection for new-technology enterprises. Often the disputes concern computers and computer applications. Does copyright protection extend to computer programs? Should it? What parts of the program are subject to copyright protection? And in what form? What if the program is "written" on a chip or other component of the machine? What can others do with a program once it's in their hands? How can they be stopped? This chapter addresses many of these questions. Perhaps more important, it also strives to make one sensitive to copyright policy and the ways copyright policy likely will satisfy the yet undefined set of future issues.

As the overview provided in Exhibit 6.1 demonstrates, the chapter does not focus only on computers, however. Concerns about copyright protection have a wide scope. With increasing frequency, design and style constitute the creativity that sells products. Can copyright protect product designs? Should it? New technologies now have the capacity to easily manipulate traditional art forms. Digital sampling and computerized photograph scanning equipment are two examples. What does copyright policy have to say about the futures of these industries? Interactive CD-ROM technology is now breaking into the marketplace. Through developments in this technology, individuals can selectively view and adapt databases of existing works. What hurdles does a manager in the CD-ROM-technology industry face? This chapter investigates some of the important questions arising in these developing contexts.

## COPYRIGHT POLICY AND COMPUTER PROGRAMS

When the computer industry was in its infancy in the mid-1960s, there was tremendous uncertainty about whether computer programs could be protected under the copyright laws. On one hand, such programs, especially when written in high-level source code, have all the earmarks of a creative literary-style document. On the other, computer programs are an integral part of an operational machine—just the type of thing excluded from the reaches of copyright. In 1976, Congress substantially revised the Copyright Act after an almost 20-year process of debating the parameters of change. Although Congress was aware of various problems that new technologies such as computers posed to copyright policy, it recognized that it would not be able to adequately address them in the pending legislative effort. Therefore, it created the National Commission on New Technological Uses of Copyrighted Works (CONTU) to make recommendations about changes to copyright policy that might be required in order to accommodate new technological developments.[1]

In 1978, after almost three years of deliberations, CONTU released its final report. CONTU's most definitive recommendation was that copyright protection should be available to computer programs. It stated:

> The cost of developing computer programs is far greater than the cost of their duplication. Consequently, computer programs . . . are likely to be disseminated only if . . . [t]he creator can spread its costs over multiple copies of the work with some form of protection against unauthorized duplication of the work. . . . The Commission is therefore satisfied that some form of protection is necessary to encourage the creation and broad distribution of computer programs in a competitive market, . . . [and] that the continued availability of copyright protection for computer programs is desirable.[2]

The final report made clear that, consistent with copyright principles in traditional contexts, protection should be offered only to the expression of computer programs. However, the report was ambiguous about what aspects of the programs should be considered expression.[3] Likewise, when Congress adopted this recommendation in 1980 by amending the Copyright Act, it failed to reveal its intentions about the limits of copyright protection for computer programs. Thus, the 1980 revisions made it clear that programs were to be protected by copyright but left it to the courts to determine the appropriate parameters for protection. How the courts have wrestled with this critical issue is illustrated by the landmark cases *Whelan v. Jaslow, Lotus Development v. Paperback Software,* and *Computer Associates v. Altai,* presented later in this chapter.

The debate over the proper extent of copyright protection for computer programs is enormously important. Program developers, of course, want the widest

## Exhibit 6.1 Overview of Copyright Issues in the Technological Environment

### Copyright Protection of Computer Programs

- Determination of expressions and ideas
  — Abstractions analysis
- "Look-and-feel" cases
  — Protection of structure, sequence, and organization of program
  — Expression is everything within the program that is not necessary to carry out the function or purpose of the program.
  — Cases: *Whelan v. Jaslow, Lotus v. Paperback Software*
- Modern trend
  — Abstraction—Filtration—Comparison
  — Reduces degree of copyright protection for computer programs.
  — Case: *Computer Associates v. Altai*

### Copyright Protection of Product Designs

- Protection only for elements not conceived with function in mind
- Special treatment for architecture
- Case: *Brandir v. Cascade Pacific Lumber*

### Protection of Trade Secrets by Shrink-Wrap Licenses

- Contracts of adhesion
- Questionable enforceability
- Case: *Vault v. Quaid*

### Emerging Arenas of Copyright Issues

- Digital audio sampling
- Digital imaging
- Protection of multimedia works
- Case: *Campbell v. Acuff-Rose Music, Inc.*

possible protection. Thus, they advocate that almost all aspects of their programs constitute protectible expression. This would include not only the code used to implement a program but also the more conceptual aspects, such as file structures, user interfaces, and the program's basic organization. On the other side, those companies involved in making compatible software, program improvements, and/or clones argue that most aspects of a program should be considered unprotectible ideas, processes, or systems. Their position is that copyright protection of expression should be limited to the literal code only.

Many of the most important copyright disputes in the computer industry come down to the basic issue of distinguishing protectible expression from unprotectible ideas. The Lotus case was a very high profile litigation, which determined the future and profitability of that company's 1-2-3 program. Similarly, a lot of attention was focused when Intel sued NEC over use of its 8086 and 8088 chip microcodes. Apple Computer's historic lawsuit against Microsoft and Hewlett-

Packard alleging improper use of its Windows graphical computer command system also boiled down to the scope of protectible expression. These, and a huge array of other lawsuits, hold billions of dollars and entire industries in the balance. The problem is that courts have to make judgments about expressions and ideas without guidance from Congress and with little comfort or familiarity with computer technology. As one court so honestly put it, "The challenge . . . to make comprehensible for the court the esoterica of bytes and modules is daunting."[4] Therefore, the judges have taken the approach that is most natural in such circumstances: they work from familiar territory, such as traditional books and movies, and they filter their considerations through the general principles of copyright policy.

Distinguishing between ideas and expression is a task that can never be taken lightly, even in the context of literature, and even the simplest literature at that. Consider the following children's story about a kitten that wants to find its ball of string. The reader helps the kitten search by physically opening flaps on the book to see what is behind them.

### Playtime

A kitten asks, "Where is my ball of string? I want to play. Could it be inside the suitcase?" Under the flap is a lamb who says, "Naaah." "Maybe I left it in the toy box?" In the box are two mice who squeak "No" and "Way." "Is the string under the covers?" Behind the flap depicting the covers is a snake who says, "Ssss-sorry." "I know, it's in the drawer!" After opening the drawer-flap, a hamster says, "Nope." "Hey, wait, I see something in that shopping bag— That must be my ball!" Behind the flap this time is a duck who quacks, "Look in the bowl behind the plants." The kitten finds the ball of string in the bowl and exclaims in delight, "Play Ball!"

What is the idea of this story? What is the expression? A substantial amount of money may rest on your decision. So how do you decide? Although your first impulse may have been that this is a trivial matter, further reflection surely demonstrates that it is not. Here are just a few of the potentially infinite number of ways to differentiate the idea of this story from its expression:

### Playtime
### Levels of Ideas and Expressions

#### I.
#### Elements of the IDEA include:

a. A kitten searches for its ball of string because it wants to play.

b. She asks if it is inside the suitcase, and after pulling up a flap, a lamb indicates in the negative.

c. She asks if it is in the toy box, and after pulling up a flap, two mice indicate in the negative.

d. She asks if it is under the covers, and after pulling up a flap, a snake indicates in the negative.

e. And so on until a duck is informative.

f. The kitten is very excited when it finds its ball of string.

g. Some of the animals make appropriate responses to the questions by making their natural animal sounds.

Elements of the EXPRESSION include:

a. The exact words only.

## II.
### Elements of the IDEA include:

a. An animal searches for something.

b. It ultimately finds what it is looking for.

c. It looks by having the reader open flaps covering the prospects.

d. When asked, animals indicate that the sought-after item is not at that location.

e. Some of the animals make appropriate responses to the questions by making their natural animal sounds.

f. The last animal knows where the item is.

### Elements of the EXPRESSION include:

a. A kitten is searching.

b. She is looking for her ball of string.

c. The animals solicited are a lamb, two mice, a snake, a hamster, and a duck.

d. The kitten looks behind, in, or under a suitcase, a toy box, covers, a drawer, a shopping bag, and plants.

## III.
### Elements of the IDEA include:

a. An animal searches for something.

b. It ultimately finds what it is looking for.

c. It looks by having the reader open flaps covering the prospects.

### Elements of the EXPRESSION include:

a. A kitten is searching.

b. She is looking for her ball of string.

c. Animals are questioned about the location.

d. The animals solicited are a lamb, two mice, a snake, a hamster, and a duck.

e. The kitten looks behind, in, or under a suitcase, a toy box, covers, a drawer, a shopping bag, and plants.

f. Some of the animals make appropriate responses to the questions by making their natural animal sounds.

g. None of the animals except the last know where the ball of string is.

## IV.
### Elements of the IDEA include:

a. An animal searches for something.

b. It ultimately finds what it is looking for.

Elements of the EXPRESSION include:
a. The animal searches by having the reader open flaps covering prospects.
b. A kitten is searching.
c. She is looking for her ball of string.
d. Animals are questioned about the location.
e. The animals solicited are a lamb, two mice, a snake, a hamster, and a duck.
f. The kitten looks behind, in, or under a suitcase, a toy box, covers, a drawer, a shopping bag, and plants.
g. Some of the animals make appropriate responses to the questions by making their natural animal sounds.
h. None of the animals except the last know where the ball of string is.

## V.
Elements of the IDEA include:
a. To tell a story.
Elements of the EXPRESSION include:
a. Everything in the story is expression including that there is a search, an animal is searching, it opens up flaps, and it finds what it is looking for.

This list was formulated so that the idea is most concrete at level I and increasingly abstract as one moves down to level V. Which is the proper formulation? Courts have tried for decades to answer that question, but without success. The decision will be largely arbitrary and ad hoc.[5] But the choice may be dramatically important.

Following is a hypothetical story about a puppy that searches for its bone. The puppy looks with the help of the reader, who pulls up flaps where the puppy wants to search. Assume that this account was published after *Playtime* and that access can be proven. If there is a lawsuit, can one establish copyright infringement?

### The Hunt
A puppy states, "I wonder where my bone could be? Is it under this leaf?" Under the leaf-flap is a snake that says, "Sssssscram." "Is it in this pile of hay?" Under the hay-flap is a squirrel that says, "No." "Is it in the barn?" Behind the barn door-flap is a horse that says, "Naay." "Is it under this pail?" Under the pail-flap is a frog that says, "Go away." "Is it in the burlap bag?" Behind the bag-flap is a duck who says, "I saw it in the mailbox." The puppy opens the mailbox-flap, finds the bone, and screams, "Yummy."

Remember that to prove infringement, one must demonstrate substantial similarity of the works and of the protectible expression. If level I is selected, there is no infringement. Not only are the ideas of the two stories somewhat different but, more important, the expression, which constitutes no more than the words, is not at all similar. At level II, there is more chance of infringement. Now the stories have the same ideas. Also, some elements of the expression are similar. Of all the possible animals to conduct the search, a puppy may seem substantially similar to a kitten. Also, the duck in the bag is the same, and there is a snake in both stories. But still, there are a lot of differences. Most of the places searched, the animals that are questioned, and how they respond are not similar given the idea upon which they were derived.

At level III, infringement becomes more likely. There are a number of things that could be found behind the flaps besides different animals, such as people or objects. That a selection of different animals is used in both stories is somewhat similar. Also, the snake and the horse in *The Hunt* answer, to some degree, in their native tongue, just as did the snake and the lamb in *Playtime*. In addition, the last animal in both stories knows where the missing item is. Indeed, this key animal in both stories is a duck. At level IV, one is very likely to conclude that there has been unlawful copying, because the stories share even more similarities in expression. This is especially true because the flap-opening characteristic is a salient attribute of expression that is presented by both books in the same way. Finally, moving to level V, which contains the most abstract version of the idea, one finds so many substantially similar elements of expressions that the only possible conclusion is that *The Hunt* infringes *Playtime*.

It is disheartening that an ad hoc decision will determine whether *The Hunt* unlawfully appropriates protected expression from *Playtime*. Courts generally are not content with abstraction level I because it provides so little protection to the work. Likewise, they are not likely to rest with level V because that gives too much: the author of *Playtime* should not have a lock on the entire genre of happy-ending stories involving animals.

Without being too definitive, and recognizing that there is tremendous variability depending on the particular facts, courts seem most inclined to select abstraction level III or IV for literary works of this kind. For example, recall that in the H.R. Pufnstuf litigation, discussed in Chapter 5, the court assumed that the idea was a fantasyland filled with diverse and fanciful characters in action. What this means is that a large part of a novel, play, or movie likely will be considered protectible expression. And be very clear that this extends well beyond the literal words. The plot, organization, characters, mood, and many other aspects often will be viewed as elements of expression capable of copyright protection.

Although the determination of proper abstraction levels remains essentially ad hoc, courts still are guided by the underlying principles of copyright. Thus, they are mindful that copyright should provide sufficient incentives to develop and distribute works of authorship without overly stifling creativity. Clearly, level I provides too little protection from copyright. Conversely, level V grants too much in that it might allow an author to have exclusive control of an artistic market. As noted in the previous chapter, copyright never should allow one to enjoy a monopoly position in the marketplace. Rather, copyright protection acts appropriately when it bestows exclusivity to one of several suitable ways to reach the relevant consuming audience. This, then, serves as one guidepost for selecting an abstraction level. If the chosen abstraction level serves to allow the copyright owner to enjoy monopolylike power in the marketplace, then that level is not a proper level.[6] Such power may be realized when there are not several alternative ways of expressing the chosen idea that would be marketable to a recognized set of consumers. Thus, at any level of abstraction, one must ask whether sufficient alternative expressions are available that would allow others to successfully compete in the marketplace. If the answer is no, then that selected level is too abstract. The following example should help clarify this complicated concept.

A. A. Hoehling wrote a historical account of the Hindenburg disaster based on exhaustive research. In the book, he argued that all previous theories about the disaster (static electricity, St. Elmo's fire) are unconvincing except sabotage. He concluded that the saboteur was a rigger who was influenced by his communist girlfriend to place a bomb in a gas cell. Michael Mooney wrote a literary version of the Hindenberg disaster using Hoehling's sabotage theory and then sold to Universal Studios the rights to make a motion picture version of the book. After the movie was made, Hoehling sued Universal for copyright infringement. He alleged that the movie copied protectible expression from his book, including the specific sabotage plot and various scenes such as those depicting German beer hall revelry, the singing of the German national anthem, and the use of certain German greetings.[7]

Hoehling's story could be abstracted as follows.

1. The IDEA is the particular sabotage theory, embellished with a German beer hall scene, German greetings, and the singing of the German national anthem. The EXPRESSION comprises the exact words only.

2. The IDEA is to relate a theory of the Hindenberg disaster. The EXPRESSION includes Hoehling's particular theory, as well as his use of the beer hall scene, the singing, and the greetings.

3. The IDEA is to tell a story. That the story focuses on the Hindenberg disaster is part of the EXPRESSION.

In his case, Hoehling was asking the court to accept something like abstraction 2 to distinguish the idea from the expression. Obviously, level 3 would be overreaching. If the Hindenberg topic, itself, were an element of expression, then the first account might control the market since all subsequent versions likely would seem substantially similar by virtue of the common theme. Thus, there would be no alternatives available for competitors to sell to those interested in the Hindenberg incident. For this reason, that level is not proper, and a less abstract one must be selected.

There are substantial problems with level 2 as well, however. Hoehling depicts his theory as the truth, based on historical facts. Those persons interested in the Hindenberg obviously would prefer the most accurate account of the disaster. Thus, if Hoehling can obtain exclusive rights to his theory by virtue of its being protectible expression, then he will dominate the marketplace because there are no other equally suitable expressions available to competitors. For this reason, the theory must be a part of the unprotectible idea, as illustrated in abstraction level 1. This demonstration indicates another reason why facts are not copyrightable, as discussed in *Feist Publications*.

Similarly, the typical German scenes cannot be part of the expression. Although they likely were fictitious embellishments to the factual account, it would not be appropriate to allow Hoehling exclusive rights to them. Such standard literary accounts, called *scènes à faire*, are indispensable to others who wish to compete in that genre of German stories. Thus, they too must be part of the unprotectible idea. Again, abstraction level 2 provides too much market power. One must move the analysis to a less abstract level, therefore, as represented by level 1.

The case of *Aliotti v. Dakin*, presented in Chapter 4, provides another example. Not only did Aliotti allege that Dakin had usurped her confidential disclosure, but she also charged violation of her copyrights in the dinosaur dolls. The court concluded that there had been no copyright violation because most of the items copied by Dakin were part of the unprotectible idea. That both lines of dinosaurs were soft and cuddly, for instance, was deemed irrelevant because such features are indispensable to sell dolls to children. Also, the similar postures and body designs were considered indispensable to depict the various dinosaurs. Other similar characteristics, such as that the winged Pterodactyls were used in mobiles also were dismissed because they were natural and expected uses of the dolls. By the end of the analysis, all that was left as protectible expression were the eye styles and the stitching—items that were not substantially similar in Dakin's dinosaur dolls.

This is the familiar terrain upon which courts tread when they review computer copyright cases. The distinction between the ideas of computer programs and their expressions is based on the same set of guiding principles. The courts deal with an array of potential abstractions, and they make decisions that are essentially ad hoc but tailored by the basic underlying policy objectives of copyright.

In very simple terms, a word processing program could fall within the following list of abstractions:

### Word Processing Program: Levels of Ideas and Expressions

#### I.
Elements of the IDEA include:

a. The purpose of the program—to conduct word processing.
b. All the particular functions to be carried out by the program.
c. All the ways the program causes the computer to interact with the user (the user interface).
d. All the subroutine functions selected to carry out the program.
e. The exact structure of commands used within each subroutine.
f. All the ways the subroutines are organized and interact within the program.

Elements of the EXPRESSION include:

a. The exact code only.

#### II.
Elements of the IDEA include:

a. The purpose of the program—to conduct word processing.
b. Some of the functions to be carried out by the program.
c. Some of the ways the program causes the computer to interact with the user.

d. Some of the subroutine functions selected to carry out the program.

e. Some of the subroutine command structures used within certain subroutines.

f. Some of the ways the subroutines are organized and interact within the program.

### Elements of the EXPRESSION include:

a. Code.

b. Some selected functions of the program.

c. Some parts of the user interface.

d. Some of the selected subroutine functions.

e. Some of the subroutine command structures.

f. Some of the ways subroutines are organized and interact.

### III.

### Elements of the IDEA include:

a. The purpose of the program—to conduct word processing.

b. Elements of the program necessary to do word processing.

### Elements of the EXPRESSION include:

a. Code.

b. The selected functions of the program.

c. The user interface.

d. The subroutine functions selected.

e. The subroutine command structures.

f. The ways subroutines are organized and interact.

### IV.

### Elements of the IDEA include:

a. A computer program that causes a computer to do something.

### Elements of the EXPRESSION include:

a. Everything about the program, including that it performs word processing.

The level that programmers would prefer depends on the programmers' type of creative activity. Those who develop new programs argue that the correct level should be very abstract, such as that represented by level III or IV. Those who wish to build upon developments in previous programs believe that the industry is best served by level I or II. The following two cases—*Whelan v. Jaslow* and *Lotus v. Paperback Software*—are landmarks in the field. The opinions illustrate how the courts first handled computer copyright issues by drawing on their experience with literary works. This led the courts to select a somewhat abstract interpretation of a computer program's idea—similar to level III in the example above.

## WHELAN ASSOCIATES, INC. V. JASLOW DENTAL LABORATORY, INC.

*Third Circuit Court of Appeals, 1986*

### Facts

Jaslow Lab manufactured dental devices. Jaslow hired Strohl Systems Group, Inc., to create a computer program that would make its bookkeeping more efficient. Whelan, who worked for Strohl, developed the program after exhaustive research on Jaslow's business operations. The program was called Dentalab and was written in EDL language. Soon thereafter, Whelan left Strohl, and Strohl assigned its entire interest in Dentalab to Whelan's new company.

Whelan entered an agreement with Jaslow under which Jaslow was to market the new program for 35% of the gross sales price. After two years, Jaslow learned more about computers and determined that many businesses would want a program capable of achieving the same functions as Dentalab, but written in BASIC language. He developed this program and called it Dentcom. Jaslow then canceled the Dentalab agreement with Whelan and independently marketed both Dentalab and Dentcom.

Whelan charged Jaslow with copyright infringement. Jaslow Lab maintained that it owned the copyright because Dentalab had been created for it by Strohl. It also alleged that it did not copy Dentalab in creating Dentcom. The district court found for Whelan on the copyright claim. First, it concluded that Whelan owned the copyright. Second, it found that there was substantial similarity of expression based on the testimony of experts. Whelan's expert claimed that although Dentcom was not a translation of Dentalab, the programs had almost identical file structures and screen outputs, and that five particularly important subroutines performed almost identically. Jaslow's expert argued that there were substantive differences in programming style, structure, algorithms, and data structures, but that there were overall structural similarities. Third, the court ruled that there was unlawful reproduction based on clear access along with the similarities. Jaslow appealed the determination of copyright infringement to the court of appeals.

### Opinion

In this case of first impression, the court must determine whether the structure, sequence, and organization of a computer program is protectible by copyright or whether the protection of copyright law extends only as far as the literal computer code.

The coding process is a comparatively small part of programming. By far the larger portion of the expense and difficulty in creating computer programs is attributable to the development of the structure and logic of the program and to debugging, documentation, and maintenance, rather than to the coding. Because efficiency is a prime concern in computer programs (an efficient program being obviously more valuable than a comparatively inefficient one), the arrangement of modules and subroutines is a critical factor for any programmer. The evidence in this case shows that Ms. Whelan had spent a tremendous amount of time studying Jaslow Labs, organizing the modules and subroutines for the Dentalab program, and working out the data arrangements and had spent a comparatively small amount of time actually coding the Dentalab program.

To prove that its copyright has been infringed, Whelan must show two things: that it owned the copyright and that Jaslow copied Dentalab in making Dentcom. Ownership is not contested on appeal. Copying may be proven inferentially by showing that the defendant had access to the work and that the allegedly infringing work is substantially similar. It is uncontested that Jaslow had access so the sole question is whether there is substantial similarity between the two programs.

To prove substantial similarity, a two-part process is used. First, one must decide whether there is sufficient similarity between the two works to conclude that the alleged infringer used the copyrighted work in making the infringer's own. For this test, expert testimony is admissible. Second, one must decide from the perspective of the lay observer only whether the copying was an unlawful appropriation of the expression from the copyrighted work. The court believes that with complex cases involving computer programs, reliance on ordinary observers alone is too limiting, and it thus concludes that expert testimony is relevant to determine if there is unlawful copying as well.

It is well established that copyright protection extends to a program's source and object codes. In this case, however, there is no copying of these codes. Rather, there is only substantial similarity of the overall structure. One can violate the copyright of a play or book by copying its plot. Also, as in *Krofft v. McDonald's*, substantial similarity may be established by comparing the total concept and feel of two works. By analogy to other literary works, it would appear that the copyrights of computer programs can be infringed even absent copying of the literal elements of the program.

**A Rule for Distinguishing Idea from Expression in Computer Programs.** It is frequently difficult to distinguish the idea from the expression since the decision is inevitably ad hoc. Because the line between idea and expression is elusive, we must pay particular attention to the pragmatic considerations that underlie copyright policy.

A previous Supreme Court case—*Baker v. Selden*—suggests that the line between idea and expression may be drawn with reference to the end sought to be achieved by the work in question. In other words, *the purpose or function of a utilitarian work would be the work's idea, and everything that is not necessary to that purpose or function would be part of the expression of the idea.* When there are various means of achieving the desired purpose, the particular means chosen is not necessary to the purpose; hence there is expression, not idea. Also, just as with literary works, those aspects that as a practical matter are indispensable to the treatment of a topic are afforded no protection. Thus, anything necessary to effect the function is part of the idea.

The rule proposed here would provide the proper incentive for programmers by protecting their most valuable efforts while not giving them a stranglehold over the development of new computer devices that accomplish the same end. The principal economic argument against this position (and supporting that only the literal code is protectible) is that computer programs are so intricate, each step so dependent on all of the other steps, that they are almost impossible to copy except literally. Some also argue that the concept of structure in computer programs is too vague to be useful in copyright cases. In addition, others believe that computer technology is achieved by stepping-stones, a process that requires the use of much of the underlying copyrighted work. Protection of computer programs beyond the code thereby will retard progress in the field. But we are not convinced by any of these arguments.

The rule proposed here has its greatest force in the analysis of utilitarian or functional works, for the purpose of such works is easily stated and identified. Here, it is clear that the purpose of the utilitarian Dentalab program was to aid in the business operations of a dental laboratory. It is also clear that the structure of the program was not essential to that task: there are other programs on the market, competitors of Dentalab and Dentcom, that perform the same functions but have different structures and designs. The conclusion is thus inescapable that the detailed structure of the Dentalab program is part of the expression, not the idea, of that program.

**Evidence of Substantial Similarity.** Defendant argues that even if copyright protection is not limited to a program's literal elements, there still is insufficient evidence of substantial similarity of expression. Jaslow claims that file structures are not protectible and that any similarities are irrelevant. However, when file structures order information in an original fashion, as they do here, that arrangement constitutes copyrightable expression. Defendant also argues that since Whelan does not assert copyright protection in the screen outputs, any similarities in screen outputs are not relevant to whether the underlying programs are substantially similar. After all, different programs can produce the same screen outputs. However, screen outputs must bear some relation to the underlying program, and therefore they have probative value to the issue of illicit copying. Finally, defendant states that the near identity of five subroutines is not sufficient to find substantial similarity in the entire program structures since the subroutines are a small fraction of the programs. However, the court must make a qualitative, not quantitative, judgment about the character of the work as a whole and the importance of the substantially similar portions of the work. We must therefore ask whether the most significant steps of the programs are similar, and we are convinced here that they are.

We hold (1) that copyright protection of computer programs may extend beyond the programs' literal code to their structure, sequence, and organization and (2) that the district court's finding of substantial similarity is not erroneous. We therefore affirm.

*Whelan v. Jaslow* was the first of the so-called look-and-feel computer cases. This designation is derived from the court's willingness to have copyright protect the structure, sequence, and organization (SSO) of a program and its reference to the total-concept-and-feel language from *Krofft v. McDonald's*. However, those who write about computer copyright protection, especially in the popular press, often are analytically imprecise when they say that the look and feel of computer programs is protectible. Rather, the accurate scenario is as follows. A program is first analyzed to determine which parts are protectible expression. The SSO of a program constitutes protectible expression as long as that SSO is not necessary or indispensable to achieve the idea or purpose of the program. This usually is demonstrated by showing that other SSOs can achieve the same functions. Sometimes it will be recognized that only certain aspects of the SSO are protectible while others are indispensable to achieve the task. Once it is determined what aspects of the SSO are expression, then another program will infringe if its SSO has a look and feel substantially similar to those protected portions. To be precise, the comparison is only to the protected expression of the program in the allegedly infringed program. Thus, when *all* the attributes of a program besides its purpose are considered expression, then effectively the look and feel of the entire program is protected. However, be clear that this is a backdoor determination; what one is really doing is comparing the expressions of two programs to determine if they are substantially similar by virtue of having the same look and feel.

The court in *Whelan* makes reference to the relevance of screen displays. Screen displays have been protectible by copyright for some time now, but controversy has enveloped the means of protection. In the past, the computer program was considered a literary work, and its screen displays were seen as separate audiovisual works. In *Whelan v. Jaslow*, Whelan focused only on the infringement of the computer program and did not bring suit for infringement of its separate screen displays. The substantial similarity in the displays would have been infringing had Whelan registered her displays as an audiovisual work and sued for their infringement separately. But since she did not do this, and sued only on the underlying program, the question was whether similar screen displays constitute evidence that the programs were copied. And as the court correctly noted, it is probative but not conclusive because identical screen displays may be fashioned from completely different program SSOs.

When screen displays were viewed as separate from the program, the common practice was to register a program as a literary work and to separately register the screen displays as an audiovisual work. This practice protected screen displays from others who might wish their programs to depict substantially similar displays. In 1989, the Copyright Office changed this somewhat redundant exercise through a new regulation under which a program is to be registered as a literary work, and that registration extends to the visual displays as well.[8] Thus, when a computer program is registered now, substantial similarity in screen displays will infringe that program. However, as with all copyright infringement situations, one still must deal with determining what parts of the screen displays constitute the idea and what parts constitute protectible expression. And again, this requires an inquiry into what the purpose of the display is and into how many alternative ways there are to achieve that end.

You should begin to question the simplicity of the court's decision in *Whelan v. Jaslow*. Why is it so clear that the purpose is merely to aid in the business operations of a dental laboratory? Is it also part of the purpose to achieve this goal efficiently? The court noted that other programs can help a dental lab, but can they do so as efficiently as Whelan's program? When efficiency is part of the idea, then if there is a most efficient SSO, then this SSO must be part of the idea also. In other words, one must move the analysis up to a less abstract level.

The court also did not evaluate the marketability of alternative programs. What if there were some aspect of Whelan's program that buyers preferred so much that they would not consider buying the alternative dental lab assistance programs? When screen displays are at issue, what if consumers prefer the layout of one more than others? Logically, part of the idea of the program should be that consumers will buy it. Thus, if only one expression appeals to consumers, then that expression should be subsumed within the idea at a less abstract level. Unbelievably, many courts have determined that marketability is not an aspect of the idea. For instance, in a lawsuit between Apple Computer and Franklin Computer, the Court of Appeals stated that commercial and competitive objectives do not enter the metaphysical issue of whether particular expressions serve as ideas.[9] So, if only one program is marketable to consumers, then it still may be protected by copyright as long as other programs can achieve the same basic purpose.

One is left in an absurd quandary by this notion. The proper level of abstraction to distinguish ideas from expressions is supposed to limit the possibility that the copyright will yield a market monopoly. Yet, some courts in computer cases ignore the very commercial realities that determine the ultimate market power from copyright protection. This, of course, leads to the issue of standardization in the computer industry. If one expression becomes such a standard in the industry that consumers refuse or are unable to adopt alternatives, hasn't that expression become an idea? Think of it this way: You develop a word processing program, which is very widely adopted. Other programs may conduct word processing, but those persons who have learned and invested in your program do not wish to take the time to learn how to use them. Wasn't your solution to the word processing "puzzle" simply a great idea, which has become extremely profitable? Shouldn't competitors now be able to share that idea and thus compete on other dimensions that are not indispensable to their survival? Now you should really be troubled because to follow this through, one's success in marketing may mean one's demise in terms of copyright protection. Courts, obviously, are cautious with evaluating market realities for just this reason. But as we shall see in the next chapter, successful trademarks may be lost by virtue of their success. Welcome to the twilight zone of intellectual property.

Do not get the impression that courts always ignore market or technical realities. For instance, one court refused to extend copyright protection to a cotton information computer system because it presented cotton information in the manner that the relevant purchasers most desired.[10] Also, in litigation between NEC and Intel, the court determined that if only one set of instructions can feasibly achieve a task within the technical constraints of the hardware, then that set must be considered part of the unprotectible idea.[11] To this author, all forms of competitive realities, be they based on market conditions or technical constraints, should be relevant to the determination of what constitutes protectible expression. However, one never knows for sure whether a court will so agree.

Not only have courts broadly interpreted the extent of copyright protection for computer programs, but they also have liberally acquiesced in the tangible forms in which such programs are found. Programs are protectible if written in source code, object code, and even microcode.[12] In addition, such codes may be protected even if they are embodied within the hardware of the computer, such as with read-only memories.[13] Although it may seem inconsistent for copyright to protect a component of a machine when the statute provides that systems and processes are off-limits, this has not stopped the courts. *Lotus Development Corp. v. Paperback Software International*, which sanctioned copyright protection for user interfaces, is a classic example of how the logic from *Whelan v. Jaslow* has been extended to new domains by certain courts.

## LOTUS DEVELOPMENT CORPORATION V. PAPERBACK SOFTWARE INTERNATIONAL

*District Court, Massachusetts, 1990*

### Facts

This case concerns two competing application programs—Lotus 1-2-3 and VP-Planner—which are primarily electronic spreadsheet programs but which also support other tasks such as limited database management and graphics creation. Like manual spreadsheets, the electronic spreadsheet presents a blank form on which numerical, statistical, financial, or other data can be assimilated, organized, manipulated, and calculated. In many spreadsheet programs, a highlighted element of the basic screen display resembles an "L" rotated 90 degrees clockwise with letters across the top to designate columns, and numbers down the left side to designate rows.

The idea for an electronic spreadsheet was first rendered into commercial practice by Daniel Bricklin, who developed VisiCalc. Although VisiCalc was a commercial success, implementational characteristics limited the scope and duration of its marketability as a spreadsheet product. Mitchell Kapor and Jonathan Sachs, the original authors of 1-2-3, exploited the opportunity. Building on Bricklin's idea for an electronic spreadsheet, they expressed the idea in a different, more powerful way, taking advantage of the IBM PC's more expansive memory and its more versatile screen display capabilities and keyboard. Built on the shoulders of VisiCalc, 1-2-3 was an evolutionary product. Microsoft later developed a different powerful spreadsheet program, called Excel, which could handle the characteristics of the Apple Macintosh.

Dr. James Stephenson formulated VP-Planner. The original version of the program had a different user interface than did 1-2-3 or Visicalc. Stephenson and Adam Osborne then created Paperback Software in 1983 to market VP-Planner. In 1984, they recognized the success of 1-2-3 and reached the conclusion that spawned this litigation: VP-Planner, in order to be a commercial success, would have to be compatible with 1-2-3. The only way to accomplish this, they believed, was to ensure that the arrangement and names of commands and menus in VP-Planner conformed to those of 1-2-3. Such compatibility would allow users to transfer spreadsheets created in 1-2-3 to VP-Planner without loss of functionality for any macros (a series of instructions designed by the user that can be implemented with one command stroke) in the spreadsheet. Also, such compatibility would allow users to switch from 1-2-3 to VP-Planner without requiring retraining in the operation of VP-Planner.

Lotus, the copyright owner of 1-2-3, sued Paperback Software, alleging that it had unlawfully copied the user interface of 1-2-3 in developing VP-Planner. According to Lotus, the user interface of 1-2-3 includes such elements as the menus (and their structure and organization), the long prompts (which provide additional information about a selected command), the appearance of the screens, the function key assignments, and the macro commands and language.

### Opinion

The expression of an idea is copyrightable. The idea itself is not. When applying these two settled rules of law, how can a decision maker distinguish between an idea and its expression? Answering this riddle is critical to determining the issues of this case: (1) whether and to what extent 1-2-3 is copyrightable and (2) whether VP-Planner is an infringing work containing elements substantially similar to the copyrightable elements of 1-2-3.

The parties agree that literal manifestations of a computer program—including both source code and object code—if original, are copyrightable. Defendants vigorously dispute, however, the copyrightability of any nonliteral elements of computer programs. Plaintiff, on the other hand, maintains that copyright protection extends to all elements of computer programs that embody original expression, whether literal or nonliteral, including any original expression embodied in the program's user interface.

Like all other works of authorship, computer programs are not entitled to an unlimited scope of copyright protection. Section 102(b) makes it clear that the *expression* adopted by the programmer is the copyrightable element in a computer program and that the actual *processes or methods* embodied in the program are not within the scope of copyright law.

With respect to such things as musical works and works of literature, it is well settled that a copyright may be infringed even if the infringer has not copied the literal aspects of the work. Infringement may be found if there is copying of the work's expression of setting, characters, or plot with resulting substantial similarity.

The court's task is governed by the object and policy of copyright law. Courts should not draw the line between copyrightable and noncopyrightable elements of computer programs in such a way as to harm the public welfare, nor should courts ignore the accommodation struck by Congress in choosing to advance the public welfare by rewarding authors. Drawing the line too liberally in favor of copyright protection would bestow strong monopolies over specific applications upon the first to write programs performing those applications and would thereby inhibit other creators from developing improved products. Drawing the line too conservatively would allow a programmer's efforts to be copied easily, thus discouraging the creation of all but modest incremental advances.

Defendants suggest that the user interface of Lotus 1-2-3 is a useful, functional object, like the layout of gears in an "H" pattern on a standard transmission, the functional assignment of letters to keys on a standard QWERTY keyboard, and the functional configuration of controls on a musical instrument. This court, concludes that defendant's contentions are inconsistent with the legislative history of the Copyright Act. The bulk of the creative work is in the conceptualization of a computer program and its interface rather than in its encoding. Defendants' contentions would preclude from protection the most significant creative elements of the process, a result inconsistent with statutory mandates.

Defendants contend that useful articles are not protected by copyright (see discussion in following section). It is true that the utilitarian aspects of useful articles are not copyrightable and that things that merely utter work, such as the cam of a drill, are not copyrightable. This does not mean, however, that every aspect of a user interface is not copyrightable. The mere fact that an intellectual work is useful or functional—be it a dictionary, directory, map, or computer program—does not mean that none of the elements of the work are copyrightable. Elements of expression, even if embodied in useful articles, are copyrightable if they may be recognized and identified separately from the functional ideas that make the article useful.

Three concepts are embedded in the idea/expression dichotomy. The first, noted previously, is that expression must embody more than functional elements in the utilitarian sense. The second is that expression must go further than the obvious. The third is that the expression must be one of several possible ways of expressing the idea for it to be copyrightable. If the expression of an idea has elements that go beyond all functional elements of the idea itself, and beyond the obvious, and if there are numerous other ways of expressing the noncopyrightable idea, then those elements of expression, if original, are copyrightable.

In making a determination of copyrightability, the court first must conceive a scale of abstractions along the scale from the most generalized conception to the most particularized and then choose some formulation for distinguishing the idea from its expression. Next the court must decide whether the alleged expression is one of only a few ways of expressing the idea.

In the context of computer programs, nonliteral elements have often been called the look and feel of a program. One may argue that the phrase is analogous to the total-concept-and-feel test developed in *Krofft*. In this case, however, the test was not invoked to determine what nonliteral elements were copyrightable. Rather, the court used the concept in applying the substantial similarity test to determine whether forbidden copying of copyrightable material had occurred.

The user interfaces of 1-2-3 and VP-Planner have many similarities. They both have the rotated "L" characteristic. They utilize a two-line moving-cursor menu structure, which presents the user with a list of command choices and a moving cursor to use in entering the choice. With each, the menu is called up to the screen by pressing the slash ("/") key. The top line of the two-line menus contains a series of words representing different commands, and the second line displays a long prompt, which contains further information about a selected command. In addition to having the option of selecting commands with the cursor, a user may instead press the key representing the first letter of the command word. VP-Planner uses the same words or words beginning with the same letters to designate commands, and their placements are identical to 1-2-3 in the menu structure. Function keys are also utilized similarly by the two programs to make command selections. Both programs also utilize macros, which by their nature are related to the structure, sequence, and organization of the menu structures and the first letters of the command choices. Although there are some differences in the menu structures and displays of the two programs, VP-Planner is designed to work like Lotus 1-2-3, keystroke for keystroke.

As the starting point, the idea is a computer program for an electronic spreadsheet. A two-line moving-cursor menu also is part of the idea since it is functional, obvious, and used in various types of computer programs. Nevertheless, not every possible method of designing a menu system that includes a two-line moving cursor is noncopyrightable. The rotated "L" characteristic is also part of the idea since there is a rather low limit on the number of ways of making a computer screen resemble a spreadsheet. In addition, the use of the slash key to invoke the command system is part of the idea. There are not many keystrokes available to perform this task because letters and numbers are used to input spreadsheet cell values. Also, since this function is used so often, it should be easily accessible without the need to hit two keys. Only the slash and the semicolon fit these requirements. Because it is one of only two options, the slash key cannot be expression. Finally, certain commands are obvious such as the use of the "+" key to indicate addition.

The court concludes that a menu command structure is capable of being expressed in many if not an unlimited number of ways and that the command structure of 1-2-3 is an original and nonobvious way of expressing a command structure. Accordingly, the menu structure of 1-2-3 taken as a whole—including the choice of command terms, the structure and order of those terms, their presentation on the screen, and the long prompts—is expression. This is made clear because there are several other spreadsheet programs with different structures, including VisiCalc and Excel. Obviously, 1-2-3's particular expression of a menu structure is not essential to the electronic spreadsheet idea. The order of commands in each menu line; the choice of letters, words, or symbolic tokens to represent each command; the method of presentation of the symbols on the screen; and the long prompts could be expressed in literally unlimited number of ways. Also, the fact that some command terms are obvious does not preclude copyrightability if they have been brought together in an original way.

Comparison of VP-Planner with the copyrightable expression of 1-2-3, from the perspectives of both experts and ordinary viewers, demonstrates that the similarities overwhelm any differences. Even though there are some differences, there are substantial similarities in the qualitatively important aspects of protectible expression. Therefore, defendant has impermissibly copied 1-2-3, and its liability has been established.

Defendants argue that the computer industry requires more legal certainty than the foregoing method of analysis provides. However, hard-and-fast rules, despite their initial attractiveness and false promises of certainty, have consequences that offend one's sense of justice. Defendants also argue that if copyright protection is extended to user interfaces and other nonliteral elements of computer programs, then there will be disastrous consequences for the computer industry. However, this prediction was disregarded by Congress in 1980, has not been proven by the evidence, and therefore is disregarded here as well.

Finally, defendants maintain that needs for compatibility and standardization in the industry require a less expansive role for copyright protection. They state that some expressions may be so effective or efficient that they become standardized throughout the field, even though the idea is capable of being expressed in other ways. However, this court is not persuaded that this is relevant to the issue of copyright protection. Defendants also argue that 1-2-3 is pervasively used and that users who have been trained on it and have written elaborate macros to run on it would be unwilling to switch to VP-Planner unless the task were simplified. Again the court is not persuaded. First, defendants ignore the success of Excel, an innovative spreadsheet that is not compatible with 1-2-3. Also, defendants could have achieved compatibility without copying. For instance, translation devices could have been used to read and convert macros written for 1-2-3 into those that could run on VP-Planner.

Defendants' standardization argument is flawed for another reason as well: By arguing that 1-2-3 was so innovative that all should be free to copy its expression, defendants flip copyright on its head. Copyright protection would be perverse if it protected only mundane increments while leaving unprotected those advancements that are more strikingly innovative.

For all of these reasons, defendants are liable for infringement of Lotus 1-2-3.

---

*Lotus v. Paperback Software* makes it clear that some courts are willing to extend copyright protection to almost all aspects of computer programs. Regrettably, this court, like so many others, intelligently discussed the role of copyrights in the intellectual property system but overlooked it when making its ultimate decision. A copyright should provide incentives to support creative activities. However, since copyright generates its stimulus within the private marketplace, its effects must be policed according to market realities. This is what the defense tried to illustrate to the court in *Lotus*, but without success.

Apparently, the courts are worried that if copyrights do not provide sufficient protection for software and other computer-related creations, then these developments will not be forthcoming. The stunning gap in this logic, however, is the emergence of patent protection for software inventions. The various components of the intellectual property system are not mutually exclusive. Under proper circumstances, one can simultaneously protect the ideas of a particular program with trade secret laws, and its expressions by copyright. Similarly, there is no restriction on obtaining protection for a computer program through both patents and copyrights. Thus, one can immediately protect software expression via copyright and protect the software idea through the patent procedures discussed in Chapters 2 and 3.

Before the 1981 decision of *Diamond v. Diehr*, patents provided little coverage for computer programs. However, since that case, the PTO has shown greater willingness to issue patents for an ever-widening range of software inventions, and the courts have upheld them. For instance, utility and/or design patents have issued for business application programs, operating systems software, expert systems, user interface systems, and data processing programs. At times, however, some courts in copyright cases seem stuck in pre-1981 patent law, thereby ignoring the role that patents legitimately should play in stimulating computer-related inventions. By allowing the subject matter of copyright to extend to what is almost undeniably software systems and processes, these courts have merged the current roles of patents and copyrights. This author believes that courts should step back and view the computer copyright cases from a vantage where they clearly distinguish the subject matter of programs for which patent protection is suitable and available. The courts then should include these aspects within the unprotectible idea, comfortably knowing that creative incentives can be properly maintained through the patent process.

Until recently, there seemed to be little chance that courts would heed this advice and retreat from the sweeping expanse of copyright protection in the computer industry. However, starting in 1992, some courts charted what may be a more sophisticated approach to copyrights in the computer field. The Second Circuit Court of Appeals, in *Computer Associates v. Altai*, was the first to take this important step.

## COMPUTER ASSOCIATES INTERNATIONAL, INC. V. ALTAI, INC.
*Second Circuit Court of Appeals, 1992*

### Facts

Both of the firms Computer Associates and Altai design, develop, and market various types of computer programs. CA-SCHEDULER is a job-scheduling program designed by Computer Associates for IBM mainframe computers. Its functions are first to create a schedule specifying when the computer should run various tasks and then to control the computer as it executes the schedule. CA-SCHEDULER contains a subprogram entitled ADAPTER, which was also developed by Computer Associates. ADAPTER is an operating system compatibility component. The IBM System 370 family of computers, for which CA-SCHEDULER was created, is designed to contain one of three operating systems (DOS/VSE, MVS, or CMS). ADAPTER's function is to translate the language of a given program, in this case CA-SCHEDULER, into the particular language that the computer's own operating system can understand. In this way, ADAPTER allows a computer user to change or use multiple operating systems while maintaining the same software. This is highly desirable since it saves the user the costs, in both time and money, that otherwise would be expended in purchasing new programs, modifying existing systems to run them, and gaining familiarity with their operation.

Starting in 1982, Altai began marketing its own scheduling program, entitled ZEKE. The original version of ZEKE was designed for use in conjunction with a VSE operating system. By late 1983, in response to customer demand, Altai decided to rewrite ZEKE so that it could be run in conjunction with an MVS operating system. At that time, James Williams, an employee of Altai, approached Claude Arney, a computer programmer who had worked for Computer Associates. Arney was a programmer who had worked on ADAPTER for Computer Associates and was intimately familiar with various aspects of ADAPTER. Arney left Computer Associates in 1984 to work for Altai and took copies of ADAPTER's source code with him. He did this in knowing violation of employee confidentiality agreements that he had signed.

Rather than redesigning ZEKE, Arney convinced Williams that the best way to make the switch to MVS was to introduce an operating system compatibility component into ZEKE. Arney created the component program, which was called OSCAR 3.4. To this end, Arney copied 30% of the OSCAR 3.4 code from Computer Associates' ADAPTER program. In late July 1988, Computer Associates first learned that Altai may have appropriated parts of ADAPTER, and it brought suit for copyright infringement and trade secret misappropriation. It was at this time that Williams first received actual knowledge that Arney had copied much of the OSCAR 3.4 code from ADAPTER.

Williams initiated a project to rewrite OSCAR so as to preserve as much as could be legitimately saved and to excise those portions copied from ADAPTER. Arney was excluded from the project, and his source code locked away. The rewrite was entitled OSCAR 3.5. From this time on, Altai shipped only OSCAR 3.5 to new customers and offered it as a free upgrade for its previous customers using OSCAR 3.4.

The district court determined that Altai infringed Computer Associates' copyrights with its OSCAR 3.4 program and awarded $364,000 in damages. However, it found that Altai was not liable for copyright infringement in developing OSCAR 3.5. In addition, the district court determined that Altai was not liable for trade secret misappropriation in developing either program. Computer Associates appealed the copyright decision involving OSCAR 3.5 and the dismissal of the trade secret claims.

## Opinion

In recent years, the growth of computer science has spawned a number of challenging legal questions, particularly in the field of copyright law. As scientific knowledge advances, courts endeavor to keep pace, and sometimes—as in the area of computer technology—they are required to venture into less than familiar waters. The copyright law seeks to establish a delicate equilibrium. On one hand, it affords protection to authors as an incentive to create, and on the other, it must appropriately limit the extent of that protection so as to avoid the effects of monopolistic stagnation. In applying the federal act to new types of cases, courts must always keep this symmetry in mind.

**Computer Program Design.** A computer programmer works from the general to the specific. The first step in programming is to identify a program's ultimate purpose. Next, a programmer breaks down the ultimate function into simpler constituent subtasks, which are also known as subroutines or modules. A programmer then arranges the subroutines into flow charts, which map the interactions between the subroutines. To accomplish these interactions, the programmer must pay careful attention to the form and content of information, called parameter lists, that is passed between modules.

The functions of the modules in a program together with each module's relationships to other modules constitute the structure of the program. In fashioning the structure, a programmer normally attempts to maximize the program's speed, efficiency, and simplicity for user operation while taking into consideration certain externalities such as the memory constraints of the computer upon which the program will be run. This stage of program design often requires the most time and investment.

Once all the necessary modules have been identified and designed and their relationships to the other modules have been laid out conceptually, then the resulting program structure must be coded. After coding is completed, the program is tested for errors. Once these are corrected, the program is complete.

**Copyright Infringement.** After OSCAR 3.4 was rewritten into OSCAR 3.5, none of the ADAPTER source code remained. Computer Associates argues that OSCAR 3.5 remained substantially similar to the structure of its ADAPTER program. As discussed before, a program's structure includes its nonliteral components such as general flow charts as well as the more specific organization of intermodule relationships and parameter lists. In addition, Computer Associates contends that OSCAR 3.5 is also substantially similar to ADAPTER with respect to the list of services that both programs obtain from the operating systems.

Congress intended computer programs to be considered literary works. A powerful syllogism therefore emerges: Since the nonliteral structures of literary works are protected by copyright and since computer programs are literary works, as we are told by Congress, then the nonliteral structures of computer programs are protected by copyright. We have no reservation in joining those courts that have already ascribed to this logic.

*Idea-versus-Expression Dichotomy.* It is a fundamental principle of copyright law that a copyright does not protect an idea, but only the expression of the idea. Drawing the line between idea and expression is a tricky business. The essential utilitarian nature of a computer program further complicates the task of distilling its idea from its expression. In the context of computer programs, the Third Circuit's noted decision in *Whelan* has, thus far, been the most thoughtful attempt to accomplish this end.

So far, in the courts, the *Whelan* rule has received mixed reception. Whereas some decisions have adopted its reasoning, others have rejected it. *Whelan* has fared even more poorly in the academic community, where its standard of distinguishing idea from expression has been widely criticized for being conceptually overbroad. The crucial flaw in *Whelan*'s reasoning is that it assumes that only one idea underlies any computer program and that once a separable idea can be identified, everything else must be expression. As we have already noted, a computer program's ultimate function or purpose is the composite result of interacting subroutines. Since each subroutine is itself a program and thus may be said to have its own idea, *Whelan*'s general formulation that a program's overall purpose equates with the program's idea is descriptively inadequate.

*Substantial Similarity Test for Computer Program Structure: Abstraction— Filtration—Comparison.* We think that *Whelan*'s approach to separating idea from expression in computer programs relies too heavily on metaphysical distinctions and does not place enough emphasis on practical considerations. The following approach breaks no new ground; rather it draws on such familiar copyright doctrines as merger, *scènes à faire*, and public domain. In ascertaining substantial similarity, a court should first break down the allegedly infringed program into constituent structural parts. Then, by examining each of these parts for such things as incorporated ideas, expression that is necessarily incidental to those ideas, and elements that are taken from the public domain, a court would then be able to sift out all nonprotectible material. Left with a kernel, or, possibly, kernels, of creative expression after following this process of elimination, the court's last step would be to compare the material with the structure of an allegedly infringing program. The result of that comparison will determine whether the protectible elements of the programs at issue are substantially similar so as to warrant a finding of infringement.

Step One—Abstraction: A court should dissect the allegedly copied program's structure and isolate each level of abstraction contained within it. This process begins with the code and ends with an articulation of the program's ultimate function.

Step Two—Filtration: Filtering entails examining the structural components at each level of abstraction to determine whether their particular inclusion at that level was indeed idea or was dictated by considerations of efficiency so as to be necessarily incidental to that idea; required by factors external to the program itself; or taken from the public domain and hence is nonprotectible expression.

In the context of computer program design, the concept of efficiency is akin to deriving the most concise logical proof. Thus, the more efficient a set of modules is, the more closely it approximates the idea or process embodied in that particular aspect of the program's structure. Although, hypothetically, there may be a myriad of ways in which a programmer may effectuate certain functions within a program (i.e., express the idea embodied in a given subroutine), efficiency concerns may so narrow the practical range of choice as to make only one or two forms of expression workable options. A court must inquire whether the use of a particular set of modules is necessary to implement efficiently that part of the program's process being implemented.

In many instances, it is virtually impossible to write a program to perform particular functions in a specific computing environment without employing standard techniques. This is a result of the fact that a programmer's freedom of design choice is often circumscribed by extrinsic considerations such as (1) the mechanical specifications of the computer on which a particular program is intended to run, (2) the compatibility requirements of other programs in conjunction with which a program is designed to operate, (3) computer manufacturers' design standards, (4) the demands of the industry being served, and (5) widely accepted programming practices within the computer industry. We conclude that a court must examine the structural content of an allegedly infringed program for elements that might have been dictated by external factors.

In addition, material found in the public domain is free for the taking and cannot be appropriated by a single author even though it is included in a copyrighted work. Thus a court must also filter out this material from the allegedly infringed program before it makes the final inquiry in its substantial similarity analysis.

Step Three—Comparison: Once a court has sifted out all elements that are ideas, or are dictated by efficiency or external factors, or are taken from the public domain, there may remain a core of protectible expression. At this point, the court's substantial similarity inquiry focuses on whether the defendant copied any aspect of this protected expression, as well as on an assessment of the copied portion's relative importance with respect to the plaintiff's overall program.

**Policy Considerations.** Computer Associates argues against the type of approach that we have set forth on the grounds that it will be a disincentive for future computer program research and development. It claims that if programmers are not guaranteed broad copyright protection for their work, they will not invest the extensive time, energy, and funds required to design and improve program structures.

*Feist* teaches that substantial effort alone cannot confer copyright status on an otherwise uncopyrightable work. Despite the fact that significant labor and expense often go into computer program flowcharting and debugging, that process does not always result in inherently protectible expression. Thus, *Feist* implicitly undercuts the *Whelan* rationale, which allowed copyright protection beyond the literal computer code in order to provide the proper incentive for programmers by protecting their most valuable efforts.

Furthermore, we are unpersuaded that the test we approve today will lead to the dire consequences for the computer program industry that Computer Associates predicts. To the contrary, serious students of the industry have been highly critical of the sweeping scope of copyright protection engendered by the *Whelan* rule, in that it enables first comers to lock up basic programming techniques as implemented in programs that perform particular tasks.

Generally, we think that copyright registration is not ideally suited to deal with the particularly dynamic technology of computer science. Thus far, many of the decisions in this area reflect the courts' attempt to fit the proverbial square peg into a round hole. The district court suggested that patent registration, with its exacting up-front novelty and nonobviousness requirements, might be the more appropriate rubric of protection for intellectual property of this kind. However, Congress has made clear that computer programs are literary works entitled to copyright protection. Of course, we shall abide by these instructions, but in so doing we must not impair the overall integrity of copyright law.

**The District Court Decision.** We agree with the district judge's systematic exclusion of nonprotectible elements in ADAPTER. The judge found that virtually no lines of code were identical after the rewrite of OSCAR. The judge also determined that most of ADAPTER's parameter lists were either in the public domain or dictated by the functional demands of the program. A few of OSCAR's parameter lists were similar to some of the remaining protectible lists from ADAPTER, but the amount of similarity was *di minimis* and not enough for infringement. The judge also concluded that the overlap exhibited between the list of services required for both programs was determined by the demands of the operating system and of the applications program to which it was linked through OSCAR and ADAPTER. Finally, the district judge accorded no weight to the similarities between the two programs' organizational charts because the charts were so simple and obvious to anyone exposed to the operation of the programs. This is but one formulation of the *scènes à faire* doctrine, which we have endorsed as a means of weeding out unprotectible elements.

We emphasize that infringement cases that involve computer programs are extremely fact specific. The amount of protection due structural elements will vary according to the protectible expression found to exist within the program at issue. The judgment by the district court that OSCAR 3.5 does not infringe the copyright in ADAPTER is affirmed.

**Trade Secret Issues.** The district court determined that the state trade secrets claim was preempted by the federal copyright statute. We disagree.

With respect to OSCAR 3.4, Altai may have had constructive notice that Arney had misappropriated trade secrets. For OSCAR 3.5, which was written after Altai received actual notice of the misappropriation, it must be determined if any trade secrets were incorporated.

The trade secret claims are remanded for determination of these trade secret issues.

---

*Computer Associates* is important for several reasons. Its most important contribution probably is the recognition that the idea of any computer program likely comprises a host of features and attributes of the program rather than simply a generalized statement of the program's purpose. In other words, the idea is viewed in less abstract terms than it was in *Whelan*. According to the Second Circuit, elements of the program dictated by efficiency and market demand are part of the idea. In addition, standard programming techniques must be filtered out as a component of the idea before the expressions are compared. The case also clearly states that copyrights may not be the most appropriate medium to protect the dynamic aspects of computer science. Rather, patents may be more

**Exhibit 6.2   Degree of Copyright Protection for Computer Programs**

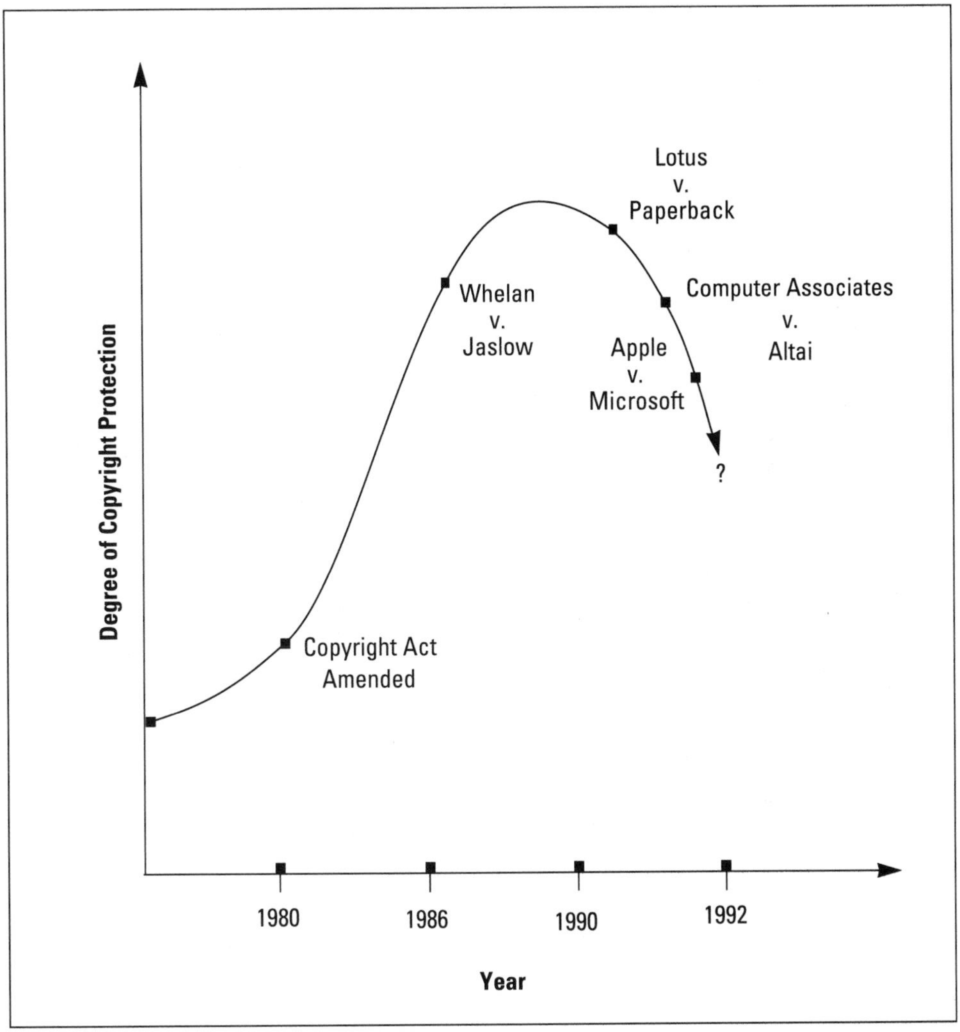

suitable. Although *Computer Associates* by no means sounds a death knell for copyright in the computer realm, it clearly demonstrates that the pendulum may now swing back in the other direction, thereby reducing the extent of copyright protection.[14]

Soon after *Computer Associates* was decided, other courts adopted its philosophy about the role of copyrights in protecting computer programs. The Federal Circuit, for instance, explicitly relied on the case in 1992 to resolve a dispute between Atari and Nintendo.[15] Also, in 1992, the historic litigation brought by Apple Computer against Microsoft and Hewlett-Packard came to a close at the district court level.[16] Although much of that case ultimately was decided on the basis of contract provisions, the judge also evaluated the degree of protection that copyright afforded to graphic interfaces. The overriding tone of the judge focused on the functionality of the user interface and the realistic needs of other companies wishing to compete. The judge determined that the arrangement of attributes in Apple's visual screen displays was designed to make the computer more utilitarian, in the same way that the interface of a car, which includes the dashboard displays, steering wheel, gear shift, and accelerator, allows a driver to operate a car.[17] As will be discussed in the next section, this analogy helps lead to the conclusion that copyright is an inappropriate means of protection. In addition, the judge put substantially more weight on the importance of standardization than did the court in *Lotus*. The result of this new trend is that computer companies are beginning to depend more on patents and trade secrets to protect their software.[18] As stated before, that approach is welcomed by this author. However, one should not get the idea that the debate about copyright protection has been completely resolved. Even as these cases were being decided, Lotus won a copyright infringement case against Borland for the user interface in its popular Quattro spreadsheet.[19] Therefore, all that can be said for now is that the dust has not settled, and only time will tell how legal policies ultimately will handle this critical technology.

The new trend started by *Computer Associates v. Altai* may have far-reaching implications for the protection of the computer program embedded in the Audio Enhancement System. As with many other classes of products, computer programs may be protected in a variety of ways. As discussed in Chapter 2, patent protection may be a viable means to protect a computer program. But assume that we have strong reservations about the prospects for meaningful patent protection for the AES program. Thus, our preference is to use trade secret protection, even though the AES will be a widely distributed consumer product. We now know, following the principles of *Sega*, that under certain circumstances found to be legitimate, competitors may be able to legally decompile the program in order to determine its ideas. Prior to *Computer Associates*, this might not have posed too severe a problem because the idea probably would have been viewed quite abstractly, as perhaps to alter the digital characteristics of audio information to improve sonic qualities. Such an interpretation would have kept most of the program in the realm of protectible expression, thereby keeping it out of the hands of any clean-room personnel instructed to design a competing product. With the advent of the *Computer Associates* line of reasoning, however, those who reverse-engineer the AES program may be able to use substantially more of what they learn through decompilation. For instance, those elements that are dictated by the mechanical specifications of the AES, or that are required to make the system work with other components, or that allow the system to operate more efficiently, now may be fair game for competitors. Thus, our trade secret protection program, implemented in conjunction with copyright, ultimately may not protect the commercially valuable aspects of the AES program. If this is the case, then maybe we should reconsider our initial decision to forgo patents.

The debate about copyright protection for computer programs becomes even more heated when one peers into the international environment. Some countries rely on duplicating software to enhance their economic status. Thus, they are reluctant to pass or enforce laws that extend copyright protection to programs in any meaningful way. Increasingly, nations are including computer programs within the reach of their copyright systems, but there are substantial variations on the degrees of protection that they offer. For these reasons, an important goal of U.S. trade negotiators is to bring international copyright standards for protecting computer programs into conformity with principles used in the United States.

In 1991, the European Union Council adopted a comprehensive Directive designed to harmonize copyright policies regarding computer programs among the EU nations.[20] With some exceptions, the guiding principles of this Directive are very similar to those applied in the United States. As in the United States, copyright protection extends to the expression of a program, including the user interface, but not to the ideas and principles underlying it.[21] Copyright privileges include exclusive rights to reproduce, adapt, translate, distribute, run, load, display, transmit, and store the program.[22] The term of protection is lengthy, ranging from a minimum of 50 years to the life of the author plus 50 years.[23] The Directive provides that the owner or licensee of a program has the right to make a backup copy and, unless a contract provides otherwise, may use the program for its intended purpose and may correct errors.[24] In the forthcoming discussion of shrink-wrap licenses, we shall see that the U.S. Copyright Act contains similar provisions, although they may apply only to owners and not licensees.[25] The Directive explicitly provides that users may engage in reverse analysis of a program to determine its underlying ideas and may decompile parts of the code when necessary to achieve interoperability.[26] These provisions are reminiscent of the principles articulated in *Sega*. In sum, the Directive clearly articulates that copyright plays a key role in protecting computer software in the European Union (EU). Such recognition by the EU should prove to be an important step in the quest to raise and harmonize copyright standards for computer programs in the broader international community.

The Japanese government also has been focusing renewed attention on elements of software protection.[27] The Japanese Agency for Cultural Affairs has formed an advisory committee to review laws regarding copyright protection of software. One issue under consideration by that committee is whether there should be a broad right of decompilation in Japan. If the advisory committee recommends adoption of this right, then the Agency for Cultural Affairs likely would endorse the concept and introduce a bill in the Diet, the Japanese legislature. Software developers in the United States are very concerned because they fear this proposal extends the decompilation right beyond that found in the EU, which permits it in the context of achieving interoperability. Similarly, they feel that the right to decompile articulated in *Sega* is limited by the fair-use doctrine to a small set of legitimate uses, such as interoperability of video games with game consoles. In 1993, the U.S. commerce secretary and the U.S. trade representative jointly wrote a letter protesting the proposal on the grounds that it might run counter to agreements previously made by the Japanese government to ease the ability for U.S. and other foreign companies to penetrate Japanese markets.[28] By so doing, the U.S. government has made it abundantly clear that protecting the international commercial interests of computer business enterprises is a top priority item.

## COPYRIGHT PROTECTION OF PRODUCT DESIGNS

Consumers buy products to satisfy needs. Most products appeal to customers because they present an appropriate balance of critical factors, including utility, appearance, warranties, and price. There are occasions when purchase decisions are made solely with utilitarian considerations in mind without regard to aesthetics. However, more typically, customers are concerned not only with how a product works but also with how it looks. Thus, a lighting fixture will be selected by reviewing its ability to illuminate a driveway along with its potential appearance to those passing by. Similarly, an exercise bicycle may be chosen as much for its dynamic shape and ergonomics as its ability to provide an aerobic workout. Likewise, purchasers of audio equipment, such as the AES, are motivated to some degree by the stylish appearances of competing components.

Marketers of many kinds of products, including those in technology industries, are focusing increased attention on the designs of their goods. As companies have channeled more and more investment dollars into the design aspects of product sales, however, concern has arisen over their protection. Design patents have always been a possibility, but they require one to hurdle the expensive and time-consuming obstacles discussed in Chapter 3. We will also see in the next chapter that trademarks offer another possible opportunity for protection, but there are a number of troubling concerns with that avenue as well. Therefore, product designers have begun looking seriously at copyright or copyrightlike protection for their creative investments.

Those who advocate the application of copyright protection to product designs emphasize that some products have reached the status of being works of art and should be treated as such by copyright. If a sculpture may be protected by copyright, why should a stunning-looking exercise bike or light fixture be treated any differently? The problem is that the Copyright Act has an explicit condition that brings protection of useful items into doubt. Section 102 provides that pictorial, graphic, and sculptural works are capable of copyright protection. However, this is qualified in Section 101 by the definition of what constitutes pictorial, graphic, or sculptural works under the act. Section 101 states:

> The design of a useful article, as defined in this section, shall be considered a pictorial, graphic, or sculptural work only if, and only to the extent that, such design incorporates pictorial, graphic, or sculptural features that can be identified separately from, and are capable of existing independently of, the utilitarian aspects of the article.

The meaning of these words has sparked a substantial debate and confusing precedents in the courts. For instance, statues that served as bases for lamps were held to be protectible by copyright.[29] However, a modern outdoor lighting fixture was denied protection because of the intimate and inseparable association with being a useful article.[30] On the other hand, belt buckles with sculptured designs cast in precious metals were deemed suitable for copyright.[31] Although they were clearly useful articles, and the artistic elements could not be physically separated from the belt attaching mechanisms, the court determined that the act requires only that the artistic aspects be "conceptually separable" from the utilitarian ones. The notion of "conceptual separability" opened the door to a host of puzzling questions about the reach of copyright. *Brandir International v. Cascade Pacific Lumber* is a recent and important case that thoughtfully considers conceptual separability and the limits to copyright protection under the existing terms of the Copyright Act.

## BRANDIR INTERNATIONAL, INC. V. CASCADE PACIFIC LUMBER CO.

*Second Circuit Court of Appeals, 1987*

### Facts

David Levine created wire sculptures shaped like sine waves, or continuous undulating ribbons, and displayed them at home. A friend who was a bicycle buff suggested that the sculptures would make excellent bicycle racks, by allowing the bikes to be parked below the overloops and on top of the underloops. Levine modified the designs slightly to accommodate the task of holding bicycles and changed the materials to heavy-gauged, tubular, rustproof galvanized steel. His company, Brandir, began marketing the bike rack, called the RIBBON Rack, in September 1979. By 1982, the bike rack had been heavily advertised, had been featured in several design and architecture magazines, and had won awards and recognition from industrial design organizations. By 1985, sales were in excess of $1.3 million.

In November 1982, Levine discovered that Cascade Pacific was selling a similar product. In December 1982, Brandir filed an application for copyright registration, but the Copyright Office refused to register the rack, stating that the sculptural aspects were not capable of independent existence apart from the shape of the useful article. Brandir sued Cascade and the Register of Copyrights, alleging that registration was improperly denied, that Cascade infringed copyright protection in the rack, and that Cascade was confusing consumers. The district court found for the defendants on all points and Brandir appealed.

### Opinion and Reasoning

In passing the Copyright Act of 1976, Congress attempted to distinguish between protectible "works of applied art" and "industrial designs not subject to copyright protection." The courts, however, have had difficulty framing tests by which the fine line establishing what is and what is not copyrightable can be drawn. Once again we are called upon to draw such a line, this time in a case involving the RIBBON Rack.

In a previous case involving belt buckles, this court accepted the idea that copyrightability can adhere in the conceptual separation of an artistic element.

Conceptual separability is thus alive and well, at least in this appellate circuit. The problem, however, is determining exactly what it is and how it is to be applied. One possible test, termed the "temporal displacement test," proposes that aesthetic features are conceptually separable if the article stimulates in the mind of the beholder a concept that is separate from the concept evoked by its utilitarian function. However, this court previously rejected that test as a standard so ethereal that it would be impossible to administer or apply. Other possible tests include (1) whether the primary use is as a utilitarian as opposed to an artistic work, (2) whether the aesthetic aspects of the work can be said to be "primary," and (3) whether the article is marketable as art. But again, none of these is very satisfactory.

We are impressed by a recently published article written by Professor Denicola, who views the statutory language in Section 101 as an attempt to identify elements whose form and appearance reflect the unconstrained perspective of the artist. Professor Denicola suggests that the dominant characteristic of industrial design is the influence of nonaesthetic, utilitarian concerns and he hence concludes that copyrightability ultimately should depend on the extent to which a work reflects artistic expression uninhibited by functional considerations. Where design elements can be identified as reflecting the designer's artistic judgment exercised independently of functional influences, conceptual separability exists. We believe that this approach provides the best test for conceptual separability and accordingly adopt it.

Applying this test to the RIBBON Rack, we find that the rack is not copyrightable. It seems clear that the form of the rack is influenced in significant measure by utilitarian concerns, and thus any aesthetic elements cannot be said to be conceptually separable from the utilitarian elements. This is true even though the sculpture that inspired the RIBBON Rack may well have been copyrightable.

Brandir argues correctly that a copyrighted work of art does not lose its protected status merely because it subsequently is put to a functional use. This explains why statues made into lamp bases retain their copyright protection. Thus, the commercialization of the rack is not relevant to determining the status of copyright protection.

Had Brandir merely adopted one of the existing sculptures as a bicycle rack, neither the application to a utilitarian end nor commercialization of that use would have caused the object to forfeit its copyrighted status. Comparison of the RIBBON Rack with the earlier sculptures, however, reveals that whereas the rack was derived from works of art, it is in its final form essentially a product of industrial design. The design clearly was adapted for utilitarian purposes. The upper loops were widened to accommodate bikes more efficiently, vertical elements were straightened to improve installation, and the materials were altered for strength and to sustain the weather.

Brandir argues that its RIBBON Rack can and should be characterized as a sculptural work of art within the minimalist art movement, which is marked by simplicity and clarity. It is unnecessary to determine whether to the art world the RIBBON Rack properly would be considered an example of minimalist sculpture. The result under the copyright statute is not changed. Using the test we have adopted, it is not enough that the rack may stimulate in the mind of the observer an artistic concept separate from the bicycle rack concept. While the RIBBON Rack may be worthy of admiration for its aesthetic qualities, it remains nonetheless the product of industrial design. Accordingly we affirm the decision that the RIBBON Rack is not protected by copyright.

Contrary to the decision of the lower court, however, we find that this rack could possibly be protected by federal and state trademark laws, and we remand to the lower court for further proceedings on this issue alone.

---

This decision rendered by the very influential 2nd Circuit Court of Appeals substantially shut the door on whatever life the conceptual separability notion may have had. Design elements of useful products are not protectible by copyright unless those elements were conceived without function in mind. Few product characteristics beyond merely external artistic flourishes will satisfy this test. Thus, the prospects for using copyrights to protect external visual characteristics of the AES seem remote.

Before 1991, limitation on the protection of industrial designs had a curious effect on the application of copyright to architecture. Architectural blueprints and models can be protected by copyright as pictorial, graphic, or sculptural works. Thus, one who copies a protected blueprint in drafting another blueprint infringes the copyright. However, that was about the extent of the protection afforded architects. A blueprint basically depicts an idea for a functional article: a house or a building. Thus, without some special statutory exception, the copyright in the blueprint could not extend to the construction of the functional architectural idea. This means that although one could not make a copy of a blueprint to help construct the depicted structure, one still would be free to erect the structure if one only took a permissible glance at that blueprint.[32] In addition, once a building were constructed, it falls within the definition of an industrial design. Thus, there would be nothing to stop an architect from viewing a home and then creating an identical abode.

In June 1989, the Copyright Office issued a special report on copyright protection for works of architecture. The report indicated that the United States had to afford greater protection to architectural works to stay in conformity with the Berne Convention.[33] Based on this study, Congress passed the Architectural Works Copyright Protection Act of 1990, which became effective in June 1991. The amendment specifically added architectural works to the Section 102 list of protectible subject items. A definition of what constitutes an architectural work also was included within Section 101, which now states:

> An architectural work is the design of a building as embodied in any tangible medium of expression, including a building, architectural plans, or drawings. The work includes the overall form as well as the arrangement and composition of spaces and elements in the design, but does not include individual standard features.

In addition, the 1991 amendments added Section 120 to the Copyright Act, which limits the scope of protection for architectural works in certain instances. For example, a person is allowed to take a picture of a building that can be viewed from a public place without gaining permission from the copyright holder (often the architect). Also, the owner of the building may make alterations or destroy the work without obtaining permission from the owner of the copyright.

Computer programs and architectural works both are specific exceptions to the rule that copyright protection does not extend to expressions that are intimately related to functional or utilitarian articles. For instance, computer programs certainly are functional, and the expressions cannot be physically separated from the functional aspects. Also, following the conceptual separability approach of the Second Circuit, it is hard to imagine that program codes are written without functional considerations in mind. This has led designers of other functional articles to push for legislation that would similarly extend copyright protection to their creative endeavors. Why, for instance, should the user interface of a computer program be protected by copyright, while the layout, controls, and shape of a radio are not?[34] What logical rationale is there for this seeming act of discrimination? Indeed, designers point out that industrial designs are protected in several other countries.[35]

For over a decade, bills have been introduced in Congress to extend copyrightlike protection to the designs of useful articles. The most current version is titled the Design Innovation and Technology Act.[36] Under most of these proposals, designs of useful articles would be treated very much like computer programs. For instance, the bills state that protection would not extend to any idea, process, system, or method of operation. Also, designs that are dictated solely by utilitarian functions are not covered. In addition, protection would not be given to ordinary and standard features. The main difference is that these bills would provide only 10 years of protection to such designs. However, in the world of rapid technological change, the markedly shorter term of protection usually will not be consequential. Although these bills are introduced annually, none so far have reached the president's desk. One primary reason is opposition by automobile replacement-part manufacturers, insurance companies and consumer groups, which fear that original-equipment automobile manufacturers would be given a lock on the aftermarkets for their cars if the designs of their components were protected. By the late 1980s, those advocating copyrightlike protection for industrial designs seemed to be gathering momentum, and the prospects for passage of the Design Innovation and Technology Act appeared promising.[37] However, by 1994, this momentum had stalled, and for now, all one can say is that the future of this legislation is in doubt.[38]

As a final note, those who oppose broad copyright protection for computer programs might gain ammunition from the industrial design debate. After all, copyright protection for computer programs really is evaluated in a way similar to the temporal displacement test considered by the Second Circuit in *Brandir*. Interestingly, in the design context, the court called that test so ethereal as to be almost impossible to apply. One thereby could draw analogies from ordinary everyday products, concrete things that judges understand very well, and demonstrate the misguided paths being taken in the less understood realm of computer technology. As mentioned earlier, this approach was followed by the district court judge in Apple's case against Microsoft and Hewlett-Packard.

## COPYRIGHTS, TRADE SECRETS, AND SHRINK-WRAP LICENSES

Section 301 of the Copyright Act provides that all state laws granting rights equivalent to those established by the federal statute are preempted but that those state laws dealing with subject matter not within the purview of the federal act may remain in force. Thus, any state law that protects expressions in tangible forms is ineffective. However, state laws that cover other subject matters, such as oral expressions or personal rights, are not preempted by the Copyright Act. In addition, any state law that otherwise conflicts with a specific provision of the Copyright Act will fall prey to preemption, as discussed in Chapter 1.

Trade secrets are protected by state law. Thus, federal preemption must be considered. Often, trade secrets are written in tangible media of expression, such as paper or magnetic disks. In addition, the purpose of trade secret laws is to restrict public access and use, a rationale exactly opposite to that of the Copyright Act, which is designed to stimulate disclosure. Does this mean that state trade secret laws are preempted by the Copyright Act? Obviously, trade secret laws walk a fine line through federal preemption principles. However, trade secret laws, especially when they are designed to offer protection in a limited distribution context, have been found free from preemption. This is primarily because trade secret laws are aimed at protecting ideas and information, not the ways they may be expressed. Since ideas are outside the purview of the Copyright Act, they are a legitimate source of state regulation, unless preemption is based on some other federal statute, such as the Patent Act. Therefore, a typical practice for a technology concern is to protect ideas through state trade secret policies and to protect the expressions of those ideas by means of the federal Copyright Act.

One trade secret protection practice with which you may be acquainted is the shrink-wrap license. A shrink-wrap license is a device used on mass-distribution products, such as computer software, by which consumers implicitly agree to contractual terms when they break the seals of the products' wrappers. A shrink-wrap license is really an offer a customer accepts upon opening the package. A typical shrink-wrap offer, this one used by Vault Corporation and the subject of substantial litigation, reads as follows:

> Important! Vault is providing the enclosed materials to you on the express condition that you assent to this software license. By using any of the enclosed diskette(s), you agree to the following provisions. If you do not agree with these license provisions, return these materials to your dealer, in original packaging within 3 days of receipt, for a refund.

> This software is licensed to you, the end-user, for your own internal use. Title to the licensed software and all proprietary rights in it shall remain with Vault.

You may not transfer, sublicense, rent, lease, convey, copy, modify, translate, convert to another language, decompile or disassemble the licensed software for any purpose without Vault's prior written consent.

In the landmark decision *Vault v. Quaid*, an appellate court determined that shrink-wrap licenses may not be enforceable. Before you read this case, it is necessary to review a few preliminary matters. First, contracts are governed by state laws, through either statutes or common law precedents. Usually, state laws provide that agreements produce binding contracts only when (1) the parties are in an equal position to understand the binding nature of their actions and (2) each party has a realistic choice whether to enter the agreement or not. If these conditions are not met, then the agreement, called a contract of adhesion, ordinarily will be viewed by a court as against the public policy of the state and therefore will not be binding. However, under certain circumstances, state legislatures will expressly provide in a statute that such an agreement conforms to public policy in spite of these conditions. Assuming that statute is not itself unlawful or unconstitutional, then the contract of adhesion will be enforceable in the state.

The other preliminary aspect deals with Section 117 of the Copyright Act, a provision passed in 1980, which limits the rights provided by the act to those who own copyrights to computer programs. Section 117 states in part:

Notwithstanding the provisions of Section 106, it is not an infringement for the owner of a copy of a computer program to make or authorize the making of another copy or adaptation of that computer program provided:

(1) that such a new copy or adaptation is created as an essential step in the utilization of the computer program in conjunction with a machine and that it is used in no other manner, or

(2) that such new copy or adaptation is for archival purposes only and that all archival copies are destroyed in the event that continued possession of the computer program should cease to be rightful.

The fascinating case of *Vault v. Quaid* examines the scope of this special provision dealing with computer programs, as well as the enforceability of shrink-wrap licenses.

## VAULT CORPORATION V. QUAID SOFTWARE LIMITED

*Fifth Circuit Court of Appeals, 1988*

### Facts

Vault produces a computer diskette called PROLOK containing a protective device that prevents unauthorized duplications of programs placed on it. The protective device consists of a small mark physically placed on the magnetic surface of the disk (the fingerprint) and a permanent computer program, which tells the computer not to run a customer's program unless the computer finds the fingerprint on the disk. Thus, although a customer's program placed on PROLOK could be copied to another blank floppy disk, it would not run because that disk would not have the appropriate fingerprint. Vault sells its PROLOK diskettes with shrink-wrap licenses, prohibiting copying, modifying, translating, decompiling and disassembling of its program.

Quaid sells a diskette called CopyWrite, which contains a feature termed "RAMKEY" that has the ability to unlock PROLOK. Ramkey essentially is a computer program that fools a computer into believing that a PROLOK diskette is being used with the appropriate fingerprint. Thus if a computer program is copied from PROLOK onto CopyWrite, the computer will run the program. In this way, pirates can make unlimited copies of programs protected by PROLOK simply by using CopyWrite diskettes.

CopyWrite was developed solely to unlock PROLOK, and it has no market value outside of this capability. Quaid developed CopyWrite by copying Vault's protection program into the memory of a computer and by analyzing the manner in which the program operated.

Vault sued Quaid for an injunction and for $100 million in damages based on several theories. Three of these were:

1.  That Quaid violated the copyright in PROLOK by copying it into the computer memory without permission;
2.  That Quaid is a contributory infringer of Vault's copyright in PROLOK and of its customers' programs placed on PROLOK by selling CopyWrite, which is used by CopyWrite's buyers to make unauthorized copies of these programs; and
3.  That Quaid breached the shrink-wrap license agreement by copying, decompiling, and disassembling PROLOK against the explicit terms of that agreement.

The district court found for Quaid, and Vault appealed to the Court of Appeals.

### Opinion and Reasoning

**Theory #1: Direct Infringement.** In order for a computer to use a program stored on an instrument such as a diskette, that program must be loaded or copied into the computer's memory. Thus, without a special exception for computer programs, one who purchases a program could not use it, for the act of loading it into the computer would violate the copyright owner's rights under Section 106. Section 117 was drafted with this in mind. Also, Section 117 allows an owner of a program to make archival copies to guard against destruction or damage by mechanical or electrical failure.

Vault contends that Quaid copied its PROLOK program into computer memory not to use the program but to discover ways of defeating its purpose. It alleges that this purpose is outside the scope of the Section 117 exception, and thus the copying violates its Section 106 rights. It substantiates this claim with the statutory language that the copy be an essential step to utilize the program and that it be "used in no other manner."

We decline to construe Section 117 in this manner. Even though the copy of Vault's program made by Quaid was not made to facilitate the use intended by Vault, it still was created as an essential step for Vault to utilize the program, albeit in a way that Vault did not desire. Section 117 contains no language to suggest that the copy it permits must be employed for a use intended by the copyright owner, and, absent clear congressional guidance to the contrary, we refuse to read such limiting language into this exception. We therefore hold that Quaid did not infringe Vault's exclusive right to reproduce its program in copies under Section 106.

**Theory #2: Contributory Infringement.** Vault contends that Quaid sells Copy-Write so that those who want to duplicate programs placed on PROLOK diskettes can use the RAMKEY feature to make unauthorized copies. Vault argues that Quaid's sale of CopyWrite thus violates the Copyright Act by contributing to the infringement of Vault's copyrights and the copyrights of its PROLOK customers. Although a purchaser of a program on a PROLOK diskette violates Section 106 by making and distributing unauthorized copies of the program, the Copyright Act does not expressly render anyone liable for the infringement committed by another. The Supreme Court in *Sony*, however, ruled that there is contributory infringement when one sells a product one knows may be used for infringing activities and there are no substantial noninfringing uses of that product. Although Quaid admits its knowledge that CopyWrite with the RAMKEY feature is used for infringing activities, it also alleges that the diskettes serve substantial noninfringing uses by allowing purchasers of programs on PROLOK diskettes to make archival copies as permitted under Section 117.

Experts for Quaid testified that software programs placed on floppy disks are subject to damage by physical and human mishap and that RAMKEY protects a purchaser's investment by providing a fully functional archival copy that can be used if the original program on the PROLOK protected disk, or the disk itself, is destroyed.

Vault contends that Section 117 allows the making of archival copies only when the program is stored on a medium that is subject to electrical or mechanical failure. A diskette, it claims, is not such a vehicle. Also, it demonstrated that copies made on regular diskettes could serve archival purposes without RAMKEY. If an electrical surge damaged a program on PROLOK, an archival copy saved on a regular diskette could then be transferred back to the PROLOK diskette and be functional. Only if the PROLOK diskette were physically damaged would a fully operational copy using RAMKEY be necessary.

Although the legislative history mentions fears about mechanical and electrical failure, the statutory language is not so limited. We believe that Congress would have been more specific had it wished the archival exception to apply only to these forms of failure. Therefore, an owner of a program is entitled under Section 117 to make an archival copy of that program in order to guard against all types of risks, including physical and human mishap as well mechanical and electrical failure.

Because Section 117 permits the making of fully functional archival copies and because CopyWrite with the RAMKEY feature can be used for this substantial noninfringing purpose, we find that Quaid has not engaged in contributory infringement by its sale of CopyWrite.

**Theory #3: Shrink-Wrap Licenses.**   The state of Louisiana has a statute, the Louisiana License Act, which permits a software producer to impose a number of contractual terms upon software purchasers provided that the terms are set forth in a license agreement that conforms to the act. Enforceable terms under the statute include the prohibition of (1) any copying and (2) modifying the program in any way, including adaptation by reverse engineering, decompilation, or disassembly. Vault's shrink-wrap license conforms to the Louisiana License Act.

Vault's license agreement is a contract of adhesion, which can be enforceable only if the Louisiana License Act is a valid and enforceable statute. The Supreme Court has held that when state law touches upon the area of patent or copyright statutes, the federal policy may not be set at naught or its benefits denied by the state law. Section 117 of the Copyright Act permits an owner of a computer program to make an adaptation of that program provided that the adaptation is either an essential step in the utilization of the program with the machine or is for archival purposes. The provision in Louisiana's License Act, which permits a software producer to prohibit the adaptation of its licensed computer program by decompilation or disassembly, conflicts with the rights of computer program owners under Section 117 and clearly touches upon an area of federal copyright law. For this reason, we hold that at least this provision of Louisiana's License Act is preempted by federal law and thus that the restriction in Vault's license agreement against decompilation or disassembly is unenforceable.

Since *Vault v. Quaid*, the legality of shrink-wrap licenses is in grave doubt. As the case indicates, the debate comes down to two issues. First, do consumers have the bargaining power to buy programs without the offending shrink-wrap terms? In Vault's situation, at least, the court concluded that the answer was no. Second, can a state statute save an otherwise unenforceable contract of adhesion? The Fifth Circuit Court of Appeals thinks not because of preemption by federal copyright policy.

The decision by the Fifth Circuit is not without its opponents. One glaring problem not addressed by the court is that Section 117 applies only to *owners* of copies of programs. The Louisiana License Act, however, deals with licensees of programs, not owners. Under Vault's contract, Vault retained ownership in the copy and merely allowed a licensee, such as Quaid, to use it. Thus, its restrictions, which have the approval of the state government, do not affect owners of programs. Following this logic, the state statute that protects this practice does not conflict with Section 117: one statute deals with owners while the other does not.[39]

Another issue not clearly considered by the court is whether the Louisiana License Act would have been preempted by patent policy had it not been preempted by copyright. This author, for one, believes that shrink-wrap licenses and statutes that condone them more clearly run afoul of patent policy than copyright. Shrink-wrap licenses are designed to protect ideas and information from getting into public hands. As you know, state trade secret laws are not preempted by federal patent policy when they are applied either internally or in a limited-distribution context. However, state policies that allow companies to control unpatented product ideas in a mass-market scenario likely would conflict with the disclosure principles of the federal patent laws. Thus, even if one can make a convincing argument that state shrink-wrap protection laws are not preempted by copyright, the patent hurdle, which may be even more serious, still remains.

The future of shrink-wrap licenses is cloudy, at best. Possibly, statutes can be written that avoid conflicts with the federal laws. However, states have been slow in making the attempt. The Illinois legislature, for instance, passed a shrink-wrap law in 1987, but it was repealed by the legislature in 1988.[40] Also, there may be scenarios in which shrink-wrap licenses do not conflict with federal law, such as in more limited distribution contexts or when the parties have equal bargaining power. Only further litigation and legislative activity are likely to answer these difficult questions.

## COPYRIGHT ON THE NEW TECHNOLOGICAL FRONTIER

Technological advances in digital and information systems have put further stress on copyright policy, adding fuel to the debate about whether the Copyright Act soon will have to be revamped. Three emerging technologies that raise serious copyright questions are digital audio sampling, digital imaging, and multimedia products. This section takes a brief look at how these new technologies fit within current copyright policies.

### Digital Audio Sampling

Digital audio sampling is a technique whereby prerecorded sounds are manipulated to form new sounds.[41] Digital samplers have the capabilities to slow down or speed up rhythms, hold notes, lower or raise pitch, change the order of notes, patch different sounds together, and layer different sounds simultaneously.[42] Digital samplers break down analog recordings into discrete, equally spaced segments of time, called samples. The samples are translated into binary digital units of information and stored in the memory system of a computer. At this point, the information can be adjusted and manipulated electronically before being translated back to analog form. Those who use the technique claim that sampling is a new instrument of creativity, but those whose sounds are used often regard the practice as blatant theft of their copyrights.[43] Numerous lawsuits, aimed particularly at rap-music artists, have been filed challenging the practice. Notable disputes include those between Jimmy Castor and the Beastie Boys and between the Turtles and De La Soul.[44] The debate raises far-reaching intellectual property questions, not only as to copyrights but regarding other realms as well.

Before we specifically address the copyright concerns of digital sampling, it is necessary to focus on how the Copyright Act protects audio artists. One who writes an original musical composition clearly enjoys copyright protection in the song. Thus, except for one particular important exception, anyone who wishes to distribute, record, or perform that song or who wants to arrange a new composition based on it must receive permission from the copyright owner in the song. The notable exception, provided in Section 115, states that after an artist distributes records, tapes, or CDs ("recordings") of the song, any other person may make and distribute separate recordings of that song as long as a statutorily defined license fee, called a compulsory license, is paid to the copyright owner of the composition.

Suppose Joe Wiseman writes a musical composition and then licenses to Elton John's recording company the right to make a sound recording of the composition and to distribute copies of it. Elton John's studio invests substantial time and creative energies to perform the song and to perfect technical sonic conditions such as the placement of microphones and the mixing of audio signals. These efforts, although based on Wiseman's song, are distinct and personal to Elton John's studio. Thus, the Copyright Act provides the recording company with certain rights in its particular recording of Wiseman's song. Specifically, Section 114 grants the studio the exclusive right to duplicate its recorded version, to distribute it, and to prepare derivative works "in which the actual sounds fixed in the sound recording are rearranged, remixed, or otherwise altered in sequence or quality."[45]

With these principles in mind, we now can examine the legal consequences of using digital samplers under the Copyright Act.[46] When a recording is transferred into the memory of a digital sampler, it is hard to say that an actual copy has been made, because the sampler translates the information into digital bits prior to storage. Clearly, the 1's and 0's look and feel substantially different from the original song. However, this is also true when an English version of a novel is translated into another language, such as French. The only difference is that whereas typical language translations are made so that other people can read compositions, samplers make translations so that works can be understood by computers. Logically, copyright law treats both forms of translations in the same way—as derivative works. And, equally in both cases, the right to make derivative works is held exclusively by the copyright owners unless special exceptions apply.

Suppose one transfers an entire existing sound recording into a digital sampling machine and then manipulates certain sounds for integration into a new song destined for commercial distribution.[47] As has probably occurred to you already, problems abound. First, storing a digital version of the whole recording without permission likely infringes the rights of the copyright owners in the composition and the sound recording. Unlike with computer programs, there is no special privilege granted to an owner of a recording to make a copy or derivative work which may be essential in order to use a digital sampler. One might raise the fair-use defense, but this rarely succeeds when an entire work is copied. Possibly a reference could be made to *Sega* in some oblique fashion to support a fair-use argument. However, sampling is not required either to learn the ideas of the song or to make alternative arrangements using those ideas. Thus, this theory seems far-fetched. One might believe that the since the initial translation of the entire work is only temporary or transitory, it would not violate the Copyright Act. However, *Sega* instructs that even interim copying is unlawful unless there is an exception such as fair use. Also, although copies must be fixed in order to infringe, this does not mean that the digital translation must be preserved in long-term memory. The act of copying the entire recording into the sampler can be analogized to copying a computer program into the random-access memory of a computer. In 1993, a court confirmed that this practice violates the copyright in the program unless authorized by the copyright owner or otherwise sanctioned by Section 117.[48] From all this, it follows that copying an entire recording into a digital sampler for ultimate commercial purposes is unlawful when undertaken without requisite copyright permissions.

If only a small portion of the original recording is translated by the digital sampler without permission, then infringement is less clear. This is because the fair-use defense becomes more credible. As we know, fair use depends on a number of factors. One key component in the analysis is the amount and substantiality of the portion that is transferred into the sampling machine. Thus, if the snippet that is copied is quantitatively small, the sampler might have a plausible fair-use argument. Of course, substantiality must be measured in qualitative terms as well. Since persons engaged in sampling often select prerecorded material for qualitative reasons—such as to bring the previous work to mind or because the segment is particularly dynamic—the substantiality factor may not be a plus, even if only small portions are used. The commercial nature of most sampling enterprises also is especially troublesome in the fair-use context. However, as we know, the negative weight that commercial activity brings to the fair-use analysis may be overcome with persuasive arguments. The best option here is for the sampler to claim that the material is being copied for integration into a song that is intended to serve as a critical parody of the original song or, possibly (although less likely), to provide some other form of social commentary.[49] Such a use may receive heightened protection under the fair-use doctrine since the defense is considered most appropriate for situations involving comment or criticism. This is especially true when the new song will not have negative effects on potential markets for the original composition. Thus, the act of copying a small portion of a recording into a digital sampler may be lawful under particularly circumscribed scenarios involving social commentary. However, it should be clear that there are a lot of ifs in this approach. Obtaining permissions from the requisite copyright owners, if possible, is by far the safer approach.

*Campbell v. Acuff-Rose Music, Inc.* is an important Supreme Court case that discusses how parodies and social commentaries should be addressed in a fair-use analysis. As noted before, these considerations are likely to be important for determining how much artistic license may be given to digital sampling. As we shall see, these fair-use principles also will be relevant to other emerging technologies, such as digital imaging.

## CAMPBELL V. ACUFF-ROSE MUSIC, INC.
### *United States Supreme Court, 1994*

### Facts

In 1964, Roy Orbison and William Dees wrote a rock ballad called "Oh, Pretty Woman" and assigned their rights to Acuff-Rose. In 1989, 2 Live Crew wrote a song entitled "Pretty Woman," which it claimed to be a parody of "Oh, Pretty Woman." For "Pretty Woman," 2 Live Crew copied the characteristic opening bass riff and the first line of the lyrics of "Oh, Pretty Woman." After the opening, 2 Live Crew's version quickly degenerates into a play on words, substituting predictable lyrics with shocking ones. The 2 Live Crew manager informed Acuff-Rose of the group's song, stating that the group would credit Acuff-Rose with ownership of the original song and would pay a fee for the use the group wished to make of "Oh, Pretty Woman." Acuff-Rose refused to grant permission. Nonetheless, 2 Live Crew released records, cassettes, and CDs of "Pretty Woman" in 1989 in an album titled "As Clean as They Wanna Be."

In 1990, Acuff-Rose sued 2 Live Crew for copyright infringement. The district court judge granted summary judgment for 2 Live Crew based on fair use. This means that given certain uncontroverted facts, the judge determined that a trial was not necessary to reach the judgment that 2 Live Crew did not violate the copyright in "Oh, Pretty Woman." The Court of Appeals reversed, ruling that 2 Live Crew's use of material from "Oh, Pretty Woman" could not constitute a fair use. The group 2 Live Crew appealed to the Supreme Court.

### Opinion

It is uncontested that 2 Live Crew's song would be an infringement of Acuff-Rose's rights in "Oh, Pretty Woman" but for a finding of fair use through parody. The task of evaluating fair use is not to be simplified with bright-line rules, for Section 107 calls for case-by-case analysis. The statute employs the terms "including" and "such as" in the preamble to indicate the illustrative function of the examples given. Also, the four statutory factors are not to be treated in isolation, one from another. All are to be explored, and the results weighed together in light of the purposes of copyright.

**Purpose and Character.** The first factor in a fair-use inquiry consists of the purpose and character of the use, including whether such use is of a commercial nature or is for nonprofit educational purposes. The inquiry here may be guided by the examples given in the preamble to Section 107, looking at whether the use is for criticism or comment or news reporting and the like. The central purpose of this investigation is to see whether the new work merely supersedes the objects of the original creation or instead adds something new with a further purpose or different character. In other words, it asks whether and to what extent the new work is transformative. Although such transformative use is not absolutely necessary for a finding of fair use, the goal of copyright is generally furthered by the creation of transformative works. The more transformative the new work, the less will be the significance of other factors, such as commercialism, that may weigh against a finding of fair use.

Parody has an obvious claim to transformative value. Parody can provide social benefit by shedding light on an earlier work and in the process creating a new one. We thus believe that parody, like other forms of comment and criticism, may claim fair use under Section 107.

For the purposes of copyright law, the heart of the parodist's claim to quote from existing material is the use of some elements of a prior author's composition to create a new one that, at least in part, comments on the original author's work. If the commentary has no critical bearing on the substance or style of the original composition, and the alleged infringer merely uses it to get attention or to avoid the drudgery in working up something fresh, the claim to fairness in borrowing from another's work diminishes accordingly (if it does not vanish), and other factors, such as the extent of its commerciality, loom larger. Parody needs to mimic the original to make its point, and so has some claim to use the creation of its victim's imagination, whereas satire can stand on its own two feet and so requires justification for the very act of borrowing. Still, looser forms of parody, and perhaps even satire, may come within the scope of fair-use analysis. For instance, when there is little or no risk of market substitution for the original (or licensed derivative works), whether because of the large extent of transformation of the earlier work, the new work's minimal distribution in the market, the small extent to which the new work borrows from the original, or other factors, then taking parodic aim at the original is a less critical factor in the analysis.

The fact that parody can claim legitimacy for some appropriation does not, of course, tell the parodist or judge where to draw the line. The suggestion by 2 Live Crew that any parodic use is presumptively fair is not justified. Parody, like any other use, has to work its way through the relevant factors and be judged case by case in light of the ends of the copyright law.

The district court held and the Court of Appeals assumed that 2 Live Crew's "Pretty Woman" contains parody, commenting on and criticizing the original work, whatever it also may have to say about society at large. The district court found that 2 Live Crew's song demonstrates how bland and banal the Orbison song seems to the members of 2 Live Crew. The dissenting judge in the Court of Appeals concluded that "Pretty Woman" was clearly intended to ridicule the white-bread original and to remind us that sexual congress with nameless streetwalkers is not necessarily the stuff of romance and is not necessarily without its consequences. Although the majority in the Court of Appeals had difficulty discerning any criticism of the original, it assumed that there was some.

We have less difficulty in finding the critical element in 2 Live Crew's song than the Court of Appeals majority did, although having found it, we will not take the further step of evaluating its quality. Whether parody is in good taste or bad does not matter to fair use. However, one still must assess whether the par-

odic element is slight or great and whether the copying is small or extensive in relation to the parodic element, for a work with only slight parodic element and
extensive copying will be more likely to merely supersede the objects of the original. While we might not assign a high rank to the parodic element here, we think
it fair to say that 2 Live Crew's song reasonably could be perceived as commenting on the original or criticizing it, to some degree: 2 Live Crew juxtaposes
the romantic musings of a man whose fantasy comes true with degrading taunts,
a bawdy demand for sex, and a sigh of relief from paternal responsibility; the
later words can be taken as a comment on the naïveté of the original of an earlier day, as a rejection of its sentiment that ignores the ugliness of street life and
the debasement it signifies.

The Court of Appeals cut short the inquiry into 2 Live Crew's fair-use claim
by confining its treatment of the first factor essentially to the commercial nature
of the use and then by overinflating its significance. In giving virtually dispositive
weight to the commercial nature of the parody, the Court of Appeals erred.

The mere fact that a work is educational and not for profit does not insulate
it from a finding of infringement, any more than the commercial character of a
use may bar a finding of fairness. The fact that a publication is commercial as opposed to nonprofit is a separate factor that tends to weigh against a finding of fair
use. But that is all. One should see that a bright-line rule forbidding commercial
use is not sensible, for the negative weight of this aspect depends on its context.
For example, the use of a copyrighted work to advertise a product, even in a
parody, will be entitled to less indulgence under the first factor than the sale of
the parody for its own sake.

**Nature.** The second factor, the nature of the copyrighted work, recognizes that
some works are closer to the core of intended copyright protection than others.
We believe that Orbison's original creative expression for public dissemination
falls within the core of the copyright's protective purposes. That fact, however,
is not much help in this case, nor is it ever likely to help much in separating the
fair-use sheep from the infringing goats in a parody case, since parodies almost
invariably copy publicly known, expressive works.

**Amount and Substantiality.** The third factor asks whether the amount and substantiality of the portion used in relation to the copyrighted work as a whole are
reasonable in relation to the purpose of the copying. Here, attention turns to the
persuasiveness of a parodist's justification for the particular copying done, and
the inquiry will harken back to the first of the statutory factors, for we recognize
that the extent of permissible copying varies with the purpose and character of
the use.

The Court of Appeals is correct that this factor calls for thought not only
about the quantity of the materials used but about their quality and importance,
too. Where we part company with the lower court is in applying these guides to
parody, and in particular to parody in the song before us. Parody presents a difficult case. Parody's humor, or in any event its comment, necessarily springs from
recognizable allusion to its object through distorted imitation. When parody
takes aim at a particular original work, the parody must be able to conjure up at

least enough of that original to make the object of its critical wit recognizable. What makes for that recognition is quotation of the original's most distinctive or memorable features, which the parodist can be sure the audience will know. Once enough has been taken to ensure identification, how much more is reasonable will depend, say, on the extent to which the song's overriding purpose and character are to parody the original or, in contrast, the likelihood that the parody may serve as a market substitute for the original.

We think the Court of Appeals was insufficiently appreciative of parody's need for the recognizable sight or sound when it ruled that 2 Live Crew's use was unreasonable as a matter of law. It is true, of course, that 2 Live Crew copied the characteristic opening bass riff, and true that the words of the first line copy the Orbison lyrics. But if quotation of the opening riff and the first line may be said to go to the heart of the original, the heart is also what most readily conjures up the song for parody, and it is the heart at which parody takes aim. If 2 Live Crew had copied a significantly less memorable part of the original, it is difficult to see how its parodic character would have come through.

This is not, of course, to say that those who call themselves parodists can skim the cream and get away scot-free. In parody, context is everything, and the question of fairness asks what else the parodist did besides go to the heart of the original. It is significant that 2 Live Crew not only copied the first line of the original but thereafter also departed markedly from the Orbison lyrics for its own ends; 2 Live Crew not only copied the bass riff and repeated it but also produced otherwise distinctive sounds, interposing scraper noise, overlaying the music with solos in different keys, and altering the drum beat. This is not a case in which a substantial portion of the parody itself is composed of a verbatim copying of the original.

As to the lyrics, we think that no more was taken than necessary, even though that portion may be the original's heart. As to the music, we express no opinion whether repetition of the bass riff is excessive copying, and we remand to permit evaluation of the amount taken in light of the song's parodic purpose and character, its transformative elements, and considerations of the potential for market substitution.

**Market Effect.** The fourth fair-use factor concerns the effect of the use upon the potential market for or value of the copyrighted work. The inquiry must take account not only of harm to the original but also of harm to the market for derivative works. The Court of Appeals assumed such harm because 2 Live Crew's intended purpose of its song was for commercial gain.

No presumption of market harm is applicable to a case involving something beyond mere duplication for commercial purpose. When a commercial use amounts to mere duplication of the entirety of an original, it clearly supersedes the objects of the original and serves as a market replacement for it. But when the second use is transformative, market substitution is at least less certain, and market harm may not be so readily inferred. Indeed, as to parody pure and simple, it is more likely that the new work will not affect the market for the original in a way cognizable under this factor, that is, by acting as a substitute for it.

This is because the parody and the original usually serve different market functions. The market for potential derivative uses includes only those that creators of original works would in general develop or license others to develop. Yet the unlikelihood that creators of imaginative works will license critical reviews or lampoons of their own productions removes such uses from the very notion of a potential licensing market. On the other hand, we make no opinion here as to the derivative markets for works using elements of an original merely as vehicles for satire or amusement, without making comment or criticism of the original.

Although there is no recognizable derivative market for critical works under this factor, 2 Live Crew's song is more complex, comprising not only parody but also rap music—and the derivative market for rap music constitutes a proper focus of inquiry. Although 2 Live Crew submitted uncontroverted affidavits on the question of market harm to the original, neither the group nor Acuff-Rose introduced evidence addressing the likely effect of 2 Live Crew's parodic rap song on the market for a nonparody rap version of "Oh, Pretty Woman." Although another rap group sought a license to record a rap derivative, there is no evidence that a potential rap market was harmed in any way by 2 Live Crew's parody rap version. Since the court record is silent on this subject, 2 Live Crew is not entitled to summary judgment in its favor. This evidentiary hole doubtless will be plugged on remand.

We reverse the judgment of the Court of Appeals and remand for further proceedings consistent with this opinion.

---

*Acuff-Rose* is an important victory for parodists because it instructed lower courts to apply a more flexible approach to the fair-use doctrine than some theretofore were using. However, it is not clear that it gives the practice of digital sampling much breathing space. The Supreme Court's direct pronouncement that the commercial nature of the work does not negate a possible finding of fair use obviously is critical since most sampling exercises will have a commercial objective. However, the rest of the opinion may not bring much relief to what are likely to be the more prevalent uses of digital sampling. Some key aspects are worth keeping in mind. Probably the most central proposition of the opinion is that the more the sampled work serves to comment on or criticize the original work, the more liberty the sampler will have to copy the original without permission. As the sampler's critical aim broadens to elements that are not specifically tied to the work utilized, the fair-use arguments weaken. And of course, if the sampler is simply trying to create a new work from preexisting materials without having any particular social commentary function in mind, the Supreme Court makes it clear that the fair-use argument virtually disappears. Because such is indeed the objective of many digital samplers, they have to be careful indeed. The other major fork of *Acuff-Rose* instructs that the more the sampled work serves as a substitute in a market that the original copyright owner would be willing to tap, the less persuasive the fair-use arguments will be. This principle also does not bode well for digital samplers who wish to use preexisting material without permission for purposes other than criticizing the original. Seemingly, in these situations, the sampler will have to rest on the small amount of material taken and the degree of transformation that ultimately results.

The digital sampler faces other copyright issues as well. Once the recording is altered by the sampler, the resultant audio work also might infringe various copyright privileges. For instance, the final version may infringe the rights of the owner in the composition. One important issue here involves substantial similarity. After a recording has been digitally manipulated, it may not bear a significant resemblance to the original composition. If typical listeners cannot hear much similarity in the works after the sampling, then the sampled song does not infringe the original composition. But, as we know from cases such as *Whelan v. Jaslow*, adoption of even a relatively small portion of qualitatively important material can yield a determination of substantial similarity. And, as previously mentioned, those engaged in sampling often find it necessary to leave qualitatively important aspects in a recognizable state. In those cases, reliance then would have to rest on the equitable principles of the fair-use defense, as expressed in *Acuff-Rose*.

The final version also might infringe the exclusive rights in the sound recording. This is made clear from the specific rights granted under Section 114, which, as related previously, include mixing, altering, and resequencing sounds.[50] Although this language seems to condemn all acts of sampling, it is likely there would not be infringement unless the song using the sampled snippet ended up sounding substantially similar to the original recording. Therefore, the analysis here probably would mirror the substantial-similarity principles involved with the rights of the composition's copyright owner. In any event, whether substantial similarity is required or not, the rights of the sound recording copyright owner also are subject to the fair-use defense. So again, the sampler conceivably can avoid infringement by conforming to the equitable principles of this doctrine. Thus, there may be occasions, such as when very small segments are sampled for the purpose of creating a parody (or perhaps a more general form of social commentary), that the rights in the sound recording will not be infringed.

From this entire discussion, one should recognize that digital sampling raises difficult copyright issues. Individuals who sample preexisting material are strongly advised to obtain appropriate copyright licenses from the copyright owners in the musical composition and the sound recording. Without doing so, there are substantial risks of infringement. It is no wonder that most persons who use sampling techniques in their songs gain the necessary copyright permissions in advance.[51]

Digital sampling raises other intellectual property issues besides those from copyright. For instance, if you heard a David Bowie riff within a sampled song, you might believe that David Bowie had been involved in the creation and production of that song. This brings up issues of trademark and unfair competition, based on the possible confusion that listeners will have about the source or sponsor of the song. One example is provided by a dispute between Chuck D, of the band Public Enemy, and McKenzie River Corporation, which markets St. Ides malt liquor. An advertisement for St. Ides used a recognizable sampled segment of Chuck D's voice without the rapper's permission.[52] Chuck D is an outspoken opponent of malt liquors because they target black consumers. It can be argued that the association of his voice with the malt liquor product might confuse listeners into believing that he endorses the St. Ides product.

Various other state laws also may protect the artists who perform in songs that are sampled. For instance, California, New York, and a host of other states have statutes protecting personal rights, such as the "right of privacy" and the "right of publicity." Generally, the right of privacy protects an individual's interest in avoiding public scrutiny, and the right of publicity protects a person's right to profit from such attention.[53] In California, a right-of-publicity statute provides that anyone who knowingly uses another person's name, *voice*, signature, photograph, or likeness in any manner on products or for the purpose of advertising or selling without first gaining consent is liable for damages.[54] Such terms clearly apply to Chuck D's dispute with McKenzie, given the commercial nature of his claim. A sampler may try to avoid liability for violating personal rights by imitating an artist's voice before sampling, rather than sampling the exact version. However, certain state courts broadly protect the right of publicity, allowing it to cover a vocalist's distinctive and recognizable voice even when imitated by another singer.[55] Therefore, even if a sampler is so careful as to license or purchase the copyrights to both the underlying composition and the sound recording, permission may still be required from the vocalist under certain circumstances. And this may even be true if the sampler goes so far as to imitate the voice prior to digitally manipulating it. Clearly, one should give great attention to the wide spectrum of rights of various copyright owners and artists before engaging in digital sampling. We will take another look at these personal rights in Chapter 8.

### Digital Imaging

The revolution in digital technology has not been restricted to the audio spectrum; visual media have been greatly affected as well. Any person who has seen the movie *Terminator 2* has an excellent feel for the power that this new technology bears. Called digital imaging, the technique utilizes digital equipment to scan film images and to convert the images into electronic signals. These then can be manipulated by graphic artists via computers to alter the shape, color, and density of images and to combine various images in virtually limitless ways.[56] Combinations can even be made with images that are invented totally within the computer. On a simpler level, but using the same technology, single photographs can be scanned into computers and similarly manipulated to created altogether new pictures.[57] One prominent example is the cover of *A Day in the Life of America*, which depicts a cowboy scene. The editors faced a problem when deciding on the dramatic scene for the cover because it was shot horizontally but had to appear vertically for the book. The dilemma was solved through computer technology, which altered the scene so that it emerged vertically without loss of any important elements in the scene.[58]

Digital imaging raises numerous legal and moral issues. Not surprisingly, many of these mirror those with digital sampling, given that the techniques are so similar. In terms of copyright, the photographer stands in the same position as the musical composer. Therefore, when a complete image is scanned into computer memory, an illegal derivative work probably has been made. As with digital sampling, one might argue that the "copy" stored in the computer is only transitory or will be erased, but these positions are not very compelling. A fair-use defense is possible but likely will not be available if the entire original picture is scanned prior to digital manipulation.

The resultant altered version may be infringing also, if it is substantially similar to the original photo. This may be a difficult issue to resolve. One can create a seascape by taking bits and pieces from different photographs—a sail from one, a boat from another, a rainbow from still another—altering their respective characteristics, and merging them. The result may be a picture that is very different from the originals. Still, if qualitatively important and recognizable elements are pulled from a photograph, there likely will be substantial similarity. Under these circumstances, one would have to rely on the fair-use defense by, for instance, arguing that the new composite picture integrates no more of the preexisting copyrighted works than is necessary to comment on or criticize the original works. Again, the complicated equitable balance articulated in *Acuff-Rose* will likely come into play.

One other copyright issue pertains more to digital imaging than to audio digital sampling. Many photographs, especially those depicting natural objects and scenes, are somewhat akin to literary works based on factual information. A photograph of a sunset taken from a remote location in Tibet, for example, may be copyrighted. However, the copyright protection does not extend to the elements given to the public by nature. Rather, the copyright protects only the individual creative aspects added by the photographer, such as composition, filtering, exposure, film selection, camera placement, and lighting. Therefore, a direct copy of the Tibetan sunset photograph infringes not because the natural sunset or landscape is reproduced but because the photographer's creative components are taken. With digital imaging, this analysis becomes complicated because the natural elements of the Tibetan scenery may be digitally appropriated while all the creative elements can be digitally altered or removed. If such steps were taken by digital imaging with the Tibetan sunset, then the photographer, who likely invested a huge amount of time and effort to reach the remote locale, may rightfully feel angry that the digital imager could access the scene simply by scanning the image into a machine. However, as we learned in *Feist v. Rural Telephone*, copyright does not protect information, facts, or natural elements even when tremendous energies are devoted to acquiring them. Although the Supreme Court recognized that the result may be harsh in some circumstances, copyright does not provide protection simply because of the sweat of the brow involved in the enterprise. This doctrine is directly applicable to the nature photographer. Therefore, the emergence of digital imaging could change the incentives to engage in nature photography expeditions. In addition, as with databases, the technology may require photographers to reconsider the techniques they use to distribute their works.

Photographers also worry that computer technology will remove their control over their pictures. If a photo is sent to a magazine for review but is rejected by the editors, how can the photographer be sure that the image was not scanned into computer memory so that portions could be used later?[59] The burden of policing likely will soon be overwhelming. Also, an intriguing development is the purchase by Kodak of Image Bank, the largest stock-photo house in the United States. Kodak plans to use its new photo CD technology to put Image Bank's entire photo library on compact discs so that the library's contents can be viewed and edited on computers and television.[60] Such simple access to so many photographs in digitized form potentially could explosively magnify the problems photographers will have in policing copyright violations. Whether these problems are handled through technical, contractual, or legal means is an interesting question. For instance, Kodak may be able to encode the compact discs so that customers are billed each time an image is downloaded.[61]

The issue of moral rights may be relevant here also. Even if the copyright to a photograph is owned by someone other than the photographer (copyright ownership, for instance, may have been assigned), the artist still retains personal moral rights to ensure proper attribution and to protect the integrity of an original piece of art. Those engaged in digital photo manipulation cannot disregard these claims. The adoption of the Berne Convention by the United States should elevate the status of moral rights in that country. Indeed, the Copyright Act was amended in 1991 to explicitly protect the moral rights of an author of a work of visual art, which, under the act, includes among other things "a still photographic image produced for exhibition purposes only, existing in a single copy that is signed by the author, or in a limited edition of 200 copies or fewer that are signed and consecutively numbered."[62] Although most practices involving digital imaging likely will not infringe moral rights as they are currently protected under the terms of the Copyright Act, one still needs to be mindful of future developments to these rights as they become further assimilated within U.S. copyright policies. In addition, one must be aware that legal principles involving moral rights are substantially more developed in various other regions of the globe, such as Europe.

Finally, there are a host of ethical issues that may be raised when viewers believe that an altered photograph depicts reality. For instance, *Time* magazine, for a cover shot, electronically merged pictures of Nancy Reagan and Raisa Gorbachev under the heading "Nancy Meets Raisa," although the two had not yet ever met.[63] More recently, a cover photograph for *New York Newsday* run prior to the 1994 Winter Olympics made it appear that figure skaters Tonya Harding and Nancy Kerrigan were skating side by side when in fact they had not done so.[64] Clearly, those engaged in manipulating photos must be concerned with the potential personal effects that their resultant work may have on artists, viewers, and subjects. One can only speculate whether these issues will be addressed through ethical codes, litigation, or state and federal legislation.

## Multimedia Works

On the very near horizon are multimedia interactive computer products using CD-ROM technology.[65] These products utilize computer database management systems that allow one to control large data banks of textual, audio, and visual images in an interactive manner. Multimedia works differ from traditional ones in that (1) the information is stored digitally; (2) the format allows one to instantaneously jump from one point to another in a work or to merge various portions of a work, rather than being forced to review it from beginning to end; (3) multimedia works are interactive—the product is capable of answering and refining questions about the existence of data; and (4) the appearance of multimedia works is likely to differ substantially each time the work is used.[66] Since so much copyrighted material is being gathered for use in potentially so many ways, the developing and offering of these products can be a legal nightmare.[67] A brief look at some of the difficult issues for multimedia works serves to demonstrate the significant legal and practical hurdles such new technologies face.

Suppose you want to market a multimedia product dealing with education in the United States. The product will offer customers interactive access to huge banks of textual, visual, audio, and statistical information dealing with the subject. For instance, a large number of books will be available, such as *Piaget for Teachers*. There will be photographs of all kinds of things related to education such as schools, great teachers, and facilities. *Blackboard Jungle*, *Goodbye Mr. Chips*, and *Stand & Deliver*, among other movies, will be provided. Music, such as "School's Out" and "Another Brick in the Wall" also will be included. In addition, you plan to collect and offer as much data as you can about education from almanacs and other sources.

Without question, every item that you want to collect requires a large array of copyright permissions. However, this also would be true if you were compiling a traditional collection of these various works. What makes multimedia works different is the various unpredictable ways that the material may viewed and used. For instance, one who licenses a photograph for a book knows the single location that the photograph will appear in the book. However, when photographers license a photograph for storage on a CD-ROM, they do not know how many times the picture will be called up by a user or with what material it might appear. This raises difficult contractual questions about fee structures, amounts, and technical monitoring. In addition, the user may be able to manipulate the photo, as discussed earlier, raising all the legal and ethical concerns attendant with that practice.

Use of the music and films raises even more problems. For the audio material, licenses will have to be negotiated with copyright owners of the compositions and the recordings. Since the audio portions may be synchronized with video images, you will need to be careful about the extent of the rights obtained in the contract. Owners of audio copyrights often demand greater fees for such uses.[68] If there is a chance that the product will be shown in a public setting, then performance rights will also have to be negotiated with the composition's copyright owners or one of the performance societies, such as ASCAP, BMI, or SESAC. And, of course, there are legal risks if the music can be sampled by the user.

Films can be very tricky because so much copyrighted audio and video material may be combined in them. Determining exactly what parties have the rights to license particular activities may be troublesome.[69] Also, the actors may have rights, either through their contracts, or based on moral principles, to control the uses of their names and likenesses.

The pitfalls of using databases was covered in *Feist v. Rural Telephones*. If you plan to integrate a database that was collected by someone else and is displayed in an original way, then you will need permission for it. Again, lack of knowledge about how the base will ultimately be used by customers may make negotiations intriguing.

Other issues abound. Since films and pictures will be used, you have to be careful about the potential for invasions of privacy and rights of publicity. What happens if your product is capable of merging sights and sounds in such a way that a person's reputation is harmed? Will you be subject to a defamation charge? The copyright owners of the material you use very likely will demand credit for their works.[70] Given that you do not know when or in what order users will call up various works, where should you include such credits? The list of potential legal issues in this new and important area is staggering. Obviously, one needs the very careful advice of an experienced attorney before embarking on such a venture.

## CONCLUSION

You have now been exposed to some of the fundamental legal controversies surrounding copyright protection of technological products. This chapter did not provide exhaustive coverage of copyright topics, however. For example, there was no mention of how new technological advancements in telecommunications may affect traditional copyright doctrines.[71] Also, this chapter limited its focus to the nature and ownership of legal rights in technological developments. One must constantly be aware, however, of practical realities. One is not always a winner just because the law is on one's side. For example, it is clearly unlawful to purchase copyrighted software and make a copy for a friend. But only a fool would believe that the law has stood as a substantial impediment to those who want inexpensive software. Indeed, as noted in Chapter 1, the laws of several countries even sanction the practice. As the uses of copyrighted material become more decentralized and the costs of duplication continue to fall, copyright enforcement becomes increasingly difficult. The challenge facing managers of technology is how to effectively and profitably market their creations in light of the new state of affairs. Possibly there will be new technical solutions, which will prevent uncompensated access to information or will somehow bill users for access.[72] Maybe there will be new legal solutions. The only thing that is certain is that change must come to this arena, and it must happen soon.

## NOTES

1. Pub. L. 93-573, §201(b)-(c), 88 Stat. 1873, 1873-74 (1974).
2. Lotus Dev. Corp. v. Paperback Software Int'l., 740 F. Supp. 37 (D. Mass. 1990) quoting CONTU, Final Report at 20-21.
3. Whelan Associates v. Jaslow Dental Lab., 797 F. 2d 1222, 1241 (3d Cir. 1986).

4. Q-Co Industries, Inc., v. Hoffman, 625 F. Supp. 608, 610 (S.D.N.Y. 1985).

5. Nicholas v. Universal Pictures Corp., 45 F. 2d 119, 121 (2d Cir 1930).

6. An important aspect of judging the power of the firm is defining the marketplace in which it competes for sales. For example, if the marketplace consists of all books, then *Playtime* will not have monopoly power, no matter what level of abstraction is selected. As the marketplace narrows, however, the relative size and power of *Playtime* grow. Under antitrust law, the appropriate competitive market is called the relevant market. Here, one must decide if the relevant market is (1) all recreational products, (2) all books, (3) all fictitious books, (4) all children's books, (5) all children's books with flaps, (6) all children's books with flaps and animals, and so on. The relevant market is determined by considering such things as customer buying habits and the willingness of purchasers to buy alternative types of products in response to price changes.

7. Hoehling v. Universal City Studios, Inc. 618 F. 2d 972 (2d Cir. 1980).

8. 53 FR 21817.

9. Apple Computer, Inc. v. Franklin Computer Corp., 714 F. 2d 1240, 1253 (3d Cir. 1983).

10. Plains Cotton Co-op v. Goodpasture Computer Service, 807 F. 2d 1256, 1263 (5th Cir. 1987).

11. NEC Corp. v. Intel Corp., 10 U.S.P.Q. 2d (BNA) 1177 (N.D. Cal. 1989).

12. See, e.g., Whelan (source code copyrightable); Apple Computer, Inc., v. Franklin, (object code copyrightable); NEC v. Intel (microcode copyrightable).

13. Williams Elecs., Inc., v. Artic Int'l., Inc. 685 F. 2d 870 (3d Cir. 1982).

14. The abstraction-filtration-comparison procedure used in *Computer Associates* is open to criticism. For instance, once an idea is identified, it might not be appropriate to filter it out of the comparison analysis completely. *Feist* makes it clear that the selection and arrangement of ideas may be protectible. *Computer Associates* does not deal clearly with this possible complication.

15. Atari Games v. Nintendo, 975 F. 2d 832 (Fed Cir., 1992).

16. Apple appealed the decision of the district court to the 9th Circuit Court of Appeals. Oral arguments were presented to the appellate court in July 1994. See V. Slind-Flor, "A Puzzled 9th Circuit Panel Hears Apple v. Microsoft," National L.J. (July 25, 1994) at A9.

17. Apple Computer, Inc. v. Microsoft Corp. and Hewlett-Packard Co., 799 F. Supp. 1006 (ND CA, 1992).

18. J. Moses, "When Copyright Law Disappoints, Software Firms Find Alternatives," Wall Street J. (May 4, 1993) at B6.

19. Lotus Development Corp., v. Borland International Inc., 799 F. Supp. 203 (D. Mass. 1992). This case has been appealed to the 1st Circuit Court of Appeals, and arguments are expected to be heard in mid-1994. The appeal is being watched closely by industry observers because the court may use *Altai* as a springboard to cut back on the copyright protection extended to Lotus by the lower court in the cases against Paperback Software and Borland. If this happens, there likely will be another strong judicial statement that copyright protection should not be available for features that have become industry standards or that

are necessary for interoperability. See V. Slind-Flor, "Battle's On for the Soul of Software," National L.J. (March 28, 1994) at A1.

20. O.J. Eur. Comm. (No. L 122) 42 (1991) (hereinafter called "Software Directive"). For a thorough discussion of the Directive, see H. Pearson, C. Miller & N. Turtle, "Commercial Implications of the European Software Copyright Directive," 8 Computer Lawyer (November 1991) at 13-21.

21. Software Directive, Article 1.

22. Software Directive, Article 4(a).

23. Software Directive, Article 8.

24. Software Directive, Article 5(1), 5(2).

25. 17 U.S.C., §117.

26. Software Directive, Article 5(3), 6.

27. See A. Pollack, "U.S. Protesting Japan's Plan to Revise Software Protection," New York Times (November 22, 1993) at D2.

28. Ibid.

29. Mazer v. Stein, 347 U.S. 201 (1954).

30. Esquire, Inc., v. Ringer, 591 F. 2d 796 (D.C. Cir. 1978).

31. Kieselstein-Cord v. Accessories by Pearl, Inc., 632 F. 2d 989 (2d Cir. 1980).

32. Demetriades v. Kaufmann, 680 F. Supp. 658 (S.D.N.Y., 1988).

33. Copyright Office Report on Works of Architecture (June 19, 1989).

34. See Burgunder, "Product Design Protection after Bonito Boats: Where It Belongs and How It Should Get There," 28 American Business L.J. 1 (1990).

35. E.g., U.K. Design Right Law (1989). On July 28, 1993, the EU Commission proposed a set of regulations and directives intended to unify product design protection within the EU. See "EC to Harmonize Design Protection," J. of Proprietary Rights (October 1993) at 36.

36. H.R. 1790 (1991).

37. See, 3 J. of Proprietary Rights (June 1991) at 35.

38. J. Pierson, "Hopes Fade for Designs on Stronger Protection," Wall Street J. (March 22, 1993) at B1.

39. A 1993 case determined that the distinction between owners and licensees is important when considering the applicability of Section 117. According to the 9th Circuit, in a case dealing with program maintenance, the privileges provided by Section 117 extend to owners but not necessarily licensees. MAI Systems Corp. v. Peak Computer Inc., 26 U.S.P.Q. 2d (BNA) 1458 (9th Cir. 1993).

40. Zanger, "Shrink Wrap License Voided by U.S. Circuit Court," Chicago Computer Guide (1991) at 16.

41. For thorough discussions of the legal issues involved with digital sampling, see J. Brown, "They Don't Make Music the Way They Used To: The Legal Implications of Sampling in Contemporary Music," 1992 Wisc. L. Rev. 1941; T. Bryam, "Digital Sound Sampling and a Federal Right of Publicity: Is It Live or Is It Macintosh?" 10 Computer L.J. 365 (1990); T. C. Moglovkin, "Original Digital: No More Free Samples," 64 S. Cal. L. Rev. 135 (1990); B. McGiverin, "Digital Sound Sampling, Copyright and Publicity: Protecting against the Electronic Appropriation of Sounds," 87 Colum. L. Rev. 1723 (1987).

42. Tomsho, "As Sampling Revolutionizes Recording, Debate Grows over Aesthetics, Copyrights," Wall Street J. (November 5, 1990) at B1.
43. "Sampling: A Creative Tool or License to Steal?" L.A. Times (August 6, 1989) at Calendar 61.
44. Ibid.
45. Sound recording copyright owners do not have rights in public performances of their works. Therefore, radio stations must make financial arrangements with composition copyright owners to air songs but do not have to deal with the sound recording copyright owners. Copyright owners of sound recordings fear that new digital technologies will allow listeners to make home recordings from the broadcast media, which will substitute for the purchase of CDs. If this concern materializes, then sound recording copyright owners may experience a diminution of income. The Home Audio Recording Act alleviates the situation somewhat by making sound recording owners a recipient class of statutory royalties. Nonetheless, legislation has been proposed to amend the Copyright Act to grant performance rights to sound recording copyright owners.
46. For a comprehensive discussion of the legal issues involved with digital sampling, see Brown, "They Don't Make Music the Way They Used To: The Legal Implications of Sampling in Contemporary Music," 1992 Wisconsin L. Rev. 1941.
47. The Audio Home Recording Act of 1992 might protect users of digital samplers that make copies of digital and analog audio material for noncommercial purposes. The act prevents infringement actions based on the noncommercial use by a consumer of a digital audio recording device. 17 U.S.C. §1008. The act defines "digital audio recording device" quite broadly, and the term conceivably could cover digital samplers. 17 U.S.C. §1001(3).
48. MAI Systems Corp., v. Peak Computer Inc., 26 U.S.P.Q. 2d (BNA) 1458 (9th Cir. 1993).
49. There is substantial debate in this context about the types of social commentary that are protected by the fair-use defense. Some courts believe the defense is most suited to parodies that offer criticism about the original works themselves. See, e.g., Acuff-Rose Music, Inc., v. Campbell, 972 F. 2d 1429 (6th Cir. 1992), rev'd and remanded 1994 U.S. Lexis 2052 (1994); Rogers v. Koons, 960 F. 2d 301 (2d. Cir.), cert. denied, 113 S. Ct. 365 (1992). However, many scholars argue that the equitable nature of the fair-use defense, backed up by First Amendment considerations, demands a broader and more flexible approach. See, e.g., E. Ames, "Beyond Rogers v. Koons: A Fair Use Standard for Appropriation," 93 Columbia L.R. 1473 (1993); M. Smith, "The Limits of Copyright: Property, Parody, and the Public Domain," 42 Duke L.J. 1233 (1993). The Supreme Court clarified the issue in *Acuff-Rose* by articulating that parodies deserve possibly a wider berth of protection than other forms of social commentary, such as satire. However, the Court did not rule out the possibility of limited protection in other contexts.
50. One way to avoid infringement of the copyright in the sound recording is to record an independent version that sounds the same and then sample from that. The copyright in the sound recording extends only to uses of the sounds fixed by that owner (Section 114[b]). This will relieve the sampler from having to deal with the owner of the sound recording, but the sampler still will need permission

from the copyright owner in the musical work, unless the resultant sampled song is not substantially similar to the original version.

51. See R. Sugarman and J. Salvo, "Sampling Gives Law a New Mix," National L.J. (November 11, 1991) at 21; Soocher, "License to Sample," National L.J. (February 3, 1989) at 1.

52. Harrington, "Rapper Sues Malt Brewer," Washington Post (August 28, 1991) at D7.

53. For a complete discussion of these rights and how they may apply to artistic ventures, see D. Burman and A. Leiner, "When the Right of Publicity Meets the Right of Free Expression," 4 J. of Proprietary Rights (March 1992) at 2-5.

54. Ca. Civ. Code, §3344.

55. Midler v. Ford Motor Co., 849 F. 2d 460 (9th Cir. 1988). See Marks, "An End to Judicial Resistance toward Vocal-Imitation Claims?" National L.J. (February 20, 1989) at 20.

56. Kaplan, Duignan-Cabrera, Wright, and Yoffe, "Lights! Action! Disk Drives!" Newsweek (July 22, 1991) at 54.

57. Ansberry, "Alterations of Photos Raise Host of Legal, Ethical Issues," Wall Street J. (January 26, 1989) at B1.

58. Ibid.

59. Ibid.

60. "Photographers Call for Boycott of Kodak Film," Wall Street J. (November 5, 1991) at B1.

61. Ibid.

62. 17 U.S.C. §§101, 106A.

63. C. Ansberry, "Alterations of Photos Raise Host of Legal, Ethical Issues," Wall Street J. (January 26, 1989) at B1.

64. K. Sawyer, "Down to a Photo Refinish," Washington Post National Weekly Edition (February 28–March 6, 1994) at 38.

65. For a thorough discussion of new media works and the important legal and contractual issues related to them, see A. Grogan, "Acquiring Content for New Media Works," Computer Lawyer (January 1991) at 2. See also Burgess, "Mixing Up a Revolution?" Washington Post (July 28, 1991) at H1.

66. A. Grogan, "Acquiring Content for New Media Works," Computer Lawyer (January 1991) at 3.

67. The difficulty of handling intellectual property issues when developing multimedia products has not escaped the popular business press. See M. Cox, "In Making CD-ROMs, Technology Proves Easy Compared with Rights Negotiations," Wall Street J. (June 28, 1993) at B1.

68. A. Grogan, "Acquiring Content for New Media Works," Computer Lawyer (January 1991) at 3.

69. Ibid. at 6.

70. Ibid. at 8.

71. For instance, digital broadcasting has raised issues about performance rights in sound recordings. See, e.g., "Performance Right in Sound Recording," American Bar Association, Section of Patent, Trademark and Copyright Law, Annual Report (1990–1991) at 187-188.

72. See P. Goldstein, "Copyright in the Information Age," Stanford L.J. (1991).

# 7

# TRADEMARK POLICY AND THE PROTECTION OF PRODUCT DESIGNS

## INTRODUCTION

Before distributing the Audio Enhancement System to the public, we have to consider how consumers will identify our product. If we are the only seller of such a system, perhaps this issue is not of great immediate concern. Perhaps we obtained an extremely broad patent covering the entire audio improvement process. However, even in the unlikely event of such comprehensive patent protection, it would be foolish to assume that competition will not appear. If the product is at all successful, engineers will find other ways to improve audio quality. And, of course, the patent will someday expire, allowing competitors to freely use the technology in their products.

Trademark protection for high-technology goods should not be taken lightly. Trademarks are an integral part of the marketing and distribution strategy. Our investments in developing and producing a high-quality product will pay off only if consumers are able to identify such quality in the marketplace. With complex technological products, such as computers or advanced audio equipment, it is not always possible to recognize the value of superior components and processes until after the product is used for some time. However, if the product carries an identifier exclusively associated with a source known for consistently high standards, then a consumer who desires that quality can easily find it. "IBM," for instance, is a classic example of the assurances a trademark can provide.

We also must consider whether there are strategic implications to the identifier we select. The phrase "Audio Enhancement System" has interesting marketing possibilities because it provides information about the purpose of the product. However, there are pitfalls that must be considered to staking one's reputation on such a descriptive designator. We might even consider whether the overall shape of the product and the arrangement of external features might be a suitable means of identification. If we can get consumers to associate a unique ergonomic design of the control panel, for instance, with our company, then maybe we can use trademark policy to keep competitors from using similar displays. This might even be advantageous if the arrangement is important for using the equipment easily.

This chapter provides a feel for how trademark considerations fit within the overall strategic plan of marketing technological products. We will consider the fundamental purposes of a trademark and evaluate the range of names and characteristics that may serve in that capacity. The chapter also reviews how one obtains trademark rights and what limitations there may be to protection. The focus then moves to the international arena. Here, we will look at gray market issues as well as international mechanisms to facilitate foreign trademark protection.

## FUNDAMENTAL PRINCIPLES OF TRADEMARK PROTECTION

Trademark policies coexist at the federal and state levels. Federal trademark law resides in the Lanham Act, which provides for the protection of words, names, symbols, or devices that serve to distinguish the sources of goods or services. One of the main attributes of the Lanham Act is the availability of federal registration, which, among other things, provides nationwide notice of the use and ownership of a trademark. However, federal protection extends to unregistered trademarks as well.

Trademark protection at the state level is very similar to federal protection, but with more limited geographical reach. For this reason, companies involved in interstate commerce usually concentrate on obtaining federal rights. However, some state laws grant certain trademark rights beyond those available under federal law. Protection of a trademark from dilution, for example, is a feature of some state laws, but it is not yet clearly available under federal law.

As discussed in Chapter 1, the conceptual bases for trademark protection are somewhat different from those for the other components of the intellectual property system. With patents, trade secrets, and copyrights, legal rights are provided to stimulate creative energies. The goals of trademark policies, on the other hand, are to combat unethical marketing practices, protect goodwill, and enhance distributional efficiency.

### Trademarks and Competitive Ethics

Federal and state trademark policies are rooted on principles of unfair competition originally developed through common law by state courts. As the name sug-

**Exhibit 7.1 Fundamental Purposes of Trademark Protection**

### Combat Unethical Marketing Practices

- Deter palming off.

### Protect Goodwill

- Reward investments in quality.

### Enhance Distributional Efficiency

- Reduce search costs.
- Must consider potential negative effects on competition.
  — Generic marks
  — Descriptive marks
  — Functional marks

gests, unfair competition is aimed at competitive practices that unfairly take advantage of honest businesspersons. Let's suppose that we have developed a high-resolution computer monitor, which is extremely reliable and will not cause eye fatigue. We stamp the name "HiLiter" on all the monitors so that consumers can readily differentiate our monitors from others in the marketplace. After a successful advertising campaign, sales begin to rise rapidly. But to our misfortune, we are then beset with a menacing competitive presence. Another company begins to sell a substantially inferior computer monitor that from external comparisons looks just like ours. Indeed, the competitor had the nerve to go so far as to stamp the name "HiLiter" on its monitors in exactly the same way as we do. Sales growth falls off dramatically; apparently customers who wanted our product are buying the competitor's product by mistake. By copying our name and design, the competitor is engaging in a deliberate and conscious scheme to palm off its inferior monitors to unsuspecting consumers who believe they are purchasing our reputable product. Even worse, we find that buyers of the competitor's monitors are calling us to complain that our screens do not function as we promised. All of a sudden, the trust and goodwill that we worked so hard to establish for our monitors are severely jeopardized.

Unfair competition doctrines are aimed at preventing the unfair consequences that arise when competitors make it difficult for consumers to locate the goods they want. Normally, when courts review business behavior to determine if it amounts to unfair competition, they look for three characteristics: (1) that the product or service of the first company employs a symbol or device—a trademark—which consumers use to identify its source; (2) that a competitor uses a symbol or device that is so similar that consumers might confuse it with that of the first company; and (3) that the competitor adopted that symbol or device having known, or under circumstances that it should have known, about the prior use by the first company. The most important remedy for unfair competition usually is an injunction, preventing the competitor from using the identifying trademark. In essence, this means that unfair competition policies legally entitle the first company, such as ours with selling HiLiter, to have exclusive rights to use that identifier—be it a name, symbol, or product attribute—in its competitive region.

Let's see how application of the three unfair competition factors may work in practice. To make things interesting, assume that our company is rather small and that we decided to advertise and sell the HiLiter monitor only in the Greater San Francisco, California, region. The competitor this time adopts the slightly revised name "HiLighter." Now, consider four scenarios: (1) the competitor sells in San Francisco and we can prove it knew about our previous use of HiLiter; (2) the competitor sells in San Francisco but it alleges that it adopted its name innocently; (3) the competitor sells in Reno, Nevada, and we can prove it knew about our previous use of HiLiter; and (4) the competitor sells in Reno, Nevada; it alleges it adopted the name innocently; and we cannot prove otherwise.

The first two situations are the easiest to assess. Scenario 1 is the classic case of palming off in which the company clearly intends to deflect customers by purposely adopting a confusingly similar identifying mark. Scenario 2 really is little different; although we may not have concrete evidence that the competitor knew about our previous use, it's hard to believe that the competitor entered our region using such a similar name without knowing about our presence. Even if the competitor did not actually know that we were using the name "HiLiter" on monitors, it would have, and should have, known had it engaged in minimal market research before entering the region. Finally, if the competitor is given every benefit of the doubt about its innocence, then we still should prevail in asking for an injunction, for otherwise consumers will be confused by the presence of two similar marks in the same area. In effect, the court will have to make a choice; equitably, the logical course is to prefer the first user in the region. Thus, the results of scenarios 1 and 2 are the same. The first user in the region gets to use the mark and can prevent competitors from subsequently adopting confusingly similar marks in that same competitive area.

Scenario 3 is somewhat different because the subsequent user is not really a competitor. We do not yet sell in the Reno area and thus none of our prospective customers will be misled by use of the similar name. At the same time, one has to be suspicious of the manufacturer's motivations for employing the term "HiLighter," having known about our success with HiLiter in San Francisco. Although no immediate harm may come to us, it's hard to say that the maker of Hilighters was acting in good faith. With the infinite number of possible names to use as a mark for identification, why did this manufacturer select a name that it knew was being used by another company elsewhere? Likely, the Hilighter company opted for the name, hoping that it might benefit in the future if we should someday decide to expand into Reno. Courts will balance the equities of this situation in the following way. As long as we do not intend to sell in Reno and consumers are not being confused, the subsequent user will be allowed to use the Hilighter name in that region. However, as soon as we can prove that we intend to expand into that region, we will be able to have a court enjoin the use of "Hilighter" in order to prevent customer confusion. Thus, we ultimately have

## Exhibit 7.2  Unfair Competition vs. Federal Registration

### Principles of Unfair Competition

- Identification of source
- Likelihood of confusion
- Notice
- Regional priority

### Advantages of Federal Registration

- Constructive notice
- National priority

rights not only in regions where we first used the name but also in others where potential competitors used the name first, but with knowledge of our previous use in another area.

In the fourth scenario, the other business adopted the name HiLighter in Reno without knowledge of our usage in San Francisco. This is not totally unbelievable. The Reno company may argue, for instance, that the term was chosen to provide insights into the high-resolution and superior lighting features of the computer screen. This is probably no different from what we were thinking when we selected our name. This business, which acted in good faith, soon will build up its own goodwill in the Reno area. If we later decide to sell HiLiters in Reno, customers might be confused by the presence of two trademarks that are so similar. This time, though, the equitable balance leans toward the Reno company, and it will be able to prevent our use of the name "HiLiter" in that region. The result is that we are allowed to use the name in the competitive regions where we first used the name, and the Reno company has priority where it was first. In other words, assuming good faith, unfair competition is a regional doctrine, granting trademark rights to the first user in a competitive area so as to prevent consumer confusion.

Federal registration under the Lanham Act is designed to turn scenario 4 into scenario 3 for the first to use a mark in the United States. According to the Lanham Act, registration of a mark provides constructive notice of the registrant's rights, which among other things, includes nationwide priority to use the registered mark as of the date that the trademark application was filed.[1] In other words, registration notifies everybody in the United States that there already is a user of a particular mark for certain types of goods or services. The notice is considered constructive, because the awareness is assumed no matter if one actually knows of the registration or not. Thus, if we had filed the registration application for HiLiter before the Reno company used "HiLighter," and we ultimately were granted the registration, then the Reno company could not claim that it unknowingly adopted the confusingly similar name. This is true even if the company otherwise was acting in good faith and really did not know about our use of, or application for, "HiLiter." Therefore, the situation will be treated the same as scenario 3 when the subsequent adoption takes place with knowledge. The benefit for us is that now when we intend to roll into the Reno area, we can demand that the Reno company take whatever steps are required to alleviate customer confusion. Remember that without the registration, the burden was on us to make the necessary changes.

## Trademarks and Distributional Efficiency

Besides enforcing standards of marketing ethics, trademark policies also further economic goals of efficiency. Trademarks provide consumers a shorthand way for finding the goods or services they desire. If the law did not protect a company's exclusive right to an identification mark, then consumers might have to contend with a marketplace where products from different sources look identical, at least from a quick visual inspection. Customers who want our computer screens might have a hard time locating them if there are competitive screens that have copied to the minutest detail our external features, including any names, colors, or symbols that we attached. Some buyers will not realize that the screens originate from different sources—those who buy monitors from competitors by mistake simply will attribute any performance differences to poor quality control. Those purchasers who are aware of the competition in the market will have to undertake measures to "search" for our monitors. They might, for instance, negotiate for trial-use periods or, together with the retailer, trace down the sources of particular shipments. Whatever method is used, consumers are forced to spend additional time and possibly money to locate the goods they desire.

In its purest form, trademark protection relieves consumers from search expenditures and guards a firm's reputation without interfering with free competition. Competitors are free to copy a product along any dimension they choose except for the exclusive identification mark. Assuming that this mark has no intrinsic value to consumers and is used by them only for identification, other companies will not suffer any competitive disadvantages. The only thing they may want but cannot have is the ability to deceive consumers about the sources of products. To put this another way, trademarks enhance market efficiency by lowering the costs of getting desired product to consumers. As long as their role is solely for identification, trademarks will have no negative effect on the efficiencies resulting from free competition. The result can be only a net plus to the competitive marketplace.

Unfortunately, trademarks are not always selected with such pure identification motivations in mind. Even our choice of the name "HiLiter" was not entirely innocent. Clearly we did not arrive at this word solely for identification purposes. Rather we carefully picked the word so that it would provide some information about the qualities of the product as well. When focusing on the net effect of trademark protection on economic efficiency, the question then becomes whether adding this informational component may negatively impact competition. If so, then it becomes less clear that trademark protection must be beneficial. Under these circumstances, one will have to be more cautious before extending trademark protection.

## Generic Marks

Suppose that instead of "HiLiter," we desired trademark protection for "computer monitor" and "video display terminal." If we obtained rights to these names, then we might obtain a competitive advantage in the marketplace. Due to our trademark rights, competitors now would have to market their products as, say, "screens" or "pads" or by some other term. What they will not be able to do is to call their products by the names that customers ordinarily use for them because we already have exclusive rights to those words. Uncertain customers may not readily buy computer pads because they may not be absolutely sure that a pad is the same as a monitor or a terminal. Thus, although the products are the same, customers may lean toward our offerings simply because the products are clearly identified as computer monitors and video display terminals, just what they knew they wanted. To offset that advantage, competitors will have to engage in additional expenditures to educate consumers that a pad is the same as a computer monitor.

This example demonstrates that one cannot always perfunctorily assume that there are no social costs from trademark protection. In this instance, in which we selected the generic terms for the product, it is clear that protection raises barriers to competition. In addition, one might wonder whether consumers really could associate a generic term with only one particular source of products. After all, generic terms are supposed to apply to a class of products, not an individual provider. For both of these reasons, unfair competition policies do not allow protection for generic words. Likewise, registration for generic terms is unavailable under the Lanham Act. It is for this reason that protection was not available for "shuttle" to identify an airline route,[2] for "cola,"[3] for "386" with respect to a computer chip,[4] or for "windows" in connection with graphical user interface operating systems.[5]

What is perhaps more interesting and dangerous is a corollary: marks that become generic over time will lose their protected status. This policy, coined "genericide," is premised on the same unfairness as before; the only thing different is the timing. For example, Bayer originally chose the somewhat creative term "aspirin" for its headache pain reliever. At first, customers recognized that aspirin was one brand of a type of pain reliever (salicylic acid). However, for a variety of reasons, consumers started to think that "aspirin" referred to the entire class of those pain relievers rather than to one particular brand in that class. This placed other makers of that headache medicine at a disadvantage—they could not call their product "aspirin," yet that is the product that customers wanted. To correct such unwarranted market power, Bayer's trademark registration for aspirin was canceled.[6] Other notable fatalities to genericide include "thermos,"[7] "trampoline,"[8] "monopoly,"[9] "escalator,"[10] and "Loglan."[11]

Obviously, genericide can be devastating to a company that has built years of goodwill in a name. All of a sudden, what once was the company's exclusive trademark is available for competitors to use. Compounding the problem is that many customers recognized that the word had brand significance and thus will be confused by the presence of new users of that term. The trademark "Sanka" provides a good example. Many people ordering Sanka simply want decaffeinated coffee. To them, the term is generic, representing the product class of decaffeinated coffees. Others, however, understand that Sanka is a brand of decaffeinated coffee. If a decision were made to allow competitors to refer to their decaffeinated coffees as "sanka," these consumers might be confused. For this reason, courts are reluctant to remove trademark protection and will do so only when convinced that the set of those likely to be confused is not substantial.

The reasons that a trademark might become generic vary depending on the situation. However, the trademark owner does have some ways to control the situation. For instance, the manner that a product is marketed can affect consumer understanding of a mark. If the makers of Rollerblade skates tell the public to try Rollerblade-brand in-line skates, then they have made it clear that Rollerblade is only one brand within its product class, clearly defined as in-line skates. However, if the slogan simply is to try Rollerblades, then customers may interpret and use the term more broadly. The problem is especially acute for a company that introduces a new class of products. Until competition materializes, consumers often use trademarks in a generic fashion since there is no need to be specific about the desired source. Just think a few years back, and consider whether you ever asked to go windsurfing, a term derived from the first brand of sailboards. As you can imagine, a company with a patented product must be very careful, because there may not be competitors for 17 years. The makers of shredded wheat learned the hard way. By the time their patent expired, the name had long since entered the general vocabulary for that type of cereal.[12]

All of this bears directly on our introduction of the Audio Enhancement System. Since this will be a new product introduction, we have to be very careful to ensure that consumers distinguish between our brand name and the common name for the product class. Indeed, since the product class does not yet exist, it is incumbent on us to develop both names. This is especially true if we receive a patent on the invention, for competitors will not be introducing similar offerings for a long time. The term "audio enhancement system" probably is not a good choice for a brand name, for if it is so used, what should we call the product class? Do we market our product as the Audio Enhancement System, the new breed of LP crystalizers? It seems very likely that Audio Enhancement System will be the generic term of choice. Therefore, it is probably better to rely on another term to represent our brand of audio enhancement system. "AES" or "StatFree," for example, should have more longevity. In addition, we should take steps to ensure that retailers and publishers do not use our brand name in a generic fashion. This will require us to scan major newspapers and magazines and to hire investigators to police how retailers treat our brand name. The Coca-Cola Company, for instance, must periodically check to make sure that when a customer asks for a Coke, Coca-Cola is provided rather than just any brand of cola. This measure is designed to prevent retailers from legitimizing the tendency of some consumers to use that trademark as a generic term for cola.

## Descriptive Marks

Trademark policies are intended to prevent consumer confusion without imposing unwarranted barriers to free competition. The restraint that could be imposed by allowing exclusivity to generic marks is too great to ever justify trademark protection. Since generic terms are more valuable for marketing purposes than other options open to competitors, the result would be an undue competitive advantage. In effect, the company would profit because it had rights to the best, or one of the very few optimal, trademark choices. As explained in *Bonito Boats*, this might be appropriate for patents, copyrights, or trade secrets, but not for trademarks.

From this, we recognize that generic marks are off-limits for naming our computer monitors. However, we still want our mark to provide information by describing its attributes. Thus, we decide to use the name "Clearvision," a word that directly indicates that our screens have high resolution. As with our choice of a generic term, this selection is meant to do more than simply allow consumers to distinguish our product. However, the selection of "Clearvision" will be less of a burden to competitors. This is because there probably are several equally informative ways to describe high-resolution monitors, such as "Sharpview" and "Superscope." But still, the various ways to describe the product are not endless. Thus, there may be competitive dangers, albeit not as great and definite as with generic marks.

Another aspect of descriptive marks is that consumers may not readily recognize that they serve as identifiers. At first, consumers may focus more on the descriptive qualities and not be sensitive to the identification function. For instance, when Clearvisions are first introduced, consumers may wonder how many companies make the monitors that provide clear visions. But assuming that we are the only company to sell Clearvisions, over time consumers will come to understand that there is only one source of Clearvisions. At this point, Clearvision serves to distinguish our product, and consumers would be confused if other companies were allowed to use it.

The Lanham Act does not allow protection of descriptive terms unless they have become distinctive of the goods from a particular source. Once they become distinctive, the terms are said to have secondary meaning; the primary meaning is the descriptive information, and the secondary meaning is the identification function. Once secondary meaning is proven, then one can register the mark or otherwise protect it through unfair competition policies. Also, under the Lanham Act, proof that a company has been the only user of a term for five years is prima facie evidence that the descriptive term has secondary meaning.[13]

That descriptive terms may receive delayed protection under the Lanham Act conforms to economic analysis. Exclusivity to a descriptive term may raise some competitive barriers simply because the available number of equally suitable descriptive words may not be enough to satisfy every potential competitor. However, there are enough to ensure substantial competitive recourse. Thus, the dangers are lower than from generic makers. Once secondary meaning arises,

**Exhibit 7.3  Protection Spectrum for Trademarks**

| Generic Marks |
| --- |
| • No protection |
| • Genericide |

| Descriptive Marks |
| --- |
| • Protection if secondary meaning |
| • Fair use |

| Suggestive Marks |
| --- |
| • Immediate protection |

| Fanciful Marks |
| --- |
| • Immediate protection |

| Case: *Abercrombie & Fitch v. Hunting World* |
| --- |

customer confusion may result if others use that descriptive term to identify their goods. Using an equitable balancing test, the economic inefficiency resulting from the confusion here outweighs the potential competitive dangers from allowing only one company to have access to the word.

The next case, *Abercrombie & Fitch v. Hunting World*, clearly presents the different ways various kinds of marks are treated by the Lanham Act. The case discusses two other aspects of the Lanham Act that must be clarified to fully appreciate it. One involves the ability to challenge the propriety of registered marks. Later in this chapter, we will review registration procedures. For now, it is enough to know that the PTO's decision to register a mark may be reviewed by a court. For instance, a company wanting to use a registered word may believe that protection is improper because the mark is descriptive and does not have secondary meaning. Most challenges to registration, such as this, must be made within five years of registration. Otherwise, according to the Lanham Act, the registration becomes incontestable.[14] One of the few exceptions to a mark's incontestable status after five years is based on genericism.[15] That is, one can challenge a registration at any time on the grounds that the mark always was or has become generic.

The other issue raised in the case involves fair use of a registered mark. When a company registers a descriptive mark, competitors may want to use the term, not to take advantage of consumers, but rather simply to describe their goods.[16] For example, although "Joy" is a registered mark for perfume, a competitor may use that word fairly to describe the nature of its perfume. What is forbidden is for the competitor to use the word in a trademark sense to identify its goods.

## ABERCROMBIE & FITCH V. HUNTING WORLD, INC.

*Second Circuit Court of Appeals, 1976*

### Facts

Abercrombie & Fitch (A&F) sued Hunting World in 1970 alleging infringement of its registered trademarks for the word "Safari" as applied to clothing and sporting goods. In particular, A&F had ten federal registrations of the word "Safari" for such items as hats, shoes, swim trunks, shirts, pants, belts, luggage, grills, ice chests, tents, axes, and smoking tobacco. A&F alleged that it had spent large sums of money in advertising and promoting products identified with its mark "Safari" and in policing its right in the mark. A&F complained that Hunting World engaged in the retail marketing of sporting apparel, including hats and shoes, some identified by the use of "Safari" alone or by expressions such as "Minisafari" and "Safariland." A&F argued that continuation of these uses would confuse the public, and it thus sought an injunction, as well as damages.

Hunting World alleged that the word "Safari" is an ordinary, common, descriptive, geographic, and generic word that is commonly used and understood by the public to mean and refer both to a journey or expedition, especially for hunting or exploring in East Africa, and to the hunters, guides, animals, and equipment forming such an expedition. Hunting World alleged that A&F may not exclusively appropriate such a term and sought cancellation of all of A&F's registrations using the word "safari."

After lengthy judicial proceedings, the district court ruled broadly in Hunting World's favor. The judge determined that "safari" is merely descriptive and does not serve to distinguish A&F's goods from anybody else's. The district court dismissed A&F's complaint and canceled all of A&F's registered "Safari" trademarks. A&F appealed.

### Opinion

The cases, and in some instances the Lanham Act, identify four different categories of terms with respect to trademark protection. Arrayed in an ascending order that roughly reflects their eligibility to trademark status and the degree of protection accorded, these classes are (1) generic, (2) descriptive, (3) suggestive, and (4) arbitrary or fanciful. The lines of demarcation, however, are not always bright. Moreover, the difficulties are compounded because a term that is in one category for a particular product may be in quite a different one for another (e.g., "ivory" is generic for a product made from elephant tusks, but arbitrary for soap), because a term may shift from one category to another in light of differences in usage through time (e.g., "elevator" originally was suggestive but became generic), because a term may have one meaning to one group of users and a different one to others ("aspirin" is generic for consumers but not for druggists), and because the same term may be put to different uses with respect to a single product (e.g., a term, such as "joy," may be used by one detergent company for identification, but by another to describe the product). In various ways, all of these complications are involved in this case.

A generic term is one that refers, or has come to be understood as referring, to the genus of which the particular product is a species. No matter how much money and effort the user of a generic term has poured into promoting the sale of its merchandise and no matter what level of success it has achieved in securing public identification, it cannot deprive competitive product manufacturers of the right to call an article by its name. The persuasiveness of this principle is illustrated by a series of well-known cases holding that when a suggestive or fanciful term has become generic as the result of a manufacturer's own advertising efforts, trademark protection will be denied.

A descriptive term forthwith coveys an immediate idea of the ingredients, qualities, or characteristics of the product. Such a term stands on a better basis than one that is generic. Although Section 1052(e) of the Lanham Act forbids the registration of a mark that is "merely descriptive," Section 1052(f) removes a considerable part of the sting by providing that such a mark may be registered if the mark has become distinctive of the applicant's goods (i.e., attains secondary meaning). For generic terms, any claim to an exclusive right must be denied because this in effect would confer a monopoly not only of the mark but of the product by rendering a competitor unable effectively to name what it was endeavoring to sell. However, for descriptive terms, the law strikes the balance between (1) the hardships to a competitor in hampering its use of an appropriate word and (2) the hardships of the owner, who, having invested money and energy to endow a word with the goodwill adhering to that owner's enterprise, would be deprived of the fruits of the enterprise's efforts.

A term is suggestive if it requires imagination, thought, and perception to reach a conclusion as to the nature of the goods. The reason for restricting protection accorded descriptive terms, namely, the undesirability of preventing an entrant from describing a product, is much less forceful when the trademark is a suggestive, because the ingenuity of the public relations profession may supply new words and slogans as needed. If a term is suggestive, it is entitled to registration without proof of secondary meaning.

It need hardly be added that fanciful or arbitrary terms, which are chosen solely for identification, enjoy all the rights accorded to suggestive terms—and without the need of debating whether the term possibly is only "merely descriptive."

We have reached the following conclusions: (1) applied to specific types of clothing, "safari" has become a generic term, and "minisafari" may be used for a smaller-brimmed hat; (2) "safari" has not, however, become a generic term for boots or shoes: it is either suggestive or merely descriptive and is a valid trademark even if merely descriptive, because it has become incontestable under the Lanham Act; (3) "Camel Safari," "Hippo Safari," and "Safari Chukka" were used by Hunting World in a purely descriptive way on its boots, and based on fair use, it thus has a defense against infringement.

It is common ground that A&F could not apply "Safari" as a trademark for an expedition into the African wilderness. This would be a clear example of the use of "Safari" as a generic term. What is perhaps less obvious is that a word may have more than one generic use. The word "Safari" has become part of a family of generic terms, which, although deriving from the original use of the word and reminiscent of its milieu, have come to be understood not as having to do with hunting in Africa, but as terms within the language referring to contemporary American fashion apparel. These terms name the components of the safari outfit, well-known to the clothing industry and its customers: the "safari hat," a broad, flat-brimmed hat with a single, large band; the "safari jacket," a belted bush jacket with patch pockets and a buttoned shoulder loop; and the "safari suit," the name given to the combination when the jacket is accompanied by matching pants. Typically, these items are khaki colored.

This outfit and its components were doubtless what the district court judge had in mind when he found that the word "safari" is widely used by the general public and people in the trade in connection with wearing apparel. It is clear that many stores have advertised these items despite A&F's attempts to police its mark. In contrast, no one besides A&F and Hunting World uses the term "Safari" on the other kinds of merchandise subject to A&F's registrations.

The foregoing supports the dismissal of A&F's complaint with respect to many of the uses of "Safari" by Hunting World. Describing a publication as a "Safariland Newsletter," containing bulletins as to safari activity in Africa, was a generic use. A&F also was not entitled to an injunction against Hunting World's use of the word in advertising goods of the kind included in the safari outfit. And if Hunting World may advertise a hat of the kind worn on safaris as a safari hat, it may also advertise a similar hat with a smaller brim as a minisafari. Although the issue may be somewhat closer, the principle against giving trademark protection to a generic term in turn sustains the denial of an injunction against Hunting World's use of "Safariland" as the name of a portion of its store devoted to the sale of clothing for which the term "Safari" has become generic.

A&F stands on stronger ground with respect to Hunting World's use of "Camel Safari," "Hippo Safari," and "Safari Chukka" as names for boots imported from Africa. There is no evidence that "Safari" has become a generic term for boots. Since A&F's registration of "Safari" for use on its shoes has become incontestable, it is immaterial whether A&F's use of "Safari" for boots was "suggestive" or "merely descriptive."

Hunting World contends that even if "Safari" is a valid trademark for boots, it is entitled to the defense of fair use provided in Section 1115(b)(4) of the Lanham Act. This section offers such a defense even against incontestable marks when the term charged to be an infringement is not used as a trademark "and is used fairly and in good faith only to describe to users the goods or services of such party, or their geographic origin."

The parent company of Hunting World has been engaged in arranging safaris to Africa since 1959. The president of both companies has written a handbook on safaris, booked persons on safaris, and purchased clothing in Africa for resale in America. These facts suffice to establish, absent a contrary showing, that Hunting World's use of "Safari" with respect to boots was in the context of hunting and traveling expeditions and not as an attempt to garner A&F's goodwill. The district court judge found that Hunting World's use of the term on its boots was intended to apprise the public of the type of product by referring to its origin and use. A plaintiff who has chosen a mark with some descriptive qualities cannot altogether exclude some kinds of competing uses, even when the mark is properly on the register. It is significant that Hunting World did not use "Safari" alone on its shoes, as it doubtless would have done if confusion had been intended. We thus hold that the district court was correct in dismissing the complaint.

We find much greater difficulty in the district court's broad invalidation of A&F's trademark registrations. When a term becomes the generic name of a product to which it is applied, grounds for cancellation exist, even if the registration is otherwise incontestable. The relevant registrations of that sort are Nos. 358,781 and 703,279. The whole of registration No. 358,781, which covers "safari" apparel was properly canceled. With respect to registration No. 703,279 only a part has become generic (to wit, pants, jackets, coats, and hats), and cancellation on that ground should be correspondingly limited.

Some of A&F's other trademark registrations, including the portions of No. 703,279 that are not generic, have become incontestable by virtue of the filing of affidavits indicating five years' continuous use after the respective registrations. There is nothing to suggest that the uses included in these registrations are the generic names of either current fashion styles or African expeditions. The generic term for A&F's "safari cloth Bermuda shorts," for example, is "Bermuda shorts," not "safari"; indeed one would suppose this garment to be almost ideally unsuited for the jungle, and there is no evidence that it has entered into the family for which "Safari" has become a generic adjective. The same holds for luggage, portable grills, and the rest of such suburban paraphernalia, from the swim trunks and raincoats to the belts and scarves included in these registrations.

We also hold that the other registrations, which have not become incontestable, should not have been canceled. "Safari" as applied to ice chests, axes, tents, and smoking tobacco does not describe such items. Rather, it is a way of conveying to affluent patrons of A&F a romantic notion of high style, coupled with an attractive foreign allusion. Such uses fit into the category of suggestive marks.

The district court is instructed to enter a new judgment consistent with this opinion.

## FUNCTIONALITY

The Lanham Act allows registration for words, names, symbols, and/or devices that serve to distinguish goods or services. Product shapes, characteristics, colors, sounds, and smells are all capable of registration. However, companies often do not attempt to register these product aspects, choosing instead to rely on general principles of unfair competition to protect them when necessary. The typical scenario involves a competitor's copying a prominent product characteristic followed by a lawsuit alleging that the characteristic is used by consumers to identify and distinguish the goods. This action may be brought under state unfair competition laws or under Section 43(a) of the Lanham Act, which, among other things, extends federal protection to unregistered marks according to basic unfair competition principles.

So, let's assume that our Audio Enhancement System is designed with two extralarge control dials in the center of the front panel. At the time of the product's introduction, this placement was unique to stereo equipment. It also made the equipment easy to use and gave the product a modern technological flair. We decided not to pursue the possibility of a design patent for this arrangement. Could we use the trademark laws to prevent competitors from copying it?

As trademark law moves into the arena of protecting product designs and attributes, it creates additional tension with the basic notions of design patent policies and the underlying principles of free competition. When product designs are not protected by a design patent, then they are supposed to be available for competitors to use freely. However, there is a limited exception to this basic notion, allowing trademark protection when necessary to protect consumers from confusion and under circumstances that will not yield competitive barriers.[17] This, of course, is the same philosophy used to analyze names and words. However, the analysis of product features is more complicated because they are actual components of the functioning product. Thus, one not only must be concerned whether the feature is generic or serves to identify source but also must consider whether the attribute somehow makes the product more useful or desirable than can alternatives available to competitors.

The determination of whether a product feature may be protected by trademark laws usually breaks down into two investigations. The first requires proof that consumers associate the feature with one source and use it to distinguish the product in the marketplace. This inquiry is very similar to that used for words. That is, it may be assumed that inherently distinctive features have source identification properties.[18] On the other hand, the more common the attribute, the heavier the burden one will bear to prove source significance. The logical extreme is with generic features, which may not receive protection at all. For example, a company should not be able to appropriate the color green for mint mouthwash, because this feature is generic for the product. Clearly, such protection would put the competition at a severe disadvantage because consumers might not readily believe that other colors of mouthwash could have a minty taste. Likewise, it would not be proper to allow trademark protection for the expected shape of the standard desk telephone.

The other, and usually more critical, consideration for product features is determining whether they are functional. The concept of functionality is not consistently treated by the courts and is the subject of much confusion. There is no debate that the doctrine is intended to ensure that trademark protection does not unduly interfere with the free availability of unpatented product designs. However, some courts address this goal in a more limited fashion than others.

Almost all courts would agree that a product design should not be protected as a trademark if that design allows the product to achieve its function in a way that is cheaper to produce than other possible methods. This was the reason, for example, that Schwinn was denied protection for a bicycle rim design that was simpler and less expensive than other possibilities.[19] Protection would be unfair in this instance because the manufacturer would have a cost advantage in supplying useful aspects of the product. For that reason, this type of functionality may be properly called utility supply functionality.

There is also widespread agreement that a product feature or design is functional and not protectible as a trademark if it enables the product to function better than a large set of alternative arrangements. Thus, Bose was denied trademark protection for the hexagonal shape of its speakers because that arrangement was important to the superior performance of that system.[20] On the other hand, the spray bottle design used by Morton-Norwich for such products as Fantastik was not considered functional because there were a large number of spray bottle forms that were equally suitable to perform the function of discharging liquid ingredients.[21] Similarly, a court more recently ruled that the exterior shapes and appearances of two Ferrari automobile models were not functional because they did not contribute to performance.[22] In all of these situations, the focus of the inquiry is whether trademark protection of a design will cause consumers to demand the product more than competitive offerings because the design is more useful to them for achieving their tasks. For this reason, one might properly call this type of functionality utility demand functionality.

The most debated aspect of functionality involves the relevance of what is called aesthetic demand functionality. This doctrine prohibits trademark protection for a product design that increases customer demand because it makes the product more aesthetically pleasing. The rationale behind the aesthetic functionality doctrine is no different from that covering the other aspects of functionality: it is intended to ensure that trademark protection does not bestow a competitive advantage. Those who support application of the doctrine perceive no reason to distinguish between protecting utilitarian advantages and protecting aesthetic

### Exhibit 7.4  Trademark Protection of Product Designs: Requirements

- Identification of Source
- Likelihood of Confusion
- Lack of Functionality
  - Utility functionality
    = Supply: cheaper to produce than potential alternative designs
    = Demand: more useful than potential alternative designs
  - Aesthetic functionality
    = Demand: more attractive than potential alternative design
- Case: *Rogers v. Keene*

ones. In both instances, trademark protection empowers the owner with more than a means to distinguish its goods. The only difference is that with utility functionality, the inquiry is on the capabilities of the product, whereas with aesthetic functionality, it is on the product's beauty.

The conceptual difficulty with aesthetic functionality is that the doctrine was misapplied by some courts leading to what appears to be an overreactive backlash by others. Aesthetic functionality is a problem if it makes the product more desirable. Based on this, the approach taken by some courts was to deny protection to a design if consumers purchased the product in part because they liked and wanted that design. In other words, aesthetic functionality came down to whether the design contributed to the commercial success of the product.[23] As recognized by other courts, this approach meant that one could not get trademark protection for anything attractive, since appearance frequently is an important aspect for commercial success. However, to make manufacturers rely solely on design patents to introduce interesting new designs might make the marketplace extremely dull. Thus, these courts rejected the doctrine. Where they went wrong, at least in the opinion of this author, is by denouncing aesthetic functionality entirely, rather than simply this incorrect application, for the proper methodology is not simply to determine whether a design makes the product more attractive but whether one design enhances attractiveness more than other designs that might be adopted by competitors. *W. T. Rogers v. Keene* provides a thorough and intelligent exposition of the functionality doctrine, as well as the legitimacy of aesthetic functionality when approached in the correct manner.

## W. T. ROGERS COMPANY V. KEENE

*Seventh Circuit Court of Appeals, 1985*

### Facts

Rogers and Keene are competing manufacturers of office supplies. In 1969, Rogers began to manufacture a molded plastic stacking office tray for letters and documents. The sides of the tray are hexagonal and have little holes on the top and "feet" on the bottom so that trays can be clamped together with other trays to form a stack. The Rogers tray was for long the only tray with hexagonal end panels; competing trays had rectangular panels. Whether because the hexagonal design was pleasing to customers or for other reasons, the Rogers tray was a big success, and by 1985 Rogers had sold about a million of the trays each year.

Wendell Keene worked for Rogers before he founded his own company in 1983. When he went to a plastics firm to get a mold made for his company's plastic stacking trays, he gave the molder a Rogers tray to make a virtually identical tray. Before Keene began competing with Rogers, Rogers had not affixed a trade name to its tray, but afterward it stamped "Stak-Ette" on the tray.

Rogers never tried to get a design patent for the hexagonal end panels that are the most distinctive feature of its tray; nor did it ever try to register the feature as a trademark. Nevertheless, it contends that the feature identifies stacking office trays made by Rogers. Rogers sued Keene under Section 43(a) [15 U.S.C. 1125(a)] of the Lanham Act.

The case was tried in the district court before a jury. The district judge asked the jury to answer two questions: (1) whether the hexagonal end panels on Rogers's tray were nonfunctional and (2) if nonfunctional, whether they served to identify the Rogers trays. The jury determined that the end panels were functional, and the district judge entered judgment for Keene. Rogers appealed.

## Opinion

Functionality is a defense to a suit under Section 43(a). The importance of recognizing a defense of functionality is to head off a collision between trademark law and patent law. The concept of functionality is intended to screen out from the protection of trademark law certain design features even if they have become so far identified with the manufacturer of a particular brand that consumers may be confused about the origin of the good if another producer is allowed to adopt the feature.

The purpose of trademark law is to reduce the cost of information to consumers by making it easy for them to identify the products or producers with which they have had either good experiences, so that they want to keep buying the product (or buying from the producer), or bad experiences, so that they want to avoid the product or the producer in the future. This purpose is achieved by letting a producer pick an identifying name or symbol for a brand and by forbidding competing producers to use the same or a confusingly similar name or symbol on their brands. Since the supply of distinctive names and symbols usable for brand identification is very large, competition is not impaired by giving each manufacturer a perpetual "monopoly" of an identifying mark; such marks are not a scarce input into the production of goods. But if instead of picking some distinctive mark for a brand a manufacturer tries to appropriate the generic name of the product, then it is trying to monopolize a scarce input. In such a case, trademark protection is denied.

The same principle apples if the trademark is part of the design of the product rather than a word or logo affixed to the product. Ornamental, fanciful shapes and patterns are not in short supply, so appropriating one of them does not take away from any competitor something it needs in order to make a competing brand. But if the feature is not ornamental or fanciful or whimsical or arbitrary but is somehow intrinsic to the entire product consisting of this manufacturer's brand and the rivals' brands, trademark protection will be denied. The name of this principle is functionality. Thus, the first company to make an airplane cannot use the characteristic shape of an airplane as its trademark, thereby condemning its rivals to build planes that won't fly. A firm that makes footballs could not use as its trademark the characteristic oval shape of a football, thereby forcing its rivals to find another shape for their footballs; since they wouldn't be able to sell any round or hexagonal footballs, the firm would have, not an identifying mark, but a product monopoly, and a product monopoly not for a term of years as under the patent laws but forever.

A functional feature is unlike those dispensable features of a particular brand that rivals do not need in order to compete effectively. If the feature asserted to give a product distinctiveness is the best design, or one of a few superior designs, for its de facto purpose, it follows that competition is hindered.

The difficult cases, and this is one, are cases in which the feature sought to be trademarked can be said to be functional by giving aesthetic pleasure. It is apparent that trade names, symbols, and design features often serve a dual purpose, one part of which is to make the product attractive along with identifying the brand to the consumer. On one hand, it would be unreasonable to deny trademark protection to a manufacturer who had the good fortune to have created a trade name, symbol, or design that became valued by the consuming public for its intrinsic pleasingness as well as for the information it conveyed about the maker of the product, unless the feature in question had become generic and therefore costly to engineer around. But it would also be unreasonable to let a manufacturer use trademark law to prevent competitors from making pleasing substitutes; yet that would be the effect of allowing the manufacturer to appropriate the most pleasing way of configuring the product.

Before Rogers began selling its tray, molded plastic office stacking trays came with rectangular end panels rather than hexagonal ones. So evidently, the hexagonal shape was not something intrinsic to the product, as the oval shape of a football is. Of course, products change, and if the hexagonal end panel made the tray substantially more useful, or substantially cheaper to produce, competing manufacturers would be entitled to copy it. But there is no suggestion here of this. The hexagonal shape does nothing to enhance the tray's utility in holding papers. And there is no suggestion that it makes a tray cheaper to produce; if anything, it makes it more expensive, albeit trivially.

It is only when the term "functional" is expanded to embrace the aesthetic that it becomes possible to argue that the hexagonal shape is functional. An identifying mark does not get thrust into the public domain just because the buying public finds it pleasing. If effective competition is possible without copying that feature, then, by analogy to the distinction between arbitrary and generic brand names, it is not a functional feature. That may well be the case here since Rogers is outsold by Eldon, the maker of a rectangular tray—though, of course, other factors could explain Eldon's success while Rogers could have the superior design.

Even if competing manufacturers of molded plastic stacking office trays could not use any form of hexagonal end panel without infringing Rogers's trademark, that would not confine them to the rectangular shape, which we may assume is too drab to be a good substitute for a fancier shape. For even with the hexagon appropriated, an infinity of geometrical patterns would remain open to competitors. Keene could have chosen an oval, a pentagon, a trapezoid, a parallelogram, an octagon, a rectangle covered with arabesques, or machicolated, or sawtoothed.

Keene argues that the decor compatibility of stacked trays requires that any manufacturer be allowed to use the same-shaped end panel as any other. The premise is that a stack of trays with differently shaped end panels would be ugly.

Thus, whatever shape the first manufacturer adopted would establish a norm from which other manufacturers could not depart with any hope of competitive success. There is only superficial appeal to this claim. For one thing, Rogers was not the first maker of stacking trays. For another, such trays are cheap items, and if someone came along with a more elegant design, office managers would be willing to replace an entire stack on some, perhaps all, of the desks in the office. For a third, as an office's stack wears out or as new companies spring up, opportunities exist for new manufacturers using different-shaped panels.

The biggest objection to decor compatibility is that it is an open sesame to trademark infringement. It is not enough that a person who owns two items with that feature wants a matched pair. Otherwise, we might be forced to admit that General Motors can duplicate the Rolls Royce, because a person who had one Rolls Royce might think a second Rolls would look good next to it in the garage.

To summarize this discussion, the jury has to determine whether the feature for which trademark protection is sought is something that other producers of the product in question would have to have as part of the product in order to be able to compete effectively in the market or whether it is the kind of merely incidental feature that gives the brand some individual distinction but that producers of competing brands can readily do without. A feature can be functional not only because it helps the product better achieve the objective for which the product would be valued by a person indifferent to matters of taste, charm, elegance, and beauty but also because it makes the product more pleasing to people not indifferent to such things. But the fact that people like the feature does not by itself prevent the manufacturer from being able to use it as a trademark. The manufacturer is prevented only if the feature is functional as defined earlier, that is, only if without it other producers of the product could not compete effectively.

Though a producer does not lose a design trademark just because the public finds it pleasing, there may come a point where the design feature is so important to the value of the product to consumers that continued trademark protection would deprive manufacturers of competitive alternatives, and at that point protection ceases. This situation is no different from that of the producer of a brand that is so popular that the brand name has become the generic name. Because trademarks do not have fixed time limits like copyrights and patents, other and vaguer methods are used to cut them off at the point where their value as information about product origin is exceeded by their cost in impeding competition. It is just another example of how firms that have the good fortune to succeed may find themselves put under restrictions; but the successful firms have at least the consolation of success. It is not a disaster for the owner of the trademark; should Rogers lose this case in the end and have to share its hexagonal design with competitors, it can (as it has begun to do) imprint a verbal or other trademark more emphatically in order to identify its brand to consumers who can no longer look to the hexagon for identification of source. What Rogers may fear of course is not the loss of an identifying mark but the loss of a competitive advantage stemming from the exclusive possession of a popular design, but for this a manufacturer must seek the aid of the design patent law, with its stringent requirements and its 14-year limitation, and not the aid of the trademark laws.

The case is remanded to the district court for a new trial with jury instructions consistent with this opinion.

---

We now can return to the issue of whether the exterior design of our Audio Enhancement System, especially the placement of the two control dials, may be protected by federal and/or state trademark laws. We need to show, first of all, that when consumers are confronted with products having that control panel design, they believe those products all come from the same source. The more unique and distinctive the design, the easier this will be for us to prove. However, we must keep one possibility, alluded to in *Rogers v. Keene*, in mind. Consumers, over time, may come to believe that a product can be an Audio Enhancement System only if it has two control dials such as ours. In other words, that feature, albeit unique, may become generic to the entire product class. Clearly, this is most likely to happen if we are the only seller of the system for a long period of time. However, as with words and names, our marketing and distribution strategies may also be pertinent.

The other set of relevant issues involves questions of functionality. Utility supply functionality likely will not be of concern unless the two-dial design is somehow the cheapest way to have the system perform the functions of those dials. Utility demand functionality may be of some concern, especially if the layout is the most ergonomically sound approach. Perhaps the location of the two dials is most convenient for proper adjustments and tuning. However, this seems very unlikely. On the other hand, we may claim that consumers associate the mere existence of two large wheels, no matter where located, with us. We may encounter more resistance if we try to extend trademark protection this far because large tuning wheels may be the best way for consumers to make the proper adjustments. Or, consumers may become so conditioned to make adjustments with two wheels that their very existence becomes a necessary standard that all companies must use to effectively compete. Just as words may become generic, so too can designs become functional by serving as industry standards. Under these circumstances, trademark protection is inappropriate since competitors would be forced to retrain customers in order to sell their products.[24] Finally, aesthetic demand functionality also may be a factor on the theory that our layout is one of the only ways to make the product attractive, either in and of itself or in conjunction with other components. As with utilitarian supply functionality, though, this possibility seems very remote.

These same principles can be applied in any high-technology context. The computer industry provides just one example. Trademark protection is available for the shape and appearance of a computer hardware product, for instance, if the design is used to identify the source and is not functional. The analysis for hardware essentially mirrors that just used for the Audio Enhancement System (AES). As with the AES, the important issues likely will be whether the hardware has sufficiently unique features to allow customers to distinguish it and whether those attributes are somehow superior for the ways customers use the product.[25] Again, one also must consider whether the product has been accepted by customers as an industry standard. For instance, a unique computer keyboard design, although initially based primarily on aesthetic considerations, was denied trademark protection because it had become an industry standard.[26] In spite of this example, there clearly will be situations when computer hardware products can satisfy all the relevant concerns, especially when they include unique ornamental features. Thus, unlike with copyrights, wherein protection for computer hardware designs is next to impossible, trademarks offer at least some realistic possibility for coverage.

The more controversial questions in the computer field involve the potential application of trademark protection to the graphical user interface of computer software.[27] The analysis for an interface should involve the same principles, thereby leading to the conclusion that it may be protected by trademarks under the right circumstances. As always, the first question will be whether the interface actually serves an identification function. The more unique the look of the interface, the easier will be the burden to prove that this requirement is satisfied. For example, some have argued that when Apple first introduced its user interface for the Macintosh system, it was sufficiently unique to serve an identification function.[28] However, whatever special attributes it may have originally had were lost over time as other companies introduced interfaces with similar visual appearances. The utility demand functionality concerns may be the real challenge for graphical user interfaces because of the serious potential that they may become standards in the industry. As mentioned before, when this happens, trademark protection should not be available. Computer software companies are just now beginning to assert trademark rights in the graphical displays of their products.[29] It will be interesting to see how receptive the courts will be to this practice when litigation inevitably ensues.

Members of the European Union (EU) have been taking a somewhat different approach to product design protection. In EU countries as well as others around the world, design protection is based on sui generis registration systems. In 1993, the EU Commission issued a draft Proposal dealing with product design protection in the union.[30] Under the Proposal, product designs would be capable of receiving union-wide protection if they have a character that is significantly different from other available designs. Such designs may be protected even if they have functional attributes. However, generic or commonly found designs would be excluded from protection. The Proposal establishes a union registration system for product designs. Registration lasts for five years and could be renewed for up to 25 years. Under the Proposal, a registrant would have the exclusive rights to apply the design to any product. The Proposal also extends protection to unregistered designs, but the term lasts only three years from the time the design is first made available to the public.

As discussed in Chapter 6, there are efforts to expand product design protection in the United States. However, opposition from groups such as the automobile replacement-parts manufacturers have prevented passage so far. The EU Proposal contains certain exceptions, which reflect some of the concerns of these groups. For instance, a parts design is not entitled to protection if a consumer is not interested in the appearance of the part. Also, the Proposal excludes protection for designs that must be copied exactly to allow interchangeability with products made by other manufacturers. Finally, it is important to note that computer programs and semiconductor topographies are not subject to this Proposal. Rather, protection for them must come solely from other existing laws.

## FEDERAL REGISTRATION: STANDARDS AND PROCEDURES

As previously discussed, federal trademark registration is desirable primarily because it provides constructive notice of the registrant's rights to exclusively use the mark. However, it carries other benefits as well. For instance, registration is prima facie evidence of the validity of the mark, its ownership, and the registrant's exclusive rights to use the mark. What this means is that a person wishing to challenge the propriety of protection has the burden of proof. In addition, once a mark has been registered for five years, a person may no longer contest the validity or ownership of the mark, except in certain special situations, such as that the mark had become generic. Registration also entitles one to take advantage of enhanced remedies for trademark counterfeiting, a topic to be taken up later in this chapter. Finally, trademark registration provides certain advantages in the international arena, such as by deterring infringing imports and by providing priority in foreign trademark applications.

The Lanham Act defines a registrable trademark very broadly. It provides that a trademark "includes any word, name, symbol or device, or any combination thereof . . . [which has been or is intended to be used by a person] . . . to identify and distinguish his or her goods, including a unique product, from those manufactured and sold by others to indicate the source of goods, even if that source is unknown."[31] A service mark is defined similarly with respect to services.[32] Just to get some flavor for the range of marks that may be registered, consider that the following have all been registered: the design of a container for household spray cleaner,[33] the color pink for fibrous glass residential insulation,[34] the smell of plumeria blossoms for yarn,[35] and three musical notes for a television network.[36] The definition makes it clear that the trademark does not have to indicate the name of the company that is the source of the goods or services. Rather, it is enough that the mark be recognized by consumers as a means to identify that the goods or services come from the same source.

Section 2 of the Lanham Act states that "no trademark by which the goods [or services] of the applicant shall be distinguished from the goods [or services] of others shall be refused registration" unless it falls in particular categories.[37] The criterion for trademark protection, thus, is provided in terms of what may not be protected. For instance, deceptive marks are impermissible.[38] Also, as discussed before, descriptive marks may not be registered until they become distinctive of the applicant's goods or in other words, have obtained secondary meaning.[39] On this score, the act further provides that five years of exclusive and continuous use of a descriptive mark is prima facie evidence of secondary meaning.[40]

The most essential negative condition is provided in Section 2(d), which disallows registration when the mark "so resembles a mark registered in the Patent and Trademark Office or a mark or trade name previously used in the United States by another as to be likely, when used on or in connection with the goods [or services] of the applicant, to cause confusion, or to cause mistake, or to deceive." There are two essential elements to this provision. The first relates to trademark priority. Since one cannot register a mark after there is evidence of previous use by another, the first to use a trademark has the upper hand in terms of registration priority. The second key aspect is based on the likelihood-of-confusion standard, the fundamental cornerstone of trademark policy. Since trademarks are supposed to help consumers clearly distinguish the sources of products and to deter palming off, registration is not allowed when it might result in two or more companies' legitimately providing products with such similar marks that customers are likely to be confused. As we shall see later, likelihood of confusion also is the standard by which infringement is measured. Thus, the same issue is raised in both contexts: what are the circumstances and factors that are relevant in determining whether two marks are likely to cause confusion? How likelihood of confusion is analyzed, both for registration and for infringement, will be demonstrated later in this chapter in *AMF, Inc., v. Sleekcraft Boats.*

Prior to the Trademark Revision Act of 1988, a person could apply for trademark registration only after using the trademark in interstate commerce. Now, however, a business may file for trademark registration under the Lanham Act without having actually used the mark as long as there is a bona fide intention to use the mark.[41] Assuming the application eventually results in a registered trademark, then nationwide priority to use the mark is provided from the time of filing the trademark application.[42] Thus, the trademark registrant has rights against anyone who adopts a confusingly similar mark after the filing date of the registration application.

Issues sometimes arise when two companies have innocently used confusingly similar trademarks in distinct trading areas prior to an application for registration. Here, the nationwide notice of registration must interface with common law unfair competition principles. The basic rule in this situation is that the first user is allowed to register the mark. However, the subsequent user retains exclusive rights in the areas where it did business prior to the application for federal registration.[43] The Lanham Act even provides for the possibility of concurrent registrations of similar marks in these situations when consumer confusion is not likely to result.[44]

Although it is not required, it is a good idea to conduct a trademark search prior to filing an application for registration. A trademark search reviews prior trademark registrations and other sources, such as trade periodicals, to determine if any other company is using a similar trademark. One reason a search is recommended is that applicants must allege in their application that to their information and belief, there are no confusingly similar marks being used in commerce.[45] A thorough search can go a long way to demonstrate the good faith of the applicant. The more important reason, though, is to ensure the strength of the mark prior to making substantial investments in goodwill around it. Companies using similar marks have opportunities during the application process to oppose registration; after registration, they are entitled to contest the validity, at least for five years. In a worst-case scenario, a business could actually receive a registration and build substantial goodwill in a name, only to face cancellation several years later because another company can prove that it was the first user of the mark.

An application for registration may be based on interstate use or a bona fide intent to use. The basic parameters of the registration process are the same, no matter which path is used, although there are some procedural differences. The first part of the registration process is the examination by the PTO to ensure that the mark meets the statutory mandates. In this regard, the PTO evaluates whether registration should be denied because the mark is confusingly similar to one previously registered at the federal level. In addition, it considers whether registration should be refused for other reasons listed in Section 2, such as because it is immoral, deceptive, generic, or descriptive without secondary meaning. This initial review normally takes between four and six months, a period that may seem long until one realizes that the PTO evaluates over 125,000 applications per year.[46] As with patents there is a procedure in which the applicant defends or amends its application to satisfy objections by the PTO. In addition, the applicant has the right to appeal decisions by PTO examiners to the Trademark Trial and Appeal Board and ultimately to the federal courts.

Currently, one can expect the total examination process with the PTO to take about 13 months.[47] Once the PTO is satisfied that registration is appropriate, the mark is published for four weeks in the Official Gazette of the PTO so that any person who believes that damage might result from the registration may oppose it.[48] Since the PTO reviews only prior registrations, this is the opportunity for those who are using similar marks but who have not sought federal registrations to be part of the process. Assuming the mark makes it through the opposition process, then it is ready for registration. At this juncture, there is a difference depending on whether the application was based on use or a bona fide intent to use the mark. In the former situation, when the application is based on actual use in interstate commerce, the mark will be routinely registered by the PTO. In 1991, 52% of trademark registration filings followed this route.[49]

The other method now available for registration is to file an application before actual use, when one has only a bona fide intention to use the mark in interstate commerce in the future. The main advantage of this course is that a company may stake a claim to a mark and complete the examination process before investing resources into product packaging and distribution. Because the filing date is interpreted to be the constructive date of first use, the application effectively grants nationwide priority to the mark unless it is rejected by the PTO or successfully opposed by a member of the public. Thus, the name is reserved on the date of filing while its suitability for registration is being tested. Assuming it overcomes the usual examination and opposition hurdles, the PTO issues a Notice of Allowance. After receiving the Notice of Allowance, the applicant effectively has 12 months to file a Statement of Use with the PTO, wherein the applicant certifies that the mark is being used in interstate commerce in a way that is commercially typical for that product or service.[50] The filing period for the Statement of Use may be extended for up to 24 additional months upon sufficient showing of good cause. According to PTO regulations, a good cause request for an extension must demonstrate ongoing efforts to make use of the marks, such as research and development, market research, manufacturing activities, promotional activities, steps to acquire distributors, steps to obtain governmental approvals, or other similar activities.[51] Once the Statement of Use is filed, the registration usually will be issued in due course by the PTO, although the statute provides for further examination and acceptance of the Statement of Use.[52] Given the advantages of the intent-to-use registration method, one can predict that the proportional number of intent-to-use applications will rise markedly in the near future from its 1991 level of around 48%.

A trademark owner cannot totally relax once registration is obtained. As mentioned before, the registration may be canceled on various grounds for up to five years after registration. Someone might allege, for instance, that the mark is descriptive and has insufficient secondary meaning to support registration or that there was prior use of the mark. In addition, the mark can always be canceled if it becomes generic. In this regard, a trademark owner always has to police advertising and usage of the mark to ensure that it not be used in a generic fashion. Companies such as Xerox, Polaroid, Coca-Cola, and Kleenex have to be constantly vigilant about how their marks are being used. Finally, registered trademarks have to be renewed every ten years verifying that they are still being used in commerce. Exhibit 7.5 summarizes the most important requirements for federal trademark registration.

## TRADEMARK INFRINGEMENT AND REMEDIES

### Likelihood of Confusion

The essence of a trademark infringement action is proving that consumers are likely to be confused about the sources of products or services in the marketplace. Suppose that we adopt the word "StatFree" as the trademark for our Audio Enhancement System, and we obtain a federal registration for it. Another company then uses "HissFree" as the mark for its line of digital audiotapes. If we bring an infringement action, we will have to show that we own the StatFree mark and that consumers are likely to be confused because a tape manufacturer is using a confusingly similar name. The maker of HissFree likely will forward a number of arguments in its defense. For instance, it may claim that "StatFree" is a descriptive name with insufficient secondary meaning to permit trademark protection. Or it may allege that it used the name before we did. Since this is a registered mark, these arguments have to be raised within five years of registration; other-

## Exhibit 7.5  Requirements for Federal Trademark Registration

### Identification of Source

- Words or names
- Symbols or devices
  - Colors
  - Smells
  - Sounds
  - Shapes
  - Designs

### Distinguishes Goods of Applicant from those of Others

- Likelihood of confusion standard
  - Case: *AMF v. Sleekcraft*
- Priority based on use

### Use Requirements for Application

- Actual use in interstate commerce
- Bona fide intent to use in interstate commerce

### Registration Process

- Application
- Examination by PTO
  - Amendments
  - Appeals
- Publication
- Opposition
- Registration
  - Intent-to-use Applications
    = Notice of allowance
    = Statement of use in interstate commerce
      •• Within 12 months of notice of allowance
      •• Extensions for good cause
  - Nationwide priority from date of filing application

### Renewal

- Every ten years

wise, the validity of the mark becomes incontestable on these grounds. Possibly the company will raise the argument that the word "free" or "statfree" is generic for background noise removal equipment. Or, it may establish some inequitable conduct that makes our actions in this matter look as bad as what *it* did. Maybe we knew about the company's use of "HissFree" for a long time but did not bring suit until after it made a huge investment in marketing and distributing the product.

The most likely position that the other company will take, however, is that customers are not likely to be confused. In other words, the company will deny that purchasers of HissFree digital audiotapes are likely to believe that the tapes come from the same source as StatFree Audio Enhancement Systems. The analysis of whether customers are likely to be confused is unexpectedly complex, depending on a number of pertinent variables. *AMF v. Sleekcraft* provides a comprehensive discussion of the issues involved in a likelihood-of-confusion analysis.

## AMF INCORPORATED V. SLEEKCRAFT BOATS
*Ninth Circuit Court of Appeals, 1979*

### Facts

AMF's predecessor used the name "Slickcraft Boat Company" from 1954 to 1969, when it became a division of AMF. The mark "Slickcraft" was federally registered on April 1, 1969. Slickcraft boats are distributed and advertised nationally. From 1964 to 1974, promotional expenditures averaged $200,000 annually, and gross sales approached $50 million.

In 1968, Nescher Boats adopted the name "Sleekcraft" for its high-performance boats. The name was selected without knowledge of AMF's use of "Slickcraft." After AMF notified Nescher of alleged trademark infringement, Nescher adopted a distinctive logo and added the identifying phrase "Boats by Nescher" on plaques affixed to the boat and in much of its advertising. The Sleekcraft mark still appears alone on some of Nescher's stationery, signs, trucks, and advertisements. Nescher's gross sales of Sleekcrafts grew quickly—to over $6 million in 1975.

Slickcraft boats are advertised primarily in general circulation magazines. Nescher advertises primarily in racing enthusiast magazines. Both exhibit product lines at boat shows, sometimes the same show.

AMF sued Nescher for trademark infringement and requested that the court issue an injunction prohibiting use of the term "Sleekcraft." Nescher did not argue at trial that it was entitled to the limited geographical defense available to those who innocently adopt an infringing mark after the trademark owner begins use but prior to registration. The district court found that Nescher had not infringed AMF's trademark and denied AMF's request for injunctive relief. AMF appealed this ruling.

### Opinion

When the goods produced by the alleged infringer compete for sales with those of the trademark owner, infringement usually will be found if the marks are sufficiently similar that confusion can be expected. When the goods are related but not competitive, several other factors are added to the calculus. If the goods are totally unrelated, there can be no trademark infringement because confusion is unlikely.

AMF contends these boat lines are competitive: Both lines comprise sporty fiberglass boats often used for waterskiing, and the sizes of the boats are similar as are the prices. Nescher contends his boats are not competitive with Slickcraft boats because his are true high-performance boats intended for racing enthusiasts.

The district court found that although there was some overlap in potential customers for the two product lines, the boats appeal to separate submarkets. Slickcraft boats are for general recreation, such as fishing, waterskiing, pleasure cruises, and sunbathing. Sleekcraft boats are low-profile racing boats designed for persons who want high-speed recreation. The district court thus concluded that competition between the lines is negligible. We affirm this ruling that the two lines are not competitive. Accordingly, we must consider all the relevant circumstances in assessing the likelihood of confusion.

**Factors Relevant to Likelihood of Confusion.** In a determination of whether confusion between related goods is likely, the following factors are relevant:

1. Strength of the mark
2. Proximity of the goods
3. Similarity of the marks
4. Evidence of actual confusion
5. Marketing channels used
6. Type of goods and the degree of care likely to be exercised by the purchaser
7. Defendant's intent in selecting the mark
8. Likelihood of expansion of the product lines

We discuss each serially.

*1. Strength of the mark*
A strong mark, one that is arbitrary or fanciful, is inherently distinctive and will be afforded the widest ambit of protection from infringing uses. AMF asserts that "Slickcraft" is a fanciful mark that is entitled to wide protection. This is incorrect. Whether "Slickcraft" is suggestive or descriptive is a close question. The distinction is based somewhat on how immediate and direct the thought process is from the mark to the particular product. From the word "Slickcraft," one might readily conjure up the image of AMF's boats, yet a number of other images might also follow. Another criterion is whether the mark is actually viewed by the public as an indication of the product's origin or as a self-serving description of it. We think buyers probably understand that "Slickcraft" is a trademark, particularly since it is used in conjunction with the mark "AMF." We thus hold that "Slickcraft" is a suggestive mark when applied to boats.

Although AMF's mark is protectible and may have been strengthened by advertising, it nonetheless is a weak mark entitled to a restricted range of protection. Thus, only if the marks are quite similar and the goods closely related will infringement be found.

*2. Proximity of the goods*
For related goods, the danger presented is that the public will mistakenly assume there is an association between the producers, though no such association exists.

The more likely the public is to make such an association, the less similarity in the marks is required to a finding of likelihood of confusion. Thus, less similarity between the marks will suffice when the goods are complementary (such as drill bits and drill bushings), the products are sold to the same class of purchasers, or the goods are similar in use and function.

Although these product lines are noncompeting, they are extremely close in use and function. Their uses overlap in some aspects. Their functional features, for the most part, are also similar: fiberglass bodies, outboard motors, and open seating. Even though the Sleekcraft boat serves a different submarket, the two product lines are so closely related that a diminished standard of similarity must be applied when comparing the marks.

### 3. Similarity of the marks

Similarity of the marks is tested on three levels: sight, sound, and meaning. Each must be considered the way each is encountered in the marketplace.

Standing alone, the words "Sleekcraft" and "Slickcraft" are the same except for two inconspicuous letters in the middle of the first syllable. To the eye, the words are similar. Nescher points out that the distinctive logo on his boats and brochures negates the similarity of the words. We agree: the names appear dissimilar when viewed in conjunction with the logo, but the logo is often absent, such as when used in trade journals, stationery, and various advertisements.

Another argument pressed by Nescher is that we should disregard the common suffix "craft" and compare "Slick" and "Sleek" alone. Although these are the salient parts of the two marks, we must consider the entire mark. "Craft," a generic term frequently used in trademarks on boats, is not itself protectible, yet the common endings do add to the marks' similarity.

Sound is also important because reputation is often conveyed by word-of-mouth. We recognize that the two sounds can be distinguished, but the difference is only in a small part of one syllable.

The final criterion reinforces our conclusion. Closeness in meaning can itself substantiate a claim of similarity of trademarks. Here, the words are virtual synonyms.

Despite the district court's findings, we hold that the marks are quite similar on all three levels.

### 4. Evidence of actual confusion

Evidence that use of the two marks has already led to confusion is persuasive proof that future confusion is likely. The district court found that in light of the number of sales and the extent of the parties' advertising, the amount of past confusion was negligible. Because of the difficulty in garnering such evidence, the failure to prove instances of actual confusion is not dispositive. Consequently, this factor is weighed heavily only when there is evidence of past confusion.

### 5. Marketing channels used

Convergent marketing channels increase the likelihood of confusion. The boat lines were not sold under the same roof except at boat shows. However, the marketing channels are parallel. Each sells through authorized retail dealers. The same sales methods are employed. The price ranges are almost identical. Different national magazines are used for advertising, yet the retail dealers use similar local means. Although different submarkets are involved, the general classes of boat purchasers exposed to the products overlap.

### 6. Type of goods and care by purchaser

Both parties produce high-quality, expensive goods. The boats are purchased only after purchasers make thoughtful, careful evaluation of the product and the performance expected.

In assessing the likelihood of confusion to the public, the standard is the typical buyer exercising ordinary caution. When the buyer has expertise in the field, a higher standard is proper. When the goods are expensive, the buyer can be expected to exercise greater care in purchasing. Here, the care exercised by the typical purchaser, though it might virtually eliminate mistaken purchases, does not guarantee that confusion as to association or sponsorship is unlikely. The district court also found that trademarks are unimportant to the average boat buyer. Common sense and the evidence indicate that this is not the type of purchase made only on general impressions. This inattention to trade symbols does reduce the possibilities for confusion.

The hallmark of a trademark owner's interest in preventing use of that owner's mark on related goods is the threat such use poses to the reputation of the owner's own goods. When the alleged infringer's goods are of equal quality, there is little harm to the reputation earned by the trademarked goods. Yet this is no defense, for present quality is no assurance of continued quality.

### 7. Intent

Nescher was unaware of AMF's use of the Slickcraft mark when he adopted Sleekcraft, and he designed a distinctive logo after notification by AMF. Nescher's good faith cannot be questioned.

When the alleged infringer knowingly adopts a mark similar to another's, the courts presume that the defendant can accomplish its purpose, that is, to deceive the public. Good faith is less probative of the likelihood of confusion, yet may be given considerable weight in fashioning a remedy.

### 8. Likelihood of expansion

A strong possibility that either party may expand its business to compete with the other will weigh in favor of finding that the present use is infringing. The evidence shows that both parties are diversifying their product lines. The potential that one or both of the parties will enter the other's submarket with a competing model is strong.

**Remedy.** Based on the preceding analysis, we hold that Nescher has infringed the Slickcraft mark. A complete prohibition against Nescher's use of the Sleekcraft name is unnecessary to eliminate public confusion. Rather, a limited injunction will suffice.

AMF has a substantial investment in the Slickcraft name, but Nescher also has expended much effort and money to build and preserve the goodwill of its mark. Nescher adopted the Sleekcraft name in good faith and has taken steps to avoid confusion. Use of the Nescher logo in all facets of the business would ensure that confusion would not occur.

In balancing the conflicting interests both parties have in the unimpaired continuation of their trademark use, and the interest the public has in avoiding confusion, we conclude that a limited mandatory injunction is warranted. Upon remand, the district court should consider the foregoing interests in structuring appropriate relief. At minimum, the logo should appear in all advertisements, signs, promotional materials, and business forms. A specific disclaimer of any association with AMF or Slickcraft seems unnecessary, nor do we think it necessary to enjoin Nescher from expanding the product line. In its discretion, the district judge may allow Nescher sufficient time to consume supplies at hand and to add the logo to more permanent assets, such as business signs.

The decision of the district court is reversed.

*AMF v. Sleekcraft* demonstrates that application of the likelihood-of-confusion standard is not susceptible to hard-and-fast rules. Rather, the evaluation is dependent on the commercial realities of particular situations. It is not possible, a priori, to determine which factors are most important or which ones should be controlling. This explains, somewhat, why this issue is almost always a point of contention.

Likelihood of confusion is an issue not only after the fact in infringement actions, but it also is pertinent on the front end in registration decisions. The evaluation that the PTO must conduct depends on a similar case-by-case analysis of the applicant's mark in light of marks that were previously registered or used. This often leads to similar frustrations and arguments. Just as an example, litigation ultimately resulted when Kenner Parker Toys, owner of the registered trademark "PLAY-DOH," opposed the registration of the mark "FUNDOUGH" for children's modeling clay. The Trademark Trial and Appeal Board dismissed the opposition, but the Federal Circuit, on appeal, analyzed the facts differently. Based on the strength of the PLAY-DOH mark, the low cost of the product, the similar meanings of the words "fun" and "play," the identical sounds of the suffixes, and the identity of the products and channels of distribution, the Federal Circuit determined that there would be a likelihood of confusion and that registration of FUNDOUGH therefore should be denied.[53]

Two other aspects regarding the confusion component in trademark policy should be noted. First, although likelihood of confusion usually is measured with reference to purchasers, nonpurchasers also may be relevant. For example, a competitor that makes an audio enhancement system that looks very similar to ours might put removable tags on the equipment clearly explaining to purchasers that the product does not come from the company making StatFree. This tag may successfully keep purchasers from being confused, but others who come in contact with the audio equipment after the explanatory labels are removed may be confused about the source of the product. Assuming that those subsequent listeners are potential future customers, such confusion could negatively affect our goodwill, especially if the competitor's product is inferior.

A related doctrine is called dilution. Dilution potentially occurs when a very distinctive and well-known mark, such as Kodak, is used by another company on an unrelated service or product, such as stereo speakers. Likelihood of confusion is not a central issue because the products and their distribution channels are so dissimilar. In other words, those buying or hearing the Kodak speakers are not likely to believe that the photography company made them. However, Kodak still may be injured by the dilution of its name. For one thing, if enough companies start using the Kodak name in various commercial contexts, then the distinctiveness of the name may become blurred or whittled away. This may lead Kodak to lose control of the overall high-quality image of its name. As one commentator has suggested, there is need to protect "the immense but fragile commercial magnetism values of trademarks."[54] Dilution may be especially relevant if the other companies make inferior goods or services. In effect, the name "Kodak" will be tarnished by these inferior, albeit unrelated, uses.

Currently, the federal Lanham Act does not extend to dilution. Likelihood of confusion remains as its fundamental principle. An attempt to expand coverage of the Lanham Act to protect famous trademarks from dilution failed to be included in the 1988 Trademark Revision Act. However, the common law and statutes in at least 22 states, including California, Illinois, New York, and Pennsylvania, do protect marks from dilution. Although these laws vary, protection is most often afforded to strong trademarks that are generally well-known by the general public and that have been distributed for some time in a large area. A highly publicized dilution battle recently pitted Mead Data Central, which owns LEXIS computer database services, against Toyota, maker of the Lexus automobile. The district court in New York, on a dilution rationale, enjoined Toyota from using the Lexus name. However, this decision was reversed on appeal. The appellate court reasoned that although lawyers were very familiar with LEXIS, the general public was not aware of it.[55]

## Remedies for Infringement

The most powerful remedy available to trademark owners for infringement is the injunction. The Lanham Act provides that a court "shall have the power to grant injunctions, according to the principles of equity and upon such terms as the court may deem reasonable."[56] Injunctions may take many forms. The most typical is a prohibition against the infringing use. These may vary in strength depending on the equities of the circumstances. For instance, as mentioned in *Sleekcraft*, the court may allow the infringer to use up existing stock of offending items before making corrections, or it may require their immediate destruction. Other types of injunctions include product recalls, corrective advertising, and disclaimers of association.

The Lanham Act also provides for monetary relief. As with patents and copyrights, monetary relief may be calculated in various ways. The act states that the trademark owner can recover, subject to the principles of equity, (1) the infringer's profits, (2) actual damages suffered by the trademark owner, and (3) the costs of bringing suit.[57] For profits, the trademark owner need prove only the infringer's sales; it is up to the infringer to prove its costs and deductions. Damages may be measured in a variety of ways such as by the extent that sales did not live up to reasonable marketing forecasts or in relation to reasonable royalties. The court also has the discretionary power to increase the actual damages by up to three times, not as a penalty, but because the amount of damages the trademark owner could prove seems inadequate given the harm sustained. Indeed, punitive damages ordinarily may not be recovered under the Lanham Act, although they may be under some state laws for egregious conduct. The final item, court costs, are routinely given; however, attorney's fees are provided only in exceptional cases involving deliberate infringement.

Another remedy available to federal trademark owners is having the U.S. Customs Service seize infringing merchandise.[58] As mentioned in Chapter 1, being able to bar imports at the door is a powerful tool, since otherwise, actions may have to be brought in several courts. To benefit from this remedy, a trademark must be recorded with the Customs Office according to regulations issued by that agency.[59]

There is no question that the Customs Office can and should seize infringing merchandise manufactured overseas by totally unrelated companies that have no authority to sell goods using the trademark. However, international commerce is not always so clean and easy, often involving subsidiaries and foreign licensed companies. Whether importation of goods produced by these entities should be barred is a subject of considerable controversy. This issue, which deals with what is called the gray market, will be discussed further in the next section.

In 1984, Congress amended the Lanham Act to attack what it perceived to be an explosive rise in trademark counterfeiting.[60] Counterfeiting is considered the most egregious form of trademark infringement because it involves the deliberate intent by unscrupulous businesses to mislead consumers. Acts of counterfeiting are not simply situations in which consumers are likely to be confused because similar marks are applied to related goods. Rather, businesses engaged in counterfeiting purposefully capitalize on the reputations, development costs, and advertising efforts of honest businesses by employing nearly identical marks on virtually the same types of goods and services. Testimony provided at congressional hearings indicated that the normal civil remedies noted previously were too weak to deter the counterfeiting of a vast array of products such as chemicals, watches, luggage, sporting goods, electronic equipment, computer components, automobile parts, and medical devices.[61] Substantial evidence showed that the enormous profit potential of counterfeiting far exceeded the magnitude of harm that ultimately might be imposed by a court if a case were ever brought. In this way, the prospect of damage awards and even injunctions were viewed by counterfeiters as merely acceptable costs of engaging in their unlawful businesses.

The 1984 amendments were designed to raise the stakes for trademark counterfeiters by making them subject to mandatory treble damage and attorney's fees awards and by imposing criminal penalties for their actions.[62] Thus, unlike the remedies that are available to be used against more typical trademark offenders, punishment is an explicit characteristic for dealing with counterfeiters. The Lanham Act defines a counterfeit as a "spurious mark which is identical with, or substantially indistinguishable from, a registered mark."[63] Thus, the additional remedial actions against counterfeiters provided by the 1984 amendments are available only if a mark is registered. This aspect, therefore, provides one more reason to seek federal registration. There are other requirements under the act that must be sustained before counterfeiting penalties can be applied.[64] For instance, the counterfeit mark must be used with the same type of goods or services for which the legitimate mark is registered. In addition, the registered mark must actually be in use at the time the counterfeit merchandise appears.[65] Also, a mark can be a counterfeit only if it is applied without the authority of the trademark owner.[66] As we shall see in the next section, this is principally designed to distinguish counterfeit goods from gray market goods. Finally, to be subject to counterfeiting penalties, one must intentionally use a mark knowing that it is a counterfeit. If all of these elements are shown to exist, then the Lanham Act requires a court to impose treble damages and attorney's fees, barring certain unusual extenuating circumstances.

## INTERNATIONAL ASPECTS OF TRADEMARK PROTECTION

The internationalization of the business environment now requires most high-technology companies to take steps to protect their goodwill in several countries outside the United States. What companies find is that trademark protection often follows different principles in those countries, sometimes jeopardizing their investments if the proper steps are not taken with the utmost urgency. Also, since trademark rights are strengthened, if not dependent, on registration, the business has to contend with the procedural demands of registering in all the selected foreign regions. In addition, once trademark rights are established in a foreign country, the product may be altered or priced differently to meet particular local conditions or needs. The question that often arises is whether the trademark owner may prevent those goods from entering the United States. This section reviews developments in these key areas of international trade.

### International Trademark Registration

Although steps are being taken to harmonize the trademark protection policies of individual countries, especially within the European Union and through WIPO and GATT, the current reality is that trademark laws vary considerably among the various jurisdictions. One mistake that managers of U.S. companies often make is assuming that they will ultimately have rights to their trademarks in foreign countries because they were the first in the international trading arena to use them. However, their complacency may have serious consequences. Unlike in the United States, where priority is based on use (or intent to use), in most countries, trademark rights are granted to the first person to file for registration. Coupled with this, one must consider that protection in the majority of countries does not depend on use, or even an intent to use. Thus, in many countries, the first to file a trademark registration obtains trademark rights, no matter whether that person has used or intends to use the mark within those borders.

So, assume that the introduction of our StatFree Audio Enhancement System is a tremendous success. A substantial advertising campaign, excellent quality control, a thoroughly informed sales staff, and top-flight product features all lead to StatFree's wide acceptance. When we finally make the decision to expand distribution outside the United States, we may have a rude awakening. Persons or companies in certain countries where we want to do business may have already registered the name "StatFree" for audio equipment, even though they have never made an audio product. What motivated their registration? Given the use and priority rules of those countries, some companies simply register names they might like to use on products if they ever decide to manufacture them. Such a practice, called warehousing, is not possible in the United States because one must have a bona fide intent to use the name in the near future. The more likely explanation in this case, though, is that the registrant perceived the success of our product in the United States and anticipated that we would soon want to internationalize operations. By registering the name "StatFree," this person now holds us hostage if we want to do business in the person's country. Our choice is to use a different name in that region, or to buy the pirate out. Given the tremendous goodwill built in the name, the first option is not very attractive. Thus, we ultimately are forced to negotiate with the pirate simply to use our name on our product in that country.

In addition, we must consider the possibility that our trademark may be registered in certain countries by companies that intend to manufacture counterfeit goods for worldwide distribution. If we register in those countries first, then we can focus enforcement at the counterfeiting source, assuming we can get the local authorities to police their laws. Otherwise, we will be forced to block the counterfeit merchandise through all the distribution channels in nations where we have ownership rights in the mark. Thus, it is often a good idea for a company to consider registration in certain nations where counterfeiting prevails, even if it has no intention of doing business within those borders.[67] The bottom line from all of this is that international trademark strategies must be considered early in product life cycles.

The essential steps for obtaining registrations in foreign countries are similar to those in the United States. It makes sense to perform a search before filing to see if the name is available. Searching normally is less extensive overseas than in the United States because only prior registrations and applications are relevant, whereas in the United States, any use must be considered. There are numerous private commercial sources that can aid in carrying out these searches. In addition, a search can be conducted at WIPO for international registrations that have been obtained under the Madrid Agreement, an important multilateral treaty that facilitates the registration process. Confusing similarity is the guiding principle in all regions, but one must be wary of the peculiar local customs. For instance, in Germany, vowel sequences have elevated importance, even if the marks do not sound or look alike.[68] If a search uncovers conflicts in important areas, then the firm must consider either purchasing the rights or developing another mark.

In some countries, there is no examination for registration. Rather almost all marks filed will be registered, leaving parties with similar registrations to fight it out in court later to determine who filed first. Most nations, though, provide for some examination followed by opposition periods. Also, as in the United States, most foreign registrations have limited terms but may be renewed indefinitely.

The real obstacles in this process are similar to those encountered by businesses pursuing international patent strategies. Because individual applications must be filed for each separate country, an international strategy requires a litany of agents, lawyers, and translators to faithfully protect trademark rights in foreign lands. This, of course, not only presents a procedural nightmare but becomes very expensive in time and money as well.

Certain international developments are now occurring that should soon prove to facilitate international trademark protection for high-technology companies with U.S. trademarks. As noted in Chapter 1, the United States is a member of the Paris Convention, which applies to trademarks as well as patents. However, this treaty provides only that U.S. citizens will be accorded the same trademark rights in a signatory country as are the nationals of that country. In addition, there is no enforcement authority to ensure that those rights are actually provided. The recently concluded Uruguay Round of GATT, which is scheduled to become effective in 1995, should add some uniformity to the international forum. Under GATT, any sign that is capable of distinguishing the goods or services of one business from those of another shall be eligible for trademark protection and registration. The Agreement further provides that the owner of a registered mark shall have the exclusive right to prevent others from using similar signs in ways that would result in a likelihood of confusion. Registrations must be for terms of at least seven years and must be renewable. In addition, although a country may require that use be a requirement for registration, use may not be a prerequisite for filing an application for trademark registration.

The major international trademark accord is the Arrangement of Madrid Concerning the International Registration of Trademarks (Madrid Agreement), joined by 29 commercial nations, but not the United States. The Madrid Agreement greatly facilitates the procedures for filing trademark applications in the signatory countries, in a way similar to the Patent Cooperation Treaty. Under the agreement, after a trademark registration is received in its home country, a business may file centrally with the World Intellectual Property Organization (WIPO) for an international registration. The international registration designates any or all of the signatory countries in which protection is sought. The extension of protection to each selected member state is automatic, unless the country refuses the registration within one year based on its own examination and opposition procedures. For this phase, local agents and attorneys may be required if objections are raised. The principal advantages, therefore, consist of the ease of filing a single application in one's native language and of obtaining priority in several nations based on the filing of the international registration.

The principal reason that the United States has refused to sign the Madrid Agreement is that the treaty requires that an international application be based on an issued national registration. This provision is viewed as discriminatory by the United States because national registrations are easier to obtain in other countries. This is because use is usually not required in order to receive foreign registrations. Even after the 1988 intent-to-use changes, the United States does not actually register marks until after use. Thus, under the Madrid Agreement, foreign firms have a substantial advantage in gaining international priority.

On June 27, 1989, WIPO adopted the Madrid Protocol to address the concerns with the Madrid Arrangement that were shared by the United States and other countries, such as Japan and Great Britain. Under the Madrid Protocol, international registrations may be granted on the basis of pending applications in the home country. Coupled with the intent-to-use provisions now available under U.S. law, this change substantially erases U.S. concerns about discrimination.

Another important issue addressed by the Protocol involves the effect upon the international registration (and the national registrations based thereupon) when the home country either rejects the application to register a mark or cancels a registered mark. According to the Protocol, an international registration will lapse (as will the territorial extensions) if the home country application or registration is rejected or canceled within five years of its date. By itself, this basic provision would be unfair to U.S. registrants because the use requirement of U.S. law makes rejections much more likely there than in other countries. Lack of use, therefore, by causing the international application to totally lapse, would wipe out all the advantages, including the priority date, of the international application for U.S. applicants. For others, because use does not affect their home registrations, the only repercussion from nonuse is that they would not obtain an extension of protection to the United States. The Protocol alleviates this problem, however. It provides that when a home country application is rejected or canceled, the owner of the international application may file, within three months, national applications in the countries to which the international application extended and may claim the priority date of the international application for them. Thus, although the international registration will lapse, there will be no loss of substantive rights. Given that the Madrid Protocol has resolved the major concerns of the United States, one can expect the United States to become a party to it relatively soon.[69] This will be a tremendous procedural step for owners of U.S. trademarks, since it is expected that as many as 100 nations may ultimately become parties to the Madrid Protocol.[70]

Other negotiations are occurring on the international front that ultimately may yield positive benefits. For instance, discussions are taking place within WIPO to streamline trademark registration procedures used by the trademark offices of the participating nations.[71] Also, the European Union (EU) is very active. In 1988, the Council of the European Union adopted a Trademark Law Harmonization Directive, which strives to unify the national laws of the members in the union.[72] Specifically, the Directive specifies the types of symbols and devices that can be registered as trademarks, establishes the grounds on which member nations may refuse or invalidate registrations, and defines the rights conferred by registration upon trademark owners.[73] In addition, the EU Council approved a regulation in December 1993 that establishes a European Union Trademark System.[74] Under this regulation, a trademark applicant may centrally register for an EU Trademark with the European Union Trademark Office and have trademark rights throughout the EU.[75] The European Union Trademark System works concurrently with the existing national systems, in a way that is analogous to the interplay between the federal and state trademark systems in the United States.

## The Gray Market

Suppose that our StatFree Audio Enhancement System is so well accepted in the United States that we decide to expand our operations into Europe. We, of course, take all the appropriate steps to obtain patent rights within the EU and to register our mark there. While investigating the strategic ways to penetrate the European markets, we begin discussions with a manufacturer in Spain that is willing to pay royalties for the rights to make and distribute StatFrees in Spain. Ultimately we enter a contract allowing the Spanish firm to manufacture and market StatFree Audio Enhancement Systems in Spain only. In the contract, we license to this company the rights to use our patented technologies, copyrighted computer programs, and certain necessary trade secrets. In addition, we grant the company the rights to attach the trademark "StatFree" to the goods.

For a number of reasons, StatFrees may be sold in Spain at a relatively cheaper price than in the United States. The laws and customs of Spain may require less warranty protection. Competitive conditions in the wholesale and retail audio markets as well as labor practices may be different in Spain from those in the United States. Also, relative national economic conditions such as interest rates and growth may lead to fluctuations in exchange rates, making goods from Spain relatively attractive. Whatever the reason, any resultant price differentials between Statfrees in Spain and Statfrees in the United States will lead to profitable opportunities for those importing StatFree Audio Enhancement Systems from Spain into the United States. These goods are called parallel imports and lead to what is coined the gray market.

The problem is that we never intended those StatFrees to compete with our distribution and marketing system in the United States. In a sense, they are not the legitimate StatFrees for the U.S. market. In addition, those selling the Spanish Statfrees in the United States are taking advantage of our investments in promotion, distribution, and service within the United States without sharing in those costs. Their free-riding could have a detrimental impact on our goodwill, especially if there are any differences in the product, such as with warranty terms. On the other hand, we did authorize the manufacture and sale of these goods with our trademark, and we did exercise control of the manufacturing process. Thus, these goods clearly are different from counterfeit goods made by unscrupulous parties. The question is whether the sale of these StatFrees in the United States violates our trademark rights, allowing us either to block their importation or to sue for infringement.

The foregoing situation demonstrates only one of several possible ways that foreign-manufactured products legitimately carrying U.S. trademarks might compete with their U.S. counterparts in the United States. Another scenario is somewhat the reverse from that just described. A foreign manufacturer sells to an independent U.S. distributor the exclusive rights to register its foreign trademark and market its goods in the United States. If the foreign goods bearing that trademark make their way into the United States through other channels, then the domestic firm's goodwill in the U.S. mark may be jeopardized.

Even another set of possibilities occurs when there is an affiliation between a foreign manufacturing firm and a U.S. distributor that owns the U.S. trademark

**Exhibit 7.6 Gray Market Scenarios**

<table>
<tr><td colspan="1" align="center">Definition</td></tr>
</table>

### Definition

A foreign-manufactured good, bearing a valid U.S. trademark, imported into the U.S. without the permission of the U.S. trademark holder.

### I.

A domestic U.S. trademark holder authorizes an independent foreign manufacturer to use its trademark, and the manufacturer agrees not to export to the U.S. A gray market is created when:
1. The foreign manufacturer exports to the U.S.
2. A third-party purchaser exports to the U.S.

### II.

An independent foreign manufacturing company sells the U.S. trademark rights to a domestic U.S. company. A gray market is created when:
1. The foreign manufacturer exports to the U.S.
2. A third-party purchaser exports to the U.S.

### III.

A foreign manufacturing company is affiliated with a domestic U.S. company that owns the U.S. trademark rights.
A. The foreign firm incorporates the U.S. subsidiary to distribute products in the U.S., and the U.S. subsidiary owns the U.S. trademark rights. A gray market is created when:
   1. The foreign manufacturer exports to the U.S.
   2. A third-party purchaser exports to the U.S.
B. The domestic U.S. trademark owner establishes a foreign manufacturing subsidiary or division. A gray market is created when:
   1. A third-party purchaser exports to the U.S.

registration for the foreign-manufactured product. For instance, a foreign manufacturer may incorporate a subsidiary in the United States and license to it the U.S. trademark rights so that the subsidiary can distribute the foreign-made products in the United States. Or, a U.S. company that has a registered U.S. trademark could establish a foreign subsidiary or division to manufacture goods that are intended to be sold in the United States by the U.S. firm. In either case, if third parties buy the goods in the foreign nations and then export them to the United States, there will be unwelcome gray market competition with the products distributed by the U.S. trademark owner.

Two laws empower the Customs Service to block imports that infringe trademarks registered in the United States: Section 526(a) of the Tariff Act and Section 42 of the Lanham Act.[76] Section 526(a) prohibits the unconsensual importation into the United States of "merchandise of foreign manufacture" that bears a U.S. registered trademark that is "owned by" a U.S. citizen or organization. Until 1988, the Customs Service interpreted Section 526 very narrowly with respect to gray market goods, blocking parallel imports only when an independent U.S. distributor purchased the rights to the U.S. registration for the foreign trademark (Scenario II in Exhibit 7.6). In 1988, the Supreme Court determined that this reading was too restrictive.[77] The statute also requires the Customs Service to stop imports when the U.S. trademark owner has authorized an independent foreign firm to manufacture goods bearing the trademark (Scenario I in Exhibit 7.6). However, the court found that ambiguities in certain terms in the statute, such as "of foreign manufacture" and "owned by," adequately supported the Customs Service's policy of allowing gray market imports of goods manufactured by affiliated foreign firms. In other words, gray market imports will not be blocked by the Customs Service under Section 526 if the foreign firm that manufactures the goods is affiliated with the owner of the registered U.S. trademark (Scenario II in Exhibit 7.6).

Section 42 of the Lanham Act requires the Customs Office to block imports of articles that copy or simulate trademarks registered in the United States. The Customs Service has interpreted Section 42 in the same way as Section 526 of the Tariff Act; that is, if the foreign manufacturer is affiliated with the U.S. trademark owner, then the gray market goods will not be denied entry into the United States. However, in 1989, the Circuit Court of Appeals for the District of Columbia questioned whether this exception for affiliated firms could be read into Section 42 of the Lanham Act. In that case, Lever Brothers Co. requested that the court order the Customs Service to block imports of Shield soap and Sunlight dishwashing liquid, which were made by its British affiliate, Lever Brothers Ltd. The British products had the same names and appearance as the U.S. products but had different fragrances and colors and produced fewer suds. The Circuit Court stated that the "natural, virtually inevitable reading of Section 42 is that it bars foreign goods bearing a trademark identical to a valid U.S. trademark but physically different, regardless of the trademark's genuine character abroad or affiliation between producing firms."[78] In 1992, the district court ordered the Customs Service to block the imports made by the affiliated British firm. That the products were physically different was an important aspect leading the court to reach its conclusion. Whether the affiliate exception would apply to Section 42 if the goods were substantially identical was not resolved in this litigation.

Debate about the gray market is heated, leading to the confusion about its legality and propriety in various contexts. U.S. trademark owners, of course, want all imports bearing similar marks to be blocked. Certain discount retailers and consumers, on the other hand, find the lower prices of gray market goods to be very attractive. As just illustrated, the courts have not provided clear direction. Questions about affiliations and the physical similarity of the goods still need to be resolved. In addition, there is controversy concerning whether private parties may sue gray market importers directly for infringement.[79] Attempts are ongoing in Congress to clarify existing laws. For instance, in 1991 and 1992, bills were introduced to add a section to the Lanham Act explicitly prohibiting importation of all gray market goods.[80] Since gray markets can have substantial impact on high-technology companies doing business in the United States, prompt resolution of these issues is imperative.

## CONCLUSION

We have now covered the main components of the intellectual property protection system in the United States. Keep in mind that there are other laws and statutes that protect more specific aspects of intellectual property in various high-technology contexts. The Semiconductor Chip Protection Act is a case in point. In addition, many high-technology industries, such as computers, telecommunications, and biotechnology, are specifically regulated by various government agencies. Thus, you should always consider whether there are specific laws and regulations that apply to your particular type of technology. Having stated that, however, you should feel satisfied at this point that you have a solid grounding in fundamental high-technology intellectual property protection principles.

This book now proceeds to cover two other important legal areas of concern for high-technology companies. One deals with liabilities for accidents, injuries, and other forms of unwanted personal intrusions caused by high-technology products. This section considers how careful one must be in designing, marketing, and using high-technology equipment. The final component deals with certain important contractual aspects, such as warranties, which one should consider when developing or distributing high-technology goods.

## NOTES

1. 15 U.S.C. §§1072; 1057(c) (1988).
2. Eastern Air Lines, Inc., v. New York Air Lines, Inc. 559 F. Supp. 1270 (S.D.N.Y. 1983).
3. Dixi-Cola Laboratories, Inc., v. Coca-Cola Co., 117 F. 2d 352 (4th Cir. 1941).
4. Intel Corp. v. Advanced Micro Devices, Inc., 756 F. Supp. 1292 (N.D. Cal. 1991).
5. On February 17, 1993, the Patent and Trademark Office issued an Office Action Letter affirming an initial decision to refuse registration of "windows" on the grounds that the word is generic. For a full discussion, see "PTO Refuses to Register Windows," 5 J. of Proprietary Rights (April 1993) at 25-26.
6. Bayer, Inc., v. United Drug Co., 272 F. 505 (S.D.N.Y. 1921).
7. King-Seely Thermos Co., v. Aladdin Indus., Inc., 321 F. 2d 577 (2d Cir. 1963).
8. Nissen Trampoline Co., v. American Trampoline Co., 193 F. Supp. 745 (S.D. Iowa 1961).
9. Anti-Monopoly, Inc., v. General Mills Fun Group, Inc., 684 F. 2d 1316 (9th Cir. 1982), cert. denied, 103 S.CT. 1234 (1983).
10. Haughton Elevator Co., v. Seeberger, 85 U.S.P.Q. (BNA) 80 (Comm. Pat. 1950).
11. The Loglan Institute, Inc., v. The Logical Language Group, Inc., No. 91-1254 (Fed. Cir., April 28, 1992).
12. Kellogg Co. v. National Biscuit Co., 305 U.S. 111 (1938).
13. 15 U.S.C. §1052(f).
14. 15 U.S.C. §1065.
15. 15 U.S.C. §1065 (4).

16. 15 U.S.C. §1115(b)(4)
17. See Sears, Roebuck & Co. v. Stiffel Co., 376 U.S. 225 (1964); Compco Corp. v. Day-Bright Lighting, Inc., 376 U.S. 234 (1964).
18. Two Pesos, Inc. v. Taco Cabana, Inc., 112 S. Ct. 2753 (1992).
19. Schwinn Bicycle Co. v. Murray Ohio Mfg. Co. 339 F. Supp. 973 (M.D. Tenn. 1971), aff'd. 470 F. 2d 975 (6th Cir. 1972).
20. In re Bose Corp., 772 F. 2d 866 (Fed. Cir. 1985).
21. In re Morton-Norwich Products, Inc. 671 F. 2d 1332 (C.C.P.A. 1982).
22. Ferrari S.P.A. Esercizio v. Roberts, 944 F .2d 1235 (6th Cir. 1991).
23. Pagliero v. Wallace China Co., 198 F. 2d 339 (9th Cir. 1952).
24. See U.S. Golf Assn. v. St. Andrews Systems, 749 F. 2d 1028, 1034 (3d Cir. 1984).
25. For a full discussion of trademark protection for hardware, see K. Liebman, G. Frischling, and A. Brunel, "The Shape of Things to Come: Trademark Protection for Computers," 9 Computer Lawyer (December 1992) at 1-8.
26. Digital Equip. Corp., v. C. Itoh and Co., 229 U.S.P.Q. (BNA) 598 (D.N.J. 1985).
27. See V. Slind-Flor, "Trade Dress Seen to Protect Trademarks: Computer Software Producers Seek Additional Safeguards," National L.J. (May 17, 1993) at 1, 28.
28. V. Slind-Flor, "Trade Dress Seen to Protect Trademarks: Computer Software Producers Seek Additional Safeguards," National L. J. (May 17, 1993) at 29.
29. See Engineering Dynamics Inc., v. Structural Software Inc., argued before the Fifth Circuit Court of Appeals on June 7, 1993, as reported in a letter to the National Law Journal (July 5, 1993) submitted by H. Langley Jr.
30. See "EC to Harmonize Design Protection," 5 J. of Proprietary Rights (October 1993) at 36.
31. 15 U.S.C. §1127.
32. 15 U.S.C. §1127.
33. See In re Morton-Norwich Products, 213 U.S.P.Q. 9 (C.C.P.A. 1982). The Patent and Trademark Office registers product configurations according to principles outlined in the Trademark Manual of Examining Procedure, Section 1202.03. As discussed in the text, the most important concerns regard identification and functionality.
34. See In re Owens-Corning Fiberglas Corp., 774 F. 2d 1116 (Fed. Cir. 1985). There is a substantial division of opinion in the courts whether single product colors should be accorded trademark protection. See J. Woo, "Product's Color Alone Can't Get Trademark Protection," Wall Street J. (January 5, 1994) at B5.
35. See In re Clarke, 17 U.S.P.Q. 2d (BNA) 1238 (T.T.A.B. 1990).
36. See In re General Electric Broadcasting Co., 199 U.S.P.Q. (BNA) 560 (T.T.A.B. 1978).
37. 15 U.S.C. §1052.
38. 15 U.S.C. §1052(a).
39. 15 U.S.C. §§1052 (e) and (f).
40. 15 U.S.C. §1052(f).
41. 15 U.S.C. §1051(b).
42. 15 U.S.C. §1057(c),
43. 15 U.S.C. §1115(b)(5).
44. 15 U.S.C. §1052(d).

45. 15 U.S.C. §1051.

46. PTC Newsletter, Vol. 10, No. 1 (Fall 1991), at 17.

47. The goal of the PTO is to issue an initial Office action within 3 months of the filing date, and to complete the process within 13 months. These goals are known as the PTO's "3/13" standards. In 1991, the PTO had difficulty meeting the 3-month goal, but since 1992, the office has been close to target. See J. Samuels, "Patent and Trademark Office Practice (Part II of IV)," 5 J. of Proprietary Rights (October 1993) at 16.

48. 15 U.S.C. §1062.

49. PTC Newsletter, Vol. 10, No. 1 (Fall 1991), at 17.

50. 15 U.S.C. §1051(d).

51. 37 C.F.R. §289.

52. 15 U.S.C. §1051(d).

53. Kenner Parker Toys Inc., v. Rose Art Industries, Inc., 963 F. 2d 350 (Fed. Cir. 1992), cert. denied 113 S. Ct. 181 (1992).

54. Pattishall, "Dawning Acceptance of the Dilution Rationale for Trademark-Trade Identity Protection," 74 Trademark Rep. 289, 290 (1983).

55. Mead Data Central, Inc., v. Toyota Motor Sales, U.S.A., Inc., 875 F. 2d 1026 (2d Cir., 1989).

56. 15 U.S.C. §1116(a).

57. 15 U.S.C. §1117.

58. This is authorized by Sections 42 and 43 of the Lanham Act and Section 526 of the Tariff Act.

59. 19 C.F.R. 133.2, 133.3.

60. Trademark Counterfeiting Act of 1984, codified at 15 U.S.C. §§1116-1118 and 18 U.S.C. §2320.

61. S. Rep. No. 526, 98th Cong., 2d Sess. 4-5 (June 21, 1984) reprinted in U.S. Code Cong. and Admin. News 3627, 3630-31.

62. 15 U.S.C. §1117(b), 18 U.S.C. §2320.

63. 15 U.S.C. §1127.

64. For a thorough discussion of these factors, see J. Dratler, Intellectual Property Law: Commercial, Creative and Industrial Property, L.J. Seminars-Press (1993) at ¶11.09[3].

65. 15 U.S.C. §1116(d)(1)(B)(i).

66. 15 U.S.C. §1116(d)(1)(B)(ii).

67. See B. Keller, A. Haemmerli, and A. Hsuan, "National Laws Play a Role in International Protection," National L.J. (December 14, 1992) at 19.

68. M. Feldman, "Trademark Hazards Are Varied," National L.J. (June 17, 1991) at 18. It is prudent to consider the meaning of trademarks in different languages as well. For instance, "No va" means in Spanish "Does not go." B. Keller, A. Haemmerli, and A. Hsuan, "National Laws Play a Role in International Protection," National L.J. (December 14, 1992) at 19.

69. The Protocol addresses other concerns as well. For instance, the one-year period for a national office to refuse extension of the international application was considered too short for countries that provide thorough examinations. The Protocol therefore extends the period to 25 months.

70. W. Cohrs, "Trademark Bar Looks to Accords," National L.J., (May 11, 1992) at S11.

71. See R. Taylor, "Proposed Treaty Would Streamline International Trademark Procedures," National L.J. (May 17, 1993) at S13-S16.

72. First Council Directive to Approximate the Laws of the Member States Relating to TradeMarks, EEC (89) 104; O.J. 1989 (l40) 32.

73. For a thorough analysis of the Trademark Law Harmonization Directive, see B. Neelman, B. Ezring, and C. Shore-Sirotin, "Trademark Rights in Europe: The EC Moves to Uncomplicate the Process," 5 J. of Proprietary Rights (April 1993) at 11-21.

74. See 6 J. of Proprietary Rights (February 1994) at 32; 6 J. of Proprietary Rights (March 1994) at 36.

75. To be eligible to register for an EU Trademark, one must be a national or domiciliary of (1) an EU member nation, (2) a country that is a party to the Paris Convention, or (3) a country that affords national treatment to the EU and that recognizes the EU Trademark. Businesses also are eligible if they have commercial establishments in the EU or in a nation that is a party to the Paris Convention.

76. The Customs Service also is empowered to block importation of unregistered marks by Section 43 of the Lanham Act.

77. K Mart Corp., v. Cartier, Inc., 486 U.S. 281 (1988).

78. Lever Bros. Co., v. U.S., 877 F. 2d 101 (D.C. Cir. 1989).

79. D. Bender and D. Gerber, "In Wake of High Court Decision, the Gray Market Gets Grayer," National L.J. (September 19, 1988).

80. The Trademark Protection Bill, S626, 101st Cong.

# 8

# TECHNOLOGY AND ISSUES OF TORT LIABILITY

## INTRODUCTION

One cannot be involved in a high-technology enterprise without being concerned about possible tort liability. The term "tort" has a wide umbrella, covering a number of personal harms. In fact, it is hard to phrase a concise definition that would capture the entire spectrum of what a tort may entail. However, as a starting point, one may consider a tort as an unwanted intrusion on a protected personal right, which causes physical, economic, or psychological injury.

For those conducting business with new technologies, the potential for tort liability is tremendous. Some technologies use or harness substantial power, thereby increasing the possibility for significant physical harm if something goes wrong. In addition, when society becomes dependent on the continuing operation of technological devices, such as it has with computers, the economic effects of even a temporary shutdown can be substantial. Also, new technologies may create new and previously uncontemplated ways to intrude on the rights of individuals. Modern methods, for instance, to record, store, and transmit personal data have raised an emotional debate about the future of privacy rights in the United States and around the world.

This chapter reviews the fundamental concepts of tort liability, and it highlights some interesting new tort issues raised by developing technologies. We will first take a brief look at negligence policies and how they apply to the management of technology. Negligence issues arise when one is less careful than a reasonable person should be, resulting in harm to another. We then will move on to strict products liability, an area that is now especially important to all purveyors of products. Here, we will focus special attention on the difficult controversies regarding tort liability for suboptimal product designs. In addition, we will consider some new areas of concern particular to the computer field, such as liabilities for defective programs, poor advice from expert diagnostic systems, and injuries from repetitive keyboard practices.

Our discussion next will focus on what are called intentional torts. A tort is intentional when one intends to intrude on another, although often without the desire to inflict harm. We will first consider fraud because of its importance when one enters into sales contracts. Next, we will review some interesting issues affecting computers, such as computer viruses, computer program bombs, and libelous statements made on bulletin boards. Then, we will briefly note some other developing contexts, such as those involving sound-alike commercials and personal rights to the unique cell lines in one's body. The chapter concludes with a discussion of privacy rights—an increasingly sensitive topic for high-technology businesses. Here, we will evaluate the propriety of certain managerial and commercial practices, such as the interception of electronic mail messages that are transmitted on company systems.

## UNINTENTIONAL TORTS: NEGLIGENCE AND STRICT PRODUCTS LIABILITY

### Negligence

Suppose that in advance of the 1992 Christmas holiday season, our Audio Enhancement System (AES) company was barraged with orders for the AES. In order to meet this unexpected surge in demand, we hired several temporary factory personnel so that we could add another production shift. We quickly trained them on their respective jobs and put them to work. Our rapid response apparently was successful, since we increased output by 30% and filled all of our orders by Christmas.

In March, we were notified that one of our customers received a serious electrical shock when moving the AES from one location to another. The incident occurred because the unit, which was picked up from its underside, had a loose metal bottom plate. This plate had come into contact with an uninsulated portion of the AC power cord, resulting in electrical shock. Several other similar incidents arose before we were able to recall the products and correct the problem. We determined that the accidents must have occurred because one of our new employees failed to verify the torque on the electronic screwdriver one evening, thereby yielding insufficient pressure on certain screws, including some of those on the bottom of the units.

The foregoing scenario demonstrates a classic case of negligent behavior. Our company and the new employee clearly were not as careful as one would expect.

It may be hard to pinpoint exactly why the employee forgot to check the screwdriver torque. Possibly our procedures for checking were not sufficient given the potential severity of the repercussions. Maybe we overloaded the employee with excessive information in insufficient time for the person to assimilate it all. Or maybe it's more simple. Possibly the employee got too little sleep the previous night or was talking while working. Whatever the reason, the company and/or its employee was negligent that evening by failing to take reasonable steps to protect users of the AES.[1] The negligence became tortious when the carelessly screwed bottoms caused the shocks that injured certain users.

Liability for negligence, for the most part, is governed by state law. Fortunately, there is some degree of uniformity in the ways negligence principles are applied from state to state due to the efforts of the American Law Institute, an organization composed of lawyers, judges, and teachers, which distilled the basic common law principles of tort liability into a treatise called the Restatement of Torts. Although the Restatement itself is not law, the principles enunciated in it are frequently followed by judges to decide cases and by state legislatures in enacting statutes. In this way, the policies of the Restatement are translated into state laws by legal authorities within the various states, leading to a high degree of consistency among the states.

The Restatement defines negligence as "conduct which falls below the standard established by law for the protection of others against unreasonable risk of harm." Accordingly, the key issues for evaluating negligence are determining the proper standard of care required under the circumstances and whether the conduct met that standard. If a person was not as careful as the law deems the person should have been, then there has been negligence. Negligence alone is not a tort, however. For tort liability to arise, three other aspects are required: (1) the negligent conduct must cause injury; (2) social policy must make the person responsible for the harm caused by the negligence; and (3) there must be no defenses for limiting tort liability.

It is normally easy to determine that the negligent conduct caused injury. In the AES situation, for example, the negligence led to the bottom plate's striking the power cord, resulting in the shock and injury to the user. Intuitively, you concluded that the negligence caused the injury because the user would not have been shocked had the negligence not occurred. In other words, causation is established because the injury would not have happened but for the negligent act. Just to make this clear, assume again that the screws were inappropriately tightened, but that this time injury resulted when an infant pulled off a knob and swallowed it. In this scenario, the negligence regarding the screws did not cause the injury to the baby. That is, the baby would have swallowed the knob even if the screws had been tightened with sufficient care. This is not to say that we may not be responsible for what happened to the baby. Possibly we were negligent in installing the knobs or by making them too small. Nonetheless, the negligence regarding the loose screws was not the cause of what happened to the baby.

Another important issue regarding causation of damages arises when the negligence of two different parties causes the injuries to an innocent victim. For instance, assume that although the loose screws caused the shock, the injuries would not have been so dramatic had there not been a power surge at the same time, resulting from negligent conduct at the electrical utility. Under the laws of many states, the injured user may sue either or both of us for the entire extent of the damages, based on a doctrine called joint and several liability. Our fear, of course, is that if the utility is not sufficiently solvent to pay for its share of the responsibility, then we will have to pay for all the damages, even though they were not all our fault. That possible result, which may be extremely onerous on businesses in certain situations, has led some states, in the name of tort reform, to limit liability to the proportionate extent of one's fault only. In those states, we therefore would be relieved from paying for the utility's share of the fault, even when the utility is unable to sufficiently compensate the user for the additional harms caused by the power surge. To the innocent user, this likely will seem unfair. From the user's vantage, none of this would have happened had we tightened the screws appropriately. Yet the user will not be totally compensated for losses, even though we may have the financial means to cover them.

Social policies recognize that humans are not infallible—all people make mistakes. Every time you wake up, you surely recognize that there is a good chance that you will do something during the day without being totally careful. Perhaps this will be the day that you don't close the door after UPS arrives with a package while your untrained dog watches from the stairs. Clearly, this is negligent; you even considered the possible repercussions while you carried the package inside. But little did you know that the dog would run outside, chase a cat down the sidewalk, cross the street in front of a fire engine, and cause it to swerve and hit a pole, resulting in the total destruction of the home to which it was bound.

People in their everyday lives take calculated risks with their behavior, including negligent behavior. Think how you would act if you were forced to pay for all the repercussions of negligent conduct, no matter how unpredictable or remote they might be. Likely, you would prefer to sit in your room wearing a straitjacket. Similarly, one would never own a dog because of incidents like the one described. So that normal social behavior can be undertaken, the law will not hold a negligent person responsible for all the consequences resulting from negligence. Rather, liability extends only to the persons and property to which harm from the negligence is reasonably foreseeable. Under negligence law, the principle of reasonable foreseeability is called *proximate cause*. In the dog situation, you might thus be liable for the harm to the fire truck because it was reasonably foreseeable that your untrained dog would dart across a street and disrupt traffic, resulting in damage to vehicles. However, you would never reasonably consider that the dog might cause the destruction of a home. Therefore, you would not be liable to pay for those damages, even though your negligence caused it to burn down. This policy makes sense since you reasonably should have considered the risk to those on the streets when deciding to leave the door open. However, the harm to the home clearly should not have entered your intuitive risk analysis.

The issue of proximate cause might arise with the loose AES screws. Suppose that the user who is shocked is thrown back against a plastic water pipe and drops the unit on a couch. The electrical sparks ignite the couch, causing the home and the neighboring water utility station to burn. The broken pipe starts a flood, which becomes uncontrollable due to the fire next door at the utility. The flood enters the underground subway, wreaking havoc within the city before the situation is contained. Our little AES company could be sued by just about everybody in the city for harms to them and their properties. After all, none of this would have happened but for the loose screws. However, our negligence is not the proximate cause of all that occurred, and our liability will be appropriately limited. In this situation, injury to the user is reasonably foreseeable. Also, since sparks and fire are a distinct possibility, damage to the house and its contents likely would be considered reasonably foreseeable. Even damage to the neighboring utility may be in the zone of reasonable danger. However, that should be the outside reach of our responsibility. We likely will not be liable for most, if any, of the damages caused by the flood. Clearly, this provides a good reason for all of those property owners to carry insurance.

The issue of defenses often is important in negligence situations as well. Typically the negligent party will disclaim some or all responsibility for harms to the person bringing suit (the plaintiff) because the plaintiff was negligent too, thereby contributing to the harm. For instance, maybe we placed a warning on the AES alerting users not to hold the unit from the bottom due to the risk of shock. When the user who was shocked ignored this warning, we might allege that the user assumed the risk of harm or at least deserves some of the blame for what happened. Even without a warning, we might claim that it is negligent to pick up an electrical unit from the bottom while it is plugged in, because most careful people understand the potential for shock. The legal systems of different states vary widely on how they treat defenses to negligence. In most situations, however, the usual result is that the comparative fault of the parties is assessed, with the damage recovery's being reduced by the degree of one's blame. So, assume that a jury determines that a person is negligent for picking up the unit from the bottom after reading the warning, but not as negligent as we are for not screwing the bottom as tightly as we should have. The jury weighs the relative faults and concludes that we are 75% negligent and the user is 25% negligent. If the user suffers $60,000 of damages, we will be liable for 75% of that, or $45,000. Had the jury thought that the user was totally at fault for ignoring the warning, then we would have been totally relieved from liability for negligence.

We have yet to address how it is determined whether conduct is negligent in the first place. Recall that actions are negligent if they fall below the applicable standard of care. How does one determine the proper standard of care? The simple answer, and the one that generally applies, is that one should exercise the care that a reasonable person would use under the same circumstances. However, such a statement somewhat begs the question, because it does not address what a reasonable person would do. The following case struggles with this issue.

## VUONO V. NEW YORK BLOOD CENTER, INC.

*U.S. District Court, Massachusetts, 1988*

### Facts

On May 16, 1983, Frank Vuono was hospitalized at the New England Deaconess Hospital in order to undergo coronary bypass surgery. On May 22 and 23, Vuono received an infusion of serum albumin, which is a fractionated blood plasma derivative. One vial of the serum albumin administered to Vuono was contaminated at the time of the infusion, and as a result, he became ill, suffered both septic shock and herpes simplex, and subsequently was prevented from undergoing open heart surgery. The contaminated vial had been processed by New York Blood Center (the Blood Center), a federally licensed blood fractionation facility.

Fractionation at the blood processing facility involves separating the serum albumin from the blood plasma, dispensing the serum albumin into glass vials, sealing the vials with rubber stoppers, covering the vials with protective aluminum foil, and packaging the vials in a series of cardboard containers. This process also includes filtering out any bacteria in the blood plasma and subjecting the serum albumin to a heat bath for the purpose of killing any contaminants that may elude the filtration procedure. The vial that is the subject of this lawsuit was part of the Blood Center's lot number 5D33A and was processed in August 1982.

Although there is no evidence that the Blood Center failed to follow its standard procedures for processing the serum albumin in this case, there is evidence that the particular glass vial, manufactured by Wheaton Industries, contained a flaw. Specifically, there was a narrow fold in the glass surface, known as a line over. Evidence also exists that this flaw is visually identifiable and that the glass fold in the vial is sufficient to catch a fingernail. Further, there is evidence that this defect interfered with the integrity of the sealed vial and thus permitted contamination from ambient sources.

Vuono sued the Blood Center and several other parties, alleging numerous contractual violations and torts, including negligence. In this proceeding, the Blood Center asked the court to dismiss before trial the action against it for negligence, by way of a procedure called summary judgment. Under the standards for summary judgment, the court is to dismiss the negligence count if the evidence that Vuono hopes to show at trial is insufficient to prove negligence.

### Opinion

In the law of torts, negligence is commonly recognized as either the omission of doing something that a prudent and reasonable person, guided by those considerations that ordinarily regulate the conduct of human affairs would do or the commission of doing something that a prudent and reasonable person would not do. In other words, the standard of conduct in determining the existence of negligence is whether the actor exercised the duty of care that an ordinarily prudent person would exercise under the same or similar circumstances. There is, however, no absolute liability for all harmful conduct; an actor is not an insurer for all of one's acts.

Applying the negligence standard often requires that the actor's conduct be tested against a background of ordinary usage and custom. The customs of the community, however, although relevant on the issue of negligence, are not conclusive, especially when such customs are clearly dangerous and careless. Judge Learned Hand eloquently explained:

> There are, no doubt, cases where courts seem to make the general practice of the calling the standard of proper diligence; we have indeed given some currency to the notion ourselves. Indeed, in most cases reasonable prudence is in fact common prudence; but strictly it is never its measure; a whole calling may have unduly lagged in the adoption of new and available devices. It never may set its own tests, however pervasive be its usages. Courts must in the end say what is required; there are precautions so imperative that even their universal disregard will not excuse their omission.

In this respect, the negligent standard of the ordinarily prudent person may be a higher standard of care than the standard followed by a particular community or industry. The fact that a certain device or practice is in common use is evidence that its use is not negligent, but such a fact is not conclusive evidence of due care because a large number of persons may fail to exercise due care in their usual practices. The plaintiff may still try to show that the practice of the entire industry is unreasonable; that the community custom lacks ordinary care.

In the present case, Blood Center argues that Vuono's negligence claims cannot survive on the grounds that Vuono fails to set forth facts demonstrating that the Blood Center breached the prevailing standard of care applicable to blood product manufacturers. Specifically, the Blood Center contends that the standard of care that the Blood Center owed to Vuono is that standard established by the blood products manufacturing industry and the applicable FDA regulations. Moreover, the quality control procedures used in testing lot 5D33A, the batch that contained the vial of serum albumin administered to Vuono, equalled or exceeded both the standard of care of the industry and FDA regulations.

As previously discussed, however, conformity with the customs and standards of the industry does not establish conclusively the absence of negligence. Rather, the court must evaluate any evidence that either the industry custom or the Blood Center's conduct was unreasonable under the circumstances. Given all the facts presented by Vuono, the court rules that a genuine issue exists concerning the Blood Center's duty to inspect and test the glass vials containing the serum albumin.

The court's opinion is founded on two sources. First, Dr. Martin Stryker testified in a deposition that:

1.  When it's time to fill the vials, the person who loads the vials onto the conveyor belt going into the vial washing and sterilization equipment is instructed to look at the vials.
2.  The defect in the glass vial that contained the serum albumin administered to Vuono existed at the time of the visual inspection.

3. The defect in the vial is fairly apparent if you look closely at it.
4. The Blood Center had experienced problems with the quality of the Wheaton glass vials, problems which initially occurred in 1980 and resurfaced in April 1983.
5. The Blood Center ceased purchasing the Wheaton 250-milliliter vials for packaging of serum albumin in late 1983.

Second, the Wheaton report on the glass vial stated, "the bottle . . . did have a line over which is a narrow fold in the glass surface. The line over extended across the top of the finish and on the inside past the sealing contact areas of the rubber stopper. . . . Depth of the glass fold was sufficient to catch a fingernail *which is the factory guideline for rejection of this defect*" (emphasis supplied by the court).

Since the attendant dangers of manufacturing and packaging serum albumin may constitute a hazard to human life, the standard of care required of the Blood Center in this case is extremely high. In this context, the Blood Center's duty of care may be viewed as a matter of the following variables:

1. The probability that a defective vial will be used in packaging serum albumin
2. The resulting injuries if such a vial is used
3. The burden of adequate precautions

Given the facts that (1) in late 1980, the Blood Center was dissatisfied with the quality of Wheaton vials; (2) an unsterile product caused by a defective vial may constitute a hazard to human life; (3) the person who loads the vials onto the conveyor is instructed to look at the vials; and (4) the defect in this vial is allegedly "fairly apparent if you look closely," this court cannot rule, as a matter of law, that the Blood Center was not negligent in testing and inspecting the glass vials that contain the serum albumin. Accordingly, the court denies the motion of the Blood Center for summary judgment on the negligence claim.

As *Vuono* makes clear, negligent conduct cannot be defined in terms of hard-and-fast rules. What a reasonable person should do under the circumstances depends on a number of factors particular to the situation. Behaving as others do when faced with the same situation is evidence that one is acting like a reasonable person. This is why industry custom is so relevant. In addition, complying with state or federal laws, as the Blood Center did, suggests that one is being reasonable. However, the case makes it clear that these considerations are not conclusive. If industry custom were an absolute standard, then industry participants might have incentives to collectively act irresponsibly, comfortable with the knowledge that they protect themselves with a low industry standard. Legal standards, too, can only be a minimum benchmark of what should be expected from reasonable persons. That is, failure to follow legal requirements may conclusively show negligent behavior, but compliance is merely evidence of reasonableness.

Other formulations of what a reasonable person should do have more of an economic foundation. One of these, which also was raised in *Vuono*, was formulated by Judge Learned Hand in 1947 in a case dealing with a barge that broke from its moorings.[2] In that case, Judge Hand stated that negligence depended on three variables: (1) the probability that the boat would break away, (2) the gravity of the resulting loss if it did, and (3) the burden of adequate precautions. Putting this into algebraic terms—with the probability called P, the loss called L, and the burden called B—liability depends on whether B is less than L multiplied by P. In other words, one acts unreasonably and is negligent if B < L × P. Alternatively, one's conduct is reasonable if B > L × P.

Another economic formulation weighs both the conduct of the person causing the injury (the injurer) and that of the victim. In very simple terms, this analysis asks which of the two parties could have avoided the accident with the least social costs. Saying this differently, the party who was in the best position to avoid the accident with the cheapest cost should be responsible to pay for the damages created from it.[3] Hypothesizing with Learned Hand's barge, assume that the probability of breaking away is 10%, the expected injury to a dock when it is smashed is $30,000, and the burden to moor the boat more securely is $2,000. Under Learned Hand's test, the boat owner would be negligent if the boat breaks away and causes damage because the burden of prevention ($2,000) is less than the risk-adjusted expected injury ($3,000 = $30,000 × 10%). However, if the dock could have been protected with a rubber wrap costing $200, then under the alternative formulation, the dock owner would bear the responsibility, since the dock owner's cost of prevention is less than that required of the boat owner. This makes economic sense because society is better off with a decision rule that motivates people to incur $200 of prevention costs rather than $2,000 of prevention.

Negligence is a growing concern for computer software and database developers. For example, an airline inadvertently corrupted its database of passenger reservations while using new software that turned out to have bugs. Eventually, the programmers fixed the bugs, but the false reservations were not eliminated. As a result, the airline had planes flying partially empty for several months because of the false bookings.[4] Given society's growing dependence on computers, there now are tremendous possibilities that huge economic and physical injuries could result from systems that do not perform adequately. Just consider the repercussions of an airline control computer system that incorrectly handles information. The standard of care owed by computer programmers in developing software and databases is a controversial and critical issue. In some professions, such as law and medicine, the professionals are held to a high standard of care because clients rely so heavily on their expertise. Many argue that computer programmers should be treated similarly, given that individuals and businesses now often entrust their livelihoods to the alleged computer experts. Certainly following Learned Hand's formulation, there is reason to expect programmers to exercise extreme care in software design, because the potential repercussions from system failure often will outweigh the burdens of thoroughly testing the software. As we shall see in the next chapter, many (but not all) of software developers' concerns regarding possible negligence can be handled with clients through contractual provisions. However, these measures will not be effective against third parties who suffer harm. Therefore, computer specialists must be

**Exhibit 8.1  Negligence Analysis Issues**

| Duty of Care |
| --- |

- Reasonable-person standard
- Community standards
- Legal standards
- Professional standards
- Economic formulations
  — Prevention costs vs. expected loss from injury
  — Cheapest cost avoider

| Causation |
| --- |

- But-for analysis
- Joint and several liability

| Proximate Cause |
| --- |

- Liability extends to persons and property to which harm from negligence is reasonably foreseeable.

| Defenses |
| --- |

- Assumption of risk
- Comparative fault

wary of the extreme care that now may be expected from them in developing and testing their wares.

### Strict Products Liability

For those companies involved in the manufacture or distribution of products, as opposed to services, the development of strict products liability principles has somewhat usurped the importance of negligence. The area of strict liability is where most of the current controversies lie and where most of the large, publicized money judgments derive. Just think of the public attention given to the defective design of the Ford Pinto gas tank.[5] Strict liability is so far-reaching because liability does not depend on the propriety or reasonableness of a person's conduct. Rather, the focus is on the condition of the product. In a nutshell, under principles of strict products liability, a seller of a product will be liable for damages resulting from an unreasonably dangerous product defect, whether that seller was negligent or not.

Why public policy has moved from negligence to strict liability principles can be understood from the following simple example. Suppose the Coca-Cola Company uses the most advanced bottling techniques, employing more state-of-the-art equipment than any competitor worldwide. Although the machinery and systems used are the best available, 1 bottle per 10,000 produced will have a flaw that creates a weakness that possibly could cause an explosion when the bottle is pressurized. Assume that one of these bottles explodes while being lifted by a consumer, causing severe injuries to the face. If the consumer sues Coca-Cola alleging negligence, the consumer will lose because the company, if anything, exceeded its standard of care in bottling its beverages. Therefore, even though an innocent victim, this consumer, under negligence principles, will be forced to absorb the losses.

There are a number of policy reasons for creating a legal system requiring Coca-Cola to compensate the consumer for injuries even though the company has not been negligent. Simply out of a sense of justice, we might yearn for a policy that favors the victim over the manufacturer. After all, Coca-Cola has derived profits from its business and thus should be liable for any negative consequences from its operations. This is especially compelling when compared to the innocent victim, who did not even derive the benefits expected from the product since it proved to be defective. Economic efficiency also may favor placing liability on the company. Under negligence principles, all those who might come near Coca-Cola products, which admittedly are conscientiously made, must take out insurance if they want to be protected from the possible tragic consequences of an exploding bottle. However, if legal rules required Coca-Cola to be responsible for the defective bottles, the company could protect itself by taking out one insurance policy to cover the less than 1 in 10,000 chance that an accident might occur. The cost of this policy, then, could be spread over the millions of bottles of soda sold. Another benefit from holding Coca-Cola strictly liable without fault is that there is a constant incentive for the company to continue improving its manufacturing systems to reduce the risks to customers. The fundamental negative from holding Coca-Cola strictly liable is the traditional cultural antipathy in the United States and elsewhere for making someone take responsibility for a tragedy when that person is not blameworthy for what occurred. Yet, this is just what strict products liability does. More than anything, the notion of liability without blame may be what continually fuels the flame that calls for products liability reform.

As with negligence, the Restatement of Torts provides guidance on when product sellers should be liable without fault. Section 402A of the Restatement states:

1. One who sells any product in a defective condition unreasonably dangerous to the user or consumer or to his property is subject to liability for physical harm thereby caused to the ultimate user or consumer, or to his property, if (a) the seller is engaged in the business of selling such product, and (b) it is expected to and does reach the consumer without substantial change in the condition in which it was sold.

2. The rule stated in Subsection 1 applies although (a) the seller has exercised all possible care in the preparation and sale of his products, and (b) the user or consumer has not bought the product from or entered into any contractual relation with the seller.

The key component of this provision is that liability attaches when the product is in a defective condition unreasonably dangerous to the user. The most difficult aspect is what constitutes a product defect, something we will consider at some length shortly. That the defect must make the product unreasonably dangerous may have struck you as akin to a negligence standard, and indeed, as the next case, *Barker v. Lull Engineering*, demonstrates, many commentators and courts have questioned what it means. The best explanation is that the manufacturer is not to be an insurer for every harm that may result from product use. For instance, it is common that users of hammers smash their thumb. Without some clarification, one might conclude that a hammer is defective when it imparts injury on the user. The term "unreasonably dangerous" was included to clarify that something more than harm is required to judge a product defective. Thus, with the hammer, the fact that the product performs as safely as the ordinary consumer expects clearly should be relevant in concluding that the product is not defective. However, as explained in *Barker v. Lull Engineering*, this may not be the end of the inquiry.

Before evaluating what it means for a product to be defective, it is worth noting some of the other components of strict products liability mentioned in the Restatement. First, Section 402A does not confine liability to manufacturers; rather, liability attaches to *sellers* of the defective product. Thus, any business in the distribution chain is a potential target of a strict products liability suit. Second, the doctrine applies only to sellers who are regularly engaged in distributing the product. This conforms to the risk-spreading and profit-making aspects of strict liability by ensuring that the seller is significantly involved with and derives sufficient revenues from the product. Third, the condition of the product must not be substantially changed by another party before the injuries take place. Thus, if an automobile purchaser makes substantial alterations to a car to jack it up, for instance, this may relieve the seller-manufacturer from liability for injuries caused by problems with the rear axle. This makes sense since the buyer's actions are totally out of the control of the seller. Strict products liability provides substantial incentives to ensure the safety of the product, but those incentives obviously can extend only to elements within the seller's control. Fourth, any person who sustains injury from a product defect may sue any seller of that product within the distribution chain, whether that person has dealt directly with the particular seller or not. Thus, sellers may be sued by purchasers, other persons who use the product, and bystanders. Also, as mentioned before, any seller in the distribution chain who is regularly engaged with the product, including the manufacturer, wholesalers, and retailers, may be liable for product defects.

The Coca-Cola scenario provides the easiest and least controversial form of product defect that subjects sellers to strict products liability. The bottle is easily identified as defective since it did not leave the manufacturing facility in the condition that the manufacturer intended. This form of product defect therefore is called a *manufacturing defect*.

When the AES machines were sold with loose screws on the bottom, this also constituted a manufacturing defect since we did not intend for the models to be distributed in that condition. Consider now how much more powerful strict products liability is for the injured consumer. Although they likely would win a negligence suit under the facts provided, the customers who received electric shocks would have to prove that we breached our duty of care in making their particular machine. Under strict products liability, their job is much simpler, since all they must do is demonstrate the defective condition of their machine. Clearly, this should be easy under the circumstances, for all they must do is present their AES unit with the insufficiently torqued screws. This process thus skips the often difficult task of delving into the reasonableness of the business behavior that led to the deficiencies in the units.

The reach of strict products liability may begin with manufacturing defects, but it definitely does not end there. A product may be defective—even when manufactured exactly as intended—if the design of the product is not adequately safe. In other words, a product may be defective because it should have been designed with more attention to user safety. Logically, this form of defect is termed a *design defect*. The famous Ford Pinto case is a clear example of the design defect situation. The location and condition of the gas tank, which was subject to exploding in a rear-end collision, was manufactured exactly as Ford intended. However, its susceptibility to explosion made the automobile unreasonably dangerous, thereby leading to the conclusion that it had a design defect.

Design defect situations are more difficult than those involving manufacturing defects for two reasons. First, they are harder to identify. Manufacturing defects are readily apparent because the particular unit deemed defective is different from others being produced. With design defects, the allegedly defective unit is no different from any other being made. The second difficulty, which is much more troubling, is determining the standards that should be used to judge a design defective. Is it defective only when the product is more dangerous than expected by an ordinary consumer, or is there more to it? Also, can a product be defective only when used as intended, or must it be designed safely for unintended uses as well? For example, if a ladder manufacturer is aware that some painters will bounce on their ladders to move them from one location to another, must the ladder be strong enough to sustain such use/abuse? The following case comprehensively discusses how strict products liability is handled in California for design defects.

## BARKER V. LULL ENGINEERING CO.

*State of California Supreme Court, 1978*

### Facts

Barker sustained serious injuries as the result of an accident that occurred while he was operating a Lull High-Lift Loader at a construction site. The loader is designed to lift loads up to 5,000 pounds to a maximum height of 32 feet. It is designed so that the load can be kept level even when the loader is being operated on sloping terrain. The leveling of the load is controlled by a lever that is positioned between the operator's legs and is equipped with a manual lock to prevent accidental slipping of the load level. The loader was not equipped with seat belts or a roll bar. A wire-and-pipe cage over the driver's seat afforded the driver some protection from falling objects.

On the day of the accident, Barker, who had previously had only limited instruction and practice on the loader, was filling in for the regular operator. The accident occurred while Barker was attempting to lift a load of lumber to a height of approximately 20 feet and to place it on the second story of a building. The lift was particularly difficult because the terrain was sharply sloped in several directions. During the lift, Barker felt some vibration. When it appeared to several coworkers that the loader was about to tip, they shouted to Barker to jump from the loader. Barker heeded these warnings, but while scrambling away, he was struck by a piece of falling lumber and was seriously injured.

Barker alleged that the accident was attributable to one or more design defects of the loader. An expert testified at trial that the loader was unstable due to its narrow base and had a tendency to roll over when lifting loads to considerable heights. The expert stated that the loader should have been equipped with outriggers to compensate for its instability. Cranes and some high-lift loader models are equipped with outriggers or offer them as optional equipment. Also, the expert testified that the loader was defective since it was not equipped with a roll bar or seat belts. In the absence of this equipment, according to the expert, Barker had no reasonable choice but to leap from the loader as it began to tip. In addition, pointing to the absence of an automatic leveling device and the placement of the lever such that it is vulnerable to inadvertent bumping, the expert stated that the accident may have been caused by the defective design of the leveling mechanism.

Lull denied that the loader was defective, and it claimed the accident resulted from Barker's lack of skill with or misuse of the loader. Lull's experts testified that the loader was not unstable when utilized on the terrain for which it was intended. If the accident did occur as a result of the tipping of the loader, then it happened because Barker had operated the loader on terrain that was too steep. The experts stated that outriggers were not necessary when the loader was used for its intended purposes and that no competitive loaders with similar-height lifting capacity were so equipped. They testified that a roll bar was unnecessary because the loader could not roll over completely given its bulk. They also stated that seat belts would have increased the danger by impairing the operator's ability to leave quickly in emergencies. As for the leveling device, they testified that the position was the safest and most convenient for the operator and that the manual lock provided adequate protection.

Lull argued that the accident probably was caused by Barker's own inexperience. If the lumber had begun to fall during the lift, it was because Barker had failed to lock the leveling device prior to the lift. In addition, Lull hypothesized that the lumber had fallen off only after Barker had leaped from the machine and that *he* was responsible because he had failed to set the hand brake, thereby permitting the loader to roll backward.

The trial court instructed the jury that strict liability for a defect in the design of a product is based on the finding that a product was unreasonably dangerous for its intended use. Based on this instruction, the jury returned a verdict in favor of the defendant. Barker appealed.

## Opinion

California courts have frequently recognized that the defectiveness concept defies a simple, uniform definition applicable to all sectors of the diverse domain of products liability. Although in many instances—as when one machine in a million contains a cracked or broken part—the meaning of the term "defect" will require little or no elaboration, in other instances, as when a product is claimed to be defective because of an unsafe design or an inadequate warning, the contours of the defect concept may not be self-evident. The formulation of a satisfactory definition of "design defect" has proven a formidable task. This court concludes that a product is defective in design either (1) if the product has failed to perform as safely as an ordinary consumer would expect when used in an intended or reasonably foreseeable manner or (2) if the benefits of the challenged design do not outweigh the risk of danger inherent in the design. This dual standard for design defects ensures an injured plaintiff protection from products that either fall below ordinary consumer expectations as to safety or that, on balance, are not as safely designed as they should be. At the same time, the standard permits a manufacturer who has marketed a product that satisfies ordinary consumer expectations to demonstrate the relative complexity of design decisions and the trade-offs that are frequently required in the adoption of alternative designs. Finally, this test reflects continued adherence to the principle that the focus of products liability actions is on the *product*, not on the *manufacturer's conduct*, and that in order to prevail, the plaintiff need not prove that the manufacturer acted unreasonably or negligently.

The drafters of the Restatement adopted the term "unreasonably dangerous" primarily as a means of continuing the application of strict tort liability to an article that is "dangerous to an extent beyond that which would be contemplated by the ordinary consumer who purchases it, with the ordinary knowledge common to the community as to its characteristics." However, in a previous case, this court flatly rejected the suggestion that recovery in a products liability action should be permitted *only* if a product is more dangerous than contemplated by the average consumer, refusing to permit the low esteem in which the public might hold a dangerous product to diminish the manufacturer's responsibility for injuries caused by that product. The flaw in the Restatement's analysis is that it treats consumer expectations as a ceiling on a manufacturer's responsibility rather than as a floor.

The defectiveness concept has embraced a great variety of injury-producing deficiencies ranging from products that cause injury because they deviate from the manufacturer's intended result (e.g., the 1 soda bottle in 10,000 that explodes without explanation) to products that, though perfectly manufactured, are unsafe because of the absence of a safety device (e.g., a paydozer without rearview mirrors) and including products that are dangerous because they lack adequate warnings or instructions (e.g., a telescope that contains inadequate instructions for assembling a sun filter attachment). The cases demonstrate that the concept of defect raises considerably more difficulties in the design defect context than it does in the manufacturing defect case.

In general, a manufacturing defect is readily identifiable because a defective product unit is one that differs from the manufacturer's intended result or from other ostensibly identical units. For example, when a product comes off the assembly line in a substandard condition, it has incurred a manufacturing defect. A design defect, by contrast, cannot be identified simply by comparing the injury-producing product with the manufacturer's plans or with other units, because by definition, the plans and all such units will reflect the same design. Rather than employing any sort of deviation-from-the-norm test in determining if a design is defective, our cases have applied two alternative criteria in ascertaining whether there is something wrong—if not in the manner of production, at least in the product.

First, our cases establish that a product may be found defective in design if the product fails to perform as safely as an ordinary consumer would expect when the product is used in an intended or reasonably foreseeable manner. Note here that the instruction to the jury is erroneous because it suggested that only the intended use of a product is relevant in evaluating defectiveness rather than the product's reasonably foreseeable use. The design and manufacture of products should not be carried out in an industrial vacuum but with recognition of the realities of their everyday use. It may be that use of a loader by a relatively inexperienced worker is not an intended use, but it still is a reasonably foreseeable use.

The expectations of the ordinary consumer cannot be viewed as the exclusive yardstick for evaluating design defectiveness because in many situations the consumer would not know what to expect, having no idea how safe the product could be made. Thus, a product may be found defective in design—even if it satisfies ordinary consumer expectations—if through hindsight the jury determines that the product's design embodies excessive preventable danger or in other words, if the risk of danger inherent in the design outweighs the benefits of the design. In evaluating the adequacy of a product's design pursuant to this standard, a jury may consider, among other relevant factors, (a) the gravity of the danger posed by the design, (b) the likelihood that such danger would occur, (c) the mechanical feasibility of a safer alternative design, (d) the financial cost of an improved design, and (e) the adverse consequences to the product and to the consumer that would result from an alternative design. Because most of the evidence relevant to the risk-benefit standard involves technical matters particularly within the knowledge of the manufacturer, we conclude that the plaintiff must show only that the injury was proximately caused by the product's design. The burden then is on the manufacturer to prove that the product is not defective in light of the relevant factors.

The technological revolution has created a society that contains never-before-contemplated dangers to the individual. The individual must face the threat to life and limb not only from the car on the street but from a massive array of haz-ardous mechanisms and products as well. The radical change from a compara-tively safe, largely agricultural society to this unsafe, industrial one has been re-flected in decisions that formerly tied liability to fault but that now are more concerned with the safety of the individual who suffers the loss. The change has been from fault to defect. Plaintiffs are no longer required to impugn the maker; they are required to impugn the product.

The jury may have interpreted the erroneous instruction as requiring plaintiff to prove that the high-lift loader was more dangerous than the average consumer contemplated. Also, the instruction additionally misinformed the jury that the de-fectiveness of the product must be evaluated in light of the product's "intended use" rather than its "reasonably foreseeable use." Therefore, judgment in favor of defendants is reversed.

As alluded to in *Barker*, there is a third kind of product defect, which poten-tially can subject a manufacturer to strict products liability: the failure to provide *adequate warnings* about possible hazards. Attention focuses on the sufficiency of the warnings when the product is manufactured correctly and designed ap-propriately. Keep in mind that a product may be manufactured and designed in a defect-free condition—and still be dangerous. Strict products liability does not mandate absolute safety. Rather, it requires that an article be designed safely within the parameters of the risk-benefit analysis described in *Barker*. Therefore, an electrical appliance, such as the AES, invariably may cause severe injury in cer-tain situations because of the high voltages used. A do-it-yourself home mechanic who dismantles the machine to fix it will be exposed to potential danger. One who plugs in the cord after it has been gnawed by the dog or exposed to mois-ture may be injured. One who uses the machine in the bathroom and tips it into the bathtub while soaking may be shocked. As a manufacturer, we may not have a duty to design around these potential hazards based on a risk-benefit analysis. Maybe the cost of designing into the AES a manageable dogproof electric cord, for example, is simply too expensive to warrant its inclusion. However, since we are aware of the potential for harm in these situations, we may have a duty to warn the user about them so as to minimize the potential for injury. That is, we have a responsibility to ensure that the user may easily recognize the various risks inherent in the product. Otherwise, the product would have a defect making it unreasonably dangerous. This time the defect regards the ability of the consumer to appreciate the spectrum of product uses that may be hazardous. In this regard, courts balance various factors such as (1) the normal expectations of the con-sumer as to how the product will perform, (2) the degrees of simplicity or com-plication in the operation or use of the product, (3) the nature and magnitude of the danger to which the user is exposed, (4) the likelihood of the injury, and (5) the feasibility and beneficial effect of including a warning.[6]

Three current examples further illustrate the difficult social and managerial is-sues raised by strict products liability. The first situation involves BIC Corporation, which has been sued for damages sustained by children who played with cigarette lighters that the company manufactured.[7] BIC argued that it should not be liable for the injuries, because the lighters were misused by individuals who were not even supposed to have them. These cases are especially difficult because the dangers of cigarette lighters are obvious to the adults who purchase them. Children, however, may not fully appreciate the hazards of playing with lighters. Following the consumer expectation test, plaintiffs have alleged that BIC should be liable because the company could reasonably foresee that children would misuse the product in a dangerous way. As stated in *Barker*, a manufacturer may be liable when it is reasonably foreseeable that its product will be used by one who is relatively inexperienced. BIC, on the other hand, states that it has a duty to protect only purchasers—in this case, adults—from unreasonable risks of harm. Otherwise, it claims, manufacturers of products such as knives and hammers also would be liable for injuries sustained by children who handle them inappropriately. Plaintiffs also have argued that regardless of consumer expectations, the lighters should have been manufactured with child-resistant features because the benefits of such attributes outweigh their cost. According to this theory, if the risks of harm are sufficiently high and if enhanced child-resistant features could have been included at a reasonable cost without overly impinging on the utility of the lighter, then liability could result. Finally, plaintiffs have complained that BIC had a responsibility to warn parents of the possible dangers to young children, even if the lighters otherwise were adequately designed. This claim, however, has not been persuasive, for the company did instruct purchasers to "keep out of reach of children"—language that a court found sufficient under the circumstances.[8]

Another interesting scenario involves the responsibility of video game manufacturers toward individuals who have a special medical condition such as epilepsy. Epilepsy is a neurological disorder that affects about 1% of the U.S. population. Around 3% of epileptics have a variety known as photosensitive epilepsy. These individuals may have seizures triggered by swiftly flashing lights, such as strobes or sunlight bouncing off water. Since the early days of television, it has also been recognized that video images can cause seizures in photosensitive epileptics, especially when the images cycle at certain frequencies. In addition, such epileptics may be especially affected by certain light wavelengths, such as that which causes the color red. In 1991, a lawsuit was brought against Nintendo in the United States by a teenager who had suffered a seizure after playing a Nintendo video game. Obviously, there may be enormous problems in proving causation in such a case. But more important, the case raises interesting questions about the range of people for whom a product must be made safe. It may be argued that Nintendo could have taken steps to prevent the reaction. For instance, maybe Nintendo could have altered the cycling frequency of the images in some of its products or avoided the color red in its games. It also could have provided a warning with its products informing consumers that flashing lights on the video screen may trigger epileptic seizures. The key policy question is how the risks to intended, but unique, individuals should be factored into the risk/utility calculus.

## Exhibit 8.2  Strict Products Liability Analysis Issues

### Manufacturing Defect

- The unit causing injury was not manufactured as safely as the manufacturer intended.

### Design Defect

- Consumer expectation: The product fails to perform as safely as an ordinary consumer would expect.
  — Intended uses
  — Reasonably foreseeable unintended uses
- Risk-benefit analysis: The risk of danger in the design outweighs the benefits in the design. Important factors are:
  — Gravity of danger
  — Likelihood of danger
  — Feasibility of alternative designs
  — Cost of alternative designs
  — Comparative utility of alternative designs

### Failure to Warn

- Factors
  — Normal expectations by consumer
  — Complexity of product
  — Potential magnitude of dnager
  — Likelihood of injury
  — Feasibility and effect of including a warning

### Manufacturers and Sellers Liable

- If regularly engaged in that business
- To anyone injured by defective product
- If product condition not substantially changed

Interestingly, Nintendo began to distribute warnings with certain products in the United States shortly after this lawsuit was brought and later in Europe and Japan. In 1992, Sega also introduced package warnings about the dangers to epileptics.[9]

A third rising area of controversy involves the possibility that cancer may be caused by exposure to electromagnetic fields (EMF) that are emitted from electric current.[10] A small set of studies have shown a link between EMF and leukemia. Most of these involve individuals who are constantly exposed to very high levels of EMF radiation, such as power-line repair technicians. However, in 1992, a Swedish study found that children living near power lines had leukemia rates that were four times normal. In addition, as of 1993, at least three lawsuits had been filed in U.S. federal courts alleging that cancers had been caused by exposure to utility lines. The public has reacted to this scant preliminary evidence with sub-stantial uneasiness. What should electric utilities do in the wake of this concern about EMF? Should they take steps to bury their existing lines, even at substan-tial cost? Wouldn't that be a tremendous waste of resources if it is later proven that there is no link between EMF and cancer? What if the link is established later? Should utilities be liable for the cancers caused by its power lines before the dangers were recognized? Recall that *Barker* asks the jury to make the risk/utility analysis using hindsight. This suggests that the utilities do indeed have to be con-cerned with this possibility. Thus, it makes sense for them to take preventive steps now, even before the dangers are proven, just in case. The question is, How far should utilities go to protect consumers from this scientifically uncertain danger?[11]

Liability for product defects is controlled mostly by state law. However, man-ufacturers of technology products also must be conscious of applicable federal policies. The most important federal regulatory body in this regard is the Con-sumer Product Safety Commission (CPSC). The CPSC's mission is to protect the public against unreasonable risks of injury from consumer products. To this end, the CPSC has established numerous rules mandating standards for various con-sumer products. For example, the CPSC has safety standards for lawn mowers that require, among other things, that they automatically shut off within three seconds after the operator's hands leave the normal operating position and that they carry specifically designed labels warning of the dangers of blade contact. In addition, the CPSC can take corrective actions against particular products to pro-tect consumers.

Firms also are required to disclose to the CPSC any information about possible product defects.[12] The primary rationale for such reports is to furnish informa-tion to the CPSC about the need for new safety standards or other corrective reg-ulatory actions in order to protect consumer safety. A firm must notify the CPSC about potential product hazards in three situations: (1) when information rea-sonably supports the conclusion that a product fails to comply with an applicable CPSC safety regulation or a voluntary industry standard upon which the CPSC relies in lieu of making its own rule, (2) when a product contains a defect that could create a substantial product hazard, or (3) when a product has been sub-ject to three civil lawsuits within two calendar years that result in settlements or judgments in favor of the plaintiffs.[13] A defect is defined broadly by the CPSC, not unlike the interpretation given in *Barker*. Thus, a manufacturer must report to the CPSC when it has information about a product's manufacturing errors, de-sign defects, or insufficient warnings.[14] Failure to report as required exposes a manufacturer to potentially costly civil penalties and may carry criminal reper-cussions as well.[15] Even with these potential penalties, companies often are reluc-tant to report possible defects. Their worries include the belief that a report might constitute an admission that the product actually is hazardous; that the public will find out about the report, thereby leading to adverse publicity; and that the CPSC will respond with draconian measures.[16] However, the law is clear that such reports are confidential and do not have to constitute an admission.[17] Nonetheless, many authorities believe that the annual number of reports received, which averages between 150 and 200, is substantially below what should be filed.[18]

## Tort Reform Measures

Many business groups believe that negligence and strict products liability policies place an unfair burden on manufacturers and distributors in the United States. Various aspects particularly concern them. Liability without fault is a key point of contention, especially with design defects. Under the principles articulated in *Barker*, businesses continually face the burden of financial responsibility if a jury makes an after-the-fact determination that more precautions or warnings should have been provided. Coupled with this is the belief that juries tend to be sympathetic with damage victims and will use the opportunity in court to reward them too generously for their injuries. In addition, firms believe that joint and several liability is unfairly burdensome when a business that was only slightly responsible for a victim's suffering is required to bear an unfair proportion of the financial burden. Other issues, such as the extent of attorney's fees and the exposure to high punitive damage awards, are also on the agenda.

Business groups have been actively working to reform the tort system at the state and federal levels. So far, there has been some moderate success in various states. For instance, many states have eliminated joint and several liability or have limited it to those situations when the actions of a business were a substantial contributing factor to the victim's damages. In addition, damage limitations and restrictions on punitive damages and attorney's fees have been enacted by several state legislatures. Even though there has been some relief in many states, business groups are still very dissatisfied with the overall national picture. The hodgepodge of state laws exposes business defendants to forum shopping, whereby injured victims seek out the state with the most generous tort policies to bring suit. Business groups, therefore, have attempted for several years to convince Congress to pass a federal products liability reform act, which would clarify tort standards and reduce potential burdens on a unified national basis. Certain consumer groups and the trial lawyers association vigorously oppose those efforts at the federal level. However, a tort reform package nearly passed in 1992.[19] Although it is too early to predict how the Democratic administration will contribute to these efforts, the momentum seems to be swinging toward the business groups, and ultimate passage of a federal tort policy, albeit possibly in a watered-down version, now appears likely.

As we evaluate tort reform measures in the United States, it is instructive to consider the experiences of other countries employing different tort liability systems. Japan may provide the most extreme example.[20] The Japanese tort system does not give individuals who are injured by products the ability to sue based on strict liability principles. Rather, the sole means of recovery is through negligence. This reflects a prevailing philosophy in Japan that safety is best achieved when consumers are required to be more careful, rather than when manufacturers are forced to protect them. The difficulties for injured consumers in Japan are further complicated by a legal system that is burdensome on plaintiffs. For instance, in Japan, litigants have only limited rights to discovery, a process liberally allowed in the United States by which an injured party can learn information that is in the hands of the defendant. This means that it is difficult to prove what a company might have known about the safety of a product. In addition, regulatory oversight of unsafe products in Japan is weaker than in the United States. The result is that products sold in Japan are less safe and carry fewer safety warnings than their counterparts in the United States. Indeed Japanese companies that sell in both markets often design the goods destined for the United States with greater safety precautions than those they sell in Japan. Thus, televisions shipped to the United States are encased with fireproof materials whereas those offered in Japan may be protected less effectively. Automobiles exported to the United States contain more expensive steel reinforcements in the frame and more expensive nonflammable materials than those made for sale in Japan. Of course, all this perturbs U.S. manufacturers, who believe the Japanese legal system gives its manufacturers a comparative advantage. This is not only because Japanese companies may need to spend less on research and legal costs but also because they have the freedom to test the safety of their products in the Japanese marketplace without incurring substantial risks of lawsuits. In the final analysis, one cannot say that one system is better than the other. The contrasting legal rules offer different incentives to manufacturers regarding the safety of their products. The proper formulation can be judged only with reference to one's social preference. However, as noted, the fact that product lability laws in Japan are inconsistent with those in the United States may lead to serious international trade issues. As the international community becomes more interdependent, a certain amount of compromise to lessen the variations in the two approaches likely will be necessary. Indeed, as this book goes to press in 1994, substantial efforts are under way in Japan to reform its tort system, which may bring some form of strict liability to that country within the next few years.[21]

Policies in the European Union (EU), in contrast, have moved more consistently in lockstep with those in the United States.[22] In 1985, the Council of the European Union passed a strict liability Directive requiring the member states to pass legislation in conformity with its principles.[23] The philosophical underpinnings of the Directive are similar to those found in the United States. For instance, the Directive defines a defective product as one that "does not provide the safety which a person is entitled to expect, taking all circumstances into account."[24] This language parallels the consumer expectation test followed in the United States. The Directive places primary responsibility on the producers of the goods.[25] However, if the goods are imported into the EU, then the importers also bear liability for defective products.[26] In addition, when the producers and importers cannot be identified, other distributors and suppliers within the EU may be subject to liability.[27] This ensures that those suffering injuries from defective products sold in the EU will have recourse against some identifiable source engaged in the distribution of the defective products within community borders. The Directive also restricts producers from disclaiming or waiving their liabilities for injuries resulting from the use of defective consumer goods.[28] As we shall see in Chapter 9, this policy conforms to that already prevalent in the United States.

## Strict Products Liability and Computers Systems

**Strict Liability for Computer Programs.**  As previously mentioned, designers of computer systems have to be increasingly concerned about their duties under negligence principles. However, attention to negligence would quickly be eclipsed by strict products liability if the latter were held applicable to computer systems. Until recently, computer software developers have believed that they were immune from strict liability doctrines. For one, there is a substantial issue whether software is even a product. Especially for custom-designed programs, a strong argument can be made that the programmer is providing the service of making a computer function as desired by the client. Services are not subject to principles of strict products liability.[29] This means that if problems develop, only the programmers should be judged regarding their duties of care; the software should not be evaluated in terms of defectiveness. This argument is eroding, however, as more and more software is sold off-the-shelf. The more standardized the program, the more it has the appearance of a product rather than a service.

Another aspect that might immunize software programmers from strict products liability is that the doctrine traditionally has been applied to tangible objects. Software essentially instructs a user how to attain a desired result with a computer. In this way it may considered little different from a guidebook, which instructs the reader about, for instance, how to select safe mushrooms. Courts have been unwilling to extend strict products liability to most books, even those that guide the reader through potentially dangerous activities.[30] Besides the tangibility aspects, courts fear that enforcing strict liability on what could be considered defective instruction would have a chilling effect on freedom of expression. However, courts have been willing to view certain kinds of guidance materials in a different light. For instance, a company that converted government data into aeronautical charts was held responsible under strict products liability when certain charts were designed with improperly converted data.[31] In defending the distinction between these charts and other materials, one court recently stated:

> Aeronautical charts are highly technical tools. They are graphic depictions of technical, mechanical data. The best analogy to an aeronautical chart is a compass. Both may be used to guide an individual who is engaged in an activity requiring certain knowledge of natural features. Computer software that fails to yield the result for which it was designed may be another.[32]

The last sentence, although it is only conjecture by the court, has effectively unnerved computer programmers. Clearly, computer programmers have reasons to worry if defects in their programs cause damages. Liability may rest not only on substandard programming expertise but also on the simple fact that the program did not perform as an ordinary user would expect. So, for example, if an error in an architectural design program caused a structure to be built with a deficiency ultimately leading to a collapse and injuries, then the programmer possibly could be sued under strict products liability and might lose even after being extremely careful in designing the program.

**Expert Systems and Medical Treatment.**  An important new development with computer technology involves what are called expert systems.[33] Expert systems represent a new frontier of computer technology that attempts to have the machines rise above simple data manipulation to the level of making reasoned judgments. In effect, the computer is programmed with judgment rules so that it can draw upon its enormous data banks of experience and then apply logic, inference, and intuition to reach a reasoned solution to a particular problem. The programming of expert systems is extremely complicated, relying on professionals in the field, on experts who synthesize decision rules, and on sophisticated computer programmers. Currently, the medical community is making the greatest inroads in using expert systems. One example is the HELP system employed at the Latter-day Saints Hospital in Salt Lake City. HELP's database contains information on thousands of diseases, symptoms, blood chemistry, and drug therapies. It uses patient records in conjunction with this knowledge to issue warnings and recommend appropriate treatment.[34] Other types of expert systems are built into operational medical devices, such as an insulin-infusion pump, which when implanted in the skin, can adjust the insulin drip rate as needed by the patient.[35]

For obvious reasons, the medical community is excited about the prospects of better treatment with the aid of expert systems. However, there also is substantial concern about potential tort liabilities. Doctors who rely on information from expert systems or recommend medical devices utilizing them have to be concerned with their respective standards of care. How far can a doctor go in trusting the diagnosis or suggested treatment by an expert system? Conversely, one might pose the alternative question: If an expert system is available, would it be negligent for a doctor not to use the system in some advisory capacity?

Those involved in developing the system also must be concerned with tort liabilities. Under negligence principles, the various manufacturers, programmers, and experts must fulfill their appropriate standards of care. Whether the applicable standard is elevated to a professional level in this context is not yet settled, but as discussed before, one should expect it shall be the trend. More threatening, of course, is the very clear potential that the system will be subject to strict products liability. The issue of whether the expert system is most like a textbook or an aeronautical chart comes alive in this context, and as at least one court has suggested, the resolution likely will be to apply strict liability. In that event, if the expert system provides an inaccurate diagnosis or treatment that leads to detrimental medical complications, then it should not be hard to prove that the system had a defect making it unreasonably dangerous.

**Repetitive Motion Injuries.**  "Repetitive motion injuries" is an umbrella term that applies to any painful condition of the neck, shoulder, arm, or hand that occurs in a worker engaged in repetitive physical duties.[36] Recently, there has been an explosion of complaints about repetitive motion injuries in the United States stemming particularly from uses of consoles, keyboards, and video display terminals associated with computers. Indeed, according to the U.S. Bureau of Labor Statistics, repetitive motion injuries are now the leading cause of occupational illness in the United States.[37] For this reason, Robert Reich, secretary of the Department of Labor under President Clinton, called these ailments "the occupational diseases of the information age."[38] Of the variety of forms of repetitive motion injuries, the most prominent is carpal tunnel syndrome, a wrist disorder alleged to be caused by computer keyboards. Other forms of trauma allegedly are caused by inappropriate layout of equipment, seating, and lighting.

Evidence on the causes of repetitive motion injuries is now being collected, and no conclusive studies have been completed to date. Nonetheless, there is activity in the legislative arenas. Labor organizations and women's rights groups, among others, have lobbied vigorously at the federal, state, and local levels for workplace protection. So far, the greatest response has been at the state and local levels. Proposed legislation has been introduced in a host of states to deal with the growing concerns about repetitive motion injuries and computers. Typical proposals would require businesses to install appropriate lighting, adjustable chairs, and proper workstations, as well as to provide more frequent rest breaks for employees. To date, policies have actually been enacted by state, county, or city governments in only a handful of regions.[39] At the federal level, the Occupational Safety and Health Administration (OSHA) announced in 1993 that it had begun to develop standards to deal with the explosive rise in problems related to ergonomic designs.[40] In addition, bills have been introduced in Congress that would require OSHA to issue these pertinent rules.[41]

The other front where workers have raised the issue of repetitive motion disorders is in the courts. Hundreds of lawsuits have been brought alleging that the designs of data processing equipment, particularly keyboards, are defective and unreasonably dangerous.[42] The lawsuits claim that the companies knew, or should have known, that the design of their products was defective and that the companies failed to adequately warn the workers who eventually used the products. Defendants include such companies as Northern Telecom, Apple Computer, Compaq, AT&T, Eastman Kodak, IBM, and Wang Laboratories. One of the important points of contention is whether it is indeed the design of the keyboards or the work environment that is responsible for the injuries. As this book is being written, only one case has been decided on the merits, and it sided with the computer keyboard manufacturer.[43] Other disputes have been settled or dismissed. For example, legal action brought by directory assistance operators in Colorado was settled for a sum of less than $50,000 per employee affected.[44] Also, a lawsuit against IBM was dismissed in August 1992 based on insufficient evidence that the design had caused the injuries.[45]

An interesting development based on concern about repetitive motion injuries is renewed interest in redesigning the basic QWERTY keyboard.[46] Many concepts reconfigure the keys and adjust the angles of the keyboards. Some even go so far as to eliminate keys altogether. One project, for instance, has each finger rest in a padded finger well and operate switches by moving to selected positions within the well.[47] Ultimately, one can surmise that equipment will not require touch for operations, relying on voice instead. This, of course, should eliminate repetitive motion injuries, but it may raise a host of new office problems when employees work in close proximity.

## INTENTIONAL TORTS

Negligence and strict products liability both deal with unintentional torts. One is negligent not because one meant to intrude on a protected right, but rather because one failed to use sufficient care. Similarly, with strict products liability, intent is not at issue. Rather, one is liable because the product has a defect that makes it unreasonably dangerous.

One commits an intentional tort when one intends to violate a protected right, and the intrusion results in injury.[48] One does not have to intend to cause harm; in fact, one may have a noble rationale for violating the protected right. For a simple example, consider the intentional tort battery; "battery" can be defined as intentionally touching another in a way a reasonable person would find harmful or offensive without consent. Suppose your neighbor in class is talking to the person behind him. Unbeknownst to him, the professor has entered the room, and you perceive the professor is becoming irritated at your neighbor's discussion. With only the best interests of your neighbor in mind, you intentionally give him a soft kick to the knee so that he will turn around and notice the presence of the professor. Unfortunately, you kicked the neighbor where he had sustained a previous wound, and serious injury resulted. This action constitutes a battery for which you will be liable if the neighbor sues.[49] Notice that you have committed a tort even though your motives were good. Also, you will be liable for all the damages that flowed from your actions even though the extent was not foreseeable. In other words, when you commit an intentional tort, you bear the risk that the affected person may be extremely sensitive to your conduct.

### Fraud

Suppose that our AES salespeople, who work on a commission basis, negotiated a contract for the sale of a substantial number of AES units to the state of New York for use in kindergarten through twelfth-grade music classrooms. A major issue for the state of New York was whether the AES could satisfactorily improve the sound of records played at 78 RPM because the state educational system has a large historical library. Your sales staff assured the state negotiators that the AES performed just as well with 78's, and the salespeople even demonstrated the system's abilities with a 78 RPM record. The fact of the matter was, though, that we had not yet perfected the AES for use with 78's. Under certain very common circumstances, the frequencies from 78's cannot be adjusted correctly by the AES, thus leading to warbles and inaccurate reproductions. The sales staff, however, found a 78 that did not trigger this deficiency, and it used that one to falsely prove effectiveness. After landing the huge contract, we richly rewarded the sales personnel involved, plowing the earnings into a large plant-and-equipment-expansion effort. Several months after the sale, the sales staff received complaints from various New York school districts about the performance of their AES units. The sales staff blamed the problems on unusual record quality, which they said would be correctable with expert service. They even convinced the districts to enter service contracts for long-term maintenance. The complaints and problems increased markedly over the next year, and the state of New York, alleging that we had engaged in fraud, demanded all of its money back. In addition, the state insisted on extra compensation both for the time and energy spent by its teachers and administrators in dealing with the units and for the resultant reduction in the level of educational quality received by students. Our managers, who did not know what the sales staff had promised or demonstrated, were shocked by the allegations. A lawsuit ensued, which we ultimately lost. The consequences were devastating, since we had to liquidate plant, equipment, and inventory to satisfy it.

The actions of the sales staff personnel constituted fraud because (1) they intended to deceive the state of New York (2) by making statements they knew or reasonably should have known were false (3) about an issue that was material to the buyers (4) under circumstances in which the buyers had justifiably relied on the truth of the statements. Since the sales personnel work for our company, the company can be held responsible for their actions, even if they were not authorized and even if top management did not know what they were doing. Fraud often can be a problem for aggressive new companies if sales personnel are not thoroughly briefed on the permissible scope of statements that can be made in the furtherance of sales. The next case provides a thorough example of how fraud is treated by courts.

## DUNN APPRAISAL COMPANY V. HONEYWELL INFORMATION SYSTEMS, INC.

*Sixth Circuit Court of Appeals, 1982*

### Facts

The plaintiffs are Dunn Appraisal Company (DAC) and its subsidiary Systems Information Services, Inc. (SIS). DAC is engaged in the automobile damage appraisal business, and its president is Robert Dunn. SIS, which is located in Cleveland, furnishes computer services to various business clients. Its president throughout most of the period of this dispute was James Saneholtz. The defendants are Honeywell, Inc., and its subsidiary Honeywell Information Systems, Inc. (HISI), which manufactures, sells, leases, and services computer equipment.

In early 1975, Saneholtz became friends with Philip Reimer, a salesman at HISI. At that time, SIS was leasing Honeywell Model 12/50 computers, but Saneholtz was interested in acquiring more modern equipment with additional capabilities. He turned to his friend Reimer for advice. At the same time, HISI was preparing to introduce a new line of computers.

On June 9, 1975, Saneholtz met with Reimer and Clark Simpson, a systems manager at HISI. At this meeting, there was a general discussion about the equipment needs of SIS and the relative merits of the forthcoming Honeywell Models 62/40 and 64/20 computers. Saneholtz allegedly told Simpson and Reimer that SIS had about 400 programs it was currently using on the 12/50 computers in order to serve its customers. This was important in deciding which new computer to acquire because the Model 12/50 programs could be run on the 64/20 with little or no change, but they would have to be converted considerably in order to be used on the 62/40. Reimer expressed the opinion that the 62/40 was better suited for what Saneholtz had in mind.

Following this meeting, Simpson privately expressed to Reimer serious reservations about going from a 12/50 to a 62/40 because of the conversion problem. He estimated that it would take 16 man-hours to convert just one program and that 400 programs would take two to four man-years to convert. He felt that such a massive conversion would not be worth the effort and that it would be better for SIS to acquire a 64/20 even though the model would not be available as soon as the 62/40. In any event, it turned out that either model was too expensive for SIS, so the matter was dropped.

By the fall of 1975, HISI had not yet made any sale of a 62/40 in the Cleveland market and was eager to do so. It was therefore willing to give a substantial price concession to the first Cleveland customer for a 62/40. Accordingly, the original parties resumed discussions in November. This time, Dunn joined Saneholtz on behalf of SIS, and Mike Mahoney, HISI's Cleveland branch manager, accompanied Reimer.

In these meetings, Reimer and Mahoney described the features of the 62/40 and the 64/20 and recommended that the 62/40 was the better choice for SIS. When the question of program conversion came up, Saneholtz told Reimer that they had between 300 and 400 programs. Dunn and Saneholtz testified at trial that Reimer and Mahoney had assured them that HISI would convert all of SIS's programs at no charge if SIS leased a 62/40.

Dunn and Saneholtz had little knowledge of computers. Therefore, following the discussions with Reimer and Mahoney, Dunn had a telephone conversation with a person knowledgeable about computers, who advised against acquiring a 62/40. The person stressed the difficulty of converting from a 12/50 to a 62/40, stating that such a transition was not a logical step because the 62/40 was not designed to replace the 12/50. Nevertheless, Dunn and Saneholtz chose to rely on Reimer, whom they knew and trusted. Reimer was familiar with SIS's business operations, and Saneholtz believed that Reimer had the best interests of SIS at heart.

In December 1975, Dunn signed a contract with HISI for the lease of a 62/40 computer and associated equipment. Although the contract specified that HISI would convert only 250 programs, Saneholtz testified that Reimer and Mahoney both told him not to worry, that the number 250 was just put there to satisfy their front office and that they would convert all of SIS's programs.

Work on converting the programs began in January 1976, and almost from the very beginning the project was an unmitigated disaster. Although the contract called for a projected installation date of March 1, 1976, this was postponed until September because the conversion process was proceeding so slowly. At the end of March, HISI informed SIS that it would not convert all of the programs— only 250 of them. Consequently, SIS was forced to hire an independent contractor to complete the job. Even by the fall of 1976, HISI had not delivered all of its 250 converted programs, and many of those delivered were not correct.

It turned out that the 62/40 as installed did not have all of the capabilities it was supposed to have without the purchase of substantial additional accessories. At HISI's request, SIS hired a full-time employee to act as a liaison for the conversion effort. Nevertheless, by October 1976, the conversion was so botched up that SIS could use neither the old machine nor the new one to conduct its business with its customers. In December 1976, DAC terminated the agreement.

DAC and SIS sued HISI and Honeywell for fraud and breach of contract. The district court dismissed the breach of contract claim for technical reasons. The evidence presented at trial was sharply conflicting, especially concerning what representations had been made regarding conversion of the programs and who was to blame for the breakdown of the conversion effort. Reimer and Mahoney denied that they had promised to convert all of SIS's programs, and Reimer denied that Simpson had ever advised him against selling a 62/40 to SIS. There was testimony by HISI personnel that at least part of the conversion problems were due to disorganization at SIS.

The trial court chose to credit the testimony of the plaintiffs and their witnesses. It determined that Reimer and Mahoney had made the following material misrepresentations in order to induce DAC to enter the contract:

1. The 62/40 computer was best suited for the SIS operation and its projected expansion.
2. Delivery and operational installation could be accomplished by March 1, 1976.
3. Conversion of the 400 programs could be accomplished with minor modifications and could be completed with little disruption to SIS customer services.
4. Honeywell would convert all 400 programs at its expense by March, although, for business expediency, the written agreement guaranteed only 250 conversions.
5. The 62/40 had more capabilities than the 12/50 and would improve SIS's efficiency in serving customers by 25 to 50%.
6. Transition to the 62/40 could be accomplished without additional formal training of SIS's employees and/or labor costs.
7. Operation and maintenance costs of the 62/40 would be substantially less than for the 12/50.
8. No additional hardware or software would be needed to meet the projected SIS growth pattern.

The district court found in favor of the plaintiffs on the fraud count. The court awarded DAC $61,573.56 compensatory damages and $30,768.78 punitive damages, plus attorney's fees of $24,628.

Honeywell and HISI appealed. They claimed that (1) the district court's findings of fraudulent misrepresentations by HISI were clearly erroneous; (2) the district court had erred in concluding that HISI had a duty to disclose to DAC the
misgivings expressed by Clark Simpson to Reimer concerning the suitability of
the 62/40; and (3) the damage award was clearly erroneous.

## Opinion

The elements of fraud are as follows: (1) there must be an actual or implied representation of a matter of fact (2) that relates to the present or past, (3) which
was material to the transactions and (4) which was false when made. (5) The
statement must be made with knowledge of its falsity or with reckless disregard
for whether it is true or not and (6) with the intent to mislead the other party in
relying upon it. (7) The other party must be ignorant of the fact averred, causing
(8) justifiable reliance and (9) injury.

The first finding made by the district court was that the Honeywell 62/40 was
"best suited for the SIS operation and its projected business expansion." HISI argues that no such statement was made, that it is an opinion about the future
rather than a statement concerning a past or present fact, and that if the statement were made, there was no proof it was false.

It is true that there was no testimony that such a verbatim statement was made
by Reimer or Mahoney. However, the trial court was not reporting a verbatim
quotation but was summarizing the fair import of the vague statements made by
HISI's agents. A false representation may be implied as well as actual. The evidence supports the trial court's finding that HISI made an implied representation
that the 62/40 would be the best computer for SIS's needs.

We also agree with the district court that the implied representation that the
62/40 would be suitable for the intended use at SIS was a statement regarding a
present fact rather than an opinion about the future because it was a statement
regarding the inherent, existing capabilities of the product. General representations that data processing equipment will be suitable for a customer's operations,
based upon familiarity with both the equipment's capabilities and the customer's
needs, are statements concerning present facts.

There is also evidence in the record, from which the trial court could have concluded that the representation was false when made because two other knowledgeable individuals recommended against using the 62/40. The fact that Reimer
did not disclose Clark Simpson's doubts about the 62/40 to Dunn and Saneholtz,
or at least modify his own recommendations in light thereof, supports the trial
court's inference of willful disregard for the truth. It is not necessary that the defendant have actual knowledge that a statement is false. It is sufficient if the statement were made with utter and reckless disregard for whether it is true or not.

Another major representation was the promise to convert all of SIS's programs. Although the general rule is that fraud cannot be predicated upon a representation concerning a future event, a statement concerning what the speaker
intends to do in the future stands upon a different footing. A promise made with
a present intention not to perform it is a misrepresentation of an existing fact

(i.e., the speaker's present state of mind), and if such a false representation induces the other party to enter into a contract, the contract may be avoided. The district court's finding that Reimer and Mahoney falsely promised to convert all of SIS's programs and that this promise was one of the factors that induced DAC to enter into the contract, was not clearly erroneous.

HISI and Honeywell also take issue with the amount of damages, totaling $61,573.56, that the district court awarded to DAC. Those damages were as follows:

1.  Cost of management time and expense devoted to installation of the 62/40 and the conversion of computer programs.
    a.  The amount of $20,000 is a reasonable monetary value for the time Robert Dunn devoted to the conversion effort.
    b.  A liaison was employed by SIS upon the advice of Mahoney at the cost of $8,389.10.
    c.  There is insufficient evidence that DAC and SIS are entitled to damages for the services of other in-house employees in the conversion process.
2.  Labor and 400 hours of machine time to prepare test data for the system at $45 per hour for a total of $18,000.
3.  DAC and SIS incurred the following expenses directly connected with the installation of the 62/40: $1,242 for the wiring of the new computer and $300 for the rental of a transformer.
4.  Lease and purchase costs of disks and tapes for the 62/40 equaled $745.93.
5.  The amount of $11,175 was paid to the independent contractor who completed the conversion of computer programs for the 62/40, and $1,721.53 was paid to another firm for tape conversions needed to service a customer account.
6.  No other items of damage were established with the requisite certainty.

Robert Dunn testified that he was paid a salary of $100,000 per year at the time of this contract and that he devoted one-fifth of his time during 1976 to the computer problem. Accordingly, the district court awarded $20,000 for the value of the time Robert Dunn devoted to the conversion effort. HISI and Honeywell argue that executive lost time is not compensable, reasoning that a chief executive officer assumes the risk of all corporate problems. We find this unpersuasive. A chief executive officer is a salaried employee like any other, and a distinction between that person and other, lower-level executives is unjustified. In either case, the corporation is paying for the executive's time. We therefore hold that the $20,000 award for time spent by Robert Dunn was proper.

HISI and Honeywell do not challenge the amounts of the punitive damages and attorney's fees awarded by the trial court.

The judgment of the district court is affirmed.

The best protection against allegations of fraud is to ensure that sales personnel do not overblow the capabilities of a product in order to finalize a deal that otherwise might not be acceptable. Thus, one should concentrate on adopting appropriate management techniques and incentives programs that discourage fraudulent representations. However, it may not always be possible to avoid disputes with dissatisfied clients over promises allegedly made by sales personnel, whether they actually made them or not.

In the next chapter, we will discuss product warranties and other contractual provisions. An additional way to protect our company from disputes over what might have been promised by sales personnel is through contractual provisions that are clearly understood by the client. As will be discussed in Chapter 9, the company should expressly specify, or warrant, in the contract any capabilities that it promises the AES will achieve. Thus, for the AES, the warranty should promise improvement only for 33 RPM records. The contract also should have a provision that states:

1. No express or implied representations have been made other than those contained in the express warranty.
2. The client has not relied on any representations that are not contained in the express warranty.

By signing contracts with this provision, customers, in essence, are giving up the right to claim that they were fraudulently induced to enter agreements based on false allegations made prior to sale by company personnel. A customer, therefore, should be very careful before accepting such a provision unless it is, in fact, accurate. If the sales personnel have promised more than is related in the express warranty, then the customer should attach an appendix to the contract that lists all important additional allegations made in the sales discussions. The language of the contract also should be appropriately amended to specifically state that the express warranty includes the allegations provided in the appendix.

### Recent High-Technology Intentional Tort Issues

Probably the most pressing concerns about new technologies involve their capacities to obtain and store information about individuals. This has led to rapidly rising attention to the proper scope of individual privacy and the limits the law should take in protecting it. These issues will be addressed in the next section. Here, however, we look at some of the other recent controversies resulting from the application of new technologies.

A number of intentional torts specially relate to the use of computers. Unlawful conduct with computers can take many forms. For example, a computer system can be either the object of the intrusion or the instrumentality to carry it out. The earliest forms of harms usually included the alteration or removal of data, such as with financial information. Recently, however, the forms of computer torts have become more sophisticated.[50] Probably the most well-known involves the intentional spread of computer viruses. A computer virus, on one hand, is like any other computer program in that it carries out the instructions programmed within it. However, a virus is special in that it can create copies of itself. Often a virus is embedded in an applications program, but it may simply be a separate program. A virus may spread whenever it comes into contact with a computer system. Thus, a virus program may replicate and be transmitted over telephone lines or cable, or from disk to disk. Most viruses are developed only in good fun, so as, for instance, to relay comic messages, but some may have potentially widespread catastrophic effects if preventive steps are not taken. The Michelangelo virus, which was programmed to destroy computer files on the anniversary of Michelangelo's birthday in 1992, is a salient example. Even when a virus is not maliciously designed to destroy or damage files, it can be a nuisance by taking up file space or otherwise interfering with normal computer operations.

The introduction of a computer virus may be a crime under federal and/or state laws. For instance, the Federal Computer Fraud and Abuse Act makes it a crime to intentionally access and cause damage to any computer used substantially for U.S. government purposes or by financial institutions. The first conviction under this statute was against a Cornell University graduate student who crippled the Internet computer network with a virus in 1988. The virus affected systems at universities and military installations and cost as much as $15 million for systems operators to eradicate.[51] Violation of this statute carries a maximum sentence of five years in prison and substantial fines. Almost all states also have laws making it a crime to damage or disrupt computer systems intentionally through viruses or otherwise.

An intentional intrusion into a computer system with a virus is little different from battery or trespassing. As with every intentional tort, those responsible for the spread of the virus may be liable for all damages caused by the virus, no matter whether the amount of damages were foreseeable or even whether harm were an objective at all. Unlike other more traditional intentional torts, however, the victim of a computer virus likely will have an extremely difficult, if not impossible, task proving where the virus originated and who the responsible parties were.

A couple of examples will demonstrate some of the other novel forms of intentional torts now being committed with computers. In one case, a computer consultant was hired by a law firm to install a new computer system and to modify its insurance claims processing software. The programmer installed a bug in the program so that the system would stop working once claim number 56789 was processed. The bug was planted by the consultant so that the law firm would be forced to retain him once again to correct the problem. In litigation by the law firm against the consultant, the court awarded the $7,000 the firm had to pay to correct the problem and an additional $18,000 in punitive damages.[52]

In another series of cases, purveyors of computer systems have been held liable for damages caused by drop-dead or time-bomb devices installed in the software. A drop-dead device causes the program to shut down at the instruction of the programmer, and a time bomb automatically locks up the program at a particular time unless the programmer deactivates it beforehand. Some computer specialists who have installed these devices have allowed them to shut down systems when clients have failed to pay appropriately, at least in the programmers' mind, according to contracts made for their services. For example, in a payment dispute between the Clayton X-Ray Company and a computer systems vendor (Professional Systems Corporation), the computer company installed a program that disabled the computer and then showed a message on the screen saying "Call Professional Systems Corporation About Your Bill."[53] In essence, when contract disputes over computer services arise, the specialists use the devices to extort payment from the clients. Courts have not looked favorably on these devices, holding the installers liable for damages and punitive damages.[54] However, one should note that in these situations, the clients were unaware that their system had disabling devices installed. If a client has agreed in the contract to the installation of a disabling device that could be activated against defined operations with reasonable notice, then it is likely that use of the device would not give rise to liability.[55]

Another recent topic involving computers affects computer bulletin boards. In a 1991 case, CompuServe Inc. was sued for reprinting allegedly defamatory material contained in a newsletter it made available on its Journalism Forum. Defamation is an intentional tort that consists of a false communication to the public that injures a person's reputation. Businesses that publish or republish false statements, such as newspapers and magazines, clearly are subject to defamation laws. For them, the greatest protection is from a policy that excludes liability for false statements about public officials and public figures unless the statements are made with reckless disregard for the truth. The issue for CompuServe and computer bulletin board companies regards their duties to police the veracity of information disseminated over their electronic networks. In CompuServe's case, the court held that a bulletin board, which does not exercise editorial control, is more like a library or a bookstore than a publishing house. As such, it is not liable for selling or transmitting publications containing defamatory statements unless it knew or had reason to know about the defamation. Since CompuServe did not review the contents of the publications it carried, it was not liable for statements made in those publications.[56] Of course, this leaves open the possibility that bulletin boards may be liable if they prescreen messages prior to distribution to members. In addition, the decision does not address the potential liability of bulletin board companies when members create and transmit the defamatory statements over the network.[57]

A recently resolved controversy outside the computer area had tremendous repercussions for the medical research community. In 1976, John Moore received treatment for a rare form of sickle-cell anemia at the University of California Medical Center in Los Angeles. As part of the therapy, Moore's spleen was removed. Prior to the operation, the physicians had arranged to obtain portions of Moore's spleen for medical research purposes. Moore was never informed of the physicians' plans to use the spleen for medical research. Unique cells from Moore's spleen ultimately were used to develop a novel and ultimately patented cell line that had potential for the treatment of cancer and immune system diseases. While the patent was pending, the physicians licensed the cell line to Genetics Institute and Sandoz Pharmaceutical Corporation for 75,000 shares of Genetics Institute stock (worth several million dollars at the current stock price) and $440,000 in research grants. Moore sued the physicians, the University of California, and the private corporations, alleging, among other things, that he had a property right in his own cells. Under this theory, anyone using Moore's property for research or otherwise would need permission from Moore. Without such consent, an intentional tort called conversion occurs. The result is that Moore would have an ownership interest in anything derived from his property, including the patented cell line.

The California Court of Appeals agreed that Moore had a property right in his cells. That decision, if it had stood on appeal, could have been potentially devastating to the research industry. This is because it would be difficult for researchers to trace the sources of all their biological materials in order to ensure that the originating patients had granted permission in broad enough terms to cover the researchers' activities. Based primarily on this policy rationale, the California Supreme Court determined that individuals do not have property interests in their own human tissues.[58] Thus, researchers cannot be liable for the tort of conversion, even without consent. However, the Supreme Court did not totally sanction the actions of the physicians. It noted that personal physicians may have conflicts of interest when opting for procedures that may yield personal financial gain. Thus, physicians have a fiduciary duty to disclose any possible economic interests that might affect their medical judgment, and they must receive informed consent from the patient. Moore therefore might be able to recover damages for inadequate disclosure. However, most important to the research community, the patient did not retain an ownership interest in the patented cell line or in any other discoveries in which the cells someday might be used.

## Intrusions on Privacy

Personal privacy is sacred within the culture of the United States. One only has to review the Bill of Rights to get a feel for U.S. reverence for individual privacy. The Fourth Amendment specifically protects individuals from government search and seizure. The Fifth Amendment prevents government from requiring self-incriminating testimony by a criminal suspect, thereby protecting from government intrusion or manipulation what one knows. Even the Fourteenth Amendment, which protects liberty from government interference, has been interpreted by some to include elements of privacy. It is no wonder, therefore, that there has been a strong public reaction to the assault on privacy that new technologies have wrought.

The concept of privacy is elusive because one often does not think about it in concrete terms until the usual and expected patterns of conduct change. For example, experience with the common telephone has led the pubic to expect that a conversation is private between the acknowledged participants. Anyone who listens in without permission or without some compelling overriding interest violates a recognized right to privacy. New phone technologies have raised novel issues, however. Consider the case of new parents who monitor their infant from another room by using a baby monitor. Sometimes these monitors pick up the frequencies emitted by portable phones, thus allowing the parents to overhear the phone conversations of their neighbors. Should the parents be expected to turn off the monitor when such a phone conversation is received? The whole point of using the monitor is to maintain constant contact with the infant, so this requirement does not seem fair or appropriate. Can we expect the parents to pay attention for baby noises but ignore all other sounds they hear? That seems impractical. At the same time, many people who use portable phones think of them as no different from traditional phones. They therefore expect that their conversations are just as private with one instrument as with the other. However, clearly the new technology must challenge accepted norms of privacy. Now, one has to consider whether the privacy of a conversation is dependent on the type of phone used. One also must reflect, in a more discriminating manner than before, about the kinds of behavior that might inappropriately interfere with privacy expectations. For example, whereas listening with the baby monitor might seem permissible under the circumstances, actively scanning the airwaves for the purpose of intercepting calls likely would appear less acceptable.

**Privacy of Self.** Traditional concepts of privacy are being tested in ways that are much too numerous to consider here. However, there are some defined groupings of privacy issues. One set of concerns involves new scientific and technological techniques that can be used to discover personal attributes or conditions. Polygraph testing provides one example. By monitoring certain physiological parameters, such as pulse rates, respiration, and perspiration, a trained technician may use a polygraph to test the veracity of one's answers given in response to questions. Such testing, especially in the employment context, has come under fire for two reasons. First, there are questions about the reliability of polygraph testing. Second, there is substantial criticism about the types of information an employer or other interrogator strives to obtain through polygraph tests. Questions about previous drug and alcohol use, criminal fantasies, gambling activities, and prior personal relationships are just a few of the topics commonly probed. Before the advent of the polygraph, it was not necessary to consider whether employers or others had a right to learn this information, because it was not technologically possible to obtain it reliably. However, with the introduction of polygraph testing, the debate surfaced about the types of information an inquirer could access and the conditions under which such information could be obtained. Those concerns resulted in substantial regulation of polygraph testing, first at the state level and more recently by federal law. The latter policy prohibits polygraph testing by private employers in almost all industries and under most circumstances, including preemployment evaluations.[59]

Modern technological methods have led to other ways to probe personal attributes. Drug (and alcohol) testing procedures have become more sophisticated, allowing detection of more types of drugs in less minute quantities. Privacy concerns have led to a patchwork of state regulation of drug testing, with some states strictly limiting the opportunities for testing and others being more permissive.[60] The U.S. Constitution, too, has been interpreted as providing protection from drug testing by government officials and employers.[61] Even more on the cutting edge are genetic testing techniques that may allow employers and insurers to identify individuals especially prone to developing certain diseases and health risk conditions, such as Alzheimer's disease, cystic fibrosis, cancer, or heart disease.[62] Although such testing is not widely used at this time, incentives to use the new techniques seem likely to increase as the tests become cheaper and more accurate while the costs of employee health benefits keep rising. Wisconsin and Oregon, among a few other states, have already responded with laws to prevent genetic screening under certain circumstances. In addition, a federal bill has been introduced in Congress, called the Human Genome Privacy Act, that restricts the ways in which federal government agencies may utilize genetic information.[63]

**Privacy of Personal Information.** A second group of privacy issues involves uses of new technologies to collect, organize, and disseminate personal information. Information on such seemingly private attributes as a person's financial status, personal interests, and buying behaviors are constantly being collected and sold to those who might find the information valuable. For instance, applicants often disclose substantial personal information in order to obtain credit cards or insurance. The data then may be sold without the applicant's knowledge or consent. Some companies develop lists of persons who have, say, filed workers' compensation claims or medical malpractice suits. Such information could be used to screen out prospective employees or medical patients based on their possible inclinations to sue.[64] Direct marketing firms can fine-tune their target marketing campaigns by purchasing lists containing the names of, for instance, magazine subscribers, elite retail shoppers, highly affluent consumers, or contributors to particular charitable groups. With cash register scanners and computers, supermarkets now have the means to precisely record every item a customer purchases. When the name of the customer can be established, as when a house discount card is used, the supermarket accumulates a wealth of data, which may be valuable for marketing purposes. For instance, makers of Ragu spaghetti sauce might use the information in a marketing campaign that targets individuals who recently purchased Prego sauce. The spread of personal information has gone so far that almost every medical, financial, or commercial transaction engaged in by an individual now can find its way into a computer system, often without restrictions on how the data may be used.

Although legal protection is growing, there currently are not a substantial number of federal laws in the United States protecting the privacy or accuracy of personal information.[65] The federal Fair Credit Reporting Act, for example, limits access to credit reports but has a notable exception in place for those with a legitimate business need for the information. The federal Right to Financial Privacy Act restricts the federal government from reviewing bank account records but does not cover state agencies or private employers.[66] Momentum now is building in the United States for the establishment of greater federal privacy protections for personal information. For instance, consumer advocates have been pushing for revisions to the Fair Credit Reporting Act that would explicitly ban the sale of credit data to direct marketers. However, as of mid-1994, these efforts have yet to be successful.[67] On the other hand, the Federal Trade Commission began to take steps in 1992 to limit credit-reporting agencies, such as TRW and Trans Union, from using financial and personal data to create target lists for marketing firms.[68] Following a complaint by the Federal Trade Commission (FTC), TRW entered an agreement with the agency, promising that it would not use credit data in its mailing list business. However, Trans Union refused to settle. According to Trans Union, the data it provided did not constitute a credit report because the data were not credit related. In particular, its list of upscale retail consumers merely included individuals who had two or more credit accounts. In 1993, an FTC administrative law judge determined that the Trans Union lists were indeed credit reports because they had a direct bearing on a consumer's creditworthiness, credit standing, or credit capacity. The judge determined that distribution of the lists was not authorized by the Fair Credit Reporting Act and therefore ordered Trans Union to stop furnishing the data to direct mail marketers.[69]

The European Union (EU) may be taking the lead in comprehensively reforming this area of privacy concerns.[70] In 1992, the EU Commission proposed a Draft Directive intended to harmonize the policies of the EU members regarding the protection and privacy of personal data collected by public and private entities.[71] Under the Directive, "personal data" encompasses all the information that can be directly or indirectly linked to an identifiable individual. The primary topics dealt with in the Directive are the permitted uses of personal data, the rights of the individual, the accuracy and quality of the information, and conditions for international transfer of the data. A basic tenet of the Directive is that personal information must be processed fairly and lawfully.[72] This principle places strong emphasis on the informed consent of the subject and prohibits surreptitious conduct.[73] The Directive lists five situations wherein consent may not be required, such as compliance with law or carrying out a public duty.[74] There is also an exception to consent when data are processed pursuant to the legitimate interests of the collector or a third party, but only if those interests are not overridden by those of the subject individual. This provision may prove to be important for direct marketers.[75] When the data are collected, individuals must be told, among other things, the purposes of the files into which the data are to go.[76] The Directive requires that collected data be relevant to the intended purposes of the file, and that data be stored no longer than the time needed to carry out those purposes.[77] In addition, the individuals must be informed when the data are first communicated to others or when the possibility of on-line access first arises.[78] Individuals will enjoy a wide array of other rights, including the right to have personal data erased from commercial or advertising list files.[79] Also, under the Directive, individuals are entitled to access their data files for purposes of verification and correction.[80] Finally, the Directive places limitations on the transfer of data to countries outside the EU that do not provide an appropriate level of protection.[81]

**Privacy of Employee Actions and Conversations.** Another area of concerns about privacy involves the monitoring of personal actions and conversations. Advancements in technology have allowed employers and others to monitor behavior that heretofore was free from close scrutiny. Electronic monitoring systems, as they are called, allow employers to measure employee efficiency in conducting routine duties. For instance, word processing and data entry tasks can be monitored for speed and errors through electronic systems that count keystrokes. The efficiency of phone operators can be checked by systems that clock the duration or count the number of calls in a given unit of time.[82] Such monitoring may be worrisome as a managerial tool because it may lead to such high performance standards that undue employee stress will result. Employees, too, may feel an undue intrusion on their personal privacy. Before electronic monitoring, supervision was likely to be periodic and with the knowledge of the employee. Electronic systems, on the other hand, may be operated remotely and constantly. In this way, there may be no way to engage in any private personal behavior—even rest—without employer awareness. In 1993, proposed federal legislation dealing with many of the concerns regarding electronic monitoring was introduced in Congress.[83] The proposal, called the Privacy for Consumers and Workers Act, garnered substantial political momentum and likely will be passed soon, if it has not become law already.

Possibly even greater attention has been given to the technical ability to monitor conversations. Concern about telephone wiretapping, for instance, led to significant regulation of wiretapping in the federal Omnibus Crime Control and Safe Streets Act. The next case discusses the federal wiretapping law and explains two important exceptions to the general prohibitions against the monitoring of phone conversations: (1) the consent of one party to the conversation and (2) monitoring in the ordinary course of business.

## WATKINS V. L. M. BERRY & COMPANY

*Eleventh Circuit Court of Appeals, 1983*

### Facts

Carmie Watkins was employed as a sales representative by Berry & Company ("Berry"). Berry was under contract with South Central Bell to solicit Yellow Pages advertising from South Central Bell's present and prospective Yellow Pages advertisers. Much of this solicitation was done by telephone, and Watkins was hired and trained to make those calls.

All employees of Berry are informed of its established policy of monitoring calls as part of its regular training program. The monitored calls are reviewed with employees to improve sales techniques. Employees are permitted to make personal calls on company telephones, and they are told that personal calls will not be monitored except to the extent necessary to determine whether a particular call is of a personal or business nature.

In April or May 1980, during her lunch hour, Watkins received in her office a call from a friend. At or near the beginning of the call, the friend asked Watkins about an employment interview Watkins had had with another company (Lipton) the evening before. Watkins responded that the interview had gone well and expressed strong interest in taking the Lipton job. Unbeknownst to Watkins, Martha Little, her immediate supervisor, was monitoring the call from her office and heard the discussion about the interview. After hearing the conversation, Little told her supervisor, Diane Wright, about the call. Later that afternoon, Watkins was called into Wright's office and was told that the company did not want her to leave. Upon discovering that the supervisor's questions had been prompted by Little's interception of the call, Watkins became upset and tempers flared. Wright fired Watkins the next day, but after Watkins complained to Wright's supervisor, she was reinstated with apologies from Little and Wright. Nonetheless, within a week, Watkins left Berry to work for Lipton.

Watkins sued Berry, Little, and Wright for violating Title III of the Omnibus Crime Control and Safe Streets Act. The district court judge granted summary judgment against Watkins and dismissed her claim. Watkins appealed.

## Opinion

Title III forbids, among other things, the interception, without judicial authorization, of the contents of telephone calls. Section 2511(1)(b) provides:

> Except as otherwise specifically provided in this chapter, any person who . . . willfully uses . . . any electronic, mechanical, or other device to intercept any oral communication . . . shall be fined not more than $10,000 or imprisoned not more than five years, or both.

In addition to criminal remedies, Title III Section 2520 provides for civil remedies. The person whose communication is unlawfully intercepted may recover actual damages or statutory damages of $100 for each day of violation up to a maximum of $1,000. In addition, one is entitled to punitive damages, attorney's fees, and litigation costs.

It is not disputed that Little's conduct violates Section 2511(1)(b) unless it comes within an exemption "specifically provided in" Title III. The defendants claim the applicability of two such exemptions. The first is the consent exemption set out in section 2511(2)(d):

> It shall not be unlawful under this chapter for a person not acting under color of law to intercept a wire or oral communication . . . where one of the parties to the communication has give prior consent to the interception. . . .

The defendants argue that, by using Berry's telephones and knowing that monitoring was possible, Watkins consented to the monitoring. The second exemption claimed is the business extension exemption in Section 2510(5)(a)(i), which defines the terms "electronic, mechanical, or other device," thereby establishing the kinds of monitoring subject to liability under Section 2511(1)(b). According to Section 2510(5)(a)(i), "electronic, mechanical, or other device" means:

> any device or apparatus which can be used to intercept a wire or oral communication other than any telephone or telegraph instrument, equipment, or facility . . . furnished to the subscriber or user by a communications common carrier in the ordinary course of its business and being used by the subscriber or user *in the ordinary course of its business* . . . [emphasis supplied].

Defendants argue that the monitoring of Watkins's call was in the ordinary course of Berry's business, that the interception therefore was not by an "electronic, mechanical, or other device" as defined in Section 2510, and that it therefore does not fall within Section 2511(1)(b).

The consent and business extension exemptions are analytically separate. Consent may be obtained for any interceptions, and the business or personal nature of the call is entirely irrelevant. Conversely, the business extension exemption operates without regard to consent. So long as the requisite business connection is demonstrated, the business extension exemption represents the circumstances under which nonconsensual interception is not violative of Section 2511(1)(b). Accordingly, we will first consider the scope of Watkins's consent to the monitoring of this call and then move to the question about whether the interception was justified as being in the ordinary course of Berry's business, notwithstanding the absence of consent.

Defendants argue that Watkins's acceptance of employment with Berry, with knowledge of the monitoring policy, constituted her consent to the interception of this call. This is erroneous with respect to Watkins's actual and implied consent.

It is clear that Watkins did not actually consent to interception of *this particular* call. Furthermore, she did not consent to a *policy* of general monitoring. She consented to a policy of monitoring sales calls but not personal calls. That consent included the inadvertent interception of a personal call, but only for as long as necessary to determine the nature of the call. So, if Little's interception went beyond the point necessary to determine the nature of the call, it went beyond the scope of Watkins's actual consent.

Consent under Title III is not to be cavalierly implied. Title III expresses a strong purpose to protect individual privacy by strictly limiting the occasions on which interception may lawfully take place. Stiff penalties are provided for its violation. It would thwart this policy if consent could routinely be implied from circumstances. Thus, knowledge of the *capability* of monitoring cannot alone be considered implied consent.

The cases that have implied consent from circumstances have involved far more compelling facts than those presented here. In one case, a police officer whose call was intercepted knew or should have known that the line he was using was *constantly* taped for police purposes; furthermore, an unmonitored line was provided expressly for personal use. (The police station had ten lines: eight were recorded continuously with an audible warning sound, one was recorded continuously without a sound, and one was not monitored.) In another case, the plaintiff made a personal call on telephones that were to be used exclusively for business calls and that he knew were regularly monitored. He had been warned on previous occasions to stop making personal calls from his business telephone; other telephones were specifically provided for personal use. In both cases, the employee was fully aware of the extent of the monitoring and deliberately ignored the strong probability or certainty of monitoring.

Such situations are worlds apart from Watkins's case, since Watkins had consented to a scheme of limited monitoring. We hold that consent within the meaning of Section 2511(2)(d) is not necessarily an all-or-nothing proposition; it can be limited. It is up to the judge or jury to determine the scope of the consent and to decide whether and to what extent the interception exceeded that consent.

If, as appears from the undisputed facts, there was no consent to the interception of the call beyond what was initially required to determine its nature, defendants must rely on the business extension exemption to shield them from liability for any listening beyond that point. It is not enough for Berry to claim that its general policy is justifiable as part of the ordinary course of business. The question, rather, is whether the interception of *this* call was in the ordinary course of business.

The general rule is that if the intercepted call was a business call, then monitoring is in the ordinary course of business. If it was a personal call, the monitoring was probably, but not certainly, *not* in the ordinary course of business. The undisputed evidence strongly suggests that the intercepted call here was not a business call, but rather was a personal call. Defendants argue, however, that the topic was Watkins's interview with another employer. Since this was obviously of interest and concern to Berry, defendants claim it was in the ordinary course of business to listen.

The phrase "in the ordinary course of business" cannot be expanded to mean "anything that interests the company." Berry might have been curious about Watkins's plans, but it had no legal interest in them. Watkins was at liberty to resign at will and so at liberty to interview with other companies. Her interview was thus a personal matter, neither in pursuit of nor to the legal detriment of Berry's business. To expand the business extension exemption as broadly as defendants suggest would permit monitoring of obviously personal calls on the grounds that the company was interested in, say, whether Watkins's friends were nice or not. We therefore conclude that the subject call was personal.

Whereas a business call is dispositive in one direction, a personal call is not dispositive in the other. In general, it is hard to see how intercepting a call involving nonbusiness matters could be "in the ordinary course of business," since such activity is unlikely to further any legitimate business interest. However, as an example, interception of calls reasonably suspected to involve nonbusiness matters might be justifiable by an employer who had had difficulty controlling personal use of business equipment through warnings. Thus, if interception of personal calls is permitted at all, it is permitted only for a very limited purpose. This might apply, for instance, to the situation in which monitoring occurs when personal calls are not allowed on business telephones.

Even in that limited situation, however, one is not entitled to monitor the contents of the entire call. We hold that a personal call may not be intercepted in the ordinary course of business under the exemption in Section 2510(5)(a)(i), except to the extent necessary to guard against unauthorized use of the telephone or to determine whether a call is personal or not. In other words, a personal call may be intercepted in the ordinary course of business to determine its nature but never its contents. The limit of this exemption for Berry's business was the policy that

Berry in fact instituted. It thus appears that Little was justified in listening to that portion of the call that indicated it was not a business call; beyond that, she was not.

The violation of Section 2511(1)(b) is the interception itself, not the interception of particular material. It is not necessary to the recovery of damages that the violator hear anything in particular; she need do no more than listen. Thus, the reinstatement of Watkins and her subsequent departure, though they may affect the amount of actual damages, do not render her claim moot. Watkins's right to recover at least the minimum statutory damages flows from the interception, not from the actual damage caused.

We hold that this case should not have been disposed by summary judgment. Among the factual questions that should be considered are: What was the monitoring policy to which Watkins had consented? Did Little know that Watkins had received the call, and if so, did that necessarily indicate a personal call? How long was the call? When was the interview discussed? Were other subjects discussed? For how long did Little listen? How long does it take to discover that a call is personal? For example, is there an immediately recognizable pattern to a sales call? This list is not exhaustive, but it points out the directions in which further inquiries should be pursued.

The judgment of the district court is reversed.

The original wiretapping law was passed in 1968. Obviously, technology has changed substantially since then. Means of communication and ways to intercept are substantially different. Nowadays, traditional phone conversations may be carried through airwaves rather than wires. New developments in electromagnetic, photoelectronic, and photooptical systems have led to a variety of new methods to transmit information. In addition, and more significantly, the computerization of offices and homes has led to an entirely new system of communication: electronic mail (E-Mail). This revolution in communications technologies led to passage of the Electronic Communication and Privacy Act (ECPA) in 1986, which amended the 1968 law to conform it to the new realities of technology.[84]

A complete discussion of the ECPA is well beyond the scope of this book. Essentially, it carries over the privacy protection discussed in *Watkins* to electronic communications of various types, including interstate electronic mail systems such as CompuServe and MCI-Mail. There are certain exceptions, most notably one for conversations over cordless phones.[85] However, as this book is being written, the rising prevalence of cordless phones is stirring debates in Congress to extend the ECPA's privacy protection to them also. One also should be aware that certain states have greater privacy protection for conversations than provided by federal law. For example, policies in some states require consent by all parties to a conversation rather than simply by one of the conversants.

The real battlefield consists of how the ECPA and state policies will be applied to E-mail, particularly when messages are reviewed by employers.[86] Several lawsuits have been filed by employees alleging employer misconduct in reading

E-mail messages.[87] Recognizing the realities of modern E-Mail technologies, the ECPA deals not only with intercepting electronic messages, as discussed in *Watkins*, but also with obtaining messages that are stored in electronic form by E-Mail service facilities pending receipt.[88] According to the act, operators of public electronic communications systems may establish through their contracts with customers the amount of privacy that will be accorded E-Mail messages.[89] Thus users of E-Mail systems who are concerned with the privacy of their messages should always refer to agreements made with the system operators. Also, the ECPA gives system operators the right to release the contents of messages under a defined set of circumstances, such as with the consent of either the sender or recipient, or to governmental authorities when appropriate.[90] In addition, the ECPA provides that it is unlawful for one to obtain messages through unauthorized access to an electronic communications facility.[91]

Having noted all this about the ECPA, one must be aware that the applicability of the ECPA to internal corporate E-mail systems is not altogether clear. However, even when the federal act does not cover private internal E-mail systems, there are state statutes, constitutions and common laws that could be relevant. On such occasions, one might expect them to be based on principles similar to those that underlie the ECPA. Therefore, the best general advice that can be given to an employer who wants the ability to intercept or obtain employee E-mail messages is that the employer should follow the philosophical content of *Watkins*. For instance, the employer might consider instituting a policy that E-mail is to be used only for business purposes. This reduces an employee's claim that it had some expectation of personal privacy and strengthens the employer's allegation that there was a legitimate business purpose for its actions. The employer should also notify all employees that E-mail messages may be intercepted and read by the employer. Acceptance of work responsibilities by the employee with knowledge of this general review policy may be construed as implied consent. In addition, the employer should consider a requirement that all employees provide written consent for their E-mail messages to be monitored. Finally, employers must always carefully review their intentions to read E-mail messages in light of specific applicable state policies. As mentioned, relying on consent solely from the employee may not be sufficient in states that require consent from both the sender and the recipients.[92] Similarly, employers should conscientiously monitor pressures emerging at the federal level to more comprehensively protect personal privacy in the workplace. In particular, it appears likely that the Privacy for Consumers and Workers Act will be passed by Congress and signed by the president, possibly as early as 1995. In addition to treating the other forms of monitoring activities noted earlier, this law will require employers to notify employees about E-mail monitoring policies, and it may provide other specific safeguards to protect the privacy of E-mail messages.[93]

**Technological Advancements Protecting Privacy.** We have seen that advances in technology have created new methods to intrude on personal privacy. However, technological innovations also may serve to protect privacy from unwanted scrutiny. For example, sophisticated data encryption systems now can be integrated into phones so that conversations and data are translated into codes before transmission. Some of these systems now are designed around algorithms that are so complex that it is virtually impossible for an eavesdropper to decipher the code without knowing the proper key to the algorithm used in the transmission. There are many legitimate reasons why companies and individuals may want to maintain the privacy of their conversations. Protecting valuable trade secrets is one clear rationale. However, parties may have more nefarious purposes for scrambling transmissions, such as evading law enforcement. On April 16, 1993, the Clinton Administration announced that it was studying a policy, advocated by the National Security Agency, which would effectively require those wishing to secure conversations to rely on a particular data encryption chip, called the Clipper Chip.[94] The purpose of the plan is to ensure that the government would have the capability to decode messages if necessary in the conduct of criminal investigations or in protecting national security. To ensure the highest degree of security, the algorithm keys, which essentially are long strings of numbers, would be divided into two pieces and held in escrow by separate government agencies. One could gain access to the keys only with a wiretap warrant.

Civil libertarians and industry executives, among others, are not content with the plan.[95] To them, there is something wrong with an arrangement under which a person is permitted to lock items up for security, but only if the government is given a copy of the key. Some worry that the government computers storing the keys might be violated, thereby allowing the keys to get into the wrong hands. Others do not trust the government to use the keys responsibly. Nonetheless, the government's national security and criminal enforcement justifications are somewhat compelling. As is many times the case, the controversy boils down to reaching the proper balance between the government's need to know and an individual's personal privacy. It is not yet clear how this traditional debate will be resolved in its new technological context. What is certain, however, is that it will be fascinating to follow this privacy issue as it unfolds in the 1990s.

**Privacy of Identity.**   There is one final arena involving personal privacy that is now becoming increasingly important. Few things can be considered so personal as one's individual identity. In a very real sense, the special attributes that make you who you are belong only to you. This includes your appearance, your personality, your voice, the way you walk, and your individual style. How would you feel if others somehow took or mimicked these special attributes and put them on public display without your permission? What if those others went so far as to make money from their appropriation? Likely, you would feel that your personal privacy had been violated. Fortunately, the law recognizes that individuals have rights to their personal identity, and it protects them from intentional invasions by others. This is especially true when commercial advantage is to be gained from such appropriation. In many states, these rights in identity are often collected together under an umbrella phrase, such as the "right of publicity."

So far, issues about identity rights have arisen predominantly in two contexts: advertising and digital manipulation. The following is just a short list of recent disputes involving possible misappropriation of privacy rights in identity:

1. The vocal imitation of Bette Midler's voice in an advertisement for Ford's Mercury Sable automobiles developed by the agency Young & Rubicam.[96]
2. The use of a guitar riff almost identical to one played by Chris Isaak in his hit song "Wicked Game," for a Nissan commercial for its Infiniti automobile.[97]
3. Imitation of the stage persona of the rap group the Fat Boys, by Joe Piscopo in a Miller beer commercial.[98]
4. Imitation of Bobby Darin's rendition of "Mack the Knife," including the singer's inflections, phrasings, and arrangement, in a McDonald's "Mac Tonight" advertising campaign.[99]
5. A robot recognizable as Vanna White used in a portrayal of the future in an advertisement for Samsung VCRs.[100]
6. An imitation of Tom Waits's raspy singing voice by Frito-Lay, Inc., in a radio commercial.[101]

Disputes involving privacy rights in identity sometimes are associated with copyright disputes. This happens when an actual recording or picture is used in creating the allegedly offending work. Digital sampling and digital imaging are two frequent contexts for this occurrence. As discussed in Chapter 6, when one uses digital means to alter portions of songs or pictures, copyright infringement likely takes place. However, invasions of publicity rights also may be alleged, as when Chuck D of the band Public Enemy sued McKenzie River Corporation, the maker of St. Ides malt liquor, after the firm used a sampled version of his voice for a commercial.[102] Privacy rights in identity clearly take on added importance when one simply imitates a voice, likeness, or style, as opposed to copying a song or a picture. This is because there may be no copyright privileges upon which one can rely for damages. Based on all this, the best advice is to get permission before copying or imitating the distinctive style, voice, or appearance of a well-known individual.

## CONCLUSION

This chapter should have made you more sensitive to the wide range of personal and social obligations that one incurs when offering a new product or service. Not only must one be careful, but one must ensure that the technology does not cause harm when used in foreseeable ways. Also, one has to consider that uses of advanced technologies may arouse public action leading to new forms of protection of personal rights.

In the next chapter, we will explore some important contracting issues for those managing technology. As we shall see, some of the concerns over torts may be handled through contract provisions. However, one usually cannot negotiate absolute protection from tort liabilities when dealing with knowledgeable parties.

In addition, although contracts may resolve liability issues between the parties to agreements, they do not offer relief when others suffer damage from use of the technology. Also, the more the context involves consumers rather than sophisticated commercial businesses, the less protection contracts can provide. Torts, therefore, will always be a critically important concern for those doing business in the technological world.

## NOTES

1. Employees who are negligent may be held personally liable for damages to those injured. Employers also may be held responsible to pay for the damages that result from an employee's negligence under a doctrine called *respondeat superior*. In addition, employers may be directly liable if they do not exercise due care in supervising the employees who caused the harm.
2. U.S. v. Carroll Towing Co., 159 F. 2d 169 (2d Cir. 1947).
3. Calabresi & Hirschoff, "Toward a Test for Strict Liability in Torts," 81 Yale L.J. 1055 (1972).
4. W. Buckley, "Databases Are Plagued by Reign of Error," Wall Street J. (May 26, 1992) at B6.
5. R. Harris Jr., "Why the Pinto Jury Felt Ford Deserved $125 Million Penalty," Wall Street J. (1978).
6. Cavers v. Cushman Motor Sales, Inc., 95 Cal. App. 3d 338, 348 (1979).
7. Todd v. Société BIC S.A., 9 F. 3d 1216 (7th Cir. 1993); Griggs v. BIC Corp., 981 F. 2d 1429 (3d Cir. 1992). In October 1993, Griggs lost its case because it was unable to prove that a BIC lighter caused the fire. However, the plaintiff may appeal. See "BIC Not Liable for Torched Child," National L.J. (November 29, 1993) at 9. For a general discussion of these cases, see M. Middleton, "Second Court Burns BIC on Lighter Liability," National L.J. (May 17, 1993).
8. Todd v. Société BIC S.A., 9 F. 3d 1216 (7th Cir. 1993).
9. The information about photosensitive epileptics was derived from M. Chase, "Nintendo to Issue Warning on Epilepsy in Europe, Japan," Wall Street J. (January 18, 1993) at B5.
10. The information about EMF is based on the following articles: B. Richards, "Electric Utilities Brace for Cancer Lawsuits Though Risk Is Unclear," Wall Street. J. (February 5, 1993) at 1; F. Rose, "Utilities React to Electromagnetic Fields," Wall Street J. (April 11, 1991) at B1.
11. The EMF issue may not be confined to electric utilities. In 1992, there was a brief flurry of public attention to the allegation that cellular phones may cause brain tumors, although most scientists disagree due to the phones' very low EMF emission levels. There also has been some concern with EMF emitted from electric razors. Thus, sellers of electricity-based products that are used in close proximity to the human body should pay careful attention to developments in EMF research.
12. Consumer Product Safety Act, 15 U.S.C. §2064(b) (1982).
13. 15 U.S.C. §§2064(b)(1), 2064(b)(2), 2084.

14. Substantial Product Hazard Reports, 16 C.F.R. 1115.4 (1991).

15. Civil penalties may be as high as $1.25 million. 15 U.S.C. §2069. Willful disregard of the reporting requirements can give rise to a one-year prison term. 15 U.S.C. §2070.

16. M. Lemov and M. Woolf, "Underreporting Defects Is Risky," National L.J. (December 14, 1992) at S6.

17. 16 C.F.R. 1115.12(a); 15 U.S.C. §2055(b)(5).

18. M. Lemov and M. Woolf, "Underreporting Defects Is Risky," National L.J. (December 14, 1992) at S6.

19. J. Davidson, "Bill to Limit Product-Liability Lawsuits by Consumers Fails in Senate, but Barely," Wall Street J. (September 11, 1992) at A4.

20. The information provided on the tort system in Japan was reported in L. Helm, "It's Buyer Beware in Japan," L.A. Times (February 6, 1993).

21. See E. Danaher, "Products Liability Overhaul," National L.J. (February 7, 1994) at 25.

22. See, e.g., S. Hurd and F. Zollers, "Product Liability in the European Community: Implications for United States Business," 31 American Business L.J. 245 (September 1993).

23. Council Directive of July 25, 1985 on the approximation of the laws, regulations, and administrative provisions of the member states concerning liability for defective products, 28 O.J. Eur. Comm. (No. L 210) 29 (1985) [hereinafter EU Products Liability Directive]. As of 1993, only France, Ireland, and Spain had not passed national legislation to comply with this Directive.

24. EU Products Liability Directive, Article 6(1).

25. EU Products Liability Directive, Article 3(1).

26. EU Products Liability Directive, Article 3(2).

27. EU Products Liability Directive, Article 3(2).

28. EU Products Liability Directive, Article 12.

29. Some services, however, are treated under strict liability principles if they are deemed ultrahazardous activities.

30. Winter v. G. P. Putnam's Sons, 938 F. 2d 1033 (9th Cir. 1991).

31. Aetna Casualty & Surety Co. v. Jeppsen & Co., 642 F. 2d 339 (9th Cir. 1981).

32. Winter v. G. P. Putnam's Sons, 938 F. 2d 1033, 1035 (9th Cir. 1991).

33. This discussion on expert systems is based on the paper B. Knowles, "Artificial Intelligence and Legal Liability: Some Observations," American Business L. Assoc. National Proceedings, 1989 at 545.

34. Marbach, Conant, and Hager, "Doctor Digital, We Presume," Newsweek (May 20, 1985) at 83.

35. B. Knowles, "Artificial Intelligence and Legal Liability: Some Observations," American Business L. Assoc. National Proceedings, 1989, at 554.

36. L. Chesler, "Repetitive Motion Injury and Cumulative Trauma Disorder: Can the Wave of Products Liability Litigation Be Averted?" Computer Lawyer (February 1992) at 13.

37. Ibid. According to the Bureau of Labor Statistics, repetitive motion injuries compose more than 60% of all occupational injuries. See K. Salwen, "White House to Proffer Ergonomic Rule for Workplaces, Employers' Liabilities," Wall Street J. (November 22, 1993) at B6.

38. B. Fellner and E. Scalia, "Ergonomic Rules May Jump the Gun," National L.J. (October 25, 1993) at 17.

39. Some examples of where video display terminal policies exist include New Mexico, Maine, New Jersey, San Francisco, and New York City. Activity is also extremely high in the state of California. Computer Lawyer, Vol. 9 (February 1992) at 21-23.

40. See K. Salwen, "White House to Proffer Ergonomic Rule for Workplaces, Employers' Liabilities," Wall Street J. (November 22, 1993) at B6.

41. See B. Fellner and E. Scalia, "Ergonomic Rules May Jump the Gun," National L.J. (October 25, 1993) at 17.

42. J. Moses, "Carpal-Tunnel Lawsuits Are Consolidated," Wall Street J. (June 3, 1992) at B8.

43. Heard v. Compaq, 91-38733 (334th Dist. Ct., Harris Co., Texas, 1994). See K. Pope, "Keyboard Users Say Makers Knew of Problems," Wall St. J. (May 4, 1994) at B1; G. Taylor, "Loss in First RSI Trial Viewed as First Step," National L.J. (March 21, 1994) at A9.

44. J. Moses, "Carpal-Tunnel Lawsuits Are Consolidated," Wall Street J. (June 3, 1992) at B8.

45. Mastalaski v. Int'l. Bus. Machines Corp., No. 92-1016 (4th Cir. August 28, 1992).

46. E. Leonard, T. Namuth, and M. Hager, "Typing without Keys," Newsweek (1992) at 63.

47. This design, called Datahand, is under development by Industrial Innovations, Inc. Ibid.

48. The protected rights include such things as (1) freedom to exist without physical interference to one's physical stature; (2) freedom of movement; (3) freedom from physical interference with one's real or personal property; and (4) freedom from interference with certain nonphysical personal interests, such as one's personal psychological constitution, personal privacy, and personal reputation.

49. These facts are based on the facts of Vosburg v. Putney, 80 Wis. 523, 50 N.W. 403 (1891).

50. Criminal Justice Manual of the Department of Justice, in S. Lipner and S. Kalman, Computer Law, Merrill Pub. Co., 1989, at 512-516; 531-539.

51. D. Johnson, T. Olson, and D. Post, "Computer Viruses: Legal and Policy Issues Facing Colleges and Universities," J. of Proprietary Rights (February 1990) at 5.

52. Werner, Zaroff, Slotnick, Stern and Askenazy v. Lewis, N.Y. Super. Ct. (August 3, 1992).

53. Clayton X-Ray Co., v. Professional Systems Corp., No. WD43583 (Mo. Ct. App., W.D. August 6, 1991).

54. Ibid. W. Bulkeley, "Drop Dead Function Gets the Ax in Court," Wall Street J. (May 8, 1989) at B1.

55. Shaw, Pittman, Potts, and Trowbridge, Technology Law Notes, (Summer 1991).

56. Cubby, Inc., v. CompuServe, Inc., No. 90 Civ. 6571 (PKL) (S.D.N.Y., October 29, 1991).

57. J. Moses and M. Miller, "Ruling Spares CompuServe from Libel Suits," Wall Street J. (October 31, 1991) at B1.

58  Moore v. Regents of the University of California, 793 P. 2d 479, 51 Cal. 3d 120 (Cal. 1990).

59. Employee Polygraph Protection Act of 1988, 29 U.S.C. §§2001 et seq. (1988).

60. Rhode Island laws bar drug testing unless drug use appears to be impairing an employee's job performance. The laws of Utah allow employers more leeway to test employees and applicants for drugs and permits them to fire employees who refuse to be tested or who test positive. W. Green, "Drug Testing Becomes Corporate Mine Field," Wall Street J. (November 21, 1989) at B1.

61. Skinner v. Railway Labor Executives' Assoc., 109 S. Ct. 1402 (1989); National Treasury Employees Union v. Von Raab, 109 S. Ct. 1384 (1989).

62. S. Sugawara, "When Privacy Goes to the Core of an Individual's Being," Washington Post Weekly, (July 13-19, 1992). See also M. Rothstein, "Discrimination Based on Genetic Information," 33 Jurimetrics (Fall 1992) at 13-18.

63. Human Genome Privacy Act of 1991, H.R. 2045.

64. A. Miller, J. Schwartz, and M. Rogers, "How Did They Get My Name?" Newsweek (June 3, 1991) at 41.

65. As of the end of 1993, privacy protection in the United States was probably more advanced under state laws and constitutions than under federal law. See, e.g., R. Boehmer and T. Palmer, "The 1992 EC Data Protection Proposal: An Examination of Its Implications for U.S. Business and U.S. Privacy Law," 31 American Business L.J. 265, 306 (September 1993).

66. A. Miller, J. Schwartz, and M. Rogers, "How Did They Get My Name?" Newsweek (June 3, 1991) at 42.

67. In 1992, a bill to enhance the privacy of consumer credit information reached the floor of the House of Representatives, but amendments weakened it so much that it was no longer acceptable to consumer advocates. In 1993, a similar legislative proposal was introduced that would have established safeguards to ensure the accuracy of credit information and would have prohibited credit bureaus from selling marketing lists to retailers and others without permission from the consumer. See A. Crenshaw, "When a Computer Error Renders You a Deadbeat," Washington Post Weekly Edition (November 1–7, 1993) at 17. In February 1994, the Consumer Reporting Reform Act of 1994 (H.R. 1015) was approved by the House of Representatives Banking Committee. However, again, the proposal represented a weakened version of what consumer advocates desired. See K. Kristof, "Credit-Reporting Reform Goes Astray in Bill," L.A. Times (March 13, 1994) at D4.

68. M. Miller, "FTC Takes Aim at Trans Union, TRW Mail Lists," Wall Street J. (January 13, 1993) at B1.

69. M. Geyelin, "Judge Tells Trans Union to Cease Giving Financial Data to Direct-Mail Marketers," Wall Street J. (September 27, 1993) at B2.

70. For thorough discussions of efforts to protect the privacy of data in Europe, see, e.g., R. Boehmer, "The 1992 EC Data Protection Proposal: An Examination of

Its Implication for U.S. Business and U.S. Privacy," 31 American Business L.J. 265 (September 1993); H. Pearson, "Data Protection in Europe," 8 Computer Lawyer (August 1991) at 24-29; J. Rosenbaum, "The European Commission's Draft Directive on Data Protection," 33 Jurimetrics (Fall 1992) at 1-12.

71. Amended Proposal for a Council Directive on the Protection of Individuals with Regard to the Processing of Personal Data and on the Free Movement of Such Data, COM(92)422 final 1992 [hereinafter 1992 EU Data Proposal]. The 1992 EU Data Proposal builds on guidelines, adopted in 1980 by the Organization for Economic Co-Operation and Development, that less comprehensively deals with the protection of privacy and transborder flows of personal data. Organization for Economic Co-Operation and Development (O.E.C.D.), "Recommendation of the Council Concerning Guidelines Governing the Protection of Privacy and Transborder Flows of Personal Data, O.E.C.D. Doc C(80) 58 final (October 1, 1980), reprinted in 20 I.L.M. 422 (1981). The United States is a member of the O.E.C.D.

72. 1992 EU Data Proposal, Article 6.

73. 1992 EU Data Proposal, Article 2(g) and Commentary 15.

74. 1992 EU Data Proposal, Article 7.

75. See R. Boehmer and T. Palmer, "The 1992 EC Data Protection Proposal: An Examination of Its Implications for U.S. Business and U.S. Privacy," 31 American Business L.J. 265 (September 1993) at 299.

76. 1992 EU Data Proposal, Article 11.

77. 1992 EU Data Proposal, Article 6.

78. 1992 EU Data Proposal, Article 12.

79. 1992 EU Data Proposal, Article 15.

80. 1992 EU Data Proposal, Article 13.

81. 1992 EU Data Proposal, Article 26.

82. J. Chalykoff and N. Nohria, "Note on Electronic Monitoring," Harvard Business School, Note #9-490-044 (2/15/90).

83. The Privacy for Consumers and Workers Act. For a thorough discussion of the provisions of this federal proposal, see J. Waks and C. Brewster, "Privacy Bill Targets Work Site Monitoring," National L.J. (January 18, 1993) at 20.

84. Pub. L. No. 99-508 (1986) codified at 18 U.S.C. §§2510 et seq.

85. 18 U.S.C. §2510 (12). Communication privacy laws of some states, such as Connecticut, protect cordless phone conversations as well. See State v. McVeigh, 224 Conn. 593, 620 A.2d 133 (1993).

86. See G. Rifkin, "Do Employees Have Right to Claim Electronic Privacy?" New York Times (December 8, 1991) at C8.

87. R. Resnick, "The Outer Limits," National L.J. (September 16, 1991) at 32-33.

88. For an excellent discussion of the ECPA and the responsibilities of system operators, see D. Johnson, "Electronic Communications Privacy: Good Sysops Should Build Good Fences," 6 Computer Lawyer (January 1989) at 26.

89. 18 U.S.C. §2701(c).

90. 18 U.S.C. §2702(b).

91. 18 U.S.C. §2701.
92. J. Olinern "An Employer's Right to Access an Employee's E-Mail," Technology Law Notes, Shaw Pittman, Potts and Trowbridge (Fall 1992).
93. See, e.g., R. Danca, "Privacy Act Would Force Firms to Inform Their Employees about E-Mail Monitoring," PC Week (June 28, 1993) at 203.
94. Manufacturers of communications equipment might be required, by law, to use only the Clipper Chip in their products. Or the government might make the use permissive but provide disincentives to select alternative chips. For instance, those not using the Clipper Chip could be denied government contracts or export licenses.
95. See, e.g., R. Hotz, "Demanding the Ability to Snoop," L.A. Times (October 3, 1993) at A1; S. Begley, M. Liu, and J. Ramo, "The Code of the Future," Newsweek (June 7, 1993) at 70; W. Schwartau, "Crypto Policy and Business Privacy," PC Week (June 28, 1993) at 207.
96. Midler v. Ford Motor Co., 849 F. 2d 460 (9th Cir. 1988), cert. denied, 112 S. Ct. 1513 (1992).
97. J. Lipman, "Soundalike Ads Should Sound Alarms in Wake of Court Ruling," Wall Street J. (March 26, 1992) at B8.
98. Ibid.
99. M. Rubiner, "Style Is One Thing, Defining It Is Another," New York Times (July 5, 1992) at H23.
100. D. Savage, "Letter of the Law: Court Says Vanna's Fame Is Her Fortune," L.A. Times (June 2, 1993) at A19; S. Barnett, "In Hollywood's Wheel of Fortune, Free Speech Loses a Turn," Wall Street J. (September 28, 1992) at A12.
101. Waits v. Frito-Lay, Inc., 978 F. 2d 1093 (9th Cir. 1992) cert. denied 113 S. Ct. 1047 (1993).
102. R. Harrington, "Rapper Sues Malt Brewer," Washington Post (August 28, 1991) at D7.

# 9

# KEY CONTRACT ISSUES FOR HIGH-TECHNOLOGY COMPANIES

## INTRODUCTION

This final chapter presents important issues which high-technology companies must consider when entering into contracts. The intent of the chapter is not to provide an exhaustive treatment of the subject. An entire book dedicated to the topic of contracts would barely suffice to cover even the most fundamental aspects of contract principles. The attempt, here, therefore is simply to familiarize the reader with a carefully selected set of the most pressing contract-related issues typically encountered by high-technology enterprises.

We first consider product warranties, a topic of critical importance for all sellers of high-technology goods. What are the standards of performance that the goods should be expected to meet? How can the seller precisely define the limits of those expectations in the contract? This section will address these important concerns. In addition, we will evaluate contract techniques that may be used to reduce the seller's monetary risks when the goods do not live up to standards promised under the warranty.

We will next review some representative contract issues raised when firms work together in what is often called a strategic alliance to develop, manufacture, and/or distribute high-technology products. Among other things, we will have an opportunity here to pull together certain of the intellectual property concepts that have been raised throughout this book. In addition, we will briefly examine alternative dispute resolution techniques. These methods, which strive to avoid litigation, have now proven their effectiveness, especially in situations when long-term business relationships are essential.

Following this discussion, we will take a look at how various contractual relationships typically entered by high-technology concerns may raise substantial antitrust concerns. Clearly, the antitrust scrutiny recently received by such firms as Microsoft, Intel, and Nintendo highlights the potential implications that antitrust may have on high-technology business strategies. Also, we will consider some of the special antitrust problems that may be raised when a company enjoys exclusive intellectual property rights in the marketplace.

For reference throughout this chapter, a very simplified sample software development agreement is provided in Appendix F. That sample is intended merely to demonstrate how some of the issues discussed in this chapter might be resolved in contractual form. The reader must understand that a comprehensive agreement would address many more topics, treating all of the relevant considerations with substantially more specificity than does this sample. Thus, one must take care not to rely on the sample as a checklist of all the important aspects of a software development contract. In addition, the language used in the sample has been greatly simplified so as to enhance its role as an educational tool. Therefore, neither its format nor any of its provisions should be used to draft legal documents.

## WARRANTIES, LIMITATIONS, AND REMEDIES

Purchasers of the AES will be very excited about the new addition to their home entertainment system. They likely will have a host of expectations about the product including what the capabilities of the product may be, under what conditions it will perform, and its durability. Some of these presumptions just come with the territory. One who buys an Audio Enhancement System naturally will expect it to improve the sound of a record collection to some reasonable degree. In addition, the purchaser will rightfully assume such things as that the product will not be damaged and that it will hold up under normal operating conditions. Other expectations may be derived from our statements and actions. Perhaps we made specific oral or written promises about how the AES would perform. Or maybe the sales staff gave certain assurances after learning what the customer wanted. It is even possible that salespeople demonstrated the performance of various features of the AES in a listening room environment, leading the customer to assume that the AES would perform the same at home. All of these scenarios involve implicit or explicit promises made to customers about the performance, qualities, and characteristics of the AES. Such promises are called warranties.

As mentioned in Chapter 1, contractual relationships are governed primarily by state law. Fortunately, all fifty states have adopted the Uniform Commercial Code (UCC) which was developed by legal experts to simplify, clarify, and modernize policies governing commercial transactions.[1] For this discussion regarding warranties, the important provisions are within Article 2, which deals with sales and licenses of goods.[2] In addition to Article 2, many states also have adopted more particularized legal codes dealing with warranties for consumer goods. For instance, when we sell the AES in California, not only must we be cognizant of the UCC, but also we must consider the Song-Beverly Consumer Warranty Act. Finally, sellers of consumer products, such as AES, are subject to federal law under the Magnuson-Moss Warranty Act, which imposes additional requirements when written warranties are made.[3] Magnuson-Moss is enforced by the Federal Trade Commission.

With respect to international transactions, the United States is a party to the Convention on Contracts for the International Sale of Goods (CISG), which has over 40 participants. The CISG applies to commercial contracts for the sale of goods when made between companies having their places of business in different nations that have ratified the convention.[4] The provisions of the CISG often are somewhat similar to those in the UCC. However, there are many technical differences that may be important, such as with risk of loss and the acceptance of offers. In addition, application of the CISG is limited to commercial transactions, whereas the UCC applies also to consumer sales. Warranties under the CISG are governed by Article 35. For the most part, warranties are treated the same under the CISG as with the UCC. Once again, though, there are some variations that could prove to be important. For example, the CISG provides merchants more flexibility in disclaiming implied warranties than does the UCC. The forthcoming treatment of warranties does not include consideration of the CISG. However, it should be clear that those engaging in international transactions must consult the CISG whenever it is applicable to their international dealings.

## Express Warranties

Express warranties consist of the actual promises made by the seller, whether communicated orally, in writing, by description, or through a demonstration. Article 2, Section 313, of the UCC explains that express warranties may arise in three ways. It provides:

1. Any affirmation of fact or promise made by the seller to the buyer which relates to the goods and becomes part of the basis of the bargain creates an express warranty that the goods shall conform to the affirmation or promise;

2. Any description of the goods which is made a part of the basis of the bargain creates an express warranty that the goods shall conform to the description;

3. Any sample or model which is made part of the basis of the bargain creates an express warranty that the whole of the goods shall conform to the sample or model.

Express warranties typically are incorporated in the written sales agreement or provided in writing with the goods. For instance, we may include with the AES written assurances that the product will exceed certain defined technical specifications, that it will be free of material defects for a specified length of time, or that it will improve the audio quality of certain types of recordings. However, this may not be the total extent of our express promises. The UCC provides that we do not have to formally declare that a promise is a warranty for it to serve as one. Thus, oral allegations made by salespersons that are more definitive than mere opinions come within the definition of express warranties. In addition, the aforementioned items (1) and (2) make it clear that descriptions in promotional literature and demonstrations of units at trade shows or in showrooms may lead to express warranties.

Providers of high-technology products and services prize a dedicated and hard-working sales staff. Often, remuneration schemes, such as those based on commissions, are established to ensure that marketing personnel have sufficient incentives to push the merchandise aggressively. Those involved in sales and marketing must be carefully trained about the statements and promises they make, for such allegations ultimately may bind the company as express warranties. However, even with careful training programs, there will be the occasional incident—such as an oral assurance that a desired objective can be obtained or a promotional booklet that highlights an unproven feature—resulting from an overwhelming desire to close a sale. Thus, most sophisticated sellers take steps to reduce their legal exposure from statements or demonstrations made by sales staff. High-technology sellers must understand how these steps might serve to protect the company. Purchasers in turn must be aware of them to ensure that promises made in the negotiation process actually survive the sale.

When we manufacture and market the AES, we have a strong desire to satisfy the expectations of our customers. We hope that our salespeople and distributors do not promise more than we can deliver, but we can never be sure, and in all likelihood some substantial mistakes or misunderstandings will arise. Our goal, therefore, is to maintain as much control as possible over the potential legal liabilities we may have to customers who allege that we have not fulfilled our promises. Our best means for accomplishing this is to clearly express in a written agreement precisely what the customer should expect from the AES and what our obligations are to fulfill these commitments.

One of the most important lessons about contract negotiations is to document in writing all the important aspects of a deal. In almost all negotiations, various issues are raised and discussed but not always clearly answered prior to closure of the transaction. Invariably, some of these issues will arise later on, leading to honest disputes about what the contracting parties actually promised each other. Although it may take more time to finalize the deal, it is far better for the parties to definitively address every conceivable issue that might affect their business relationship and clearly write down how they intend to handle those issues should they eventually materialize. Although this exercise may not reduce the physical problems that might occur, the clarity that it lends to expectations should result in more congenial solutions.

Beyond this practical reason for memorializing a deal in writing, there are legal reasons as well. The legal system has a strong preference for written contracts. Because proof about the existence and terms of oral agreements may come only from the memories and allegations of the individuals involved in the deal, oral arrangements raise the specter of dishonesty and fraud. For this reason, all states have passed laws that require certain types of contracts to be in writing if the parties wish to bring lawsuits regarding them.[5]

Far more important for this discussion, however, is how written contracts affect oral and even written statements made prior to finalization of a deal. In general terms, the policy is that once the parties finalize their agreement in writing, the writing takes substantial precedence over all previous promises. All prior (or contemporaneous) contradictory statements will be thrown out by a court if a dispute arises. A court might consider a supplementary promise, such as when a salesperson orally makes an additional warranty pledge, if the promise is otherwise consistent with the written terms in the final contract. However, if the parties indicate that the written contract is to be treated as the exclusive statement of the terms of the agreement, then even consistent statements made prior to the contract will be ignored by the courts.[6] Such contracts, called *integrated contracts*, are the key for the company to help control its warranty obligations. If the parties agree that their written contract is integrated, then the buyer cannot later allege that the seller made warranty promises that are not somehow contained within the four corners of the contract. This effectively means that statements and demonstrations made by salespersons may not be considered part of the express warranty terms of the deal if a dispute arises.

The following type of language in written contracts makes it clear that the agreement is to be treated as an integrated expression:

> This contract constitutes the complete and exclusive statement of the agreement between the parties and it supersedes all proposals, oral or written, and all other communications between the parties relating to the subject matter of this contract.

Companies intending to rely on integrated written contracts to control express warranties must always remember that the law ultimately will strive to protect the reasonable expectations of the parties. If one's goal is to take advantage of unsophisticated buyers by luring them with promises that are ultimately taken away in the final written agreement, then the purchasers likely will have legal recourse. Fraud, which was discussed in Chapter 8, provides one theory of liability, notwithstanding the integration clause in the written contract. In addition, some courts in egregious situations might decide that it is unconscionable to enforce the integration clause, thereby giving them the freedom to evaluate whether other promises were made that might not have been included in the final written expression.

The message from all this for the buyer should be very clear. When there is a written contract specifying the terms of an agreement—and there always should be—then the buyer should take care to ensure that the contract includes all important promises made by the seller during the sales negotiation process. Since the seller often uses a standard form contract, the buyer should require that an appendix be attached that clearly specifies any promises the seller made that the buyer considers to be a key aspect of the deal. Such allegations may have been made orally by salespeople, claimed in sales brochures, or indicated through sales demonstrations. Whatever the source, failure to include them in the written agreement may raise substantial obstacles if a dispute ever arises.

## Implied Warranties

In addition to any express warranties made by the seller, the UCC provides that the seller makes certain implied warranties simply by virtue that the transaction occurred. According to UCC Section 2-314, merchants who enter into a contract for the sale (or license) of goods imply in the contract that the goods will be merchantable. Here, a merchant is a person who regularly deals in the goods under consideration, a definition that clearly covers our company when we sell the AES.[7] In order for AES units to be considered merchantable, they should meet at least the following standards:

1. Be fit for the ordinary purposes for which such audio equipment is used.
2. Be adequately contained and packaged.
3. Conform to any promises made on the packaging.
4. Meet other standards expected from the way we deal with the AES or that ordinarily arise in the audio trade.

Besides the implied warranty pertaining to merchantability, we also may make an implied warranty that the goods are fit for a particular need or purpose expressed to us by the customer. UCC Section 2-315 states:

> Where the seller at the time of contracting has reason to know any particular purpose for which the goods are required and that the buyer is relying on the seller's skill or judgment to select or furnish suitable goods, there is . . . an implied warranty that the goods shall be fit for such purpose.

This situation could easily arise with the AES, as with all audio equipment. For instance, customers may explain to our salesperson that they are searching for a way to improve the sound quality of special records or that they will need to store the audio equipment in a very hot or moist environment or that the unit must be compatible with certain types of components. In all likelihood, the salesperson will know that customers are relying on the salesperson's superior knowledge and judgment about audio equipment to guide their decision. If the salesperson ultimately recommends and sells the AES knowing about these special needs, then by implication we have promised that the AES will satisfy them.

One final kind of implied warranty that may be important to sellers of high-technology goods is the warranty of title and against infringement.[8] When a company sells products incorporating intellectual property, then it implyingly promises that the product does not infringe the intellectual property rights of another. A purchaser of the AES, for instance, could be liable for patent infringement when using the machine if the machine contains patented technology owned by someone other than our company. If this ultimately damages certain customers, they could sue us for compensation.

Implied warranties are unattractive to manufacturers and sellers who wish to maximize control of potential liabilities stemming from alleged deficiencies in their products. Anytime a court has the flexibility to infer a promise from actions or a course of dealing, sellers are susceptible to unfavorable interpretations. This is particularly true with the implied warranty of fitness for a particular purpose, wherein liability can depend on the believability of testimony regarding the knowledge of the seller about the needs of the purchaser. Thus, manufacturers often strive to exclude the implied warranties so that they may be committed only to their express promises.

Under the UCC, all three kinds of implied warranties may be excluded. However, one must be careful to communicate the exclusion clearly to the purchaser by using appropriate language. In addition, one also must be mindful of state and federal consumer warranty laws that may affect one's ability to limit or exclude implied warranties.

One method to disclaim all implied warranties is to clearly state in the contract that the goods are sold "as is" or "with all faults." Generally, such language is used when the seller makes no warranties, either express or implied, regarding the products. However, this is not the method of choice, especially for sellers of new merchandise, for purchasers usually expect some level of warranty protection. You can imagine the response if we tried to sell new AES units "as is." The more common method is to clearly state express warranties and then particularly exclude the implied warranties. The most important requirement when using this method is that the exclusion be conspicuous. This means that a reasonable person in the buyer's position would not be surprised if later shown that the exclusion is in the contract. Typically, it is a good idea to print the exclusion close to the signature line, using a larger-size typeface than the rest of the contract and in bold print. The UCC also requires that the disclaimer of the implied warranty of merchantability must actually mention the word "merchantability." The following clause provides an example of how the implied warranties of merchantability and fitness can be effectively excluded in the contract:

TO THE EXTENT ALLOWED BY LAW, SELLER HEREBY DISCLAIMS ALL IMPLIED WARRANTIES, INCLUDING, BUT NOT LIMITED TO, THE IMPLIED WARRANTIES OF MERCHANTABILITY AND FITNESS FOR A PARTICULAR PURPOSE.

Since the AES is a consumer product, we will have to comply with the federal Magnuson-Moss Act and possibly state consumer warranty laws if we wish to reduce our exposure to implied warranties. The Magnuson-Moss Act states that if we make a written express warranty, then that warranty must be either a Full Warranty or a Limited Warranty, as those terms are defined by the act. For our purposes, the major difference is that implied warranties may not be limited or excluded if a Full Warranty is provided. Thus, assuming we wish to control this aspect, we will have to provide a Limited Warranty. Even with this, however, we are not able to fully exclude the implied warranties. Rather, we may only limit their duration to either the length of our express warranty or a reasonable amount of time, whichever is longer. In addition, we must indicate in a conspicuous way that the laws of certain states may give different rights with respect to limitations on implied warranties. In California, for instance, the Song-Beverly Consumer Warranty Act allows implied warranties to be coextensive in duration with the express warranties, but in no event less than 60 days. Other states may be even more restrictive, possibly not allowing any limitation at all. According to the Magnuson-Moss Act, our disclaimer of implied warranties must conspicuously inform purchasers of their potential rights under state laws with the following language:

> SOME STATES DO NOT ALLOW LIMITATIONS ON HOW LONG AN IMPLIED WARRANTY LASTS, SO THE ABOVE LIMITATION MAY NOT APPLY TO YOU.

In sum, the best course is to provide written express warranties and to disclaim implied warranties as much as possible. With consumer products, however, one will have to conform this strategy both to the federal Magnuson-Moss Act and to appropriate state consumer warranty laws.

## Remedies for Breach of Warranties and Limitations of Remedies

**Compensatory Damages.** When an AES unit does not work as warranted, the buyer likely will suffer damages. For instance, one important warranted feature of the AES is that it improves sound quality to a defined degree according to some technical measure. If that improvement is not achieved with a purchased machine, then the buyer has not received the product for which that buyer bargained and paid. In this case, our company should have to compensate for this damage. For instance, assume a consumer could have purchased a competing brand for $500. However, the customer opted for our StatFree brand, even with its $1,300 price tag, because we warranted that it could achieve a 14-ptu quality boost while the competitor's model could yield an improvement of only 10 ptus. If it turns out that our customer's StatFree delivers only a 10-ptu increase, then the buyer clearly has suffered damage. The extent of the damage depends on how one looks at the situation. On one hand, the buyer paid $800 more for the machine than it is worth. On the other, the buyer paid $1,300 with the expectation of receiving a 14-ptu quality improvement. Damages could be considered the difference between what was promised and what actually was received. If it turns out that in reality, a 14-ptu machine is worth something much more than $1,300, say $5,000, then the buyer has suffered $4,500 in damages, representing the difference in the value of what was expected ($5,000) and the value of what was obtained ($500).

Damages for breach of warranty are covered by the UCC in Article 2, Section 714, which provides that the measure of damages for breach of warranty is the difference between the value of the goods accepted and the value they would have had if they had been as warranted. Thus, the calculation of damages under the UCC is based on the expectations raised by the warranty. In the foregoing situation, this amount could be $800, assuming our sales price represented the actual market value of a 14-ptu machine. However, as noted before, the figure could be somewhat higher, if what we promised actually is worth more than the $1,300 we charged.

You probably can begin to see how this could be troublesome for our small company, especially if a large number of units end up being distributed with this deficiency. If numerous claims for $800 or more arise, we may not have the cash available to satisfy them. Proceeds from sales may have already been spent to satisfy creditors and investors or may have been invested in new inventory. Under these circumstances, replacing the unit would be a better alternative, assuming the customer would allow us to remedy the situation in this way. It also is possible that we could fix the units fairly easily if the customers simply sent them back to us and waited a week or two. And, of course, if that nightmare occurs wherein only models costing $5,000 will perform as we warranted, then we will be liable for far more than even our total sales proceeds. However, according to the UCC, the customer may seek the monetary award unless we take steps in the contract to control the remedies for breach of warranty.

As a seller, we certainly would like to come to some understanding about the ways that a dissatisfied customer may remedy the situation. For instance, we would want the customer to agree that we should have the opportunity to repair or replace the model rather than our having to pay monetary compensation. Presumably, if those efforts cannot achieve the performance warranted, then we would have to satisfy the customer with money. Our fear then is what the value of the warranted product ultimately may be determined to be—potentially $5,000 as described earlier. To alleviate this concern, we also want the customer to agree that our maximum responsibility is to return the purchase price should we fail in our efforts to repair or replace the unit satisfactorily.

Fortunately, the UCC, in Section 719, allows us to reach such agreements with our customers. Section 719 provides that the agreement may provide for other types of remedies such as (1) return of the goods and repayment of the purchase price or (2) repair and replacement of nonconforming goods. This section also allows us to limit the available remedies solely to those provided for in the agreement as long as we expressly provide that they are exclusive. Thus, we are given a lot of room to fashion the purchaser's remedies to meet our needs. However, this right is not unlimited. Section 719 provides that when circumstances cause an exclusive or limited remedy *to fail of its essential purpose*, then the buyer may resort to the remedies normally available under the code. In other words, we ultimately must be able to satisfy the buyer in a reasonable fashion. For instance, our contract might provide that we will repair or replace the unit so that the customer receives the performance warranted. If after a reasonable number of attempts we are unable to provide a unit conforming to the warranty, then our remedy has failed of its essential purpose. In this case, the buyer is entitled to the compensation needed to fulfill expectations under the bargain.

One way to soften the sting of this result is to provide a fallback remedy in the agreement that becomes effective if our efforts to repair or replace fail. Again, though, one must keep in mind that the fallback must be reasonable. Therefore, to be somewhat extreme, one might consider a clause stating that if repairs are not effective, the buyer is entitled to $1. Clearly, this would be unreasonable and would make the entire remedy fail of the essential purpose. Obviously, by doing this, we are trying to make the buyer bear the total responsibility for the deficiency in our product. This is the type of solution we must avoid. Rather, our fallback remedy should provide for the return of the entire purchase price or of some amount of compensation that is reasonable under the circumstances. The following is an example of an effective remedy limitation with a reasonable fallback provision:

> If the product does not conform to the warranty, Seller shall at its sole and absolute option repair the product at no charge or replace the product with the same model or its equivalent at no charge. If, after repeated efforts, Seller is unable to provide correction for the nonconformity, then Buyer's exclusive remedy and Seller's entire liability is to refund the amounts paid by Buyer to Seller upon return of the product to Seller.

**Consequential Damages.** The foregoing discussion focused on damages to the buyer because the AES we delivered was not worth as much as we promised. However, there are other ways that a purchaser could be damaged that potentially could be far more costly. For example, suppose some of the AES machines somehow erased or damaged records even though we promised that the machine would have no effect on prerecorded material. Unfortunately, one of the purchasers just happened to have a particularly treasured collection of old classical and jazz LPs and did not discover the problem until most of them had been played. Clearly, this buyer not only will demand that the defect be repaired but also will want to be compensated for the other dire consequences from our breach of warranty—and under the circumstances, this could total thousands of dollars, even though we received only $1,300 in payment for the machine. As another example, consider a buyer who made it clear to the salesperson that the StatFree was going to be the central feature of a new kind of '50s nightclub premised on the premier sound quality of music performed by the original artists. Since much of this music is available only on LP format, the concept depends on the StatFree's working as warranted. If the Statfree does not perform adequately and the nightclub fails, the owner may blame us for the demise and expect compensation for all the losses on the project. One final illustration involves a buyer who is severely electrocuted by a damaged power cord, even though we warranted that the product would be free of material safety defects. Obviously, damages of these kinds, which are called consequential damages, may be staggering.

Section 714 provides that a buyer not only is entitled to compensation for loss of the benefit of the bargain but also may receive incidental and consequential damages. Of these, consequential damages is by far the most important and threatening. According to Section 715 of the UCC, consequential damages include:

1. losses resulting from general or particular requirements and needs of the buyer about which the seller had reason to know and which could not be reasonably prevented by the buyer; and
2. injuries to persons or property which the seller knew or reasonably should have known would have resulted from any breach of warranty.

This definition covers all of the scenarios presented earlier. Therefore, we could be liable by our breach of warranty for potentially enormous consequential damage awards unless we are able to limit or exclude our exposure to them through the contract. Again, the UCC provides us some flexibility in this regard. Section 719 provides:

> Consequential damages may be limited or excluded unless the limitation or exclusion is unconscionable. Limitation of consequential damages for injury to the person in the case of consumer goods is prima facie unconscionable but limitation of damages where the loss is commercial is not.

Following this, we do have the ability to limit or exclude our liability for consequential damages. However, we need to keep a few issues in mind. First, the limitation cannot be *unconscionable* under the circumstances. The types of scenarios that might make the limitation unconscionable are hard to classify. However, one might envision a spectrum running from "certainly unconscionable" to "clearly not unconscionable." The clause defines one scenario that is certainly unconscionable: that involving a consumer good that causes personal injury. Therefore, we will not be able to limit our exposure for the power cord mishap with the AES. At the other extreme would be situations involving agreements between commercial parties having equal bargaining power. For those situations in the middle ground, characteristics that are often relevant include (1) the sophistication of the buyer, (2) whether the buyer read and understood the ramifications of the limitation, and (3) how much power the buyer was able to exercise in bargaining for changes in the contract.

The second issue to consider regarding consequential damages is that some states have adopted laws that are more restrictive than the UCC, especially when dealing with consumer goods. A seller has to pay attention to particular state laws, such as the Song-Beverly Act in California, before attempting to limit the ability of buyers to recover consequential (or incidental) damages. Indeed, the federal Magnuson-Moss Act requires the following statement to conspicuously appear on the face of a warranty for consumer products:

> SOME STATES DO NOT ALLOW THE EXCLUSION OR LIMITATION OF INCIDENTAL OR CONSEQUENTIAL DAMAGES, SO THE ABOVE LIMITATION OR EXCLUSION MAY NOT APPLY TO YOU.

Sellers who wish to limit their exposure to consequential damages must deal with one other area of uncertainty. Section 719 of the UCC is somewhat ambiguous about what happens to a consequential damage limitation if an exclusive remedy fails of its essential purpose. For instance, it is typical for a seller to have an exclusive remedy of repair or replacement along with a limitation of consequential damages. If the seller ultimately is unable to repair or replace the product satisfactorily, then that remedy has failed of its essential purpose. Does that mean that the limitation of consequential damages has also failed? After all, the buyer may have agreed to the restriction on consequential damages on the assumption that the unit ultimately would work as warranted. Under these circumstances, one might argue that it is unconscionable to enforce the limitation on consequential damages. The courts vary widely on this issue. Some are inclined to package the exclusive remedy with the limitation on consequential damages, so that when the exclusive remedy fails, the consequential damage limitation is thrown out with it.[9] Others treat the subjects more discretely. In these courts, there are circumstances in which an exclusive remedy could fail of its essential purpose while a limitation on consequential damages remains conscionable. The following case, which takes this latter position, thoughtfully explores the interrelationships between exclusive remedies and consequential damage limitations.

## CHATLOS SYSTEMS, INC. V. NATIONAL CASH REGISTER CORPORATION

*Third Circuit Court of Appeals, 1980*

### Facts

Chatlos Systems designs and manufactures cable pressurization equipment for the telecommunications industry. NCR designs, manufactures, and sells computer systems, programming, and services. In 1974, Chatlos wished to purchase a computer system to modernize its control of data. After Chatlos discussed its business operations with Sam Long, an NCR salesman, Long recommended that Chatlos acquire the NCR 399 Magnetic Ledger Card System (399 MAG). Long represented that the 399 MAG could provide six functions: accounts receivable, payroll, order entry, inventory deletion, state income tax, and cash receipts. NCR also informed Chatlos that the 399 MAG could be upgraded with a more advanced disc storage system while still being able to perform the same functions as the 399 MAG. NCR also represented that the more advanced disc system was a good investment, would be programmed by capable NCR personnel, and would be "up and running" within six months.

Relying on these statements, Chatlos decided, in 1974, to acquire the disc system. To finance the system, a bank purchased the computer and then leased it to Chatlos for $70,162.09, which was to be paid in 66 equal payments. Chatlos also entered a service agreement for $5,621.22. Based on the representations of NCR, Chatlos expected the machine to be fully operational by March 1975.

The payroll program became operational in March 1975. When NCR next attempted to install the inventory deletion and order entry programs, incompatibilities with the disc system made these functions inoperative. After some personnel changes, NCR assured Chatlos that the computer would be fully operational. In March 1976, NCR analysts attempted to demonstrate the order entry and accounts receivable functions, but the test revealed substantial problems. In August 1976, Chatlos experienced problems with the payroll function, the only job the computer had been performing. This problem was corrected. In September 1976, NCR announced that it was ready to install the order entry program. Chatlos would not accept the program and sent a letter to NCR asking that the lease be canceled and that the computer be removed. NCR refused, stating that the computer was owned by the bank. Chatlos sued NCR for breach of warranty and fraud.[10]

The district court determined that NCR had breached express warranties. The equipment contract specifically warranted the equipment for "12 months after delivery against defects in material workmanship and operational failure from ordinary use." Also, the service agreement provided, "NCR warrants that the services will be performed in a skillful and workmanlike manner." In addition, Mr. Long, the NCR salesperson, had made verbal warranties that were memorialized in the written contract as follows: "Since the above goods are purchased by us expressly for the use of the Lessee [Chatlos], you [NCR] further warrant that the goods are in good working order, fit for the use for which the Lessee intends them."

NCR also made an implied warranty of fitness by recommending the disc system for Chatlos's purposes, under circumstances wherein it was well aware that Chatlos was relying on NCR's skill and judgment. This implied warranty of fitness also was breached, according to the district court.

The contract had an exclusive remedy clause, which stated that "NCR's obligation is limited to correcting any error in any program as appears within 60 days after such has been furnished." The contract also provided that "in no event shall NCR be liable for special or consequential damages from any cause whatsoever." The district court determined that NCR's remedy had failed of its essential purpose and had deprived Chatlos of the substantial value of its bargain. It therefore found NCR liable for damages from breach of warranty and consequential damages.

The district court determined that the damages from breach of warranty were $57,152.76. This was determined by subtracting the value of the goods received from the value that the goods would have had without a breach. The district court found that the expected value of the goods equaled their cost, including interest embedded in the bank lease ($75,783.31). The value of the goods received was $18,630.55. The district court also awarded consequential damages of $63,558.16, consisting mostly of employee, executive, and profit losses.

## Opinion

An exclusive or limited remedy must be viewed against the backdrop of U.C.C. 2-719(2), which provides, "Where circumstances cause an exclusive or limited remedy to fail of its essential purpose, remedy may be had as provided in this Act." This section requires analysis of the applicable remedy so as to determine its essential purpose and whether it has failed of that purpose. Several goals of the limited remedy of repair may be envisioned, but its primary objective is to give the seller an opportunity to make the goods conform while limiting exposure to risk by excluding liability for damages that otherwise might be due. Viewed from the buyer's standpoint, the repair remedy's aim is to provide goods that conform to the contract for sale and do so at an appropriate time. A delay in supplying the remedy can just as effectively deny the purchaser the product expected as can the total inability to repair. In both instances, the buyer loses the substantial benefit of the purchase.

To be effective, the repair remedy must be provided within a reasonable time after discovery of the defect. It is not necessary to show negligence or bad faith on the part of the seller. The detriment to the buyer is the same whether the seller diligently but unsuccessfully attempts to honor the promise or acts negligently or in bad faith.

This case considers a product programmed specifically to meet a customer's individual needs. Time was of substantial importance. Chatlos realized that the increasing scale of its operations required computerization and it undertook the investment in 1974 because added efficiency was needed at that time. NCR represented to Chatlos that a six-function system would be up and running by March 1975. Yet, more than one year later than that, only one of the functions was in operation, and by September 1976, less than half of the desired capabilities of the system was available to Chatlos.

NCR repeatedly attempted to correct the deficiencies in the system; but nevertheless, a year and a half after Chatlos had reasonably expected a fully operational computer, NCR still had not provided the product warranted. In these circumstances, the delay made the correction remedy ineffective, and it therefore failed of its essential purpose. Consequently, the contractual limitation was unenforceable and did not preclude recovery of damages for the breach of warranty.

This conclusion, however, does not dispose of the contractual clause excluding consequential damages. Section 2-719(3) provides:

> Consequential damages may be limited or excluded unless the limitation or exclusion is unconscionable. Limitation of consequential damages for injury to the person in the case of consumer goods is prima facie unconscionable but limitation of damages where the loss is commercial is not.

Several cases have held that when a limited remedy fails of its purpose, an exclusion of consequential damages also falls, but approximately the same number of decisions have treated the preclusion as a separate matter. It appears to us that the better-reasoned approach is to treat the consequential damage disclaimer as an independent provision, valid unless unconscionable.

The limited remedy of repair and a consequential damage exclusion are two discrete ways of attempting to limit recovery for breach of warranty. The U.C.C., moreover, tests each by a different standard. The former survives unless it fails of its essential purpose, while the latter is valid unless it is unconscionable.

Whether the preclusion of consequential damages should be effective in this case depends upon the circumstances involved. The repair remedy's failure of essential purpose, while a discrete question, is not completely irrelevant to the issue of the conscionability of enforcing the consequential damages exclusion. The latter term is merely an allocation of unknown or undeterminable risks. Recognizing this, the question here narrows to the unconscionability of the buyer's retaining the risk of consequential damages upon the failure of the essential purpose of the exclusive repair remedy.

One fact in this case that becomes significant under the U.C.C. is that the claim is not for personal injury but for property damage. Limitations on damages for personal injuries are not favored, but no such prejudice applies to property losses. It is also important that the claim is for commercial loss and the adversaries are substantial business concerns. We find no great disparity in the parties' bargaining power or sophistication. Apparently, Chatlos, a manufacturer of complex electronic equipment, had some appreciation of the problems that might be encountered with a computer system. Nor is there a surprise element here. The limitation was clearly expressed in a short, easily understandable sales contract. This is not an instance of an ordinary consumer's being misled by a disclaimer hidden in a linguistic maze.

From the perspective of the later events, it appears that the type of damage claimed here came within the realm of expectable losses. Some disruption of normal business routines, expenditure of employee time, and impairment of efficiency cannot be considered highly unusual or unforeseeable in a faulty computer installation. Moreover, this is not a case where the seller acted unreasonably or in bad faith. In short, there is nothing in the formation of the contract or the circumstances resulting in the failure of performance that makes it unconscionable to enforce the parties' allocation of risk. We conclude, therefore, that the provision of the agreement excluding consequential damages should be enforced, and the district court erred in making an award of such losses.

Chatlos argues that, in assessing damages, the district court erred by equating the value of the goods accepted with their cost. Chatlos contends that the correct standard is market value, an amount its expert testified was substantially in excess of the contract price. To use contract price, in this case, Chatlos argued, deprives it of the benefit of its bargain. We agree that fair market value is the most appropriate measure of the value of the goods as guaranteed. The district court also erred by including the interest paid to the bank in its determination of the value of the goods as warranted. In the absence of special circumstances, interest is not a proper factor to be considered.

Accordingly, the judgment of the district court is affirmed insofar as it imposes liability on NCR to pay damages to Chatlos. The case is remanded for a redetermination of the amount of damages.

---

Companies that provide exclusive remedies along with consequential damages limitations certainly want a court to enforce the consequential damage restriction when the exclusive remedy fails. Certain steps can make it more likely that a court will do this. The best means is to ensure that the exclusive remedy does not fail. Having an effective backup remedy may be helpful in this regard. Also, the seller should make it very clear in the contract that the two issues are considered to be separate and discrete aspects of the deal. To this end, the contract should provide the consequential damage limitation in a clause that is separate from the one providing the exclusive remedy. Packaging them in the same paragraph may lead a court to believe that the two should be treated together. Also, the consequential damage limitation should expressly state that the parties intend the limitation to remain effective even if the exclusive remedy fails. Such language clearly demonstrates how the parties intended to allocate the risks of the venture, especially if they are both sophisticated in commercial matters.

**Exhibit 9.1  Warranties: Important Considerations**

## Applicable Laws

- Uniform Commercial Code (UCC), Article 2
- Magnuson-Moss Warranty Act
  — Federal Trade Commission
- State consumer warranty laws
- International laws and conventions
  — Convention on Contracts for the International Sale of Goods

## Express Warranties

- UCC, 2-313
- Importance of integrated contracts

## Implied Warranties

- Merchantability
  — UCC, 2-314
- Fitness for a particular purpose
  — UCC, 2-315
- Title and against infringement
  — UCC, 2-312

## Exclusion of Implied Warranties

- UCC, 2-316
  — Conspicuous
- Consumer products
  — Magnuson-Moss Warranty Act
    = Limited warranty
    = Implied warranties may be limited in duration but not excluded
  — State consumer warranty law

## Remedies

- Compensatory damages
  — UCC, 2-714
  — Benefit of the bargain
- Consequential damages
  — UCC, 2-715

## Limitation of Remedies

- UCC, 2-719
- Alternative remedy may not fail of its essential purpose.
  — Repair or replacement
  — Fallback remedy
    = Return of payments made
- Limitation of consequential damages may not be unconscionable.
  — Consumer goods and personal injuries
- State consumer warranty laws

## STRATEGIC ALLIANCES: INTELLECTUAL PROPERTY AND OTHER CONCERNS

There are numerous business concepts that currently have aroused the interest of the press. "Competitiveness" and "total quality management" provide two notable illustrations. Another favorite is the growing importance of "strategic alliances" or "strategic partnering." As with the other terms, the notion of a strategic alliance is somewhat vague. On one level, people often are simply referring to a spirit of working together. However, on a more important plane, strategic alliances constitute a growing trend by companies to join forces in relatively long term formal ventures to pursue common goals.

The move toward forming strategic alliances appears to be especially important in high-technology industries. A 1992 survey of CEOs in the electronics industry states that "[a]lliance building now is fundamental to the way U.S. electronics companies conduct business."[11] According to this survey, around 80% of the electronics companies have entered alliances, and most CEOs are planning or negotiating new ones. One of the most consistent headline business topics of 1993 was the formation of strategic alliances between telecommunications, computer, and media corporate giants with the goal of developing interactive multimedia capabilities.[12] Visionaries in this field anticipate an information superhighway that will be utilized most successfully by those companies involved in the development, coordination, and control of three essential components of the multimedia arena: media content (e.g., films, books, photographs), delivery (e.g., cable, cellular, satellite), and interactive technologies (e.g., software, control devices). A sample of these budding multimedia business relationships includes alliances between: (1) Sega, Time Warner, and Tele-Communications, Inc. (TCI); (2) Microsoft, Intel, and General Instrument; (3) 3DO, MCA, AT&T, and Time Warner; (4) QVC, TCI, and Liberty Media; and (5) US West and Time Warner.[13]

The computer field has been a source of alliances for years, including the notable links between (1) Apple Computer, IBM, and Motorola to develop a new family of microprocessors called PowerPC as well as an operating system called Taligent; (2) Apple Computer and Sharp Electronics to develop a handheld computer called a Personal Digital Assistant; (3) Texas Instruments, Hewlett-Packard, Canon, and the Singapore Economic Development Board to manufacture dynamic random-access memory chips (DRAMs); (4) Motorola and Toshiba, also to develop DRAMs; and (5) IBM, Toshiba, and Siemens AG, once again to develop DRAMs. SEMATECH, a consortium consisting of 14 U.S. computer chip makers, is another important example of a high-technology strategic venture.

High-technology concerns may enter strategic alliances for a variety of reasons. The following list indicates just some of the possible benefits that a company might seek from a strategic alliance.[14] It should be clear from the list that a partner likely is attempting to benefit from a few, but not all, of the items on the list. In addition, each partner may be entering a particular strategic relationship to achieve different long-term goals.

- *Acquisition of technology*: An alliance may be formed to gain access to technologies or to combine technologies.

- *Tapping of manufacturing capacity*: One may prefer to use the existing plant and equipment of another firm rather than make the investment independently.
- *Access to Distribution*: The importance of distribution channels for high-technology products may lead one to seek out a partner with established networks.
- *Risk and Cost Sharing*: With a particularly risky venture, it might make sense to join forces with other firms to share the costs of the enterprise.
- *Access to Capital*: The need for money often is a motivation for strategic alliances.
- *Geographic Expansion*: A strategic alliance with firms doing business in other regions may be a way to more quickly and easily enter these areas. In the international environment, this may be especially helpful in countries that have concerns about ventures run by foreigners.
- *Marketing*: Strategic alliances may further marketing objectives in various ways. Joining forces with a company having a solid reputation may improve the chances of raising public awareness and acceptance of the technology. Or one might expand the product line with complementary products or services to better meet the needs of consumers.
- *Reduction of Infringement Risks*: Uncertainties about the extent of intellectual property rights owned by another company, for example in software, may make an alliance with that company attractive. This may prevent that company from bringing a costly litigation action when one plans to develop or sell similar technology.
- *Prevention of Competitors' Access to Technology*: One might consider an alliance as a defensive measure in order to keep competitors from being able to use important technologies.

When one enters a strategic alliance, there are a whole spectrum of legal issues that must be considered. What business structure will the alliance take? The partners may choose to stay separate, forming the team solely through contract. Or they may opt to unify the relationship under the umbrella of a more formal structure, such as a partnership, joint venture, or corporation. The decision will rest on such variables as tax considerations, liability concerns, the expected length of the relationship, the manner that resources may be pooled, and the extent that risks will be shared. For some of these forms, securities laws will have to be consulted. In addition, as we shall see later in this chapter, the parties should review how the antitrust laws might bear on the arrangement. As you surmised, the allocation of risks and liabilities between the parties, including such things as warranties and limits on liabilities, will be crucial decisions in forming a successful alliance. Also, since intellectual property rights undoubtedly will be involved, substantial decisions will have to be made regarding their ownership and protection. In addition, since partners often have the expectation of entering the alliance for the long haul, they should give serious thought about the ways disputes will be resolved should they arise. And, of course, if the alliance plans to move into international circles, an overlay of additional complex issues arises, such as customs regulations, export and technology transfer controls, foreign ownership restrictions, and foreign political practices.

When considering these legal issues, those involved in the alliance must never lose sight of the strategic business concerns and objectives that led the parties to contemplate the union in the first place. For example, if the goal of the alliance is to create a new technological standard upon which other companies will build their products, then it might make sense to make the technology freely available rather than tightly controlling it through intellectual property protection licenses. Also, the partners must be very wary of the distinct corporate cultures of each of the participants in the alliance. One only has to look at the computer industry to understand how these differences can affect the relationship between partners in an alliance. Some companies in the computer field have a culture that supports trade secret protection and the substantial security measures required to implement it. Employees in these firms generally accept the importance of various security measures and are willing to put up with certain physical impediments and intrusions on privacy. Other companies take more of a maverick approach, encouraging employees to freely share and use their ideas with little corporate scrutiny. Such differences must be recognized before these companies form a strategic alliance, especially if they will need to share trade secrets in the arrangement. As you can imagine, employees in the maverick company are likely to reject and ignore the demands for security that the more protective company naturally will want implemented. Clearly, the participants in a successful strategic alliance must not only grasp the business and economic issues supporting the effort but also must fully consider the human and cultural implications of the partnership as well.

Suppose we decide that our company cannot develop, manufacture, market, and distribute audio components using the AES technology successfully on its own. In particular, we need help in developing the software, and we require partners for product design, manufacturing, and sales. After extensive negotiations, we determine that SoftWave Corporation is best suited to develop the software that will control certain basic functions of the AES and that Scherer Audio Company has the skill and capacity to design, manufacture, and market AES products using our technology and SoftWave's software. We decide that we will keep our business entities separate and will handle the partnering through contracts.

There are a multitude of contract issues that must be evaluated by all three parties to this arrangement. Indeed, the contracts should spell out with great detail how the parties expect to handle every aspect of the deal. What specific tasks is each supposed to perform for the others? When are the tasks supposed to be completed? When is payment required? Is there a period for testing the products, and how will it be determined if the tests have been passed? Is one party responsible for training the others to use or install software or components? How, from where, and by whom will ultimate products be distributed to consumers? When does the relationship end? The parties should have answered these and a litany of other questions in their contracts before engaging in operations. Although all of these considerations are vitally important, they are not the subject of this discussion. Rather, the attempt here will be to resurrect some of the intellectual property and liability issues already raised in previous chapters of this book. In addition, we will consider alternative methods to resolve disputes other than formal litigation in the traditional court systems. Such possibilities, called alternative dispute resolution (ADR) techniques, have become an increasingly important aspect of strategic partnering arrangements in high-technology fields.

## Patent Issues

We learned in Chapters 2 and 3 that we can receive patents for computer software and machines that use software. In developing the AES, many patent issues may arise, particularly between SoftWave and ourselves. If SoftWave develops patentable software, that company likely will be considered the inventor. Thus, SoftWave will have to file the patent applications. However, we still must deal with the very important issue of ownership. If we wish to control the patent on the software, then SoftWave will have to agree to assign the patent to us. This will be very important if we integrate the software into a patentable AES machine or process. If SoftWave owns the patent on the software, then we will have to negotiate a license to use the invention in the AES. Otherwise, our product or process, although patentable, would infringe SoftWave's patent. Similarly, we need to address with SoftWave which company will own any software improvements that might be created in the future.

Since we are dealing with potentially patentable inventions, all the parties should agree to take the requisite steps to verify dates of invention and diligent conception to practice. In addition, we need to work out who will undertake the responsibility to file for and obtain the patents in the United States and abroad. Obviously, as part of this, we must address how the parties expect to pay for the expenses that will be incurred in these efforts. In addition, we have to take care in the contracts to ensure that the participants do not carelessly destroy the chances for international patent protection. For instance, we might want to put certain constraints on Scherer to not market the product until an international application is filed with the PTO.

In our arrangement, the technology essentially is developed by SoftWave and our company, while Scherer is in charge of product design and marketing. A typical transaction might have our company (along with SoftWave, if necessary) license the technology to Scherer with the understanding that Scherer is to pay a sizable royalty based on a percentage of its ultimate sales revenues. Disputes often arise from this form of agreement when the marketing firm ends up shelving the technology, thereby yielding no return to the inventors. This is especially true when the technology license is given exclusively, because then the inventors are dependent solely on the success of the marketer. The inventors may feel aggrieved, believing that the marketer failed to try hard enough to push the technology. Perhaps other projects overburdened the firm, causing it to neglect the invention. The following case points out how the courts attempt to handle the equities of these situations.

## PERMANENCE CORPORATION V. KENNAMETAL, INC.

*Sixth Circuit Court of Appeals, 1990*

### Facts

In the 1970s, Permanence conducted research and manufactured products in the tungsten carbide field. In 1977, Permanence obtained a patent (Patent 902) for a process to form an alloy by incorporating tungsten carbide into a steel matrix.

On February 8, 1979, Permanence signed an agreement with Kennametal, a corporation specializing in the manufacture of tools, tooling systems, and supplies for the metalworking industry. In the contract, Permanence granted Kennametal the nonexclusive right to the Patent 902 and others that were pending. For that nonexclusive license, Kennametal agreed to pay Permanence a $150,000 fee and a royalty rate of 2¾% on the net sales price of products made by Kennametal using processes that fell under valid claims of the licensed patents. The contract also required Kennametal to pay $100,000 in advance royalties for the nonexclusive license.

The agreement additionally provided that Kennametal had the option to obtain an exclusive license to the patents, which could be exercised within 24 months. Kennametal agreed that to exercise the option, it would pay Permanence a second $150,000 fee and a second $100,000 in advanced royalties. Under the exclusive license, the royalty rate would be 3½%. Kennametal also agreed that if the option were not exercised within 24 months, it would pay a royalty rate of 3½% for the continuation of nonexclusive license rights.

On February 8, 1979, Kennametal paid the up-front fee of $150,000 and $100,000 as advance royalties for the nonexclusive license. On February 5, 1981, Kennametal exercised its option and paid an additional $250,000 for the grant of the exclusive license—$150,000 for the exercise of the option and another $100,000 in advance royalties.

Seven years later, in 1988, Permanence sued Kennametal, alleging that it had breached the contract by not fulfilling an obligation to use best-efforts to exploit the patents. As there was no best-efforts provision in the contract, Permanence argued that the grant of an exclusive license imposed on Kennametal an implied duty to use best efforts. Kennametal asked the district court judge to dismiss the case, arguing that it had spent $500,000 for the use of the patented technology and that a best-efforts obligation had specifically been negotiated out of the agreement. The district court judge determined that a best-efforts obligation could not be implied from the contract and dismissed the case. Permanence appealed this ruling.

### Opinion

Although the term "best efforts" is often used to describe an implied duty of activity, a more accurate description of the obligation owed would be the exercise of "due diligence" or "reasonable efforts." Permanence's basis for its legal theory that Kennametal had a best-efforts obligation is founded on the landmark case

*Wood v. Lucy, Lady Duff-Gordon.* There, a fashion designer gave the plaintiff the exclusive privilege of marketing its designs. The court implied an obligation to exploit the design, although there was not an express obligation to do so in the contract, because the designer's sole revenue from the exclusive grant was to be derived from plaintiff's clothing sales. The designer, thus, was at plaintiff's mercy. In subsequent cases, an obligation to employ best efforts has generally been implied in contracts in which the only consideration for a grant of property lies in the payment of royalties.

In cases such as *Wood*, courts have found it necessary to imply a covenant to employ best efforts because otherwise the contract would be inequitable. It would be inherently unfair to place the productiveness of the licensed property solely within the control of the licensee, thereby putting the licensor at the licensee's mercy, without imposing a reciprocal obligation upon that licensee. However, the existence of a best-efforts obligation should not be lightly inferred, for such an obligation subjects licensees to significant litigation exposure and deprives them of the fundamental power of determining for themselves the reasonableness of their marketing efforts.

Permanence argues that in order to give effect to the meaning of the contract, a best-efforts obligation must be implied because the contract provides for royalties to be paid to Permanence by Kennametal on products produced by the processes of the licensed patents to which Kennametal had exclusive rights. Permanence argues that the district court erred in determining that Permanence had received sufficient consideration—$500,000—in exchange for its rights to the patents because $250,000 of the money paid by Kennametal was for the grant of the nonexclusive license. We agree with Permanence on this score that only $250,000 was paid for the exclusive license. Permanence contends that in spite of the additional $250,000 paid for the option and advance royalties on the exclusive license, a best-efforts obligation must be implied because royalties under an exclusive license will be generated only if the licensee is under a duty to exploit the patented processes. Permanence contends that because of the grant of the exclusive, rather than the nonexclusive, right to the patented processes, Permanence bargained for and received an increase in the rate of royalty from 2¾% to 3½%.

Permanence's argument that it received an increase in the royalty rate as consideration for the exclusive license is negated by the terms of the contract. The contract stated that if the option were not exercised with 24 months and Kennametal chose instead to continue the nonexclusive license, the royalty rate would increase from 2¾% to 3½%. This fact bolsters Kennametal's argument that the consideration given for the exclusive, as opposed to the nonexclusive, right to the patented processes consisted of the $150,000 fee paid up front for the exercise of the option and the additional $100,000 paid in advance royalties under the exclusive license.

Permanence concedes that there was no best-efforts obligation to exploit the nonexclusive license initially granted to Kennametal for a $150,000 fee and $100,000 in advance royalties. Yet royalties were also to be paid on products manufactured under the nonexclusive license.

Courts have held that by imposing a substantial minimum or advance royalty payment, licensors—in lieu of obtaining an express agreement to use best efforts—have protected themselves against the possibility that the licensee will do nothing. Rather than leaving the licensor at the mercy of the licensee, the demand for a substantial up-front or advance royalty payment creates an incentive for the licensee to exploit the invention or patent. In the present case, Permanence received a substantial total advance payment of $250,000 for its right to the exclusive license and, unlike the licensor in the majority of cases wherein a duty to exploit has been implied, did not depend for its consideration solely on Kennametal's sale of products developed under the patents.

Although the advance royalty clause and up-front payment alone might not preclude the finding of an implied obligation to exploit, these provisions of the contract must be considered with the other express provisions already discussed. Moreover, the contract contained a merger or integration clause. By emphasizing that the formal contract, which contained no express agreement by Kennametal to exploit the patents, constituted the entire agreement between the parties, this clause further negates the implication that a duty to use best efforts was assumed.

Permanence relies on two cases in which the courts implied a covenant to employ best efforts despite the payment of other consideration for the grant of the exclusive license. We believe that these cases have misapplied the doctrine articulated in *Wood* where it was necessary to imply best efforts in order to save the agreement. In *Wood*, the court stated:

> [The designer's] *sole* compensation for the grant of an exclusive agency is to be one-half of all the profits resulting from the plaintiff's efforts. *Unless he gave his efforts, she could never get anything.* Without an implied promise, the transaction cannot have such business efficacy, as both parties must have intended that at all events it should have (emphasis added).

It is not necessary for a court to interject—into every contract in which there is an exclusive license—a covenant to employ best efforts. Especially, as is true in the present case, when an inventor grants a license to patented technology, the application of which is unknown, a commitment on the part of the licensee to devote best-efforts to the development of the technology is a substantial commitment, which should not be automatically inferred.

We do not believe that Kennametal impliedly promised to perfect an incompletely developed technology, which is what, in effect, Permanence asserts. The total payment of $250,000 for the exclusive license to the patents provided sufficient incentive and demonstration of good faith that Kennametal would attempt to commercialize and market the Permanence process. Moreover, we find that if Permanence wished to bind Kennametal to a best-efforts commitment in the circumstances of this case, it was incumbent upon Permanence to spell out this obligation in the formal written agreement. The decision of the district court is affirmed.

As with all contract matters, the best way to avoid such disputes is to fully address all potential outcomes at the beginning of the relationship. Thus, from our point of view, we would like the contract to specifically state that Scherer will use best efforts to market the technology. In the alternative, we would probably be satisfied with a substantial up-front payment for an exclusive license to market. Scherer likely will not want to leave it up to a court to determine if it used best efforts, especially if sales turned out to be somewhat dismal. On the other hand, it likely will desire an exclusive license. Its best option, therefore, is to have the contract explicitly say that it does not have to use best efforts. However, we likely will not buy into that. If sufficient advance compensation is not possible, then Scherer might consider discussing the possibility of terms that allow it to terminate the relationship on short notice. In this way, Scherer could end our dependency on its efforts should those efforts not be resulting in satisfactory sales.[15]

## Trade Secret Issues

As part of this development and distribution partnership, the participants probably will be exchanging numerous trade secrets. In our dealings with SoftWave, we will have to disclose information about our technology and the ultimate product concept so that SoftWave can develop the appropriate software. After creating the software, SoftWave will have to provide us with sufficient information about the functional parameters of the program so that we can utilize it in the product. Also, since we are relying on Scherer to manufacture and distribute the ultimate AES products, we will have to disclose an enormous amount of information to that company about the attributes and constraints of the technologies we created along with SoftWave. Much of this information will be valuable as long as it is not in the hands of competitors. Also, we likely will not rely on patent protection for some, if not all of it, either because of perceived negative strategic implications with the patent system or because the information does not meet the standards for patentability. Therefore, the partners will all have to be very conscious of how the trade secrets will be protected as they are passed among themselves.

The two most important considerations for dealing with trade secrets are (1) ownership of the secrets and (2) ensuring that the secrets are the subject of reasonable measures to preserve their secrecy. The ownership issue is little different from the one that applies with patents. Since much of the valuable information and ideas will be jointly developed, it is important for the parties to determine at the beginning of the relationship how the fruits of the innovations should be shared. For instance, if we expect that all secrets ultimately should belong to us, then we must take care in the contracts to provide for this outcome. The final determination about ownership will depend on a number of factors, such as the relative importance of each company's technological contributions, each party's relative bargaining strengths, the most efficient ways to control and improve the technologies, and compensation schemes.

As we know, once the ownership issues are ironed out, then the trade secret owners, as determined under the agreements, must take measures that are reasonable under the circumstances to protect the secrecy of their information. We have already seen in Chapter 4 how difficult this can be simply within the confines even of one's own firm. Confidentiality agreements in conjunction with a host of physical measures are always required. Such steps are just as important when other companies are entrusted with the information. However, the problems are multiplied. When we furnish trade secrets to SoftWave, for instance, we have to watch over that company to ensure that it handles the information as we do within our own enterprise. To this end, our agreements should very specifically enumerate (1) whom the information can be shared with, both within and outside SoftWave; (2) that confidentiality agreements must be signed by all who have access to the information; (3) any physical security measures that must be undertaken by SoftWave; (4) that SoftWave must ensure that reasonable security measures be taken by those who are allowed access to the information outside SoftWave; (5) whether other protections such as enforcing covenants not to compete with particular individuals are necessary; and (6) what measures we will take to monitor SoftWave's compliance with these terms. The last item is important not to overlook. Part of our responsibility in preserving the secrecy of the valuable information is engaging in periodic audits, not only within our company but also within the confines of all businesses entrusted with the secrets. Thus, our agreement with SoftWave should ensure that we have permission to inspect its operations under mutually agreed-to terms so that we are satisfied SoftWave is adequately preserving the secrecy of our technologies.

Clearly, this all becomes more and more complicated as the number of parties and trade secret owners increases. If SoftWave owns trade secrets in its software, then it will want similar assurances from us and rights to ensure our compliance. Likewise, we both will have to extend these protections over to Scherer's operations. And, of course, both companies will have to work very closely with Scherer, once distribution begins, in order to make sure that the distributors and retailers take whatever steps we think are necessary to preserve the secrecy of information given to them to help explain, sell, and maintain the products.

### Copyright Issues

It is likely that the copyright laws will be used to protect portions of the computer program utilized in the AES.[16] Also, various written documents, such as manuals, instructions, and sales brochures are susceptible to copyright protection. As previously discussed, however, protection for just about any other facet of the AES will not be possible via the copyright laws in the United States.

A particularly important issue will again be ownership. In this regard, we must follow the principles laid down in *CCNV v. Reid*. Unless we come to some other understanding in the contract, it is likely that SoftWave will be the owner of the copyright to the AES program. This is despite the fact that we came to SoftWave with the idea to create the program. We would not even be a joint owner in this situation since we did not contribute to the expressive portions of the ultimate program. Thus, if we expect to be the owner of the copyright in the program used by the AES, then in the contract, SoftWave will have to assign its copyright in the program to us. As for all the other copyrightable materials, we will have to be similarly conscious of copyright ownership principles, especially those applying to works made for hire.

The owners of the copyrights in these various items will have to license to developers and marketers the rights to copy and/or distribute the works. For instance, if we design an instruction booklet to explain the AES to users, then Scherer will need permission to duplicate it for inclusion with each AES it produces. In addition, some participants in the sales channels, including Scherer, may need permission to distribute the copies along with the product. In this regard, the first-sale doctrine of Section 109 should be consulted to determine if permissions are necessary.

Similar principles will apply to the computer program. Scherer will need to receive from the copyright owner, whether it is us or SoftWave, the authority to duplicate the program if it must make copies in order to manufacture the product. Of course, if we provide Scherer with components that already integrate the program, then Scherer will not require a license to copy. Also, if Scherer wishes to improve the AES, necessitating changes in the program, then permission from the copyright owner will be required to make derivative works. In this regard, another possibility is that the copyright owner may commit itself to make these updates so that they can be integrated into Scherer's new products. Beyond these issues, Scherer and possibly others involved in distribution may need licenses to carry out their marketing duties, just as was necessary with the instruction booklet. As you can see, the copyright owner has tremendous flexibility in determining how to allocate its rights, requiring the parties to give tremendous thought to their allocation, preferably at the beginning of the deal. Failure to clearly come to grips with all the potential ways that the relationship might develop may inevitably lead to tensions between the parties. Part of the dispute between Apple and Microsoft, for instance, questioned whether Apple's license allowing Microsoft to sell Windows 1.0 extended to Microsoft's improved version, Windows 2.03.[17]

## Trademark Issues

Trademark issues are usually somewhat easier to resolve. Assuming that the alliance has chosen the word "StatFree" to serve as a trademark, the first question again centers on ownership. Likely, our company or Scherer will own the trademark and will be responsible for federal registration. If we are the owner of the trademark, we will need to consider what persons involved in manufacturing, marketing, and distributing the product might need permission to use the trademark to carry out their responsibilities. This obviously will include Scherer but likely will encompass others as well. Another issue involves the steps the parties will take in policing use of the trademark to ensure that it does not lose trademark significance, such as by becoming generic. For instance, we may require those involved in marketing the product to follow certain guidelines specifying linguistic dos and don'ts when promoting the product. In addition, we may want those involved in distribution and sales to police improper customer usage, by perhaps correcting customers when they use the word "statfree" in a product sense rather than with brand significance. Finally, the parties need to resolve whether they should have rights to use the name on other products they may develop. Scherer, for instance, may want to ensure that it has the right to use the StatFree name on a line of AES accessory products that it later may choose to manufacture and distribute.

## Liability Issues

When parties undertake a strategic alliance, it is crucial that they fully comprehend the potential risks of the relationship and appropriately divide responsibility for negative outcomes should those consequences materialize. Clear definitions of what each party should expect from the others in the alliance lead to unambiguous solutions to the problems and disappointments that inevitably occur. This is not to say that such understandings will reduce the financial pain when a party is obligated to bear the costs. However, such clarity does tend to narrow the extent of disagreements among the parties, leading to less contentious outcomes to problems. This, in turn, can help ensure the harmony that is necessary for a successful long-term strategic relationship.

To this end, it is common for commercial parties to articulate very specifically in the contract exactly what types and levels of performance should be expected from their products and services. In other words, sophisticated businesspersons will make somewhat elaborate express warranties and usually will disclaim the implied warranties of merchantability and fitness. Keep in mind that the restrictions on disclaiming implied warranties discussed earlier in this chapter applied only to the sale of consumer goods. This conforms to the philosophy that commercial parties (who in theory do not need such extensive protections of the law to look after their interests) should have the flexibility to structure a deal according to their particular needs.

Similarly, commercial contracts can be quite specific about the types and extent of remedies that one party can assess against another. For instance, Softwave must be very concerned about its financial exposure if a defect in its software causes distributed AES units to fail. In its contract negotiations with us, SoftWave may try to come to some mutually agreeable outcome that allows it to limit its exposure to potentially enormous consequential damages. Of course, any reduction of SoftWave's ultimate responsibility to pay for these consequential damages means that we must absorb the losses, even though the error was committed by SoftWave. However, we can reduce the risk of such an outcome by requiring certain specific tests to be passed by the computer software before we accept it. In addition, assuming responsibility for consequential damages might be the price we have to pay to allow the alliance to come together in the first place.

Likewise, commercial parties may allocate the risks from potential tort liabilities through contracts. For instance, there may be some concern that the components we supply to Scherer may cause severe electrical shocks when being installed and tested by Scherer employees. If these shocks were to materialize and employees were thereby injured, we could be liable through negligence or strict liability principles. Given that we are a small company, such potential tort liabilities should give us pause. Indeed, the risks may be so high that we might not be willing to enter the deal at all. The members of the strategic alliance may reallocate these risks through the contract so as to reduce our uncertainty, thereby allowing the deal to go forward. For instance, we may agree that Scherer should bear the total responsibility for injuries caused by the shocks should they occur.

An important element of risk allocation among strategic partners is the ability to seek indemnification against other participants. Indemnification is the right to be reimbursed for payments made to third parties to satisfy their legal claims. For instance, assume a third party alleges that Scherer violates the third party's copyright in a computer program when Scherer copies and distributes the program designed by SoftWave. Not only will Scherer have to pay for its defense in court, but should the court find that the program does unlawfully infringe, then Scherer would be liable for damages as well. Clearly, Scherer was depending on SoftWave to create a program that would not cause legal problems. Indeed, among the participants to the alliance, SoftWave is in the best position to control whether the software violates the rights of any third party. Under circumstances such as this, the partners will want the contract to clearly specify that SoftWave will indemnify them should legal problems arising from the software require payments to third parties.

Since SoftWave ultimately is responsible to pay these third-party claims, it naturally will want to have the opportunity to control the litigation. Thus, indemnification clauses normally allow the responsible party, here SoftWave, to have a say in the selection of legal counsel, the choice of litigation strategies, and the course of settlement negotiations. Such input usually is not absolute, however, for the party being sued has a stake in the outcome if the indemnifier does not have the financial means to satisfy the ultimate judgment. For example, Scherer may want to accept a settlement offer while SoftWave would prefer to fight in court. Suppose the offer is turned down according to SoftWave's wishes. If the defense fails in court and the losses are much larger than the settlement offer, then Scherer is on the hook should SoftWave not be able to pay the damages fully. Thus, indemnification clauses should be given tremendous forethought and must be carefully tailored according to the needs and financial means of the parties involved.

Indemnification clauses are essential to high-technology alliances. The previous example illustrates that when companies are making and distributing products dependent on intellectual property, there are enormous risks of infringement. Thus, indemnification clauses often deal with potential copyright, patent, trade secret, and trademark issues. However, indemnification clauses may be broader, depending on the context. For instance, they may extend to potential tort and contract liabilities, as well as to more specialized issues, such as the possible violation of particular rules, regulations, and statutes applicable to the situation at hand.

## Alternative Dispute Resolution

From the simple overview of contractual matters presented in this chapter, you can recognize the varied scope of issues that arise in any strategic venture. You also should be aware that it is simply impossible to address every potential problem up front in a contract. One certainty when entering any long-term strategic alliance is that disputes invariably will arise. Many of these disagreements may be settled through discussions and negotiations. However, when these measures fail, then the parties will require more formal channels to resolve their differences.

The traditional avenue for resolving disputes is by litigation in the state or federal court systems. However, litigation presents a number of problems, particularly for high-technology strategic ventures. Possibly the biggest drawback to litigation hinges on its very nature, based on confrontation, hostility, and distrust. One fairly certain outcome of litigation is that the parties will not be friendly once it concludes. Such a state of affairs, of course, is hardly consistent with a strategic venture, which depends on long-term working relationships among the participants. A second pitfall with litigation is the time frame for handling disputes. Depending on the jurisdiction, it may take years before a civil case comes to trial. In the fast-paced world of high technology, in which firms must move quickly and decisively, delays of this magnitude to the smooth operation of the partnership may doom the venture. Another drawback with litigation is that the decision makers often are inexperienced with the subject matter underlying the dispute. We have already seen what happens to computer copyright disputes when they are resolved by judges and juries who do not fully appreciate the technology. High-technology litigants often invest substantial resources into teaching the decision maker about the technology, with little assurance that the intricacies can be assimilated in a relatively short amount of time. This often leads to poor decisions that only increase the frustration surrounding the dispute. An additional deficiency with litigation is the public nature of the proceedings. This can lead to substantial hardships when the dispute involves modern technologies, especially those consisting of trade secrets. Although there are ways for the litigants to preserve the confidentiality of their trade secrets during litigation, the course may be perilous. Finally, litigation can be extremely expensive, mostly because of high attorney's fees and extensive discovery requirements.

Alternative dispute resolution (ADR) techniques are designed to help the parties reach a satisfactory decision while minimizing the deficiencies inherent in the traditional litigation system. The key to ADR is that it can be tailored to the special needs of the parties involved. Many firms now specialize in advising firms on the proper forms and implementation of ADR.[18] The techniques being used are extremely varied, ranging from highly informal to very formal. However, some attributes are fairly consistent. For instance, the process is private, thereby alleviating fears of trade secret disclosure. Also, selection of the decision maker(s) is up to the parties. This means that the parties are free to find people who have expertise in the matters under dispute. Other key aspects, such as time and expense, vary considerably, depending on the technique being used. We will now take a brief look at three types of ADR that have received substantial attention in high-technology contexts. They are mediation, the minitrial, and arbitration.

**Mediation.** In mediation, the parties engage a neutral person to help them resolve their differences. The mediator is not a decision maker. Rather, the role of the mediator is to facilitate settlement of the dispute by removing obstacles and helping the parties explore avenues of potential agreement. More than anything else, the effectiveness of the mediator depends on trust. The mediator is like a shuttle diplomat, working between the parties to resolve their differences. The mediator's goal is to buffer the animosity between the disputants and to find ways to have them overcome their differences so that an effective working relationship can be restored. The mediator often is able to identify the key issues, allowing the parties to see through their hostility to the real points of disagreement. An effective mediator may render impartial assessments of positions, highlight the consequences of not reaching a settlement, and explore mutually acceptable bases for agreement. From the foregoing, one can tell that mediators must have skills in diplomacy more than anything else. However, to be most effective, it also is helpful when the mediator has expertise in the particular field of the dispute. Organizations such as the Center for Public Resources and the American Arbitration Association maintain panels of highly qualified mediators and should be consulted if mediation is pursued.

The entire mediation process is consensual and informal and can be terminated by any party at any time. Because there is no binding commitment and, thus, little downside to its use, mediation often is selected as a first crack at finding a solution to the problem. If it fails, then the parties can resort to more formal methods of dispute resolution. With this in mind, commercial parties entering a long-term relationship should consider including the following form of provision in their agreement:

> In the event that there is a dispute or claim relating to this contract, and the parties are not able to resolve it through direct negotiations, then the parties hereby agree that they will attempt to settle the dispute or claim first by means of mediation according to the Commercial Mediation Rules of the American Arbitration Association. The parties further agree that they will proceed to litigation, arbitration or any other resolution procedure only if they fail to resolve their differences through mediation.

This provision is just one example of a very simple type of mediation agreement. Often the strategic partners will want to be much more specific in the agreement about the mediation process if it becomes necessary to use it. For instance, they may specify the number, qualifications, and possibly the identity of the mediators. They also may be more concrete about what resolution process might follow mediation should it fail, such as by requiring arbitration in lieu of litigation.

**Minitrial.** A minitrial is not really a trial; rather it is a test run so that the disputing parties may explore what might happen if they pursued litigation all the way through the trial process. The procedure is relatively informal, and like mediation, it is confidential and has no binding affect on the parties. Often minitrials are pursued when mediation is unable to bring the sides to agreement—usually because the parties have widely divergent views about the probabilities of success at trial or the amounts of money that might be recovered.

A minitrial neither takes place in a courtroom nor uses a judge to render a decision. However, it has attributes that mirror a trial setting. The parties make presentations of their views about the situation to "juries" consisting of business executives with settlement powers from both of the contesting corporations. Often the case is facilitated by a neutral third party, who has expertise in mediation. The goal of the minitrial is to have the executives get a realistic feel for what might happen at trial should that avenue be followed. The presentations are informal without the constraints of rules of evidence. However, in complex cases, such as those involving patents, realism is ensured by allowing experts to "testify" and by allowing the parties flexibility to learn various facts from each other (called "discovery") prior to the proceeding. The neutral participant facilitates the proceeding and may ask questions during the presentations. After the presentations, the neutral party may be asked to give the executives an advisory opinion about the risks each side would face at trial and a prediction of the outcome. The jury of executives then "deliberates," sometimes with the neutral individual mediating the discussions. If the minitrial is successful, the sides will see the merits of each other's arguments, substantiated by the independent thoughts of the neutral participant. These insights may lead the parties to reach a settlement in a relatively swift, inexpensive, and consensual manner.

**Arbitration.** Arbitration essentially is a private, trial-type proceeding that is conducted according to the wishes of the disputing parties. Although the parties may choose a nonbinding form of arbitration, it is far more common that they opt for binding arbitration. Binding arbitration means that the parties agree to be bound by the decision of the arbitrator, an aspect that marks an important difference from the preceding styles of ADR, in which voluntary resolution was the goal. With binding arbitration, the parties have determined that the neutral will decide the outcome of their dispute and fashion the appropriate relief. And there is little recourse if a party is dissatisfied with the decision. Although one might appeal the determination to the appellate courts, the grounds for any appeal are extremely limited, to, say, fraud or illegality. More typical reasons for dissatisfaction, such as that the arbitrator did not understand the facts or did not apply the law correctly to those facts, normally will not be reviewed by the courts. Thus, the choice to use arbitration must be made with the understanding that binding really does mean binding.

Arbitration is increasingly preferred by high-technology firms over litigation because it is private, relatively fast, and decisive. Also, the participants may fashion the ground rules for the arbitration in their contractual relationship so that it is tailored to their specific needs. Typical issues that must be resolved involve who will serve as the arbitrator or arbitrators, how much discovery will be allowed, what rules of evidence will control the arbitration, and what types of relief may be granted.

Normally, an arbitration agreement will specify how many arbitrators will be used and how they will be selected. Obviously, it is less expensive to use only one arbitrator to make the decision. But many times, companies prefer panels of arbitrators, most often consisting of three individuals. There are several explanations for this preference. Probably of most importance, the parties may disagree about what types of expertise an arbitrator should have. For instance, in a software dispute, one party may want a software engineer while the other prefers an intellectual-property attorney.[19] A panel containing both kinds of experts solves the impasse. Another important virtue of panels is that they may be perceived as more able to impart a fair decision than a single arbitrator could.

The arbitration agreement should establish not only the number of arbitrators but also the methods whereby each will be selected. The American Arbitration Association maintains lists of arbitrators who have expertise in a variety of areas, such as the National Panel of Patent Arbitrators and the National Panel of Commercial Arbitrators. These can be very useful in filling the slots. The selection techniques range anywhere from methods of chance to specification of the particular arbitrators in the agreement. One typical arrangement is for each party to select an arbitrator of its choice and leave it to those two individuals to select a third.

One of the principal advantages of arbitration is that the parties may specify simplified rules about discovering information prior to trial and about trial procedures. Discovery of information in traditional litigation can be very expensive and time-consuming. The parties may control discovery in arbitration by limiting or even prohibiting it in their arbitration agreement. Indeed, in some states, discovery is restricted by law unless the agreement provides that increased discovery will be used.[20] Similarly, the rules of evidence used to conduct the hearing may be tailored by the parties. Usually these are more relaxed than civil trial procedures. Often the parties will agree to use the American Arbitration Association's Commercial Arbitration rules or will follow the Center for Public Resource's Model ADR Procedures for technology disputes.[21]

One other key issue is the type of relief the arbitrator is empowered to grant. Typically, the arbitrators are given the authority to decide the appropriate relief based on their own discretion. This flexibility is no different from what exists in normal civil litigation. Sometimes, the arbitrators are more constrained in fashioning relief. One example is called "final offer arbitration" or "baseball arbitration." When this approach is used, each party submits to the arbitrator a single proposed award. After hearing the evidence at the hearing, the arbitrator is required to pick one of the two submitted alternatives without modification. This procedure tends to discourage the sides from taking extreme positions since the arbitrator is not likely to accept an unreasonable recommendation.[22] In addition, the narrowing of the differences in this manner may help lead to an early settlement.

ADR certainly presents a lot of potential advantages to high-technology firms. This explains the explosive growth in the use of ADR procedures by businesses in the past few years.[23] In fact, more than half of the Fortune 500 have signed a pledge to explore alternatives to litigation whenever possible.[24] However, ADR is not a universal panacea. Sometimes it can turn out to be more expensive and time-consuming than litigation. Also, ADR techniques may disclose certain weaknesses if the dispute ultimately gets to trial. In addition, some observers contend that arbitrators have a tendency to pursue the middle ground, a possible negative if your rights are the ones being sacrificed. Other factors, such as the publicity surrounding civil trials and the desire to have juries consider sympathetic cases also may trigger a preference for traditional channels of litigation.[25] In sum, firms conducting business in the technology field should seriously consider the potential benefits of ADR techniques when devising strategic partnerships, but they should not perfunctorily assume that ADR is the way to go. The decision is a crucial one that demands substantial consideration.

## ANTITRUST AND ANTICOMPETITIVE CONDUCT

When high-technology firms enter contractual or other business arrangements, they need to assess what effect they might have on competition and whether those consequences will be acceptable to the public and to key policymakers. The barrage of media attention recently given to Microsoft and Nintendo, among others, for engaging in practices that some say may be unduly anticompetitive, points out the importance of this policy area.[26] Usually competition policy comes within the broad umbrella of what is called antitrust. An associated policy forum also relevant to firms dealing with intellectual property is termed "misuse." This chapter closes by providing a sense of how high-technology firms might be affected by these important competition policies.

### Antitrust

**Overview.** Antitrust policy in the United States has its roots in the Industrial Revolution. The time was marked by a substantial shift in economic and political power from the once-dominant farming community to the emerging industrialists. There also was a notable change in the way economic power was controlled. Whereas before the Industrial Revolution, economic wealth was diffused over a multitude of owners of small businesses and entrepreneurs, the era brought with it new breeds of empires that sometimes controlled substantial economic assets and power. The result was a populist reaction around the turn of the 20th century. It was during this tumultuous period that antitrust policies were born.

The fundamental antitrust statutes are the Sherman Act, the Clayton Act, and the FTC Act. The Sherman Act, which serves as the cornerstone of antitrust policy, prohibits contracts, combinations and conspiracies in restraint of trade. In addition, it states that monopolizing is unlawful. The Clayton Act deals with a number of practices such as price discrimination. However, its major thrust is its merger clause prohibiting mergers that may substantially lessen competition. The FTC Act empowers the Federal Trade Commission to prohibit unfair methods of competition.

A notable similarity between these statutes is how vague they are in describing unlawful conduct. What does it mean to restrain trade? What kind of conduct constitutes monopolizing? Under what circumstances will a merger have the possible effect of lessening competition? What kinds of business methods are unfair? One frightening aspect of antitrust is that there is no clear guidance about the meanings of these terms, leaving businesses constantly exposed to the vagaries of the policymakers in charge of interpreting them.

Those responsible for giving meaning to the vague terms of antitrust generally search the historical origins of the policy to determine the philosophical constructs from which it evolved. Unfortunately, such historical analyses have led to two substantially different notions of what antitrust is designed to achieve. One school of thought attaches a populist philosophy to antitrust. According to this approach, antitrust arose to protect small farms and businesses from the powerful industrial enterprises. Antitrust was conceived to ensure a vital system of small producers and sellers, thereby ensuring that American entrepreneurial ingenuity thrives through the incentives of universal opportunity. Following this line of reasoning, antitrust is based on a generalized distrust of big business. Although one legitimately might make arguments that big business can be more efficient in the production and distribution of goods and services, that notion is viewed with skepticism, especially when taking a long-term perspective. Those advocating the importance of small business to society believe that any economic benefits that might conceivably be achieved through size ultimately will be enjoyed by the large-business powerhouses to the detriment of consumers and society. The small-business supporters therefore are inclined to use antitrust to attack the formation and growth of big business, even when faced with convincing arguments that greater size might yield lower costs. From all of this, one should not be surprised that those entertaining a small-business philosophy to antitrust usually support an active program of antitrust enforcement.

One can review the history of antitrust and reach an entirely different construct about the purposes of antitrust. One of the concerns of the Industrial Revolution was the rise of true economic monopolies that faced little if any competition in their industries and that had the means to deter any firm that might consider entering the field. Economists consider monopolies to be inefficient not only because they transfer wealth from consumers but also because they impose an unrecoverable cost on society through the income redistribution process. Thus, it makes sense for the government to interfere with the free market when the unfettered market otherwise would result in monopoly power. Here, monopoly power does not mean that the business is big. Rather, it is related to the capability of the business to dominate firms that compete with it.

Following this line of reasoning, the other philosophical approach to antitrust is founded on the principle of maintaining economic efficiency. Those supporting this view of antitrust policy believe that enforcement is proper only when the free market, left to its own devices, would not render an efficient outcome. However, this scenario is considered the exception rather than the rule. Decisions and arrangements normally made by business firms through the natural forces of the competitive process are viewed as serving the public interest by increasing economic efficiency. The strategies adopted by firms are to do better than their rivals, ultimately leading to lower prices or better products for consumers. If the process leads to more powerful firms, then it likely is because their added scope enhances certain economic efficiencies that allow those businesses to be more formidable competitors. Big business, therefore, is not seen as something that is necessarily bad. In fact, it may be viewed positively, as long as there are market forces in place to ensure competitive practices, such as with pricing. Therefore, those advocating the efficiency objectives to antitrust, based on these observations, normally call for a hands-off or passive approach to antitrust enforcement, under the assumption that the free market normally will result in the most efficient outcome.

Antitrust policy initially derives from Congress through statutes. However, as already noted, Congress has been somewhat vague in articulating antitrust standards. On occasion Congress has been more forceful, providing greater clarity for certain specific areas of antitrust concern. For example, in 1984, Congress reduced the antitrust exposure for companies engaging in joint research and development projects when it passed the National Cooperative Research Act.[27] This move stimulated a number of joint research efforts that otherwise may not have occurred for fear of antitrust enforcement.[28] For example, thanks somewhat to this amendment to the antitrust laws, the big three automakers jointly developed a manufacturing process for a lightweight material that could someday substitute for steel. In addition, they received a joint patent for the process in 1993.[29] Nonetheless, for most arrangements, congressional statutes remain vague about the potential applicability of antitrust. Under circumstances such as these, policymaking shifts from Congress to administrative agencies, the president, and the courts.

The Federal Trade Commission and the Antitrust Division of the Justice Department are charged with enforcing the antitrust laws for the public. As you can imagine, the degree of scrutiny these agencies give to various business practices is a function of the philosophies held by their top administrators. In the 1960s, for instance, these agencies were ruled by the small-business philosophy, thereby leading to somewhat aggressive enforcement practices. However, in the 1980s, both agencies were much more passive, due in large part to philosophical shifts that at that time supported the efficiency approach. Since the top administrators are appointed by the president, one can quickly see one way the president can influence antitrust policy. The marked change in enforcement activity, for instance, can be ascribed somewhat to the different philosophical approaches held by the Democratic administrations in the 1960s compared to President Reagan's in the 1980s.

When the administrative agencies bring enforcement actions, the cases either are initially heard in the federal courts or may ultimately be reviewed by them. In addition, private parties may bring antitrust actions in the federal courts when they believe they have been damaged by violations of the antitrust laws. When such cases are brought, the federal courts must interpret the vague language of the statutes to answer the question at hand. For example, if a case is brought against a company and it is shown that the company fixed prices with a competitor, then the court must determine if this practice is the type of restraint that Congress intended to be unlawful under the Sherman Act. As with administrative agencies, the decision of the court likely will be influenced by the antitrust philosophies held by the residing judges. Looking at the 1960s and the 1980s, we see a marked difference in the approaches taken by courts. Whereas in the 1960s there was concern for the protection of small business, in the 1980s, the focus was on maintaining economic efficiency. This change again can be ascribed somewhat to the influence of the president, who is responsible for nominating federal judges when vacancies occur.

Violation of the antitrust laws may carry severe penalties. When private parties are successful in antitrust litigation, they are entitled to three times their proven damages (treble damages), plus attorney's fees and court costs. Also, the Justice Department may bring criminal proceedings against alleged violators of the Sherman Act. In addition, the FTC and the Justice Department may initiate civil cases, asking the tribunal to impose injunctions and possibly to order the payment of damages. The potential degree of liability, coupled with uncertainty about how the law will be enforced and interpreted, can make antitrust litigation a very frightening prospect indeed.

**Application of the Antitrust Laws.** Section 1 of the Sherman Act prohibits contracts, combinations, and conspiracies that unreasonably restrain trade. The ambit of this provision is so broad that firms must evaluate any contemplated business transaction with other companies in terms of its reasonableness. What makes an arrangement reasonable, therefore, is the key question for the Sherman Act, Section 1. When cases are brought to the federal courts, judges use what is termed the "rule of reason" to make this analysis. The rule of reason can be likened to a scale, balancing how the arrangement might harm competition against the possible ways it could benefit competition. If the likely harms to competition outweigh the benefits, then the transaction is unreasonable and unlawful; if the benefits outweigh the harms, then it is reasonable and lawful.

For example, a common distribution practice is for manufacturers to provide retailers the exclusive rights to sell in particular regions. Such an arrangement may harm consumers because they will not be able to comparison shop for the manufacturer's goods at different retail outlets in the area. On the other hand, the exclusive privilege might encourage the retailer to more aggressively push the manufacturer's brand since the retailer knows that customers, once persuaded, have no choice but to buy the brand from it. Other manufacturers may be forced to match the increased promotion with vigorous competitive responses, such as with lower prices or enhanced services, thereby benefiting consumers. Whether the arrangement is reasonable depends on the particular facts and the relative weights given to each possibility by the courts. *Eastman Kodak v. Image Technical Services*, presented later in the chapter, also illustrates how arrangements conceivably may have both positive and negative effects on competition.

The rule of reason raises significant ambiguity for businesses. One never knows which arguments, information, or expert testimony ultimately will per-

**Exhibit 9.2  Rule of Reason**

| Possible harms to "competition: | ∧ | Possible benefits to "competition" |
| --- | --- | --- |

suade the court. In addition, as mentioned earlier, "competition" may be defined in different ways by different judges. Some may evaluate the transaction by considering the effects on economic efficiency. Other judges may be more concerned with how the transaction might impact the ability of small businesses to survive.

The courts have developed one shortcut that adds more certainty to their judgment about certain kinds of transactions. Those sitting in the courts have concluded that some arrangements are potentially so harmful that no alleged benefits could ever outweigh their dangers in a rule-of-reason analysis. Rather than wasting everyone's time by reviewing evidence regarding the reasonableness of such deals, the courts skip the weighing analysis and jump directly to the conclusion that they are unlawful. In other words, to be successful, all the plaintiff must do is prove that the defendant engaged in one of these arrangements. This is substantially easier and more predictable than in the typical rule-of-reason scenario wherein the plaintiff must prove not only the existence of the transaction but also that it is unreasonable on balance. Since unreasonableness is assumed, these transactions are called illegal per se (literally, illegal in and of itself).

As you might imagine, those advocating the small-business approach to antitrust are more inclined to support illegal-per-se determinations than are those who favor efficiency. This is because they are more suspicious of business arrangements that might increase the competitive power of firms in the marketplace. For this reason, numerous arrangements were judged illegal per se in the 1960s when small-business proponents dominated the courts. However, by the 1980s, the efficiency-minded judges then in place were more inclined to fully review the economic effects of particular transactions rather than perfunctorily deem them illegal. Thus, the list of illegal-per-se offenses began to shrink. The most important change was in vertical nonprice restrictions, which were illegal per se prior to 1977. However, the Supreme Court changed its mind in that year, ruling that these important arrangements should be fully evaluated under the rule of reason.[30] Currently, certain practices are still illegal per se, but the courts often are very particular about the circumstances that make a practice unlawful out of hand. For instance, tying arrangements, which are the primary subject of *Eastman Kodak v. Image Technical Services*, are illegal per se, but only if (1) there are two products and (2) the company has appreciable market power in the tying product.[31] If these aspects are not found, then the arrangement is judged under the rule of reason. Vertical price fixing, in which parties at different levels of the distribution chain make agreements about resale prices, is illegal per se, but again, the courts have substantially narrowed the kinds of conduct that come within the definition of vertical price fixing.[32] A few practices, such as price agreements between competitors, have remained steadfastly illegal per se. What will happen throughout the 1990s of course depends greatly on the types of judges appointed by President Clinton and the presidents who follow him.

The Sherman Act, Section 2, prohibits monopolizing. In the 1940s and 1950s, a company seemingly could run afoul of this provision simply by obtaining a market share that was too large.[33] However, with the shift toward efficiency considerations, being too large became only a prerequisite to illegality. Now, not only must one's market share be excessive, but one also must engage in business practices that cannot be explained satisfactorily through efficiency considerations.[34] *Eastman Kodak v. Image Technical Services*, which follows, explains how the courts evaluate monopolization charges.

*Eastman Kodak v. Image Technical Services* deals with a critical subject for high-technology firms: the contractual provision, imposed by some manufacturers of high-technology equipment, requiring purchasers to have their products serviced by the manufacturers. In antitrust terms, this may be likened to a tying arrangement, a situation wherein the manufacturer limits the right of customers to purchase a product they desire (the tying product) without also buying some item they do not necessarily want (the tied product). For this arrangement to be illegal per se, one must show that repair services are distinct from the equipment and that the manufacturer has appreciable market power in the desired equipment. Keep in mind that if the arrangement is not illegal per se for want of one of these elements, then it still might be unlawful under the more extensive rule-of-reason analysis.

The tying of service to hardware has become somewhat common in the computer industry. One can point to a number of reasons why such tying arrangements might be reasonable under certain circumstances.[35] For instance, some customers prefer a turnkey solution to computer problems, which includes hardware, software, software updates, and maintenance. For some manufacturers, it may not be feasible to offer all these features unless the features are packaged in some attractive way. Another important consideration is that vendors of computer software often have substantial trade secrets that they wish to protect in their products. Maintenance agreements ensure that the software developer does not have to relinquish source code to the customer or third-party maintenance firms so that problems can be corrected. Also, customers who experience substantial problems in the servicing of their computer products may attribute the problems to the products, when poor service may actually be the problem. Thus, service maintenance agreements can preserve a company's goodwill and make it a more respected competitor with other firms. On the other hand, tying arrangements requiring service may have certain pernicious effects. For instance, the requirement may simply be a way for the manufacturer to force third-party service providers out of business so that the manufacturer can raise service prices and sustain a high-level stream of future income. Those adhering to the small-business philosophy to antitrust naturally would be especially sensitive to this possibility.

*Kodak* is a 1992 Supreme Court decision that evaluates some of the important antitrust issues respecting service maintenance agreements. This case discusses service contracts both as tying arrangements under Section 1 of the Sherman Act and as a means for monopolizing under the Sherman Act, Section 2. Given the propensity of the Supreme Court in the early 1990s to favor the efficiency role of antitrust, there was some expectation that the court would side with the defendant, Kodak, in the proceeding. As you will see, however, there always are surprises lurking in the world of antitrust.

## EASTMAN KODAK COMPANY V. IMAGE TECHNICAL SERVICES, INC.

*United States Supreme Court, 1992*

### Facts

Kodak manufactures and sells technologically complex, high-volume photocopiers and micrographics equipment. This equipment is serviced by Kodak and by independent service organizations (ISOs), such as Image Technical Services (ITS). ITS and other ISOs sued Kodak after Kodak adopted policies limiting the availability of parts to ISOs, thus making it harder for the ISOs to compete with Kodak in servicing Kodak equipment. The ISOs alleged that Kodak's policies amounted to illegal-per-se tying and monopolization, as prohibited by Sections 1 and 2 of the Sherman Act. The district court granted summary judgment for Kodak. This means that even if all the facts alleged by the ISOs were true, the ISOs would not prevail after a trial. According to the District Court, since Kodak did not have market power in the equipment market, it could not have market power for service or parts. Consequently, it could not have engaged in illegal-per-se tying or unlawful monopolization. The Court of Appeals reversed, and Kodak appealed to the Supreme Court.

Summary judgment is improper, and the case should go to trial if the ISOs could potentially win at trial based on their version of the facts. To determine the propriety of summary judgment, the Supreme Court assumes that the facts alleged by the ISOs are true. If the ISOs persuade the Supreme Court that summary judgment is improper, then the case proceeds to trial both for determination of the actual facts and for proper resolution of the dispute based on those facts. Thus, the "facts" presented in this case are only the allegations of the ISOs.

Kodak provides to its customers service and parts for its equipment. It produces some of the parts itself; the rest are made to order for Kodak by independent original equipment manufacturers (OEMs). Kodak provides service after an initial warranty period either through annual service contracts, which include all necessary parts, or on a per-call basis.

Beginning in the early 1980s, ISOs began repairing and servicing Kodak equipment at substantially lower prices than Kodak. Some of the ISO customers purchased their own parts and hired ISOs only for service. Others chose ISOs to supply both service and parts. ISOs kept an inventory of parts, which were purchased either from Kodak or from other sources, primarily OEMs.

In 1985, Kodak implemented a policy of selling replacement parts for equipment only to buyers of Kodak equipment who use Kodak service or who repair their own machines. Kodak also sought to limit ISO access to other sources of Kodak parts. Kodak and the OEMs agreed that the OEMs would not sell to anyone other than Kodak those parts fitting Kodak equipment. Kodak also pressured Kodak equipment owners and independent parts distributors not to sell Kodak parts to ISOs. In addition, Kodak took steps to restrict the availability of used machines. Due to these actions, ISOs were unable to obtain parts from reliable sources, and many were forced out of business.

## Opinion

**Tying Arrangements.** The ISOs allege that Kodak unlawfully tied the sale of service of Kodak machines to the sale of parts. A tying arrangement is an agreement by a party to sell one product but only on the condition that the buyer also purchase a different (or tied) product or at least agree not to purchase that different product from any other supplier. Such an arrangement violates Section 1 of the Sherman Act if the seller has tied the sale of two products and has appreciable economic power in the tying product.

For service and parts to be considered two distinct products, there must be sufficient consumer demand so that it is efficient for a firm to provide service separately from parts. Evidence in the record indicates that service and parts have been sold separately in the past and still are sold separately to self-service equipment owners. Indeed, the development of the entire high-technology service industry is evidence of the efficiency of a separate market for service.

Kodak insists that because there is no demand for parts separate from service, there cannot be separate markets for service and parts. By that logic, we would be forced to conclude that there can never be separate markets, for example, for cameras and film, computers and software, or automobiles and tires. We have often found arrangements involving functionally linked products at least one of which is useless without the other to be prohibited tying devices.

Also, the ISOs have presented evidence that service was tied to parts. The record indicates that Kodak would sell parts to third parties only if they agreed not to buy service from ISOs.

Having found sufficient evidence of a tying arrangement, we now consider whether there was appreciable economic power in the tying market. Market power is the power to force purchasers to do something they would not do in a competitive market. It has been defined as the ability of a single seller to raise price and restrict output. The existence of such power ordinarily is inferred from the seller's possession of a predominant share of the market.

The ISOs allege that Kodak's control over the parts market has excluded service competition, boosted service prices, and forced unwilling consumption of Kodak service. The ISOs have offered evidence that consumers have switched to Kodak service even though they preferred ISO service, that Kodak service was of higher price and lower quality than the preferred ISO service, and that ISOs were driven out of business by Kodak's policies.

Kodak counters that even if it concedes monopoly *share* of the relevant parts market, it cannot actually exercise the necessary market *power* because competition exists in the equipment market. Kodak argues that it could not have the ability to raise prices of service and parts above the level that would be charged in a competitive market because any increase in profits from a higher price in the aftermarkets at least would be offset by a corresponding loss in profits from lower equipment sales as consumers began purchasing equipment with more attractive service costs.

The extent to which one market prevents exploitation of another market depends on the extent to which consumers will change their consumption of one product in response to a price change in another. Although competition in the equipment market may impose a restraint on prices in the aftermarkets, this by no means disproves the existence of power in those markets. There is no immutable law—no basic economic reality—that competition in the equipment market cannot coexist with market power in the aftermarkets.

Significant information and switching costs constitute one possible explanation of this potential coexistence. For the service market price to affect equipment demand, consumers must inform themselves of the total cost of the package— being equipment, service, and parts—at the time of purchase; that is, consumers must engage in accurate life-cycle pricing. Life-cycle pricing of complex, durable equipment is difficult and costly. In order to arrive at an accurate price, a consumer must acquire a substantial amount of raw data and undertake sophisticated analysis. The necessary information would include data on price, quality, and availability of products needed to operate, upgrade, or enhance the initial equipment, as well as service and repair costs, including estimates of breakdown frequency, nature of repairs, price of service and parts, length of downtime, and losses incurred from downtime.

Much of this kind of information is difficult—some of it impossible—to acquire at the time of purchase. Moreover, even if consumers were capable of acquiring and processing the complex body of information, they may choose not to do so. Acquiring the information is expensive. If the costs of service are small relative to the equipment price, or if consumers are more concerned about equipment capabilities than service costs, they may not find it cost-efficient to compile the information.

As Kodak notes, there likely will be some large-volume, sophisticated purchasers who will undertake the comparative studies and insist that Kodak charge them competitive prices. Kodak contends that these knowledgeable customers will hold down the package price for all other customers. There are reasons, however, to doubt that sophisticated purchasers will ensure that competitive prices are charged to unsophisticated purchasers too. As an initial matter, if the number of sophisticated customers are relatively small, the amount of profits to be gained by supracompetitive pricing in the service market could make it profitable to let the knowledgeable consumers take their business elsewhere. More important, if a company is able to price-discriminate between sophisticated and unsophisticated consumers, the sophisticated will be unable to prevent the exploitation of the uninformed. Therefore, it makes little sense to assume, in the absence of any evidentiary support, that equipment-purchasing decisions are based on an accurate assessment of the total cost of the equipment, service, and parts over the lifetime of a machine.

A second factor undermining Kodak's claim that supracompetitive prices in the service market lead to ruinous losses in equipment sales is the cost to current owners of switching to a different product. If the cost of switching is high, consumers who already have purchased the equipment, and are thus locked-in, will tolerate some level of service-price increases before changing equipment brands. The ISOs have offered evidence that the heavy initial outlay for Kodak equipment, combined with the required support material that works only with Kodak equipment, makes switching costs very high for existing Kodak customers.

In sum, there is a question of fact whether information costs and switching costs foil the simple assumption that the equipment and service markets act as pure complements to one another. We conclude, then, that Kodak has failed to demonstrate that the ISOs' inference of market power in the service and parts market is unreasonable. Kodak thus is not entitled to summary judgment on the tying claim.

Kodak contends that despite the appearance of anticompetitiveness, its behavior actually favors competition because its ability to pursue innovative marketing plans will allow it to compete more effectively in the equipment market. A pricing strategy based on lower equipment prices and higher aftermarket prices could enhance equipment sales by making it easier for the buyer to finance the initial purchase. It is undisputed that competition is enhanced when a firm is able to offer various marketing options, including bundling of support and maintenance service with the sale of equipment. Nor do such actions run afoul of the antitrust laws. But the procompetitive effect of the specific conduct here—elimination of all consumer parts and service options—is far less clear.

**Monopolization.** The offense of monopolization under Section 2 of the Sherman Act has two elements: (1) the possession of monopoly power in the relevant market and (2) the willful acquisition or maintenance of that power as distinguished from growth or development as a consequence of a superior product, business acumen, or historical accident.

The existence of the first element—possession of monopoly power—is easily resolved. As has been noted, the ISOs have presented the plausible claims that service and parts are separate markets and that Kodak has the power to control prices or exclude competition in service and parts. Monopoly power under Section 2 requires something greater than market power under Section 1. The ISOs' evidence that Kodak controls nearly 100% of the parts market and 80% to 95% of the service market, with no readily available substitutes, is sufficient, however, to survive summary judgment under the more stringent monopoly standard of Section 2.

Kodak contends that a single brand of a product or service can never be a relevant market under the Sherman Act. We disagree. The relevant market, for antitrust purposes, is determined by the choices available to Kodak equipment owners. Prior cases support the proposition that, in some instances, one brand of a product can constitute a separate market.

The second element of a Section 2 claim is the use of monopoly power to foreclose competition, to gain a competitive advantage, or to destroy a competitor. Liability turns, then, on whether valid business reasons can explain Kodak's actions. Kodak claims that it has three valid business justifications for its actions: (1) to promote interbrand equipment competition by allowing Kodak to stress the quality of its service; (2) to improve asset management by reducing Kodak's inventory costs; and (3) to prevent ISOs from free riding on Kodak's capital investment in equipment, parts, and service. Factual questions exist, however, about the validity and sufficiency of each claimed justification, making summary judgment inappropriate.

As to the quality of service, there is evidence that ISOs provide quality service that is preferred by some Kodak equipment owners. With respect to asset management, Kodak's actions appear inconsistent with a need to control inventory costs. The justification fails to explain, for example, the ISOs' evidence that Kodak forced OEMs, equipment owners, and parts brokers not to sell parts to ISOs—actions that have no effect on Kodak's inventory costs. Finally, Kodak's argument that the ISOs are free-riding by not entering the equipment and parts markets is not persuasive. One of the evils proscribed by the antitrust laws is the creation of entry barriers to potential competitors by requiring them to enter two markets simultaneously.

The judgment of the Court of Appeals denying summary judgment is affirmed.

---

The foregoing discussion dealt only with fundamental principles regarding the Sherman Act. Always keep in mind that there are other federal antitrust laws and policies that also must be considered before embarking on any new venture. All 50 states have their own antitrust laws as well. As just one example, companies contemplating mergers must make evaluations in terms of the Clayton Act, Section 7, as well as relevant state statutes. Federal merger and joint venture policy has undergone substantial changes during the past 25 years. In the 1960s, mergers creating firms of just 5% market shares were attacked by the federal administrative agencies and found to be unlawful by the courts.[36] More recently, however, following the efficiency approach to antitrust, one finds that the federal enforcement agencies are much more permissive and that the courts are considerably more tolerant of mergers and joint ventures.[37] This is especially true of mergers involving companies that handle different product lines. A relatively permissive antitrust attitude could prove to be important to certain emerging high-technology industries, such as those using multimedia technologies, for those industries likely will depend on strategic relationships and mergers between existing corporate powerhouses.[38] As stated before, only time will tell whether the efficiency attitude will continue to prevail or whether there will be a resurgence of efforts to have antitrust policy protect the viability of small-business enterprises.[39] The only thing that is clear is that the course of antitrust will always be an important variable for firms doing business in high-technology fields in the United States.

**International Dimensions of Antitrust.**  Most high-technology enterprises now take on global dimensions and thus must be concerned not only with the antitrust policies of the United States but with those of other nations as well. Strategic alliances in high-technology fields increasingly involve an international host of partners.[40] For example, IBM, which has formed over 20,000 business relationships worldwide, clearly is carrying out a strategy of creating global networks of alliances for technology, marketing, and manufacturing.[41] Such an international posture is not simply for the corporate giants, however. For instance, Xilinx, a small Silicon Valley computer company, depends substantially on Japanese partners for much of its manufacturing and overseas distribution.[42]

As with all international matters, there is not a uniform standard for competition policy. Thus, a company must consider the competition policy of any nation that might be affected by its operations. This does not mean simply consulting the laws of the country where manufacturing takes place or that houses the corporate headquarters. For instance, even foreign companies that have no assets in the United States may be subject to U.S. antitrust laws if their operations have a substantial and reasonably foreseeable effect on either the import trade or the domestic commerce of the United States. Other nations, too, may have policies with similar extraterritorial effect.

The competition policies of different nations vary widely, depending on their respective philosophies toward economic relationships. Thus, one always must scrutinize local competition laws when entering new international markets. As just one example, consider the antitrust policies of the European Union (EU), which mirror those of the United States to some degree. Competition policy in the EU Common Market is governed by the Treaty of Rome. Article 85, Section 1 of the treaty prohibits agreements that prevent, distort, or restrict competition in the Common Market and affect trade among the member states. This language somewhat parallels the Sherman Act, Section 1. There are some differences, however. For instance, an EU Commission Notice states that to be subject to this provision, participating companies must reach a threshold size and hold more than 5% of the total market in the area of the EU affected by the agreement.[43] The article also lists examples of prohibited conduct, something that the Sherman Act generally fails to do. A few of these specified examples are price fixing; the limitation or control of production, markets, technical developments, or investment; the sharing of markets of sources or supply; and tying arrangements. The implication from this specific list of prohibited conduct is that EU policy is less flexible than the rule-of-reason analysis generally used in the United States.[44] However, the EU has mechanisms through which businesses may proceed with transactions, even though the transactions may fall within the list of prohibited activities. Companies wishing to engage in a particular transaction may notify the EU Commission, requesting that their deal be cleared by that body. If the EU Commission is persuaded that the transaction will improve economic progress in the EU and will not unduly restrict competition, then it may issue what is called a negative clearance or an exemption for the arrangement. It also may issue a comfort letter indicating that the EU Commission will not pursue enforcement action. This approach, not unlike agency guidelines in the United States, does not prevent others from taking legal actions, however.

Although these mechanisms give businesses an opportunity to engage in practices that otherwise are forbidden, they are mired with problems. One notable drawback is that it may take several years to receive a negative clearance or individual exemption. Another consideration is that exemptions, once given, may be limited in time.[45] To alleviate these concerns, the EU Commission has established a means to give preliminary blanket approval to sets of activities by means of block exemptions. Block exemptions have been issued for various practices such as certain patent licensing agreements, exclusive dealing situations, research and development agreements, know-how licenses (which protect trade secrets), and franchising arrangements, among others.[46] Block exemptions are divided into three categories: (1) the White List, which indicates agreements that are compatible with the spirit of Article 85(1); (2) the Gray List, which designates transactions that normally do not violate the law, but under special circumstances might run afoul of it; and (3) the Black List, which identifies agreements that are not protected by the block exemption. Viewing all of these procedures together suggests that antitrust in the EU ultimately is governed by principles akin to the rule-of-reason analysis used in the United States. However, the specific methods of applying the standards differ markedly and must be recognized before pursuing transactions within the EU.

Article 86 of the treaty prohibits the abuse of a dominant position—language that is reminiscent of Section 2 of the Sherman Act. As with the Sherman Act, it is not enough that one holds a dominant position. To be unlawful under Article 86, there also must be abusive exploitation of market power.[47] Again though, one should not be tempted by this similarity with U.S. policy to assume that EU antitrust principles always mirror those in the United States. For instance, private parties cannot bring causes of action for damages. In addition, the broad extraterritorial application of U.S. antitrust law is offensive to many European countries. Thus, the European Commission usually does not take jurisdiction over actions that are implemented outside the Common Market.[48]

A more recent addition to EU competition policy came with the adoption of the EU Merger Regulation, which became effective September 1990.[49] The Regulation provides that a concentration is incompatible with the Common Market when it "creates or strengthens a dominant position as a result of which effective competition would be significantly impeded in the common market or a substantial part of it." The focus on dominance is perhaps a little stronger than the approach used in the United States. According to the Regulation and commission interpretations of it, the resultant merger must produce a firm having over a 25% market share for it to be subject to further scrutiny.[50]

Under the Regulation, all mergers with a community dimension fall within the jurisdiction of the EU Commission. Business groups hailed the Regulation because under it, they have to deal only with the EU Commission to gain clearance throughout the EU for their mergers. However, to benefit from this attribute, the merger must meet the community dimension threshold requirements—that the merging parties have combined worldwide sales of 5 billion European Currency Units ($6.5 billion at the 1992 average annual exchange rate) and that each party has sales of 250 million European Currency Units ($324.5 million in 1992) in the EU.[51] If the merger does not meet the community dimension criteria, then it is subject to the varying standards and procedures of the member states. This can be quite onerous, especially since 9 of the 12 member countries have their own premerger clearance procedures. The EU Commission has proposed that the community dimension standards be lowered substantially to facilitate merger clearance hurdles within the community.[52] However, as of 1993, that proposal has languished.[53]

It is still too early to tell how the merger regulation will be applied. Some have entertained fears that it might be used to achieve nonmarket political objectives. However, as of 1993, the European Commission has focused substantially on economic factors, such as relevant competitive markets, synergistic potential, technological potential, and future market changes.[54]

## Intellectual Property and the Doctrine of Misuse

Those high-technology firms dealing with intellectual property must come to grips with an inherent tension between intellectual property and antitrust policies. Intellectual property laws grant exclusivity to intangible assets so that creators have sufficient economic incentives to develop and disclose their works. In effect, the laws provide a form of limited monopoly, preventing others from accessing the intellectual property in ways proscribed by statute. For instance, the patent laws prevent others from making, using, or selling an invention, while the copyright laws keep the public from copying expressions. Since the purpose of the limited monopoly is to allow creators to earn economic benefits from exclusivity, one should expect those having such legal protection to try to maximize the economic returns from the rights bestowed.

Interesting questions arise, however, since these goals must interface with antitrust policies. That a company is granted a monopoly by the law does not mean it is immune from antitrust. In fact, just the opposite may be true. Those applying the antitrust laws are most worried about firms that enjoy a position of economic strength in the marketplace. This rings true for those holding either of the philosophical foundations of antitrust. For example, in *Kodak*, we saw that tying arrangements are automatically condemned if applied by firms having market power. Otherwise, the more relaxed rule of reason is applied. Thus, firms enjoying intellectual property rights, together with the monopolylike status that attends them, must be particularly wary. This does not necessarily mean that anything these firms do is unlawful. Most transactions are not illegal per se, even for the most powerful firms, and thus may be lawful as long as they are reasonable under the circumstances. Also, just because a company has a legal monopoly, such as from a patent, copyright, or trademark, does not mean that the business has market power in an antitrust sense. For instance, an inventor who receives a patent on an autofocusing device for cameras does not necessarily have market power, because cameras using that invention arguably must compete with cameras utilizing different autofocus technologies. In addition, they may have to contend with other types of cameras, such as those having manual focus and even static focus capabilities. Therefore, one should not jump unduly to the conclusion that intellectual property rights become a straitjacket under the antitrust laws. Rather, a firm with intellectual property rights simply must refrain from engaging in anticompetitive conduct, just as all firms must do. The only proviso is that special attention must be given to how the intellectual property rights affect one's particular economic position in the market.

Firms owning intellectual property violate the antitrust laws when they use their legally bestowed rights as leverage to achieve anticompetitive ends. For example, the following practices are just a few typical intellectual property transactions that may unreasonably restrain trade under certain factual conditions: (1) tying arrangements, wherein customers are forced to purchase products they do not want in order to get the legally protected technology they do want; (2) covenants not to deal in competing goods, in which licensees promise not to deal with products using competitive technologies; (3) resale restraints, wherein certain controls are placed on the manner that purchasers of products utilizing intellectual property may sell those products; (4) price-fixing agreements, in which prices for products with protected technologies are specified; and (5) grant-back provisions, requiring licensees to assign to the licensor ownership to inventions developed by the licensees during the license term. When situations such as these arise, courts do not alter their antitrust analysis simply because intellectual property is involved. The rule of reason, or per-se illegality, if relevant, will be applied, just as if intellectual property were not the subject of the litigation. Again, though, one must always keep in mind that the courts may find that intellectual property rights bestow market power, a conclusion that may seriously tip the scales in an antitrust suit.

Having said all this, there is another, possibly more pernicious doctrine that intellectual property owners must consider when transacting business involving their legally protected rights. The doctrine, called misuse, has its roots in the patent realm. According to a long line of patent cases, patent holders who misuse their legal privileges may not enforce their patent rights until the misuse terminates. What makes this doctrine so extreme is that it applies even when others knowingly and purposively infringe the patent. Making this more extreme is the fact that others may lawfully infringe the patent even if they are not personally subject to the misuse. This means that even if the conduct amounting to misuse is restricted to only a few business dealings, all patent rights nonetheless are essentially shelved until those incidents of misuse are completely purged. As we shall see in *Lasercomb v. Reynolds*, those who infringe intellectual property rights thus can point to misuse with others to defend their own wrongful behavior.

Patent misuse arise in two contexts. From an academic sense, perhaps the least troubling is when a firm is using a patent in a way that violates the antitrust laws. At least one can take solace that the firm has done something tangibly wrong with the patent by using it to achieve anticompetitive ends. However, patent misuse has a life independent of the antitrust laws. In 1942, the Supreme Court made it clear in *Morton Salt v. Suppiger* that one may engage in misuse, even without violating the antitrust laws, by unlawfully extending the patent monopoly.[55] Some situations of this type are easy to understand. For instance, if a licensor attempts to extend the life of a patent by requiring licensees to pay royalties beyond the patent term, then there clearly is a disruption of the patent system's careful balance between incentives and disclosure. Note that this practice might pass muster under the antitrust laws. However, reference to antitrust is unnecessary because competitive effects is not the real issue. Rather, the concern is focused on the period of public exclusion and individual rights of access.

The difficulty with the independent line of misuse arises because most patent practices raise concerns only in a context of restraining competition. In these situations, it is more difficult to argue that a practice judged reasonable under the antitrust laws should nevertheless be considered too anticompetitive under the patent laws. One notable judge probably stated it best when he asked, "If misuse claims are not tested by conventional antitrust principles, by what principles shall they be tested?"[56] However, misuse based on anticompetitive conduct without reference to antitrust remains alive in the courts. As Lasercomb found to its misfortune in the case that follows, the uncertainty surrounding such a possibility may be difficult to manage.

Congress has begun to question whether there can be patent misuse without an antitrust violation. In 1988, the Senate supported new legislation that, had it become law, would have prohibited a finding of patent misuse unless the patentholder had violated the antitrust laws as well.[57] However, the House of Representatives did not go along with such a broad policy change. What resulted was the Patent Misuse Reform Act of 1988, which effectively removed refusals to deal from allegations of patent misuse and which instructed that misuse claims based on tying arrangements must conform more to antitrust principles.[58]

It was in this environment that the next case, *Lasercomb v. Reynolds*, arose. For two reasons, this case was a shock to many legal analysts in the field. First, it confirmed the continuing viability of patent misuse based on anticompetitive conduct even when the actions are reasonable under antitrust policies. Second, it extended the misuse doctrine to copyrights, which heretofore had been traditionally confined to the patent arena. This latter aspect has drawn the most attention because it raises the very real possibility that owners of copyrights in computer programs, among others, must now contend not only with antitrust but with misuse as well.

## LASERCOMB AMERICA, INC. V. REYNOLDS

*Fourth Circuit Court of Appeals, 1990*

### Facts

Lasercomb and Holiday Steel were competitors in the manufacture of steel rule dies used to cut and score cardboard for boxes. Lasercomb developed a computer-assisted design and manufacturing (CAD/CAM) program called Interact for such tasks, and it licensed copies to several businesses, including Holiday. Many of these licenses had durations of 99 years and provided, among other things, that during the license term and for one year thereafter, the licensee would not produce or sell computer-assisted die-making software. These terms were negotiable, and Holiday Steel was one of possibly a number of companies that was not bound by these provisions.

Lasercomb licensed to Holiday Steel four prerelease copies of Interact, receiving $35,000 for the first copy, $17,500 each for the next two copies, and $2,000 for the fourth. Lasercomb informed Holiday Steel that it would charge $2,000 for each additional copy Holiday Steel cared to purchase. However, rather than paying royalties for additional licensed copies, Holiday circumvented protective devices provided with the software and made three unauthorized copies. Later, Holiday Steel created a software program called PDS-1000, which was almost entirely a direct copy of Interact, and marketed it as its own CAD/CAM die-making software.

Lasercomb sued Holiday Steel on several grounds, including copyright infringement. Holiday Steel argued that recovery should be barred because the noncompete contract clauses constituted a misuse of copyright. However, the trial court rejected the defense because (1) the noncompete provisions were reasonable in light of the sensitive and delicate nature of computer software, (2) Holiday Steel was not subject to the noncompete clauses, and (3) the very existence of the copyright misuse defense is questionable. The trial court awarded Lasercomb $105,000 in damages for copyright infringement and enjoined Holiday Steel from publishing and marketing the PDS-1000 software.

### Opinion

We agree with the district court that much uncertainty engulfs the misuse of copyright defense. The misuse of a patent is a potential defense to suit for infringement, and both the existence and parameters of that body of law are well established. The origins of patent and copyright law in England, the treatment of these two aspects of intellectual property by the framers of the U.S. Constitution, and the later statutory and judicial development of patent and copyright law in the United States persuade us that parallel public policies underlie the protection of both types of intellectual property rights. We think these parallel policies call for application of the misuse defense to copyright as well as to patent law.

*Morton Salt Co. v. G.S. Suppiger* is the foundational patent misuse case. Morton Salt brought suit on the basis that defendant had infringed Morton's patent in a salt-depositing machine. Morton's agreements licensing the use of the patented machines required that licensees use only unpatented salt tablets produced by Morton. Morton was thereby using its patent to restrain competition in the sale of an item that was not within the scope of the patent's privilege. The Supreme Court held that it would not aid Morton in protecting its patent when Morton was using that patent in a manner contrary to public policy.

Since *Morton Salt*, the courts have recognized patent misuse as a valid defense and have applied it in a number of cases in which patent owners have attempted to use their patents for price fixing, tie-ins, territorial restrictions, and so forth. The patent misuse defense also has been acknowledged by Congress, in its passage of the 1988 Patent Misuse Reform Act, which limited but did not eliminate the defense.

Although the patent misuse defense has been generally recognized since *Morton Salt*, it has been less certain whether an analogous copyright misuse defense exists. The few courts considering the issue have split on whether the defense should be recognized. We are of the view that since copyright and patent law serve parallel public interests, a misuse defense should apply to infringement actions brought to vindicate either right. Both patent law and copyright law seek to increase the store of human knowledge and arts by rewarding inventors and authors with the exclusive rights to their works for a limited time. At the same time, the granted monopoly power does not extend to property not covered by the patent or copyright. Thus, we are persuaded that the rationale of *Morton Salt* in establishing the misuse defense applies to copyrights.

In declining to recognize a misuse-of-copyright defense, the district court found reasonable Lasercomb's attempt to protect its software copyright by using anticompetitive clauses in its licensing agreement. The court referred to the delicate and sensitive nature of software and that the noncompete language was negotiable. If, as it appears, the district court analogized from the rule-of-reason concept of antitrust law, we think its reliance on that principle was misplaced. A patent or copyright is often regarded as a limited monopoly—an exception to the general public policy against restraints of trade. Since antitrust law is the statutory embodiment of that public policy, there is an understandable association of antitrust law with the misuse defense. Certainly, an entity that uses its patent as the means of violating antitrust law is subject to a misuse-of-patent defense. However, *Morton Salt* held that it is not necessary to prove an antitrust violation in order to successfully assert patent misuse.

So while it is true that the attempted use of a copyright to violate antitrust law probably would give rise to a misuse-of-copyright defense, the converse is not necessarily true: a misuse need not be a violation of antitrust law in order to constitute a defense to an infringement action. The question is not whether the copyright is being used in a manner violative of antitrust law (such as whether the licensing agreement is reasonable), but whether the copyright is being used in a manner violative of the public policy embodied in the grant of a copyright.

Lasercomb undoubtedly has the right to protect against copying of the Interact code. Its standard licensing agreement, however, goes much further and essentially attempts to suppress any attempt by the licensee to independently implement the idea that Interact expresses. The misuse arises from Lasercomb's attempt to use its copyright in a particular expression—the Interact software—to control competition in an area outside the copyright (i.e., the idea of computer-assisted die manufacture) regardless of whether such conduct amounts to an antitrust violation. Although one or another licensee might succeed in negotiating out the noncompete provisions, this does not negate the fact that Lasercomb is attempting to use its copyright in a manner adverse to the public policy embodied in copyright law.

The language employed by the Lasercomb agreement is extremely broad. Each time Lasercomb sells its Interact program to a company and obtains that company's agreement to the noncompete language, the company is required to forgo utilization of the creative abilities of all its officers, directors, and employees in the area of CAD/CAM die-making software. Of yet greater concern, these creative abilities are withdrawn from the public. The period for which this anticompetitive restraint exists is 99 years, which could be longer than the life of the copyright itself.

In its rejection of the copyright misuse defense, the district court emphasized that Holiday Steel was not explicitly a party to a licensing agreement containing the offending language. However, again analogizing to patent misuse, the defense-of-copyright misuse is available even if the defendants themselves have not been injured by the misuse. In *Morton Salt*, the defendant was not a party to the license requirement that only Morton-produced salt tablets be used with Morton's salt-depositing machine. Nevertheless, suit against the defendant was barred on public policy grounds.

In sum, we find that misuse of copyright is a valid defense, that Lasercomb's clauses in its standard licensing agreement constitute misuse of copyright, and that the defense is available to Holiday Steel even though it was not a party to the standard licensing agreement. Holding that Lasercomb should have been barred by the defense-of-copyright misuse from suing for infringement of its copyright in the Interact program, we reverse the injunction and the award of damages for copyright infringement. This holding, of course, is not an invalidation of Lasercomb's copyright. Lasercomb is free to bring suit for infringement once it has purged itself of the misuse.

---

*Lasercomb* can be criticized on a number of grounds. The analogy between copyright and patents may be misplaced when evaluating anticompetitive conduct. Patents provide their owners somewhat more power in the market than do copyrights. Patents, for instance, protect against independent creation; copyrights do not. Patents protect ideas embedded in products; copyrights give rights to only one of many ways to express ideas. Also, doctrines such as scènes à faire ensure that copyrights do not stifle competition. Therefore, even if one had a heightened concern (beyond antitrust policy) about the possible competitive effects from misusing a patent, it does not readily follow that one should carry the same concerns over to copyrights. Indeed, the *Lasercomb* court should have been especially cautious in extending the misuse doctrine based on this analogy, because Congress had recently expressed some substantial concerns about misuse even with patents.

The case also appears to be hostile to trade secret protection techniques. The court places a lot of emphasis on the importance of public disclosure, and it is critical of attempts to restrict access to ideas in copyrighted works. Indeed, one might sense that the court considers trade secret protection to be incompatible with federal copyright policies. To take this thought to the logical extreme, *Lasercomb* raises the issue that state trade secret laws are preempted by the federal Copyright Act. However, this would be reading too much into *Lasercomb*. Rather, the court probably was most concerned with the manner and the length of time that the trade secrets were protected. As we have seen, covenants not to compete are viewed skeptically by the courts. They are, after all, somewhat of a hammer approach for ensuring that licensees do not use trade secrets in developing competitive products. Perhaps, then, one lesson from *Lasercomb* is that noncompete provisions may not be the safest course to take to protect trade secrets. An effective alternative would be to have a contract provision stating that any competing product made or sold by the licensee will be presumed to contain trade secrets obtained from the licensed product. This provision, which shifts the burden to the licensee to prove independent development, should be effective in deterring trade secret abuses without having the appearance of overreaching.

The length of the noncompete clauses, although found reasonable by the trial court, also disturbed the appellate court. Since Interact is a work made for hire, its copyright lasts at most for 100 years from the date of creation.[59] The licenses under review lasted for 100 years. Thus, the term of the licenses extend beyond the statutory length for the copyright, given that the licenses were signed after the date of creation. As with patents, attempts to extend protection beyond the statutory term should be criticized under copyright policy without reference to antitrust or competition. This aspect, too, certainly contributed to the finding of copyright misuse. Therefore, although copyright misuse apparently has viability, one should not overreact, as some have, from its appearance in this case. Maintaining prudent trade secret protection procedures, along with keeping a watchful eye on how courts treat future cases, seems to be the best approach.

## CONCLUSION

The message throughout this book should now be very clear. A high-technology company must fully understand what might be done before deciding what should be done. Business strategy cannot be formulated in a vacuum. Rather it must be made with reference to the possible techniques that exist to achieve various ends. Obviously, an understanding of contracts and how they are treated within the legal system is a critical component of this strategy formulation process.

You now have a sophisticated understanding of the most important legal policies that affect firms managing advanced technologies. You know what currently can be done within the policy constraints of the law. You understand the pros and cons of various approaches, including the likelihood and extent of protection, their costs, and the liabilities if things do not go as planned. The decisions about what should be done are now up to you. Part of the fun of learning about the legal frameworks is the power such learning gives you to make meaningful business strategy decisions. But always remember that with the ever-increasing pace of change in the world of high technologies, legal constructs are increasingly under pressure to adapt. Thus, what you have finished learning today may be out-of-date tomorrow. Hopefully, this book has alerted you to that very prospect. It is incumbent on you, therefore, as a manager in a high-technology enterprise, to keep constantly abreast of changes to legal policies not only in the United States but in the international environment as well. It is only with that kind of perseverance that you can be confident your business strategies are based on the most recent array of legal policies governing your decisions.

## NOTES

1. Louisiana has not adopted all the articles of the Uniform Commercial Code.
2. Although certain provisions of Article 2 specifically are directed to the sale of goods, courts in major jurisdictions, such as California and New York, have applied those provisions to licenses as well. In addition, Article 2A, which specifically applies to leases, treats warranties in a fashion similar to that under Article 2.
3. Magnuson-Moss is codified at 15 U.S.C. §§2301-2312 (1982).
4. For a multinational corporation, its place of business is the country that has the closest relationship to the contract and is closest to where it will be performed. CISG Article 10.
5. See UCC, §2-201.
6. UCC, §2-202.
7. UCC, §2-104, provides additional situations in which a person may be defined as a merchant.
8. UCC, §2-312.
9. See Milgard Tempering, Inc., v. Selas Corp. of America, 902 F. 2d 703 (9th Cir. 1990); RRX Indus. v. Lab-Con, Inc., 772 F. 2d 543 (9th Cir. 1985).
10. The district court determined that although NCR's representations were overly optimistic, they were not fraudulent. This was affirmed on appeal.
11. Survey conducted by Ernst & Young and Electronic Business magazine, reported in S. Almassy, "A New Mind-Set for Electronics Executives," Electronic Business (March 30, 1992) at 83.
12. See, e.g., B. Powell, "Eyes on the Future," Newsweek (May 31, 1993) at 39; S. Yoder and G. Zachary, "Digital Media Business Takes Form as a Battle of Complex Alliances," Wall Street J. (July 14, 1993) at 1, 6.
13. B. Powell, A. Underwood, S. Nayyar and C. Fleming, "Eyes on the Future," Newsweek (May 31, 1993) at 39.
14. This list is derived from a superb article that comprehensively explains the reasons for and forms of strategic alliances. D. Scrivner, "Strategic Alliances in the 1990s," Computer Lawyer (December 1992) at 24-32.

15. For a full discussion of best-efforts contracts, see W. Carvill and R. Campbell, "Licensing Agreements and the Obligation to Use "Best Efforts," 3 J. of Proprietary Rights 2 (January 1991).

16. If the program ultimately is embodied in a semiconductor chip, then protection may be sought not only under copyright but also under the Semiconductor Chip Protection Act. This will protect not only the program but the mask, which is used to manufacture the chip. The mask, in essence, is like the blueprint of a house in that it contains the pattern of the circuitry to be implanted on the chip. The Semiconductor Chip Protection Act thereby extends protection to the creative efforts of the engineer who designed the chip to implement the program. See Lipner and Kalman, Computer Law, (Merrill Publishing Co., 1989) at 36-40.

17. Apple Computer, Inc., v. Microsoft Corp. and Hewlett-Packard Co., No. C-88-20149 (N.D. Cal. April 15, 1992).

18. E. Pollock, "Mediation Firms Alter the Legal Landscape," Wall Street J. (March 22, 1993) at B1.

19. K. Clark and W. Fenwick, "Structuring an Arbitration Agreement for High Technology Disputes," 9 Computer Lawyer 22, 23 (September 1992).

20. See, e.g., Cal. Code Civ. P. Section 1283.

21. K. Clark and W. Fenwick, "Structuring an Arbitration Agreement for High Technology Disputes," 9 Computer Lawyer 22 (September 1992).

22. D. Bender, "Alternative Dispute Resolution and the Computer-Related Dispute: An Ideal Marriage?" 7 Computer Lawyer 9, 10 (May 1990).

23. E. Pollock, "Mediation Firms Alter the Legal Landscape," Wall Street J. (March 22, 1993) at B1.

24. V. Cundiff, "Companies Are Seeking Litigation Alternatives," National L.J.(May 17, 1993) at S25.

25. For a thorough discussion of the possible drawbacks to ADR, see D. Friedman and M. Broaddus,"Computer Contract Disputes in the 1990s: Choosing ADR or Litigation," 5 J. of Proprietary Rights 2, 5-8 (April 1993).

26. Allegations of anticompetitive conduct against Nintendo include the use of lockout chips to prevent the functioning of games that are not licensed by Nintendo, the bundling of hardware and software, restrictive software licensing agreements, and vertical price fixing. Microsoft has been under the antitrust spotlight for, among other things, allegedly failing to disclose important aspects of its operating system to licensees, thereby placing them at a competitive disadvantage. See, e.g., S. Sugawara, "Microsoft: Hot Rod or Road Hog," Washington Post (August 2 1993) at H1; J. Markoff, "Microsoft Confronts Its Success," New York Times (August 23, 1993) at D1.

27. National Cooperative Research Act of 1984, 15 U.S.C. §§4301 et seq. Congress currently is considering legislation that would extend this act to joint production ventures as well.

28. C. Chipello, "Joint Ventures Are Encouraged by Government," Wall Street J. (June 23, 1989).

29. O. Suris, "Big Three Win Joint Patent, Marking a First," Wall Street J. (April 13, 1993) at B1.

30. Continental T.V., Inc. v. GTE Sylvania Inc., 433 U.S. 36 (1977).

31. Jefferson Parish Hospital District No. 2 v. Hyde, 104 S. Ct. 1551 (1984).

32. Business Electronics Corp. v. Sharp Electronics Corp., 485 U.S. 717 (1988).

33. See U.S. v. Aluminum Company of America, 148 F. 2d 416 (2d Cir. 1945).

34. Aspen Skiing Co. v. Aspen Highlands Skiing Corp., 105 S. Ct. 2847 (1985).

35. See J. Yates and A. DiResta, "Software Support and Hardware Maintenance Practices: Tying Considerations," 8 Computer Lawyer 17 (June 1991).

36. See Brown Shoe Co. v. U.S., 370 U.S. 294 (1962).

37. U.S. Department of Justice and Federal Trade Commission Horizontal Merger Guidelines (April 2, 1992), reprinted in 4 Trade Reg. Rep. (CCH) 13,104.

38. For a full discussion of antitrust issues facing high-technology companies considering mergers, see M. Ostrau, "When High-Tech Companies Join Forces," Business Law Today (January/February 1993) at 56.

39. For a discussion suggesting that enhanced antitrust enforcement may be around the corner, see E. Gellhorn and W. Kovacic, "Anti-Competitive Forces May Stir Anew," National L.J. (May 24, 1993) at 19-21.

40. For a summary of this trend, and a comment on its antitrust ramifications, see C. Compton, "Cooperation, Collaboration, and Coalition: A Perspective on the Types and Purposes of Technology Joint Ventures," 61 Antitrust L.J. 861 (Spring 1993).

41. J. Markhoff, "Unable to Beat Them, IBM Now Joins Them," New York Times (July 6, 1992) at C1.

42. C. Compton, at 862. See D. Hamilton, "U.S., Japan Focusing on Electronic Gear," Wall Street J. (July 12, 1993) at 1.

43. Commission Notice Concerning Agreements of Minor Importance, O.J. Eur. Comm. (No. C 231) 2 (1986).

44. M. Powell, "Software Licenses and the Application of the EC Competition Rules," 8 Computer Lawyer (July 1991) at 15.

45. R. Tritell, "The Application of Block Exemptions to Intellectual Property Licensing in the European Community," 5 J. of Proprietary Rights (July 1993) at 12.

46. Ibid.

47. W. Ryba Jr., "The New European Community Merger Law: Competition Policy and Its Application," Business & the Contemporary World (Autumn 1992) at 75.

48. R. Schaffer, B. Earle, and F. Agusti, "International Business Law and Its Environment. West Publishing Co. (1990) at 462, 464.

49. Council Regulation (EEC) No. 4064/89 of December 21, 1989 on the control of concentrations between undertakings.

50. F. Fine, "The Substantive Test of the EEC Merger Control Regulation: The First Two Years," 61 Antitrust L.J. (Spring 1993) at 711.

51. EC Merger Regulation, Art. 1(2). See J. Winterscheid, "E.C. Merger Rules Remain Snarled," National L.J. (September 6, 1993) at S11.

52. Community dimension standards would have been lowered under the proposal to 2 billion European Currency Units in combined worldwide sales and 100 million European Currency Units for each party in EC sales. "Notes on Council Regulation (EEC), 4064/89," Bull. EC Supp. 2/90 at 23.

53. J. Winterscheid, "E.C. Merger Rules Remain Snarled," National L.J. (September 6, 1993) at S11.
54. W. Ryba Jr, at 84; See F. Fine, "The Substantive Test of the EEC Merger Control Regulation: The First Two Years," 61 Antitrust L.J. (Spring 1993) at 735.
55. 314 U.S. 488 (1942).
56. USM Corp., v. SPS Technologies, Inc., 694 F. 2d 505, 512 (7th Cir. 1982) (opinion written by Justice R. Posner).
57. The Intellectual Property Antitrust Protection Act of 1988, S. 438.
58. Patent Misuse Reform Act of 1988, amending 35 U.S.C. 271(d).
59. The duration of copyright protection for works made for hire is 75 years from the date of publication or 100 years from the date of creation, whichever expires first. 17 U.S.C. §302(c).

# APPENDIXES

§100. Definitions.

When used in this title unless the context otherwise indicates—

(a) The term "invention" means invention or discovery.

(b) The term "process" means process, art or method, and includes a new use of a known process, machine, manufacture, composition of matter, or material.

(c) The terms "United States" and "this country" means the United States of America, its territories and possessions.

(d) The word "patentee" includes not only the patentee to whom the patent was issued but also the successors in title to the patentee.

§101. Inventions Patentable.

Whoever invents or discovers any new and useful process, machine, manufacture, or composition of matter, or any new and useful improvement thereof, may obtain a patent therefor, subject to the conditions and requirements of this title.

§102. Conditions for Patentability; Novelty and Loss of Right to Patent.

A person shall be entitled to a patent unless—

(a) the invention was known or used by others in this country, or patented or described in a printed publication in this or a foreign country, before the invention thereof by the application for patent, or

(b) the invention was patented or described in a printed publication in this or a foreign country or in public use or on sale in this country, more than one year prior to the date of the application for patent in the United States, or

(c) he has abandoned the invention, or

(d) the invention was first patented or caused to be patented, or was the subject of an inventor's certificate, by the applicant or his legal representatives or assigns in a foreign country prior to the date of the application for patent in this country on an application for patent or inventor's certificate filed more than twelve months before the filing of the application in the United States, or

(e) the invention was described in a patent granted on an application for patent by another filed in the United States before the invention thereof by the applicant for patent, or on an international application by another who has fulfilled the requirements of paragraphs (1), (2), and (4) of section 371(c) of this title before the invention thereof by the applicant for patent, or

(f) he did not himself invent the subject matter sought to be patented, or

(g) before the applicant's invention thereof the invention was made in this country by another who had not abandoned, suppressed, or concealed it. In determining priority of invention there shall be considered not only the respective dates of conception and reduction to practice of the invention, but also the reasonable diligence of one who was first to conceive and last to reduce to practice, from a time prior to conception by the other.

## §103. Conditions for Patentability; Non-Obvious Subject Matter.

A patent may not be obtained though the invention is not identically disclosed or described as set forth in section 102 of this title, if the differences between the subject matter sought to be patented and the prior art are such that the subject matter as a whole would have been obvious at the time the invention was made to a person having ordinary skill in the art to which said subject matter pertains. Patentability shall not be negatived by the manner in which the invention was made.

Subject matter developed by another person, which qualifies as prior art only under subsection (f) or (g) of section 102 of this title, shall not preclude patentability under this section where the subject matter and the claimed invention were, at the time the invention was made, owned by the same person or subject to an obligation of assignment to the same person.

## §111. Application for Patent.

Application for patent shall be made, or authorized to be made, by the inventor, except as otherwise provided in this title, in writing to the Commissioner. Such application shall include (1) a specification as prescribed by section 112 of this title; (2) a drawing as prescribed by section 113 of this title; and (3) on oath by the applicant as prescribed by section 115 of this title. The application must be accompanied by the fee required by law. The fee and oath may be submitted after the specification and any required drawing are submitted, within such period and under such conditions, including the payment of a surcharge, as may be prescribed by the Commissioner. Upon failure to submit the fee and oath within such prescribed period, the application shall be regarded as abandoned, unless it is shown to the satisfaction of the Commissioner that the delay in submitting the fee and oath was unavoidable. The filing date of an application shall be the date on which the specification and any required drawing are received in the Patent and Trademark Office.

## §112. Specification.

The specification shall contain a written description of the invention, and of the manner and process of making and using it, in such full, clear, concise, and exact terms as to enable any person skilled in the art to which it pertains, or with which it is most nearly connected, to make and use the same, and shall set forth the best mode contemplated by the inventor of carrying out his invention.

The specification shall conclude with one or more claims particularly pointing out and distinctly claiming the subject matter which the applicant regards as his invention.

A claim may be written in independent or, if the nature of the case admits, in dependent or multiple dependent form.

Subject to the following paragraph, a claim in dependent form shall contain a reference to a claim previously set forth and then specify a further limitation of the subject matter claimed. A claim in dependent form shall be construed to incorporate by reference all the limitations of the claim to which it refers.

A claim in multiple dependent form shall contain a reference, in the alternative only, to more than one claim previously set forth and then specify a further limitation of the subject matter claimed. A multiple dependent claim shall not serve as a basis for any other multiple dependent claim. A multiple dependent claim shall be construed to incorporate by reference all the limitations of the particular claim in relation to which it is being considered.

An element in a claim for a combination may be expressed as a means or step for performing a specified function without the recital of structure, material, or acts in support thereof, and such claim shall be construed to cover the corresponding structure, material, or acts described in the specification and equivalents thereof.

## §113. Drawings.

The applicant shall furnish a drawing where necessary for the understanding of the subject matter sought to be patented. When the nature of such subject matter admits of illustration by a drawing and the applicant has not furnished such a drawing, the Commissioner may require its submission with a time period of not less than two months from the sending of a notice thereof. Drawings submitted after the filing date of the application may not be used (i) to overcome any insufficiency of the specification due to lack of an enabling disclosure or otherwise inadequate disclosure therein, or (ii) to supplement the original disclosure thereof for the purpose of interpretation of the scope of any claim.

## §116. Joint Inventors.

When an invention is made by two or more persons jointly, they shall apply for patent jointly and each make the required oath, except as otherwise provided in this title. Inventors may apply for a patent jointly even though (1) they did not physically work together or at the same time, (2) each did not make the same type or amount of contribution, or (3) each did not make a contribution to the subject matter of every claim of the patent.

If a joint inventor refuses to join in an application for patent or cannot be found or reached after diligent effort, the application may be made by the other inventor on behalf of himself and the omitted inventor. The Commissioner, on proof of the pertinent facts and after such notice to the omitted inventor as he prescribes, may grant a patent to the inventor making the application, subject to the same rights which the omitted inventor would have had if he had been joined. The omitted inventor may subsequently join in the application.

Whenever through error a person is named in an application for patent as the inventor, or through error an inventor is not named in an application, and such error arose without any deceptive intention on his part, the Commissioner may permit the application to be amended accordingly, under such terms as he prescribes.

## §119. Benefit of Earlier Filing Date in Foreign Country; Right of Priority.

An application for patent for an invention filed in this country by any person who has, or whose legal representatives or assigns have, previously regularly filed an application for a patent for the same invention in a foreign country which affords similar privileges in the case of applications filed in the United States or to citizens of the United States, shall have the same effect as the same application would have if filed in this country on the date on which the application for patent for the same invention was first filed in such foreign country, if the application in this country is filed within twelve months from the earliest date on which such foreign application was filed; but no patent shall be granted on any application for patent for an invention which had been patented or described in a printed publication in any country more than one year before the date of the actual filing of the application in this country, or which had been in public use or on sale in this country more than one year prior to such filing.

No application for patent shall be entitled to this right of priority unless a claim therefor and a certified copy of the original foreign application, specification and drawings upon which it is based are filed in the Patent and Trademark Office before the patent is granted, or at such time during the pendency of the application as required by the Commissioner not earlier than six months after the filing of the application in this country. Such certification shall be made by the patent office of the foreign country in which filed and show the date of the application and of the filing of the specification and other papers. The Commissioner may require a translation of the papers filed if not in the English language and such other information as he deems necessary.

In like manner and subject to the same conditions and requirements, the right provided in this section may be based upon a subsequent regularly filed application in the same foreign country instead of the first filed foreign application, provided that any foreign application filed prior to such subsequent application has been withdrawn, abandoned, or otherwise disposed of, without having been laid open to public inspection and without leaving any rights outstanding, and has not served, nor thereafter shall serve, as a basis for claiming a right of priority.

Applications for inventors' certificates filed in a foreign country in which applicants have a right to apply, at their discretion, either for a patent or for an inventor's certificate shall be treated in this country in the same manner and have the same effect for purpose of the right of priority under this section as applications for patents, subject to the same conditions and requirements of this section as apply to applications for patents, provided such applicants are entitled to the benefits of the Stockholm Revision of the Paris Convention at the time of such filing.

## §122. Confidential Status of Applications.

Applications for patent shall be kept in confidence by the Patent and Trademark Office and no information concerning the same given without authority of the applicant or owner unless necessary to carry out the provisions of any Act of Congress or in such special circumstances as may be determined by the Commissioner.

## §131. Examination of Application.

The Commissioner shall cause an examination to be made of the application and the alleged new invention; and if on such examination it appears that the applicant is entitled to a patent under the law, the Commissioner shall issue a patent therefor.

## §154. Contents and Term of Patent.

Every patent shall contain a short title of the invention and a grant to the patentee, his heirs or assigns, for the term of seventeen years, subject to the payment of issue fees as provided for in this title, of the right to exclude others from making, using, or selling the invention throughout the United States and, if the invention is a process, of the right to exclude others from using or selling throughout the United States, or importing into the United States, products made by that process, referring to the specification for the particulars thereof. A copy of the specification and drawings shall be annexed to the patent and be a part thereof.

## §161. Patents for Plants.

Whoever invents or discovers and asexually reproduces any distinct and new variety of plant, including cultivated sports, mutants, hybrids, and newly found seedlings, other than a tuber propagated plant or a plant found in an uncultivated state, may obtain a patent therefor, subject to the conditions and requirements of this title.

The provisions of this title relating to patents for inventions shall apply to patents for plants, except as otherwise provided.

## §171. Patents for Designs.

Whoever invents any new, original and ornamental design for an article of manufacture may obtain a patent therefor, subject to the conditions and requirements of this title.

The provisions of this title relating to patents for inventions shall apply to patents for designs, except as otherwise provided.

## §173. Term of Design Patent.

Patents for designs shall be granted for the term of fourteen years.

## §181. Secrecy of Certain Inventions and Withholding of Patent.

Whenever publication or disclosure by the grant of a patent on an invention in which the Government has a property interest might, in the opinion of the head of the interested Government agency, be detrimental to the national security, the Commissioner upon being so notified shall order that the invention be kept secret and shall withhold the grant of a patent therefor under the conditions set forth hereinafter.

Whenever the publication or disclosure of an invention by the granting of a patent, in which the Government does not have a property interest, might, in the opinion of the Commissioner, be detrimental to the national security, he shall make the application for patent in which such invention is disclosed available for inspection to the Atomic Energy Commission, the Secretary of Defense, and the chief officer of any other department or agency of the Government designated by the President as a defense agency of the United States.

Each individual to whom the application is disclosed shall sign a dated acknowledgement thereof, which acknowledgement shall be entered in the file of the application. If, in the opinion of the Atomic Energy Commission, the Secretary of Defense Department, or the chief officer of another department or agency so designated, the publication or disclosure of the invention by the granting of a patent therefor would be detrimental to the national security, the Atomic Energy Commission, the Secretary of a Defense Department, or such other chief officer shall notify the Commissioner and the Commissioner shall order that the inventions be kept secret and shall withhold the grant of a patent for such period as the national interest requires, and notify the applicant thereof. Upon proper showing by the head of the department or agency who caused the secrecy order to be issued that the examination of the application might jeopardize the national interest, the Commissioner shall thereupon maintain the application in a sealed condition and notify the applicant thereof. The owner of an application which has been placed under a secrecy order shall have a right to appeal from the order to the Secretary of Commerce under the rules prescribed by him.

An invention shall not be ordered kept secret and the grant of a patent withheld for a period of more than one year. The Commissioner shall renew the order at the end thereof, or at the end of any renewal period, for additional periods of one year upon notification by the head of the department or the chief officer of the agency who caused the order to be issued that an affirmative determination has been made that the national interest continues so to require. An order in effect, or issued, during a time when the United States is at war, shall remain in effect for the duration of hostilities and one year following cessation of hostilities. An order in effect, or issued, during a national emergency declared by the President shall remain in effect for the duration of the national emergency and six months thereafter. The Commissioner may rescind any order upon notification by the heads of the departments and the chief officers of the agencies who caused the order to be issued that the publication or disclosure of the invention is no longer deemed detrimental to the national security.

## §184. Filing of Application in Foreign Country.

Except when authorized by a license obtained from the Commissioner a person shall not file or cause or authorize to be filed in any foreign country prior to six months after filing in the United States an application for patent or for the registration of a utility model, industrial design, or model in respect of an invention made in this country. A license shall not be granted with respect to an invention subject to an order issued by the Commissioner pursuant to section 181 of this title without the concurrence of the head of the departments and the chief officers of the agencies who caused the order to be issued. The license may be granted retroactively where an application has been filed abroad through error and without deceptive intent and the application does not disclose an invention within the scope of section 181 of this title.

The term "application" when used in this chapter includes applications and any modifications, amendments, or supplements thereto, or divisions thereof.

The scope of a license shall permit subsequent modifications, amendments, and supplements containing additional subject matter if the application upon which the request for the license is based is not, or was not, required to be made available for inspection under section 181 of this title and if such modifications, amendments, and supplements does not change the general nature of the invention in a manner which would require such application to be made available for inspection under such section 181. In any case in which a license is not, or was not, required in order to file an application in any foreign country, such subsequent modifications, amendments, and supplements may be made, without a license, to the application filed in the foreign country if the United States application was not required to be made available for inspection under section 181 and if such modifications, amendments, and supplements do not, or did not, change the general nature of the invention in a manner which would require the United States application to have been made available for inspection under such section 181.

## §262. Joint Owners.

In the absence of any agreement to the contrary, each of the joint owners of a patent may make, use or sell the patented invention without the consent of and without accounting to the other owners.

## §271. Infringement of Patent.

(a) Except as otherwise provided in this title, whoever, without authority makes, uses or sells any patented invention, within the United States during the term of the patent therefor, infringes the patent.

(b) Whoever actively induced infringement of a patent shall be liable as an infringer.

(c) Whoever sells a component of a patented machine, manufacturer, combination or composition, or a material or apparatus for use in practicing a patented process, constituting a material part of the invention, knowing the same to be especially made or especially adapted for use in an infringement of such patent, and not a staple article or commodity of commerce suitable for substantial noninfringing use, shall be liable as a contributory infringer.

(g) Whoever without authority imports into the United States or sells or uses within the United States a product which is made by a process patented in the United States shall be liable as an infringer, if the importation, sale, or use of the product occurs during the term of such process patent. In an action for infringement of a process patent, no remedy may be granted for infringement on account of the noncommercial use or retail sale of a product unless there is no adequate remedy under this title for infringement on account of the importation or other use or sale of that product. A product which is made by a patented process will, for purposes of this title, not be considered to be so made after—

(1) it is materially changed by subsequent processes; or

(2) it becomes a trivial and nonessential component of another product.

§283. Injunction.

The several courts having jurisdiction of cases under this title may grant injunctions in accordance with the principles of equity to prevent the violation of any right secured by patent, on such terms as the court deems reasonable.

§284. Damages.

Upon finding for the claimant the court shall award the claimant damages adequate to compensate for the infringement but in no event less than a reasonable royalty for the use made of the invention by the infringer, together with interest and costs as fixed by the court.

When the damages are not found by a jury, the court shall assess them. In either event the court may increase the damages up to three times the amount found or assessed.

The court may receive expert testimony as an aid to the determination of damages or of what royalty would be reasonable under the circumstances.

§285. Attorney Fees.

The court in exceptional cases may award reasonable attorney fees to the prevailing party.

§287. Limitation on Damages and Other Remedies; Marking and Notice.

(a) Patentees, and persons making or selling any patented article for or under them, may give notice to the public that the same is patented, either by fixing thereon the word "patent" or the abbreviation "pat", together with the number of the patent, or when, from the character of the article, this can not be done, by fixing to it, or to the package wherein one or more of them is contained, a label containing a like notice. In the event of failure so to mark, no damages shall be recovered by the patentee in any action for infringement, except on proof that the infringer was notified of the infringement and continued to infringe thereafter, in which event damages may be recovered only for infringement occurring after such notice. Filing of an action for infringement shall constitute such notice.

(b)(1) An infringer under section 217(g) shall be subject to all the provisions of this title relating to damages and injunctions except to the extent those remedies are modified by this subsection or section 9006 of the Process Patent Amendments Act of 1988. The modifications of remedies provided in this subsection shall not be available to any person who—

(A) practiced the patented process;

(B) owns or controls, or is owned or controlled

by, the person who practiced the patented process; or

(C) had knowledge before the infringement that a patented process was used to make the product the importation, use, or sale of which constitutes the infringement.

(2) No remedies for infringement under section 271(g) of this title shall be available with respect to any product in the possession of, or in transit to, the person subject to liability under such section before that person had notice of infringement with respect to that product. The person subject to liability shall bear the burden of proving any such possession or transit.

(3)(A) In making a determination with respect to the remedy in an action brought for infringement under section 271(g), the court shall consider—

(i) the good faith demonstrated by the defendant with respect to a request for disclosure,

(ii) the good faith demonstrated by the plaintiff with respect to a request for disclosure, and

(iii) the need to restore the exclusive rights secured by the patent.

(B) For purposes of subparagraph (A), the following are evidence of good faith:

(i) a request for disclosure made by the defendant;

(ii) a response within a reasonable time by the person receiving the request for disclosure; and

(iii) the submission of the response by the defendant to the manufacturer, or if the manufacturer is not known, to the supplier, of the product to be purchased by the defendant, together with a request for a written statement that the process claimed in any patent disclosed in the response is not used to produce such product.

The failure to perform any acts described in the preceding sentence is evidence of absence of good faith unless there are mitigating circumstances. Mitigating circumstances include the case in which, due to the nature of the product, or like commercial circumstances, a request for disclosure is not necessary or practicable to avoid infringement.

(4)(A) For purposes of this subsection, a "request for disclosure" means a written request made to a person then engaged in the manufacture of a product to identify all process patents owned by or licensed to that person, as of the time of the request, that the person then reasonably believes could be asserted to be infringed under section 271(g) if that product were imported into, or sold or used in, the United States by an unauthorized person. A request for disclosure is further limited to a request—

(i) which is made by a person regularly engaged in the United States in the sale of the same type of products as those manufactured by the person to whom the request is directed, or which includes facts showing that the person making the request plans to engage in the sale of such products in the United States;

(ii) which is made by such person before the person's first importation, use, or sale of units of the product produced by an infringing process and before the person had notice of infringement with respect to the product; and

(iii) which includes a representation by the person making the request that such person will promptly submit the patents identified pursuant to the request to the manufacturer, or if the manufacturer is not known, to the supplier, of the product to be purchased by the person making the request, and will request from that manufacturer or supplier a written statement that none of the processes claimed in those patents is used in the manufacture of the product.

(B) In the case of a request for disclosure received by a person to whom a patent is licensed, that person shall either identify the patent or promptly notify the licensor of the request for disclosure.

(C) A person who has marked, in the manner prescribed by subsection (a), the number of the process patent on all products made by the patented process which have been sold by that person in the United States before a request for disclosure is received is not required to respond to the request for disclosure. For purposes of the preceding sentence, the term "all products" does not include products made before the effective date of the Process Patent Amendments Act of 1988.

(5)(A) For purposes of this subsection, notice of infringement means actual knowledge, or receipt by a person of a written notification, or a combination thereof, of information sufficient to persuade a reasonable person that it is likely that a product was made by a process patented in the United States.

(B) A written notification from the patent holder charging a person with infringement shall specify the patented process alleged to have been used and the reason for a good faith belief that such process was used. The patent holder shall include in the notification such information as is reasonably necessary to explain fairly the patent holder's belief, except that the patent holder is not required to disclose any trade secret information.

(C) A person who receives a written notification described in subparagraph (B) or a written response to a request for disclosure described in paragraph (4) shall be deemed to have notice of infringement with respect to any patent referred to in such written notification or response unless that person, absent mitigating circumstances—

(i) promptly transmits the written notification or response to the manufacturer or, if the manufacturer is not known, to the supplier, of the product purchased or to be purchased by that person; and

(ii) receives a written statement from the manufacturer or supplier which on its face sets forth a well grounded factual basis for a belief that the identified patents are not infringed.

(D) For purposes of this subsection, a person who obtains a product made by a process patented in the United States in a quantity which is abnormally large in relation to the volume of business of such person or an efficient inventory level shall be rebuttably presumed to have actual knowledge that the product was made by such patented process.

(6) A person who receives a response to a request for disclosure under this subsection shall pay to the person to whom the request was made a reasonable fee to cover actual costs incurred in complying with the request, which may not exceed the cost of a commercially available automated patent search of the matter involved, but in no case more than $500.

### §301. Citation of Prior Art.

Any person at any time may cite to the Office in writing prior art consisting of patents or printed publications which that person believes to have a bearing on the patentability of any claim of a particular patent. If the person explains in writing the pertinency and manner of applying such prior art to at least one claim of the patent, the citation of such prior art and the explanation thereof will become a part of the official file of the patent. At the written request of the person citing the prior art, his or her identity will be excluded from the patent file and kept confidential.

### §302. Request for Reexamination.

Any person at any time may file a request for reexamination by the Office of any claim of patent on the basis of any prior art cited under the provisions of Section 301 of this title. The request must be in writing and must be accompanied by payment of a reexamination fee established by the Commissioner of Patents pursuant to the provisions of Section 41 of this title. The request must set forth the pertinency and manner of applying cited prior art to every claim for which reexamination is requested. Unless the requesting person is the owner of the patent, the Commissioner promptly will send a copy of the request to the owner of record of the patent.

## APPENDIX B
### Selected Provisions of The Uniform Trade Secrets Act

#### §1. Definitions.
As used in this Act, unless the context requires otherwise:

(1) "Improper means" includes theft, bribery, misrepresentation, breach or inducement of a breach of a duty to maintain secrecy, or espionage through electronic or other means;

(2) "Misappropriation" means:

(i) acquisition of a trade secret of another by a person who knows or has reason to know that the trade secret was acquired by improper means; or

(ii) disclosure or use of a trade secret of another without express or implied consent by a person who

(A) used improper means to acquire knowledge of the trade secret; or

(B) at the time of disclosure or use, knew or had reason to know that his knowledge of the trade secret was

(I) derived from or through a person who had utilized improper means to acquire it;

(II) acquired under circumstances giving rise to a duty to maintain its secrecy or limit its use; or

(III) derived from or through a person who owed a duty to the person seeking relief to maintain its secrecy or limit its use; or

(C) before a material change of his [or her] position, knew or had reason to know that it was a trade secret and that knowledge of it had been acquired by accident or mistake.

(3) "Person" means a natural person, corporation, business trust, estate, trust, partnership, association, joint venture, government, governmental subdivision or agency, or any other legal or commercial entity.

(4) "Trade secret" means information, including a formula, pattern, compilation, program, device, method, technique, or process, that:

(i) derives independent economic value, actual or potential, from not being generally known to, and not being readily ascertainable by proper means by, other persons who can obtain economic value from its disclosure or use, and

(ii) is the subject of efforts that are reasonable under the circumstances to maintain its secrecy.

#### §2. Injunctive Relief.
(a) Actual or threatened misappropriation may be enjoined. Upon application to the court, an injunction shall be terminated when the trade secret has ceased to exist, but the injunction may be continued for an additional reasonable period of time in order to eliminate commercial advantage that otherwise would be derived from the misappropriation.

(b) In exceptional circumstances, an injunction may condition future use upon payment of a reasonable royalty for no longer than the period of time for which use could have been prohibited. Exceptional circumstances include, but are not limited to, a material and prejudicial change of position prior to acquiring knowledge or reason to know of misappropriation that renders a prohibitive injunction inequitable.

(c) In appropriate circumstances, affirmative acts to protect a trade secret may be compelled by court order.

#### §3. Damages.
(a) Except to the extent that a material and prejudicial change of position prior to acquiring knowledge or reason to know of misappropriation renders a monetary recovery inequitable, a complainant is entitled to recover damages for misappropriation. Damages can include both actual loss caused by misappropriation and the unjust enrichment caused by misappropriation that is not taken into account in computing actual loss. In lieu of damages measured by any other methods, the damages caused by misappropriation may be measured by imposition of liability for a reasonable royalty for a misappropriator's unauthorized disclosure or use of a trade secret.

(b) If willful and malicious misappropriation exists, the court may award exemplary damages in an amount not exceeding twice any award made under subsection (a).

#### §4. Attorney's Fees.
If (i) a claim of misappropriation is made in bad faith, (ii) a motion to terminate an injunction is made or resisted in bad faith, or (iii) willful and malicious misappropriation exists, the court may award reasonable attorney's fees to the prevailing party.

#### §5. Preservation of Secrecy.
In an action under this Act, a court shall preserve the secrecy of an alleged trade secret by rea-

sonable means, which may include granting protective orders in connection with discovery proceedings, holding in-camera hearings, sealing the records of the action, and ordering any person involved in the litigation not to disclose an alleged trade secret without prior court approval.

### §6. Statute of Limitations.

An action for misappropriation must be brought within 3 years after the misappropriation is discovered or by the exercise of reasonable diligence should have been discovered. For the purposes of this section, a continuing misappropriation constitutes a single claim.

### §7. Effect on Other Law.

(a) Except as provided in subsection (b), this Act displaces conflicting tort, restitutionary, and other law of this State providing civil remedies for misappropriation of a trade secret.

(b) This Act does not affect:

(1) contractual remedies, whether or not based upon misappropriation of a trade secret;

(2) other civil remedies that are not based upon misappropriation of a trade secret; or

(3) criminal remedies, whether or not based upon misappropriation of a trade secret.

## APPENDIX C
## Selected Provisions of The Copyright Act

### §101. Definitions.

An "architectural work" is the design of a building as embodied in any tangible medium of expression, including a building, architectural plans, or drawings. The work includes the overall form as well as the arrangement and composition of spaces and elements in the design, but does not include individual standard features.

"Audiovisual works" are works that consist of a series of related images which are intrinsically intended to be shown by the use of machines or devices such as projectors, viewers, or electronic equipment, together with accompanying sounds, if any, regardless of the nature of the material objects, such as films or tapes, in which the works are embodied.

A "compilation" is a work formed by the collection and assembling of preexisting materials or of data that are selected, coordinated, or arranged in such a way that the resulting work as a whole constitutes an original work of authorship. The term "compilation" includes collective works.

A "computer program" is a set of statements or instructions to be used directly or indirectly in a computer in order to bring about a certain result.

"Copies" are material objects, other than phono-records, in which a work is fixed by any method now known or later developed, and from which the work can be perceived, reproduced, or otherwise communicated, either directly or with the aid of a machine or device. The term "copies" includes the material object, other than a phonorecord, in which the work is first fixed.

A "derivative work" is a work based upon one or more preexisting works, such as a translation, musical arrangement, dramatization, fictionalization, motion picture version, sound recording, art reproduction, abridgment, condensation, or any other form in which a work may be recast, transformed, or adapted. A work consisting of editorial revisions, annotations, elaborations, or other modifications which, as a whole, represent an original work of authorship, is a "derivative work".

To "display" a work means to show a copy of it, either directly or by means of a film, slide, television image, or any other device or process or, in the case of a motion picture or other audiovisual work, to show individual images nonsequentially.

A work is "fixed" in a tangible medium of expression when its embodiment in a copy or phonorecord, by or under the authority of the author, is sufficiently permanent or stable to permit it to be perceived, reproduced, or otherwise communicated for a period of more than transitory duration. A work consisting of sounds, images, or both, that are being transmitted, is "fixed" for purposes of this title if a fixation of the work is being made simultaneously with its transmission.

A "joint work" is a work prepared by two or more authors with the intention that their contributions be merged into inseparable or interdependent parts of a unitary whole.

"Literary works" are works, other than audiovisual works, expressed in words, numbers, or other verbal or numerical symbols or indicia, regardless of the nature of the material objects, such as books, periodicals, manuscripts, phonorecords, film, tapes, disks, or cards, in which they are embodied.

"Pictorial, graphic, and sculptural works" include two-dimensional and three-dimensional works of fine, graphic, and applied art, photographs, prints and art reproductions, maps, globes, charts, diagrams, models, and technical drawings, including architectural plans. Such works shall include works of artistic crafts-manship insofar as their form but not their mechanical or utilitarian aspects are concerned; the design of a useful article, as defined in this section, shall be considered a pictorial, graphic, or sculptural work only if, and only to the extent that, such design incorporates picto-rial, graphic, or sculptural features that can be identified separately from, and are capable of ex-isting independently of, the utilitarian aspects of the article.

"Publication" is the distribution of copies or phonorecords of a work to the public by sale or other transfer of ownership, or by rental, lease, or lending. The offering to distribute copies or phonorecords to a group of persons for pur-poses of further distribution, public performance, or public display, constitutes publication. A public performance or display of a work does not of itself constitute publication.

To perform or display a work "publicly" means—

(1) to perform or display it at a place open to the public or at any place where a substantial number of persons outside of a normal circle of a family and its social acquaintances is gathered; or

(2) to transmit or otherwise communicate a performance or display of the work to a place specified by clause (1) or to the public, by means of any device or process, whether the members of the public capable of receiving the performance or display receive it in the same place or in sepa-rate places and at the same time or at different times.

"Sound recordings" are works that result from the fixation of a series of musical, spoken, or other sounds, but not including the sounds ac-companying a motion picture or other audiovi-sual work, regardless of the nature of the mate-rial objects, such as disks, tapes, or other phonorecords, in which they are embodied.

A "useful article" is an article having an in-trinsic utilitarian function that is not merely to portray the appearance of the article or to convey information. An article that is normally a part of a useful article is considered a "useful article".

A "work of visual art" is—

(1) a painting, drawing, print, or sculpture, ex-isting in a single copy, in a limited edition of 200 copies or fewer that are signed and consecutively numbered by the author, or, in the case of a sculpture, in multiple cast, carved, or fabricated sculptures of 200 or fewer that are consecutively numbered by the author and bear the signature or other identifying mark of the author; or

(2) a still photographic image produced for ex-hibition purposes only, existing in a single copy that is signed by the author, or in a limited edi-tion of 200 copies or fewer that are signed and consecutively numbered by the author.

A work of visual art does not include—

(A)(i) any poster, map, globe, chart, technical drawing, diagram, model, applied art, motion picture or other audio-visual work, book, maga-zine, newspaper, periodical, data base, electronic information service, electronic publication, or similar publication;

(ii) any merchandising item or advertising, promotional, descriptive, covering, or packaging material or container;

(iii) any portion or part of any item described in clause (i) or (ii);

(B) any work made for hire; or

(C) any work not subject to copyright protec-tion under this title.

A "work made for hire" is—

(1) a work prepared by an employee within the scope of his or her employment; or

(2) a work specially ordered or commissioned for use as a contribution to a collective work, as a part of a motion picture or other audiovisual work, as a translation, as a supplementary work, as a compilation, as an instructional text, as a test, as answer material for a test, or as an atlas, if the parties expressly agree in a written instru-ment signed by them that the work shall be con-sidered a work made for hire. For the purpose of the foregoing sentence, a "supplementary work" is a work prepared for publication as a secondary adjunct to a work by another author for the pur-pose of introducing, concluding, illustrating, ex-plaining, revising, commenting upon, or assisting in the use of the other work, such as forewords, afterwords, pictorial illustrations, maps, charts, tables, editorial notes, musical arrangements, an-swer material for tests, bibliographies, appen-dixes, and indexes, and an "instructional text" is a literary, pictorial, or graphic work prepared for publication and with the purpose of use in sys-tematic instructional activities.

## §102. Subject Matter of Copyright; In General.

(a) Copyright protection subsists, in accor-dance with this title, in original works of author-ship fixed in any tangible medium of expression, now known or later developed, from which they can be perceived, reproduced, or otherwise com-municated, either directly or with the aid of a ma-chine or device. Works of authorship include the following categories:

(1) literary works;

(2) musical works, including any accompanying words;

(3) dramatic works, including any accompanying music;

(4) pantomimes and choreographic works;

(5) pictorial, graphic, and sculptural works;

(6) motion pictures and other audiovisual works;

(7) sound recordings; and

(8) architectural works.

(b) In no case does copyright protection for an original work of authorship extend to any idea, procedure, process, system, method of operation, concept, principle, or discovery, regardless of the form in which it is described, explained, illustrated, or embodied in such work.

## §103. Subject Matter of Copyright; Compilations and Derivative Works.

(a) The subject matter of copyright as specified by section 102 includes compilations and derivative works, but protection for a work employing preexisting material in which copyright subsists does not extend to any part of the work in which such material has been used unlawfully.

(b) The copyright in a compilation or derivative work extends only to the material contributed by the author of such work, as distinguished from the preexisting material employed in the work, and does not imply any exclusive right in the preexisting material. The copyright in such work is independent of, and does not affect or enlarge the scope, duration, ownership, or subsistence of, any copyright protection in the preexisting material.

## §106. Exclusive Rights in Copyrighted Works.

Subject to sections 107 through 120, the owner of copyright under this title has the exclusive rights to do and to authorize any of the following:

(1) to reproduce the copyrighted work in copies or phonorecords;

(2) to prepare derivative works based upon the copyrighted work;

(3) to distribute copies or phonorecords of the copyrighted work to the public by sale or other transfer of ownership, or by rental, lease, or lending;

(4) in the case of literary, musical, dramatic, and choreographic works, pantomimes, and motion pictures and other audiovisual works, to perform the copyrighted work publicly; and

(5) in the case of literary, musical, dramatic, and choreographic works, pantomimes, and pictorial, graphic, or sculptural works, including the individual images of a motion picture or other audiovisual work, to display the copyrighted work publicly.

## §106A. Rights of Certain Authors to Attribution and Integrity.

(a) Rights of Attribution and Integrity. Subject to section 107 and independent of the exclusive rights provided in section 106, the author of a work of visual art—

(1) shall have the right—

(A) to claim authorship of that work, and

(B) to prevent the use of his or her name as the author of any work of visual art which he or she did not create;

(2) shall have the right to prevent the use of his or her name as the author of the work of visual art in the event of a distortion, mutilation, or other modification of the work which would be prejudicial to his or her honor or reputation; and

(3) subject to the limitations set forth in section 113(d), shall have the right—

(A) to prevent any intentional distortion, mutilation, or other modification of that work which would be prejudicial to his or her honor or reputation, and any intentional distortion, mutilation, or modification of that work is a violation of that right, and

(B) to prevent any destruction of a work of recognized stature, and any intentional or grossly negligent destruction of that work is a violation of that right.

(b) Scope and Exercise of Rights. Only the author of a work of visual art has the rights conferred by subsection (a) in that work, whether or not the author is the copyright owner. The authors of a joint work of visual art are co-owners of the rights conferred by subsection (a) in that work.

(c) Exceptions.

(1) The modification of a work of visual art which is a result of the passage of time or the inherent nature of the materials is not a distortion, mutilation, or other modification described in subsection (a)(3)(A).

(2) The modification of a work of visual art which is the result of conservation, or of the public presentation, including lighting and placement, of the work is not a destruction, distortion, mutilation, or other modification described in subsection (a)(3) unless the modification is caused by gross negligence.

(3) The rights described in paragraphs (1) and (2) of subsection (a) shall not apply to any reproduction, depiction, portrayal, or other use of a work in, upon, or in any connection with any item described in subparagraph (A) or (B) of the definition of "work of visual art" in section 101, and any such reproduction, depiction, portrayal, distortion, mutilation, or other modification described in paragraph (3) of subsection (a).

(d) Duration of Rights.

(1) With respect to works of visual art created on or after the effective date set forth in section 610(a) of the Visual Artists Rights Act of 1990, the rights conferred by subsection (a) shall endure for a term consisting of the life of the author.

(2) With respect to works of visual art created before the effective date set forth in section 610(a) of the Visual Artists Rights Act of 1990, but title to which has not, as of such effective date, been transferred from the author, the rights conferred by subsection (a) shall be coextensive with, and shall expire at the same time as, the rights conferred by section 106.

(3) In the case of a joint work prepared by two or more authors, the rights conferred by subsection (a) shall endure for a term consisting of the life of the last surviving author.

(4) All terms of the rights conferred by subsection (a) run to the end of the calendar year in which they would otherwise expire.

(e) Transfer and Waiver.

(1) The rights conferred by subsection (a) may not be transferred, but those rights may be waived if the author expressly agrees to such waiver in a written instrument signed by the author. Such instrument shall specifically identify the work, and uses of that work, to which the waiver applies, and the waiver shall apply only to the work and uses so identified. In the case of a joint work prepared by two or more authors, a waiver of rights under this paragraph made by one such author waives such rights for all such authors.

(2) Ownership of the rights conferred by subsection (a) with respect to a work of visual art is distinct from ownership of any copy of that work, or of a copyright or any exclusive right under a copyright in that work. Transfer of ownership of any copy of a work of visual art, or of a copyright or any exclusive right under a copyright, shall not constitute a waiver of the rights conferred by subsection (a). Except as may otherwise be agreed by the author in a written instrument signed by the author, a waiver of the rights conferred by subsection (a) with respect to

a work of visual art shall not constitute a transfer of ownership of any copy of that work, or of ownership of a copyright or of any exclusive right under a copyright in that work.

## §107. [Effective June 1, 1991] Limitations on Exclusive Rights: Fair Use.

Notwithstanding the provisions of sections 106 and 106A, the fair use of a copyrighted work, including such use by reproduction in copies or phonorecords or by any other means specified by that section, for purposes such as criticism, comment, news reporting, teaching (including multiple copies for classroom use), scholarship, or research, is not an infringement of copyright. In determining whether the use made of a work in any particular case is a fair use the factors to be considered shall include—

(1) the purpose and character of the use, including whether such use is of a commercial nature or is for nonprofit educational purposes;

(2) the nature of the copyrighted work;

(3) the amount and substantiality of the portion used in relation to the copyrighted work as a whole; and

(4) the effect of the use upon the potential market for or value of the copyrighted work. The fact that a work is unpublished shall not itself bar a finding of fair use if such finding is made upon consideration of all the above factors.

## §109. Limitations on Exclusive Rights: Effect of Transfer of Particular Copy or Phonorecord.

(a) Notwithstanding the provisions of section 106(3), the owner of a particular copy or phonorecord lawfully made under this title, or any person authorized by such owner, is entitled, without the authority of the copyright owner, to sell or otherwise dispose of the possession of that copy or phonorecord.

(b) (1) (A) Notwithstanding the provisions of subsection (a), unless authorized by the owners of copyright in the sound recording or the owner of copyright in a computer program (including any tape, disk, or other medium embodying such program), and in the case of a sound recording in the musical works embodied therein, neither the owner of a particular phonorecord nor any person in possession of a particular copy of a computer program (including any tape, disk, or other medium embodying such program), may, for the purposes of direct or indirect commercial advantage, dispose of, or authorize the disposal of, the possession of that phonorecord or computer program (including any tape, disk, or other medium embodying such program) by rental, lease, or lending, or by any other act or practice in the nature of rental, lease, or lending. Nothing in the preceding sentence shall apply to the rental, lease, or lending of a phonorecord for nonprofit purposes by a nonprofit library or nonprofit educational institution. The transfer of possession of a lawfully made copy of a computer program by a nonprofit educational institution to another nonprofit educational institution or to faculty, staff, and students does not constitute rental, lease, or lending for direct or indirect commercial purposes under this subsection.

(B) This subsection does not apply to—

(i) a computer program which is embodied in a machine or product and which cannot be copied during the ordinary operation or use of the machine or product; or

(ii) a computer program embodied in or used in conjunction with a limited purpose computer that is designed for playing video games and may be designed for other purposes.

## §114. Scope of Exclusive Rights in Sound Recordings.

(a) The exclusive rights of the owner of copyright in a sound recording are limited to the rights specified by clauses (1), (2), and (3) of section 106, and do not include any right of performance under section 106(4).

(b) The exclusive right of the owner of copyright in a sound recording under clause (1) of section 106 is limited to the right to duplicate the sound recording in the form of phonorecords, or of copies of motion pictures and other audiovisual works, that directly or indirectly recapture the actual sounds fixed in the recording. The exclusive right of the owner of copyright in a sound recording under clause (2) of section 106 is limited to the right to prepare a derivative work in which the actual sounds fixed in the sound recording are rearranged, remixed, or otherwise altered in sequence or quality. The exclusive rights of the owner of copyright in a sound recording under clauses (1) and (2) of section 106 do not extend to the making or duplication of another sound recording that consists entirely of an independent fixation of other sounds, even though such sounds imitate or simulate those in the copyrighted sound recording. The exclusive rights of the owner of copyright in a sound recording under clauses (1), (2), and (3) of section 106 do not apply to sound recordings included in educational television and radio programs (as defined in section 397 of title 47) distributed or transmitted by or through public broadcasting entities (as defined by section

118(g): *Provided,* That copies or phonorecords of said programs are not commercially distributed by or through public broadcasting entities to the general public.

(c) This section does not limit or impair the exclusive right to perform publicly, by means of a phonorecord, any of the works specified by section 106(4).

(d) On January 3, 1978, the Register of Copyrights, after consulting with representatives of owners of copyrighted materials, representatives of the broadcasting, recording, motion picture, entertainment industries, and arts organizations, representatives of organized labor and performers of copyrighted materials, shall submit to the Congress a report setting forth recommendations as to whether this section should be amended to provide for performers and copyright owners of copyrighted material any performance rights in such material. The report should describe the status of such rights in foreign countries, the views of major interested parties, and specific legislative or other recommendations, if any.

## §115. Scope of Exclusive Rights in Nondramatic Musical Works: Compulsory License for Making and Distributing Phonorecords.

In the case of nondramatic musical works, the exclusive rights provided by clauses (1) and (3) of section 106, to make and to distribute phonorecords of such works, are subject to compulsory licensing under the conditions specified by this section.

(a) Availability and Scope of Compulsory License.

(1) When phonorecords of a nondramatic musical work have been distributed to the public in the United States under the authority of the copyright owner, any other person may, by complying with the provisions of this section, obtain a compulsory license to make and distribute phonorecords of the work. A person may obtain a compulsory license only if his or her primary purpose in making phonorecords is to distribute them to the public for private use. A person may not obtain a compulsory license for use of the work in the making of phonorecords duplicating a sound recording fixed by another, unless: (i) such sound recording was fixed lawfully; and (ii) the making of the phonorecords was authorized by the owner of copyright in the sound recording or, if the sound recording was fixed before February 15, 1972, by any person who fixed the sound recording pursuant to an express license from the owner of the copyright in the musical work or

pursuant to a valid compulsory license for use of such work in a sound recording.

(2) A compulsory license includes the privilege of making a musical arrangement of the work to the extent necessary to conform it to the style or manner of interpretation of the performance involved, but the arrangement shall not change the basic melody or fundamental character of the work, and shall not be subject to protection as a derivative work under this title, except with the express consent of the copyright owner.

## §117. Limitations on Exclusive Rights: Computer Programs.

Notwithstanding the provisions of section 106, it is not an infringement for the owner of a copy of a computer program to make or authorize the making of another copy or adaptation of that computer program provided:

(1) that such a new copy or adaptation is created as an essential step in the utilization of the computer program in conjunction with a machine and that it is used in no other manner, or

(2) that such new copy or adaptation is for archival purposes only and that all archival copies are destroyed in the event that continued possession of the computer program should cease to be rightful.

Any exact copies prepared in accordance with the provisions of this section may be leased, sold, or otherwise transferred, along with the copy from which such copies were prepared, only as part of the lease, sale, or other transfer of all rights in the program. Adaptations so prepared may be transferred only with the authorization of the copyright owner.

## §120. Scope of Exclusive Rights in Architectural Works.

(a) Pictorial Representations Permitted. The copyright in an architectural work that has been constructed does not include the right to prevent the making, distributing, or public display of pictures, paintings, photographs, or other pictorial representations of the work, if the building in which the work is embodied is located in or ordinarily visible from a public place.

(b) Alterations to and Destruction of Buildings. Notwithstanding the provisions of section 106(2), the owners of a building embodying an architectural work may, without the consent of the author or copyright owner of the architectural work, make or authorize the making of alterations to such building, and destroy or authorize the destruction of such building.

## §201. Ownership of Copyright.

(a) Initial Ownership. Copyright in a work protected under this title vests initially in the author or authors of the work. The authors of a joint work are co-owners of copyright in the work.

(b) Works Made for Hire. In the case of a work made for hire, the employer or other person for whom the work was prepared is considered the author for purposes of this title, and, unless the parties have expressly agreed otherwise in a written instrument signed by them, owns all of the rights comprised in the copyright.

(c) Contributions to Collective Works. Copyright in each separate contribution to a collective work is distinct from copyright in the collective work as a whole, and vests initially in the author of the contribution. In the absence of an express transfer of the copyright or of any rights under it, the owner of copyright in the collective work is presumed to have acquired only the privilege of reproducing and distributing the contribution as part of that particular collective work, any revision of that collective work, and any later collective work in the same series.

(d) Transfer of Ownership.

(1) The ownership of a copyright may be transferred in whole or in part by any means of conveyance or by operation of law, and may be bequeathed by will or pass as personal property by the applicable laws of intestate succession.

(2) Any of the exclusive rights comprised in a copyright, including any subdivision of any of the rights specified by section 106, may be transferred as provided by clause (1) and owned separately. The owner of any particular exclusive right is entitled, to the extent of that right, to all of the protection and remedies accorded to the copyright owner by this title.

## §202. Ownership of Copyright as Distinct From Ownership of Material Object.

Ownership of a copyright, or of any of the exclusive rights under a copyright, is distinct from ownership of any material object in which the work is embodied. Transfer of ownership of any material object, including the copy of a phonorecord in which the work is first fixed, does not of itself convey any rights in the copyrighted work embodied in the object; nor, in the absence of an agreement, does transfer of ownership of a copyright or of any exclusive rights under a copyright convey property rights in any material object.

## §302. Duration of Copyright: Works Created on or After January 1, 1978.

(a) In General. Copyright in a work created on or after January 1, 1978, subsists from its creation and, except as provided by the following subsections, endures for a term consisting of the life of the author and fifty years after the author's death.

(b) Joint Works. In the case of a joint work prepared by two or more authors who did not work for hire, the copyright endures for a term consisting of the life of the last surviving author and fifty years after such last surviving author's death.

(c) Anonymous Works, Pseudonymous Works, and Works Made for Hire. In the case of an anonymous work, a pseudonymous work, or a work made for hire, the copyright endures for a term of seventy-five years from the year of its first publication, or a term of one hundred years from the year of its creation, whichever expires first. If, before the end of such term, the identity of one or more of the authors of an anonymous or pseudonymous work is revealed in the records of a registration made for that work under subsections (a) or (d) of section 408, or in the records provided by this subsection, the copyright in the work endures for the term specified by subsection (a) or (b), based on the life of the author or authors whose identity has been revealed. Any person having an interest in the copyright in an anonymous or pseudonymous work may at any time record, in records to be maintained by the Copyright Office for that purpose, a statement identifying one or more authors of the work; the statement shall also identify the person filing it, the nature of that person's interest, the source of the information recorded, and the particular work affected, and shall comply in form and content with requirements that the Register of Copyrights shall prescribe by regulation.

## §401. Notice of Copyright: Visually Perceptible Copies.

(a) General Provisions. Whenever a work protected under this title is published in the United States or elsewhere by authority of the copyright owner, a notice of copyright as provided by this section may be placed on publicly distributed copies from which the work can be visually perceived, either directly or with the aid of a machine or device.

(b) Form of Notice. If a notice appears on the copies, it shall consist of the following three elements:

(1) the symbol © (the letter C in a circle), or the word "Copyright", or the abbreviation "Copr."; and

(2) the year of first publication of the work; in the case of compilations or derivative works incorporating previously published material, the year date of first publication of the compilation or derivative work is sufficient. The year date may be omitted where a pictorial, graphic, or sculptural work, with accompanying text matter, if any, is reproduced in or on greeting cards, postcards, stationery, jewelry, dolls, toys, or any useful articles; and

(3) the name of the owner of copyright in the work, or an abbreviation by which the name can be recognized, or a generally known alternative designation of the owner.

(c) Position of Notice. The notice shall be affixed to the copies in such manner and location as to give reasonable notice of the claim of copyright. The Register of Copyrights shall prescribe by regulation, as examples, specific methods of affixation and positions of the notice on various types of works that will satisfy this requirement, but these specifications shall not be considered exhaustive.

(d) Evidentiary Weight of Notice. If a notice of copyright in the form and position specified by this section appears on the published copy or copies to which a defendant in a copyright infringement suit had access, then no weight shall be given to such a defendant's interposition of a defense based on innocent infringement in mitigation of actual or statutory damages, except as provided in the last sentence of section 504(c)(2).

## §407. Deposit of Copies or Phonorecords for Library of Congress.

(a) Except as provided by subsection (c), and subject to the provisions of subsection (e), the owner of copyright or of the exclusive right of publication in a work published in the United States shall deposit, within three months after the date of such publication—

(1) two complete copies of the best edition; or

(2) if the work is a sound recording, two complete phonorecords of the best edition, together with any printed or other visually perceptible material published with such phonorecords.

Neither the deposit requirements of this subsection nor the acquisition provisions of subsection (e) are conditions of copyright protection.

(b) The required copies or phonorecords shall be deposited in the Copyright Office for the use or disposition of the Library of Congress. The Register of Copyrights shall, when requested by the depositor and upon payment of the fee prescribed by section 708, issue a receipt for the deposit.

(c) The Register of Copyrights may be regulation exempt any categories of material from the deposit requirements of this section, or require deposit of only one copy or phonorecord with respect to any categories. Such regulations shall provide either for complete exemption from the deposit requirements of this section, or for alternative forms of deposit aimed at providing a satisfactory archival record of a work without imposing practical or financial hardships on the depositor, where the individual author is the owner of copyright in a pictorial, graphic, or sculptural work and (i) less than five copies of the work have been published, or (ii) the work has been published in a limited edition consisting of numbered copies, the monetary value of which would make the mandatory deposit of two copies of the best edition of the work burdensome, unfair, or unreasonable.

(d) At any time after publication of a work as provided by subsection (a), the Register of Copyrights may make written demand for the required deposit on any of the persons obligated to make the deposit under subsection (a). Unless deposit is made within three months after the demand is received, the person or persons on whom the demand was made are liable—

(1) to a fine of not more than $250 for each work; and

(2) to pay into a specially designated fund in the Library of Congress the total retail price of the copies or phonorecords demanded, or, if no retail price has been fixed, the reasonable cost of the Library of Congress of acquiring them; and

(3) to pay a fine of $2,500, in addition to any fine or liability imposed under clauses (1) and (2), if such person willfully or repeatedly fails or refuses to comply with such a demand.

## §408. Copyright Registration in General.

(a) Registration Permissive. At any time during the subsistence of copyright in any published or unpublished work, the owner of copyright or of any exclusive right in the work may obtain registration of the copyright claim by delivering to the Copyright Office the deposit specified by this section, together with the application and fee specified by sections 409 and 708. Such registration is not a condition of copyright protection.

(b) Deposit for Copyright Registration. Except as provided by subsection (c), the material deposited for registration shall include—

(1) in the case of an unpublished work, one complete copy or phonorecord;

(2) in the case of a published work, two complete copies or phonorecords of the best edition;

(3) in the case of a work first published outside the United States, one complete copy or phonorecord as so published;

(4) in the case of a contribution to a collective work, one complete copy or phonorecord of the best edition of the collective work.

Copies or phonorecords deposited for the Library of Congress under section 407 may be used to satisfy the deposit provisions of this section, if they are accompanied by the prescribed application and fee, and by any additional identifying material that the Register may, by regulation, require. The Register shall also prescribe regulations establishing requirements under which copies or phonorecords acquired for the Library of Congress under subsection (e) of section 407, otherwise than by deposit, may be used to satisfy the deposit provisions of this section.

(c) Administrative Classification and Optional Deposit.

(1) The Register of Copyrights is authorized to specify by regulation the administrative classes into which works are to be placed for purposes of deposit and registration, and the nature of the copies or phonorecords to be deposited in the various classes specified. The regulations may require or permit, for particular classes, the deposit of identifying material instead of copies or phonorecords, the deposit of only one copy or phonorecord where two would normally be required, or a single registration for a group of related works. This administrative classification of works has no significance with respect to the subject matter of copyright or the exclusive rights provided by this title.

## §409. Application for Copyright Registration.

The application for copyright registration shall be made on a form prescribed by the Register of Copyrights and shall include—

(1) the name and address of the copyright claimant;

(2) in the case of a work other than an anonymous or pseudonymous work, the name and nationality or domicile of the author or authors, and, if one or more of the authors is dead, the dates of their deaths;

(3) if the work is anonymous or pseudonymous, the nationality or domicile of the author or authors;

(4) in the case of a work made for hire, a statement to this effect;

(5) if the copyright claimant is not the author,

a brief statement of how the claimant obtained ownership of the copyright;

(6) the title of the work, together with any previous or alternative titles under which the work can be identified;

(7) the year in which creation of the work was completed;

(8) if the work has been published, the date and nation of its first publication;

(9) in the case of a compilation or derivative work, an identification of any preexisting work or works that it is based on or incorporates, and a brief, general statement of the additional material covered by the copyright claim being registered;

(10) in the case of a published work containing material of which copies are required by section 601 to be manufactured in the United States, the names of the persons or organizations who performed the processes specified by subsection (c) of section 601 with respect to that material, and the places where those processes were performed; and

(11) any other information regarded by the Register of Copyrights as bearing upon the preparation or identification of the work or the existence, ownership, or duration of the copyright.

## §410. Registration of Claim and Issuance of Certificate.

(a) When, after examination, the Register of Copyrights determines that, in accordance with the provisions of this title, the material deposited constitutes copyrightable subject matter and that the other legal and formal requirements of this title have been met, the Register shall register the claim and issue to the applicant a certificate of registration under the seal of the Copyright Office. The certificate shall contain the information given in the application, together with the number and effective date of the registration.

(b) In any case in which the Register of Copyrights determines that, in accordance with the provisions of this title, the material deposited does not constitute copyrightable subject matter or that the claim is invalid for any other reason, the Register shall refuse registration and shall notify the applicant in writing of the reasons for such refusal.

(c) In any judicial proceedings the certificate of a registration made before or within five years after first publication of the work shall constitute prima facie evidence of the validity of the copyright and of the facts stated in the certificate. The evidentiary weight to be accorded the certificate of a registration made thereafter shall be within the discretion of the court.

(d) The effective date of a copyright registration is the day on which an application, deposit, and fee, which are later determined by the Register of Copyrights or by a court of competent jurisdiction to be acceptable for registration, have all been received in the Copyright Office.

## §411. Registration and Infringement Actions.

(a) Except for actions for infringement of copyright in Berne Convention works whose country of origin is not the United States and an action brought for violation of the rights of the author under section 106A(a), and subject to the provisions of subsection (b), no action for infringement of the copyright in any work shall be instituted until registration of the copyright claim has been made in accordance with this title. In any case, however, where the deposit, application, and fee required for registration have been delivered to the Copyright Office in proper form and registration has been refused, the applicant is entitled to institute an action for infringement if notice thereof, with a copy of complaint, is served on the Register of Copyrights. The Register may, at his or her option, become a party to the action with respect to the issue of registrability of the copyright claim by entering an appearance within sixty days after such service, but the Register's failure to become a party shall not deprive the court of jurisdiction to determine that issue.

(b) In the case of a work consisting of sounds, images, or both, the first fixation of which is made simultaneously with its transmission, the copyright owner may, either before or after such fixation takes place, institute an action for infringement under section 501, fully subject to the remedies provided by sections 502 through 506 and sections 509 and 510, if, in accordance with requirements that the Register of Copyrights shall prescribe by regulation, the copyright owner—

(1) serves notice upon the infringer, not less than ten or more than thirty days before such fixation, identifying the work and the specific time and source of its first transmission, and declaring an intention to secure copyright in the work; and

(2) makes registration for the work, if required by subsection (a), within three months after its first transmission.

## §412. Registration as Prerequisite to Certain Remedies for Infringement.

In any action under this title, other than an action brought for a violation of the rights of the author under section 106A(a) or an action instituted under section 411(b), no award of statutory damages or of attorney's fees, as provided by sections 504 and 505, shall be made for—

(1) any infringement of copyright in an unpublished work commenced before the effective date of its registration; or

(2) any infringement of copyright commenced after first publication of the work and before the effective date of its registration, unless such registration is made within three months after the first publication of the work.

## §501. Infringement of Copyright.

(a) Anyone who violates any of the exclusive rights of the copyright owner as provided by sections 106 through 118 or of the author as provided in section 106A(a), or who imports copies or phonorecords into the United States in violation of section 602, is an infringer of the copyright or right of the author, as the case may be. For purposes of this chapter (other than section 506), any reference to copyright shall be deemed to include the rights conferred by section 106A(a). As used in this subsection, the term "anyone" includes any State, any instrumentality of a State, and any officer or employee of a State or instrumentality of a State acting in his or her official capacity. Any State, and any such instrumentality, officer, or employee, shall be subject to the provisions of this title in the same manner and to the same extent as any nongovernmental entity.

## §502. Remedies for Infringement: Injunctions.

(a) Any court having jurisdiction of a civil action arising under this title may, subject to the provisions of section 1498 of title 28, grant temporary and final injunctions on such terms as it may deem reasonable to prevent or restrain infringement of a copyright.

(b) Any such injunction may be served anywhere in the United States on the person enjoined; it shall be operative throughout the United States and shall be enforceable, by proceedings in contempt or otherwise, by any United States court having jurisdiction of that person. The clerk of the court granting the injunction shall, when requested by any other court in which enforcement of the injunction is sought, transmit promptly to the other court a certified copy of all the papers in the case on file in such clerk's office.

## §503. Remedies for Infringement: Impounding and Disposition of Infringing Articles.

(a) At any time while an action under this title is pending, the court may order the impounding, on such terms as it may deem reasonable, of all copies or phonorecords claimed to have been made or used in violation of the copyright owner's exclusive rights, and of all plates, molds, matrices, masters, tapes, film negatives, or other articles by means of which such copies or phonorecords may be reproduced.

(b) As part of a final judgment or decree, the court may order the destruction or other reasonable disposition of all copies or phonorecords found to have been made or used in violation of the copyright owner's exclusive rights, and of all plates, molds, matrices, masters, tapes, film negatives, or other articles by means of which such copies or phonorecords may be reproduced.

## §504. Remedies for Infringement: Damages and Profits.

(a) In General. Except as otherwise provided by this title, an infringer of copyright is liable for either—

(1) the copyright owner's actual damages and any additional profits of the infringer, as provided by subsection (b); or

(2) statutory damages, as provided by subsection (c).

(b) Actual Damages and Profits. The copyright owner is entitled to recover the actual damages suffered by him or her as a result of the infringement, and any profits of the infringer that are attributable to the infringement and are not taken into account in computing the actual damages. In establishing the infringer's profits, the copyright owner is required to present proof only of the infringer's gross revenue, and the infringer is required to prove his or her deductible expenses and the elements of profit attributable to factors other than the copyrighted work.

(c) Statutory Damages.

(1) Except as provided by clause (2) of this subsection, the copyright owner may elect, at any time before final judgment is rendered, to recover, instead of actual damages and profits, an award of statutory damages for all infringements involved in the action, with respect to any one work, for which any one infringer is liable indi-

vidually, or for which any two or more infringers are liable jointly and severally, in a sum of not less than $500 or more than $20,000 as the court considers just. For the purposes of this subsection, all the parts of a compilation or derivative work constitute one work.

(2) In a case where a copyright owner sustains the burden of proving, and the court finds, that infringement was committed willfully, the court in its discretion may increase the award of statutory damages to a sum of not more than $100,000. In a case where the infringer sustains the burden of proving, and the court finds, that such infringer was not aware and had no reason to believe that his or her acts constituted an infringement of copyright, the court in its discretion may reduce the award of statutory damages to a sum of not less than $200. The court shall remit statutory damages in any case where an infringer believed and had reasonable grounds for believing that his or her use of the copyright work was a fair use under section 107, if the infringer was: (i) an employee or agent of a nonprofit educational institution, library, or archives acting within the scope of his or her employment who, or such institution, library, or archives itself, which infringed by reproducing the work in copies or phonorecords; or (ii) a public broadcasting entity which or a person who, as a regular part of the nonprofit activities of a public broadcasting entity (as described in subsection (g) of section 118) infringed by performing a published nondramatic literary work or by reproducing a transmission program embodying a performance of such a work. Leg.H. October 31, 1988, P.L. 100-568 §10(b), 102 Stat. 2860.

## §505. Remedies for Infringement: Costs and Attorney's Fees.

In any civil action under this title, the court in its discretion may allow the recovery of full costs by or against any party other than the United States or an officer thereof. Except as otherwise provided in this title, the court may also award a reasonable attorney's fee to the prevailing party as part of the costs.

## §506. Criminal Offenses.

(a) Criminal Infringement. Any person who infringes a copyright willfully and for purposes of commercial advantage or private financial gain shall be punished as provided in section 2319 of title 18.

(b) Forfeiture and Destruction. When any person is convicted of any violation of subsection (a), the court in its judgment of conviction shall, in addition to the penalty therein prescribed, order the forfeiture and destruction or other disposition of all infringing copies or phonorecords and all implements, devices, or equipment used in the manufacture of such infringing copies or phonorecords.

(c) Fraudulent Copyright Notice. Any person who, with fraudulent intent, places on any article a notice of copyright or words of the same purport that such person knows to be false, or who, with fraudulent intent, publicly distributes or imports for public distribution any article bearing such notice or words that such person knows to be false, shall be fined not more than $2,500.

(d) Fraudulent Removal of Copyright. Any person who, with fraudulent intent, removes or alters any notice of copyright appearing on a copy of a copyrighted work shall be fined not more than $2,500.

(e) False Representation. Any person who knowingly makes a false representation of a material fact in the application for copyright registration provided for by section 409, or in any written statement filed in connection with the application, shall be fined not more than $2,500.

(f) Rights of Attribution and Integrity. Nothing in this section applies to infringement of the rights conferred by section 106A(a).

## §511. Liability of States, Instrumentalities of States, and State Officials for Infringement of Copyright.

(a) In General. Any State, any instrumentality of a State, and any officer or employee of a State or instrumentality of a State acting in his or her official capacity, shall not be immune, under the Eleventh Amendment of the Constitution of the United States or under any other doctrine of sovereign immunity, from suit in Federal court by any person, including any governmental or nongovernmental entity, for a violation of any of the exclusive rights of a copyright owner provided by sections 106 through 119, for importing copies of phonorecords in violation of section 602, or for any other violation under this title.

(b) Remedies. In a suit described in subsection (a) for a violation described in that subsection, remedies (including remedies both at law and in equity) are available for the violation to the same extent as such remedies are available for such a violation in a suit against any public or private entity other than a State, instrumentality of a

State, or officer or employee of a State acting in his or her official capacity. Such remedies include impounding and disposition of infringing articles under section 503, actual damages and profits and statutory damages under section 504, costs and attorney's fees under section 505, and the remedies provided in section 510.

### §602. Infringing Importation of Copies or Phonorecords.

(a) Importation into the United States, without the authority of the owner of copyright under this title, of copies or phonorecords of a work that have been acquired outside the United States is an infringement of the exclusive right to distribute copies or phonorecords under section 106, actionable under section 501. This subsection does not apply to—

(1) importation of copies or phonorecords under the authority or for the use of the Government of the United States or of any State or political subdivision of a State, but not including copies or phonorecords for use in schools, or copies of any audiovisual work imported for purposes other than archival use;

(2) importation, for the private use of the importer and not for distribution, by any person with respect to no more than one copy or phonorecord of any one work at any one time, or by any person arriving from outside the United States with respect to copies or phonorecords forming part of such person's personal baggage; or

(3) importation by or for an organization operated for scholarly, educational, or religious purposes and not for private gain, with respect to no more than one copy of an audiovisual work solely for its archival purposes, and no more than five copies or phonorecords of any other work for its library lending or archival purposes, unless the importation of such copies or phonorecords is part of an activity consisting of systematic reproduction or distribution, engaged in by such organization in violation of the provisions of section 108(g)(2).

(b) In a case where the making of the copies or phonorecords would have constituted an infringement of copyright if this title had been applicable, their importation is prohibited. In a case where the copies or phonorecords were lawfully made, the United States Customs Service has no authority to prevent their importation unless the provisions of section 601 are applicable. In either case, the Secretary of the Treasury is authorized to prescribe, by regulation, a procedure under which any person claiming an interest in the copyright in a particular work may, upon payment of a specified fee, be entitled to notification by the Customs Service of the importation of articles that appear to be copies or phonorecords of the work.

## APPENDIX D
### Selected Provisions of The Lanham Act—Title 15

### §1051. Registration of Trademarks on Principal Register; Requirements of Application for Same; Intent-to-Use Applications; Designation of United States Resident by Foreign Applicant.

(a) Trade-Marks Used in Commerce. The owner of a trademark used in commerce may apply to register his or her trade-mark under this chapter on the principal register established:

(1) By filing in the Patent and Trademark Office—

(A) a written application, in such form as may be prescribed by the Commissioner, verified by the applicant, or by a member of the firm or an officer of the corporation or association applying, specifying applicant's domicile and citizenship, the date of applicant's first use of the mark, the date of the applicant's first use of the mark in commerce, the goods in connection with which the mark is used and the mode or manner in which the mark is used in connection with such goods, and including a statement to the effect that the person making the verification believes himself, or the firm, corporation, or association in whose behalf he makes the verification, to be the owner of the mark sought to be registered, that the mark is in use in commerce, and that no other person, firm, corporation, or association, to the best of his knowledge and belief, has the right to use such mark in commerce either in the identical form thereof or in such near resemblance thereto as to be likely, when used on or in connection with the goods of such other person, to cause confusion, or to cause mistake, or to deceive: Provided, That in the case of every application claiming concurrent use the applicant shall state exceptions to his claim of exclusive use, in which he shall specify, to the extent of his knowledge, any concurrent use by others, the goods on or in connection with which and the areas in which each concurrent use exists, the periods of each use, and the goods and area for which the applicant desires registration;

(B) a drawing of the mark; and

(C) such number of specimens or facsimiles of the mark as used as may be required by the Commissioner.

(2) By paying into the Patent and Trademark Office the prescribed fee.

(3) By complying with such rules or regulations, not inconsistent with law, as may be prescribed by the Commissioner.

(b) Trade-Marks Intended for Use in Commerce. A person who has a bona fide intention, under circumstances showing the good faith of such person, to use a trademark in commerce may apply to register the trademark under this chapter on the principal register hereby established:

(1) By filing in the Patent and Trademark Office—

(A) a written application, in such form as may be prescribed by the Commissioner, verified by the applicant, or by a member of the firm or an officer of the corporation or association applying, specifying applicant's domicile and citizenship, applicant's bona fide intention to use the mark in commerce, the goods on or in connection with which the applicant has a bona fide intention to use the mark and the mode or manner in which the mark is intended to be used on or in connection with such goods, including a statement to the effect that the person making the verification believes himself or herself, or the firm, corporation, or association in whose behalf he or she makes the verification, to be entitled to use the mark in commerce, and that no other person, firm, corporation, or association, to the best of his or her knowledge and belief, has the right to use such mark in commerce either in the identical form of the mark or in such near resemblance to the mark as to be likely, when used on or in connection with the goods of such other person, to cause confusion, or to cause mistake, or to deceive; however, except for applications filed pursuant to section 1126 of this title, no mark shall be registered until the applicant has met the requirements of subsection (d) of this section; and

(B) a drawing of the mark.

(2) By paying in the Patent and Trademark Office the prescribed fee.

(3) By complying with such rules or regulations, not inconsistent with law, as may be prescribed by the Commissioner.

(c) Amendment of Application Under Subsection (b) to Conform to Requirements of Subsection (a). At any time during examination of an application filed under subsection (b) of this section, an applicant who has made use of the mark in commerce may claim the benefits of such use for purposes of this chapter, by amending his or her application to bring it into conformity with the requirements of subsection (a) of this section.

(d) Verified Statement That Trade-Mark Is Used in Commerce.

(1) Within six months after the date on which the notice of allowance with respect to a mark is issued under section 1063(b)(2) of this title to an applicant under subsection (b) of this section, the applicant shall file in the Patent and Trademark Office, together with such number of specimens or facsimiles of the mark as used in commerce as may be required by the Commissioner and payment of the prescribed fee, a verified statement that the mark is in use in commerce and specifying the date of the applicant's first use of the mark in commerce, those goods or services specified in the notice of allowance on or in connection with which the mark is used in commerce, and the mode or manner in which the mark is used on or in connection with such goods or services. Subject to examination and acceptance of the statement of use, the mark shall be registered in the Patent and Trademark Office, a certificate of registration shall be issued for those goods or services recited in the statement for use for which the mark is entitled to registration, and notice of registration shall be published in the Official Gazette of the Patent and Trademark Office. Such examination may include an examination of the factors set forth in subsections (a) through (e) of section 1052 of this title. The notice of registration shall specify the goods or services for which the mark is registered.

(2) The Commissioner shall extend, for one additional 6-month period, the time for filing the statement of use under paragraph (1), upon written request of the applicant before the expiration of the 6-month period provided in paragraph (1). In addition to an extension under the preceding sentence, the Commissioner may, upon a showing of good cause by the applicant, further extend the time for filing the statement of use under paragraph (1) for periods aggregating not more than 24 months, pursuant to written request of the applicant made before the expiration of the last extension granted under this paragraph. Any request for an extension under this paragraph shall be accompanied by a verified statement that the applicant has a continued bona fide intention to use the mark in commerce and specifying those goods or services identified in the notice of allowance on or in connection with which the applicant has a continued bona fide intention to use the mark in commerce. Any request for an extension under this paragraph shall be accompanied by payment of the prescribed fee. The Commissioner shall issue regulations setting forth guidelines for determining

what constitutes good cause for purposes of this paragraph.

(3) The Commissioner shall notify any applicant who files a statement of use of the acceptance or refusal thereof and, if the statement of use is refused, the reasons for the refusal. An applicant may amend the statement of use.

(4) The failure to timely file a verified statement of use under this subsection shall result in abandonment of the application.

## §1052. Trademarks Registrable on the Principal Register.

No trademark by which the goods of the applicant may be distinguished from the goods of others shall be refused registration on the principal register on account of its nature unless it—

(a) Consists of or comprises immoral, deceptive, or scandalous matter; or matter which may disparage or falsely suggest a connection with persons, living or dead, institutions, beliefs, or national symbols, or bring them into contempt, or disrepute.

(b) Consists of or comprises the flag or coat of arms or other insignia of the United States, or of any State or municipality, or of any foreign nation, or any simulation thereof.

(c) Consists of or comprises a name, portrait, or signature identifying a particular living individual except by his written consent, or the name, signature, or portrait of a deceased President of the United States during the life of his widow, if any, except by the written consent of his widow.

(d) Consists of or comprises a mark which so resembles a mark registered in the Patent and Trademark Office, or a mark or trade name previously used in the United States by another and not abandoned, as to be likely, when used on or in connection with the goods of the applicant, to cause confusion, or to cause mistake, or to deceive: Provided, That if the Commissioner determines that confusion, mistake, or deception is not likely to result from the continued use by more than one person of the same or similar marks under conditions and limitations as to the mode or place of use of the marks or the goods on or in connection with which such marks are used, concurrent registrations may be issued to such persons when they have become entitled to use such marks as a result of their concurrent lawful use in commerce prior to (1) the earliest of the filing dates of the applications pending or of any registration issued under this chapter; (2) July 5, 1947, in the case of registrations previously issued under the Act of March 3, 1881, or

February 20, 1905, and continuing in full force and effect on that date; or (3) July 5, 1947, in the case of applications filed under the Act of February 20, 1905, and registered after July 5, 1947. Use prior to the filing date of any pending application or a registration shall not be required when the owner of such application or registration consents to the grant of a concurrent registration to the applicant. Concurrent registrations may also be issued by the Commissioner when a court of competent jurisdiction has finally determined that more than one person is entitled to use the same or similar marks in commerce. In issuing concurrent registrations, the Commissioner shall prescribe conditions and limitations as to the mode or place of use of the mark or the goods on or in connection with which such mark is registered to the respective persons.

(e) Consists of a mark which, (1) when used on or in connection with the goods of the applicant is merely descriptive or deceptively misdescriptive of them, or (2) when used on or in connection with the goods of the applicant is primarily geographically descriptive or deceptively misdescriptive of them, except as indications of regional origin may be registrable under section 1054 of this title, or (3) is primarily merely a surname.

(f) Except as expressly excluded in paragraphs (a)–(d) of this section, nothing in this chapter shall prevent the registration of a mark used by the applicant which has become distinctive of the applicant's goods in commerce. The Commissioner may accept as prima facie evidence that the mark has become distinctive, as used on or in connection with the applicant's goods in commerce, proof of substantially exclusive and continuous use thereof as a mark by the applicant in commerce for the five years before the date on which the claim of distinctiveness is made.

## §1053. Service Marks Registrable.

Subject to the provisions relating to the registration of trademarks, so far as they are applicable, service marks shall be registrable, in the same manner and with the same effect as are trade-marks, and when registered they shall be entitled to the protection provided in this chapter in the case of trade-marks. Applications and procedure under this section shall conform as nearly as practicable to those prescribed for the registration of trademarks.

## §1057. Certificates.

(a) Issuance and Form. Certificates of registration of marks registered upon the principal register shall be issued in the name of the United States of America, under the seal of the Patent and Trademark Office, and shall be signed by the Commissioner or have his signature placed thereon, and a record thereof shall be kept in the Patent and Trademark Office. The registration shall reproduce the mark, and state that the mark is registered on the principal register under this chapter, the date of the first use of the mark, the date of the first use of the mark in commerce, the particular goods or services for which it is registered, the number and date of the registration, the term thereof, the date on which the application for registration was received in the Patent and Trademark Office, and any conditions and limitations that may be imposed in the registration.

(b) Certificate as Prima Facie Evidence. A certificate of registration of a mark upon the principal register provided by this chapter shall be prima facie evidence of the validity of the registered mark and of the registration of the mark, of the registrant's ownership of the mark, and of the registrant's exclusive right to use the registered mark in commerce on or in connection with the goods or services specified in the certificate subject to any conditions or limitations stated in the certificate.

(c) Application to Register Mark Considered Constructive Use. Contingent on the registration of a mark on the principal register provided by this chapter, the filing of the application to register such mark shall constitute constructive use of the mark, conferring a right of priority, nationwide in effect, on or in connection with the goods or services specified in the registration against any other person except for a person whose mark has not been abandoned and who, prior to such filing—

(1) has used the mark;

(2) has filed an application to register the mark which is pending or has resulted in registration of the mark; or

(3) has filed a foreign application to register the mark on the basis of which he or she has acquired a right of priority, and timely files an application under section 1126(d) of this title to register the mark which is pending or has resulted in registration of the mark.

### §1058. Duration.

(a) Affidavit of Continuing Use. Each certificate of registration shall remain in force for ten years: *Provided*, That the registration of any mark under the provisions of this chapter shall be canceled by the Commissioner at the end of six years following its date, unless within one year next preceding the expiration of such six years the registrant shall file in the Patent and Trademark Office an affidavit setting forth those goods or services recited in the registration on or in connection with which the mark is in use in commerce and attaching to the affidavit a specimen or facsimile showing current use of the mark, or showing that any nonuse is due to special circumstances which excuse such nonuse and is not due to any intention to abandon the mark. Special notice of the requirement for such affidavit shall be attached to each certificate of registration.

### §1059. Renewal.

(a) Period of Renewal; Time for Renewal. Each registration may be renewed for periods of ten years from the end of the expiring period upon payment of the prescribed fee and the filing of a verified application therefor, setting forth those goods or services recited in the registration on or in connection with which the mark is still in use in commerce and having attached thereto a specimen or facsimile showing current use of the mark, or showing that any nonuse is due to special circumstances which excuse such nonuse and it is not due to any intention to abandon the mark. Such application may be made at any time within six months before the expiration of the period for which the registration was issued or renewed, or it may be made within three months after such expiration on payment of the additional fee herein prescribed.

(b) Notification of Refusal of Renewal. If the Commissioner refuses to renew the registration, he shall notify the registrant of his refusal and the reasons therefor.

### §1062. Publication.

(a) Examination and Publication. Upon the filing of an application for registration and payment of the prescribed fee, the Commissioner shall refer the application to the examiner in charge of the registration of marks, who shall cause an examination to be made and, if on such examination it shall appear that the applicant is entitled to registration upon the acceptance of the statement of use required by section 1051(d) of this title, the Commissioner shall cause the mark to be published in the Official Gazette of the Patent and Trademark Office: *Provided*, That in the case of an applicant claiming concurrent use, or in the case of an application to be placed in an interference as provided for in section 1066 of this title, the mark, if otherwise registrable, may be published subject to the determination of the rights of the parties to such proceedings.

(b) Refusal of Registration; Amendment of Application; Abandonment. If the applicant is found not entitled to registration, the examiner shall advise the applicant thereof and of the reasons therefor. The applicant shall have a period of six months in which to reply or amend his application, which shall then be re-examined. This procedure may be repeated until (1) the examiner finally refuses registration of the mark or (2) the applicant fails for a period of six months to reply or amend or appeal, whereupon the application shall be deemed to have been abandoned, unless it can be shown to the satisfaction of the Commissioner that the delay in responding was unavoidable, whereupon such time may be extended.

## §1063. Opposition.

(a) Any person who believes that he would be damaged by the registration of a mark upon the principal register may, upon payment of the prescribed fee, file an opposition in the Patent and Trademark Office, stating the grounds therefor, within thirty days after the publication under subsection (a) of section 1062 of this title of the mark sought to be registered. Upon written request prior to the expiration of the thirty-day period, the time for filing opposition shall be extended for an additional thirty days, and further extensions of time for filing opposition may be granted by the Commissioner for good cause when requested prior to the expiration of an extension. The Commissioner shall notify the applicant of each extension of the time for filing opposition. An opposition may be amended under such conditions as may be prescribed by the Commissioner.

(b) Unless registration is successfully opposed—

(1) a mark entitled to registration on the principal register based on an application filed under section 1051(a) or pursuant to section 1126 of this title shall be registered in the Patent and Trademark Office, a certificate of registration shall be issued, and notice of the registration shall be published in the Official Gazette of the Patent and Trademark Office; or

(2) a notice of allowance shall be issued to the applicant if the applicant applied for registration under section 1051(b) of this title.

## §1064. Cancellation.

A petition to cancel a registration of a mark, stating the grounds relied upon, may, upon payment of the prescribed fee, be filed as follows by any person who believes that he is or will be damaged by the registration of a mark on the principal register established by this chapter, or under the Act of March 3, 1881, or the Act of February 20, 1905:

(1) Within five years from the date of the registration of the mark under this chapter.

(3) At any time if the registered mark becomes the generic name for the goods or services, or a portion thereof, for which it is registered, or has been abandoned, or its registration was obtained fraudulently or contrary to the provisions of section 1054 of this title or of subsection (a), (b), or (c) of section 1052 of this title for a registration under this chapter, or contrary to similar prohibitory provisions of such prior Acts for a registration under such Acts, or if the registered mark is being used by, or with the permission of, the registrant so as to misrepresent the source of the goods or services on or in connection with which the mark is used. If the registered mark becomes the generic name for lees than all of the goods or services for which it is registered, a petition to cancel the registration for only those goods or services may be filed. A registered mark shall not be deemed to be the generic name of goods or services solely because such mark is also used as a name of or to identify a unique product or service. The primary significance of the registered mark to the relevant public rather than purchaser motivation shall be the test for determining whether the registered mark has become the generic name of goods or services on or in connection with which it has been used.

(5) At any time in the case of a certification mark on the ground that the registrant (A) does not control, or is not able legitimately to exercise control over, the use of such mark, or (B) engages in the production or marketing of any goods or services to which the certification mark is applied, or (C) permits the use of the certification mark for purposes other than to certify, or (D) discriminately refuses to certify or to continue to certify the goods or services of any person who maintains the standards or conditions which such mark certifies:

*Provided,* That the Federal Trade Commission may apply to cancel on the grounds specified in paragraphs (3) and (5) of this section any mark registered on the principal register established by this chapter, and the prescribed fee shall not be required.

## §1065. Requirements for Right to Use of Mark to Become Incontestable.

Except on a ground for which application to cancel may be filed at any time under paragraphs (3) and (5) of section 1064 of this title, and except to the extent, if any, to which the use of a mark registered on the principal register infringes a valid right acquired under the law of any State or Territory by use of a mark or trade name continuing from a date prior to the date of registration under this chapter of such registered mark, the right of the registrant to use such registered mark in commerce for the goods or services on or in connection with which such registered mark has been in continuous use for five consecutive years subsequent to the date of such registration and is still in use in commerce, shall be incontestable: *Provided*, That—

(1) there has been no final decision adverse to registrant's claim of ownership of such mark for such goods or services, or to registrant's right to register the same or to keep the same on the register; and

(2) there is no proceeding involving said rights pending in the Patent and Trademark Office or in a court and not finally disposed of, and

(3) an affidavit is filed with the Commissioner within one year after the expiration of any such five-year period setting forth those goods or services stated in the registration on or in connection with which such mark has been in continuous use for such five consecutive years and is still in use in commerce, and the other matters specified in paragraphs (1) and (2) of this section; and

(4) no incontestable right shall be acquired in a mark which is the generic name of the goods or services or a portion thereof, for which it is registered.

## §1072. Registration is Notice.

Registration of a mark on the principal register provided by this chapter or under the Act of March 3, 1881, or the Act of February 20, 1905, shall be constructive notice of the registrant's claim of ownership thereof.

## §1111. Notice of Registration.

Notwithstanding the provisions of section 1072 of this title, a registrant of a mark registered in the Patent and Trademark Office, may give notice that his mark is registered by displaying with the mark the words "Registered in U.S. Patent and Trademark Office" or "Reg. U.S. Pat. & Tm. Off." or the letter R enclosed within a circle, thus ®; and in any suit for infringement under this chapter by such a registrant failing to give such notice of registration, no profits and no damages shall be recovered under the provisions of this chapter unless the defendant had actual notice of the registration.

## §1114. Remedies.

(1) Any person who shall, without the consent of the registrant—

(a) use in commerce any reproduction, counterfeit, copy, or colorable imitation of a registered mark in connection with the sale, offering for sale, distribution, or advertising of any goods or services on or in connection with which such use is likely to cause confusion, or to cause mistake, or to deceive; or

(b) reproduce, counterfeit, copy, or colorably imitate a registered mark and apply such reproduction, counterfeit, copy, or colorable imitation to labels, signs, prints, packages, wrappers, receptacles or advertisements intended to be used in commerce upon or in connection with the sale, offering for sale, distribution, or advertising of goods or services on or in connection with which such use is likely to cause confusion, or to cause mistake, or to deceive shall be liable in a civil action by the registrant for the remedies hereinafter provided. Under subsection (b) of this section, the registrant shall not be entitled to recover profits or damages unless the acts have been committed with knowledge that such imitation is intended to be used to cause confusion, or to cause mistake, or to deceive.

## §1115. Registration on Principal Register as Evidence of Validity and Exclusive Right to Use Mark; Defenses to Incontestable Registration.

(a) Evidentiary Value; Defenses. Any registration issued under the Act of March 3, 1881, or the Act of February 20, 1905, or of a mark registered on the principal register provided by this chapter and owned by a party to an action shall be admissible in evidence and shall be prima facie evidence of the validity of the registered mark and of the registration of the mark, of the registrant's ownership of the mark, and of the registrant's exclusive right to use the registered mark in commerce on or in connection with the goods or services specified in the registration subject to any conditions or limitations stated therein, but shall not preclude another person from proving any legal or equitable defense or defect, including those set forth in subsection (b) of this section, which might have been asserted if such mark had not been registered.

(b) Incontestability; Defenses. To the extent that the right to use the registered mark has become incontestable under section 1065 of this title, the registration shall be conclusive evidence of the validity of the registered mark and of the registration of the mark, of the registrant's ownership of the mark, and of the registrant's exclusive right to use the registered mark in commerce. Such conclusive evidence shall relate to the exclusive right to use the mark on or in connection with the goods or services specified in the affidavit filed under the provisions of section 1065 of this title, or in the renewal application filed under the provisions of section 1059 of this title if the goods or services specified in the renewal are fewer in number, subject to any conditions or limitations in the registration or in such affidavit or renewal application. Such conclusive evidence of the right to use the registered mark shall be subject to proof of infringement as defined in section 1114 of this title, and shall be subject to the following defenses or defects:

(1) That the registration or the incontestable right to use the mark was obtained fraudulently; or

(2) That the mark has been abandoned by the registrant; or

(3) That the registered mark is being used, by or with the permission of the registrant or a person in privity with the registrant, so as to misrepresent the source of the goods or services on or in connection with which the mark is used; or

(4) That the use of the name, term, or device charged to be an infringement is a use, otherwise than as a mark, of the party's individual name in his own business, or of the individual name of anyone in privity with such party, or of a term or device which is descriptive of and used fairly and in good faith only to describe the goods or services of such party, or their geographic origin; or

(5) That the mark whose use by a party is charged as an infringement was adopted without knowledge of the registrant's prior use and has been continuously used by such party or those in privity with him from a date prior to (A) the date of constructive use of the mark established pursuant to section 1057(c) of this title, (B) the registration of the mark under this chapter if the application for registration is filed before the effective date of the Trademark Law Revision Act of 1988, or (C) publication of the registered mark under subsection (c) of section 1062 of this title: Provided, however, That this defense or defect shall apply only for the area in which such continuous prior use is proved; or

(6) That the mark whose use is charged as an infringement was registered and used prior to the registration under this chapter or publication under subsection (c) of section 1062 of this title of the registered mark of the registrant, and not abandoned: Provided, however, That this defense or defect shall apply only for the area in which the mark was used prior to such registration or such publication of the registrant's mark; or

(7) That the mark has been or is being used to violate the antitrust laws of the United States; or

(8) That equitable principles, including laches, estoppel, and acquiescence, are applicable.

## §1116. Injunctions to Prevent Infringement; Enforcement of Same; Seizure of Goods in Counterfeiting Cases.

(a) Jurisdiction; Service. The several courts vested with jurisdiction of civil actions arising under this chapter shall have power to grant injunctions, according to the principles of equity and upon such terms as the court may deem reasonable, to prevent the violation of any right of the registrant of a mark registered in the Patent and Trademark Office or to prevent a violation under section 1125(a) of this title. Any such injunction may include a provision directing the defendant to file with the court and serve on the plaintiff within thirty days after the service on the defendant of such injunction, or such extended period as the court may direct, a report in writing under oath setting forth in detail the manner and form in which the defendant has complied with the injunction. Any such injunction granted upon hearing, after notice to the defendant, by any district court of the United States, may be served on the parties against whom such injunction is granted anywhere in the United States where they may be found, and shall be operative and may be enforced by proceedings to punish for contempt, or otherwise, by the court by which such injunction was granted, or by any other United States district court in whose jurisdiction the defendant may be found.

(d) Civil Actions Arising Out of Use of Counterfeit Marks.

(1)(A) In the case of a civil action arising under section 1114(1)(a) of this title or section 380 of Title 36 with respect to a violation that consists of using a counterfeit mark in connection with the sale, offering for sale, or distribution of goods or services, the court may, upon ex parte application, grant an order under subsection (a) of this section pursuant to this subsection providing for the seizure of goods and counterfeit marks involved in such violation and the means of making such marks, and records documenting the manufacture, sale, or receipt of things involved in such violation.

(B) As used in this subsection the term "counterfeit mark" means—

(i) a counterfeit of a mark that is registered on the principal register in the United States Patent and Trademark Office for such goods or services sold, offered for sale, or distributed and that is in use, whether or not the person against whom relief is sought knew such mark was so registered; or

(ii) a spurious designation that is identical with, or substantially indistinguishable from, a designation as to which the remedies of this chapter are made available by reason of section 380 of Title 36;

but such term does not include any mark or designation used on or in connection with goods or services of which the manufacture or producer was, at the time of the manufacture or production in question authorized to use the mark or designation for the type of goods or services so manufactured or produced, by the holder of the right to use such mark or designation.

### §1117. Monetary Recovery for Infringement: Attorney's Fees; Costs; Prejudgment Interest.

(a) Profits; Damages and Costs; Attorney Fees. When a violation of any right of the registrant of a mark registered in the Patent and Trademark Office, or a violation under section 1125(a) of this title, shall have been established in any civil action arising under this chapter, the plaintiff shall be entitled, subject to the provisions of sections 1111 and 1114 of this title, and subject to the principles of equity, to recover (1) defendant's profits, (2) any damages sustained by the plaintiff, and (3) the costs of the action. The court shall assess such profits and damages or cause the same to be assessed under its direction. In assessing profits the plaintiff shall be required to proved defendant's sales only; defendant must prove all elements of cost or deduction claimed. In assessing damages the court may enter judgment, according to the circumstances of the case, for any sum above the amount found as actual damages, not exceeding three times such amount. If the court shall find that the amount of the recovery based on profits is either inadequate or excessive the court may in its discretion enter judgment for such sum as the court shall find to be just, according to the circumstances of the case.

Such sum in either of the above circumstances shall constitute compensation and not a penalty. The court in exceptional cases may award reasonable attorney fees to the prevailing party.

(b) Treble Damages for Use of Counterfeit Mark. In assessing damages under subsection (a) of this section, the court shall, unless the court finds extenuating circumstances, enter judgment for three times such profits or damages, whichever is greater, together with a reasonable attorney's fee, in the case of any violation of section 1114(1)(A) of this title or section 380 of Title 36 that consists of intentionally using a mark or designation, knowing such mark or designation is a counterfeit mark (as defined in section 1116(d) of this title), in connection with the sale, offering for sale, or distribution of goods and services. In such cases, the court may in its discretion award prejudgment interest on such amount at an annual interest rate established under section 6621 of Title 26, commencing on the date of the service of the claimant's pleadings setting forth the claim for such entry and ending on the date such entry is made, or for such shorter time as the court deems appropriate.

### §1124. Importation Forbidden of Goods Bearing Infringing Marks or Names.

Except as provided in subsection (d) of section 1526 of Title 19, no article of imported merchandise which shall copy or simulate the name of the any domestic manufacture, or manufacturer, or trader, or of any manufacturer or trader located in any foreign country which, by treaty, convention, or law affords similar privileges to citizens of the United States, or which shall copy or simulate a trademark registered in accordance with the provisions of this chapter or shall bear a name or mark calculated to induce the public to believe that the article is manufactured in the United States, or that it is manufactured in any foreign country or locality other than the country or locality in which it is in fact manufactured, shall be admitted to entry at any customhouse of the United States; and, in order to aid the officers of the customs in enforcing this prohibition, any domestic manufacturer or trader, and any foreign manufacturer or trader, who is entitled under the provisions of a treaty, convention, declaration, or agreement between the United States and any foreign country to the advantages afforded by law to citizens of the United States in respect to trademarks and commercial names, may require his name and residence, and the name of the locality in which his goods are manufactured, and a copy of the certificate of registration of his trademark, issued in accordance with the provisions of this chapter, to be recorded in books which shall be kept for this purpose in the Department of the Treasury, under such regulations as the Secretary of the Treasury shall prescribe, and may furnish to the Department facsimiles of his name, the name of the locality in which his goods are manufactured, or of his registered trademark, and thereupon the Secretary of the Treasury shall cause one or more copies of the same to be transmitted to each collector or other proper officer of customs.

## §1125. False Designation of Origin and False Description Forbidden.

(a) Any person who, on or in connection with any goods or services, or any container for goods, uses in commerce any word, term, name, symbol, or device, or any combination thereof, or any false designation of origin, false or misleading description of fact, or false or misleading representation of fact, which—

(1) is likely to cause confusion, or to cause mistake, or to deceive as to the affiliation, connection, or association of such person with another person, or as to the origin, sponsorship, or approval of his or her goods, services, or commercial activities by another person, or

(2) in commercial advertising or promotion, misrepresents the nature, characteristics, qualities, or geographic origin of his or her or another person's goods, services, or commercial activities,

shall be liable in a civil action by any person who believes that he or she is or is likely to be damaged by such act.

(b) Any goods marked or labeled in contravention of the provisions of this section shall not be imported into the United States or admitted to entry at any customhouse of the United States. The owner, importer, or consignee of goods refused entry at any customhouse under this section may have any recourse by protest or appeal that is given under the customs revenue laws or may have the remedy given by this chapter in cases involving goods refused entry or seized.

## §1127. Construction and Definitions.

In the construction of this chapter, unless the contrary is plainly apparent from the context—

The United States included and embraces all territory which is under its jurisdiction and control.

The word "commerce" means all commerce which may lawfully be regulated by Congress.

The term "principal register" refers to the register provided for by sections 1051 to 1072 of this title, and the term "supplemental register" refers to the register provided for by sections 1091 to 1096 of this title.

The term "person" and any other word or term used to designate the applicant or other entitled to a benefit or privilege or rendered liable under the provisions of this chapter includes a juristic person as well as a natural person. The term "juristic person" includes a firm, corporation, union, association, or other organization capable of suing and being sued in a court of law.

The terms "applicant" and "registrant" embrace the legal representatives, predecessors, successors and assigns of such applicant or registrant.

The term "Commissioner" means the Commissioner of Patents and Trademarks.

The term "related company" means any person whose use of a mark is controlled by the owner of the mark with respect to the nature and quality of the goods or services on or in connection with which the mark is used.

The terms "trade name" and "commercial name" mean any name used by a person to identify his or her business or vocation.

The term "trademark" includes any word, name, symbol, or device, or any combination thereof—

(1) used by a person, or

(2) which a person has a bona fide intention to use in commerce and applies to register on the principal register established by this chapter,

to identify and distinguish his or her goods, including a unique product, from those manufactured or sold by others and to indicate the source of the goods, even if that source is unknown.

The term "service mark" means any word, name, symbol, or device, or any combination thereof—

(1) used by a person, or

(2) which a person has a bona fide intention to use in commerce and applies to register on the principal register established by this chapter,

to identify and distinguish the services of one person, including a unique service, from the services of others and to indicate the source of the services, even if that source is unknown. Titles, character names, and other distinctive features of radio or television programs may be registered as service marks notwithstanding that they, or the programs, may advertise the goods of the sponsor.

The term "certification mark" means any word, name, symbol, or device, or any combination thereof—

(1) used by a person other than its owner, or

(2) which its owner has a bona fide intention to permit a person other than the owner to use in commerce and files an application to register on the principal register established by this chapter, to certify regional or other origin, material, mode of manufacture, quality, accuracy, or other characteristics of such person's goods or services or that the work or labor on the goods or services was performed by members of a union or other organization.

The term "collective mark" means a trademark or service mark—

(1) used by the members of a cooperative, an association, or other collective group or organization, or

(2) which such cooperative, association, or other collective group or organization has a bona fide intention to use in commerce and applies to register on the principal register established by this chapter, and includes marks indicating membership in a union, an association, or other organization.

The term "mark" includes any trademark, service mark, collective mark, or certification mark.

The term "use in commerce" means the bona fide use of a mark in the ordinary course of trade, and not made merely to reserve a right in a mark. For purposes of this chapter, a mark shall be deemed to be in use in commerce—

(1) on goods when—

(A) it is placed in any manner on the goods or their containers or the displays associated therewith or on the tags or labels affixed thereto, or if the nature of the goods makes such placement impracticable, then on documents associated with the goods or their sale, and

(B) the goods are sold or transported in commerce, and

(2) on services when it is used or displayed in the sale or advertising of services and the services are rendered in commerce, or the services are rendered in more than one State or in the United States and a foreign country and the person rendering the services is engaged in commerce in connection with the services.

A mark shall be deemed to be "abandoned" when either of the following occurs:

(1) When its use has been discontinued with intent not to resume such use. Intent not to resume may be inferred from circumstances. Nonuse for two consecutive years shall be prima facie evidence of abandonment. "Use" of a mark means the bona fide use of that mark made in the ordinary course of trade, and not made merely to reserve a right in a mark.

(2) When any course of conduct of the owner, including acts of omission as well as commission, causes the mark to become the generic name for the goods or services on or in connection with which it is used or otherwise to lose its significance as a mark. Purchaser motivation shall not be a test for determining abandonment under this paragraph.

The term "colorable imitation" includes any mark which so resembles a registered mark as to be likely to cause confusion or mistake or to deceive.

The term "registered mark" means a mark registered in the United States Patent and Trademark Office under this chapter or under the Act of March 3, 1881, or the Act of February 20, 1905, or the Act of March 19, 1920. The phrase "marks registered in the Patent and Trademark Office" means registered marks.

The term "Act of March 3, 1881", "Act of February 20, 1905", or "Act of March 19, 1920," means the respective Act as amended.

A "counterfeit" is a spurious mark which is identical with, or substantially indistinguishable from, a registered mark.

Words used in the singular include the plural and vice versa.

The intent of this chapter is to regulate commerce within the control of Congress by making actionable the deceptive and misleading use of marks in such commerce; to protect registered marks used in such commerce from interference by State, or territorial legislation; to protect persons engaged in such commerce against unfair competition; to prevent fraud and deception in such commerce by the use of reproductions, copies, counterfeits, or colorable imitations of registered marks; and to provide rights and remedies stipulated by treaties and conventions respecting trade-marks, trade names, and unfair competition entered into between the United States and foreign nations.

# APPENDIX E
## Selected Provisions of The Uniform Commercial Code

§2-201. Formal Requirements; Statute of Frauds.

(1) Except as otherwise provided in this section a contract for the sale of goods for the price of $500 or more is not enforceable by way of action or defense unless there is some writing sufficient to indicate that a contract for sale has been made between the parties and signed by the party

against whom enforcement is sought or by his authorized agent or broker. A writing is not insufficient because it omits or incorrectly states a term agreed upon but the contract is not enforceable under this paragraph beyond the quantity of goods shown in such writing.

(2) Between merchants if within a reasonable time a writing in confirmation of the contract and sufficient against the sender is received and the party receiving it has reason to know its contents, it satisfies the requirements of subsection(1) against such party unless written notice of objection to its contents is given within ten days after it is received.

(3) A contract which does not satisfy the requirements of subsection (1) but which is valid in other respects is enforceable

(a) if the goods are to be specially manufactured for the buyer and are not suitable for sale to others in the ordinary course of the seller's business and the seller, before notice of repudiation is received and under circumstances which reasonably indicate that the goods are for the buyer, has made either a substantial beginning of their manufacture or commitments for their procurement; or

(b) if the party against whom enforcement is sought admits in his pleading, testimony or otherwise in court that a contract for sale was made, but the contract is not enforceable under this provision beyond the quantity of goods admitted; or

(c) with respect to goods for which payment has been made and accepted or which have been received and accepted (§2-606).

## §2-202. Final Written Expression: Parol or Extrinsic Evidence.

Terms with respect to which the confirmatory memoranda of the parties agree or which are otherwise set forth in a writing intended by the parties as a final expression of their agreement with respect to such terms as are included therein may not be contradicted by evidence of any prior agreement or of a contemporaneous oral agreement but may be explained or supplemented

(a) by course of dealing or usage of trade (Section 1-205) or by course of performance (Section 2-208); and

(b) by evidence of consistent additional terms unless the court finds the writing to have been intended also as a complete and exclusive statement of the terms of the agreement.

## §2-302. Unconscionable Contract or Clause

(1) If the court as a matter of law finds the contract or any clause of the contract to have been unconscionable at the time it was made the court may refuse to enforce the contract, or it may enforce the remainder of the contract without the unconscionable clause, or it may so limit the application of any unconscionable clause as to avoid any unconscionable result.

(2) When it is claimed or appears to the court that the contract or any clause thereof may be unconscionable the parties shall be afforded a reasonable opportunity to present evidence as to its commercial setting, purpose and effect to aid the court in making the determination.

## §2-312. Warranty of Title and Against Infringement; Buyer's Obligation Against Infringement.

(1) Subject to subsection (2) there is in a contract for sale a warranty by the seller that

(a) the title conveyed shall be good, and its transfer rightful; and

(b) the goods shall be delivered free from any security interest or other lien or encumbrance of which the buyer at the time of contracting has no knowledge.

(2) A warranty under subsection (1) will be excluded or modified only by specific language or by circumstances which give the buyer reason to know that the person selling does not claim title in himself or that he is purporting to sell only such right or title as he or a third person may have.

(3) Unless otherwise agreed a seller who is a merchant regularly dealing in goods of the kind warrants that the goods shall be delivered free of the rightful claim of any third person by way of infringement or the like but a buyer who furnishes specifications to the seller must hold the seller harmless against any such claim which arises out of compliance with the specifications.

## §2-313. Express Warranties by Affirmation, Promise, Description, Sample.

(1) Express warranties by the seller are created as follows:

(a) any affirmation of fact or promise made by the seller to the buyer which relates to the goods and becomes part of the basis of the bargain creates an express warranty that the goods shall conform to the affirmation or promise.

(b) Any description of the goods which is made part of the basis of the bargain creates an express warranty that the goods shall conform to the description.

(c) Any sample or model which is made part of the basis of the bargain creates an express warranty that the whole of the goods shall conform to the sample or model.

(2) It is not necessary to the creation of an express warranty that the seller use formal words such as "warrant" or "guarantee" or that he have a specific intention to make a warranty, but an affirmation merely of the value of the goods or a statement purporting to be merely the seller's opinion or commendation of the goods does not create a warranty.

## §2-314. Implied Warranty: Merchantability; Usage of Trade.

(1) Unless excluded or modified (Section 2-316), a warranty that the goods shall be merchantable is implied in a contract for their sale if the seller is a merchant with respect to goods of that kind. Under this section the serving for value of food or drink to be consumed either on the premises or elsewhere is a sale.

(2) Goods to be merchantable must be at least such as

(a) pass without objection in the trade under the contract description; and

(b) in the case of fungible goods, are of fair average quality within the description; and

(c) are fit for the ordinary purposes for which such goods are used; and

(d) run, within the variations permitted by the agreement, of even kind, quality and quantity within each unit and among all units involved; and

(e) are adequately contained, packaged, and labeled as the agreement may require; and

(f) conform to the promises or affirmations of fact made on the container or label if any.

(3) Unless excluded or modified (Section 2-316) other implied warranties may arise from course of dealing or usage of trade.

## §2-315. Implied Warranty: Fitness for Particular Purpose.

Where the seller at the time of contracting has reason to know any particular purpose for which the goods are required and that the buyer is relying on the seller's skill or judgment to select or furnish suitable goods, there is unless excluded or modified under the next section an implied warranty that the goods shall be fit for such purpose.

## §2-316. Exclusion or Modification of Warranties.

(1) Words or conduct relevant to the creation of an express warranty and words or conduct tending to negate or limit warranty shall be construed wherever reasonable as consistent with each other; but subject to the provisions of this Article on parol or extrinsic evidence (Section 2-202) negation or limitation is inoperative to the extent that such construction is unreasonable.

(2) Subject to subsection (3), to exclude or modify the implied warranty of merchantability or any part of it the language must mention merchantability and in case of a writing must be conspicuous, and to exclude or modify any implied warranty of fitness the exclusion must be by a writing and conspicuous. Language to exclude all implied warranties of fitness is sufficient if it states, for example, that "There are no warranties which extend beyond the description on the face hereof."

(3) Notwithstanding subsection (2)

(a) unless the circumstances indicate otherwise, all implied warranties are excluded by expressions like "as is", "with all faults" or other language which in common understanding calls the buyer's attention to the exclusion of warranties and makes plain that there is no implied warranty; and

(b) when the buyer before entering into the contract has examined the goods or the sample or model as fully as he desired or has refused to examine the goods there is no implied warranty with regard to defects which an examination ought in the circumstances to have revealed to him; and

(c) an implied warranty can also be excluded or modified by course of dealing or course of performance or usage of trade.

(4) Remedies for breach of warranty can be limited in accordance with the provisions of this Article on liquidation or limitation of damages and on contractual modification of remedy (Sections 2-718 and 2-719).

## §2-318. Third Party Beneficiaries of Warranties Express or Implied.

Note: If this Act is introduced in the Congress of the United States this section should be omitted. (States to select one alternative).

### Alternative A

A seller's warranty whether express or implied extends to any natural person who is in the family or household of his buyer or who is a guest in his home if it is reasonable to expect that such person may use, consume or be affected by the goods and who is injured in person by breach of the warranty. A seller may not exclude or limit the operation of this section.

## Alternative B

A seller's warranty whether express or implied extends to any natural person who may reasonably be expected to use, consume or be affected by the goods and who is injured in person by breach of the warranty. A seller may not exclude or limit the operation of this section.

## Alternative C

A seller's warranty whether express or implied extends to any person who may reasonably be expected to use, consume or be affected by the goods and who is injured by breach of the warranty. A seller may not exclude or limit the operation of this section with respect to injury to the person of an individual to whom the warranty extends.

## §2-714. Buyer's Damages for Breach in Regard to Accepted Goods.

(1) Where the buyer has accepted goods and given notification (subsection (3) of Section 2-607) he may recover as damages for any non-conformity of tender the loss resulting in the ordinary course of events from the seller's breach as determined in any manner which is reasonable.

(2) The measure of damages for breach of warranty is the difference at the time and place of acceptance between the value of the goods accepted and the value they would have had if they had been as warranted, unless special circumstances show proximate damages of a different amount.

(3) in a proper case any incidental and consequential damages under the next section may also be recovered.

## §2-715. Buyer's Incidental and Consequential Damages.

(1) Incidental damages resulting from the seller's breach include expenses reasonably incurred in inspection, receipt, transportation and care and custody of goods rightfully rejected, any commercially reasonable charges, expenses or commissions in connection with effecting cover and any other reasonable expense incident to the delay or other breach.

(2) Consequential damages resulting from the seller's breach include

(a) any loss resulting from general or particular requirements and needs of which the seller at the time of contracting had reason to know and which could not reasonably be preventing by cover or otherwise; and

(b) injury to person or property proximately resulting from any breach of warranty.

## §2-719. Contractual Modification or Limitation of Remedy.

(1) Subject to the provisions of subsections (2) and (3) of this section and of the preceding section on liquidation and limitation of damages,

(a) the agreement may provide for remedies in addition to or in substitution for those provided in this Article and may limit or alter the measure of damages recoverable under this Article, as by limiting the buyer's remedies to return of the goods and repayment of the price or to repair and replacement of non-conforming goods or parts; and

(b) resort to a remedy as provided is optional unless the remedy is expressly agreed to be exclusive, in which case it is the sole remedy.

(2) Where circumstances cause an exclusive or limited remedy to fail of its essential purpose, remedy may be had as provided in this Act.

(3) Consequential damages may be limited or excluded unless the limitation or exclusion is unconscionable. Limitation of consequential damages for injury to the person in the case of consumer goods is prima facie unconscionable but limitation of damages where the loss is commercial is not.

## §2-725. Statute of Limitations in Contracts for Sale.

(1) An action for breach of any contract for sale must be commenced within four years after the cause of action has accrued. By the original agreement the parties may reduce the period of limitation to not less than one year but may not extend it.

(2) A cause of action accrues when the breach occurs, regardless of the aggrieved party's lack of knowledge of the breach. A breach of warranty occurs when tender of delivery is made, except that where a warranty explicitly extends to future performance of the goods and discovery of the breach must await the time of such performance the cause of action accrues when the breach is or should have been discovered.

## APPENDIX F

### Simplified Sample Software Development Contract

*[NOTE: This sample agreement is intended solely to demonstrate how a few important issues might be addressed in a written contract. Although it presents several topics which typically are covered in development agreements, this highly simplified exposition should not be used as a checklist of pertinent considerations. In addition, it's form and language should not be used in any way to draft legal agreements.]*

THIS AGREEMENT is made this _____ day of _____ 19 ___ between Optico Imaging Company (hereinafter referred to as "Client") and the Neptune Corporation (hereinafter referred to as "Developer").

*WITNESSETH:*

WHEREAS, Client requires computer software to control Client's specialized machinery used to grind mirrors for optical telescopes; and

WHEREAS, the operations and characteristics of Client's machinery are carefully guarded as trade secrets; and

WHEREAS, Client requires the software to achieve a detailed set of defined tasks; and

WHEREAS, Developer has the expertise to develop said software to meet the defined tasks;

IT IS, THEREFORE, AGREED as follows:

1. DEFINITIONS

   (a) *Software.* "Software" means all computer programs, subroutines, translations, and any other specialized software produced or provided by Developer to satisfy its obligations under this Agreement.

   (b) *Functional Specifications.* "Functional Specifications" means (1) the set of tasks and functions that must be performed by the Software to fulfill the needs of Client, and (2) the design specifications which indicate the way the Software must be organized to accomplish those tasks and functions.

   (c) *Documentation.* "Documentation" means the instructions necessary for Client to operate the Software and its features.

   (d) *Services.* "Services" means all tasks provided by Developer under this Agreement, including, but not limited to analysis, design, programming, testing, consulting, and installation.

   (e) *Modifications.* "Modifications" means (a) changes to Software allowing it to be used on hardware other than for that which the Software was initially designed, and (b) any changes to source code resulting from the addition of a substantial feature or capability not present in the original Software.

   (f) *Proprietary Information.* "Proprietary Information" means all information relating to the Software, including, but not limited to, source code, object code, listings, printouts, flow charts, research materials, programming notes, operational and performance specifications, test results, and Documentation.

2. SCOPE OF SERVICES

   (a) PART I. In consultation with Client, Developer will analyze Client's business and machinery, and create the Functional Specifications for Software intended to meet the set of Client needs specified in Exhibit A.

   (b) PART II. Upon acceptance of the Functional Specifications by Client, Developer will code, test and debug Software that meets the Functional Specifications, prepare the Documentation, and install the Software on the equipment specified in Exhibit A. Delivery of the Software and Documentation under PART II must be made within 180 days of the day that this Agreement is signed.

   (c) Modifications. Client shall provide Developer the opportunity to develop any modifications to the Software and Documentation created under this Agreement.

3. PAYMENT

   (a) PART I. Developer shall be paid for the Functional Specifications developed under Part I on a fixed fee basis, in the amounts and according to the timetable specified in Exhibit B.

   (b) PART II. Developer shall be paid for the Software and Documentation developed under Part II according to the fixed fee and royalty schedules provided in Exhibit B.

(c) Modifications. Developer will be paid to develop modifications according to the schedule provided in Exhibit B.

## 4. ACCEPTANCE

(a) PART I. Upon delivery of the Functional Specifications due under Part I of this Agreement, Client shall have 15 business days to examine the Functional Specifications to determine if they conform to this Agreement. If the Functional Specifications conform, Client shall notify Developer of acceptance in writing within the acceptance period. If they do not conform to this agreement, Client shall notify Developer within 15 days of delivery and specify the deficiency. Client shall have the opportunity to correct the deficiency within a reasonable time and to deliver the Functional Specifications for acceptance as specified herein.

(b) PART II. Upon delivery of the Software and Documentation due under PART II, Client shall have 30 business days to conduct the acceptance tests, listed in Exhibit C, on the Software on Client's hardware and machinery in its facilities to determine if the Software meet the terms of this Agreement.

(b.1) If the Software passes all acceptance tests, based on reasonable judgment when necessary, Client shall notify Developer in writing within 5 business days from the date that the last test is fulfilled.

(b.2) If the Software does not pass all acceptance tests listed in Exhibit C, then Client shall notify Developer in writing within 5 business days of failure, and Developer shall have a reasonable time to correct the Software so that it can meet the acceptance tests. Thereafter, Client shall have 20 business days to conduct the acceptance tests. This process may be repeated as many times as required until the Software meets the acceptance tests; provided, however, that if the Software does not successfully pass all acceptance tests within 180 days after initial delivery of the Software under PART II, Client shall be entitled to consider Developer to be in default of this Agreement.

## 5. WARRANTIES

(a) *Limited Software Warranty.* Developer warrants that the Software delivered under this Agreement, excluding Modifications, will conform to the Functional Specifications and any other requirements described in this Agreement, and will be free of defects that materially affect the performance of such features. The warranty is effective for 180 days following the acceptance date of PART II. This warranty shall not apply to nonconformities or defects due to any of the following:

(i) misuse or modification of the Software by the Client or a third party;
(ii) failure of the Client or third party to maintain proper operating conditions;
(iii) hardware equipment defects or operating system software error; or
(iv) interaction with software not provided by Developer.

(a.1) *Remedies For Breach of Limited Software Warranty*

If at any time during this 180 day Limited Software Warranty period Client notifies Developer in writing of any nonconformity or defect, Developer shall at its sole and exclusive option either (1) provide all reasonable programming services to repair such nonconformity or defect, or (2) replace the nonconforming Software with conforming Software. If Developer reasonably is unable to repair or replace the nonconforming or defective Software, Developer shall refund to Client all sums paid by Client to Developer under this Agreement for the Software.

THESE REMEDIES ARE THE SOLE AND EXCLUSIVE REMEDIES FOR BREACH OF THE LIMITED SOFTWARE WARRANTY PROVIDED HEREIN.

(b) *Noninfringement Warranty.* Developer warrants that the Software will not infringe any United States copyright, trademark, or patent or misappropriate any trade secret of any third persons.

(b.1) *Remedies for Breach of Noninfringement Warranty and Indemnification*

(b.1.A) In the event that a lawsuit is brought against Client claiming that the Software infringes a United States patent, copyright or trademark, or misappropriates trade secrets:

(i) Client must give prompt notice to Developer of the lawsuit;
(ii) Developer shall have the option to defend the lawsuit at its expense. Under this circumstance, Client agrees to (a) give Developer the right to control and direct the investigation, preparation, defense and settlement of the claims, and (b) fully cooperate with Developer in the investigation, preparation, defense and settlement of the claims; and

(iii) Developer will indemnify Client for all damages and costs awarded against Client, except that Developer will not be responsible for any cost or expense paid, or settlement made, by Client without Developer's written consent.
Client agrees that Developer will not be liable if the claims of infringement or misappropriation result from modifications to the Software made by the Client or any third party, or are based on the use of the Software in combination with software not developed by the Developer.

(b.1.B) If Client receives notice regarding the Software of any alleged infringement of any United States copyright, trademark, or patent, or any alleged misappropriation of trade secrets, Developer may at its option and expense:

(i) obtain for Client the right to continued use of the Software for the purposes intended under this Agreement,

(ii) replace the Software with functionally equivalent and noninfringing Software, or

(iii) modify the Software so that it no longer infringes or misappropriates said rights.

THESE REMEDIES ARE THE SOLE AND EXCLUSIVE REMEDIES FOR BREACH OF THE NONINFRINGEMENT WARRANTY PROVIDED HEREIN.

(c) Client expressly acknowledges that no representations or warranties other than those contained in this Agreement have been made respecting the Software, Modifications, Documentation or Services to be provided, and that Client has not relied on any representation not expressly set out in this Agreement.

## 6. WARRANTY DISCLAIMER
TO THE EXTENT ALLOWED BY LAW, DEVELOPER EXPRESSLY DISCLAIMS ALL IMPLIED WARRANTIES, INCLUDING WARRANTIES OF MERCHANT-ABILITY AND FITNESS FOR A PARTICULAR PURPOSE. SHOULD A COURT DETERMINE THAT THE PRODUCTS ARE "CONSUMER PRODUCTS" UNDER THE MAGNUSON-MOSS WARRANTY ACT, THEN IMPLIED WARRANTIES ARE LIMITED IN DURATION TO A PERIOD OF 180 DAYS AFTER ACCEPTANCE. AFTER SUCH 180 DAY PERIOD, ALL IMPLIED WARRANTIES ARE EXPRESSLY DISCLAIMED. SOME STATES DO NOT ALLOW LIMITATIONS ON HOW LONG AN IMPLIED WARRANTY LASTS, SO THE ABOVE LIMITATION MAY NOT APPLY TO CLIENT.

## 7. LIMITATION OF LIABILITY
DEVELOPER'S LIABILITY TO CLIENT ON ANY CLAIM FOR DAMAGES ARISING OUT OF THIS AGREEMENT SHALL BE LIMITED TO DIRECT DAMAGES AND SHALL NOT EXCEED THE AMOUNT OF THE FEES PAID BY CLIENT UNDER THIS AGREEMENT. IN NO EVENT SHALL DEVELOPER BE LIABLE FOR ANY SPECIAL OR CONSEQUENTIAL DAMAGES, INCLUDING, BUT NOT LIMITED TO LOST PROFITS, LOSS OF GOODWILL, OR LOSS OF BUSINESS OPPORTUNITIES, EVEN IF DEVELOPER HAS BEEN ADVISED OF THE POSSIBILITY OF SUCH DAMAGES. IN NO EVENT SHALL DEVELOPER BE LIABLE FOR ANY SPECIAL OR CONSEQUENTIAL DAMAGES BASED UPON NEGLIGENCE OR STRICT PRODUCTS LIABILITY. SOME STATES DO NOT ALLOW THE EXCLUSION OR LIMITATION OF SPECIAL OR CONSEQUENTIAL DAMAGES SO THE ABOVE LIMITATION OR EXCLUSION MAY NOT APPLY TO CLIENT.

## 8. MAINTENANCE
Following expiration of the warranty, Developer agrees to provide all maintenance services necessary to correct and resolve any errors or defects which appear in the Software as a result of its use by Client. Developer's obligation to provide such maintenance services is contingent upon payment of the maintenance fees, as specified in Exhibit B, and the accurate and timely reporting of any problems with the Software. Maintenance services shall not apply to any problems resulting from modifications to the Software by Client or any third party.

## 9. OWNERSHIP
All Software developed pursuant to this Agreement, and all corresponding copyrights, Proprietary Information, and patents, shall be owned by Client. Developer agrees to take all actions and execute all documents and assignments reasonably necessary to carry out this intent.

## 10. CONFIDENTIALITY
(a) Each party acknowledges that, during the course of this Agreement, it will be entrusted with trade secrets relating to the business and products of the other party. Each party agrees that it will not use such trade secrets for any purpose except for the performance of this Agreement, and that it will

not disclose any such trade secrets to any person unless such disclosure is authorized by the other party in writing.

(b) Developer agrees to comply with the trade secret protection measures provided in Exhibit D. Developer hereby grants to Client the right to visit Developer's site during normal business hours upon reasonable notice for the purpose of verifying that the trade secrets and Proprietary Information are being protected in accordance with this Agreement.

## 11. TERMINATION

Client may, for any reason, terminate this Agreement at any time effective upon Developer's receipt of written notice. In the event of termination, Client will pay all sums due to Developer, including pro-rata fees and expenses for items partially complete at the time of termination, as well as any expenses associated with termination. After receipt of the payment of such sums, Developer will deliver to client copies of its work product completed to that date.

## 12. MEDIATION AND ARBITRATION

(a) In the event that there is a dispute or claim relating to this Agreement, and the parties are not able to resolve it through direct negotiations, then the parties hereby agree that they will attempt to settle the dispute or claim first by means of mediation according to the Commercial Mediation Rules of the American Arbitration Association.

(b) If mediation fails to resolve any dispute or claim arising under this Agreement, then it shall be submitted to binding arbitration. The procedures for conducting binding arbitration are detailed in Exhibit E.

(c) Except where clearly prevented by the area in dispute, both parties agree to continue performing their respective obligations under this Agreement while the dispute is being resolved.

## 13. ENTIRE AGREEMENT

This Agreement constitutes the complete and exclusive statement of the agreement between the parties with respect to the subject matter herein, and supersedes all prior proposals, agreements, negotiations, representations and communications, whether oral or written, between Developer and Client.

## 14. ATTORNEY'S FEES

In the event that any action or proceeding is brought by either party in connection with this Agreement, the prevailing party shall be entitled to recover its costs and reasonable attorney's fees.

## 15. AMENDMENTS

This Agreement may not be changed except by a written agreement, executed on behalf of Developer and Client.

## 16. EXHIBITS

Exhibits A, B, C, D, E and F, which are attached, are included in this Agreement. No other exhibits or appendices form a part of this Agreement.

IN WITNESS WHEREOF, the parties hereto, intending to be bound hereby, have caused this Agreement to be executed by their duly authorized representatives as of the day and year hereinabove set forth.

Attest:                  Optico Imaging Company

_____     By _____


Attest:                  Neptune Corporation

_____     By _____

# INDEX